CLASSICAL PRESENCES

General Editors

LORNA HARDWICK   JAMES I. PORTER

CLASSICAL PRESENCES

Attempts to receive the texts, images, and material culture of ancient Greece and Rome inevitably run the risk of appropriating the past in order to authenticate the present. Exploring the ways in which the classical past has been mapped over the centuries allows us to trace the avowal and disavowal of values and identities, old and new. Classical Presences brings the latest scholarship to bear on the contexts, theory, and practice of such use, and abuse, of the classical past.

Frontispiece. Richard Busby, headmaster of Westminster School 1638–95, was seen as a prime example of the flogging classical headmaster who might be promoted to a bishopric (hence the birch and the hoped-for (*spero*) mitre). The ornamentation of the chair displays different aspects of Latin and Greek grammar and syntax. This 1802 satirical print alludes to the promotions of classical scholars to ecclesiastical office in the early nineteenth century, the age of the 'Greek play bishop'. See the List of Illustrations, p. xxi.

Image reproduced courtesy of Elizabeth Wells, Westminster School archives.

Classics in Britain

Scholarship, Education,
and Publishing 1800–2000

Christopher Stray

WITH AN INTRODUCTION BY
Constanze Güthenke

OXFORD
UNIVERSITY PRESS

OXFORD
UNIVERSITY PRESS

Great Clarendon Street, Oxford, OX2 6DP,
United Kingdom

Oxford University Press is a department of the University of Oxford.
It furthers the University's objective of excellence in research, scholarship,
and education by publishing worldwide. Oxford is a registered trade mark of
Oxford University Press in the UK and in certain other countries

Published in the United States of America by Oxford University Press
198 Madison Avenue, New York, NY 10016, United States of America

British Library Cataloguing in Publication Data
Data available

Library of Congress Control Number: 2018949662

ISBN 978-0-19-956937-3

Printed and bound by
CPI Group (UK) Ltd, Croydon, CR0 4YY

This book is dedicated to the memory of Ian Jackson
27 October 1951–18 February 2018

Preface

This volume brings together articles on various aspects of classical teaching and scholarship in nineteenth- and twentieth-century Britain. Most have been previously published in books and journals in a range of different subject areas; two are published here for the first time.[1] Collecting these pieces in a single volume has made it possible to correct errors, remove overlaps, and update references; but in addition, the texts have been rewritten to make an organized whole which is intended to be more than the sum of its constituent parts. Reshaping and retrospection have gone together, to make a corpus which is unified both by its subject matter and by research interests whose thematic coherence was not always originally apparent to the researcher.

The initial impulse to look at the past came from a study of the present, an MSc thesis in sociology based on interviews with Classics teachers in and around Swansea (1977: note that in this volume, my own work is cited by date alone). Its explicit focus was on their response to the introduction of the radically new Cambridge Latin Course, introduced in the later 1960s, which all but abandoned the formal grammar that had formed the basis of their own training. In order to understand the teachers' responses, I asked them about their own schooling: in their responses, most of my interviewees looked back nostalgically to a lost paradise in the interwar years, when Latin reigned supreme as the prime exemplar of rigorous humanist learning in grammar schools. While this was understandable, I was surprised that these teachers showed no awareness of, or interest in, the Victorian Hellenism which had played such a central role in nineteenth-century British culture, and which maintained a high profile in the twentieth century through the work of men like Gilbert Murray and Sir Richard Livingstone. This puzzlement prompted an investigation of Classics in nineteenth- and twentieth-century Britain, and a PhD thesis, again in sociology (1994), was later published as *Classics Transformed* (1998).[2] The book was intended to complement two earlier works, Richard Jenkyns' *The Victorians and Ancient Greece* (Jenkyns 1980) and Frank Turner's *The Greek Heritage in Victorian Britain* (Turner 1981). They had themselves overlapped less than their titles might have suggested, as well as representing very different intellectual and academic styles.[3] But in addition, by design neither addressed the nature of Classics as a body of organized pedagogic knowledge, its role in social formations, whether social classes or professional bodies, or its involvement

---

[1] Chapters 3 and 8 are previously unpublished. The sources of the other chapters are given in the Sources of Chapters section, pp. xv–xvi below.

[2] In both cases, my research was supervised by John Parker, to whom I owe my introduction to historically-aware sociological analysis.

[3] Turner's original title was *The Use and Abuse of Greek Antiquity in 19th Century Britain*. It was changed after Jenkyns' book appeared.

in the institutional histories of schools and universities. These topics were addressed in *Classics Transformed*, which also took the story on into the twentieth century, ending with an account of the 'age of Latin' (*c.*1920–60) to which the teachers I had interviewed belonged, and whose passing they had mourned in the 1970s.

In my PhD thesis, I had begun by offering a sociological analysis of the general phenomenon of appeals to exemplary pasts to cope with the present, and to place English Classics in a European context (1994, 11–56). We could, I suggested, define Classics as the product of a form of social action ('classicizing') in which powerful past meanings are deployed in the present for a variety of purposes, conscious or otherwise. Very often this purpose has been to hold to a set of exemplary models which enable resistance to change and relativity. Classics has often provided those models, its nearest rivals in European history being religion and nationalism.[4] 'The Classics' were a favourite study of the nineteenth-century English gentleman, though the nature of this study and the motives for practising it varied widely. Some educated men sought the esoteric meaning of Plato's works, others enjoyed turning grocers' bills and other mundane documents into Latin or Greek verse; many more turned to their favourite authors for comforting touchstones of literary and moral value.[5] In the same period, however, historicism and the growth of other subjects, both scientific and humane, eroded the claims of Classics in this area, leaving compulsory Greek, until the end of the First World War, and for forty years afterwards its successor, compulsory Latin, to soldier on as the increasingly withered and skeuomorphic remnant of what had once been the exemplar of humanistic knowledge.

This largely male world was the subject of *Classics Transformed*, focused on to some extent because of its neglect by late twentieth-century scholars whose ideological agendas emphasized the oppressed, the disempowered, women—those left out of the nineteenth-century's account of itself. For these writers, the gentlemanly scholars of Victorian England were Dead White European Males, fit only to be denounced, or simply ignored. The 'oppressors' had become the oppressed. Similarly, I was concerned to react against the disempowerment or disappearance of individuals in contemporary academic writing which emphasized structure at the expense of human agency: hence my resuscitation of forgotten minor figures like George Griffith (1998, 91–3). This interest in shadowy and marginal figures led to a search for absences and silences: absent institutions (2014a), individuals overshadowed by their celebrated colleagues (Beard, King, and Stray 1998),[6] unpublished books (2011a, b, cf. Bruni and Pettegree 2016),

---

[4] In *Classics Transformed*, this was reduced to a remark and a footnote reference: 1998a, 10 and n. 8; some of the analysis was incorporated into 2001b.

[5] As Sir Edward Cook wrote in his *More Literary Recreations* (1919):

> The call of the classics is strong upon those who make long voyages or live much in solitude. Undisturbed by the carking cares of trivial tasks, or seeking consolation in danger…men turn to the ancient writings, in which, as Professor Murray has finely said, 'stridency and clamour are forgotten in the ancient stillness…' (p. 30).

[6] In *The Birds and the Bees*, my co-authors and I were concerned to bring to light women classical scholars in 1870–1920 Cambridge who were not Jane Harrison. Similarly, the late lamented Frank Turner

expurgation (Harrison and Stray 2012). More generally, my scepticism about the ideological agendas I have just mentioned led me to focus on analysis (including comparative analysis) and empirical case studies rather than theory. I kept in mind George Fox's complaint about scholars:

These Seven Arts, Names, Terms and words have been their holes and dens where they have been hidden, and there they have hid themselves from the ignorant...through every art and science [they] make a trade, and keep the people blind by [their] high expressions.[7]

My scepticism was reinforced by observing that in some cases, ideological agendas led to narratives being constructed that were based on the distortion of evidence as well as inadequate knowledge of historical contexts (2014b; cf. Chapter 19).

Transmitting Classical Messages

In *Classics Transformed* I explored three major channels through which the messages of antiquity were transmitted to the modern world: institutions, individuals, and publications.

Institutions (Chapters 1–5, 9)

The most constructively critical review of *Classics Transformed* came from the ancient historian Oswyn Murray, who suggested that the analysis of Classics at university level was weakened by the failure to take sufficient account of Oxford.[8] The book certainly had much more to say about Cambridge, largely because the patterns of disciplinary organization which developed there were characteristic of wider social and cultural trends against which Oxford held out. Thus Oxford, while constituting then (and now) the largest single centre of classical teaching and learning in Britain, was atypical in the domination of its final honour school (Greats) by history and philosophy.[9] Murray's comments encouraged me both to investigate Oxford Classics in depth and to develop a comparison of the two ancient universities, whose interaction has displayed both collegiacy and competition (2007e, included here in revised form as Chapter 2; cf. 2001b, 2005b, 2011a, 2013c, 2013d, 2014a). The relationship between Oxford and Cambridge is not the only kind of inter-institutional link that can be explored. Another relationship explored in *Classics Transformed* was that between schools and universities. Historians of education have tended to focus on one or the other.[10] This not only

described a forthcoming book as being about 'all the Tractarians who were *not* called J. H. Newman': he was overruled by his publishers, who knew that Newman's name would sell, and the book appeared as *John Henry Newman and the Challenge to Evangelical Religion* (Yale UP 2002).

[7] Fox 1659, 4, 55; cf. Secord 2001, 518–21.

[8] Murray 2000.

[9] In 1956 the Regius Professor of Greek, E.R. Dodds, complained that Oxford did not have what almost all other British universities possessed, a 'Final Honour School of Classics' (Dodds 1956).

[10] An exception is the chapter on schooling in volume 7 of the *History of the University of Oxford* (Honey and Curthoys 2000).

diverts attention away from their interaction, but also encourages an anachronistic view of nineteenth-century schooling as a single system with graded stages. State schooling dates only from 1870 for elementary schools and 1902 for secondary schools; we cannot speak of a 'system' in the modern sense. In particular, what are now graded stages were then inchoate and overlapping. Thus provincial, metropolitan, or colonial graduates often took a second first degree at Oxford or Cambridge, while some men became fellows of their colleges while still undergraduates. Further, some schools and Oxbridge colleges were so closely linked that they were in effect single entities: Winchester College and New College, Oxford; Eton College and King's College, Cambridge. In both cases, successful pupils went up to the sister college, then returned as schoolmasters. This system was formally weakened by the Royal Commissions on Oxford and Cambridge in the early 1850s, but persisted informally for several decades.[11]

Formal educational institutions have their own individual characters; each shapes the knowledge maintained and transmitted with it in a different way. The point comes out clearly from the comparison of Oxford and Cambridge mentioned above, but also applies within each university: within a university style there are subtle variations at the collegiate level. Further, the nature of the interaction between colleges and universities affects the way such variations operate. This has been affected by size among other factors: in Cambridge, for example, Trinity and St John's dwarfed the smaller colleges, whereas inter-college variations in size were smaller in Oxford, though Christ Church and Magdalen were larger than others. Variation may also operate within colleges: they have after all historically been composed of two groups of members with different and potentially opposed interests: dons and students. Formal and informal structures sit side by side; hierarchical relationships are in tension with peer-group solidarity. Some of these patterns can be seen in school and university slang (2008a, 2012b; cf. 1998c). Comparison could also be extended to other universities; institutions I have looked at include the universities of Birmingham (Chapter 16), London (Chapters 11 and 15), Reading (Stray, Pelling and Harrison 2019), and Glasgow (Chapter 10).

Individuals (Chapters 3, 4, 10, 11, 15–18)

Institutions shape individuals, but the historian has always to allow for the empirical possibility of a dialectic between the two; and it is easy to think of individuals who have exerted powerful influences at both college and university levels, such as Benjamin Jowett of Oxford and William Whewell of Cambridge. It is remarkable that some scholars have been able to produce determinist analyses which are contradicted by

---

[11] A notable aspect of the lack of coordination between schools and universities was the repetition in the latter of what had already been learnt in the upper reaches of schools: intensive reading of texts. In stark contrast, at Oxford the shift from this kind of learning in the first part of the honours course (Mods) to the very different content and style of the second part, Greats (philosophy and ancient history) often led to failure and distress for students.

the very process of their own production by active, creative individuals.[12] A focus on individuals also helps in exploring the fine structure and micro-politics of institutional life, including the connections between institutions. Following individual life-courses, for example, helps in plotting the relationships between schools and universities.

Several individuals discussed in the following chapters exercised influence over a wide area. Thomas Gaisford, Regius Professor of Greek at Oxford 1812–55, a powerful college head (Dean of Christ Church 1831–55), was also an influential Delegate of Oxford University Press for nearly fifty years (Chapter 3). Richard Porson, Regius Professor of Greek at Cambridge 1792–1808, became a culture hero whose disciples and followers built up a scholarly cult based at Trinity College (Chapter 4). Sir Richard Jebb, Regius Professor of Greek at Cambridge 1889–1905, was revered as a Hellenist, and became the leading spokesman for the humanities in Britain in the late-Victorian decades (Chapter 10, 2013a). Sir William Smith, editor of a series of standard classical dictionaries, gave his name to several publishing series and became an institution in himself (Chapter 11). Edward Sonnenschein co-founded the Classical Association (1903) and master-minded a series of parallel grammars of European languages (Chapter 16). Benjamin Kennedy, headmaster of Shrewsbury School 1836–66 and Regius Professor Greek at Cambridge 1867–89, wrote Latin primers which dominated school classical teaching for a century and created their own mythology (Chapters 17, 18).

A focus on the individual and the idiosyncratic can bring about a retreat to the micro level, to a pointillism which loses touch with larger structures; but it can also make possible the exploration of the structural and institutional roots of idiosyncrasy, something I have discussed in my work on E. D. A. Morshead of Winchester College (1849–1912) and his idiolect, 'Mushri' (1996; cf. 1998a). More generally, it makes possible a fine-textured study of the dialectic of the individual and the institutional. For long the conventional way to write the history of scholarship was to assemble a line of biographies of great scholars. The line of great scholars—for example, Bentley, Porson, Housman, or Wolf, Boeckh, Hermann, Wilamowitz, Fraenkel—has been the spine beneath the flesh of many a narrative. The insufficiency of such an approach is now clear (see 1987, on C. O. Brink's *English Classical Scholarship*, and cf. Marchand 2011), and is discussed in Chapter 4. The conclusion to be drawn is that specificity must be sought at both individual and institutional levels, while allowing constantly for dialectic between them, within wider national contexts. Looking at individuals takes us to the micropolitics of transmission and reception, maintenance and change, in Classics. It also (literally) adds life to historical narrative.

---

[12] The title of Arthur Lovejoy's neglected paper 'The paradox of the thinking behaviorist' (Lovejoy 1922) says it all. His targets were the psychologist J.B. Watson and his followers, who painted a picture of human beings as passively reacting to external stimuli—a picture totally at variance with their own activity. For a more recent critique which targets the failure to allow for the relative autonomy of institutions in the work of Basil Bernstein and Pierre Bourdieu, see Archer 1983.

Publishing (Chapters 6–11, 15, 17)

The exploration of Victorian classical schooling in *Classics Transformed* included a detailed investigation of Benjamin Kennedy's *Public School Latin Primer*, published in 1866 and revised in 1888 (1989, 1994, 1996a, b, 2003).[13] This led me to realize that publishers' archives were a neglected source of information; any scholar might have left correspondence in such an archive, whether as an author or as a publisher's reader.[14] The discussion of textbooks (in *Classics Transformed*, also in Chapters 14–18) led to a wider exploration of different genres, including editions (Chapter 10, 2015a,b); dictionaries (Chapter 9, 2010, 2011a, 2012a, Stray, Clarke, and Katz 2019); grammars (2013b, c, 2016); and journals (Chapters 6–8, also 2016a). Just as the character of institutions (schools, universities and so on) needs to be investigated in order to understand the way Classics is taught, learned, and transmitted through them, so the material and commercial world of printing and publishing must be taken into account if we are to understand the nature of classical books and journals. Classical texts and the writing of classical scholars have been shaped since the invention of printing by the constraints and possibilities of paper, type, and printing technology (2010). In the early nineteenth century, lithography made it possible to produce cheap short runs and to print exotic (non-roman) fonts (Chapter 14). In the same period, stereotyping released type for printing by providing moulds taken from standing type (2013c). The link between text format and page size is illustrated by the stretching of a planned page width for the Loeb Classical Library to allow Greek hexameters to be printed without frequent overruns.

The range of classical study and of motivation mentioned earlier on is reflected in nineteenth-century journals (Chapters 6–8), from the *Edinburgh Review* (1809) and its Tory rivals *Blackwood's Magazine* and the *Quarterly Review*, through the *Athenaeum, Fraser's, Macmillan's* and the *Fortnightly*, to the rather different world of the *Academy* (1869). As is well known, the attacks on Oxford which led eventually to the Royal Commission of 1850 were launched by the *Edinburgh Review* in 1809 (Smith 1809). The champion who stepped forward to defend Oxford, Edward Copleston, was soon recruited by William Gifford to write for the *Quarterly Review*, and brought other scholars into the fold, including James Monk, Charles Blomfield, and Peter Elmsley (see Chapter 6).[15] The *Quarterly* became a stronghold of the conservative classical-Anglican alliance of the Church and the ancient universities, which, while willing to learn from German scholarship, was suspicious of its potential for religious scepticism. The *Academy* was established in 1869 to provide a forum for general

---

[13] Much of this work benefited from discussions with other members of the Textbook Colloquium, a research network which the late Ian Michael and I founded in 1988.

[14] The archives I have drawn on include those of George Bell, CUP, Harper and Brothers, Longman, Macmillan, John Murray, OUP, Rivingtons, and Sidgwick and Jackson.

[15] Copleston 1810. Two further editions followed in 1810 and 1811. Detailed discussions of the *Quarterly Review* and its contributors can be found in Jonathan Cutmore's Quarterly Review Archives on the Romantic Circles website (www.rc.umd.edu). Cf. Cutmore 2008, 2018.

academic discussion, though it soon split into specialized sections. In 1880 the *Journal of Hellenic Studies* was founded: the earliest British classical journal which survives to this day. The era of the academic journal had begun, and the emergence of sensational journalism and of mass newspapers in the 1880s accentuated the polarization between scholarly and mass publishing (Chapter 8, 2016a).

Scholarship and/as Reception

The study of classical reception is now a fast-growing field. Its practitioners have gained a footing in major universities and several publishers have set up dedicated book series, including the series in which this book appears. Two international journals have been founded, the *International Journal of the Classical Tradition* (1994–) and the *Classical Receptions Journal* (2009–). Yet their content is dominated by studies of literature and the visual arts, while the part played in the transmission of classical culture by scholarship and teaching is but rarely reflected in their pages. I hope that the essays collected in the present volume will encourage others to redress the balance.

Acknowledgements

I owe thanks to Hilary O'Shea, who invited me to turn my PhD thesis into a book, and retired in 2015 after building up a remarkable Classics list at OUP; to her successor Charlotte Loveridge and to Charlotte's assistant Georgina Leighton; to Christine Ranft and Kalpana Sagayanathan; to Bill Bruneau and John Henderson for their helpful suggestions on the form and content of this book; and to Constanze Güthenke for providing an introductory essay. For help with illustrations, my thanks are due to Nicolas Bell, Judith Curthoys, Fiona Haarer, Laura Irwin, James Kirwan, Peggy Smith, and Elizabeth Wells. Much of my work has benefited from the stimulus of collaboration; for that, I must thank Bob Ackerman, Mary Beard, Arthur Burns, David Butterfield, Michael Clarke, Jonathan Cutmore, Pat Easterling, Augustus Grumblecarrot, Judy Hallett, Lorna Hardwick, Margaret Harris, Stephen Harrison, Ian Jackson, Bob Kaster, Joshua Katz, Chris Kraus, Barbara McManus, Ian Michael, Mick Morris, John Parker, Chris Pelling, Jonathan Smith, Gill Sutherland, Bob Todd, Michael Twyman, Stuart Wallace, and Graham Whitaker. Last but not least, I thank Margaret Kenna for everything.

Acknowledgements

Contents

List of Illustrations

Sources of Chapters

The texts collected in this volume have all been revised from their original published forms. The sources of the chapters are listed below.

I Scholarship and Institutions

Chapter 1: 'Purity in Danger: The Contextual Life of Savants', in S. J. Harrison (ed.), *Texts, Ideas, and the Classics* (Oxford: OUP, 2001), 265–85.

Chapter 2: 'Non-Identical Twins: Classics in Nineteenth-Century Oxford and Cambridge', in C. A. Stray (ed.), *Oxford Classics* (London: Duckworth, 2007), 1–13, and 'Curriculum and Style in the Collegiate University: Classics in Nineteenth-Century Oxbridge', *History of Universities*, 16.2 (2001), 183–218.

Chapter 3: Previously unpublished; based on my Gaisford lecture, given in Oxford in 2008.

Chapter 4: 'The Rise and Fall of Porsoniasm', *Cambridge Classical Journal* 53 (2007), 40–71. Reprinted with permission.

Chapter 5: 'Renegotiating Classics: The Politics of Curricular Reform in Late-Victorian Cambridge', *Echos du Monde Classique/Classical Views* 42.3 (1998), 449–70. (Please note that the journal changed its name to *Mouseion* in 2001 and adopted a new numbering system.)

II Scholarship and Publishing

Chapter 6: 'Politics, Culture, and Scholarship: Classics in the *Quarterly Review*', in J. Cutmore (ed.), *Conservatism and the Quarterly Review* (London: Pickering and Chatto, 2007), 87–106, 233–8.

Chapter 7: 'From one Museum to another: The *Museum Criticum* (1813–26) and the *Philological Museum* (1831–3)', *Victorian Periodicals Review* 37 (2004), 289–314.

Chapter 8 is previously unpublished.

Chapters 9 and 10: 'Sir William Smith and his Dictionaries: A Study in Scarlet and Black' and 'Jebb's Sophocles: An Edition and its Maker', in C. A. Stray (ed.), *Classical Books: Scholarship and Publishing in Britain since* 1800 (London: Institute of Classical Studies, 2007), 35–54 and 75–94.

Chapter 11: *Promoting and Defending: Reflections on the History of the Hellenic Society (1879) and the Classical Association (1903)* (Classical Association, 2003).

Chapter 12: 'Scholars, Gentlemen, and Schoolboys: The Authority of Latin in Nineteenth and Twentieth-Century England', in C. Burnett and N. Mann (eds), *Britannia Latina:*

Latin in the Culture of Great Britain from the Middle Ages to the Twentieth Century (Warburg Institute Colloquia, vol. 8; London: Warburg Institute, 2005), 194–208.

III Schools and Schoolbooks

Chapter 13: 'Paper Wraps Stone: The Beginnings of Educational Lithography', *Journal of the Printing Historical Society* ns 9 (2006), 13–29.

Chapter 14: 'John Taylor and Locke's Classical System', *Paradigm* 1.20 (1996), 26–38 and 'Locke's System of Classical Instruction', *The Locke Newsletter* 22 (1991), 115–21.

Chapter 15: 'Schoolboys and Gentlemen: Classical Pedagogy and Authority in the English Public School', in N. Livingstone and Y. L. Too (eds), *Pedagogy and Power: Rhetorics of Ancient Learning* (Cambridge: CUP, 1998), 29–46. Reprinted with permission.

Chapter 16: 'Edward Adolf Sonnenschein and the Politics of Linguistic Authority in England 1880–1930', in A. Linn and N. McLelland (eds), *Flores Grammaticae: Essays in Memory of Vivien Law* (Münster: Nodus, 2004), 211–19.

Chapter 17: 'Primers, Publishing and Politics: The Classical Textbooks of Benjamin Hall Kennedy', *Papers of the Bibliographical Society of America* 90.4 (1996), 451–74. Published by the University of Chicago Press.

Chapter 18: 'The Smell of Latin Grammar: Contrary Imaginings in English Classrooms', *Bulletin of the John Rylands Library* 76.3 (1994), 201–22; 'Sexy Ghosts and Gay Grammarians: Kennedy's Latin Primer in Britten's *Turn of the Screw*', *Paradigm* 2.6 (2003), 9–13; and 'A preference for naughty boys in apple trees', *ad familiares* XX (2001), vi.

Introduction

'A Mirror does not develop...': The History of Classical Scholarship as Reception

Constanze Güthenke

E. M. Forster, reflecting on the art and technology of the novel, claimed that 'a mirror does not develop because a historical pageant passes in front of it. It only develops when it gets a fresh coat of quicksilver—in other words, when it acquires new sensitiveness.'[1] What may be true of the novel may also be true of a scholarly discipline, and the book to which my own reflections here serve as an introduction, is a call for a new sensitiveness: one not without appreciation of the historical pageant, but one that equally cares about the fresh workings of the quicksilver.

The Scottish novelist and writer Ali Smith, herself often engaged with figures and tropes from antiquity, elaborates on Forster's pronouncement in her hard-to-classify text *Artful* (2012), four chapters of a first-person narrative that were also four lectures Smith gave at Oxford University as the Weidenfeld Visiting Professor in European Comparative Literature. Smith's text does not simply slot into the category of lectures on art, literature, or poetics. Instead, this is a text that thinks with being in the disorienting and reorienting position of speaking in the role of the scholar in front of an audience of scholars. She does so by harnessing that sense of difference for her first-person narrative, which speaks from the point of view of someone whose beloved partner returns from the dead to worry about a series of unfinished lectures with the same titles as Smith's chapters. Her partial, opaque, often funny, communications force the narrator to confront, in turn, the patchiness of language, of knowing an other, and of knowing again anything thought familiar, in approaching those unfinished, alien scripts herself.

Smith's text deliberately breaks with the conventions of academic discourse, but is, at the same time, deeply philological: in its reflections on language, its enacted forms of interpretation, reading and re-reading, and correction, in its evasions (the 'artful' of

---

[1] Forster 2005 [1927], 36.

the title is also Charles Dickens's Artful Dodger) and exposures of the interpreter, in its relish of wordplay and etymology, its rattling of words, its forcing the reader to remain in and to remain aware of a state of not-knowing, of knowing incompletely. In her last lecture, 'On Offer and On Reflection', comes Smith's elaboration of Forster's comment:

All reflection involves both Narcissus and Hermes. E. M. Forster, in *Aspects of the Novel*, reminds his readers that 'a mirror does not develop because a historical pageant passes in front of it. It only develops when it gets a fresh coat of quicksilver—in other words, when it acquires new sensitiveness.' Quicksilver is another word for Mercury, is another word for a planet that looks like a grey boulder in space, is another word for an element which is both fluid and solid, can change its shape yet still hold its form, is another word for Hermes, Greek god of art, artfulness, thievery, changeability, swiftness of thought and of communication, language, the alphabet, speechmaking, emails, texts, tweets; god of bartering, trade, liaison, roads and crossroads, travellers, the stock exchange, wages, dreams; [...] God of quick-wittedness, god of the musical potential of the shells of dead things, god of getting a tune out of goat-guts, but above all god of perfect timing, god of canny slippage, god of changing the subject.[2]

Compare this Hermes, who lends his name to the art and science of hermeneutics, of interpretation, with another Oxford lecture, that, almost exactly a hundred years earlier, also invokes the dead and that is likely to be more immediately familiar to classicists. In 1908, Ulrich von Wilamowitz-Moellendorff spoke, in English, to a scholarly audience in Oxford, pronouncing what might be his most recognizable statement in the Anglophone world, that '[t]he tradition is dead; our task is to revivify life that has passed away. We know that ghosts cannot speak until they have drunk blood; and the spirits which we invoke demand the blood of our hearts. We give it to them gladly; but if they then abide our question, something from us has entered into them; something alien, that must be cast out in the name of truth!'[3] Wilamowitz's *Herzblut* emphasizes the heart's desire for proximity and the reactive need to pull back in the name of science, expressing a nostalgic, self-denying energy in the name of discipline, in the most literal sense of the word.

That Wilamowitz himself is the author of a (still readily available, and translated) history of classical scholarship, and that 'blood for the ghosts' gave the title to a collection of essays on the history of classical scholarship by Hugh Lloyd-Jones that is also still widely referenced, illuminates one end of the spectrum of how the history of classical scholarship has been approached: from within the discipline, as a history of the

---

[2] Smith 2012, 185–6. Forster's *Aspects of the Novel*, from which the quotation comes, was itself also rooted in a series of lectures, the Clark Lectures in English literature, delivered at Cambridge University in 1927, an invitation that filled Forster with some apprehension, speaking in a scholarly frame as a writer. His 'Introductory', from which the quote comes, also includes reflections on the scholar.

[3] Wilamowitz 1908, 25. The lectures were, incidentally, translated for him by Gilbert Murray. On the lectures, Fowler 2009; on their correspondence, Calder 2002; in terms of referencing Wilamowitz in the field of Reception Studies and the history of Classics, 'blood for the ghosts' might now be the equivalent of what Steven Nimis has termed the 'Wilamowitz footnote' in classical scholarship, that is, a token reference to Wilamowitz as exemplar without necessarily engaging in any critical depth with the material quoted; Nimis 1984.

self, a history of familiarity, anecdotal, yet teleological, and looking backwards in the way Seth Lerer has described the self-historicizing, self-disciplining, and self-sustaining narratives of scholarly identity as 'a form of nostalgia that lies at the heart of the rhetoric of philology'.[4]

If this is an approach to understanding the past and those who try to understand the past that is in stark contrast to the lateral, mutable, contingent, and unexpected guiding trickster spirit of Smith's Oxford lectures, then Christopher Stray's work on British Classics that is gathered in this volume and that itself often circles around Oxford, no less than around its sibling institution Cambridge, can look, Janus-faced, in more than one direction: it acknowledges, in looking back at recognized scholarly and narrative templates, the power of the individual, of the evocation of scholarly environments, of the familiar characters, but it never considers those narrative genealogies without critical examination; at the same time, and in an entirely un-nostalgic and encouragingly unsentimental way, it tells those stories not as self-sufficient exemplars, but instead suggests and describes something closer to 'sites of learning', or 'sites of knowledge' (to borrow Christian Jacob's term 'lieux de savoir'),[5] which are overlapping, open, connective, provisional, highlighting the accidental, the unstable, the surprising, and often the overlooked, whether people, objects, or technologies, each with their own agency and, often elliptical and erratic, trajectory.

*   *   *   *

The history of classical scholarship, then, has, and has had, multiple identities: on the one hand, as an established part of the study of the ancient Greek and Roman world, though often as a secondary part; as, in effect, a naming of the parts of traditions and genealogies. But, on the other hand, it has also, especially alongside new research interests in the reception of antiquity, been claiming its place as a more fully reflective and theorized field that is and ought to be integral to classical studies themselves. As a field of inquiry, it is multifaceted and multidisciplinary. It taps into larger concerns of the history of scholarship and science, and of disciplinarity in the modern research university; it encourages the meta-critical reflection of specific, historically conditioned practices, epistemologies, and ways of knowing; and it addresses, even if indirectly, the question of what forms of knowledge of antiquity lie outside the confines of the discipline and how those ways of knowing have been articulated.

---

[4] Lerer 2002, 10; likewise, '[t]he construction of academic disciplines may not be keyed to an objective subject of study but to a subjective narrative of disciplinary maintenance. Rhetoric and philology become the paradigms for such self-reflective inquiry. Recounting the history of the field effectively justifies the field; anecdotalizing the experience of its experts is the means by which one makes oneself an expert', Lerer 2002, 9.

[5] *Lieux de savoir* is a research network and book series directed by the French cultural historian and classicist Christian Jacob, with a strongly comparatist mission: Jacob 2007, Jacob 2011. The term alludes to the project on *lieux de mémoire*, 'memory sites', connected with a group of historians around Pierre Nora in the 1980s, a term that itself plays on the Roman rhetorical notion of mnemotechnics, topoi, and memory maps; Nora 1984–92.

In a 2009 review essay on recent work in the history of classical scholarship, I suggested that some of the nodal points around which new projects were emerging were disciplinarity, philology, and the figure of the scholar.[6] These were not isolated categories, and the work of the last decade has, if anything, continued to probe the porous membranes around those terms, as many scholars of scholarship have, in effect, continued to turn a philological eye on the philologists.[7] Such philological gazes have maybe been most evident in work that arises out of interaction with a turn to 'practices' in the History of Science, examining the tools, habits, and epistemological expectations of classicists in a way that is temporally and geographically expansive, and increasingly deliberately comparative.[8] This willingness to probe and extend the capacity of terms is maybe most evident in the term 'philology' itself, whose recent treatments can range from the historical and comparative technologies of textual knowledge, collection, and criticism to the philosophy and epistemologies of making meaning of text; and from philology as a way of living to philology as a means of living, spanning the ethical as much as the institutional and professional, the social as much as the epistemological.[9] Biography, likewise, is playing a newly invigorated role in this: no longer a positivist, teleological narrative, the biographical is opened in different directions:[10] the detailed intellectual biography that emphasizes self-fashioning and larger intellectual trends, yet is equally and critically attuned to the content of the scholars' work;[11] the emphasis on networks, collaborations, and harder to register forms of academic labour;[12] or new forms of experimentation with narrative altogether.[13]

[6] Güthenke 2009; see also Güthenke 2015 for an annotated bibliography.

[7] 'A double historicization is required, that of the philologist—and we philologists historicize ourselves as rarely as physicians heal themselves—no less than that of the text'; Pollock 2009, 958.

[8] For a good account, see Daston and Most 2015. For an account of the rise of *Altertumswissenschaft* in Germany that, among other things, explicitly and profitably looks to impulses from the history of science such as the history of specific disputes, see Harloe 2013. The opening of the history of classical scholarship to the history of the humanities *tout court*, or its welcome integration into it, is also reflected in such ventures as the recent journal *History of the Humanities* (University of Chicago Press).

[9] On tools and practices, for example, Most 1997, 1998, 1999, 2002. For Stray's work on practices, tools, and people, selectively and to give a sense of the range, Butterfield and Stray 2009; Hallett and Stray 2009; Stray 2010; Stray and Whitaker 2015; Kraus and Stray 2015. For histories of philology in a comparative and global frame: Pollock, Elman and Chang 2014; Grafton and Most 2016; also the research project www.zukunftsphilologie.de, a project housed at the Freie Universität, Berlin under the auspices of the Forum Transregionale Studien, and its new, associated journal and book series *Philological Encounters* (Brill). For the philosophy and theory of philology: Hamacher 2015; Schwindt 2009; Gurd 2010, Wegmann 2014. On philology as a 'way of life': a graduate seminar recently team-taught at the University of Chicago by Boris Maslov and Rocco Rubini, to be repeated at the University of Oslo in 2018; on 'ethical reading', addressing the interactions between Theology and Classics, Najman 2017. On detailed and large-scale trajectories about the rise of modern philological institutions: Clark 2006; Turner 2014. For a recent survey, Hui 2016.

[10] See Marchand 2011 on Baertschi and King 2009 for reflections on biography as a tool.

[11] For example, Rebenich 2002; Grafton and Weinberg 2011; Haugen 2011.

[12] For networks and forms of collaboration not just as a historical feature but as itself in turn encouraging new methodological and theoretical reflection, see, for example, Avlami and Alvar 2010; Bonnet, Krings, and Valentini 2010; Stockhorst, Lepper, and Hoppe 2016; Hilbold, Simon, and Späth 2017.

[13] A good example is the 'Archive of Encounters' that continues the research project on Classics and class undertaken by Edith Hall and Henry Stead at King's College London: www.classicsandclass.info; Goldhill 2017 on family biography as a narrative challenge arising from a philological dynamic.

Christopher Stray's essays collected in this volume resonate with many of those recent tendencies. Although they profess not to be explicitly oriented towards theory, nor to aim for theorizing, a good number of them gesture in that direction as one inseparable from their analytical thrust. Stray puts his emphasis, and his affinities, with fine-grained, in-depth, archive-based case studies, rich in evidence and data. At the same time, such case studies are legible not only in the familiar frames of the field's self-historicizing; in their responsiveness to the more elusive dynamic of what they describe, including that of the archive, they prove equally rich in and rich as connectors and sensors that allow for the materials to articulate new, open-ended theoretical and methodological questions and to enact a new mobility within Classics at large.[14]

In his Preface to this volume, Stray suggests a definition of Classics 'as the product of a form of social action ('classicizing') in which powerful past meanings are deployed in the present for a variety of purposes, conscious or otherwise. Very often this purpose has been to hold to a set of exemplary models which enable resistance to change and relativity. Classics has often provided those models, its nearest rivals in European history being religion and nationalism' (pp ix–xv). If stability was one purpose, in practice Stray's essays offer overlapping spheres in which the contingency of stability, compromise, and provisionality weigh heavily. If anything, the 'exemplarity' of classical models appears to be much less about stability than about a spectrum of flexibility and inflexibility, of roadblocks and sideways manoeuvers, of attempts at creating stability, and of the avowals and disavowals those attempts bring. Stray's historical frame for the nineteenth and twentieth centuries is one where priorities were themselves shifting and kept doing so: curricular reform and institutional changes interacted with the Royal Commissions of 1850, 1872, and 1922—though, again, rather than making this a determining contextual frame, Stray is clear that those changes were the result of negotiation, workable compromise, shifting constellations, and sometimes sheer accident.[15] These are essays about connectedness and its limitations, too: about in-groups and out-groups, exclusion and inclusion, schools (literally and figuratively), communities, pedagogy, and the anxieties, dynamic, and confusions that come with them.

Stray emphasizes his attention to 'micro-environments'; but this is not the work of someone who would not look up from crafting a little model university on his desk: instead, the deeper the archival exploration, the clearer also the reckoning with the kaleidoscopic contingencies and negotiations inherent in the material record. Likewise, in focusing on Classics in Britain, the essays might suggest a self-contained lens, and one that often anchors itself in the dominance of a few institutions. But there is a calculated, repeated emphasis on connectivity and messiness both at the edges and right in the centres of those institutions that Stray singles out: British Classics tends beyond Britain, it reacts, in explicit and disavowed ways to scholarly and cultural events outside

---

[14] For a reflection on Classics and the 'open field', and a call for such mobility, see Güthenke and Holmes 2018.

[15] For the instabilities, risks, and dangers of aspiring to classical models in the same period, see, for example and in a different key, Richardson 2013.

Britain; and much as a micro-ecology of in-groups in universities, colleges, and schools develops larger explicatory force, at the end of the day Stray's characters show again and again, intentionally or not, that Classics is not and cannot be done in isolation, splendid or not.[16] There are no watertight dividing lines, be they individual, institutional, disciplinary, or national. British Classics is, in its texture, about Classics in Germany, in America, in France and Holland, and about the messiness and force of mutual perception and self-perception, making it more than ever a timely book.[17]

* * * *

If, in the last twenty years or so, there has been a pendulum swing from genealogical histories of classical scholarship written by classicists, for classicists, towards critical histories of scholarly practices, institutions, and individuals written (mostly) by cultural historians and historians of scholarship and of science, then Stray's work fits that paradigm. As he explains in his Preface, when he began work on the history of classical scholarship in Britain, his interests were not in the first instance focused on the creation of meaning and understanding of textual content in the classical scholars, teachers and pupils he discussed. At the same time, and not least due to the significant collaborative energy that has seen him team up with classicists for a large number of edited volumes on practices, objects, and individuals, his work points ahead to an important shift in how text and context relate.

When Stray started on his research from an initially sociological point of view, in the late 1970s, and even when his *Classics Transformed: Schools, Universities, and Society in England, 1830–1960* was published as a monograph in 1998, there was very little like it. His work approached the history of classical knowledge in a comprehensive, institutional, cultural-historical way, and at the same time distinguished itself from both the prosopographically-focused histories of Classics written from 'within', such as those of J.E. Sandys, Rudolf Pfeiffer, or Wilamowitz,[18] and from the very fine-grained *longue durée* historical and intellectual portraits of scholars, works, and scholarly themes offered by, for example, Arnaldo Momigliano.[19] (Stray outlines in his Preface the genesis of the work, in relation to especially the related, yet different work on England by, Richard Jenkyns and Frank Turner.)[20] In the late 1990s, the book stood in dialogue with new cultural-historical work such as that of Linda Dowling on the Hellenism of Victorian Oxford, or with Suzanne Marchand's seminal study of German

---

[16] See, explicitly, Hallett and Stray 2009.

[17] New and important work is being done on émigré scholars (for example, Crawford, Ulmschneider, and Elsner 2017). But comparatively little is said about the longer back-story of exchange. To take the example of Anglo-German scholarly histories, the role of Winckelmann has rightly been emphasized, as, for example, in Evangelista 2009, or Orrells 2011. Ellis 2014 makes a case for a two-directional transnational approach. Stray's great many instances of pointing up the connectors gesture towards the need for a much more detailed and extensive study of Anglo-German classical relations, including its complex history of mutual perception, that remains to be written.

[18] Sandys 1903–8; Pfeiffer 1976; Wilamowitz 1982 [1921]. [19] Momigliano 1994.

[20] Jenkyns 1980; Turner 1981.

institutional Hellenism and Archaeology, as well as a growing body of work, especially in Germany and Italy at the time, on Classics and nationalism.[21]

If, on the one hand, Stray's work had affinities with a growing body of work by historians, rather than classicists, it also interacted strongly with the growing field of Reception Studies that, in the British context, arose from within Classics. That line of inquiry, particularly indebted to questions of the aesthetics of reception, included scholarly receptions, but tended towards reception events in the arts, literature, and wider culture. Twenty years on, both the field of the history of scholarship and of Reception Studies has expanded and changed.[22] Categories are transforming, not only in terms of the thin line between Reception Studies, the history of Classics, and Classics itself, a permeability that has arguably changed all three, but especially in the increasingly less productive or provocative binaries of historicism versus aesthetics, or the ostensibly self-evident imagination of text enveloped by but separate from context.[23]

While the language of 'context' remains important, it raises the question whether context is distinguishable from text.[24] No classicist will be surprised that texts have histories, for example, and that, therefore, textual form is interdependent with context. But there is also a deeper situatedness of any act of scholarly interpretation and knowledge, one which (still) tends to get side-lined in the name of scientific objectivity— a reprise of Wilamowitz' gesture to keep the dead, called up, at bay. Again, work in the history of science has made clear how much 'objectivity' itself is an active, changing, labour-intensive historical phenomenon, without making this insight a battle-cry for relativism.[25] Many studies, whether by classicists or historians, have left in place a distinction between historical circumstance and the ancient materials studied; as a result, it would appear that classicists can decide, on and off, to take an optional interest in the 'background' of their institutions, or figures of identification. But this is increasingly no longer the case. In this sense, Stray's findings, portraits, exempla, 'micro-environments' also feed into a new awareness that Classics as a discipline with its textual and scholarly practices, with its incorporations of value, and with the situated, embodied nature of its agents is in fact inseparable from questions of reception.[26] For a small example, we might take Stray's chapter on Jebb's Sophocles: here, Stray gives a thick description

---

[21] Dowling 1994; Marchand 1996. On Classics and nationalist ideology, Losemann 1977; Canfora 1980; Wegeler 1996; Näf 2001; Christ 2006. More recently, Stephens and Vasunia 2010, or Klaniczay, Werner, and Gecser 2011 have broken away from the emphasis on nationalism as nationalist ideology.

[22] For an account of the important place of *Redeeming the Text*, and a reflection on and encouragement of the critical developments of the field since, see the 2013 special issue of the *Classical Receptions Journal*.

[23] See, for example, the programmatic pieces by Goldhill and Martindale in Hall and Harrop 2010, for a definition and exemplification of the historicism vs aesthetics parameters, but also the ultimate limit(ation)s of the terms. Leonard 2006 and 2011, or the introduction to Butler 2016 suggest some useful correctives.

[24] This is a question generally alive in literary and cultural studies; see, for example, Felski 2011, expanded in Felski 2016.

[25] Daston and Galison 2007.

[26] For some recent formulations of this, Butler 2016; Formisano and Kraus 2018; Postclassicisms Collective (forthcoming).

that includes Jebb's cultural investment in a particular kind of Sophocles; the format of the multi-volume edition and translation; the constellations, continuities, and discontinuities that went into making 'Jebb's Sophocles'. Does this leave Sophocles' Greek intact, and out of the picture? Maybe—but when one reads Stray's account together with, say, Goldhill's *The Language of Sophocles* (2012) it becomes clear how tricky it is to try to disentangle an underlying text from hermeneutic, specifically late nineteenth-century, Christian expectations about Sophoclean style, arrangement, and notions of the tragic, and how elusive it is to treat such 'contextual', reception-oriented knowledge as optional, or forming an external, removable layer.[27]

A recurring theme across Stray's explorations is that of negotiated and interdependent rivalries: between individuals, between institutions, between nations, and between Classics and other disciplines. The sense of contested territory that Stray's classicists experienced was shared outside Britain in the changing world of the research university. The German classicist W. S. Teuffel, in a lecture of 1858 on recent developments in the study of classical antiquity, speaks of a hypothetical comparison of Classics now and then that would leave many a philologist justifiably feeling like 'an older sister in a large family', one who has 'to watch attention move away from her and towards the younger siblings many of whom she was once rocking', an older sister 'who is still amiable, and now even more experienced, well-read, and educated (*gebildet*) compared to a decade ago'.[28] Teuffel here thinks in particular of the rise of other, modern philologies who owe their techniques to classical philology. In our current moment, the relationship between Classics, Reception, and the History of Scholarship is no less part of a sibling dynamic, though we might want to think of family resemblances rather than questions of primogeniture and unidirectional nurture (besides, the implications of sibling affects may prove a useful heuristic). If scholarship is always a form of reception, then any history of scholarship is entangled with that reception—and is itself situated in a similar way. This is not to make a point or issue a warning about infinite regress, about getting stuck in a relativist loop or *mise-en-abîme* where every position is hopelessly subjective; instead it is an encouragement to show care and responsibility vis-à-vis the changeability of the field, thinking about potential rather than vertigo, articulating it as a fresh sensitivity (not least in Forster's sense), rather than making it a pronouncement on instability and crisis.

Ali Smith closes her reflection on Forster, interpretation, Narcissus, and Hermes the changeable as follows:

Because of this messenger going ahead of us, whose quickness is a reminder that alive and very fast both sometimes mean the same thing, we are able not just to know but to see where we are

---

[27] Goldhill 2012; on notions of the tragic inflecting and building structures of classical knowledge, see, e.g., Billings 2015 and Leonhard 2015.

[28] Teuffel 1871, 460. For the use of gendered imagery of a personified science and a gendered object of inquiry, too, compelling work has been done for nineteenth-century historiography (for example, Smith 1998; Schnicke 2015), including on ancient historians such as Mommsen (Müller 2010). Nothing comparable is currently available for Classics as such.

and where we're living. With this mercurial god, division comes to mean response. His presence allows transparency, protection, a seeing through something *and* an act of seeing something through.[29]

Does reflection on Classics and its history offer any form of protection? Probably no more or less than Wilamowitz's revenants drawn near by blood, then kept at bay by protesting science. Christopher Stray's essays, the people, acts, and things they circumscribe, indicate movement between stability and slippage, between promise and compromise, between familiar narratives and pointers to newly configured, mercurial pathways. They challenge any certainties about which doors are opening and which ones are closing. They do see through something, and they see something through.

[29] Smith 2012, 186.

PART I

Scholarship and Institutions

1

Purity in Danger

The Contextual Life of Savants

In her anthropological study of boundaries and pollution *Purity and Danger*, Mary Douglas redefined 'dirt' as 'matter out of place'. Impurity, she argued, is not a state intrinsic to an object or person, but stems from their being where, according to a particular system of values, they or it should not be (Douglas 1966, 35). Douglas's account of notions of boundaries and pollution is relevant to the debates between traditional and new-style critics of classical literature, since they revolve in part around the boundaries between text and context, 'literary' and other readings.[1] Behind these debates is a history of institutional separation in which literature has been set apart from history, archaeology, philosophy, and philology.

The location of these boundaries, and the way in which areas of Classics have been combined or related, has varied between institutions. For more than a century from its creation in the 1850s, the Honour Moderations ('Mods') course at Oxford, which focused on language and literature, led on to Literae Humaniores ('Greats'), in which ancient history was combined with ancient and modern philosophy. In Cambridge the Classical Tripos, originally sharing the narrow focus of Honour Mods, was split into two parts in 1879. Part I continued the traditional concentration on language and literature; Part II contained specialized courses in literature, philosophy, history, archaeology, and philology. In both places, teachers and students could be found who sought to cross these boundaries (Chapter 2). In Oxford, two successive holders of the Regius chair of Greek, Gilbert Murray (1908–36) and E. R. Dodds (1936–60), tried unsuccessfully to transcend them; through most of his period of office, Murray organized a set of contextualizing lectures as a preliminary to the Greats course (the 'Seven against Greats'). In Cambridge, the increasingly specialized nature of the Tripos was regretted by Richard Jebb, Regius Professor of Greek 1889–1905, who in 1902 urged the secretary of the new British Academy to encourage links between the committees of its different sections. 'In Cambridge', Jebb declared, 'I have long felt that the extremely rigorous specialization fostered by Part II of the Classical Tripos has had the effect of narrowing our scholarship & partitioning the field in a <u>rigid</u> manner which has

---

[1] See Harrison 2001, in which an earlier version of this chapter appeared, and Fowler 2000.

scarcely a parallel in any other University.'[2] It also prompted the reactively integrating projects of J. C. Stobart in his *The Glory that was Greece* and *The Grandeur that was Rome* (Stobart 1911, 1912).[3] In the late-Victorian and Edwardian periods Greats was regarded as Oxford University's premier course, though in the 1890s it was overtaken in numerical terms by the school of Modern History. In Cambridge in the late nineteenth century, it was Part I, the equivalent of Mods, which was successful, while Part II numbers remained very small; but classical literature was treated largely as a linguistic corpus.[4] Francis Cornford, whose pioneering book *Thucydides Mythistoricus* (Cornford 1907) brought together Greek literature, philosophy, and medicine, later wrote the elegant satire *Microsmographia Academica*.[5] This witty and much-quoted guide to academic politics was the product of a decade's participant observation of a little world in which it was almost impossible to bring about change. Much of Cornford's inspiration in his classical work came from his older colleague and friend Jane Harrison, who brought the ideas of Durkheim and Bergson to bear on the study of Greek art, myth, and literature. In the Edwardian years, Harrison's influence on both Cornford and Gilbert Murray led to the placing of Greek literature, especially drama, in a context of ritual and belief (Beard 2002, Robinson 2002). Their work held out the possibility of a fruitful alliance between Classics and the emerging study of anthropology, some of whose pioneers were working in Cambridge.[6] By the early 1920s, these possibilities had faded away; Harrison had left Cambridge for Paris and Murray, always a half-hearted supporter of 'ritualism', had become disenchanted and was in any case deeply involved in the League of Nations. Meanwhile Bronislaw Malinowski (who had been interned in Australia by Murray's brother, a colonial administrator) was preaching the gospel of anthropology through intensive fieldwork; his major rival as a disciplinary empire-builder, Alfred Radcliffe-Brown, sought to distance the subject from psychology and speculative history and to define it as a specialized natural science (Kuper 2014). Classics and anthropology went their separate ways.[7]

---

[2] Jebb to Israel Gollancz, 15 December 1902 (British Academy archives).

[3] For Jebb's regrets, see further 2013, 254. Stobart is discussed later in this chapter ('The British Academy'); cf. 1998a, 8–11.

[4] Until 1918, a degree could be obtained on the basis of Part I alone: see Chapter 5.

[5] Cornford 1908; for the local background to Cornford's skit, see Johnson 1994.

[6] The Torres Strait expedition had taken place in 1898 (A. C. Haddon, C. S. and E. Seligman): see Herle and Rouse 1998. Harrison went in 1910 to lectures given by the young A. R. Brown (later self-hyphenated as Radcliffe-Brown). On the other hand, of the two obvious individual links between Classics and anthropology, J. G. Frazer was reclusive, his privacy guarded by his fiercely protective wife, while William Ridgeway was a misogynist, Harrison being a pet hate. Henry Jackson, elected to succeed Jebb as Regius Professor of Greek in 1906, had planned to give lectures on anthropology and Classics, but they never materialized. E. E. Sikes's *Anthropology of the Greeks* (Sikes 1914) dealt with anthropology in, not of, classical Greece, unlike the Oxford collection edited by R. R. Marett, to which Arthur Evans, Gilbert Murray, and J. L. Myres contributed (Marett 1908).

[7] E. R. Dodds (1893–1979) read Frazer and Harrison as a young man in the 1910s; his work on Greek drama reflects their influence Scullion 2019, though his best-known work, *The Greeks and the Irrational* (1951) draws instead on American psychological anthropology (Parker 2019).

The subtitle of this chapter alludes to a study of anthropological analyses of Iceland by an Icelandic anthropologist. Gísli Pálsson's *The Textual Life of Savants* (Pálsson 1995) examines the role of his fellow Icelandic academics in the highlighting of linguistic purity and social equality as focal points of Icelandic identity. Pálsson's title alludes to Malinowski's anthropological classic *The Sexual Life of Savages in North-Western Melanesia* (Malinowski 1929). It suggests both that anthropologists as a tribe are amenable to the analyses they direct at others, and that the textual sphere is as central to their existence as sex has been seen to be in the life of 'savages'. Pálsson's work on patriotic theorizing is a useful reminder of what the linguist Deborah Cameron emphasized in her book *Verbal Hygiene* (Cameron 1995). Persisting concerns with linguistic purity, she argued, stem from much more than a technical or professional concern with linguistic accuracy; they reflect obsessional concerns with the marking of distinctions felt to be vital to one's personal or institutional self-image. Pálsson's study of the role of scholarship in the ideological defence of linguistic and cultural purity provides a fruitful exemplar for the British cases I discuss in this chapter.

The twist I have given to Mary Douglas's title is meant to hint at the presence of challenge and response; of a politics of 'purity'. The major weakness of Douglas's analysis is that following Durkheim she assumes that knowledge boundaries reflect logically prior societal forms. This perspective makes it difficult to account for cultural change, for power differentials, and for the role of individuals: none of these are given the analytic autonomy which would enable them to be conceived of as independent variables. There are similar weaknesses in Thomas Kuhn's analysis of scientific revolutions (Kuhn 1966). His stress on the workings of 'normal science', massively supported by shared assumptions within a knowledge community until a divergent view reaches critical mass and provokes change, is in many ways enlightening, but there are two related problems with his picture of the successive states of normal science. The first is that consensus is assumed, while dispute and disagreement are residualized. The second is that change is not adequately explained. Kuhnian paradigms, and the normal science they underpin, roll on and on, until, suddenly, they roll over; change is a gestalt switch, rather as the Roman Catholic Church moves instantly from one state of certainty to another when its policy is changed. The politics of knowledge has no place in this picture.

Similar difficulties can be found in the major sociological account of curricular content and structure developed by Basil Bernstein in the late 1960s (Bernstein 1971). Bernstein too drew on Durkheim's work, and was directly influenced by Mary Douglas; but he also took inspiration from the structuralism of Lévi-Strauss. The curriculum is thus seen as a set of units whose contents are not intrinsically significant; what is significant is the pattern constituted by their formal relations, and—here Bernstein goes beyond Lévi-Strauss—the strength with which the boundaries between them are maintained. These factors he calls 'classification and framing'. The content of subjects has no place in this analysis. Bernstein talks of the relative 'purity' of subject contents, but without a theoretical notion of content, purity can have little meaning. 'Pure' subject combinations are those drawn from a 'common universe of knowledge'—the example given is Chemistry/Mathematics/Physics—but this 'universe' is a folk-category which lies outside Bernstein's theoretical framework. Similarly, he suggests that a proposed Oxford Human Sciences degree course was a 'relatively pure combination'; again, this depends on common-sense judgements.[8] Bernstein's analysis of curriculum in fact reflected his own socialization into the ideological bases of the English curriculum (1990).

In the next section, I consider some disputes between English classical scholars in the second half of the nineteenth century in the light of the observations made above. My concern is to identify their ideological and institutional contexts, and to establish what were the nature and sources of unity and diversity among scholars. As will appear in the next three sections notions of 'purity', sometimes explicitly formulated as such, can be discerned in these disputes.

The Politics of Textual Scholarship: Shilleto vs Grote

In 1839 Robert Scott of Balliol—the Scott of 'Liddell and Scott'—wrote as follows of the eminent German classicist Gottfried Hermann:

This venerable man has long outlived the freaks which brought him under the lash of Porson... His pre-eminence cannot be disputed; pity only it is that he wishes to reign like the Turk, with no brother near the throne; and declares war against all and sundry who will not join his party... Our readers may smile at the use of such a word as party, in connexion with the dead languages and their literature. Political England has other excitements.

(Scott 1839, 371)

Not long after Scott's pronouncement appeared, party spirit was evident in a dispute about classical literature. In 1851, the Cambridge classicist Richard Shilleto issued a polemical pamphlet entitled *Thucydides or Grote?* His target was the sixth volume of Grote's *History of Greece* (1848). Most of Shilleto's charges related to alleged misunderstandings of the Greek of Thucydides, and much of his pamphlet is taken up with the detailed textual analysis for which he was renowned. But the pamphlet opens in a very different vein, expressing his disagreement with Grote's claim that Thucydides was biased against the Athenian demagogue Cleon. 'I confess', he says, 'that I opened and read throughout Mr Grote's volume with great prejudice against its author—the prejudice of one not ashamed to call himself a Tory against one not (I believe) ashamed to call himself a Republican—of one proud of an Academical Education against one disregarding such a position.'[9] Grote's offence was a double one: in seeking to rehabilitate

---

[8] The subjects involved were anthropology, sociology, psychology, and biology. The most convenient source for both his own paper and perceptive comments on it by A. H. Halsey is Hopper 1971; for the Oxford course, see p. 189 (Bernstein) and p. 267 (Halsey).

[9] Shilleto 1851, 1. The overtones of 'Republican' in mid-nineteenth century England might be compared with those of 'Communist' in the USA a century later.

Cleon, he was at once showing democratic sympathies and challenging the objectivity of Thucydides.

This was not the first time that party politics had reared its head in such scholarly disputes. The heady and (to conservatives) alarming atmosphere of Europe in the late 1840s and early 1850s could be paralleled in the England of the 1820s and early 1830s, when reformist proposals were continually being brought before Parliament. In 1825, when the Cambridge Greek chair was being filled after the death of Peter Paul Dobree, the two leading candidates were a liberal (Julius Hare) and a conservative (Hugh Rose). The first round of voting was inconclusive, but in the second round, one of Hare's supporters, John Croft, switched his vote to a third candidate, James Scholefield, who was then elected. Rose encountered Croft and Hare the next day, and Croft claimed that he had heard that the Archbishop of Canterbury had intervened on behalf of Rose; he himself had therefore 'given his vote in the generous indignation of Whig independence'.[10] The ideological polarization between Hare and Rose seems to have continued, since in 1834 the latter was widely suspected of having had a hand in the expulsion from Trinity of Hare's friend and collaborator, Connop Thirlwall.[11]

Shilleto's introduction of the question of academic status in his pamphlet had its ironic aspects. It is true that Grote was a London merchant banker without an academic position. Shilleto himself, however, occupied a somewhat marginal position in Cambridge; his marriage had debarred him from a college fellowship, and he made his living by taking private pupils. He was in fact in the position of an 'extraordinarius' (adjunct) in a German university, not directly employed by the university but living off private fee income. This will perhaps have sharpened his antagonism to the views of a successful outsider, at a time when the first inroads into the predominantly linguistic curriculum of the Classical Tripos had just been made, with the addition in 1849 of a paper on ancient history. But it is also relevant that at this time the University was being investigated by a Royal Commission which was drawing up new statutes for it; appointed in 1850 by Lord John Russell's liberal government, it included several leading Cambridge liberals.[12] The autonomy of the conservative enclaves of Oxford and Cambridge was being threatened by reforming politicians in London, and this surely has something to do with Shilleto's resentment at Grote's *History*.[13]

---

[10] The account is from the diary of Christopher Wordsworth Jr, then an undergraduate; his eponymous father, the conservative master of Trinity College, was the presumed target of the alleged archiepiscopal intervention. Young Wordsworth is quoting a letter from Rose to his father. (Trinity College Library, Cambridge, O.11.9: quoted by permission of the Master and Fellows of Trinity College.) Further detail is given in a letter from John Croft to Joseph Romilly of 2 May 1853: Cambridge University archives, CUR 39.4, 31.

[11] Thirlwall had argued publicly against compelling undergraduates to attend chapel services. After leaving Cambridge he worked on his history of Greece; it was published in eight volumes, 1835–44, but was overshadowed by Grote's history (twelve volumes, 1846–56).

[12] On the impact of the Royal Commission on Cambridge, see Winstanley 1947, 234–69; Searby 1997, 507–44.

[13] Another symbol of the invasion of Cambridge by the metropolis was the extension of the railway, which reached Cambridge in 1845 (Oxford had succumbed in 1844).

Shilleto's pamphlet represents a defensive assertion of the Porsonian tradition of close linguistic study, of which he was perhaps the last representative, against a contextualizing historiography which threatened to outflank it. The Porsonian style, sometimes referred to as 'pure' or 'definite' scholarship, was also described as 'narrow and masculine' (see Chapter 4). Its practitioners not only devoted themselves to understanding the nuances of Latin and (especially) Greek usage, but also used this understanding to compose proses and verses in both languages. In this emphasis lay the distinctive feature of the classical scholarship practised in the ancient universities and in the public schools.[14] At the same time, the dispute was about several other issues as well: marginal status within academic institutions, political allegiances, and the autonomy of universities vis-à-vis the state. The autonomy of the literary text stands for the autonomy of its interpreters. It is notable that the text of Thucydides, which cannot be as easily divorced from historical context as some others might be, is the object of attention.

Grote decided not to publish a reply to Shilleto, though he did add an appendix to a later volume of his *History*. The cudgels were taken up instead by his younger brother John, professor of moral philosophy at Cambridge (Grote 1851). He began his pamphlet by stressing that Shilleto's attack, though 'in itself worthless... may be of... interest as a specimen of... classical criticism'. In his peroration, he argues that 'pamphlets like this of Mr Shilleto's... stand in the way of good criticism... they convert discussion into recrimination, and controversy into quarrel; they discredit criticism... they stop the mouths... of many who have truth to utter' (83). Grote ends by denouncing his opponent's 'childishness... garrulity... senile narrow-mindedness' (84). Strong language for a mild-mannered cleric; but it illustrates the intensity of Grote's commitment to genuine open discussion. This ideal was carried on after his death by the 'Grote Club', whose members included two younger Trinity men, Henry Jackson and Henry Sidgwick (Gibbins 2007).

Grote's references to Shilleto may of course reflect a fraternal defensiveness, but they certainly display a more general concern about constructive criticism and its enemies. This generalizing vein re-emerged ten years later, when he sprang to the defence of William Whewell, the master of Trinity, with a pamphlet entitled *A Few Words on Criticism* (Grote 1861). The target this time was a dismissive anonymous notice in the *Saturday Review* of Whewell's *Platonic Dialogues for English Readers* (Whewell 1860).[15] Grote opens by remarking that:

It is commonly said that ours is in a very special manner a critical age. One may doubt however how far this is really the case. We are fond of reading criticism; but a good deal of the criticism we read seems to presume on [sic] readers who... are... incapable of making [a criticism] for

---

[14] It obtained less strongly at Oxford; for the contrast, see Chapter 2.

[15] The review appeared in the issue of 20 April 1861, pp. 400–1. The *Review* was edited and published in London; it is erroneously referred to as the *Cambridge Saturday Review* by J. Gibbins, 'George Grote and natural religion', in K. Demetriou (ed.), *Brill's Companion to George Grote and the Classical Tradition* (2014), 111.

themselves. There is one thing that this criticism never seems to have a notion of, and that is, the possibility of criticism on itself.

Grote goes on to claim that 'Latin and Greek scholarship is...the only branch of science or literature in which...the...impertinent assumption' he is attacking in the review 'is ever found' Part of the problem, he suggests, is the lack of academic journals in which proper discussion could take place (Grote 1861, 3, 41). The *Journal of Classical and Sacred Philology*, which J. E. B. Mayor of St John's College, Cambridge, had started in 1854, had ceased publication by the time Grote wrote his pamphlet; its successor the *Journal of Philology* did not begin to appear till 1868. The first British classical journal to appear which survives today, the *Journal of Hellenic Studies*, was not founded until 1880. (It was doubly specialized, as it focused on Greece rather than Rome, and on archaeological and historical material rather than on language and literature.) The first society devoted to classical scholarship, the Oxford Philological Society, was founded in 1870. Grote was thus writing at a time when those standard features of a developed academic community, journals, and learned societies, had not emerged.[16] For published articles and reviews, readers were largely dependent on general literary magazines like the *Saturday Review* and the *Athenaeum*. Grote raises the question, what are the conditions for successful debate? It is worth noticing that both of those defended by him from criticism were in some sense amateurs. Whewell was famous as a polymath: it was said of him that science was his forte and omniscience his weakness, but his major claim to intellectual fame is as a philosopher of science (Fisch and Schaffer 1991).

The lack of academic journals mentioned by John Grote is a symptom of the embeddedness of Classics as a gentlemanly pursuit in Victorian society. No professional academic career or community had yet emerged, and indeed had hardly done so by the end of the century (Engel 1983). As Grote put it in his essay 'Old studies and new' in 1856, knowledge of Classics constituted a 'bond of intellectual communion among civilized men' (Grote 1856, 114). This status began to be eroded in the following decade by the foundation of new honours courses in law, history, philosophy, and science at Oxford and Cambridge following the Royal Commissions of 1850. The foundation of the Oxford Latin chair in 1854 was among the consequences of the Oxford Commission's report. Reviewing the inaugural lecture of John Conington, the first incumbent, Richard Monckton Milnes declared that the appointment of a Professor of Latin at Oxford was

in itself a strong proof of the diminution of the classical spirit. This very eulogy of the Latin language reads like a funeral oration over that condition of study, when the colloquialisms of life, the banter of youth, the academic sports...the principles of philosophy, and the verities of religion, spoke the great common diction.[17]

---

[16] For a detailed account of nineteenth-century classical journals, see Chapter 8.

[17] Milnes 1857, 512. Milnes is referring to the use of Latin as an international medium of communication, but he was a keen student of 'diction' of other kinds; collections of idiosyncratic phraseology and pronunciation abound in his commonplace books (Trinity College Library, Cambridge, Houghton G. 1–16).

The Defence of the Page

The full-blown insertion of ancient history into the Cambridge curriculum had to wait until the late 1870s, when the Tripos was reorganized into two parts. As I have mentioned, Part I represented the traditional liberal education model and was devoted to language and literature; Part II consisted of a set of specialized courses, including literature (Section A) but also philosophy (B), history (C), archaeology (D), and comparative philology (E). In 1877, during the debates which led up to this reorganization, the Trinity classicist Henry Jackson characterized the traditional style of Porsonian scholarship in the following manner. 'I must go back to the old tripos', he said, 'the golden age of "pure scholarship". What... "pure scholarship" meant was this. [Undergraduates] read Thucydides, but not Grote; they studied the construction of the speeches, but did not confuse themselves with trying to study their drift. They read the Phaedrus, but had no Theory of Ideas' (Winstanley 1950, 211). 'Thucydides, but not Grote': the older members of Jackson's audience would have recognized the reference to Shilleto's pamphlet, and indeed Jackson was using 'pure scholarship' to refer to the Porsonian style of work carried on by Shilleto.[18] This style was complemented and supported by the practice of composition, which was carried on in the public schools as well as in the ancient universities. The world of the classically-educated gentleman in mid-Victorian England included both sectors; but the reform of the Tripos took the organization of classical knowledge down a road which the schools did not follow. It is unsurprising, therefore, that the most outspoken attack on the reforms of the late 1870s came from Thomas Ethelbert Page, a member of the Cambridge classical board whose active career was spent as a schoolmaster at Charterhouse. 'The proposed scheme', said Page, 'while making liberal provision for men with special knowledge of any of the sections B, C, D, E (in any of which it would be possible to take a high place with but little classical knowledge) absolutely ignores the requirements of perhaps a far more important class of students—the men, who without any desire to pursue any special branch of classical learning, are widely read in classical literature... the proposed scheme... affords men of high general attainments no opportunity to distinguish themselves'.[19] Page pursued the theme in 1888, in a review of a new edition of Orelli's Horace:

The editor follows Orelli in treating all English editions since the days of Bentley and Cunningham as if they were non-existent. Probably this is due to the fact that English editors have paid comparatively little attention to spelling, to the scholia, to MSS, and to emendations. An opinion apparently prevails in Germany, and is becoming increasingly prevalent in England, that these things constitute the most important portion of the study of classical literature. It may be so. It may be that the odes of Horace... can only be properly understood by one who is strictly orthodox on the spelling of *querella*, who has groped for treasure among the antiquarian dustheaps of Porphyrion, Acron and COMM. CRUQ., who can exactly estimate the evidential

---

[18]   He had himself been a pupil of Shilleto's. For his view of Shilleto's scholarship, see Parry 1926, 228.

[19]   Ibid., 221. Note that for Page, 'classical knowledge' refers only to knowledge of Greek and Latin.

value of ABMOSTdy... It may be so; but if it is so, then the study of the classics, long and justly considered a necessary part of liberal education, will not long withstand the vigorous attacks with which it is continually assailed.[20]

Page went on to draw a characteristic contrast between the 'dry and unprofitable details' of the transmission of texts and 'the secret of their living force' (ibid.). The supercession of 'liberal education' by 'learning' is thus allied to the subordination of teachers to professors.

Page was particularly incensed by an attempt by the archaeological brothers Percy and Ernest Gardner in 1900 to promote classical archaeology in schools.[21] Here the dirt is literally in evidence, material evidence obtruding on what had been a relaxed world in which one read Plato or Thucydides with one's feet on the fender.[22] The kind of visceral reaction such analysis could prompt is suggested by the language of Housman (an advocate of physical responses to literature), in the denunciation in his Cambridge inaugural of 1911 of the encroachment of the 'miry clay of the nineteenth century... the horrible pit of the twentieth' on 'the library of Apollo on the Palatine' (Housman 1969, 35). This is dirt as 'matter out of place', indeed. Even more visceral is the remark by Gilbert Murray's pupil Isobel Henderson that Jane Harrison's work had 'tipped [the study of Hellenism] over to the slimy side.'[23] Page was more restrained, but something of the same theme is evident in his sarcastic characterization of Percy Gardner's position that 'he who would walk with Plato must neglect ideas and tread the solid soil of the Academy'. He went on to claim that

the living, imperishable value of the classics is almost entirely independent of [archaeology] ... education is being much injured by professors... they live in a world of theory, and from it, they hold out a guiding hand to men in hourly contact with hard facts.[24]

Page's remarks summarize a reaction to shifts in curriculum content and in the social organization of scholarship: the marginalization both of the learned schoolmasters who had formerly shared a common world with their university colleagues, and of the literary texts whose eternal value they had revered. Page had shared second place in the Classical Tripos of 1873 with A. W. Verrall; in the competition for the Chancellor's medal for composition, of which two were awarded annually, they and S. H. Butcher, who came first, were so close that, uniquely, three medals were awarded. Butcher and

[20] Page 1888. Porphyrion, Actron and COMM. CRUQ. are ancient commentators and scholiasts; ABMOSTdy are manuscript sources for the text of Horace.

[21] For references and contextual detail on Page and his targets, cf. 1998a, 207–10.

[22] The saying originates with Macaulay: 'Macaulay detested the labour of manufacturing Greek and Latin verse in cold blood as an exercise; and his hexameters were never up to the best Etonian mark, nor his iambics to the highest standard of Shrewsbury. He defined a scholar as one who reads Plato with his feet on the fender' (Trevelyan 1932, r1.76. Trevelyan later noted (2.433) that his uncle read Plato in the 1602 Frankfurt edition, a massive folio 'weighing within half an ounce of twelve pounds'.

[23] Henderson, in Smith and Toynbee 1960, 140.

[24] T. E. Page, the *Times*, 2 Jan 1904, 10d. Percy Gardner was professor of classical archaeology at Oxford, his brother Ernest professor of archaeology at University College London.

Verrall went on to academic careers, Page taught at Charterhouse till he retired. Barred from a headship because he was not ordained, prevented from standing for the Cambridge Latin chair by his wife's refusal to move, he had some cause to be resentful (Rudd 1981).

As an organized academic field gradually emerged in late nineteenth-century Cambridge, we can see the beginnings of a division of labour; the staking of claims to classical authors by scholars working within a single institution. To consider only the Greek dramatists, one thinks of Jebb's Sophocles, Verrall's Euripides, Headlam's Aeschylus—the apostrophes hinting at possessiveness.[25] Alongside this pattern of specialization, however, from the later 1860s there emerged a collaborative attempt to provide organized teaching on an inter-collegiate basis (Rothblatt 1968, 205–7). The initiative of the Trinity College dons Richard Jebb, Henry Jackson, and William Currey, it was followed up at the turn of the century by a younger fellow of Trinity, Francis Cornford. Cornford was a leading light in the Cambridge Classical Society, founded in 1903 to do, in effect, what a faculty would have done had it existed. In the 1920s, when yet another Royal Commission (1922) led to the establishment of the Faculty of Classics (1926), the Society dissolved itself. These developments had to do with undergraduate teaching, not research, but they arguably encouraged prospective scholars to think of their own projects as something more than private possessions.

The British Academy

The changes Page resisted were pressed by members of a group of academic liberals whose political influence was strong in the 1860s, though it waned in the following two decades (Harvie 1976). In the late 1890s academics were offered a chance to organize intellectual life centrally and to provide, in effect, a map of knowledge, through the campaign to found a British Academy.[26] At this point the academic career was becoming established, and of the forty-eight original fellows of the Academy thirty-seven had been educated at Oxford or Cambridge and twenty-nine were teaching there. Around half the total were engaged in the study of classical or pre-classical cultures. As one might expect, the naming of sections in the new body was the subject of private negotiation. The language of successive drafts is significantly wobbly. Early texts seem to have defined 'literature' as 'the sciences of language, history, philosophy and antiquities'; later drafts enlarged this to 'modern philology' (British Academy 2002). This shows clearly how dangerous it is to read such nomenclature as an unmediated reflection of the current state of an intellectual field. The example of the British Academy illustrates how many classifications of knowledge are the products of moments

[25] It is worth noting that Bernstein acknowledged the element of possessiveness in the 'collection' (specialized) curriculum (Bernstein 1971). 'Mayor's Juvenal' was neatly inverted in the title of Henderson 1998; cf. 2013.

[26] Harvie 1976, 215–71; Collini 1991, 21–7; Drayton 2005.

in processes of negotiation—diplomatic compromises between the rhetorics of competing interest groups.

The study of English literature was at this point hardly recognized as a serious academic pursuit; the Cambridge English Tripos was founded only in 1917, and the Oxford English school had only been established in the 1890s after long and stormy debates between the advocates of modern literature and those who believed that scientific philology was the only way to approach a text (Baldick 1983). The bandying of phrases like 'chatter about Shelley' and 'novels about sunsets' indicates the fearful contempt felt by opponents of the proposed school; debates between philological and literary-critical dons led to a predictable campaign of mutual sniping and stereotyping. When a group of scholars met at the British Museum on 28 June 1901 to consider how humanities subjects could be organized at a national level, 'the general feeling of the men of letters present was evidently against the idea of the Royal Society initiating any project to secure corporate organization for the exact literary studies'.[27] Two different boundaries were being established here. The first was between science and the humanities, or as it was often called then, 'letters', the relevant areas being in this case philological, archaeological, and historical study. The second was between the academic ('exact') study of literature, largely based in philology, and the aesthetic evaluation which evoked the fears of 'chatter' and 'sunsets' mentioned above.

The foundation of the Academy ran against a powerful ideological current of decentralized autonomy in nineteenth-century England. Here the dangerous anti-exemplars were at different times the centralized French and the regimented Germans. Dean Trench, in his celebrated paper to the Philological Society of London in 1857 on deficiencies in English dictionaries—a paper which led to the production of James Murray's *New English Dictionary*, now familiar as *OED*—was typical of this current in denouncing the centralized prescription of usage. 'I cannot understand how any writer with the smallest confidence in himself' he declared, 'should consent...to let one self-made dictator, or forty, determine for him what words he should use, and what he should forbear from using'.[28] In fact the origins of the Academy lie in an international academic meeting in the mid-1890s, at which it was found that while the Royal Society represented British natural science, the humanities had no such organization (Drayton 2005) Within classical scholarship, this anti-centralist current was manifested in the glorification of the English style of tasteful, intuitive scholarship as opposed, increasingly, to what was seen as the over-organized mechanical Germanic style (*Dampfmaschiner Wissenschaft*, 'steam-engine research'). This was a stereotypical contrast which hardened as Germany, Lucifer-like, was transformed from angel to devil, and it reached its apogee, as one might expect, during the First World War (1998a, 211–12; Murray 1915). Similar stereotyping was employed in the USA (Nimis

---

[27] The sentence comes from a statement by R. C. Jebb, one of those present at the meeting: see British Academy 2002, 9.

[28] The reference to 'forty' is to the members of the Academie Française, who produced the official French dictionary. For the history of *OED*, see Gilliver 2016.

1984). The aspect of this English style I want to emphasize is its potential for the discouragement of working together. Where scholarship is a matter of individual taste, scholars are likely to work alone. Against this background, the collaboration practised by Jane Harrison and her friends—the so-called Cambridge Ritualist tendency—was a striking development. When Murray wrote to Cornford in 1914 agreeing to add his name to a book of Cornford's, he added:

There is a great satisfaction in feeling that several of us are working on the same field, helping an correcting one another, and in getting away from the horrid old tradition which made it a scholar's first business to slay and mangle the last man who had written on the subject.[29]

The English scholar was typically a gentleman, and a concern with social style often hampered the search for truth. Two American sociologists who visited the English universities in the 1930s reported that the objectives of scholarship appeared to be 'to prepare the university man to move easily and urbanely in formal social circles...to be in polite society rather than to understand social life...men are trained to argue with charm and lofty detachment rather than to investigate with precision'.[30] One has to allow for their concern with social science rather than with Classics, but the Oxbridge style rather than a specific subject is what is being described. This was, after all, at a time when there were only two graduate students engaged in classical research in Oxford.[31] Two years later, Louis MacNeice recalled in his poem *Autumn Journal* how he 'studied the classics at Marlborough and Merton'. Not everyone, he went on, 'had the privilege of learning a language that is incontrovertibly dead, and of carting a toy-box of hall-marked marmoreal phrases around in his head'. MacNeice catches the mixture of snobbism, pedagogic ritualism, and genuine concern for ideas. 'The boy on the Modern Side is merely a parasite, but the classical student is born to the purple'; but he goes on, 'And knowledge, besides, should be prized for the sake of knowledge: Oxford crowded the mantelpiece with gods—Scaliger, Heinsius, Dindorf, Bentley and Wilamowitz—as we learned our genuflections for Honour Mods' (MacNeice 1939; 1998a, 286–8). Note the slightly uneasy disjunction of elite culture and the pursuit of learning: 'and...besides ...' No mention of Liddell and Scott, of Smith's classical dictionaries (Chapter 11), or of any other collaborative projects: the gods are heroic individuals, to be celebrated, emulated, and at that stage, quoted in examinations.[32] Knowledge is a commodity to be prized and guarded in an institutional climate which fosters competition for marks and prizes, not collaboration in shared learning.

Which brings us back, in a way, to 'purity'. The 'pure scholarship' of Shilleto was a style exemplified by Porson's writings (cf. Chapter 4). It was maintained largely within the institutional context of Cambridge, where its narrow rigour was consonant with

---

[29] Gilbert Murray to Francis Cornford, 17 Feb. 1914: British Library, Add. MS 58427, F.40.

[30] Becker and Barnes 1938, 794.

[31] Nisbet 2007, 219. Nisbet commented, 'I was surprised...I had not thought there would be so many.'

[32] An example of the hero-worship of individual scholars is provided by Professor William M. Calder III, a long-term student of Wilamowitz, who named his own residence the Villa Mowitz.

the competitive, problem-solving focus of Cambridge mathematics (Warwick 2003). The motive force which underpinned this ethos was competition: between colleges and between individual candidates for honours. The strains generated by this competition were so great that mental and physical breakdown were not uncommon occurrences. It is difficult to pinpoint detailed effects of this ethos on subsequent scholarly work, but one might suspect that it discouraged the sharing of knowledge in favour of possessiveness. Within a scholarly community, there is here a potential contradiction, since publication, the act which demonstrates how much one knows, is an act of sharing: it makes my knowledge into our knowledge. Such sharing might be problematic if achieved by plagiarism. Charles Anthon of Columbia had been accused of this in the *Classical Journal* in the 1820s; and in the 1840s the charge had been made in the pamphlets exchanged by Thomas Key and John Donaldson about the latter's *Varronianus*.[33] In 1888, the Cambridge Platonist Richard Archer-Hind's edition of the *Timaeus* received a long and scathing review in the *Classical Review* at the hands of the Oxford scholar John Cook Wilson (*CR* 3 (1889), 114–23). This produced a reply from the author, a rebuttal from his tormenter, and a 'last word' from Archer-Hind. But Cook Wilson was not to be silenced: he threatened, and soon published, a lengthy pamphlet which dissected the edition at inordinate length, complete with parallel columns comparing Archer-Hind's notes with those from which he was alleged to have copied (Cook Wilson 1889). The *Cambridge Review* carried, not a review of the book, but a poem by Arthur Platt entitled 'A tribute to J. Cook Wilson, esq':

> If Cambridge scholars publish something good,
> Scream, Wilson, scream!
> In rank abuse finds envy fitting food;
> Scream, Wilson, scream!
> Stallbaum will do to cudgel Archer-Hind;
> Exalt him high;
> Though you know Stallbaum was both deaf and blind,
> 'Lie, Wilson, lie!'
> Yes, Archer-Hind's a fool—rave, rant and curse
> To crush his book;
> But what to do with facts that prove adverse?—
> 'Cook, Wilson, COOK!'[34]

The rivalry between the two universities, as this might suggest, gave added spice to this particular dispute. And this serves to remind us that the institutional contexts of such events is an important factor in their emergence and the course they take. Within

---

[33] Confident of victory, Key issued all five pamphlets in a book called *The Controversy about the Varronianus between T. H. Key and the Rev. J. W. Donaldson* (Key 1845).

[34] *Cambridge Review* 10 (1889), 278. Gottfried Stallbaum had published extensively on Plato and was the general editor of the Teubner text. The quarrel is described by A. S. L. Farquharson in his memoir of Cook Wilson: J. Cook Wilson, *Statement and Inference* (Oxford, 1926), 1.xxxiii–xxxv.

Cambridge in this period we can see the beginnings of a division of labour; not the 'patterned isolation' which Lawrence Veysey has identified in the American university of the late nineteenth century (Veysey 1965, 338), but rather the staking of claims to their authors by scholars working within a single institution. Here we must remember that in a collegiate university where only half of all college fellows had university positions, academics belonged to more than one kind of community. College loyalties were very strong, and inter-collegiate undertones could be seen in academic disputes, as with the quarrel between Walter Headlam of King's College and Arthur Verrall of Trinity. Verrall began by producing editions of Euripides, but when he published on Aeschylus, he entered ground Headlam had chosen for his own, and was greeted by a long and contemptuous pamphlet. He replied with his own pamphlet; the consensus was that Headlam was the victor as far as scholarship was concerned, but had couched his attack in ungentlemanly terms (Headlam 1892, Verrall 1892, Goldhill 2002, 232–43). Headlam's planned edition of the *Agamemnon* was never published; his declared aim of interpreting Aeschylus by reading the whole of Greek literature through to late antiquity had a predictable result for a man who was never quick to commit himself to print. Here we can see a useful function of disputes: some scholars write in anger what they would otherwise never write (let alone publish) at all.

Tensions could be found within as well as between colleges. The largest college in Cambridge, Trinity, housed both Richard Jebb and his ex-pupil Arthur Verrall, whose focus on Sophocles and Euripides reflected their very different personalities: the provocative, sceptical Verrall stood in marked contrast to the controlled poise of Jebb.[35] Verrall wrote in a memoir of Jebb that 'He could not speak of Euripides without pain in his voice, and seldom, without necessity, spoke at all. He had no strong desire, I think, to comprehend such a person.' For 'Euripides' we might read 'Verrall'. Jebb's view of Verrall can be glimpsed in his submission to the university committee to which Verrall had applied for an honorary degree in 1888. In his report, Jebb wrote:

A modern mind, of much acumen, and richly endowed with the gifts of the advocate, seems to treat the material with more keenness, perhaps, than sympathy; yet with unquestionable power, and therefore with an instructiveness of the larger sort; because, by its qualities and by their defects, it makes us think wherein the antique differs from the modern; and so helps us to appreciate the antique better.   (Cambridge University Archives, CUR 28.15.29; cf 2013a, 218)

Behind such public disputes stand not only the ghosts of disputes past but also the tensions which never became full-blown disputes. Two other fellows of Trinity shrank from publishing their views because their authors could not face the prospect of criticism. The Latinist H. A. J. Munro withdrew from publishing in the 1870s after being roughly handled in a German classical journal; Henry Jackson's planned history of Greek philosophy never appeared because he was convinced it would express a

---

[35] For Verrall, see Lowe 2005; for Jebb, see 2013a.

minority opinion. A full account of disputes would need to consider such cases, as well as the non-conflictual mutual positionings within the academic field, whose topology changes as different styles of work emerge, expand, and dwindle.

Disputes promote both division and solidarity. The most promising questions for future work concern the relationship between different kinds of division and solidarity and the nature and conduct of disputes. So far we have seen divisions emerging both within the ranks of academics, and between university and school teachers. In 1911, John Clarke Stobart lamented both of these trends in the preface to his *The Glory that was Greece*, which I mentioned at the beginning of this chapter. Himself a schoolmaster and then briefly an academic, he saw his task as the bringing together of literary and historical evidence in a form which could be appreciated by an educated public which could no longer be assumed to know Latin or Greek.[36] Scholars, he commented, were nowadays like miners tunnelling underground, out of contact with one another. The inference could be drawn, though he did not draw it himself, that they would excavate each his or her own tunnel without mutual criticism. In the era of scholarly specialization which followed, the most striking example of a broad vision which might promote argument at a general level was Marxism. Its leading proponent in Britain within Classics was George Thomson, who conducted a fierce argument with F. M. Cornford about Plato in the late 1930s and early 1940s. Their correspondence shows a Fabian Socialist and a Marxist discussing the texts and ideas of Plato, in particular the phrase often translated as 'Noble Lie'—which Cornford argued was a mistranslation.[37] Cornford's public evaluation of Thomson's views, and those of his fellow-Marxist Benjamin Farrington, was given in a forthright lecture of 1941 which again discussed the Platonic phrase.[38] The most widely-reported dispute in twentieth-century classical scholarship was sparked off by Martin Bernal, the son of Thomson's contemporary and fellow-Marxist, the crystallographer J. D. Bernal, when he brought out *Black Athena* in 1987.[39] There are striking resonances with the earlier controversy over the decipherment of Linear B (Chadwick 1958, Levin 1964). In each case an outsider challenged the profession; in each case the fundamental issues revolved around the interaction between Greek and non-Greek. In a sense the claims have been made in opposite directions: Ventris identified what was thought to be non-Greek as Greek, Bernal claimed that much of Greek culture was taken from the East. The two cases deserve to be considered together in relation to the politics of academic boundaries.

---

[36] This was also the audience aimed at by the Loeb Classical Library, whose volumes began to appear in 1912: see Horsley 2011.

[37] The correspondence is held in Thomson's papers at the Library of Birmingham, MS 2672, box 13.

[38] 'The Marxist view of ancient philosophy', in Cornford 1950, 117–37.

[39] See Berlinerblau 1999. Asked if he was anti-European, Bernal replied 'My enemy is not Europe, it's purity—the idea that purity ever exists' (Obituary, *The Independent*, 28 Aug. 2013).

Conclusions

The disputes I have been considering revolve around the ideological defence of textual scholarship against perceived challenges. Shilleto's reaction to Grote's treatment of Thucydides belongs to a period in which the introduction of modern works into discussions of classical authors was often seen as a kind of blasphemy.[40] Also at stake in this case is a particular style of scholarship. Page's conception of scholarship was not that of the Porsonians, but nevertheless the threat posed for him by archaeology and by over-professionalized textual scholarship was similar to the threat Grote posed to Shilleto's ideal. They seemed to detract from respect for a repository of ideal and eternal value, and to threaten the integrity and continuation of scholarly practices into which several generations had been socialized. As with the series of nineteenth-century *Methodenstreiten* in Germany, the text/context debate is more fruitfully seen as a dispute between absolutist and relativist views (Most 1997). It is worth emphasizing that the absolute invoked was seen as both universal and eternal: an exemplary source of value, proof against change and relativity. Texts appeared to speak to successive generations of readers in a way which transcended time—to be absolutely and unequivocally present to them in some essential sense that was not affected by quibbling over the details of individual letters or words.

By 'the contextual life of savants', I mean to refer not just to the contextualizing impact of historicism, but the wider contexts in which scholarship takes place. In Victorian England, structural changes in academic institutions and in their social contexts set up challenges to particular conceptions of Classics. The introduction of new honours courses after state intervention in the 1850s, the reorganization of university curricula after further intervention in the 1870s, the setting up of faculty structures after another wave in the 1920s, all had knock-on effects.[41] Boundaries were created within Classics, between it and other subjects, and between academics and the ordinary world. J. C. Stobart's two books of 1911–12 on Greece and Rome were intended to heal the first and last of these divisions, which Stobart himself, typical of his semi-professional generation, experienced at first hand. The asking of large cultural questions about the ideals of Hellenism went out of fashion after the Great War. In Oxford, the home of lost causes, Sir Richard Livingstone carried on the good fight (Livingstone 1941), while Alfred Zimmern's *Greek Commonwealth* of 1911 (Millett 2007) emerged from Oxford teaching blended with a concern for adult education.[42]

---

[40] This makes it all the more remarkable that in the Oxford Literae Humaniores course of the 1850s, modern philosophy was admitted (though 'not required'). A century later, tensions between special interests had become a serious problem: looking back in his autobiography, E. R. Dodds complained that the modern philosophers had 'clung tenaciously to their squatters' rights', and that Greats in the 1950s had been 'on the way to becoming in effect a bizarre combination of two wholly unrelated subjects, epigraphically based history and modern logic' (Dodds 1977, 177–8).

[41] Oxford had begun to set up faculties just before WW1.

[42] The nearest parallel to Zimmern in Cambridge was perhaps T. R. Glover, whose wide range and popularizing concerns sat uneasily with the reigning Cantabrigian ideology of academic specialization. There

From the 1920s on, a cosily fragmented intellectual field was consolidated, buttressed by the succession of compulsory Latin to the throne once occupied by compulsory Greek and, after 1945, by an expansion of secondary education in which a rise in absolute numbers of classical pupils masked the relative decline of the subject in schools. Rigour rather than imagination was at a premium. The typical classical scholar was someone who, in G. S. Kirk's formulation, was 'always looking over his shoulder'—presumably to see if he or she was about to be stabbed in the back. The staffing of the higher reaches of government and civil service by Oxbridge graduates (mostly Oxford men) provided a cushion,[43] as did the distancing of the British Academy (1902) and the University Grants Committee (1917) from government. This may have encouraged a complacency about academic freedom which left British academics ill-equipped later on to cope with bouts of state intervention.

The disputes I have described can be paralleled by those over Hellenism—another pure essence seen to be under attack. The excavations of Heinrich Schliemann and the explorations of Jane Harrison cast a shadow on the bright, serene world of Greece which so inspired and comforted scholars like Jebb. These disputes between adherents of textual/literary scholarship and their opponents are both polyvalent and embedded in social and institutional contexts. They thus raise questions about the bases and connotations of current debates and about the institutional changes which have provoked and fuelled them. In Anglo-American anthropology, the study of disputes was for long relegated to the marginal field of the anthropology of law.[44] It has been argued, however, that the dispute process may provide an essential key to the disclosure of the socio-cultural order as a whole (Comaroff and Roberts 1981). Similarly, the disputes I have discussed serve to illuminate features of the world of learning in which they occur. They reveal its fault lines, its divisions, its obsessions.

The nature and possibility of co-operation vary according to historical circumstance, institutional structures, and ideological currents. The divisions and differences which obstruct co-operation have been both both vertical (class; university vs school staff) and horizontal (textualists vs contextualists; fragmenting specialisms). The disputes which take place across their boundaries offer useful clues to the fault lines and bones of contention which underlie them. Shilleto's attack on Grote, as we have seen, was motivated by more than a concern for accurate linguistic analysis. The historical contexts which Grote evoked were not just the extra-textual world of the Greeks, but

---

are also parallels with Livingstone: e.g. in Glover's broadcasts on 'The challenge of the Greek' for the BBC in 1938.

[43] See Stray 1998a, 238 on staffing figures at the Board of Education.

[44] The study of law remains marginal to the work of students of ancient history. Its inclusion in undergraduate syllabuses usually reflects a personal interest, as with the short-lived 'Group F' in Part II of the Cambridge Classical Tripos, instigated by A. H. M. Jones c.1968 and then taught till his retirement in 1984 by John Crook.

the contested sphere of Victorian cultural politics. Similarly, the opposed views on Icelandic language which Pálsson discusses are powerfully motivated by convictions about class and nation. 'Purity' is all too often a secondary end, dependent on primary ends which are left unstated (cf. Rothblatt 1968, 97–132). As such, it tends to be the target of concerns displaced from other sites: 'hygienic obsessions'. Purity may be in danger, but there is also a danger in 'purity'.

2

Curriculum and Style in the Collegiate University

Classics in Nineteenth-Century Oxbridge

Oxford and Cambridge are as a pair unique among European universities.[1] On the continent the arts faculty had atrophied since the Middle Ages, while the professional faculties (law, religion, and medicine) had developed and expanded. In England, however, training for the church was hardly carried on seriously, although the two ancient universities were wings of the Anglican Church; legal training was dominated by the Inns of Court, which were in effect England's third university; and serious students of medicine went to Scotland or the Netherlands. On the continent the faculties ruled; in England the colleges had taken over. The conjunction of this collegiate focus and arts training produced the tutorial system, as opposed to the professorial lectures common on the other side of the Channel. In addition, continental universities had been either destroyed or reconstructed in the wake of the Enlightenment and the French Revolution, neither of which had had much direct effect in England. In the first half of the nineteenth century, Oxford and Cambridge were thus anomalous institutions which did not correspond to any of the four European models of the university: the corporate institutions of Scotland and Russia, the state universities of Austria, Spain, Holland, and Belgium, the French *Université*, and the Humboldtian idealist model of Germany. The two English universities entered the nineteenth century as conservative, collegiate, and confessional institutions, run by small bodies (the Hebdomadal Board in Oxford, the Caput Senatus in Cambridge) whose powers of veto made successful reform very hard to achieve.

These two institutions, however, despite their marked similarities, were in some ways strikingly different. This chapter explores their differences, focusing on the content, organization, and status of their classical curricula, and looking at the links between these and the social and intellectual styles characteristic of the two universities. These styles are identified both in the comparisons made within Oxford and Cambridge and in the fictional accounts which transmitted them in stereotyped form to a wider public. Such a comparison has the advantage of highlighting the extent to

---

[1] The best discussion of what follows is Brockliss 1997; see also Anderson 2004.

which transmitted knowledge is shaped by specific institutional contexts: academic politics, organizational structures, and ideological traditions, and patterns of teaching and learning. In looking at Oxford and Cambridge from this point of view, we need to remember that in the collegiate university a layer of pedagogical and political activity has to be allowed for which is absent in most other such institutions. The Oxford battles between the advocates of college-based tutorials and those of a research-oriented professoriate—between the followers of Benjamin Jowett and Mark Pattison—are well known. Throughout the nineteenth century both universities had professors, but these were not the powerful founders and controllers of seminars, the patrons of pupils who followed their style and their commands which one finds in Germany in this period.[2] In the first half of the century, indeed, many Oxbridge professors did not lecture, and some did not even reside. The university was beginning to take back the original authority which had been usurped by the colleges several centuries before, but the process was by no means complete.[3]

The recognition of 'Oxbridge' as a single institutional world was cemented by the coining of the term by Thackeray in 1849 in his novel *Pendennis*.[4] In a sense the conflated title was a timely coinage, since Lord John Russell's government had just appointed a pair of Royal Commissions to investigate the 'state, discipline, studies and revenues' of the two universities. This intervention came as the climax of a long series of intermittent attacks on Oxford and Cambridge, beginning with articles in the *Edinburgh Review* in 1809. The charges were that they were socially and religiously exclusive, had narrow curricula, and were not even very good at what they did teach. As a result of the two Commissions' reports, new honours courses were introduced and old ones reformed, and some religious restrictions were relaxed. The 1850s marked, in fact, the beginning of the period in which the state first intervened seriously in modern times in English education at all levels; Oxford and Cambridge in their present form were shaped by these Commissions and by those which followed in the 1870s and the 1920s.[5] In general this process has had a homogenizing effect; yet differences in the extent and nature of state intervention also led to continuing differences in their internal structure, and especially in the relations between colleges and university.

---

[2] For Germany, see Grafton 1983. The organization of Classics in the Netherlands in an earlier period offers a similar contrast with England: Feingold 1996, 237–8.

[3] The basic secondary sources are the two official university histories. The *History of the University of Oxford* (hereafter *HUO*) in eight multi-authored volumes, was completed in the autumn of 2000 by the publication of volume 7 (1870–1914). The *History of the University of Cambridge* (*HUC*) is on a smaller scale: four single-authored volumes, published between 1988 and 2004. Understandably, neither pays much attention to the other place. But whereas the Oxford nineteenth-century volumes (6 and 7) include chapters devoted to Classics, their Cambridge equivalents, working to a much more restrictive brief, do not.

[4] 'Camford' also appeared there for the first time, but has failed to enter public consciousness: Oxbridge is mentioned eighty-four times in the text of the *Oxford Dictionary of National Biography*, Camford not at all.

[5] Intervention in Scottish universities, however, had begun in 1826: see, for example, Davie 1961, 26–40, and for a detailed critique of Davie, Morris 2009.

Through the process of change initiated by the three Royal Commissions between 1850 and 1925, the Oxford colleges retained more independence than their counterparts in Cambridge, which thus became a more centralized institution than its sibling. It also needs to be pointed out that the 'nationalization' of the ancient universities, while promoting convergence in curriculum and organization, *ipso facto* provoked ideological celebrations of difference; and this was surely a potent factor in the publication of Oxford and Cambridge college histories at the end of the nineteenth century.[6]

In the early nineteenth century, other differences were recognizable, most of them the products of the separate routes each university had taken as it developed from its medieval beginnings. After the unsettling of the scholastic curriculum under the impact of the scientific revolution, Cambridge took up the study of mathematics and Lockean epistemology, while Oxford clung to the logic and ethics of Aristotle (Feingold 1997). The role of mathematics at Cambridge became increasingly important in the eighteenth century as Newtonian natural theology was adopted as a bulwark of the 'holy alliance' between science and Anglicanism (Gascoigne 1989, 7). The strength of latitudinarianism promoted a wider range of theological debate than was found in Oxford (Green 1964, 153). Political differences between the two places confirmed those in religion. After the accession of George III in 1760, Whig Cambridge found its relatively favoured position vis-à-vis the throne eroded, as the threat of Jacobitism faded, to be replaced by that of Jacobinism. The threats to the social order posed by Wilkes's followers, by the American rebels, and finally by the French Revolution made liberalism suspect and prompted a move to the right (Gascoigne 1989, 187).

Yet if this promoted a convergence with Tory Anglican Oxford, the timing of curricular reform in the two universities led to continuing differences between them. The dominance of mathematics in Cambridge was established by the 1750s, and changes later in the century simply increased the pressure and intensity of the examination system. The campaigns of John Jebb to widen the curriculum in the 1770s foundered partly on the revelation of his Unitarianism. Within a less contested climate of institutional debate, John Napleton's contemporary proposals for reform at Oxford were less controversial.[7] Oxford reform, however, was meditated and realized at the turn of the century, at the height of conservative fears of secularism and radicalism. The statute of 1800 which founded the modern Oxford examination system was in large part aimed at containment and control.[8] This was a time when the conservative Anglican establishment was nervous at the prospect of radical intellectual and political activity, and throughout Europe there were fears of the consequences of an overproduction of educated young men. Hence the remark of Sydney Smith in

---

[6] See Campbell 1901, and for the methodological point, 1995, 2–36. A series of college histories was published by the firm of F. E. Robinson between 1898 and 1906.

[7] For Jebb's campaigns, see Searby 1997, 163–6, Page 2003,129–50; for Napleton, Green 1986, 615–18.

[8] This was stressed by Ward 1958, 14; cf. Green 1986, 622–3, and Brock 1997, 8.

the *Edinburgh Review* article of 1809 which opened that journal's campaign against Oxford. He wrote of the Oxford dons that:

> To preserve the principles of their pupils they confine them to the safe and elegant imbecilities of classical learning. A genuine Oxford tutor would shudder to hear his young men disputing upon moral and political truth, forming and pulling down theories, and indulging in all the boldness of political discussion. He would augur nothing from it but impiety to God, and treason to Kings.   (Smith 1809, 50)

In Cambridge, resistance to French ideas focused on a disapproval of analytical (algebraic) mathematics by a Newtonian mathematical establishment which had become hidebound. Until the first Classical Tripos examination was held in 1824, the only university examination in Cambridge was the Senate House Examination, dominated by mathematics, which had been evolving since the early eighteen century, and whose lists of Wranglers, Senior Optimes, and Junior Optimes (first, second, and third class honours men) had first been published in the 1750s. The examination had begun as an add-on to the traditional oral disputations, but had gradually usurped their place, and by the late eighteenth century had become a rigorous and intensive test, centred on Newtonian mathematical physics.[9] The successful insertion of French analysis into the curriculum was accomplished in the more relaxed years after the Napoleonic Wars; the addition of Classics to the curriculum followed in the early 1820s. Again, the timing was crucial, but perceptions of the social role of knowledge also played a part. In a period of repression and suspicion, the distance of mathematical teaching and learning from social (especially political and religious) practice meant that it attracted much less controversy than Classics.[10]

Partly because of its subject matter, the Senate House Examination had become an almost entirely written examination (Gascoigne 1989, 270–99, Warwick 2003; 2005c). The atmosphere of the examination room, so familiar to us moderns but then so strange, was captured in a vivid account in the 1802 Cambridge University Calendar:

> Immediately after the University clock has struck *eight*, the names are called over... The classes to be examined are called out, and proceed to their appointed tables, where they find pens, ink, and paper provided in great abundance... The young men hear the propositions or Questions delivered by the Examiners; they instantly apply themselves... All is silence; nothing heard save

---

[9]   In a sense its history began in 1730, the year in which the new Senate House was opened; the examination had however been held before then. For a summary, see Searby 1997, 158–9; for more detailed discussions, Gascoigne 1989 and Warwick 2003; cf. 2005c. The term 'Mathematical Tripos' technically became possible only after 1824 (though it was used proleptically in Philograntus 1822), but 'Senate House Examination' continued in use for some time after that date.

[10]   References to religion can be found, however, as in the *Memoirs of the Analytical Society* (1813), written by Charles Babbage and John Herschel. The aim of the Society was to promote the continental (Leibnizian) approach to calculus (which employed a notation involving 'D') as opposed to Newtonian fluxions, which used dots. As Babbage later put it, their aim was to promote 'the principle of pure D-ism in opposition to the Dot-age of the University'. His plan to publish a translation of a French mathematical textbook without annotations was announced amid a local controversy about whether the Bible should be published with or without notes (Babbage 1864, 28–9).

the voice of the Examiners; or the gentle request of some one, who may wish a repetition of the enunciation. It requires every person to use the utmost despatch; for as soon as the Examiners perceive that any one has finished his paper, and subscribed his name to it, another Question is immediately given.   (Raworth 1802, xx)

What is being described is a vast, impersonal sorting and grading machine. Later in the century, in its developed form, it was seen by some as a kind of monster: in 1867 John Seeley declared that 'Cambridge is like a country invaded by the Sphinx. To answer the monster's conundrums has become the one absorbing occupation' (Seeley 1867, 163). But (to return to the description of 1802) like any well-oiled machine, it ran with very little noise: 'All is silence'. The implied contrast here is not only with the college examinations and the oral disputations which still preceded the written examination, but also with the Oxford examinations in Literae Humaniores, established by the 1800 statute and first held in December 1801, which were both public and entirely viva voce. The other obvious difference was that the Cambridge examinations were almost entirely mathematical, while at Oxford Classics was also tested, along with law and Hebrew; mathematics and science were hived off to a separate examination in 1807 (2005c).

Oxford undergraduates could choose which books[11] to bring up to be tested on, were examined orally, and were not in competition with one another—all or none might be in the first class, for example. There are famous stories of outstanding performances. In 1810 Sir William Hamilton offered a large number of books, was examined for twelve hours over two days, and at the end was publicly thanked by his examiners. In 1831 Gladstone's examiner tried to change the subject at one point, only to be told firmly that the examinee wanted to pursue it further.[12] Only in the late 1820s did the sheer weight of work force the introduction of printed papers and written answers. The use of 'books' contrasted strikingly with the Cantabrigian emphasis on translation into and out of Latin and Greek. Henry Fynes Clinton of Christ Church was sure that the Oxford method was better, and denounced the Cantabs' way as leading to superficiality.[13] John Conington, first holder of the Oxford Latin chair founded in 1854, had this to say in 1843:

Cambridge...imparts an education, valuable not so much for itself, as for the excellent discipline which prepares the mind to pass from the investigation of abstract intellectual truth to the contemplation of moral subjects. Oxford, on the contrary, seeks without any such medium to arrive at the higher ground at once...leading the mind, before it has been sufficiently disciplined, to investigate the highest and most sacred subjects at once.[14]

---

[11] 'Books' referred not to actual volumes, but to prescribed groups of texts.

[12] Oscar Wilde may have been riffing on this during his divinity examination in 1875, when the examiner halted his translation of the story of Judas and the thirty pieces of silver. Wilde protested that he wanted to carry on find out what happened (Ellmann 1987, 62).

[13] Clinton 1854, 74–5. Clinton's contrast was between 'author' and 'subject'; I believe this was in effect a comparison of Oxonian and Cantabrigian procedures.

[14] Letter of 19 May 1843, printed in the memoir of Conington by H. J. S. Smith: Conington 1872, 1. xviii.

That was written while Conington was still in the sixth form at Rugby; a school which was itself seen in some quarters as producing over-moralized young men—in short, prigs.

The well-oiled machine described in the 1802 Cambridge Calendar was famous, or notorious, for its rigour: it was no respecter of persons. This rigorous neutrality was one of the features emphasized in 1808 in a pamphlet by Benjamin Newton, a Cambridge man who at the time held a rural living near Bath (Newton 1808). Asked by a friend to which of the two universities he should send his son, Newton wrote him a letter designed to show the superiority of Cambridge. This he published as preface to a list of 'the names on the Cambridge triposes'—that being the title of his pamphlet. To the rule of intellect and the intense competition for tripos places in his old university, he contrasted the more leisurely pace of oral examinations at Oxford.

What of Classics in particular? Newton observes that in Cambridge 'Opportunities are afforded by Browne's Medals, and writing verses for the Triposes, of bringing undergraduates very early into repute as classical scholars' (xvii).[15] He adds that Cambridge has more prizes to give than Oxford. When Newton wrote only two awards were available in Oxford: the Craven scholarships (first awarded in 1649), tenable for fourteen years as at Cambridge, and the Chancellor's Latin verse prize, first awarded in 1769—a Latin essay prize was added in 1810. The other prizes and scholarships familiar from the curricula vitae of men like Gilbert Murray, Arthur Godley, and Tommy Higham all come later: Ireland 1825; Hertford (Latin) 1835; Gaisford (Greek) 1857. And until 1858 preference for Craven studentships was shown to founders' kin—some of whom had decidedly flimsy claims to the status (Squibb 1972, 29–30).

Now Newton is clearly not a neutral witness, but his account does show up some differences of style, and these relate to the differential status of Classics in the two universities. The paucity of prizes at Oxford can be linked to the established position of Classics; and perhaps the foundation of the later prizes for linguistic virtuosity between 1825 and 1857 can be linked to the rise of Greats, with its stress on history and philosophy. In other words, such endowments are more often made to compensate for perceived weaknesses than to celebrate existing strengths. This interpretation is strengthened by the fact Oxford had two mathematical scholarships, whereas Cambridge had none.

Oxford, Cambridge, and English Schooling

In 1800 Oxford and Cambridge were the educational wings of the Anglican Church. Many of their students were the sons of clerics; many of their graduates took orders on graduation.[16] Throughout the first half of the century, the Church took the brightest

---

[15] Commissioned verses by undergraduates were printed on the reverse of the published lists of examination results ('triposes')—or vice versa, as *OED* quaintly suggests s.v *tripos*.

[16] Theological colleges existed, but their graduates, though ordained, were not regarded as gentlemen: Haig 1986b.

and best of their bachelors. And since Latin and Greek, together with Hebrew, were the languages of the Church, what was at times referred to as 'the classical system'—the domination of elite schooling by the learning of Latin and Greek—was tightly tied to the 'Anglican system', the domination of education by the Established Church. In the elementary schools, the Anglican National Schools competed for pupils with the dissenting British Schools from around 1810. The public schools and universities of England, on the other hand, were suffused with Anglican belief and practice. When the criteria for ecclesiastical appointments began to shift, towards the end of the eighteenth century, from social connection to intellectual merit, that merit was measured by prowess in Greek scholarship. Hence that curious phenomenon the 'Greek play bishop' (Brock 1997, 15; 1998a, 39, 41; Burns and Stray 2011). Conversely, when the editors of Greek plays became bishops, they typically abandoned classical scholarship. Hence A. E. Housman's well-known reference in the preface to his edition of Manilius to the 'strokes of doom' of 1824–5 which sent Peter Dobree and Peter Elmsley to their graves, and Charles Blomfield from Cambridge to the bishopric of Chester. In fact, Blomfield had been appointed in 1819 to the rectorate of St Botolph's, Billingsgate (while retaining a rural living). Thomas Gaisford, professor of Greek at Oxford, wrote to his colleague Peter Elmsley on 13 May 1820, 'Whether Blomfield will go on with Aeschylus, or merge himself altogether in divinity is to me rather uncertain.'[17] Similarly, Julius Hare's classical publication ceased completely when he left Cambridge for a clerical living in 1832.[18]

The word 'system' may suggest a tightly integrated set of institutions, with levels through which pupils progressed. The reality was very different. In contrast with France and Germany, which both had mass schooling systems in place by the early nineteenth century, state intervention in education came very late in England (Armstrong 1973, Green 1990). The first tentative steps toward government involvement in education came in 1833, but consisted merely of establishing a committee of the Privy Council and issuing a few grants; in the 1840s a schools inspectorate was established. The basic legislation was passed only in 1870 for elementary schools, and in 1902 for secondary schools. The public (i.e., fee-paying) schools were united by the middle- and upper-class clientele to which they appealed, but it was a clientele for which they competed. Competition fostered differentiation between the schools, even as it held them together against the social groups they excluded by charging for their services.

The lack of standardized provision which resulted is evident in the attempts made to combat it in the 1830s and 1840s—the period when the expansion of the rail network and the introduction of a cheap postal system enhanced communication and mobility. In 1835 Thomas Arnold urged the production of standard Latin grammars, so that a boy who moved from one school to another would not have his schooling disrupted. The novelist Samuel Butler wrote feelingly of his difficulties in having a new Latin

---

[17] Elmsley papers, Westminster School, box 2.
[18] See the bibliography of his publications in Distad 1979.

grammar beaten into him each time he moved school (1989). Through the century, and after several waves of expansion, the public school sector gradually took shape as a coherent system. The Head Masters' Conference, founded in 1869, provided a talking shop for its leaders.[19] The Oxford and Cambridge School Examinations Board, set up four years later, promoted common standards in assessment, as well as encouraging liaison between the two universities and their feeder schools. Here, too, the pattern had been a ragged one. The schools had developed that curious institution, the sixth form, whose members' average age increased until boys were leaving at nineteen or twenty. The sixth form was almost an alternative to an undergraduate career (Reid and Filby 1982, 17–43). Indeed, there were embarrassments in the 1830s and 1840s, when sixth formers who were applying to enter Oxbridge went in for university classical prizes and won them while still at school. At the same time, the large salaries offered to classical masters at the leading schools, especially those who were in charge of boarding houses, made it difficult for the universities to compete.[20] In short, our modern assumptions about progression from one form of schooling to another do not apply in any straightforward sense.[21]

Oxford was informally integrated with this loose-knit system in a way that Cambridge was not. The elite schools taught almost nothing but Classics throughout the first half of the nineteenth century (Clarke 1959, 74–84; 1998, 31–45). They thus offered a thorough grounding for the university curriculum at Oxford, similarly dominated by Classics, but not for the Cambridge course, which consisted largely of mathematics. Those who went to Cambridge might be prepared in rural grammar schools (notably those in the north of England, like William Wordsworth's Hawkeshead School), by private tutors—some of them local clergy educated at Cambridge—or at the London colleges. Otherwise they had to begin with the rudiments after matriculating (see Warwick 2003). This informal disjunction between Classics and mathematics had a hierarchical dimension reflected in the contrast between the two largest Cambridge colleges. St John's specialized in mathematics and had many sizars (poor students who had originally earned their keep by carrying out menial tasks, but by the nineteenth century were in effect minor scholars). Trinity's strength lay rather in Classics, and it drew students, on the whole, from a higher social stratum. Even at St John's, however, the college examination system (the first to be established in Cambridge, in 1765) included thorough and regular testing of classical knowledge (2005c).

Cambridge was, however, integrated with the schools at the college level; it was the colleges which were the sole home of classical teaching and examining until the

---

[19] It is worth remembering that the HMC was founded by heads of less famous schools as a means of resisting the dominance of schools like Eton, Harrow, and Winchester. The challenge had been absorbed by the late 1880s.

[20] See, for example, Alfred Marshall's evidence to the (Aberdare) Commission on Higher Education in Wales and Monmouthshire, in Groenewegen 1996, 44 (Question no. 18,266).

[21] This may be why the matriculation rates at Oxbridge levelled off from the mid-1820s to c. 1860: adolescents went to, or stayed on at, schools in the expanding public-school sector.

foundation of the Classical Tripos in 1822, and organized inter-collegiate teaching began only in the late 1860s.[22] It is very difficult to gauge the overall relationship between the schools and the two universities, and hence to answer the question: If the two universities inhabited a competitive field in which their individual identities throve on agonistic differentiation, how did competition actually *happen*? To what extent did students (more likely, their parents and teachers) actually choose between them in the nineteenth century? The available data, scattered and heterogeneous as they are, do not offer a firm basis for generalization. In the first half of the century, many schools had close links to particular colleges—most notably, Winchester with New College, Oxford, and Eton with King's College, Cambridge. It was also common for a college to draw from a particular county or region. Such links were cut by the 1850 Royal Commissions on Oxford and Cambridge, but they took some time to wither away. Oscar Wilde's friend Robert Ross was thrown into a fountain at King's in the 1880s during a tussle between the snobbish old-Etonian clique and those they regarded as their social inferiors. The figures assembled by Honey and Curthoys on school–university links suggest a fairly stable relationship, but their comparative data point to a rather greater intake by Oxford from higher social classes—a pattern which it is reasonable to link with the university's classical bias (Honey and Curthoys 2000).

Classics at Oxford and Cambridge

In the first half of the nineteenth century, both places had curricular structures which can be described as 'sequential' rather than 'branching'. In Oxford one studied Classics, and if successful could then study mathematics; in Cambridge the reverse held true. Choice of subject was thus only available in the negative sense that having studied one subject, one could choose not to study another; or, of course, by going to one university rather than the other. The Cambridge Classical Tripos was not established until 1822, though efforts had been made in that direction by James Monk, the Regius Professor of Greek, in the 1810s. The Oxford examination, as befitted the work of cautious, even nervous, planners, included both the major areas of received high-status knowledge: Classics (*literae humaniores*) and mathematics and science (*scientiae naturales*); though the latter was as we have seen soon (1807) hived off to a separate examination, one which was only accessible to those with classical honours. The preponderance of Classics in the new examination reflected the university's existing curricular bias. In Cambridge Christopher Wordsworth, vice-chancellor of the university, master of Trinity, and the leading figure behind the Tripos's foundation, had to battle against a dominant mathematical majority. The concessions he had to make to get his measure through show

---

[22] It should not however be assumed that such integration guaranteed a progressive course of study, especially as a large proportion of students—in some cases a majority—did not proceed to honours degrees. The evidence on this for Cambridge is unclear, and the available estimates are difficult to reconcile (see Chapter 5).

how powerful the opposition was. His original proposal was for an examination to be taken after the mathematics examination, to be compulsory for all except the top ten wranglers (first-class men) in mathematics, and to include original composition in Latin and Greek. The examination which emerged in 1824 was entirely voluntary, and was open only to those who had already achieved honours in mathematics. What is more, it contained no original composition at all. It is true that the university had a series of prizes, some of which were awarded for compositional prowess. But it is probably also true that composition was seen by the mathematicians as the farther shore of Classics—the hardest to acquire in a short time, and also the most obvious example of 'taste', as opposed to the intellectual rigour and instant problem-solving on which the Cambridge mathematical establishment prided itself. The new examination, then, was handicapped from the start.

At Oxford, the oral examination in *Literae Humaniores* had by the early 1830s become primarily a written test, examined separately from mathematics and science, and with four classes. Composition in Latin and Greek, not included at first, was added in 1830.[23] The examination included history and philosophy, and candidates were allowed to illustrate their answers from modern authors. This might be said to reflect the broader vision of classical scholarship imported from Germany (*Altertumswissenschaft*) rather than the narrower textual work of men like Porson and Elmsley, Monk and Blomfield. To put it another way, it supported the Germanizing trend of the *Philological Museum*, the journal founded in 1831 by Julius Hare and Connop Thirlwall, rather than the Porsonian aims of its predecessor the *Museum Criticum*, which had ceased publication in 1826 (Chapter 7). Both journals had been run from Trinity College, Cambridge; but the broader vision of the *Philological Museum* had little effect on the Cambridge classical curriculum. By the mid-1830s, in any case, Hare had left for a rich country living and Thirlwall had been expelled from his college for criticizing compulsory chapel attendance. The tripos continued to test translation and composition, with a scattering of questions arising from the texts set. Not until 1849 was a paper on ancient history added, and by all accounts it was not taken very seriously by undergraduates.

It was also at this point that the mathematical bar on entry was relaxed, though access did not become completely free until 1854. Thus for the first thirty years of the tripos's history, those classicists who could not cope with the rigours of Cambridge mathematics were unable to sit the examination. Richard Shilleto, one of the best-known Cambridge scholars in the narrowly linguistic, Porsonian style, just scraped in: he was Wooden Spoon (last in the list of mathematical honours) in 1832 (2012b). The only compensation was that the possession of an honours degree was not then so essential to academic employment as it became later on. Thomas Evans, one of the unfortunate victims of the system, went on to teach at Shrewsbury School, then the most effective producer of classical students in England, and later became professor of Greek at

---

[23] F. W. Newman ascribed this to the influence of the university scholarships introduced in 1825 (Huber 1843, 2. 524); but it would not have been possible without the shift to written papers (2005c).

Durham. Evans was agreed to be one of the half dozen best composers of Greek and Latin in Victorian England. In 1839, while still at Cambridge, he took his revenge on the mathematicians by publishing a poem in Greek called *Mathematogonia, or the mythological birth of the nymph Mathesis*, in which he poured elegant scorn on the curriculum which had blocked his path. His poem, loosely based on Hesiod's Theogony, tells of the fashioning of mathematics from the triangle and other figures by Hephaestus at Zeus's command. It is borne by the Furies first to the Nile delta ('a country which is triangular') and eventually to the banks of the Cam. Here it is set down 'to generate disputes and sharp provocations to madden [the inhabitants'] minds...a Death destroying everything, a second Sphinx, one born to compose inscrutable riddles and generate havoc among mortal kin' (Evans 1839: note the anticipation of Seeley's reference to the Sphinx, mentioned above).

At Oxford, meanwhile, Greats had in 1850 been recast in the form which would last until 1972: dominated by ancient history and ancient and modern philosophy, and preceded by a Moderations course which concentrated on language and literature. The nature of Greats gave rise in the 1880s to the complaint by Oxford historians that a final school of Classics paid very little attention to Latin and Greek. This remained the case in the 1960s.[24] The Cambridge tripos, on the other hand, had been described in Oxford as giving extensive knowledge of those languages, but without any idea of what one might do with that knowledge. In the 1860s and 70s, however, the ancient history paper was expanded, and a paper on ancient philosophy added; but the dominant emphasis was still placed on the accurate knowledge of the wide variety of linguistic styles found in ancient authors, and an ability to reflect these in translation and manipulate them in composition. The Cantabrigian view of Oxford was that it concentrated on literature, not language, and on the rote learning of set books. The contrast was reinforced by the fact that in Oxford a student could choose which books to offer in examination; the number and choice of books offered, in effect, constituted an announcement of the class of degree at which one was aiming. Francis Newman's Oxonian comment on the Cambridge system in 1843 was that

it is not a very rare thing for students so to concentrate their attention on mere language and style, on the manual called 'The Greek Theatre', and on books on Greek and Latin Antiquities, as to be quite unacquainted with the contents of any one work; having perhaps not read a single author through.

He goes on to admit, however, that the Oxford system was liable to promote the rote learning of set books.[25]

---

[24] In 1960, Kenneth Dover refused the Regius chair of Greek because he believed reform was needed, but was convinced it could not be achieved. Sending his refusal to the then prime Minster, Harold Macmillan, he wrote that 'Oxford is the only major university which makes no provision for Classics (as normally understood) as a Final Honours School'. Dover to Macmillan, 7 March 1960; Dover family papers.

[25] Huber 1843, ii. 521. The book was translated and edited by Newman, who used his notes to supplement, correct, and often to admonish Huber. The book he refers to is presumably P. W. Buckham's *The Theatre of the Greeks* (1825), later much enlarged and revised by J. W. Donaldson (4th edn 1836, 7th edn 1859).

The modern form of the Classical Tripos dates from 1879, when it was divided into two parts. Part I, as we saw in Chapter 1, included language and literature, rather like Mods; Part II consisted of five separate courses in literature and criticism, philosophy, history, archaeology, and philology. The highly specialized nature of Part II was progressively accentuated over the next twenty years by the reduction in the number of sections which could be offered by a candidate for examination, and by the reform of 1895 by which the literature section, which had initially been compulsory, became optional. Its range was wider than that of Greats, but it was a specialized rather than an integrated course. The optional status of Part II (as we have seen, it was not needed for a degree till 1918) proved almost fatal, as its numbers by the 1890s were pathetically small—except, embarrassingly, among the women (Breay 1999). Public schoolboys came up to read Classics, went through more of what they had had at school, then took their degree after Part I, or perhaps changed to another tripos. The Tripos continues in much the same form today.[26] Group X, an interdisciplinary course, began in the 1980s.[27] In its transcending of specialization it might be thought to approach the nature of Greats, though one of its founders has referred to Greats as 'a glorious white elephant' (Beard 1999, 133). The attitude this suggests comes quite close, paradoxically enough, to the Oxonian delight in being behind the (modern) times. Matthew Arnold famously eulogized Oxford in *Essays in Criticism* (1865) as the 'home of lost causes, and forsaken beliefs, and unpopular names, and impossible loyalties'. More prosaically, the author of a guide to student life in Oxford remarked that:

It is sometimes said that our university, compared with Cambridge, is antiquated, unenterprising, and 'behind the times'. In the modicum of truth which gives force to such criticisms, may be found the secret of Oxford culture.   (Lefroy 1878, 71)

To summarize, then, the two courses had in common in the last century a basis in the teaching of language and literature; and both of them offered a path from that to the study of history and philosophy. But the status of the basis was different in each case. In Cambridge, it was in effect a full course, sufficient unto itself, to which the specialist sections of Part II were optional add-ons. In Oxford, Moderations was merely a stepping-stone to Greats. Their status also differed. In Cambridge, Classics emerged in, and long remained under, the shadow of mathematics. Not until the late 1850s was it autonomous, and even then it was never to acquire the status of Greats as the university's premier course. In Oxford, Classics dominated university examinations from their foundation. This status surely provided a fruitful basis for the expansive, integrated nature of Greats. Similarly we might suspect a link between the second-rank status of Classics in Cambridge and the more specialized curriculum which evolved there.

---

[26] In 1918 the label *section* was replaced by *group*—perhaps connoting integration rather than division. One might even detect an Oxonian influence in the new terminology—perhaps imported via Henry Jackson of Trinity College, Regius Professor of Greek 1906–21, who spearheaded the reform. See 'Comparison, Contact, and Complications', below, for Jackson's Oxford links.

[27] A characteristic product is Beard and Henderson 1995.

A Mutual Regard: Contemporary Comparisons

Comparisons between the two universities belong to their history, and have a history of their own. The opinion given by the adolescent John Conington in 1843 was quoted in Chapter 1: Cambridge aimed for discipline, Oxford for culture. It is unclear just which parts of the curriculum Conington had in mind, but in the case of Cambridge it must have included mathematics, since at that point the Classical Tripos was only accessible to those with high mathematical honours. William Whewell, master of Trinity College, Cambridge, wrote in similar terms in 1840 to his friend Julius Hare:

> You say that the Oxford men have come forwards more strenuously than we have in this attempt to purify and elevate the current principles of action. True: but they have come forwards before they know what they have to say.[28]

Both of the above comments were made in the wake of the controversy provoked by the Tractarians in Oxford, and so have to be evaluated as part of that moment.[29]

Others went into more detail on curriculum and pedagogy. Charles Merivale remarked that where 'Oxford professed to cultivate the study of the ancient literature, Cambridge's [aim] was to acquire the most accurate appreciation of the ancient languages' (Merivale 1898, 102). Merivale's testimony is supported by that of the classical archaeologist Percy Gardner, recollecting in the tranquillity of old age in the early 1930s his undergraduate career at Cambridge in the 1860s; his testimony is valuable because he had taught at both universities.

> The system of Shillito [sic] and other noted teachers of classics was to lay all the stress on words, and to neglect the subject matter of the ancient writers. Exact scholarship was the one thing they aimed at. They liked to see a man, as they put it, translate through a brick wall, turn classical phrases into elegant English, and English prose into readable Greek and Latin, without troubling oneself what was the full bearing of the passage.[30]

As we saw in Chapter 1, T. E. Page, who was at Cambridge a few years after Gardner, fiercely defended the system they had gone through against the reform proposals which led to the addition of Part II. Jackson himself had inherited a developmental conception of the Platonic dialogues based on the work of Schleiermacher, and transmitted through Julius Hare and through his own teacher William Hepworth Thompson. In the present context, it is worth noting that in one of the prefaces to his translation of Plato's dialogues the Oxford classicist Benjamin Jowett criticized

---

[28] Whewell to J. C. Hare, 5 November 1840. Trinity College Library, Add. MS a 215/52. Quoted by permission of the Master and Fellows of Trinity College, Cambridge.

[29] In 1838, when the controversy was it its height, Cambridge men referred to Oxford's 'New-mania': H. G. Liddell to H. W. Acland, 23 April 1838, Christ Church Library, MS 348.

[30] P. Gardner, *Autobiographica* (Oxford, 1933), 13. 'Translating through a brick wall' can be traced back at least as far as George Burges' article on 'English scholarship in its rise, progress and decay' in the *Church of England Quarterly Review*, 1838, 98.

Jackson for focusing too much on individual passages and thus failing to appreciate the unity of individual dialogues.[31]

The Rough and the Smooth: Oxford and Cambridge Styles

In this section the analysis is broadened to consider social and intellectual styles more generally, as identified both within the universities and without. From the 1850s on, the major focus for public comparisons of the two universities was provided by the annual Boat Race. Hence such comments as the following, which taken out of context might be thought to refer to dress styles: 'The Oxford and Cambridge styles used to be palpably different to the eye by the height of the feather'; 'The feather was cleaner than that of Cambridge.'[32] Characterizations (and stereotypes) are also to be found in fiction: first in novels, in the twentieth century also in films. In some cases these fictional representations are 'without' in more than one sense: beyond the boundaries not just of Oxbridge, but of Britain. The exploits of Oxonians abroad are better known, largely because of their involvement with the British Empire (Symonds 1986); but Cambridge examples can be found, as in the novel *The Ebb-tide* (1894) written by R. L. Stevenson and his son-in-law Lloyd Osbourne. This concerns a group of young Englishmen stranded in the South Seas: they were 'the three most miserable English-speaking men in Tahiti…yet not one of them had figured in a court of justice; two were of kindly virtues; and one had a tattered Virgil in his pocket'. From that rhetorical tricolon we might infer that the habitual reader of Virgil constitutes the moral apex of this miserable triangle. I ascribe this example to Cambridge because one of the three had a boat which he called after his 'old shop', Trinity Hall. Earlier in the book one of the three, surrounded by sailors on the Thames, meets another of the trio and recognizes the style of the university man, latching on to him with relief. The novel thus offers us vignettes of the English university man stranded on a foreign shore—socially on the Thames, geographically in the South Seas. It also reminds us of the colonization of the world by the social and cultural authority which was represented by the ancient universities; a colonization usually thought of in terms of 'Oxford and Empire', but which extended perhaps beyond both of these.

For an Oxford example we can take Edmund Clerihew Bentley's celebrated detective novel of 1913, *Trent's Last Case*. It describes Trent's first meeting with Marlowe, the young secretary of the murdered millionaire Sigsbee Manderson.

---

[31] B. Jowett, *The Dialogues of Plato* (2nd edn, Oxford, 1875),1. pp. xxix–xxxvi. There are thus three levels of analysis to consider—the corpus, the dialogue, the passage—in such debates, each receiving more or less attention depending on the interpretative strategy of individual scholars.

[32] *Pall Mall Gazette*, 16 May 1865; *St James's Gazette*, 28 March 1884. Feathering is the practice of turning oars through ninety degrees when raising them out of the water, so as to decrease wind resistance; the term was later applied to aircraft propellers.

In his carriage, inelastic as weariness had made it; in his handsome, regular features; in his short, smooth, yellow hair; and in his voice as he addressed Trent, the influence of a special sort of training was confessed. 'Oxford was your play-ground, I think, my young friend', said Trent to himself. [33]

If it had been appropriate to be more specific, Bentley might have mentioned his own college, Merton. He was himself devoted to his alma mater, his devotion apparently only increased by the sense of shame he felt at gaining only a second in history in 1898. Bentley gained his degree at just the time when the numbers graduating in modern history were overtaking those in Greats. Greats was, as I mentioned in Chapter 1, for some time after that officially regarded as the premier course in the university, but in the twentieth century it increasingly became one subject among many.

Another Oxonian writer of detective novels, Edmund Crispin (the pseudonym of Bruce Montgomery) gives us a contrast between products of the two universities. His detective, Gervase Fen, is a professor of English at Oxford, and much given to spouting lines of English literature at odd moments—rather like Michael Innes' (i.e. J. I. M. Stewart's) John Appleby, though in a less mannered way. In *Frequent Hearses* (1950), Fen investigates a death at a film studio. The victim has been starring in a historical drama about Alexander Pope, for which a 'small, futile Cambridge don' called Gresson is hired as historical adviser. His stock falls when he is unable to give the date of Queen Anne's death. His only distinction is that he is constantly pursuing starlets.[34] To this fictional film one can add a real one: Alfred Hitchcock's *The Lady Vanishes* (1938). When the smooth Ruritanian officer travelling with two Englishmen is asked where he learned such excellent English, he replies 'At Oxford'. Shortly afterwards, one of them clubs him over the head, remarking 'I'm a Cambridge man myself.'[35]

Here, then, we have two contrasted styles: the smooth confidence of Oxford, the rough energy of Cambridge.[36] Of course the Stevenson example leaves Cambridge undercharacterized, but in a way that is the point: in the shadow of its more prestigious rival, the Cambridge character is often difficult to identify, and sometimes seems to be simply a lack of Oxonian grace. No wonder Thackeray, a Cambridge man, placed his hero in Oxbridge rather than in Camford.

Comparison, Contact, and Complication

Within Oxford and Cambridge themselves, comparisons were often made of their different intellectual styles. The typical contrast which emerges from such comments

---

[33] Bentley, 1937, 48. Bentley wisely does not try to explain how Marlowe's regularity of features and hair colour can be attributed to his Oxford training.

[34] 'He conceived the studios to be a kind of stalking-ground for the pandemic Venus... [he was] immitigably ensnared by lubricious fancies.' *Frequent Hearses* (London, 1950), 58.

[35] The English 'clubman' was Caldicott, played by Naunton Wayne.

[36] The comparison has even been applied to the modes of opening a boiled egg: delicately picked apart in Oxford, sliced across in Cambridge. See the correspondence in the *Times* in November 1934.

is that Oxford men enjoyed arguing about large metaphysical questions on which they split hairs and chopped logic, while Cantabs were more down to earth. The Eton master William Johnson (later Cory), who was at Cambridge in the 1840s with Henry Maine, described in 1847 a visit Maine had just made to him at Eton, two years after they had graduated:

> We went through several hard subjects in the old Cambridge way, in that method of minute comparison of opinions, without argument which I believe to be peculiar to the small intellectual aristocracy of Cambridge.[37]

This is, I think, the first occurrence of the phrase 'intellectual aristocracy', which has been given general currency by a well-known paper by Noel Annan.[38] Johnson's account is supported, in a way which harks back to Conington's comparison, by Leslie Stephen in his biography of his friend Henry Fawcett. 'The dominant influences of Cambridge in those days', he writes, referring to the mid-1850s, 'were indeed favourable to a masculine but limited type of understanding'. Later on he offers an illuminating comparison of Fawcett with William Gladstone:

> Mr Gladstone...was as typical a representative of the Oxford which obeyed the impulse of Newman, as Fawcett of the comparatively plain, practical, and downright Cambridge. Mr Gladstone's astonishing versatility of mind...was a source of wondering amusement to Fawcett's strong, but comparatively limited intellect. He was rather scandalised than amused by the singular subtlety and ingenuity in presenting unexpected interpretations of apparently plain doctrines which makes the history of Mr Gladstone's opinions so curious a subject for the psychologist.[39]

Elsewhere, Stephen declared that Gladstone 'with his great abilities somewhat marred by over-acuteness and polish, is an excellent type of the Oxford mind'.[40] Gladstone, of course, was at Oxford at a time, around 1830, when Aristotle had still to be joined, if not dethroned, by Plato.[41] The passionate exactitude, pedantry even, which an Oxford training in Aristotelian logic could produce was exemplified in his reply when asked where the followers of Peel should sit in the House of Commons: 'Taking a seat is an external sign and pledge that ought to follow upon full conviction of the thing it is understood to betoken' (Young 1948, 55).

To mention Gladstone, however, is to invoke a unique phenomenon, and one which reminds us that individuals had their own styles. Not all Oxonians were clones of their alma mater—who was herself internally various. Another example which illustrates

---

[37] *Extracts from the Journals of W. Cory*, selected by F. W. Cornish (London, 1897), 46. The extract is headed 'Eton, 1847'.

[38] 'The intellectual aristocracy', now most easily available as the final chapter of his *The Dons* (Annan 1999).

[39] L. Stephen, *Life of Henry Fawcett* (London, 1885), 90, 244.

[40] L Stephen, *Sketches from Cambridge* (London, 1865, repr. 1932), 95.

[41] For a discussion of Coleridge's dictum that 'Every man is born an Aristotelian, or a Platonist' in relation to the contrast between Oxford and Cambridge, see Newsome 1974, 73–8.

the complicating effect of idiosyncrasy comes from a letter written by Roger Fry to his friend James Headlam in 1887. Fry was staying in Lucerne with another friend, James McTaggart, a keen Hegelian from Trinity College, Cambridge. In his letter he reports a visit from the brothers Schiller, of Balliol and Magdalen:

[they] rejoice in the title of 'intelligent Philistines' and make great capital out of McTaggart who has been staying here and whom I fear they rather hate...[There was an] incessant storm of argument...I fear poor McT. had rather a hard time of it. It is very interesting to me to find how totally different the Oxford point of view is to ours [:] it is so essentially critical in the sense rather of disbelieving in every thing than of sympathetic criticism. The elder brother believes in ghosts and scientific politics & in nothing else as far as I can see.[42]

Here Hegelian idealism, which was much more at home in Oxford, is represented by a Cambridge man, while the cutting knives of scepticism are wielded by Oxonians.[43]

These contrasts have to do with intellectual style, but of course this can be related to the social style which is so often intertwined with it. Gladstone was a remarkable orator as well as a remarkable constructor of intellectual patterns—a point hinted at in Stephen's reference to his 'presenting' interpretations. It was Oxford that had the orators; it was precisely in 'presenting' ideas that the Oxonians scored. One might say that Oxford typically produced public, Cambridge private men.

Another witness who knew both places was Alexander Macmillan, who after selling books in Cambridge for a decade became publisher to Oxford University Press in 1863. Macmillan declared in 1864 that:

There is a very marked Oxford manner...[a] fine gentlemanliness...[the] Cambridge manner—opener and more manly (aliter, rougher and less gentlemanly).[44]

Henry Jackson wrote in much the same vein in 1913, responding to a friend who had remarked what an attractive scholar Gilbert Murray was:

I think that Oxford is very successful in breeding 'attractive' scholars: more than Cambridge. And this is not surprising. For we dare not talk our shop in a mixed company, and even in a scholars' party we are very conscious of our limitations as specialists.[45]

Jackson's knowledge of Oxford came largely from his membership of the joint dining club called the Ad Eundem, a title taken from the formula with which the two universities recognized the validity of each other's degrees.[46] He had been going to its dinners since 1869, and thus had more than forty years' experience of discussions which must

---

[42] Roger Fry to James Headlam [August 1887], Headlam papers, Churchill Archives Centre, Cambridge.
[43] For another surprising contrast of this kind, see my discussion of J. W. Headlam and J. W. Mackail: 1998a, 242–6.
[44] C. L. Graves, *Life and Letters of Alexander Macmillan* (London, 1910), 228–9.
[45] Henry Jackson to J. A. Platt, 15 August 1913: Parry 1926, 184–5.
[46] The club was founded in 1864 by William Sidgwick, fellow of Merton College, Oxford, whose brother Henry was at Cambridge; their brother Arthur moved from Cambridge to Oxford . Since 1862 it had been possible to travel by rail between the two university cities.

often have included a comparing of notes—especially on the two great issues which hung over both places from the 1870s to the early 1920s, the admission of women and the status of compulsory Greek. Others also had sufficient experience of both places to compare them. Some were brothers—Charles and Christopher Wordsworth, William, Henry, and Arthur Sidgwick, for example. Some moved from one place to the other, as in the case of Percy Gardner. In other cases, the gap was bridged by friendship. Oscar Wilde and his friend Robert Ross engaged in a running argument, half serious, half jesting, about the relative merits of Oxford, Wilde's own university, and Ross's Cambridge, which Wilde referred to as 'a kind of preparatory institution for Oxford'. Ross wrote an essay called 'The Brand of Isis' which Linda Dowling has called 'the amusing protest of a Cambridge man at the Oxford ascendancy' (Ross 1909; Dowling 1994, 119 n. 18). (In the light of my comments on Gladstone, it is interesting to see that in his essay Ross claims the Grand Old Man for Cambridge: 'Mr Gladstone intellectually always seemed to me a Cambridge man in his energy, his enthusiasm, his political outlook. Only in his High Church proclivities is he suspect').[47] Further investigation on a wider front would, I think, show that this case is typical, in that the Cambridge literature talks of Oxford, while in Oxford, Cambridge is rarely mentioned. The same might also be said of the Scottish universities. During a visit to Edinburgh in 1866, Benjamin Jowett met the university's professor of Greek, John Stuart Blackie, who told him, 'I hope you in Oxford don't think we hate you.' Jowett replied, 'We don't think about you.'[48]

In 1910 Sir Frederick Pollock wrote as follows in an obituary for his friend Arthur Butler, Italian scholar and mountaineer, and Eighth Classic at Cambridge in 1867:

He was...a typical and excellent Cambridge scholar, determined that whatever he made himself answerable for should be thoroughly done as far as it went, and choosing at need rather to narrow the limits of his work than to run any risk of not knowing exactly what he was doing.[49]

A nice example of the ties which bind and which provoke comparison can be found in Gladstone's correspondence with his brother-in-law Lord Lyttelton. Gladstone had gained a double first at Oxford in 1831, Lyttelton was Senior Classic at Cambridge in 1838. In 1839 they were married to the Glynne sisters in a double wedding; later that year they were asked to act as examiners for the Newcastle scholarship at Eton, founded four years previously. On 16 November 1839, Lyttelton wrote to Gladstone:

I would prefer that you should take the Divinity paper, the Latin prose paper (I mean from Latin into English) & the general paper, which I imagine ought to be partly historical or antiquarian, partly grammatical & perhaps ought to bear in some measure upon general philosophical views of antiquity, & recognized and notable modern theories, such as Niebuhr's and Thirlwall's

[47] Ross 1909, 37. The essay was originally published in 1902.
[48] Abbott and Campbell 1897, 1.399; cf. Wallace 2006, 246, 261 n. 12.
[49] F. Pollock, 'Arthur Butler', *Cambridge Review* 31 (1909–10), 315.

on Roman and Greek history, the Homeric Question etc. It is an old quarrel of mine with the Cambridge system as at present worked, that it produces hardly any of such knowledge; & feeling my deficiency, I propose that branch to your Oxonian self.... I should then have the Greek papers, and the Latin verse.[50]

The example of Gladstone—acclaimed as Oxonian, claimed as Cantabrigian, yet triumphantly *sui generis*—should remind us not to reify the notion of institutional styles. We have already seen in Chapter 1 how Richard Jebb and J. C. Stobart reacted against Cambridge specialization. Jebb had attempted to teach modern as well as ancient Greek during his tenure of the chair of Greek at Glasgow; and though best known for his work on Sophocles, had energetically supported the foundation of the British School of Archaeology in Athens (2013a).

As a final example of the knowledge boundaries set up in Cambridge, consider the case of Francis Cornford. Cornford was inspired by Jane Harrison to look at the assumptions underlying explicit philosophical systems; his first book, *Thucydides Mythistoricus*, dealt with the influence of contemporary medical thought and terminology on Thucydides. Yet he never referred in his writing to the modern philosophical work carried on in his lifetime, some of it by fellow fellows of Trinity like Moore, Whitehead, Russell, and Wittgenstein. The next generation of Cambridge ancient philosophers (W. K. C. Guthrie, G. S. Kirk, J. E. Raven) were positively antagonistic to attempts to liaise with practitioners of philosophy.[51] In the case of Whitehead and Russell's work in mathematical logic, or of Wittgenstein's in epistemology, one could understand this; but Moore's ethics and Whitehead's writing on metaphysics and religion would surely have appealed to Cornford. We know, however, that Cornford was a reserved person who did not mix much with the other fellows of his college. In company he tended to listen rather than talk. So perhaps, as with Gladstone from whom we began, we have to allow for the relative autonomy of the individual. There are certainly Cambridge classical scholars who might have been happier at Oxford: the most obvious example is perhaps the historian, Baptist, and popularizer T. R. Glover, the nearest thing Cambridge could offer to Oxford's A. E. Zimmern.[52]

In making the kind of inter-institutional comparison I am exploring here, we are confronted with what used to be called Galton's problem: that comparison of distinct entities is contaminated by their interaction. Oxford and Cambridge dons not only interacted with each other, they also frequently compared the curricula, pedagogies, and styles of the two places. There were several mechanisms for this. I have already mentioned that some dons moved from one to another. There were joint dining clubs

[50] British Library, Add. MS 44238, 16 Nov. 1839. Drafts of the examination timetable and papers are at Add. MS 44729, ff. 1–13.

[51] This point was emphasized to me by Myles Burnyeat, another Oxbridge migrant: formerly Professor of Ancient Philosophy at Cambridge, later a fellow of All Souls College, Oxford. It had earlier been made by a Cambridge classicist turned philosopher, Renford Bambrough, in a BBC talk about Cornford entitled 'The beginning of wisdom' given on the Third Programme on 26 April 1953. (Bambrough's script is preserved at the BBC's Written Archives Centre at Caversham.)

[52] On Glover see Wood 1953; on Zimmern, see Millett 2007.

like the Ad Eundem club, mentioned above, founded by Henry and William Sidgwick and their friends in the winter of 1864–5; Henry Jackson became its mainstay after Henry Sidgwick's death in 1900. And at crucial points when curriculum change was mooted, hasty checks were carried out on the other place, to gather evidence of what might be copied, because it was a good idea, or avoided, because it was not locally practised.[53] In the extensive debates on the classical curriculum in Cambridge in the late 1860s, a standard conservative argument was that both places had their own distinctive styles of work: philosophical in Oxford, philological in Cambridge. Students could thus choose which they preferred—where they had the information and the freedom of action needed for choice—which, as I have suggested above, rather few in fact possessed.

It has been claimed that schools sent their best classicists to Oxford, the less good to Cambridge. That would have made sense while the mathematics bar was in place in Cambridge, that is, until 1854. After that, however, such decisions would have better been made on pupils' potentials for different *kinds* of work (2013a, 190–1). We have already seen that Percy Gardner lamented going to the wrong place. More famously, A. E. Housman, who failed Greats, perhaps at his own provocation, would surely have done better in Cambridge. The story is a familiar one, so I summarize: Housman gained a first in Mods, then devoted himself to textual study, and in his Greats exam sent in such pathetically inadequate answers that instead of being given a fourth, as some others were, he was failed outright (Naiditch 1988, 191–203). How good the schools were at such strategic decisions is another question. Charles Stevens was a high-achieving pupil at Winchester College, skilled at the language-centred scholarship which still dominated classical teaching there just after the First World War. In 1922, he went up to New College and gained a first in Mods, but then collapsed to a third in Greats. The austere rigours of analytic philosophy, especially as practised by his tutor H. W. B. Joseph, were too much for him. His friend the ancient historian John Myres wrote of him that the catastrophe of his Greats marks scarred him for life (1998d, 2–7). Similarly, the celebrated Greek scholar J. D. Denniston, author of a standard work on Greek particles, who narrowly missed succeeding Gilbert Murray in the Regius chair of Greek in 1936, had achieved only a second-class degree in Greats after a first in Moderations.[54] How many others suffered in this way it is hard to know, partly because the interaction between schools and universities is so little researched. But it is clear that, as in Gardner's case and probably also Stevens's, some public schools established channels of migration with one place or the other and then cultivated them. We thus have a picture of the fundamental flaws in the two systems: at Oxford you could be sucked into a curriculum which first repeated what you had done at school, then hurled you into new fields where you might wither and die. In Cambridge the mathematics requirement could prevent your even getting into classics, unless you

---

[53] See for example the correspondence between Leonard Whibley of Cambridge and Alfred Godley of Oxford on the Compulsory Greek issue in the 1900s (Whibley papers, Pembroke College, Cambridge).

[54] C. M. Bowra, 'John Dewar Denniston', *Proceedings of the British Academy* 35 (1949), 219–32.

gained a high level of knowledge of a very different subject of which you might have learned very little at school.

The picture of Oxford men as more comfortable in society fits well with the university's dominance in the public life of nation and empire. The statistics of imperial appointments, civil service personnel, and bishoprics tell their own story. To take the cabinet as an example, in the period from 1812 to 1940, only between 1828 and 1841 were there more Cambridge members than there were Oxonians (Curthoys 1997, 481). From Jowett's Balliol a conveyor belt took graduates to the higher reaches of the home civil service and to the administration of the Empire. Cambridge had a part in this, but it was both smaller and less organized. Overall, the public profile of Oxford was much higher than that of Cambridge. And from at least the 1850s until the Great War, Greats symbolized Oxford, and was regarded as its premier course. Did this lead to complacency? It is true that the Oxford classical dons managed to make changes in a way which their Cantabrigian colleagues found impossible. The obvious explanation is that the classicists were in a majority at Oxford, a minority at Cambridge. The failure of Part II of the Cambridge Classical Tripos in the 1890s was a publicly admitted fact which its teachers were powerless to do anything about: when they tried, they were outvoted.

Conclusion

I have attempted above to compare the two most prestigious and influential institutional versions of classics in nineteenth-century England. At Oxford classics was dominant, and Greats acknowledged as the university's premier course. The examination tested knowledge of set books which were chosen by students from an official list. Language and literature (Moderations or 'Mods') served as a basis for an integrated course in history and philosophy (*Literae Humaniores* or 'Greats'). The heavy emphasis on Aristotle in the earlier part of the century gave way after the 1850s to a focus on Plato. In Cambridge, the Classical Tripos emerged in the shadow of a well-established and prestigious mathematics course, and gained autonomy only in the late 1850s. Its division into two parts produced a course which superficially resembled the Oxford curriculum, but Part II, itself divided into options, was hamstrung until 1918 by the availability of a degree after Part I.[55]

The Oxford man might be seen as a reflection of Aristotle's great-souled man, of Plato's guardian, or as an amalgam of the two. In any case, he was typically comfortable with a place in the public sphere, projecting an image of effortless learning. His Cambridge counterpart preferred the back room, where he worked strenuously to fulfil restricted objectives and specialized tasks. He knew more about the classical languages, but less about literature, then his Oxonian opposite number. Here we have, then, the 'rough' and the 'smooth'. The larger picture in which such comparisons must be

[55] For a discussion of the suggestion that the Classical Tripos was a 'parochial anomaly', see 2001a.

located includes the two universities' religious history. Tractarianism, which emerged and occupied minds at Oxford in the 1830s and 40s, had little impact in Cambridge, where fervour ran in Broad Church channels and dissenters could matriculate, though not take degrees. Indeed, among the Tractarians to 'Cambridgize' became a term of opprobrium, rather like 'protestantize' or 'Miltonize' (Nockles 1997, 211).

In both cases, we need to distinguish ideological projections from reality. In Oxford, as Ian Small has suggested (Small 1991), Pater and Wilde may have been reacting against a perceived turn to professionalized scholarship, of which their writing was respectively subversive (Pater) and transgressive (Wilde). Similarly, what has been called 'Cambridge ritualism'—the work of Jane Harrison and her associates—could be seen as an attempt to raise an integrated chthonic vision against the specialized respectability of the Tripos.[56] Their path might thus be seen as parallel to that of Frazer, who began with a dissertation on Plato and went over to the wild side of antiquity when his eye was caught by the *Golden Bough*. Here again the religious context has to be taken into account: a concern to subvert conventional Christian belief was certainly present in Frazer's work, as it was in the writing of Arthur Verrall and perhaps with Harrison herself. But as in the case of Gladstone, we have to allow for individual and idiosyncratic variations on institutional themes.

---

[56] On the nature of the 'Ritualists', see Beard 2000, 109–28.

3

Thomas Gaisford

Legion, Legend, Lexicographer

Gaisford was legion, for he was many. He was in fact a pluralist (appropriately enough) in more than one sense. First, he held more than one ecclesiastical position. He was Rector of Westwell, Oxfordshire 1815–47, prebendary of St Paul's and of Llandaff 1823–55, canon of Worcester 1825–9 and of Durham 1829–31, and Dean of Christ Church, Oxford (an institution which was at once cathedral and college), 1831–55 (Figure 3.1). Secondly, he occupied several university posts in Oxford: Delegate of the Clarendon Press from 1807, and Regius Professor of Greek and Curator of the Bodleian Library from 1812. All three posts were held, along with his college headship, until his death in 1855. He thus occupied all four posts simultaneously for nearly a quarter of a century.

Gaisford was a legend: for if he is remembered today, it is for something he almost certainly never said, supposedly in the conclusion to a sermon:

Nor can I do better, in conclusion, than impress upon you the study of Greek literature, which not only elevates above the vulgar herd, but leads not infrequently to positions of considerable emolument.

This is what might be called the classical form of the anecdote, reported by William Tuckwell (New College, 1848–58) in his *Reminiscences of Oxford* (Tuckwell 1900, 124), and now enshrined in the *Oxford Dictionary of Quotations*.[1] A splendidly absurd and blasphemous supplement, 'both in this world and the next' has also circulated, and is discussed in the final section of this chapter.

The third and final term of my subtitle celebrates Gaisford's involvement with dictionary making. He brought out editions of several late-antique lexica, encouraged Liddell and Scott in the making of their *Greek-English Lexicon* (1843), and as we shall see, thought long and hard about increasing the user friendliness of dictionaries.

In 1885, Gilbert Murray, then an undergraduate at St John's College, founded a Gaisford Society, but it seems not to have lasted long and has left almost no trace.[2]

---

[1] *ODQ* has been an important carrier of such anecdotes: see Elizabeth Knowles, 'Intelligent elasticity: the early years of the *Oxford Dictionary of Quotations*', *Dictionaries* 25 (2004) 65–76; 'History of the Dictionary', *Oxford Dictionary of Quotations*, 7th edn, 2009, pp. xiii–xviii.

[2] The only reference I know is by J. U. Powell in 1932: Lehnus 2012, 268–9.

Figure 3.1 Thomas Gaisford (1779–1855), a portrait painted *c.*1847 by Henry William Pickersgill (1782–1875). Christ Church, University of Oxford, LPE 264.
By permission of the Governing Body of Christ Church, Oxford.

What keeps Gaisford's name alive in Oxford today is the succession of awards made from the fund established in his memory. One might think that in 1856, the year after his death, it was natural and appropriate to found a Greek composition prize in his memory. In fact it was singularly inappropriate, since Gaisford himself was not at all interested in such things: his own work was focused on the editing of ancient texts. When he became Dean of Christ Church, he brought a long tradition of prizes for

Latin elegiacs to an end by the simple ploy of not setting topics.[3] It was however highly convenient to found such a prize, since the existing classical prizes and scholarships were either general, or restricted to Latin. The prize thus honoured Gaisford's memory while filling a rather obvious gap. The Gaisford Prize has had a roll call of distinguished winners: in real life they include John Beazley in 1907, for his Herodotean account of a visit to the Zoo; in fiction, four years later, Max Beerbohm's lovelorn Duke of Dorset in his Oxford novel *Zuleika Dobson* (Beerbohm 1911, 26). When Beerbohm wrote, the dukedom was conveniently extinct (it had been since 1843), and he was probably unaware that the fourth Duke had been a pupil of Gaisford's, and a promising one, not long before his premature death in 1815. The recent history of the prize is complicated. In 1974, in the face of declining numbers of entries, the statute was revised: prizes were to be given for essays, and the annual Gaisford lecture was founded. A reserve clause allowed the award of a prize for composition but in practice it lapsed, to be revived in the 1990s. In 2002 another statute revision removed this clause; composition prizes have, nevertheless, continued to be awarded.

Gaisford's name, then, is heard: but little is remembered of the man and his work. My aim in this chapter is to rescue Thomas Gaisford not so much from the condescension of posterity as from a mixture of ignorance and indifference. I shall bear in mind that many readers will be more interested in his career as a classical scholar than in his work for the Clarendon Press or the Bodleian Library; but also that most of the books and manuscripts he bought and catalogued for the Bodleian, and commissioned for the Press, were classical in nature. The best existing account of Gaisford (Lloyd-Jones 1982), concentrated on its subject's classical scholarship, but also briefly discussed his work as curator, delegate, and college head. I shall cover the same ground but in different ways, asking some different questions, and using evidence which was either inaccessible to Lloyd-Jones or not used by him.[4]

Thomas Gaisford was born in Iford in Wiltshire in 1779, the son of a rich cloth merchant and a clergyman's daughter. He was schooled at Hyde Abbey School in Winchester, a private academy run by Revd Charles Richards which seems to have had a good reputation;[5] a dozen of its alumni appear in the *Dictionary of National Biography*, and Gaisford was preceded by George Canning and followed by Thomas Bowdler. Richards, known as 'Flogging Richards', was notorious for his harsh punishments; an old boy wrote home from India many years later, 'I am among savages, it is true, but none so savage as old Richards' (Bell 1846, 42). Gaisford entered Christ Church in 1797 as a commoner: what in other colleges would have been called a

---

[3] They were sent in for recitation in Lent term. The practice had flourished in the eighteenth century, when two collections of verses were published: Thompson 1900, 143.

[4] I have drawn in particular on the Order Books of the Delegates of the Clarendon Press (OUP archive), the Elmsley papers (Westminster School), the Burney family papers (Beinecke Library, Yale), and the family papers made available by Patrick Gaisford-St Lawrence: Christ Church archives, SOC xxiii.c.10.

[5] Surprisingly, it is not mentioned in A. F. Leach's chapter on education in the *Victoria County History* (Leach 1903). It went back at least to the early nineteenth century; the school accounts for 1807–28 survive in Hampshire County Record Office

pensioner, that is, an ordinary paying undergraduate, ranking above a servitor or poor student, but below a nobleman or gentleman commoner. In 1800 he was elevated to the status of student, in other words, put on the foundation, by the nomination of the Dean, Cyril Jackson.[6] He graduated in 1801, just before the first examination under the new university examination statute, held in December of that year; later he acted as a tutor, Robert Peel being among his pupils, though they do not seem to have got on very well. From 1809 to 1811, with considerable reluctance, he acted as a university examiner. In March 1809 he wrote to Charles Burney:

I have been prevailed upon to accept the office of public examiner for the coming year—much to my annoyance & discomfort. O the mountains of dialectic & such trash that I shall have to cross before the month of November next. You will I hope condole me for the amount of time which is to be so ill, so unprofitably spent.[7]

Here we catch a glimpse of a Gaisfordian leitmotiv which will reappear: the concern to be left alone to practise scholarship, free from other duties.

From 1805 a series of classical editions began to appear from his hand. The earliest were re-edited compilations of other men's work, but in 1810 came his edition of Hephaestion on metres, and in 1812 Gaisford was appointed Regius Professor of Greek by the Crown.[8] A better scholar, Peter Elmsley, six years older, was fatally disadvantaged by being a known liberal who had contributed to the *Edinburgh Review*, a journal whose attacks on Oxford in 1808–10 had not been forgotten (cf. Chapters 2 and 6). In gaining the chair, Gaisford became *ex officio* both a Curator of the Bodleian Library and a Delegate of the Clarendon Press, but he had already been appointed a Delegate in 1807, probably as a result of his making the first catalogue of the university's Greek MSS in the previous year. From 1825 to 1829 he served as canon of Worcester, and in 1829, while declining the bishopric of Oxford, felt obliged to accept a rich canonry at Durham, perhaps under pressure from his wife, whose uncle William Van Mildert was the Prince-Bishop. Two years later, he managed to exchange this position for the deanery of Christ Church. His wife, with whom he had five children, had died in 1830, and in 1832 he married Jane Jenkyns, sister of the Master of Balliol. Gaisford ruled the House

[6] Christ Church consisted at that point of a Dean, eight canons and 101 students (fellows). The co-existence of canons and students reflected Christ Church's hybrid status as both college and cathedral. For its history see Curthoys 2012, the first volume in a planned trilogy.
[7] Gaisford to C. Burney, 8 March [1809], Christ Church MS 436.
[8] The year of election has been variously reported. The *Historical Register of the University of Oxford* (1888), p. 49 dates it to 1811, followed by M. G. Brock (Brock 1997, 55); the *Gentleman's Magazine* reported the appointment to the chair in its issue of Mar. 1812 (p. 287), but in its obituary of Gaisford (July 1855, pp. 99–100) stated that he was elected in 1811. Boase's *Modern English Biography* (1.1115) dates the appointment firmly, but without a source, to 29 Feb. 1812. According to *ODNB*, Gaisford's predecessor William Jackson held the chair till 1811, but was consecrated Bishop of Oxford on 23 Feb. 1812. The matter is settled by an announcement in the *London Gazette*, no. 16578, issue of 25–9 Feb. 1812, p. 381: 'His Royal Highness [the Prince Regent] has...been pleased...to grant to the Rev. Thomas Gaisford, Master of Arts, the office or place of Reader or Professor of Greek in the University of Oxford. Whitehall, February 29th, 1812.'

till his death in 1855, when he was succeeded by his pupil and fellow-lexicographer Henry Liddell.

The Classical Scholar

As a glance at any academic library catalogue will reveal, Gaisford was very prolific— there are over thirty books to his name. The word 'chalcenteric' has been applied to him, and he certainly made a habit of tackling large and difficult projects. He began by assembling other men's work on Cicero and making school editions of Euripides for Westminster, a school with close ties to Christ Church, but then homed in, after his work on Hephaestion (1810), on ancient lexicography, focusing on the great compilations of late antiquity: *Suidas* (1834) and the *Etymologicum Magnum* (1848).[9] In the 1830s and 1840s he advised Liddell and Scott on their Greek-English lexicon, which was published in 1843.

Gaisford clearly thought hard about Greek lexicography: why did he not make his own lexicon? It is clear that he preferred dealing with ancient primary sources, like the two compilations I have mentioned; but his inability to use the Greek-German lexica of Schneider and of Passow must in any case have deterred him, since as he admitted to his friend Henry Fynes Clinton in 1825, 'Unfortunately I neglected many years ago to acquire a knowledge of that language [German], and consequently am shut out from a source of copious and valuable information.'[10]

Since 'considerable emoluments' feature largely in the most famous Gaisford anecdote, quoted above, something should be said of his salary. From 1800, as a student of Christ Church he would have received about £25 a year, rising with seniority to £80. The regius chair to which he was appointed in 1812 brought in only £40 a year; an amount unchanged since its foundation in 1546. Proposals within the college in the 1850s to raise this to £300 came to nothing, and it was not till 1865 that it was raised to £500.[11] Gaisford gained income from his Worcester and Durham canonries, especially the latter (his stall, the eleventh, was known as the Golden Stall); and his income as Dean of Christ Church was probably in excess of £2,500.[12]

---

[9] His MS transcript of the Galean MS of Photius in Trinity College Library was presented to Christ Church in 1896 and is now MS 453. It is unlikely to been made direct, since there is no record at Trinity of a loan having been made; probably he was lent a transcription by Porson, with whom he was in contact, and who visited Oxford on at least one occasion (Watson 1861, 284, 304).

[10] Gaisford to Clinton, 2 Aug. 1825 (Christ Church MS 498). Gaisford got Liddell to translate a review by Gottfried Hermann so that he could read it: Thompson 1899, 24–5.

[11] The Cambridge chair (also worth £40 p.a., since its foundation in 1540) was augmented in 1848 with an Ely canonry worth £600 p.a. The low salary of the Oxford chair was deplored by John Selby Watson as 'no great honour to so wealthy a country as this' (Watson 1861, 112: for Watson, headmaster, biographer and murderer, see 2004e).

[12] *Report of Oxford University Commission* (1852), 1.233. The Golden Stall appears to have brought in over £4000 p.a.

In his forty-three years as Regius Professor Gaisford never lectured, the last holder of the chair not to do so.[13] Within Christ Church, however, his influence can be seen in the work of four men, of whom Fynes Clinton, two years younger than Gaisford, was the oldest. Clinton recorded that amid an almost useless formal teaching system, he had gained a lot from the conversation of Gaisford and John Symmons (Clinton 1854, 8). Clinton's great works, the *Fasti Hellenici* of 1824–34 and the *Fasti Romani* of 1845–50, carried the Gaisfordian chalcenteric style into civil and literary chronology. The subject matter was new, but the principle was the same as Gaisford's, of collecting the primary evidence on which analysis could be based. To this Clinton added his own obsessive hyperempiricism—for example, he counted the number of pages of Greek and Latin read each day, recording that during his undergraduate career he had read 'about 5,223' pages (Clinton 1854, 23).

Gaisford's pupil John Cramer was fourteen years younger than his tutor. His major publications, like Clinton's, extended the Gaisford style into a new field: his geographical and historical descriptions of ancient Italy (1826), Greece (1828), and Asia Minor (1832) were based on ancient evidence and the reports of post-antique travellers. It may have been at Gaisford's prompting that in 1827 he offered the Press a translation of Schrevel's Greek-Latin dictionary; the project was abandoned three years later.[14]

George Cornewall Lewis was twenty-seven years younger than Gaisford; when he graduated in 1829, he had already translated Karl Otfried Mueller's *Die Dorier*, and went on to publish a critique of Niebuhr's account of Roman history (Lewis 1855). Gaisford wrote to Clinton commending Lewis as a promising scholar.[15] Both in his familiarity with German scholarship and in his use of comparative analysis, Cornewall Lewis represents a step beyond the Gaisford style. But the chalcenteric gathering of evidence is there, as is the sustained commitment to serious study—Lewis is said to have remarked that life would be tolerable were it not for its amusements.[16]

The fourth Christ Church man to be influenced by Gaisford was his successor as Dean, and very nearly as professor of Greek, Henry Liddell. Liddell was a very different kind of dean, and would surely have been a different kind of professor. In an elegant sketch of the two men, Peter Parsons has suggested that their portraits—'Gaisford's straight stare, Liddell's reflective profile'—reflect their contrasting characters (Parsons 2006, 104). Their politics, too, were very different, Gaisford being an extreme Tory and Liddell a pronounced Liberal. But both men were lexicographers; and as we shall see, Gaisford was involved in the production of Liddell and Scott's lexicon.

---

[13] In Cambridge, neither James Monk (1808–23) nor his successor Peter Dobree (1823–5) lectured, but James Scholefield (1825–53) did so regularly.

[14] The delegates paid him £400 for his time and for the material already printed. Delegates' Order Book, 2 Feb. 1827, 5 Mar. 1830.

[15] Gaisford to Clinton [1829–30] and 7 Feb. 1830: Christ Church library, MS 498.

[16] Cramer's works suggested 'a new level of seriousness in the study of ancient texts' (Murray 1997, 522–3); from 1823 to 1825 he was vice-principal of St Alban's Hall, when the principal was Peter Elmsley. Clinton was left a legacy on condition he did not enter the church; Lewis was independently wealthy and went into politics.

Gaisford and the Scholarly Community

So much for Gaisford's pupils: what of his peers? In 1805, the year he began to publish, Gaisford wrote to Charles Burney:

In Oxford, as you will know, there are very few who have studied the classics critically, and still fewer who have read the Greek poets with that care and accuracy which they deserve, so that on nice points I can expect neither advice nor assistance from any persons here.[17]

Gaisford's comment on the scholarship of his own university, made to a Cambridge man, is striking; not least, perhaps, as an anticipation of opinions publicized three years later by the *Edinburgh Review*, in what Edward Copleston of Oriel, the defender of Oxford, called their 'calumnies'.[18] The letter to Burney both explains and exemplifies Gaisford's contacts with scholars outside Oxford. In 1805 Richard Porson (whom he both met and corresponded with)[19] was still alive and accepted as the leading Greek scholar of the day (see Chapter 4). After his death in 1808 his disciples Dobree, Monk, and Blomfield kept the intense but narrow Porsonian style of scholarship alive. Elmsley, living in Kent when he was not travelling in France or Italy, worked in the same style but with greater breadth. Burney, who as a Cambridge undergraduate had been expelled for stealing books from the University Library, had rehabilitated himself and built up a large library of his own, from which he was happy to lend to other scholars. Such loans between individuals are a running theme of the letters of the men I mentioned above. Appeals were also made through intermediaries to grandees with large libraries, such as Thomas Grenville and Earl Spencer. On 30 December 1814 Gaisford wrote to Elmsley, 'Can you tell me where I can pick up a shabby copy of Calliergus's Theocritus.'[20] Five days later, Elmsley passed on the request to Thomas Grenville, whose nephew was a close friend.[21] Ten days after that, Gaisford wrote to Elmsley, 'Your kind offices with Mr Grenville have produced me not the loan of a copy of Calliergus, but the donation of a duplicate from Lord Spencer's library.'[22] These exchanges give us a vivid glimpse of the workings of this network of scholars, gentlemen, and bibliophiles. In 1815 Charles Blomfield remarked to Elmsley, 'Here is a strong bibliographical corps—besides Lord Spencer and Mr Grenville, we have Dr Burney and Mr Heber.'[23]

---

[17] Gaisford to Burney, 18 Jan 1805. Christ Church library, MS 436.
[18] It might be seen as significant that Gaisford did not contribute to that debate; but he was not inclined to join in public discussion.
[19] Gaisford to Porson, 20 Feb. 1807: National Art Library, Dyce Collection, MSL/1869/63/92.
[20] The edition of 1516 printed in Venice by Zacharias Kallierges.
[21] BL Add MS 41858, Elmsley to Grenville, 4 Jan 1815. Grenville was the uncle of Elmsley's school friend Charles Watkin Williams Wynn.
[22] Gaisford to Elmsley, 21 Jan. 1815: Elmsley papers, Westminster School.
[23] Blomfield to Elmsley, 3 January 1815: Elmsley papers. The relative weakness of the British Museum Library was bemoaned by Gaisford in 1819. Burney had left his library to the Museum, but the list of duplicates auctioned off was a short one: 'There were exceedingly few critical books brought to the hammer, which shows the penury of the Museum in that department.' Gaisford to Elmsley, 5 Apr. 1819, Elmsley papers. Burney had possessed forty-seven editions of Aeschylus, 102 of Sophocles and 166 of Euripides.

Blomfield's military metaphor, deployed in the year of Waterloo, serves to remind us that at this point the continental blockade was still in place, and communication with foreign scholars difficult; though some London booksellers had found ways of importing stock. After Waterloo, Gaisford visited Leyden several times, staying in 1816 with the classical scholar Daniel Wyttenbach, whose papers he helped to put in order after a fire, and the following year with another classicist, Jonas Bake, with whom he spent four months, after a three months' stay in Paris. In 1824 he was in The Hague attending the Meerman sale, where he bought books and manuscripts for the Bodleian. Later he stayed in Leipzig with Karl Wilhelm Dindorf, who on seeing him at his door, is said to have hugged and kissed him (Bake 1839, v–vii; Sandys 1908, 279). In 1847 he spent a month in Vienna inspecting a manuscript of Stobaeus.[24] For some years Elmsley carried out commissions for Gaisford on his own continental travels, inspecting manuscripts and arranging for collations to be made. We also gain a glimpse of a return visit, by an unnamed Jena professor (could it have been Gottfried Hermann?) in October 1815. The account is by an old Christ Church man, published thirty years later, and describes a conversation about the textual criticism of Euripides and Shakespeare. In his account, he and Gaisford join in supporting straightforward criticism and emendation against the over-interventionist German style (Anon. 1845).

Gaisford was thus linked not just to the Porsonian circle, but also to German and Dutch scholars who worked in a similar style. Not for them the grand designs of Wolf's Alterthumswissenschaft, as developed by Wolf's pupil August Boeckh. Indeed the Dutch ethos, carried from Wyttenbach through Bake to Cobet, resonated with Gaisford's own predilections in prolonging a traditional focus on close textual study.

Gaisford the Reviewer

One index of an individual's involvement in the scholarly community is their production of articles and reviews. When Gaisford began to publish in 1805 there were no classical journals in Britain, but articles and reviews frequently appeared in the *British Critic*, the *Monthly Review*, the *Edinburgh Review*, the *Gentleman's Magazine*, and other periodicals. It was long thought that Gaisford did not contribute to them.[25] In fact he did, though his cautious attitude to such publication was typical of the man. In February 1806, he offered Charles Burney a review of Walpole's *Comicorum Graecorum Fragmenta* (1805), for Burney to send to the *Monthly Review* if he liked.[26] A review

Richard Heber, who died in 1833, may have had 150,000 books in his collection; he was known for his generosity in lending to friends.

[24] Gaisford to Fynes Clinton, 14 Jan. 1848. Christ Church Library, MS 498.

[25] H. R. Luard wrote of Gaisford in 1856 that he had never contributed to the Reviews (Luard 1856), supplementing and correcting Barrow 1855. In his letter Luard assigned the review of Walpole's *Comicorum fragmenta* in the *Monthly Review* of Mar. 1806 to Dobree; but in his *DNB* entry on Gaisford (1889) he accepted that Gaisford was the author.

[26] Gaisford to Burney, 23 Feb. [1806]; Burney family papers, OSB MSs 3.701, Beinecke Library, Yale.

appeared in the March issue which was at last partly written by Gaisford.[27] On 6 March, he told Burney that he felt 'much obliged to you for your attention to the critique. Pray amend, alter, reject, or add what you think fit. The less of my own is in it the better shall I be pleased.' He added that he did not propose to review Schweighaeuser's *Athenaeus* (which Burney had presumably asked him to deal with): 'It would I fear be a work not compatible with the limits of a periodical journal, and particularly as the defects so far exceed its excellence.'[28] He did however contribute a brief review to the May number.[29]

In 1808, John Murray and his collaborators began to plan their conservative journal the *Quarterly Review*, designed as a counterweight to the liberal *Edinburgh Review*. Gaisford was on their list of possible contributors, and in 1811 the journal's founding editor William Gifford mentioned him to Edward Copleston of Oriel, his main Oxford adviser, and currently famous as the defender of Oxonian scholarship against the onslaughts of the *Edinburgh Review* (see Chapter 6). Gifford wrote, 'Heber once mentioned Mr Gaisford to me, as having undertaken to review Wittenbach', but nothing seems to have come of this.[30]

In 1810 Abraham Valpy founded the *Classical Journal*, later to be involved in hostilities with the *Museum Criticum*, established in Cambridge in 1812 by James Monk and Charles Blomfield (Chapters 4 and 7). Acting on their behalf, in 1815 Peter Elmsley tried to persuade Gaisford to contribute to the *Museum*; Gaisford replied:

Respecting the Museum Criticum. I have a great value for the work and indeed for all works of the same kind—but I have neither leisure nor inclination to contribute to it or to any other work of that kind, except so far as to point out some rare tract &c. I pointed out two or three such to Mr Valpy, one of which he printed, but completely spoiled my design by the manner in which he executed it. As a result, I have declined correspondence with Mr. Valpy.[31]

Once again, Gaisford's reluctance to enter the public arena is noticeable. As this letter indicates, he was also quick to withdraw if he was unhappy with the way his material

---

[27] *Monthly Review*, vol. 49 (Mar. 1806), pp. 225–36.The narrative voice refers back to the writer's previous reviews, so must be Burney's, but the frequent citations from Kuster's *Suidas* and from Stobaeus point to Gaisford.

[28] Gaisford to Burney, 6 Mar. [1806]. Christ Church library MS 436.

[29] *Monthly Review* 50 (June 1806), 130–3, a review of Bonar's 'Disquisitions on the origin and radical sense of the Greek prepositions', which had appeared in *Transactions of the Royal Society of Edinburgh* 5 (1802), and was reprinted separately in 1804. Gaisford thought it fanciful, with some unlikely ideas and some simply copied from Lennep. Gaisford was identified as author of the two reviews from the marked editorial copy in Nangle 1955, 105, 215. (Lonsdale 1963/4 is useful for context but does not mention Gaisford.)

[30] For the list of potential contributors, see Cutmore 2008, 197. The letter from William Gifford to Edward Copleston, 26 February 1811, is no. 83 in Jonathan Cutmore's forthcoming edition of letters related to the *Review* (Cutmore 2018) the original is Devon Public Record Office, 1149M, f. 83. Gifford had perhaps hoped for a review of Daniel Wyttenbach's *Bibliotheca critica*, the third and final volume of which had been published in 1808.

[31] Gaisford to Elmsley, 21 Jan. 1815: Elmsley papers. If one looks for possible earlier contributions, a tempting candidate is a review in the third number of Burney's *Tentamen de metris* (*Classical Journal* vol. 2, no. 3 (Sept. 1810), 642–56) which displays considerable metrical knowledge, and also has remarks on printers' problems and page layout (p. 648). The review is signed 'O', perhaps for 'Oxoniensis'.

had been treated. He had wanted the material he sent published in a single issue, so that readers could use it more easily; Valpy had split it between two issues. This concern for layout and for reader friendliness will recur.

Gaisford the Lexicographer

Given Gaisford's concern to produce useful editions of primary sources and his focus on the linguistic analysis of texts, it is not surprising that he spent much of his time on editions of ancient lexica. His name was included by Samuel Parr in an editorial Ministry of All the Talents for a proposed collaborative Greek lexicon:

Let the labour be thus divided: the epigrammatic school should be assigned to Gaisford, the lyric to Charles Burney exclusively, the dramatic to Elmsley, Blomfield, Maltby and Samuel Butler conjointly, the pastoral to Burney and Butler, the orators to Dobree only, the historians to Edmund Barker—and let the metaphysical and sacred be reserved to myself. Bishop Butler and Dr Routh must be consulted occasionally upon the prose-writers.[32]

Gaisford's two major achievements, the *Suidas* of 1834 and the *Etymologicum Magnum* of 1848, have already been mentioned. These two late antique lexica both demanded years of unremitting work, collating manuscripts, annotating the texts, and not least, seeing them through the press. Gaisford may have conceived them as part of a single plan of work, since in January 1824 he was paid £230 by the Delegates of the Clarendon Press for collating both *Suidas* and the *Etymologicum*.[33]

What is remarkable about these books, apart from their sheer size, is the work that went into making them user friendly by employing a page layout and a system of typographic cueing which made them easy to navigate. In 1974, in his pioneering book *The Classical Text*, E. J. Kenney discussed these aspects of book design and production, remarking that 'what I call, for want of a better name, "functional bibliography" is a field that is not merely uncultivated but apparently unperceived by bibliographers'. The name has not caught on, but the field is no longer uncultivated.[34] In January 1824, Gaisford was already thinking of how to make his books user friendly. In the following month, he wrote to his friend Henry Fynes Clinton:

my book will make...two volumes in folio...the Latin version will not appear, being as I conceive, useless, or nearly so. The size, or rather the height of the page will be shorter considerably

---

[32] 'Memoranda on Dr Parr's approval of a Greek thesaurus/lexicon, proposed by Burney'. Osborn MSS 7,482, Beinecke Library, Yale University. Burney, who had published a supplement to Scapula's lexicon in 1789 (*Appendix ad Lexicon Graeco-Latinum a Joan. Scapula Constructum*), predeceased Parr in 1817. The letter is probably to be dated to the period 1810–15, when Gaisford's *Hephaestion* had been published and Edmund Barker was living with Parr and acting as his amanuensis. The reference to 'Bishop Butler' dates the accompanying text after 1836, when Samuel Butler became Bishop of Lichfield; it is probably by Burney's son Charles Parr Burney.

[33] Delegates' Order Books, 30 Jan. 1824. This was presumably a repayment for the commissioning of MSS abroad.

[34] Kenney 1974, 153, n. 1. I have explored the topic in studies of William Smith's dictionaries and Richard Jebb's edition of Sophocles (see Chapters 9 and 10).

than that of Kuster's edition;[35] I propose to use what is called foolscap paper—a very convenient form, much used by the early printers. I shall introduce, what I cannot help but think will present many facilities to those who may consult the lexicon, a method of printing the glosses which has not hitherto been adopted in any edition of a Greek lexicon. The heads of the glosses, as they are technically termed, i.e. the word or phrase to be explained, will be printed in small capitals—the explanation in the ordinary character, & the example in another line and in a less character. In short the book will wear an appearance somewhat similar to a modern, say Johnson's, dictionary.[36]

In English dictionaries, capitalized headwords had been introduced by Nathan Bailey in 1721, and taken over by Johnson in 1755.[37] The earliest use of cueing by type size within glosses I know is by Noah Webster's American *Dictionary of the English Language* (1828)—published before the *Suidas*, but after Gaisford made his plans. Capitalized headwords remained standard in English dictionaries till the introduction of bold-face headwords in the late nineteenth century.[38]

When it appeared in 1834, the *Suidas* was indeed in two volumes, but rather larger than foolscap.[39] The page illustrated in Figure 3.2 shows the features Gaisford had planned earlier—capitalized headwords and variation in type size—but a lot more is going on. Numeration is by columns not pages; in the footnotes, headwords are bracketed off. An alphabetic sequence A–H runs down the page, to which the index is keyed.[40] Footnotes are keyed to a repeating alphabet—the traditional Latin alphabet, lacking j and w, that was also used for identifying signatures (gatherings) of pages in books.

This attention to typography and layout was a characteristic feature of Gaisford's work. In September 1819, on learning that Peter Elmsley was going to Herculanaeum with Humphry Davy to try to unroll and decipher papyri, he had written to him:

I am glad to find that you are appointed to assist Sir H[umphry] D[avy]. The experiment will now be really tried; and I have no doubt, supposing things to go on smoothly, that 12 months

---

[35] This is the Cambridge edition of 1705, which Gaisford used as his working copy; I have been able to inspect the book through the kindness of Richard Jenkyns, to whom it descended from his great-great-grandfather, Gaisford's brother-in-law. This copy was previously owned by Jonathan Toup, whose annotations it contains: 'I keep at my house Toup's copy of Kuster in which he has written many notes, and references which are not to be found in his printed Emendations': Gaisford to Fynes Clinton, 16 Feb. 1824, Christ Church library, MS 498. Kuster included a Latin translation by Aemilius Portus, and it is to this that Gaisford refers.

[36] Gaisford to Clinton, 16 February 1824. Christ Church library, MS 498. Later letters enable us to chart the progress of the edition, but we lack printing records. The contrast is striking with the evidence available for Kuster's Cambridge edition of 1705, where we know which compositors worked which sheets and how much they were paid. See Roberts 1954, 7–14, and especially Mackenzie 1966, 1.224–33.

[37] See Luna 2000. Bailey indented the headings and Johnson, *pace* Luna, did not.

[38] Luna 2005, 192. The delay is not surprising: Kenney has pointed out that several useful innovations by editors and printers were not taken up by others for some time, despite their obvious utility: Kenney 1974, 153. For bilingual dictionaries, see 'Liddell and Scott' below.on Liddell and Scott's Greek-English lexicon.

[39] The index is sometimes found bound separately as a third volume. The book overall runs to over 2,300 pages.

[40] The system is extended in Hugh Johnson's *Wine Atlas* (1971–), where the cross-references derived from mapping are applied also to text pages. For earlier uses of such alphabetic keying, see Blair 2010, 143.

142, 43   **A P**

A P   143, 2

ΑΡΙΣΚΎΔΗΣ: Ἡ ὀργίλη· παρὰ τὸ ἀρι καὶ τὸ
σκύζεσθαι, ἡ ἄγαν σκυζομένη. Οὕτως Ἀρτεμίδωρος.

45 ΑΡΙΠΡΕΠΕΕΣ: Διαπρέποντες, ἔκδηλοι.

Δεῦρο, γύναι, φέρε χηλὸν ἀριπρεπέ' ἥτις ἀρίστη.

Ἀριπρεπέα νῦν ἑνικῶς. Ἔστι δὲ καὶ οὐδετέρως
πληθυντικόν, καὶ ἀρσενικῶς.

Ὃς δ' ὅτ' ἐν οὐρανῷ ἄστρα
φαίνετ' ἀριπρεπέα.

Καὶ ἀρσενικῶς, αἰτιατικῇ,

50   Φράσσατο δ' ἵππον ἀριπρεπέα προὔχοντα.

Καὶ οὐδετέρως,

Ὡς καὶ σοὶ εἶδος·μὲν ἀριπρεπές.

Ἀριήκοος· Εὐήκοος. Ἀπολλώνιος,
[Ἴκεο πέτρας] Ῥίμφα Μελαντείοιο ἀρήκοον.
Γίνεται παρὰ τὸ ἀρι ἐπιτατικόν, καὶ τὸ ἀκούω.

55 ΑΡΙΣΤΑΛΛΟΣ: Ὄνομα παρὰ Ἀριστοφάνει. Εἴ-
ρηται δὲ ὑποκοριστικῶς, ὁ Ἀριστοκλῆς. Ὡς γὰρ
παρὰ τὸ Ἡρακλῆς, Ἤρυλλος καὶ παρὰ τὸ Θρασυ-
143 κλῆς, Θράσυλλος· καὶ παρὰ τὸ Βαθυκλῆς, Βάβυλλος,
ὄνομα κύριον, ὁ ἐράμενος Ἀνακρέοντος· οὕτως καὶ
παρὰ τὸ Ἀριστοκλῆς καὶ Ἀρίσταλλος. Οὕτως

Ἡρωδιανὸς εἰς τὴν Ἀπολλωνίου εἰσαγωγήν, ἢ περὶ
Παθῶν. Διογενιανός, ἀντὶ τοῦ ἄριστος. [Καὶ] Ἀριστοφάνης ἐν Τελμισεῦσιν.   5

ΑΡΙΣΤΟΣ: Παρὰ τὸ Ἄρης, ὁ πόλεμος, γίνεται
συγκριτικὸν, ἀρείων· ἐξ οὗ ἄριστος, κυρίως ὁ ἐν
πολέμῳ ἰσχυρός, καταχρηστικῶς δὲ καὶ ἐπὶ παντὸς
προήκοντος.

[ΑΡΙΣΤΟΣ] κυρίως ὁ ἐν πολέμῳ ἀνδραγαθῶν,
καταχρηστικῶς δὲ, ὁ ἐν οἰῳδήποτε πράγματι· παρὰ
τὸν Ἄρην ἐξ οὗ παρώνυμον, ἀριστεύς.   10

ΑΡΙΣΤΗ, ἀπὸ τοῦ ἄριστος. Τὸ ΑΡΙΣΤΟΝ, ὑπερθετικὸν ὄνομα, ἀπὸ τοῦ ἀρείων συγκριτικοῦ. Τὸ δὲ
ἀρείων, παρὰ τὸ Ἄρης, ὁ πόλεμος. Κυρίως γὰρ
ἀρείων, ὁ ἐν τῷ πολέμῳ κρείττων.

ΑΡΙΣΤΙΝΑΔΗΝ: Ἐκλελεγμένους κατὰ ἀριστείαν, 15
ἀπὸ τοῦ ἄριστος.

ΑΡΙΣΤΟΝ ἐπὶ τῆς εὐωχίας, ἀόριστόν τι ὄν· ἀόρι-
στον γὰρ κατὰ καιρόν. Ἐντεῦθεν οὖν ἔχει τὸ Α
μακρόν. Ἡ παρὰ τὸν ἄρεα· τοῖς γὰρ ἐς ἄρεα
προϊοῦσι παρασκευάζεται, ὡς καὶ τὸ δεῖπνον.

ΑΡΙΣΤΗΤΙΚΟΣ, ὁ ἔθος ἔχων ἀριστᾶν.

407

43. ΑΡΙΣΚΎΔΗΣ] Pertinet forte ad Callim. fr. Bentl.   A
CVIII.

ib. ἡ ὀργίλη om. Va.

ib. καὶ τὸ σκύζεσθαι] ἐπιτατικὸν ἐπίρρημα, καὶ τὸ σκύζω
τὸ ὀργίζομαι, ἢ ἄγαν σκυζομένη, ὅ ἐστιν ὀργιζομένη· σκύζεσθαι γὰρ τὸ ὀργίζεσθαι Va. cum οὕτως Ἀρτ. in marg.

45. ΑΡΙΠΡΕΠΕΕΣ etc.] Ἀριπρεπὴς, ὁ ἄγαν πρεπώδης,
καὶ ἀριπρεπέα ἡ αἰτιατική. ζήτει Va.

ib. Ἀριπρεπέα. διαπρέποντες, ἔκδηλοι. . . . . ἔστι
καὶ οὐδέτερον ὡς τὸ, Καὶ σὺ μὲν εἶδος ἀριπρεπές· καὶ ἀρι-
πρεπία. δεῦρο γύναι φέρε χηλὸν ἀριπρεπέ' ἥτις ἀρίστη,
ἔστι καὶ ἐπὶ ἀρσενικοῦ πτώσεως αἰτιατικῆς τῶν ἑνικῶν. ὡς
τὸ, φράσσατο δ' ἵππον ἀριπρεπέα προὔχοντα. ἐκ ἐπὶ οὐδε-
τέρου πληθυντικοῦ ὡς ὃ' ὅτ' ἐν οὐρανῷ ἄστρα φαίνεται
ἀριπρεπέα Vb. In versu ἀριπρεπέες D.

ib. Δεῦρο—ἐνικῶς om. Vb.

47. δὲ καὶ οὐδετέρως] καὶ οὐδέτερον Vb.

48. Ὡς δ' ὅτ' ἐν οὐρανῷ ἄστρα] καὶ Ὅμηρος, ἀμφὶ σελή-
νην Gud. et sic voluit Sorb.

ib. φαίνετ'] φαίνετ' D.

52. εὐήκοος] ὁ μεγάλως ἀκούων, ὁ εὐήκοος Va, ubi om.
Ἀπολλώνιος—γίνεται.

ib. Apollonii locus est Argonaut. lib.4.v.1706. SYLB.

ib. Ἀπολλώνιος—ἀρήκοον] Locus est IV. 1707. ubi
vid. Schol. Conf. Photium p. 1070, 58. et interpp.
Callimachi h. in Del. 308. ANON.

53. ἀρήκοος] ἀρυήκοος D. Call. qui om. Ἴκεο πέτρας.

ib. παρὰ τὸ ἀρι ἐπιτατικὸν] παρὰ τὴν ἐπίτασιν Va.

55. παρὰ Ἀριστοφάνει] Vid. Aristoph. Plut. 311. ibi-
que Schol. Conf. interpp. Hesych. T. I. p. 535. not. 7.
ANON.

ib. παρὰ—ὑποκοριστικῶς] ὑποκοριστικὸν cum παρ' Ἀριστοφάνει in marg. Va.

ἀριστοκλῆς

56. Ἀριστοκλῆς] ὁ ἀρακλῆς D.

57. καὶ παρὰ τὸ] καὶ βαθυκλῆς βάβυλλος. Βαθυκλῆς δὲ ὁ
ἐρώμενος Ἀνακρέοντος Va. quae om. infra, qui habet οὕτως
—Τελμισεῦσι in marg.

143, 1. Βάβυλλος] Vid. Fischer. ad Anacreont. Odyss.
θ. 8 et 9. p.43 sq. Omnino de Etymologi loco vid.
Fischer. ad Welleri Gramm. Graec. Vol. II. p. 33. ST.

3. Ἀρίσταλλος] καὶ Ἀρ. D.   408

4. Διογένης] διὸ D. ubi mox ἀρτφ* ἐν τελμί. sine καί.
Διογενιανὸν MS. Aug. ap. Tittman.

5. Ἀριστοφάνης ἐν Τελμισοῖς] Vid. Aristoph. Fragmm.
Dindorf. n. 456.

ib. Τελμισοῖς] Τελμισσεῦσι Hemst.

6. ΑΡΙΣΤΟΣ παρὰ τὸ ἀρείων. τοῦτο παρὰ τὸ Ἄρης τὸν
πόλεμον τὸ συγκριτικὸν ἀρείων καὶ ἄριστος ὑπερθετικὸν ὁ ἐν
πολέμοις ἀνδραγαθῶν. τὸ δὲ Ἄρης, ὃ σημαίνει τὸν πόλεμον,
παρὰ τὸ ῥῶ τὸ λέγω. ζήτει Va. Tum Vb. habet Ἄριστος
παρὰ τὸ—ἀρείων· κυρίως ὁ ἐν—πράγματι· ἐξ οὗ ὑπερθετικὸν ἄριστος κυρίως ὁ ἐν πολέμῳ ἰσχυρός· καταχρηστικῶς
δὲ καὶ ἐπὶ παντὸς προήκοντος· ἐκ δὲ τοῦ ἄριστος παρώνυμον
ὄνομα ἀριστεύς. Tum seq. Ἀριστίνδην. ἐκλελεγμένους κ.
C α. α. τ. ἄριστος. Et Ἀριστητικός. ἔθος ἔχει ἀριστᾶν. ἐκλελεγμένους D.P. Sumpsi Ἀριστίνδην e D. marg.

7. ἀρίων] ἀρείων D.P.

ib. Ad formam κραίων a Grammaticis fictum esse,
quanquam in nullius scriptoris loco repertum, existimo:
cujus generis exempli Etymologicis abundant. Usi-
tata comparativi forma, ἀρείων, est paulo post. v. 13. et
D 14.   Sed ex ἀρίων multo commodius et facilius, quam
ex ἀρείων, superlativus ἄριστος ducitur. ST.

ib. κυρίως ὁ ἐν πολέμῳ ἰσχυρός] Sic Helladius Chre-
stomath. p. 17. Ὅτι τὸ ἄριστος, κυρίως μὲν ἐπὶ τῶν κατὰ
πόλεμον εὐδοκιμούντων ἂν ῥηθείη. διότι καὶ ἀριστέας τούτους
καλοῦμεν.—εἰ καταχρήσει δὲ, καὶ ἐπὶ τῶν ἄλλο τι κατορ-
θούντων λέγεται. ANON.

E 8. προσήκοντος] Dedi προήκοντος cum Orione p. 25, 18.
In προσήκοντος consentiunt Gud. Sorb.

9. Sejunxi haec a praecedentibus.

11. Iterum sejunxi a praecedentibus. Vid. Crameri
Anecd. T. I. p. 50, 28.

15. Ἄριστον. ἐπὶ] Novus articulus Va. desinens cum
παρασκευάζεται.

F 16. κατὰ] ἔστι καὶ κατὰ Va.

18. προσιοῦσι] Bastius ad Gregor. de Dialectis p. 22.
edit. Schaefer. e duobus codicibus corrigi jubet προϊοῦσιν. alter mox τὸ δεῖπνον ferri posse negat, sed in
alio Etymologici Parisiensis loco reperiri ait ὁ δεῖπνος.
BE. τοῖς γὰρ εἰς·ἄρεα προϊοῦσιν παρεσκευάζετο δὲ καὶ
δεῖπνον. Sorb. τ. γ. ε. ἄ. π. π. δὲς καὶ τὸ δεῖπνον Gud.
G qui paullo supra, ἄριστος καὶ ἄριστον διχῶς ἐκφωνεῖται,
ὥσπερ καὶ τὸ (ὁ Brux.) δεῖπνος καὶ τὸ δεῖπνον. In D.
plane τὸ δεῖπνος ut vulg.

ib. Convenientius fere προϊοῦσι, prodeuntibus, ex-
euntibus. Ibidem mox in τὸ δεῖπνον duplicis scripturae
notationem intelligo, nempe τὸ δεῖπνον, et ὁ δεῖπνος. Vix
enim puto τὸ δεῖπνος ita usurpasse ut τὸ τεῖχος. SYLB.

ib. ΑΡΙΣΤΗΤΙΚΟΣ] Hoc usus est Eupolis in Δήμοις.
Vid. Bekkeri Anecd. p. 79, 22. ST.

Figure 3.2 A page from Gaisford's edition of the Byzantine encyclopaedic lexicon known as Suidas ('the fortress'), published by Oxford University Press in 1834.

will tell us whether the remains of any author worth preserving are to be recovered out of the ruins. In one thing you will assuredly acquire much information—I mean Palaeography. Of course you will be desirous of printing, as [*sic*] least of copying as fast as they are unrolled, the different books in a character similar to that to be found in the original MS. If a copy can once be accurately made, it can be multiplied any number of times, by the use of Lithography, which is now rapidly advancing to a state of perfection. A person by name Marcuard[41] who lives in Manor Place, Chelsea has printed a set of specimens, chiefly from Oriental MSS in the Museum, which will show you how nearly and exactly such representations can be made.[42] Over and above the superior accuracy it has to engraving, lithography is infinitely less expensive. I have no doubt that it may be employed with the greatest advantage in publishing the Herculaneum remains.[43]

Liddell and Scott

In 1843, five years before Gaisford's edition of the *Etymologicum Magnum* appeared, the first edition of an epoch-making Greek-English lexicon was published by the Clarendon Press, edited by two Christ Church men, Henry Liddell and Robert Scott.[44] The lexicon had been commissioned by the Oxford bookseller and publisher David Talboys in 1836.[45] Talboys himself took an interest in the makeup of complex text on the page. In 1838 he had published a volume of chronological tables of history, which combined a flexible tabular format with considerable typographic variation, including a pioneering use of bold-looking type for some headings. It is also clear that his firm was involved in printing the Greek lexicon. When the first edition came out in 1843, Liddell and Scott reported to the Delegates that they were owed £52, including £19 'due to Mr Talboys for setting up of type'.[46]

On Talboys' death in 1840, the book was taken over by Oxford University Press, doubtless on Gaisford's initiative. But he had been involved before this; indeed even before the editors had signed up with Talboys, Liddell had told a friend that Gaisford

[41] Charles Marcuard, formerly of the War Office Press, the first lithographic press in Britain, now an independent printer: see Twyman 1990, 52–3. His Oxford equivalent was Nathaniel Whittock, who lithographed Herculaneum items held by the University: Delegates' Order Books, 30 Jan. 1824.

[42] Revd. George Hunt, *Specimens of lithography* (1819, but printed in 1818, in a run of sixty impressions): see Twyman 1990, 52–3, 298. The Davy/Elmsley project foundered on the obstructiveness of the papyri's local guardians.

[43] Gaisford to Elmsley, 9 Sept. 1819 (Elmsley papers).

[44] In 1834 Scott circulated a splendid parody of the Homeric catalogue of ships, *Fragmenta e codice Barocciano*, listing the heads of colleges. Gaisford (ll.32–6) leads the Christ Church contingent, armed with two mighty lexica. William Tuckwell assumed they were *Suidas* and the *Etymologicum* (Tuckwell 1907, 309) but the latter was not published till fourteen years later; Scott was presumably referring to the two main text volumes of *Suidas*. There is a copy of Scott's parody in the Bodleian Library, G.A.Oxon 8°.659 (26); it was reprinted in Tuckwell 1907, 307–9. For the Lexicon, see Stray, Clarke, and Katz 2019.

[45] The commissioning has been variously dated, but can be securely located by a letter of 21 Nov. 1836 from Liddell to H. H. Vaughan announcing that he and Scott were 'about to close an engagement with Talboys for a lexicon founded chiefly on Passow': Bodleian Library, MS. Eng. Let. d 435.

[46] Delegates' Order Books, 27 Oct 1843. Talboys had died in May 1840; the £19 was perhaps to go to the publisher William Pickering, one of his executors. Typesetting of the book at the Clarendon Press began in 1841, but may have followed a style established by Talboys.

had 'given us a number of very valuable hints'.[47] What might these have been? Comments on the treatment of particular words, perhaps; but I think it very likely that he also made suggestions on page layout and the arrangement of glosses. The most striking feature of the first edition is the use of bold type for headwords—something we now take for granted in dictionaries of any language and in other complicated texts, but then a striking innovation.[48] That this was a tentative first step is suggested by the fact that the Press compositors clearly had no access to capitals—all the bolding is lower case, ordinary capitals being used where necessary.[49] The bolded Greek in the Lexicon, the first to be used in Britain, was one of two such founts used by the Press. It is surely significant that both of them were known within the Printing House well into the twentieth century as 'Gaisford type'.[50] Gaisford, who in the 1820s, as we have seen, was planning to modernize classical lexica by using capitals in the style of Johnson, was now well ahead of the lexicographers of English.[51]

The *Etymologicon Magnum*

Gaisford's second large-scale lexicographical edition, the *Etymologicon Magnum* of 1848, enables us to look again at his use of typography and page layout, and also to compare his practice with that of the *Suidas* of the 1830s. This is a single volume, but a substantial one, of 1,379 pages and weighing over eight kilogrammes. It must have been a lengthy task to assemble in manuscript, transfer to print, and then proofread.[52] The main text is preceded by an arabic-numbered preface and a roman-numbered section, and is followed by a series of indexes in Arabic-numbered pages. Most of the

---

[47] Liddell to H. H. Vaughan, n.d., quoted in Thompson 1899, 67. The original is in the Bodleian Library, MS Eng. Lett. d 435.

[48] Bold-looking (fattened face) lemmata were used in the 5th edn of the French Academy's dictionary (1835), but that was in roman type. A supplement to the previous edition, published in 1827, had also used such headings: see Twyman 1993. 'Gaisford type' is less specific and less memorable than 'Porson Greek', which was based on Porson's handwriting; but it deserves to be remembered. It should be noted that Gaisford knew of Talboys' *Chronological Tables*: letter to Fynes Clinton, 19 May 1835: Christ Church library, MS 498.

[49] This looks odd, though it supplies for root-forms, printed entirely in capitals, an increased differentiation which is functionally effective. Bolded capitals were used for the first time in the 5th edn (1861).

[50] 'List of ancient and modern Greek and oriental types in use at OUP' (1959: copies in OUP archive and at St Bride Printing Library); cf. Bowman 1992, 58–60; 1998, 156. Both founts were supplied by Vincent Figgins; a third Figgins fount is described in the OUP list as having been 'used for Dr Gaisford's books', implying no doubt a looser connection, for it was the two bold Greek founts that actually bore Gaisford's name.

[51] The US editions of Liddell and Scott did not have bolded headwords. In Greece, bolding as a cueing device in Greek printing began in the 1870s, but was not used in e.g. Konstantinides' translation of Liddell and Scott (Konstantinides 1901–7) W. Freund's Latin dictionary (Freund 1834–45) has no bolding; headwords are mostly lower-case, with some entries in capitals. Andrews'), based on Freund (Andrews 1850), has bolded headwords, as does William Smith's (Smith 1855); in 1856 Andrews' British publishers Sampson Low claimed that Smith had copied their typography (Stray 2007h, 48; cf. Chapter 11).

[52] Gaisford's progress can be followed in his letters to Fynes Clinton, where the book is first mentioned in 1835. In 1840 he pauses while a Paris MS is copied for him; in 1844 he hopes for publication in 1846; by 1845 it is one-third printed. By Mar. 1847 the main text was printed, and in Jan. 1848 the book was published.

book has a single numbering sequence, but the numbers belong to columns in the main text and pages elsewhere—a very curious arrangement.

The layout shows Gaisford still experimenting, and moving on from that of the *Suidas*. Column numbers persist but are now located lower down, separating the main text from the footnotes. The main text has sections and line numbers marked, and these are repeated at the top of the page. The text figures for footnotes have gone, to be replaced by line-number references which avoid cluttering the main text. The central alphabetic references (A–G) now cover only the footnotes. Gaisford may have decided that they were redundant in the main text of a lexicon, where an alphabetically-ordered text is already organized for reference. It is perhaps more likely, however, that while in the text of *Suidas* (as distinct from the notes) he was avoiding reference to Kuster's edition, which did not impress him, here he is using page and line numbers from Friedrich Sylburg's 1594 edition, of which he thought highly. Finally, and most strikingly, text in footnotes representing quotations in the sources is bolded in a Gaisford type. It can be argued that this layout is over busy; but Gaisford is still trying to make his text as reader friendly as possible; and a constant reader would surely become used to navigating the page. In the light of the evidence offered here, I find it impossible to agree with Lloyd-Jones's statement that Gaisford 'was not interested in typography' (Lloyd-Jones 1982, 99).

Delegate of the Clarendon Press

It would be an understatement to say that Gaisford was an active delegate. The extent of his activities was vividly portrayed in a 'Letter from Oxford' on the Clarendon Press published in March 1828:

Professor Gaisford has been some months absent, and the classical department has consequently remained nearly at a stand-still. It is not so generally known as it ought to be, even in the University, how much the present eminence of the Clarendon [Press] is owing to the indefatigable exertions of this consummate scholar…preparing for the Press, and publishing, those admirable editions of the Classics, for which, under his auspices, we have now become so justly celebrated…It may well be worth the consideration of His Majesty's Government, whether, in giving him such a reward as he truly merited, it would not have been more judicious to invest him with a canonry at Christ-Church, Oxford, and to retain his services in Oxford, instead of a stall at Worcester, which necessarily takes him much away from us, while the Canonry is filled (if I may so say) by a person who never occupies it.[53]

Gaisford was indefatigable not only in writing, but also in commissioning works from other scholars. In his period as a delegate, the Clarendon Press became a prime site for the publication of editions of classical authors, mostly by German scholars—Oxford

---

[53] Amicus, 'Letters from Oxford. – No. 1', *The Crypt, or Receptacle or Things Past, and West of England Magazine* 2 (1828), 168–72. Gaisford was presumably away in Worcester, where he as obliged to spend two months a year while he held a canonry from 1825 to 1829.

became, in fact, a major German place of publication. From at least 1816, he sent his fellow-delegates proposals from foreign scholars. Proposals for work by Immanuel Bekker and in particular the Dindorf brothers usually came through him, and he was regularly deputed to deal with them.[54] All was usually sweetness and light, but the Delegates were ready to reject work which was not up to their standards or in accordance with agreements. In 1819 the ageing Wyttenbach was told he would not receive a promised sum unless he returned the collations for which the Press had paid. In 1823 Bekker was severely rebuked for sending in an inadequate preface to his edition of the Attic orators. He replied with an indignant letter: 'praefationem tertiam nec debeo vobis nec dabo'. The Delegates sent him his money, with a warning that they would not take anything else from him. In 1824, Dindorf was told that he would not be paid for his notes on Sophocles, since they were so meagre. He capitulated, revised and was paid.[55]

Gaisford died on 2 June 1855. At their next meeting, the Delegates recorded their sense of the loss of a man

whose unwearied attention to the interest of the Press, and great liberality in his transactions with it, no less than his learning, sagacity and prudence, contributed so much to the prosperity of the concern, and the promotion of classical literature.[56]

This was doubtless true, though some of his books surely lost the Press money: the *Suidas*, for example, cost £3,685 to produce and rarely sold more than ten copies a year (Sutcliffe 1978, 3). A survey of his own output and the books of others he brought to the Press shows a relentless concentration on Greek texts. One could not guess from a listing of these books that Oxford had been developing, in the first half of the century, a broad-based classical curriculum which led in Gaisford's lifetime to the foundation of the Greats course. The emphasis on ancient history and philosophy, so much wider than that of the Cambridge Classical Tripos, was hardly reflected in the Press's pattern of publication.

Curator of the Bodleian Library

The curators of the Bodleian Library were the Vice-Chancellor, the two proctors, and the five regius professors. The first three were short-term incumbents who could hardly be expected to show much commitment; of the latter, only Edward Pusey,

---

[54] Gaisford's most prolific correspondent, Karl Wilhelm Dindorf, was far better known than his brother Ludwig—some claimed, indeed, that Ludwig did not exist, but was a figment invented to explain the remarkably large Dindorfian output. A proposal from Gottfried Hermann to publish his projected edition of Aeschylus with the Press was sent to Elmsley (Bodley, MS Clarendon Press, d.55 f. 68r, 18 May 1821. Elmsley surely mentioned this to Gaisford, but the offer was not conveyed to the Delegates, and the edition was in fact published only in 1852, after Hermann's death. My thanks to Giacomo Mancuso, whose edition of the correspondence is forthcoming (Mancuso 2018).

[55] All these exchanges are recorded in the Delegates' Order Books.

[56] Delegates' Order Books, 15 June 1855.

professor of divinity, and Gaisford were really interested; and Edmund Craster, the historian of the Library, declared that 'The latter in particular, with his enthusiasm for Greek MSS and his intimate knowledge of book values, was the real ruler' (Craster 1952, 83). In 1806 Gaisford brought out the first catalogue of the university's collection of Greek manuscripts, and when in 1809 the university bought the collection of the Cambridge antiquary E. D. Clarke, he added a supplement. He got on well with the sub-librarian Henry Coxe, appointed in 1839, who shared his interest in MSS. One day he found Coxe cataloguing MS 11, realized it was a text by the Byzantine scholar Michael Psellus, nudged him and chuckled (Craster 1952, 38)—a pleasantly human moment.

Ian Philip has emphasized that 'it was largely due to [Gaisford] that the Library was able to pursue a remarkably successful accessions policy for upwards of forty years, until his death in 1855'.[57] He was responsible for the purchase of the Canonici collection in 1817 and the Saibante collection in 1820, and in 1824 travelled to The Hague to bid at the sale of the Meerman collection, where he secured nearly sixty manuscripts, including the fifth-century MS of Jerome's translation of Eusebius.[58] He was however outbid several times by Sir Thomas Phillipps, the self-described 'vellomaniac' who was busy assembling the largest private collection in the country. Gaisford wrote to Fynes Clinton in 1830:

But for his silly interference I should have placed 6 years ago the whole that was valuable in Meerman's collection in our public library, but he would not consent to let me have 2 or 3 mss which I much wished—which can never be of use to him—for he is an arrant ignoramus.[59]

In 1848 Phillipps wrote that he had discovered they were distantly related, and that had he known this in 1824, he would not have bid against him so often at the Meerman sale.[60] After this Gaisford had to endure intermittent correspondence with Phillipps, who was rightly summed up by Craster (p. 83) as 'wealthy, vain, irascible'. At one point Phillipps offered Gaisford a loan of several of his manuscripts, including a Hesiod (which turned out to be a forgery).[61] In his later years he offered his collection to the university, to be housed in the Ashmolean, on condition that accommodation be provided there for him during his lifetime; another offer carried the condition that he should be made Bodley's Librarian. Not surprisingly, the negotiations collapsed.[62]

---

[57] Philip 1997, 588. Lloyd-Jones 1982, 99 declared that Gaisford was not interested in administration. This is hard to evaluate, since in Gaisford's day administrative hierarchies hardly existed in the modern sense; as with Lloyd-Jones's comment on typography, cited above, it is unclear on what evidence he was relying. The Delegates of the Press were presided over by the Vice- Chancellor; the University Registrar acted as their secretary. But it is clear that Gaisford put in a great deal of work as a Delegate, though one might not call it 'administration', and the same could be said of his activities as Dean of Christ Church.

[58] Craster 1952, 195; Anon. 1952.

[59] Gaisford to Clinton, 20 Dec. 1830: Christ Church MS 486.

[60] Phillipps' anonymous biographer claimed that Gaisford was able to secure some volumes owing to Phillipps' 'unwillingness to bid against Thomas Gaisford': De Ricci 1930, 120.

[61] A. N. L. Munby, *The Formation of the Phillipps Library from 1841 to 1872* (Phillipps Studies no.4) (1956), 126–7.

[62] This was in 1861: Craster 1952, 86–7. For an earlier attempt, see Munby, *The Dispersal of the Phillipps Library* (Phillipps Studies No. 5) (1960), 2–3.

Dean of Christ Church: Scholarship and Religion

One of the great themes of nineteenth-century English social and cultural history is the entanglement of Classics with the Anglican Church. Oxford and Cambridge were the educational wings of the church, and their curricula were fundamentally classical at the college level, and in Oxford at the university level too. Some undergraduates became fellows, and there they might stay, unless they married. In that case they might proceed to college livings, of which there were between 700 and 800 in either university. Christ Church was at once the great symbol of this entanglement of learning and religion and its great anomaly, being both an Oxford college and the cathedral of the Oxford diocese—as well as having no statutes. It was run by its dean and canons; the fellows (known as 'students') gained a share in the running of the House only in the 1860s (Bill and Mason 1970, 38–182). During Gaisford's period as Dean, he had almost unfettered power, which he used to enforce discipline rigorously and to keep the undergraduates away from university examinations. Measured by numbers of Firsts, Christ Church's record declined rapidly after his appointment.[63] Gaisford favoured the sons of the aristocracy, and resisted attempts by their social inferiors to rise (as he had himself done) through scholarship.[64] As a member of the Hebdomadal Board, he was a staunch and consistent conservative. When the Royal Commissioners wrote to the heads of houses after their appointment in 1850, several replies told them in effect to mind their own business; Gaisford went one better and did not even reply.

Several of Gaisford's contemporaries, having made a name in scholarship, were given ecclesiastical preferment, after which they almost never published on classical subjects. This was the age of the Greek play bishop, a phenomenon named only in the 1840s but which belonged to the period of Lord Liverpool's administration in the 1810s and 20s.[65] Almost all references to these bishops name James Monk or Charles Blomfield of Trinity College Cambridge; Monk became Bishop of Gloucester, Blomfield Bishop of Chester, then of London. Given that Oxford was if anything more tightly entwined with the Anglican establishment than Cambridge, it is striking that the only recusant Greek play bishops seem to have been Oxford men: Elmsley, who refused the see of Calcutta, and Gaisford himself, who rejected an offer of the see of Oxford. Peter Elmsley had inherited from his uncle of the same name, a successful bookseller and Gibbon's agent, and as a wealthy bachelor could spend his time on classical editing. Gaisford found the perfect home in Christ Church, college and cathedral,

---

[63]   The numbers of Firsts at Christ Church and Balliol in the 1820s were fifty-one and eleven; in the 1830s thirty-one and twenty-two; in the 1840s thirteen and twenty-two. Bill and Mason 1970, 24.

[64]   A tragic example is that of Theodore Buckley (1825–56), whose life was ended by drink and drugs. See the entry on Buckley by M. Nelson in Todd 2004, 116–17. The account in Richardson 2013, 29–34 is vitiated by a failure to take the social context of Christ Church into account.

[65]   See Burns and Stray 2011. Richardson 2013, 21–9 uses evidence selectively to fit a preconceived narrative; cf. 2014b, and for the general issue, 1991b, a review of Peacock 1988.

in an office which was both academic and ecclesiastical, and with the Bodleian Library and the University Press nearby. Obliged to move to Durham in 1829, he soon managed to exchange his canonry for the deanery of Christ Church. In one respect, however, his publishing career approximates to those of Monk and Blomfield: in the late 1830s he began to move from profane to sacred texts, including Eusebius and Theodoret.[66]

As with his scholarship and publishing, so as Dean of Christ Church Gaisford held to a consistent line, controlling college life and keeping the world beyond at a distance. Just as his scholarship became more obviously old-fashioned as Oxford changed, so his conservative policy as college head stood out in the age of the Royal Commission, which attempted to transfer wealth from the colleges to the University.

The best-known account of Gaisford as Dean is that of Ruskin in his *Praeterita*. Collections, the end-of-term examination, was an ordeal to be dreaded, the Dean being 'scornful at once, and vindictive, thunderous always, more sullen and threatening as the day went on, he stalked with baneful emanation of Gorgonian cold from dais to door, from door to dais of the majestic torture chamber'.[67] Ruskin's reference to Gaisford as a 'rotundly progressive terror'[68] was surely the only time the word 'progressive' (referring here, of course, to his forward locomotion) was ever applied to him. Less well known than Ruskin's memoir is a vivid picture painted in a memoir of Sir Herbert Oakeley, an undergraduate in the late 1840s:

Christ Church was at this time ... ruled—many still like to add, with a rod of iron—by the 'stern captain' of Ruskin's Praeterita, who with rounded brow and glittering dark eye led in his thunderous old Latin the responses of the morning prayer. Few Christ Church men of the time can forget the rasping and indignantly remonstrant tones of his 'Te rogamus, audi nos'. And those who, like Oakeley, were endowed with the excellent gift of the mimic, felt ... that 'this phenomenon awaked our dormant faculty; such a heaven-sent subject is not to be lighted upon every day'. So there arose quite a school of mimicry of Dean Gaisford ... and he is almost as well known to younger generations as to his own.[69]

This story takes us, I think, close to the original context of the mythicizing of Gaisford, when he began to pass from life into legend. He had first entered the world of fiction in 1814 as a result of his courtship of Helen Douglas, niece of William Van Mildert, then Regius Professor of Divinity and a canon of Christ Church. A university wit noticed the similarity of her name to that of Ellen Douglas, the girl pursued by three suitors in

---

[66] How this move might have been related to the contemporary upheaval in Oxford caused by Tractarianism is something that needs further investigation: cf. Ellis 2012; Ledger-Lomas 2013, 405, 419–22; 2019.

[67] *Praeterita* ch. 11, 'Christ Church choir', in Cook and Wedderburn, *The Works of John Ruskin*, vol. 35 (1908), 193.

[68] Ibid., 203. Ruskin was at Christ Church in the later 1830s.

[69] E. M. Oakeley, *Life of Sir H. S. Oakeley* (1904), 27; other anecdotes are told on pp. 28–30.

Walter Scott's *The Lady of the Lake* (1810); the result was 'The song of Roderick Dhu', whose first stanza ran as follows:[70]

> All hail to the maid who so graceful advances!
> Tis sweet Ellen Douglas, if right I divine;
> Cupid, thou classical god of sweet glances
> Teach me to ogle and make the nymph mine.
> Look on a Tutor true
> Ellen, for love of you,
> Just metamorphosed from Blacksmith to Beau,
> Hair combed and breeches new,
> Grace-alter'd Rhoderick Dhu;
> While ev'ry Gownsman cries Ho! Ho ho ho.

The three suitors are named as in Scott's poem, Roderick Dhu being Gaisford, and the reference to the blacksmith in the first stanza is not the only one in the Gaisford literature; it may allude to Richard Bentley's suggestion that Joshua Barnes knew as much Greek as an Athenian blacksmith. Here Gaisford is portrayed as a man more at home in the Greek he studies than in English, something which underlines the incongruity of his having ordinary human feelings. (Thirty years later, when his pupil Henry Liddell announced his engagement, Gaisford apparently commented that it showed that love and lexicography were not incompatible: Thompson 1899, 59.)

The unusual smartening of dress is confirmed in the letter Elmsley wrote to Thomas Grenville in 1815, passing on Gaisford's request for a copy of Calliergus's Theocritus:

He used to be eminently careful both of his own books and of those which he borrowed. Whether his present condition, which is that of a lover, has taken from his books that care and attention, which, as I am informed, it has added to his dress and personal appearance, I cannot pretend to say. If he is not quite altered, however, there are no hands in which a valuable book can be deposited with more security than in his.[71]

---

[70] There are three MS versions: Bodleian Library, Add MS b.83/11–12 and MS Top Cheshire e6/15–17; Lambeth Palace Library, MS 2212; the differences are minor. A text was published in the *New Monthly Magazine* (1815), 435; *Blackwood's Edinburgh Magazine* (Sept 1819), 733, repr. *Noctes Ambrosianae* (1863), 1.124–5 (see p. 13 for a reference to Gaisford); *Punch* (1869), 109. It was also given by W. Tuckwell, *Reminiscences of Oxford* (ed. 2, 1907), 126–7. The historical Rhoderick Dhu ('Black Roderick') was 38th chief of Clan Macneil; Gaisford was described at the time as 'black-a-vised': 'Gaisford, unloverlike, slovenly, black-a-vised, wooed and won his first wife' (Tuckwell 1907, 127). One of the Bodley versions names 'Hughes, of Oriel' as author; Tuckwell ascribes it to Henry Cotton, also of Oriel. A copy listed in Maggs Bros' autograph catalogue of 1931, p. 77, attributes it to Hughes and dates it to 1814; A. L. Strout, *A Bibliography of Articles in Blackwood's Magazine, 1817–1825* (1959) tentatively agrees, citing Hughes' *Lays of Past Days*, where (on p. 125) two characters called Humphrey and Buller are talking, and Humphrey says to Buller, 'Drop your inveterate trick of capping rhymes, or if you must rhyme, give us your old song of Roderic Dhu, as a reminiscence of Christopher's Tent.'

[71] Elmsley to Thomas Grenville, 4 Jan. 1815 (BL Add MS 41858, f.193). Grenville, who has already been mentioned, was a politician till his retirement in 1818, and known for his remarkable book collection; cf. n. 79 below.

In writing to ask Elmsley for a copy of the Theocritus, Gaisford had explained why he needed it: 'The Bodley is now so cold that I cannot sit there the requisite time for due collation.' This was late December 1814; in February 1813 he had told Elmsley in discussing a book held in the Bodleian Library, 'The coldness of the weather will prevent me from more thoroughly examining into the subject for some time.'[72] Clearly even the chalcenteric Gaisford's brazen bowels had their limits, in an unheated library in winter. In his will, Sir Thomas Bodley had forbidden the use of 'fire and flame', so the library was almost impossible to use in cold weather.[73] A steam heating system was installed in 1845 but found to be ineffective.[74] For Gaisford, long summer days offered not a chance for relaxation, but good working conditions; looking ahead to the annual move to Worcester at the end of May, he wrote to Fynes Clinton on 18 March 1826:

If nothing occurs to thrown an obstacle in my way by that time I shall have completed 50 or 52 sheets, which will contain according to my computation about 250 pages of Kuster's edition. I cannot take with me the books needed for illustrating this grammatical compilation, so I shall lose the long days & warm weather of the summer which is the time for working with comfort and advantage.[75]

Accompanying Gaisford's domination of Christ Church was his determination that undergraduates should be examined within the college rather than through the public examinations. The resulting insulation from the university was remarked on by Macaulay, who dined at the House in June 1853. He wrote in his diary:

After dinner the speechifying began... The Dean uttered only words of form. He seems to be a mere heavy taciturn, sluggish, pedant....What struck me most was the intensity and exclusiveness of Christ Church feeling which appeared in all that was said. One would have thought that Christ Church was Oxford.[76]

Legendary Gaisford

It will be clear by now that Gaisford was the kind of don about whom stories clustered. His uncouth personal style and his rigid discipline provided a tempting target, as we have seen, for both imitation and invention. The reputation for bluntness he acquired

[72] Gaisford to Elmsley, 30 Dec. 1814, 3 Feb. 1813 (Elmsley papers).
[73] Compare the Senate House in Cambridge, where in the eighteenth and much of the nineteenth centuries, candidates for the Mathematical Tripos sat in January without heating, and it was said that in some years, the ink in their inkwells froze solid (one of the perils of the Cambridge system of written exams).
[74] Craster, Bodleian, 25–7. One wonders if Gaisford knew that Gerard Langbaine had died on 10 February 1658 'of an extream cold taken by sitting in the University-Library whole Winter days' (ODNB s.v. G. Langbaine).
[75] Christ Church Library, MS 498.
[76] Macaulay, Journal, 8 June 1853: W. Thomas (ed.), The Journals of T. B. Macaulay (Pickering and Chatto, 2008), 4.57. In some ways Gaisford resembles William Powell, Master of St John's College, Cambridge, who on his arrival in 1765 had set up twice-yearly examinations which he supervised himself, as a way of resisting the influence of the mathematics-dominated university examinations.

as Dean was heightened in contrast with other heads of houses. A couplet compared him with the courtly Dr Sneyd, Warden of All Souls:

> Gaisford and Sneyd each others' lectures seek,
> The one learns manners, and the other Greek.[77]

An undergraduate asked for an exeat to attend the funeral of the Duke of Wellington: Gaisford shouted at him, 'No Sir!' The Marquis of Chandos wished to stay up into the vacation. 'Do you wish it?' 'Yes'. 'Does your parent wish it?' 'Yes'. 'Does your Tutor wish it?' 'Yes'. 'But I do not wish it, so you can't' (Lehnus 2012, 309). It has been claimed that when Gaisford was offered the chair of Greek in 1812 he wrote to Lord Liverpool, 'My Lord, I have received your letter and accede to its contents'; Dean Jackson of Christ Church discovered this, and persuaded him to send a flowery letter with a luxuriously bound copy of his Hephaestion. This story is recorded in Charles Wordsworth's autobiography,[78] and has often been repeated,[79] but since Gaisford was appointed to the chair in February 1812 he cannot have been writing to Liverpool, who only became Prime Minister in June, after the assassination of Spencer Perceval in the previous month. And indeed letters from Perceval show that Gaisford was offered the chair in January, given it in February and sent Perceval his Hephaestion in March. Acknowledging the gift, Perceval thanked Gaisford for his 'politeness and attention'. [80]

Another story relates to a proposed visit by Queen Victoria. Asked what accommodation she could have in the college, Gaisford replied, 'Her two rooms'—that is, the two rooms over the passage between Tom and Peckwater quads (Lehnus 2012, 310). In fact Victoria's only visit to the college as Queen seems to have been an unannounced one, in 1860, after Gaisford's death.[81] The source of the story is probably a visit by Queen Adelaide in 1835, and the surviving correspondence shows that Gaisford offered to put

---

[77] Thompson 1899, 138. In fact neither man lectured. Sneyd, a Christ Church man, was Warden of All Souls 1827–58.

[78] Wordsworth 1891, 67. These stories were attested c.1829–30. In his sequel, Wordsworth reported that Henry Liddell had confirmed the story, having heard it from a Christ Church man who had heard it from Cyril Jackson, Gaisford's predecessor as Dean (Wordsworth 1893, xxv).

[79] E.g. J. Morley, Life of Gladstone (1903), 1.49.

[80] The delays were caused first by Perceval being unwilling to send Gaisford's name to the Prince Regent before he had accepted the offer; second by his waiting till the 18th of February, when the restrictions on the regent's powers ended and Gaisford could be appointed for life and not 'during pleasure' (Perceval to Gaisford, 29 Jan.–12 Mar. 1812; Christ Church archives, SOC xxiii.c.101.2). J. E. Sandys claimed that Gaisford was appointed by 'Lord Grenville, the minister in whose hands the appointment lay' (Sandys 1908, 397); he was followed by Lloyd-Jones (Lloyd-Jones 1982, 14). But Grenville's premiership was in 1806–7; he was out of office in 1812, the leader of the Whigs from then till 1817, and Chancellor of Oxford 1809–34. H. L. Thompson refers to Grenville as Chancellor, but specifies that the Hephaestion was sent to him (Thompson 1899, 139). (It is of course possible that both Grenville and Perceval were sent copies.) Grenville was the younger brother of Thomas Grenville, the bibliophile; the Grenville Homer', the most luxurious classical production of the University Press in the period, was named for them (2013b, 441).

[81] She had visited in 1832 as Princess Victoria, but apparently without entering Christ Church: J. Morris, The Oxford Book of Oxford (Oxford, 1978), 196.

the Deanery at her disposal, but explained that it was small, with only three bedrooms. As a result, the royal party took over a nearby inn.[82] Another Laconian saying was reported by Charles Wordsworth from 1840: replying to the father of an undergraduate, Gaisford wrote, 'Dear Sir, Such letters as yours are a great annoyance to your obedient servant, T. Gaisford.'[83] His letter to Wordsworth's father, the Master of Trinity College, Cambridge, acknowledging the loan of Porson's copy of Kuster's *Suidas*, is as quoted certainly curt, replying as it did to a flowery letter of congratulation on his appointment as Dean of Christ Church; but the letters to Wordsworth's successor William Whewell, though businesslike, are not lacking in courtesy.[84]

A comparison of Gaisford with other dons who have inspired anecdotes suggests that there are two kinds of legendary figures. One is the don who cultivates epigrammatic or other striking utterance, and is thus the author of his own legend. In Oxford the leading example is William Spooner, Warden of New College 1903–24, the creator of relatively few spoonerisms, though enough to encourage the creation of many more by others.[85] In Cambridge, it is William Thompson, Master of Trinity 1866–86, who 'had an unhappy gift of epigrammatic utterance'; of the young Richard Jebb he allegedly said, 'The time that Mr Jebb takes from the neglect of his duties, he devotes to the adornment of his dress.' At a college council meeting, he remarked, 'None of us is perfect—not even the youngest among us.'[86] The other kind of don is mythicized without conscious help from himself. For example, Herbert Blakiston, President of Trinity, whose *ODNB* article ends as follows:

For much of his life, Blakiston was a recognized Oxford character, even a figure of fun. He was ugly, he wore glasses (the nickname Blinks dated from his adolescence), he was a bad driver, and he made enemies easily. After his death he was quickly reduced to a series of comic anecdotes, redolent of the Victorian common-room tradition he had himself enjoyed.[87]

Another mythicized Oxford figure was Benjamin Jowett, the subject of a well-known rhyme by Herbert Beeching in the *Masque of Balliol* (1875):

> First come I. My name is Jowett.
> There's no knowledge but I know it.
> I am the Master of this College;
> What I don't know isn't knowledge.

---

[82] Christ Church archives, SOC xxiii.c.101.31 (Oct. 1835).

[83] From a letter from Edward Pusey to Christopher Wordsworth sr, 7 Aug. 1840: Wordsworth 1891, 67.

[84] Gaisford to Whewell, 1842–1844 (six letters). Trinity College, Library, Add MS a 205, 2–7.

[85] J. Huxley, 'Doctor Spooner: the growth of a legend', *On Living in a Revolution* (1944), 90–5; R. H. Robbins, 'The Warden's wordplay: toward a redefinition of the Spoonerism', *Dalhousie Review* 46 (1966–7), 457–65; W. Hayter, *Spooner: A Biography* (1977), 136–46.

[86] Uniquely, not only can the historicity of this anecdote be verified, but even the date of the utterance: 24 Nov. 1878. See H. Jackson, 'After all, we are none of us infallible—not even the youngest of us', *Fasciculus J. W. Clark dicatus* (1909), 274–6.

[87] C. Hopkins, 'Blakiston, Herbert Edward Douglas'; cf. T. F. Higham, *Dr Blakiston Recalled* (1957).

F. W. Bateson recalled that when he went up in 1920, the current version was anapaestic:

> I am Benjamin Jowett
> Master of Balliol College
> Whatever is known I know it
> What I don't know isn't knowledge.[88]

Maurice Bowra, finally, is an especially interesting case, being both a focus of stories and a generator of them himself: one of those who turn their contemporaries into mythicized figures for later generations (see Mitchell 2009).

The Gaisford Story

I come finally to the anecdote for which Gaisford is most widely remembered, and whose 'classical form' I quoted above. There are other stories. For example, he is claimed to have begun a sermon with 'St Paul says, and I partly agree with him...'.[89] He is also alleged, again in a sermon, after listing the passages in which he thought the biblical account was confirmed by Greek and Roman authors, to have asked his hearers to give such passages of the Bible which lacked that advantage their 'fauvorable considerashion'.[90] Anecdotes of this kind spread through a kind of Chinese whispers, changing in transmission, but also elaborated by inventive narrators. But *the* Gaisford story has outstripped the rest by far, and this is surely because of the cultural centrality of its themes. Some of its versions have survived, we can assume, through their formal elegance or through the authority and accessibility of specific channels of transmission.

The Tuckwell version scores on both counts. It was the first version to appear in print in a book, it has a nicely balanced dual structure, and its wording is finely honed. Curiously, however, its main clause is clumsy: what is being impressed is surely not Greek literature, but its value. But how many of us have noticed this? This version has also benefited from inclusion in *the Oxford Dictionary of Quotations*—a book many of us possess, but whose history has yet to be written.[91] Tuckwell's version did not,

---

[88]   Bateson, *The Scholar-Critic* (1972), 118. The *Masque* was reprinted in W. G. Hiscock, ed. *The Balliol Rhymes*. Oxford: Blackwell (1939), which includes variant forms of the rhyme.

[89]   A. B. Walkley, *Pastiche and Prejudice* (1921), 94.

[90]   'Alfred Bailey...gave an amusing account of a sermon, which he had himself actually heard preached by old Dean Gaisford, in which, after enumerating the various passages in which the Biblical writers to be by Greek and Roman authors, he appealed to his hearers to give such passages of the Bible as had not that advantage their 'fauvorable considerashion'. M. E. Grant Duff, *Notes from a Diary, 1896–1901* (1905), 1.16–7 (16 Feb. 1896). The spelling of the final phrase is presumably meant to indicate regional (Wiltshire) pronunciation.

[91]   The first edition (1941) was assembled by Alice Smyth, who had previously published with OUP a *Book of Fabulous Beasts: Old Stories Retold* and *Rip van Winkle and the Flying Dutchman*. Both titles seem strangely appropriate to the present discussion. The Dictionary has been illuminatingly discussed by its editor, Elizabeth Knowles (see n. 1 above). In a foreword to the first edition, Bernard Darwin slyly suggested that the representation of W. H. Thompson of Cambridge, of whom many stories were told, by a single anecdote, might be due to the Oxonian bias of the Dictionary.

however, appear in the first edition, in which Oxonian oral tradition was drawn on for a version reported by Thomas Strong, Bishop of Oxford and previously Dean of Christ Church, who claimed to have heard it from Henry Liddon, who was at the House in Gaisford's last years:

The advantages of a classical education are two-fold—it enables us to look down with contempt on those who have not shared its advantages, and also fits us for places of emolument not only in this world, but in that which is to come.

At some point before the publication of the second edition, the definitive Tuckwell version must have been reported to the editor, and this was inserted instead, perhaps because a printed account was seen as more reliable.

So far we have two elements, which we can label 'superiority' and 'emolument', apparently the core of the anecdote; but also what I called earlier the blasphemous supplement 'next world'. The basis for this can be seen in two early twentieth-century versions. The first appeared in 1904:

the study of Greek, which not only, by the light it throws on revealed truth, prepares us for eternal happiness in the next world, but also not unfrequently leads to positions of considerable emolument in this.[92]

This was followed in 1914 by a version from the noted Oxford wit A. D. Godley:

In political and ecclesiastical circles especially, young men who had distinguished themselves at the university were much in demand. Greek scholarship, it has been said, led not only to knowledge of the means of salvation in the next world, but to positions of emolument in this. Fellows of colleges who wanted church preferment edited Greek plays. I fear bishops have other qualifications now.[93]

Here we can see the basis of 'next world', discussed below.

To complete the picture we have to add a fourth element which sometimes appears: Greek is the language of our Lord.

Every one knows Dean Gaisford's three reasons for the cultivation of the Greek language...It may not be necessary [for the scholar] 'to read the words of Christ in the original'; it may not be of absolute importance that he should 'have situations of affluence opened to him.' But it certainly is essential that he should 'look down on his fellow-creatures from a proper elevation.'[94]

This element, which we can call 'language', seems to be an alternative to 'next world'; at least I have not found them together. Perhaps the attractions of a tricolon discouraged tellers from adding both of them to the dual core of 'superiority' and 'emolument'.

---

[92] J. B. Wainewright, letter, *The Tablet*, 14 May 1904, 21. I owe this reference to Peter Rhodes.

[93] A. D. Godley, 'The present position of classical studies in England', *Lectures delivered [at] Princeton University in October* 1913 (1914), 79. Godley is remembered for his macaronic verses on omnibuses which referred first to 'motor bus' and then to 'motorem bum'. The poem was written in 1914, when motor buses were introduced in Oxford.

[94] G. Saintsbury, 'Modern English prose', *Fortnightly Review* 19 ns [25 os] Feb. 1876, 243–59, at 251.

They are of course very different, one being distinctly exotic and the other a conventional argument for the study of Greek.

Looking at the variants, what one might expect if one knew nothing of the Tuckwell version is a tricolon: the language of our Lord, superiority, and emoluments—as in Saintsbury's version, quoted above. Instead we find a curious variety of versions. Not only that, two early versions include the phrase 'even in this life', which is distinctly, and perhaps deliberately, incongruous coming after 'considerable emolument':

in the words of Dean Gaisford, virtue and industry 'lead to positions of considerable emolument even in this life'.[95]

[A] preacher at Harrow School...told his hearers that by a course of industry and uprightness they might rise to positions of considerable emolument, even in this life.[96]

Here Godley offers a nice attempt to make balanced sense.

Finally, the earliest known printed version deserves quotation:

Dr Gaisford sometimes preaches in the Cathedral of Christ Church, and the following extract from a sermon reported to have been delivered by him one Christmas Day some ten or twenty years ago, will show what kind of a divine and a Christian the Rev. Doctor is. Speaking of classical studies, he observed that one of the great advantages derived from them was, that 'they not only enabled a man to look down with calm contempt upon his less fortunate competitors, but also occasionally led to high preferments, to which considerable emoluments were attached'.[97]

Here we begin in the present tense (this comes from the year before Gaisford's death) but then move into the past. Even in the period when I believe the story emerged, it already inhabited a mythical past. We can learn from it, however, that the dual-core fable found in Tuckwell does seem to have been the original form. The inclusion of 'occasionally' gives us a glimpse of a stylistic element stripped out later on in the interest of formal economy. It also perhaps shows us a brutal frankness on Gaisford's part; but in the light of his history, which until 1831 alternated between adequately paid jobs which made scholarly work almost impossible, and poorly paid jobs which allowed time for scholarship, we might wonder if this is not frankness, but irony.

Almost nothing can be said about the transmission of the story in the 1850s and 60s. The only evidence comes from a memoir published in 1930:

A greater man [than Benjamin Symonds of Wadham] in the public eye was Gaisford, Dean of Christ Church. His comment on the value of scholarship, and particularly of Greek, is worth recalling at the present time, even for its audacity. This is what he declaimed from the University pulpit:

'The study of Greek Literature...which not only enables us to look down on others less gifted than ourselves, not only elevates above the common herd, but leads not infrequently to positions of considerable emolument.'

I know that Osborne Gordon guaranteed another version:

---

[95] Anon. review, *The Graphic* (London), 26 Feb. 1876, 210.

[96] Anon., *Irish Monthly* 5 (1877), 573.

[97] [Edward Walford], 'Oxford, its past and present, pt. II', *Dublin Review* 37 (1854), 68–96, at.85. So far no versions have come to light between 1854 and 1876.

'but also leads to posts of honour and emolument, certainly in this world, and probably in the next'.

Gordon served under the Dean, but I doubt his memory. Gaisford was pompous, and vain of his learning, but not an irreverent fool.[98]

This gives us a glimpse of the standard dual-core version, superiority plus emolument (interestingly, expanded into a tricolon), plus the 'irreverent' element, running side by side. The earlier linking of salvation in the next world and emolument in this has led to a blasphemous conflation. It also points the finger at Osborne Gordon as a transmitter and elaborator; the only version which casts any light on this process.[99] Sneyd-Kynnersley's book also has a chapter (pp. 114–30) discussing the nature of anecdotes and their transmission, though he does not use the Gaisford anecdote as an example.

To judge by the undergraduate dates of the original informants, it looks as if the story emerged in the late 1840s—when the move toward liberalization, and the growth of the examination system at Oxford, will have made Gaisford's stubborn and college-centred conservatism more and more noticeable. (I have already mentioned his refusal to recognize the Royal Commission.) It was in this period that the Dean and Chapter of Christ Church came under fire for accepting payment for giving university sermons. A flurry of pamphlets in 1847 included two defences of the Chapter by Gaisford.[100] In his second statement, he remarked of the Canons of Christ Church that 'their station and the emoluments arising therefrom seem to require the execution of this not very heavy duty ... without remuneration'.[101] If this statement had any part in the emergence of the story, then clearly Gaisford was, once again, misrepresented. The 'considerable emoluments' of the anecdote were publicly acknowledged, but as a reason for forgoing payment.

There are also points of interest in the later transmission of the story. It is striking how hard it is for some people to abandon the assumption that there was an original sermon (even Parsons nods here). In Notes and Queries in 1934, a plaintive enquirer, who had heard W. R. Inge's reference to the 'famous sermon' in his presidential address to the Classical Association earlier that year, asked when the sermon had been given, and whether it was the same as the 'sermon on verbs in –mi'. Peter Green, in his amusement at Gaisford's pretensions, retains the assumption of historicity:

Not only in this world but also in that which is to come. We may laugh at Gaisford's eschatological pretensions—the notion of professors forming a corps d'élite in heaven has its own weird charm ...[102]

---

[98] As told by 'the Dean of Zedcaster', perhaps at St John's, in the 1890s, according to E. M. Sneyd-Kynnersley, HMI's Notebook (1930), 30–1 (matric. Balliol 1860, fellow of St John's 1865–79).

[99] Lloyd-Jones thought Gordon might have been the prime source of Gaisfordian anecdotes (Lloyd-Jones 1982, 83); J. F. A. Mason (pers. comm.) thinks this unlikely. Another candidate is Henry Coxe, sub-librarian at the Bodleian from 1839, with whom as we have seen Gaisford got on very well, and who was an accomplished mimic and storyteller.

[100] See E. H. Cordeaux and D. H. Merry, A Bibliography of Printed Works Relating to the University of Oxford (1968), nos. 3776-81; Gaisford's defences are nos. 3777 and 3781.

[101] 'The subject of University Sermons ... etc.' C and M 3381. Bodley, G. A. Oxon c.63 (81); Durham University Library, Routh LXVI E 11/6.

[102] P. Green, Classical Bearings (1989), 19, 272.

But the palm, or rather the wooden spoon, for credulity goes to Michael Grant, who in 1999 felt able to distinguish between later reports and what Gaisford actually said: 'What Dean Gaisford actually said was, 'Nor can I do better ... emolument.'[103]

On the other hand, there are occasionally—very occasionally—signs of a critical stance. J. B. Skemp in 1952 quoted the first edition of the *Oxford Dictionary of Quotations*, adding, 'Let us hope that bishop Strong's memory was not perfect.'[104] But the first prize for scepticism goes to the versatile and eccentric Gilbert Bagnani of Toronto:

The study of Greek undoubtedly 'led to positions of dignity and emolument' ... It has always been attributed to Dean Gaisford, but it is so completely in the eighteenth century tradition that I suspect it to have originated much earlier. It seems the kind of remark that one would expect from someone like Parr.[105]

It was left to J. W. Mackail in 1924 to apply Matthew Arnold's doctrine of the best self. At his hands, Gaisford's utterance is not denied, but humanized:

The latter of these motives ['dignity and emolument'] cannot be offered now; but there remains as a reward the dignity of human nature ... For the former, ... Greek makes us consciously superior, not to others, but to ourselves.[106]

Conclusion

To return, finally, to the terms of my subtitle. 'Legion': Liddell wrote of Gaisford in 1852 that he was 'an unreasonable man in all things except Philology and bookselling and the management of libraries.'[107] Gaisford was indeed a hard-working and effective scholar, delegate and curator; his chair and his deanship gave him the chance to do the work he wanted to do, but the latter also embroiled him to some extent in work he did not want to do. 'Legend': I hope to have shown that much of what has been written about Gaisford is either factually wrong or influenced by the stereotype inspired by his undoubted bearishness. The four elements of the Gaisford anecdote, in their various combinations, reflect above all the entanglement of Classics and religion with each other and with social status—an entanglement also represented in Gaisford's position as professor of Greek and head of that anomalous hybrid institution, Christ Church. 'Lexicographer': Gaisford's involvement with his two large dictionaries over a quarter

---

[103] M. Grant, *The Collapse and Recovery of the Roman Empire* (1999), 106.

[104] J. B. Skemp, 'The permanent value of Greek studies', *Durham University Journal* 13 (1952), 37.

[105] G. Bagnani, 'Winckelmann and the second renaissance, 1755–1955', *American Journal of Archaeology* 59 (1955), 107–18, at 113. For Bagnani, see L. Woodbury, 'Gentleman-scholar: a memoir of Gilbert Bagnani', in *Collected Writings* (Atlanta GA, 1990), 613–19; W. J. N. Rudd, *It Seems Like Yesterday* (London: Classical Association, 2003),[18–19].

[106] J. W. Mackail, *What is the Good of Greek?* (1924), 22.

[107] Liddell to Henry Acland, Feb. 1852; quoted in C. E. Mallet, *History of the University of Oxford* (1924–7) 3.219.

of a century is not only impressive by itself, it can now also be seen as part of the prehistory of Liddell and Scott's lexicon. Among the most striking aspects of this commitment, one which brings together Gaisford the scholar, library curator, and press delegate, is his hands-on involvement in the making of books which readers could use easily and effectively. Here the social and intellectual conservative was very much an innovator. The invention of stereotyping (making moulds of movable type to facilitate cheaper reprinting) coincided with Gaisford's matriculation at Christ Church in the late 1790s. 'Stereotyping' became a metaphor for fixity of opinion just before he died in 1855, and entered psychological parlance in the 1920s. Given Gaisford's achievements in the world of scholarly books, it is appropriate, perhaps, to describe this chapter as an attempt to see what lies behind the stereotype.[108]

[108] My thanks to Chris Pelling, for inviting me to give the 2008 Gaisford Lecture, and for help of various kinds, to Judith Curthoys, Christopher Lewis and the late Janet McMullin (Christ Church, Oxford), Patrick Gaisford-St Lawrence (Dublin), Eddie Smith and Selma Thomas (Westminster School), John Bowman (UCL), David Butterfield, Chris Collard, August Imholtz jr, Richard Jenkyns, Ted Kenney, Luigi Lehnus, John Mason, Michael Reeve, Graham Whitaker, Gayle Cooper (Small Special Collections Library, University of Virginia), Karen Nangle (Beinecke Library, Yale University), Margaret McCollum (Durham University Library), Klimis Mastoridis (University of Cyprus), Martin Maw (OUP archives), Nigel Roche (St Bride Printing Library), and Michael Twyman.

4

The Rise and Fall of Porsoniasm

In 1903, in the preface to the first volume of his edition of Manilius, A. E. Housman wrote that:

we now witness in Germany pretty much what happened in England after 1825, when our own great age of scholarship, begun in 1691 by Bentley's Epistola ad Millium, was ended by the successive strokes of doom which consigned Dobree and Elmsley to the grave and Blomfield to the bishopric of Chester. England disappeared from the fellowship of nations for the next forty years.   (Housman 1903, xlii)

The scholar who lurks unnamed behind this paragraph is Richard Porson, and Dobree, Elmsley, and Blomfield, who *are* named, were all in different ways his disciples. Although Porson had no pupils and gave no lectures, in the generation just after his death he had a number of followers who cultivated his memory and emulated his style, at least before they were removed to higher spheres by death or preferment to bishoprics.[1] If the cultivation of his scholarly style can be called Porsonianism, it was the cult of Porson himself after his death in 1808, centred on Trinity College Cambridge, for which three years later the Oxford scholar Peter Elmsley coined the name 'Porsoniasm'. As one might expect, the name-giver was an outsider. Yet as his inclusion in Housman's sketch indicates, Elmsley could himself be called a Porsonian, and indeed in 1911, in his inaugural lecture as Professor of Latin at Cambridge, Housman remarked that 'scholarship meant to Elmsley what it meant to Dobree' (Housman 1969, 25; cf. n. 55 below). But though Elmsley was a Porsonian, he was not (if I may venture a hapax of my own) a Porsoniast. His original coinage occurred in a letter to Samuel Butler in August 1811:

Do you happen to know the name of the author of the Review of Blomfield's Prometheus in the Quarterly Review? He is evidently a Cantabrigian, a friend to Blomfield, a fierce enemy to you, rather hostile to me than otherwise, and, above all, initiated in the higher mysteries of Porsoniasm.   (Elmsley to Butler, 17 Aug. 1811: Butler 1896, 1.71)

Elmsley's wordplay followed a lead given by Butler himself in the previous year, in a pamphlet addressed to Blomfield. Blomfield had reviewed Butler's edition of Aeschylus

---

[1] To Housman's list we might add James Henry Monk, who succeeded Porson as Regius Professor of Greek, but he was appointed Dean of Peterborough in 1822 (too early for Housman's scheme), and became Bishop of Gloucester in 1830 (too late).

in the *Edinburgh Review*, anonymously as was then usual, and Butler's response took the common form of a published letter to a third party (Butler 1810). In this case, having found that Blomfield was the reviewer, he pretended ignorance, and in effect complained of the review to its author. In the course of his pamphlet, of whose 'dreary pleasantry' J. E. B. Mayor later complained (Mayor 1869, 911), he referred to Porson's disciples as Porsonulettes, Porsoninians, and Porsonaccians (Butler 1810, 25, 62). He also wrote that 'I know that by the freedom of my remarks I have disturbed the...whole nest of aspirants to the Porsonian throne' (ibid. 76)—one of whom was of course Blomfield himself.

Butler's edition of Aeschylus was natural prey for the Porsonians, since it was a bulky variorum edition assembled for Cambridge University Press on the basis of Thomas Stanley's seventeenth-century text—precisely the commission that Porson had famously refused to accept nearly twenty years earlier. On his asking for university support to go abroad to collate manuscripts, the Vice-Chancellor had commented, 'Let Mr Porson collect his MSS at home' (Clarke 1937, 15–16).[2]

Butler's coinages, I suggest, were the product of a nervous jocularity which welcomed solidarity with other scholars outside the magic circle but reflected anxiety at his own exclusion. They were picked up by Elmsley in a letter of November 1811 in which he commented that 'the Porsonulettes of Cambridge...are in possession of the scriptures as well as the oral tradition of Porsoniasm'.[3] I have now cited the only two occurrences of 'Porsoniasm' that I know of—only three months apart, so this flurry of wordplay was transient as well as idiolectal. It belonged to a moment in which the Porsonians asserted their scholarly authority and their collective identity through the hostile reviewing of an outsider's work.[4]

To return to Elmsley's enquiry: his anonymous reviewer was in fact James Henry Monk, who in 1808, at the age of twenty-five, had succeeded Porson as Regius Professor of Greek. He and Charles James Blomfield were not only brother-fellows of Trinity but lifelong friends, and godfathers to one another's children.[5] They both secured influential patrons and through them preferment, and having edited Greek plays, ended up as the best-known of the 'Greek play bishops' (Burns and Stray 2011). If we stick with Housman's fuzzy chronology, the mid-1820s saw not only their preferment and Dobree's

[2] Porson later referred scornfully in print to scholars who did not understand the difference between collating and collecting (Clarke 1937, 15–6).

[3] Elmsley to Butler, 14 Nov. 1811: Butler 1896, 1. 71. The 'scriptures' were Porson's notes, held in Trinity, which were published between 1812 and 1822 by Monk, Blomfield, and Dobree. 'Porsonulettes' doubly denigrates diminutive demoiselles. M. L. Clarke, in quoting from this letter, gives 'Porsonianism' (the *facilior lectio*) for 'Porsoniasm', a rare lapse by a fastidious scholar: Clarke 1937, 106. The correct reading can in both cases be confirmed from the original MSS: British Library, Add. Ms. 34583, f. 334 (Aug.), f. 342 (Nov.).

[4] The first occurrences of Porson-related terms I have found are as follows: 1810 Porsonian school, Porsonians, Porsonaccians, Porsonulettes; 1811 Porsoniasm; 1812 Porsoniana, Porsonic type; 1813 Porsonian type, Porsonianism; 1825 Porsonian canon; 1827 a Porsonian (i.e. winner of the Porson Prize); c.1830 Porsonia (Hugh Boyd's nickname for Elizabeth Barrett); 1839 Porsonunculi, Porsunculi, Porsonian article, Porsonian pause; 1854 pre-Porsonian school.

[5] Blomfield returned Monk's favour by reviewing his *Alcestis* in the *Quarterly Review* (Blomfield 1816).

death, but the demise of the journal they edited, the *Museum Criticum* (1826), and one might add, the retirement in 1824 of William Gifford, editor of the *Quarterly Review*, for which they had both written.[6] The period I am primarily concerned with thus runs from Porson's death in 1808 to the mid-1820s. The topics I focus on are the social and institutional affiliations, the inclusions and exclusions, the solidarities and conflicts, which surrounded the practice of the Porsonian style. My aims are to characterize the style of the school; to discuss what made it a school, looking especially at its institutional bases and internal structure; to investigate its relations with the outside world—including the Others who sustained its identity by disagreement or enmity; and to establish how and why it declined.

Inclusion and Exclusion: School, Group and Network

Elmsley's enquiry takes us into the heart of the world in which Porsoniasm was born: a world of scholarship practised by a network of men in colleges, schools, and rectories, with its social inclusion and exclusion, knowledge and ignorance, its mixture of friendship and enmity, of respect and jealousy. In this letter an Oxford-trained scholar living in Kent asks a Cambridge-trained scholar, the headmaster of Shrewsbury, for information about the author of an anonymous review. Elmsley lacked this information for several reasons. First, in 1811 most articles on classical topics were, like this one, published anonymously in literary and political journals. Secondly, in the politically polarized world of the reviews he was associated with the reformist *Edinburgh Review*, notorious for its recent attacks on Oxford scholarship, rather than its conservative opponent the *Quarterly Review*, for which Monk and Blomfield wrote.[7] Thirdly and finally, like Butler he was not a member of the Porsonian circle based in Trinity College, Cambridge. Butler however, unlike Elmsley, was a Cantab, and so more likely to have access to such information. The remarkable success of his pupils in Cambridge examinations was maintained in part by regular visits to his alma mater to check up on examining tendencies. Christopher Wordsworth, Master of Trinity, complained that 'Dr Butler comes here year after year, just as a first-rate London milliner makes a yearly visit to Paris to get the fashions' (Butler 1896, 1. 9).[8] Thus there were degrees of inclusion and exclusion; but in addition, as I hope to show, both men in different ways had links with the Porsonians, who were themselves linked by division as well as solidarity.

---

[6] For the *Museum Criticum*, see Chapter 7; for the role of classical articles in the *Quarterly Review*, see Chapter 6.

[7] He himself wrote for it soon afterwards (Elmsley 1812a, b) in an attempt to redeem his reputation in conservative Anglican circles.

[8] Butler's preface is separately paginated. He does not date the remark; it must have been made between Wordsworth's appointment as Master of Trinity in 1820 and Butler's retirement in 1836.

To return to Housman's artful rhetorical vignette: the picture he paints is populated only by a few individuals, with a distant backdrop of 'the fellowship of nations'. In this he is largely followed by Charles Brink in his book on English classical scholarship (Brink 1986). Brink's book is by design a study of three outstanding individuals: Bentley, Porson, and Housman (though it does include a chapter on Victorian classical education),[9] and it thus belongs to a tradition followed also by Wilamowitz, Sandys, and Pfeiffer.[10] As I suggest in my conclusion, and as I hope the chapter will demonstrate, there are serious weaknesses in a historiography of scholarship which concentrates on individuals to the neglect of groups, networks, and institutional traditions.

It is with the amorphous and somewhat neglected phenomenon of informal collaboration and scholarly networks that this paper is concerned.[11] We are familiar with formal groups such as the Oxford (1870) and Cambridge (1871) Philological Societies, the Hellenic (1879) and Roman (1910) societies, and with the German philological seminars of the eighteen and nineteenth centuries (Grafton 1983, Clark 2006, 162–79). One thinks of Heyne and Wolf, Boeckh and Hermann, and of the rebellious young Friedrich Ritschl against whom his pupil Wilhelm Wagner later rebelled (Glucker 1981). A well-known Victorian example of a network is the X Club, a group of scientific friends including J. D. Hooker and T. H. Huxley, active in the second half of the nineteenth century (Barton 2006). Historians of science have been active in discussing the features and conditions of such groups and group-styles, from Ludwik Fleck's 'Denkstil' and 'Denkkollectiv' (Fleck 1935, on syphilology) to Thomas Kuhn's 'paradigm' and 'disciplinary matrix' (Kuhn 1966, on physics).[12] The best-known case in classical scholarship is that of the 'Cambridge Ritualists'. Sometimes labelled 'the Cambridge Group', they are better seen as a collection of atoms revolving around the nucleus provided by Jane Harrison; the 'group' is the product of retrospective reification (Beard 2000, 111–15). In his recent *ODNB* group article on the Ritualists, Robert Ackerman does not discuss this aspect because he was unable to find hard evidence of usage.[13] It is worth pointing out, however, that in 1951 Gilbert Murray identified 'a certain movement in Greek studies, represented principally by J. E. H.[arrison] and me, and Cornford . . .'. He went on to assert that 'the movement is

---

[9] Brink 1986, 114–49. It was my disagreement with some of the views expressed in this chapter which prompted my own first investigation of the history of classical scholarship (1988). Cf. now 2016a.

[10] The remarks quoted above from Housman's *Manilius* preface are based on a passage in the preface to Wilamowitz's *Heracles*: quoted by Brink 1986, 215 n. 4 (German), 115 (English).

[11] Nicholas Horsfall remarked in his review of Brink's book, 'There is a good deal more to be said about the "Porsonulettes"': Horsfall (1987). *Expertus scripsit*: see Horsfall 1974, based on Elmsley's correspondence. Clarke's account (Clarke 1945, 85–101) remains useful.

[12] More recent discussions include Rouse 1987 and Warwick and Kaiser 2005. The impact of such work on practitioners of science is another matter; it has been suggested, for example, that for practising particle physicists, 'Their history of physics is a short hagiography and a list of miracles' (Traweek 1988, 77).

[13] Ackerman 2007. The earliest published reference to 'the Cambridge Ritualists' I know of is Ackerman's own article (Ackerman 1971); his doctoral thesis was entitled 'The Cambridge group and the origins of myth criticism' (Ackerman 1969).

a real one'.[14] The Porsonians, nevertheless, are rather different: they had an eponymous hero to worship and were labelled as a 'school' by their contemporaries.[15] The chronological profiles of the two phenomena were also very different. The amount of direct interaction with the hero was minimal or non-existent in the Porsonian circle, except in the case of Dobree; the Ritualists, on the other hand, were inspired by a woman who was an older contemporary of her co-workers. Porsonians and Ritualists however had this in common, that they were based in Cambridge but had Oxonian connexions.

The world of textual scholarship in early nineteenth-century England was a small and select one. In July 1813, Blomfield, editor with Monk of the new Cambridge classical journal *Museum Criticum*, told Elmsley that:

Murray [the publisher John Murray] ... committed the unaccountable folly of having 1000 copies printed! When unquestionably there are not 300 persons in England who will read the book, nor 100 who will understand it.[16]

In the previous year, he had reported the opinion of Francis Jeffrey, editor of the *Edinburgh Review*: 'having observed that my article would occupy 30 pages ... he adds, "while on a liberal computation, there are about as many persons who will understand it"' (Blomfield to Elmsley, 6 May 1812). One sympathizes with Jeffrey: the minute linguistic style of Porsonian reviews made them rebarbative contributions to general literary journals, consisting as they did of a page or so of general comments followed by a long list of detailed points.[17] In November 1811, referring to a paper on Clarendon and a 'long paper on the preface to the Hecuba', Elmsley had remarked that the former (non-classical) paper was 'the price of his [Jeffreys'] inserting the paper on Hecuba'. Two months later, he reported that his paper on Hecuba 'has been nearly three quarters of a year in the hands of the editor, who, I am afraid, begins to think that the Edinburgh Review is too learned'. Nothing daunted, however, he added, 'I shall make some curious additions to it in the next number.'[18] The great reviews were keen to cultivate the ancient universities as sources of both writers and subscribers, but their editors were aware that too much classical scholarship, like too much theology, might damage their sales.

[14] Murray to J. A. K. Thomson, 14 Feb. 1951; Bodleian Library, MSS Gilbert Murray, 175 f. 52. In his letter, Murray urged Thomson to write an article on the movement for the *Classical Quarterly* or the *Journal of Hellenic Studies*. The letter is quoted and discussed by Barbara McManus (McManus 2007, 195).

[15] Butler seems once again to be the original coiner, in his *Letter to Blomfield*: 'why should his [Porson's] disciples ... admit nothing to have the least claim to attention which is not of the Porsonian School?': Butler 1810, 14. The *Letter* is dated 9 April 1810.

[16] Blomfield to Elmsley, 17 July 1813: Elmsley papers, Westminster School. Quotations from the papers are made by permission of the Headmaster.

[17] The genre is not extinct: see for example C. S. Kraus's review of L. A. Sussman's *The Declamations of Calpurnius Flaccus* (*BMCR* 95.08.07), described by its author (pers. comm.) as 'almost a parody of the genre'; though the symphonic return to a general theme *ad fin.* distinguishes it from its early nineteenth-century ancestors.

[18] Elmsley to S. Butler, 14 Nov. 1811, 10 Jan. 1812: BL, Add. Ms. 34583, ff. 342, 357.

Elmsley himself in 1813 was even more pessimistic than Blomfield: 'The fact is, as you are well aware, there are about ten men in England who really study the <u>minutiae</u> of Greek, and of these few, four or five do not write.'[19] He went on to make a proposal which in passing offers a thumbnail sketch of the English classical world:

I propose the following scheme to you. Should the communication with the North of Germany be opened in the spring, let us collect all the classical labours of English scholars for the last five or six years, and send them as a present to Hermann, who I believe, dwells at Jena. I mean, Greek plays out of number, Burney's Tentamen, Gaisford's Hephaestion, Porsoniana, Etc. The present to be made by Gaisford and Monk (the two Professors), Burney, you, and me. I looked the other day into a new volume of Erfurdt's Sophocles. The German scholar appears to be entirely unacquainted with our labours for several years past.[20]

The Porsonian style

The style is well known: it was based on an accurate memory for detail, using knowledge of Greek usage in vocabulary, grammar, syntax, and metre to control emendation. The most famous product of all this was Porson's Law, first expounded in the preface to the revised edition of his edition of *Hecuba* (1802), in response to a review of the first edition by Hermann.[21] The Law (in fact an empirical generalization) soon acquired an almost sacred authority. In the 1870s, when an unsigned fair copy of iambics written by Henry Hayman, headmaster of Rugby, was shown to Henry Moss, headmaster of Shrewsbury, by a Rugby master, Moss raised an eyebrow at an infringement of the Law and exclaimed, 'How old is the boy?' (Wilson 1933, 73). Nearly a century later, many readers of Robert Ogilvie's book *Latin and Greek* must have been surprised to find that 'Porson's law of the final cretic is even now familiar to every schoolboy' (Ogilvie 1964, 87). Indeed some may have asked, 'Where has this man been?'—the answer being, since 1957, at Balliol College, Oxford. Ogilvie may have changed his mind on the topic after becoming headmaster of Tonbridge School in 1970.[22]

The authors worked on by the Porsonians were almost without exception Greek; something which marked the school as belonging in some sense to the tide of romantic Hellenism which had swept over England in the second half of the eighteenth century.

[19] He was perhaps thinking of Samuel Parr's decade of scholars: Porson, Kidd, Monk, Blomfield, Barker, Burges, Maltby, Butler, Dobree, Elmsley: Johnstone 1828, 1.752.

[20] Elmsley to [Blomfield], 8 Feb. 1813: Bodleian Library MS Autogr. D.24, ff. 150r–151v. Cf. the 'ministry of all the talents' referred to in Chapter 3. The addressee is not named ('Dear Sir') but is certainly Blomfield. The 'opening' refers to the spring thaw in the River Elbe. My thanks to Patrick Finglass, who told me of the letter, and to Chris Collard for transcribing it.

[21] In the nineteenth century it was usually called 'the Porsonian canon', a phrase which was still used by Hardie in *Res Metrica* (Hardie 1920); 'Porson's Law' dates from the 1880s, and by the early twentieth century had become the common form.

[22] Hayman declared that he 'did not recognise the rule of the final cretic' (Wilson 1933, 72–3). Benjamin Jowett, Regius Professor of Greek at Oxford, had shared Hayman's doubts about the infallibility of Porson's Law, to the horror of the Professor of Latin, John Conington (Abbott and Campbell 1897, 1.249).

But Porsonian scholarship was Greek rather than Hellenic—one heard little from the Porsonians of the glory that was Greece. Nothing would have been more alien to them than Gilbert Murray's insistence in his Glasgow inaugural in 1889 that we should be working for 'Greece, not Greek' (Murray 1889). Their eyes were firmly fixed on the language of the texts they edited. The issues were very well summed up in 1817 in a letter to his father written by a precocious adolescent who was being taught by another classical fellow of Trinity, James Scholefield:

There seems to be the same difference between one of the accurate Cantab scholars who compares readings and collates Editions, and gives to every Greek particle its due honours and definite significations, and an elegant scholar who tastes the beauties of the classics without condescending to those minutiae, which there is between a mixer of colours and an amateur in painting... The business of the one is to facilitate the enjoyment of the other. But to make that the end which ought only to be the means... is a truly deplorable perversion of judgement.[23]

After his death in 1808, Porson's disciples and followers tended the fire at his shrine in several ways. First, they produced editions of his unpublished notes—hence Butler's reference to their 'possessing the scriptures' in his letter to Blomfield. On 6 April 1810 the Master and Seniors of Trinity College agreed 'that the Porsonian Collection of Mss, lately purchased, be published, for the Benefit of the College'.[24] The first result was the publication of Porson's adversaria by Monk and Blomfield (Monk and Blomfield 1812). In 1815 another Trinity admirer, Thomas Kidd, published Porson's *Tracts and Miscellaneous Criticisms* (Kidd 1815). Finally, Dobree published Porson's notes on Aristophanes, and then his Photius (Dobree 1820, 1822). Second, they published editions of their own in the Porsonian style. Third, they made clear their reverence for the great man in reviews and other articles. In fact this enables us to guess at the authorship of anonymous pieces in periodicals—the running theme of laudation of Porson is common with Monk and Blomfield but not with Elmsley. The Porsonians worked mostly on Greek tragedy, and this is reflected in the way they were viewed outside their home territory. In his novel *College Life, or the Proctor's Notebook*, Joseph Hewlett wrote of two Oxford undergraduates who were expelled but given *bene discessits*:

The Senior Proctor observed that Cambridge might appreciate their histrionical taste, as it was devoted to the [Greek] drama, and thought that 'the classics' were comprehended in a [Greek] chorus.[25]

---

[23] Thomas Babington Macaulay to Zachary Macaulay [?20] October 1817: Pinney 1974, 87. Macaulay's aversion to the study of language rather than literature was also evident in his (re)definition of scholarship as a relaxed reading of classical authors: 'Macaulay detested the labour of manufacturing Greek and Latin verse in cold blood as an exercise; and his hexameters were never up to the best Etonian mark, nor his iambics to the highest standard of Shrewsbury. He defined a scholar as one who reads Plato with his feet on the fender.' G. O. Trevelyan, *Life of T. B. Macaulay*, OUP (Worlds Classics) 1932, 1.76.

[24] Trinity College, Cambridge, Conclusion Book 1646–1811, 626.

[25] Hewlett 1843, iii.60. Hewlett's account was based on his own experience as an undergraduate in Oxford from 1818 to 1822. Conversely, the tragic canon might be identified by undergraduates with

The stereotype, as one would expect, rested on over-simplification. Porson himself worked on Aristophanes and on the late lexicographer Photius, and it was claimed in some quarters that his favourite author was Athenaeus. Before they were removed from the scholarly scene by preferment, Monk and Blomfield published mostly on Euripides and Aeschylus (tending, not surprisingly, to avoid plays already edited by Porson); but they also wrote on other topics in the *Museum Criticum*, the major outlet for their shorter pieces. Elmsley and Dobree, as we shall see, were marginal in different ways. Dobree worked on Porson's Aristophanes, but was also interested in Lysias, the subject of his praelection for the Regius chair in 1823. Elmsley edited Sophocles, but was also bold enough to tackle a play recently edited by Porson.[26] Thomas Kidd, an admirer of Porson but a more marginal figure than Dobree or Elmsley, mostly collected other men's work: Bentley, Dawes, Ruhnken, and Porson. He christened one of his sons Richard Bentley Porson Kidd. Kidd's career consisted of a succession of headmaster-ships and clerical livings, so he was mostly away from Cambridge, though he spent some time in Cambridge Castle, imprisoned for debt (he had married a spendthrift).[27] Another marginal figure, George Burges, also had a chequered career which ended in poverty. Burges was notorious for his extensive emendations ('Mr. Burges has written a new play which he entitles the SUPPLICES');[28] he also invented a machine for flying across the Channel and a patent corset 'a la Venus', and urged the use of human sewage as fertilizer.

The Porsonians and their Others

The solidarity of the school was also maintained by battles with those without. Samuel Parr, 'the Whig Dr Johnson', a learned but faintly ridiculous figure with his old-fashioned buzzwig and his constant pipe-smoking, acted as the patron of a loose-knit group of opponents of the Porsonians. In his *Letter to Blomfield*, Butler wrote (Butler 1810, 3) that when the issue of the *Edinburgh Review* containing the review of his Aeschylus reached him, he was sitting in his back parlour with 'the most illustrious scholar now living, from whose friendship and society I derive no small satisfaction' (Butler 1810, 3). The reference was to Parr, and in making a lightly-coded allusion he knew would be rightly read by Blomfield, Butler was nailing his colours to the mast. Elmsley wrote to Butler in the following year, 'Dr Parr wrote me not long after Porson's death…that Porson had left his disciples scraps of Greek and cartloads of insolence.'[29]

Porsonian editions: as Thomas Short of Christ Church wrote in 1829, 'Euripides and Aeschylus are sup-posed by many undergraduates to have written those plays only which are edited by Porson, Blomfield, and Monk' (Short 1829, 34).

[26] Porson's *Medea* was published in 1801; Elmsley worked on it soon afterwards, but the edition was suppressed *c.*1805, as was a complete text of Sophocles: see Finglass 2007.

[27] For Kidd, see *ODNB* (H. R. Luard, rev. R. Smail).

[28] [Anon.], *Museum Criticum* 7 (1821), 530. For Burges, see the article on him in *ODNB* (A. Goodwin, rev. M. Curthoys), and Collard 2004.

[29] Elmsley to Butler, 4–5 Feb 1811: BL Add Ms 34583/327–8 = Butler 1896, 1.66.

Porson had stayed with Parr for some time in the early 1790s, but his behaviour had led to Mrs Parr's ejecting him, apparently by setting a commode in his place at the dinner table.[30] The most vociferous opponent of the Porsonians was Edmund Barker, who had spent several years with Parr as an amanuensis and secretary (he was one of the few who could read Parr's appalling handwriting), and later collected volumes of 'Parriana', recollections of his patron. Barker was a Trinity man, though he had left in 1809 without taking a degree. He supported himself by writing, editing, and publishing, using his large stocks of classical learning, which alas were not matched by his judgment (McKitterick 2007). One of his more endearing habits was to add after his name on title pages the letters OTN, perhaps meant to suggest such acronyms as S[anctae] T[heologiae] P[rofessor], the Latinate equivalent of DD, but in fact standing for 'Of Thetford, Norfolk' where he lived. Barker's major ally was the printer and publisher Abraham Valpy. During its lifetime, from 1810 to 1829, Valpy's *Classical Journal* contained many contributions from Barker. He also edited Valpy's edition of 'Henry Stephens" (i.e. Henri Estienne's) Greek thesaurus, published in parts between 1816 and 1828.[31] Barker, as we shall see, was a constant thorn in the side of Monk and Blomfield, especially after they started their Porsonian journal, the *Museum Criticum*, in 1813.

Relationships with German scholars were mostly cordial. Porson himself had never been abroad, and so had never 'got drunk with Brunck'. As for his rhyme on Hermann—'The Germans in Greek are sadly to seek...all except Herman, and Herman's a German': the two men shared a scholarly style and this in itself promoted rivalry.[32] Porson's followers did not share his jokey chauvinism—witness for example Elmsley's proposal to send books to Germany.

Samuel Butler, as we have seen, was a marked man for the Porsonians, having taken on for Cambridge University Press the Aeschylus which Porson turned down in the 1780s. The first volume of his bulky variorum edition, published in four volumes between 1809 and 1816, was severely reviewed by Blomfield in the *Edinburgh Review*.[33] The quarrel was eventually patched up in 1818 after Monk intervened; and it is probably significant that in the previous year Monk had met Jane Hughes, sister of

---

[30]   Butler 1896, 1.57. In a rare revelation of local oral tradition, Butler tells us that the story was transmitted from Edmund Barker to Alexander Dyce to W. H. Luard [*sic*: a conflation of H. R. Luard and W. H. Thompson, both of Trinity College?] to J. E. B. Mayor, and thence to Butler himself.

[31]   A scornful review by Blomfield (*Quarterly Review* 22, no. 44 (Jan. 1820), 302–48) led to Barker's being sidelined. It may have been at this point that J. R. Major, a recent graduate from Trinity, was hired as editor; the title page of his *Questions adapted to Mitford's* History of Greece...(Major 1827) declared that he had been editor of the Thesaurus 'for some years'. Major had the right connections: he had been to Valpy's father's school at Reading and was curate of Thetford, Barker's home town, from 1820 to 1826. In 1826 he published a school edition of the *Hecuba* which included a translation (from Latin into English) of the preface and notes from Porson's edition, whose text he used (Major 1826).

[32]   We might call this, with apologies to Durkheim, mechanical rivalry, as opposed to the organic rivalry with Boeckh and his followers, since it was based on similarity rather than difference.

[33]   Blomfield 1809–10: it was this review that prompted Butler's *Letter to Blomfield* (Butler 1810).

one of Butler's favourite pupils; they married in 1822.[34] The antagonism between the Porsonians and their critics was thus softened in one case by a mediating influence.[35]

Institutional Bases

It is remarkable that in the generation to which Monk and Blomfield belonged, the study of classical texts, especially of Greek drama, flowered in Cambridge, especially in Trinity, in a way which had almost no parallel at Oxford. Among the causes of this disparity, and for the concentration of scholars in Trinity College, were the radical internal changes which had taken place in the college in the 1780s and 1790s. In 1786 a protest over the misconduct of fellowship elections led to the institution of a public written examination for candidates. In 1790 annual examinations were introduced for first and second year undergraduates (Smith 2001). Thus by the time Monk, Blomfield, and their friends entered Trinity in the early 1800s, a merit-based system was in place, in what had since the 1780s been the largest college in Cambridge.[36] This system was reinforced by the use made of a large donation in 1810, which Monk and his brother-fellow George Pryme persuaded the College to devote to raising the value of rural livings. Since these were at the same time made more difficult to hold with a fellowship, the backlog of fellows staying in college while waiting for a living was reduced. From now on, those who stayed tended to be those with academic, not ecclesiastical ambitions.[37] Such a system was likely to encourage academic talent, just as the open examinations for fellowships did at Oriel. The Oxford statute of 1800, which had set up honours examinations, represented the extension to the university as a whole of the best practice of Christ Church, Oriel, and Balliol (Brock 1997, 7–8); but it must also have been observed and pondered in Cambridge.

College pride in Trinity was sharpened by its intense rivalry with the other large Cambridge college, its neighbour St John's. Samuel Butler, headmaster of Shrewsbury, was a fellow of St John's, and it can hardly be doubted that this exacerbated the quarrels between him and his Porsonian critics. Monk's tenure of the Greek chair, from 1808 to 1823, was marked by the resurgence of Trinity in the university, and of Classics as against the still dominant mathematical ethos both of the university and of St John's, the leading mathematics college. As a tutor, Monk built up Classics in his college until, frustrated by the lack of recognition open to his best pupils at university level, he began campaigning for the establishment of a degree examination in Classics. This was not founded till 1822, the first examination being in 1824; before then the only road to

[34] Not in 1823, as the *ODNB* article on Monk has it.

[35] Hughes's status as potential mediator dates back at least to 1810, when Butler referred to 'our common friend Hughes' in a letter to Monk: 8 June 1810 (BL, Add MS 34583, f. 305).

[36] This is also the period of the revival of the public schools, whose curriculum was almost exclusively classical; this would have benefited Trinity much more than St John's, whose strength lay in mathematics and which recruited more than Trinity did from northern grammar schools.

[37] The gift (amounting to £12,000) came from John Piggott. This point was made by Robert Robson (Robson 1967, 320–1); it has recently been challenged (Hilton 2011, 318).

recognition was through performance in college annual, scholarship or fellowship exams, or by winning one of the handful of university prizes and medals. This account I believe explains why Porsonianism flourished in Cambridge, when Classics was overshadowed by mathematics at university level, whereas in Oxford the converse obtained. The influence of Porson combined with the Trinity power base and its merit-based entry, despite the dominance of mathematics (and perhaps even spurred by it, given the role of St John's as the leading mathematical college), was at the root of the phenomenon. Cambridge politics were not like those of Oxford, where colleges were more similar in size, and intercollegiate rivalry perhaps less intense; but Monk's campaign to transfer his Trinity successes to the university arena in a way paralleled what had happened in Oxford.

Porson was not the only hero to be revered in Cambridge, and at Trinity in particular. Bentley was the acknowledged founder of British classical scholarship, and it may be that the breadth of his work explains why a Bentleian cult did not develop in the same way as Porsoniasm did. Porson's narrower and more focused style, that is, made it easier to identify and follow (cf. Brink 1986, 111, quoting Hermann). The turbulent history of Bentley's mastership of the college must also have discouraged hero-worship in some quarters, as is suggested by the rejection of Macaulay's proposal that a statue of him be placed in the ante-chapel.[38] The other local hero who needs to be mentioned is Isaac Newton, whose achievements and reputation had significant effects on the curriculum and styles of work in Cambridge. Roubiliac's marble statue of Newton (1755) stood in the antechapel of Trinity, a mute encouragement to emulation ('The marble index of a mind for ever / Voyaging through strange seas of Thought alone');[39] in 1808 it was joined by Chantrey's bust of Porson. There are interesting parallels between the two men's posthumous reputations. The Newtonian style in mathematical physics dominated Cambridge mathematics through the eighteenth century, and when towards the end of the century advanced French algebraic techniques became available, they were resisted by the local mathematical establishment. What had been the leading edge of research had become encrusted and fossilized in its institutional home. Attempts to introduce French analytic techniques began in the 1800s, but were only successful a decade later, when the autonomy of examiners enabled reformers to insert a new kind of question into the mathematical examination (Gascoigne 1989, 270–99, Warwick 2003, 1–175). The parallel with Porsoniasm is clear: the Cambridge mathematicians resisted French algebraic analysis, the classicists resisted German *Altertumswissenschaft*. The coincidence of the Revolution and its aftermath, leading to the continental blockade, not only encouraged suspicion of what was practised

[38] John Barrow was chosen instead: see Winstanley 1947, 437–9, who printed Macaulay's letter to William Whewell of 1 December 1856 recommending Bentley as the subject of a statue (cf. Pinney 1981, 67–9). Macaulay wrote that 'To this day...the scholarship of Trinity men has a peculiar character which may be called Bentleian', but did not explain what he meant by this.

[39] The couplet was added by Wordsworth to the 1850 edition of *The Prelude*. For reflections on this image of Newton, see Schaffer 2007.

across the Channel, but also promoted stereotyping through the scarcity of accurate information. The cults of Newton and of Porson thus have many features in common, though the latter's was much less long-lived.

Internal Structure

We can begin with the dynamic duo of Monk and Blomfield. Together they ran the *Museum Criticum* from its first appearance in 1813; Blomfield had left Cambridge for a rural living but Monk, as Regius Professor, stayed at Trinity and co-ordinated everything from there. The two friends were different in character, Monk being benign but pompous while Blomfield had more spark to him; one cannot help warming to a man whose first publication, in his early twenties, was 'On the dancing of the ancients' (Blomfield 1807–8). He was also a forceful writer whom Monk employed to compose polemics, especially against Edmund Barker.[40] In 1813 Monk wrote to Blomfield:

My dear friend

Something must be done respecting this pestilential cur that is eternally barking at our heels: he has exalted himself to the dignity of a nuisance, tho' he can never rise higher. We will make out an article between us; tho' to say the truth, I shall principally rely upon you. Nature has given me the dangerous powers of satire with a very sparing hand...[41]

Their correspondence in the next few years reveals that Monk was the hard-working organizer, Blomfield the more wide-ranging and talented scholar. What they share is the pride of arrogance, as fellows of Trinity and guardians of the Porsonian flame. David McKitterick has written of their 'scholarly invective and preening' (McKitterick 1998, 289–93); and both were evident in their reviews of friends and foe. George Butler, headmaster of Harrow, wrote to Samuel Butler (no relation) in 1810 denouncing the 'Ipse-dixit ism...captiousness,...hypercritical dogmatism,...bigotry of many of his [Porson's] votaries'.[42] Samuel Butler himself commented to Elmsley in 1811 that 'The mischief of the Porsonian school can only be appreciated by a residence at Trinity'.[43] A glimpse of the atmosphere there is provided by the young American scholar George Ticknor, who visited Cambridge in 1819. In his journal, Ticknor wrote that he had

met Dobree, Monk et al. The tone of this society was certainly stiff and pedantic, and a good deal of little jealousy apparent, in the manner in which they spoke of persons with whom they or their college or the university had come into collision.   (Hillard 1876, 1.224)

---

[40] Blomfield was also a witty and inventive participant in oral disputations. In 1818, assigned to respond to a thesis advanced by John Beverley, a tiresomely persistent debater, he 'kept the schools in a continual laugh at Beverley's expense, during the whole of this usually solemn, not to say gloomy exhibition' (Gunning 1855, 2.296).

[41] Monk to Blomfield, 15 July 1813. Monk papers, Trinity College Library. (This and other papers in the Library are quoted by permission of the Master and Fellows of Trinity College.)

[42] G. Butler to S. Butler, 15 July 1810: J. R. M. Butler, Trinity College Library, Cambridge, M2/1/26.

[43] Butler to Elmsley, c.4–5 February 1811; Butler 1896, 1.66.

Peter Paul Dobree, protégé of Porson and rivalled only by Elmsley as a critical scholar in the master's style, succeeded Monk as Regius Professor of Greek in 1823. Dobree is almost entirely absent from the correspondence between Monk and Blomfield, and also from that between Elmsley and the publisher John Murray which I cite below. Nicholas Horsfall, in a study of early nineteenth-century scholarship based on letters to Elmsley from Monk, Blomfield, and Gaisford, commented that Dobree is 'hardly so much as mentioned… I find the silence perplexing' (Horsfall 1974, 449). Three factors, I think, help to explain his absence. First, Dobree was a quiet and retiring man who kept to himself. Reviewing the posthumous edition of his *Adversaria*, Julius Hare wrote that Dobree 'was so fastidious, that hardly anything but death could loose his tongue, except his reverence for Porson'.[44] It should also be remembered that Dobree, who had been deprived of Porson's chair by his junior Monk, had unlike him known Porson personally.[45]

Second, he was said to have been involved in the foundation of the *Museum Criticum*'s rival the *Classical Journal*, as well as writing for it; he certainly contributed to the first number in April 1810. Not only was he, like the *Journal*'s publisher Abraham Valpy, a Channel Islander, he had been educated at Valpy's father's school at Reading before coming to Trinity. Monk's nervousness about these links is clear from a letter he wrote to John Murray in November 1813:

The British Museum trustees have given permission to transcribe Bentley's MSS—can anyone else get at them? If they fall into Valpy's hands, the British Museum permission is nugatory. Dobree is going to transcribe the notes on Aristophanes, whether for his own use or Valpy's, who he knows, I know not… it is distressing…[46]

Third, Dobree and Monk had a falling out over the plans to publish Porson's notes. Dobree wrote to Blomfield in December 1812:

Dear Blomfield

Your letter instantly set me thinking on Aristophanes, & I did not rest till I had fired off a grand proposal for a grand edition sumptibus collegii. This was Oct 1. I was civilly refused about the 30th. After much writing & talking backwards & forwards about my having the use of the papers for an edition on my own acct, I was given to understand by their High Mightinesses about a week ago, that any such plan was a deviation from their sublime intentions; which they now find to have been all along, that the notes should remain unmixed with baser matter, & be included in the college miscellany. I on my part, make my bow, & tell these

---

[44]   J. C. H[are], 'Dobree's *Adversaria*, *Philological Museum* 1(1832), 204–8, at 207.

[45]   As for Blomfield, he told Elmsley that 'With Porson himself I was totally unacquainted, never having been in his company but once; on which occasion he was exceedingly intoxicated, and I as sick of his company as he probably was of his liquour in the course of the night.' Blomfield to Elmsley, 14 October 1812 (Elmsley papers).

[46]   Monk to Murray, 27 Nov. 1813. Quoted by permission of the John Murray Archive, National Library of Scotland.

Acharnians to fare exceedingly well; & so the comic remains in the comical situation where he will probably long remain.[47]

Dobree may have resented the tightly-knit duo of Monk and Blomfield; he will certainly have jibbed at Monk's pomposity. The reference to 'High and Mightinesses' above (i.e. the Master and Senior Fellows of Trinity) suggests a dislike of authority figures; we might compare the rejection of 'the language and conduct of the P C' (i. e. the Privy Council?) in a review of Elmsley's edition of the *Oedipus Coloneus*, in 1823.[48]

Dobree sent his news to Monk too; who immediately complained to Blomfield that

Dobree's conduct has been inconceivably strange. Without intimating his design to me, who would readily have assented to it, he makes a proposition to the Seniors to publish the Aristophanes: this they decline: he then, without mentioning it to me, subjects to them another proposal for editing the notes on Aristophanes, as well as all that remains unedited (viz. on the prose writers, the Lat. writers etc.) in the form of Adversaria, or supplements to the present volume: & all this in spite of a long conversation with me before the Long Vacation, in which there was an understanding that we were to do these together.[49]

Soon afterwards Monk and Dobree were reconciled, and agreed that Dobree would edit Porson's work on Aristophanes, Monk the rest.

How is Dobree to be located within the Porsonian circle? The evidence I have quoted suggests that he could be described as an 'outside insider'. This ambivalent status can be clarified if we turn to Peter Elmsley, whom we might call an 'inside outsider'. This status is evident in a letter he wrote to Samuel Butler in February 1811:

some persons think that I have not treated Porson with sufficient respect. You must have observed the strong disposition which the school feels to convert him into an idol. The natural consequence of this idolatry is to produce in the non-initiated a disposition to bring him nearer to the pitch of common men than they are justified in doing. I am not quite sure that I have not some kind of leaning to this kind of critical Protestantism.[50]

Whether it was 'Protestantism' or not, Elmsley was prepared to criticize Porson, and not just in detail, but in relation to editorial strategy. In the preface to his edition of *Medea* (1818), he did not hesitate to declare that of the two tasks of the editor, emendation and interpretation, Porson had accomplished the former but neglected the latter.[51]

---

[47] Dobree to Blomfield 21 Dec. 1812 (corrected to 24 Dec., but postmarked 23 Dec.). Beinecke Library, Yale University, Osborn D 4452.

[48] *CJ* 28 (1823), 356: anonymous, but my conjecture, on stylistic grounds, that Dobree was the author (Finglass 2007, 105 n.8) has now been confirmed (Finglass 2009, 189 n.4).

[49] Monk to Blomfield, 25 December 1812: Monk papers, Trinity College Library. These letters were written out of term time, and it could be argued that Monk and Dobree communicated verbally in term; this letter suggests however that such communication was constrained.

[50] Elmsley to Butler, 3 Feb. 1811, BL Add ms 34583, f. 325; Butler (1896) 1.65.

[51] 'Cum duabus potissimum rebus contineatur editoris officium, lectionis scilicet emendatione et sententiarum interpretatione, illam ea felicitate gessit Porsonus, ut recensionis multo melioris exiguam sane spem reliquerit; hanc vero, si pauca hic illic in transcursu explicata excipias, omnino neglexit.' The passage is quoted more extensively by Brink (1986) 215, n. 43.

As we have seen, Elmsley was in close touch with Samuel Butler. Like Dobree he contributed to the *Classical Journal*; he also wrote for the *Edinburgh Review*, in which he reviewed Blomfield's edition of *Prometheus Vinctus* (Elmsley 1810). The nephew, as we saw in Chapter 3, of a bookseller who had acted as agent for Gibbon and later for Oxford University Press, he inherited substantially from his uncle in 1802 and often travelled to continental libraries to look at MSS. Elmsley was large and jolly (reputedly the fattest undergraduate of his time), but two clouds of allegation hung over his head. One was that he tried to seduce the affections of Harriet Lewin from George Grote after they became engaged; the other was that he plagiarized emendations from Porson. This latter allegation, which Elmsley vigorously denied in letters to Monk, was maintained in particular by Dobree, the only Porsonian who had been at all close to the master.[52] Denys Page dismissed the allegations *con brio* as 'a sordid falsehood, ridiculous to anyone who knows the character of Elmsley' (Page 1960, 230): but this is to ignore the circumstantial evidence produced at the time.[53] Both Elmsley's undoubted corpulence and his alleged plagiarism feature in George Burges's comment that he 'was not... the only scholar who got fat on the picking of Porson's brains' (Burges 1838–9, 415–16, cf. 439).[54] Elmsley's religious position was more liberal than that of Monk and Blomfield; this lost him the Oxford Regius chair of Greek in 1812, which went (as we have seen in Chapter 3) to Thomas Gaisford. He was given the Camden chair of ancient history and the headship of a small and rather disreputable college only in 1823, two years before his death.[55] The breadth of his scholarship can be glimpsed from a reference by G. H. Smith, who had attended his lectures and in his *Manual of Grecian Antiquities* acknowledged 'his obligations to the profound and elegant lectures of the principal of Alban Hall, and Camden Professor of Ancient History, for the chapter in the Appendix, on the Coinage and Currency of the Greeks' (Smith 1834, p. vi). Elmsley was an appropriate choice to accompany Humphry Davy to Herculaneum to attempt the unwrapping and decipherment of carbonized papyri.[56] Elmsley's position as an 'outside insider', then, was the product of several factors: his geographical position

---

[52] 'Dobree always spoke of Elmsley as *archikleptistatos*': Barker (1852) 2.60.

[53] The main source is George Burges, whose anonymous account (Burges 1838–9, 413–15) was cited by Watson 1861, 310–11; cf. Clarke 1937, 106. The evidence of earlier antagonism between Porson and Elmsley discovered by Patrick Finglass also needs to be taken into account: see Finglass 2007, 115.

[54] On Burges, see Christopher Collard's spirited account (Collard 2004); to his reference to Burges 1838–9, add *Church of England Quarterly Review* 4 (1838), 91–125. Burges was also the author of 'The living lamps of learning' (Burges 1840), claimed by him in *Journal of Classical and Sacred Philology* 3 (1856), 362.

[55] St Alban's Hall was notorious for taking undergraduates expelled from other colleges. Elmsley's and Dobree's lives were curiously parallel in their reaching official eminence in 1823, two years before their deaths.

[56] The attempt was thwarted by the condition of the papyri and the obstructiveness of local officials: see Davy 1821, and cf. Horsfall 1974, 477. Elmsley commented that 'we are not able to announce the discovery of a single sentence of Greek or Latin': Bodleian Library, Oxford, MS. Clarendon Press d.44, 59, kindly inspected for me by Chris Collard. Herculaneum was the ideal site for such collaboration, linking as it did the history of the earth and of human life: cf. Rudwick 2005, 185–94. A recent survey (which does not mention Davy or Elmsley) is provided by Coates and Seydl 2007.

outside Cambridge, his Oxonian allegiances, his theological views and his scholarship. An accomplished editor in the Porsonian style, he also had much wider interests.[57]

The correspondence between Elmsley, Monk, and Blomfield reveals a nervous ritual dance. The Trinity duo knew that Elmsley had published in the *Edinburgh Review* (as indeed Blomfield had for a time) and in the *Classical Journal*, and that he had links with Samuel Butler, with whom they had a chequered history. But they also recognized that he was a first-rate textual scholar, and like all editors, they needed contributions; so they continually encouraged him to contribute to *Museum Criticum*, flattering, cajoling, but never laying on the whip too hard.

The Porsonians and the Outside World

The wider political and religious context of Porsoniasm has already been hinted at. The *Classical Journal* (1810) and the *Museum Criticum* (1813) were founded at a time when several general literary journals were already in the field. The *Edinburgh Review* had been founded as a reformist organ in 1802; the *Quarterly Review* was set up in 1809 to oppose it and to defend the political establishment. General and classical journals are juxtaposed in the version of Horace Odes 1.22 composed by Sidney Walker of Trinity around 1815:

> The man, my **Moultrie**, arm'd with native strength,
> And of his own worth conscious, needs no aid
> Of venal critic, or ephemeral puff
> Prelusive, or satiric quiver stored
> With poison'd shafts defensive: fearless he
> Sends forth his work, essay, or ode, or note
> On crabb'd Greek play, or squib political.
> Him nor the fierce *Eclectic's* foaming page
> Aught troubles, nor the uncourteous *Times*, nor yet
> The *Journal*, which, misnamed of *Classics*, deals
> Its three-months' errors out.[58]

Monk and Blomfield's work for the *Quarterly* aligns them with the conservative camp; but Blomfield's contributing to the *Edinburgh* till 1813 reflects a greater flexibility than Monk possessed. Elmsley's query to Butler belongs not just to the world of scholarship, but also to this wider world of political and religious rivalry, in which the literary reviews played an important part (see further Chapter 6).

[57] Page's generous but wilful account seems to me to exaggerate the differences between Porson and Elmsley; comparing their editions of *Medea*, he concludes that 'In a single decade we move into a world very different from Porson's (Page 1960, 230). Compare Clarke's comment, 'Elmsley to us may appear scarcely distinguishable from the Porsonians' (Clarke 1937, 106); and of course Housman's remark, quoted at the beginning of this chapter, that 'scholarship meant to Elmsley what it meant to Dobree' (Housman 1969, 25).

[58] W. S. Walker, 'HOR. 1. 22, imitated': Walker 1852, 157–8. 'My Moultrie' edited his friend's *Remains* and added a memoir. (The 'Journal' referred to in the penultimate line is Valpy's *Classical Journal*—to which Walker himself contributed.)

In the first half of the nineteenth century, reviews were rarely signed, and this offered fruitful opportunities for writers to snipe at one another. The private letters of the period—and doubtless the conversations in common rooms and coffee houses— were full of enquiries like Elmsley's—'Do you know who wrote the review of X in Y?' Many of the articles in the *Quarterly* and *Edinburgh* dealt with political topics, and were written by men whose careers would have suffered had their identity been known. William Gifford, the first editor of the *Quarterly*, made it clear to Edward Copleston of Oxford how much he relied on him as a contributor and advisor by offering to reveal the identities of all his authors. Copleston, soon to be famous as the champion who defended Oxford against the 'calumnies' of the *Edinburgh Review* (Copleston 1810), brought other scholars into the fold, including Monk, Blomfield, and Elmsley. The foundation of the *Classical Journal* gave Edmund Barker a useful platform for his views. He seems to have begun as a contributor, but at some point joined in the editing, and was associated with the journal until it folded in 1829. The *Classical Journal* was an omnium gatherum of articles on classical, biblical, and oriental subjects, reviews, reports of new books, Oxford and Cambridge prize poems, newly discovered inscriptions, travellers' reports, and translations. It appealed to the scholar, the semi-learned country gentleman, the antiquarian, and the schoolmaster (see Blomfield's reference to schoolmasters, below). It may be Barker who was referred to in a cautionary letter Gaisford sent to Henry Fynes Clinton, who was concerned at the criticism of his *Fasti Hellenici* in the *Classical Journal*:

It is not unwise in a writer to pay attention, in however small a degree, to the lowest caviller:... in the new edition...it would...be as well...to insert here & there a notice or an expression which might...expound your design which may not be fully comprehended by all readers, of whom squire Valpy's man (they call him the count of Cambridge) is chief.[59]

In the previous year, Gaisford had summarized the relations between the warring parties:

The quarrel between the conductors of the Museum Criticum and Classical Journal commenced long ago at Cambridge. It is Barker and Burges versus Monk and Blomfield—who pull each other to pieces at every opportunity. You may have seen or heard of Barker's Aristarchus Anti-Blomfieldianus, a scurrilous production not dissimular [sic] from many an article in the Classical Journal. The merits of the quarrell [sic] are not worth discussing by those who are unacquainted with the parties.[60]

For much of its life the *Classical Journal* published attacks on and defences against Monk and Blomfield. Blomfield's review of the first volume of Valpy's *Greek Thesaurus* pointed out that the work was proceeding so slowly that its 1,000 subscribers would

[59] Gaisford to Fynes Clinton, 2 Aug. 1825: Gaisford papers, Christ Church, Oxford. Quotations from these papers by permission of the Fellow Librarian, Professor C. B. R. Pelling. 'The count of Cambridge' might also refer to George Burges.

[60] Gaisford to Fynes Clinton, 11 Mar. 1824: Gaisford papers, Christ Church, Oxford.

have to wait another fifty-five years before they could complete their sets (Blomfield 1820).[61] The work then proceeded faster, Barker presumably having been sidelined; he replied to his tormentor in the furious and incoherent pamphlet referred to by Gaisford, *Aristarchus Anti-Blomfieldianus* (Barker 1820).[62] More often, however, Barker took the initiative himself, having acquired a mastery of the art of literary offence and defence. Having published an anonymous article, he would send a rather feeble attack on it to another journal under a pseudonym, and then follow this with a triumphant justification of himself under his own name. The ultimate technique for engaging in controversy was thus to conduct both sides of it. In the 1810s Barker conducted a running battle with Monk and Blomfield, using the tactic I have just described, and another which infuriated Monk even more. In 1812 Barker inserted a review of a third party in the *Gentleman's Magazine*, signing it with Monk's initials, JHM. A few months later, Monk discovered the ruse:

My dear Blomfield

First Mr E. H. Barker must come upon the stage—as I wish to discharge all that occurs about that dunce. Elmsley mentioned to me that he had been deceived by an impostor who assumed my initials in the Gent[leman's] Mag[azine] and whom he suspected to be no other than E. H. Barker himself. I immediately went and searched the Numbers of the Gent. Mag. and in that for May, 1812 I found 15 columns, signed J. H. M. containing the most immoderate, fulsome, and disgusting compliments to Barker's 2 Tracts of Cicero, praising not only his learning, but his genius, his sublime mind, his judgment &c &c. but venturing occasionally to differ in some trivial points from this 'ornament to the Univ. of Cam'. In the next Number appears a letter signed E. H. Barker, graciously accepting all the compliments of the learned editor JHM and adding a few of his own, and triumphantly oversetting all his objections. Elmsley's conjecture is certain. Never was internal evidence so decisive. The style cannot be mistaken—& having pushed my enquiries somewhat further, I find that he is carrying on the same complimentary warfare in 5 or 6 periodical publications.... You will find that he is conducting a controversy between Edmund and Henry in the Class[ical] Journal. He is beginning another in the New Review, and in the Br[itish] Critic he has been reviewing and praising himself for some time. In the last number of the British Critic, he talks of some considerable advantages which Mr Barker possesses over his two Rivals, Professor Monk & Mr Blomfield, who it seems know nothing of Greek Antiquities....

What is to be done with the fellow? He will infallibly give us trouble, do what we will. My opinion is, that the best way will be to expose his ignorance presumption arrogance vanity folly—& insufferable egotism—but to do it seriously:...let it be a serious bastinado, not a school flogging.[63]

---

[61] A contemporary wrote that 'Blomfield...plied the shafts of misrepresentation, ridicule, and sarcasm, with such stunning force, as would have staggered the stoutest opponent' (Wright 1827, 2.265–6).

[62] Blomfield's annotated copy is in the Sterling Memorial Library, Yale University (my thanks to Chris Kraus for copying pages to me). Valpy issued a more temperate response, *A Reply to the Quarterly Reviewer of Stephens' Greek Thesaurus*.

[63] Monk to Blomfield, 7 Jan. 1813: Monk papers, Trinity College Library. Note the deployment of Porsonian critical analysis on contemporary English texts.

Almost a year earlier, Blomfield had written to Elmsley:

I wrote the paper on Sophron, to which you allude, in the last number of the Classical Journal—and a short Diatribe on Antimachus in the preceding No. Besides these, I have nothing in that precious ollapodrida of absurdities. I had intended to continue my remarks on S[ophron] for four or five numbers; but I think I shall drop my intention, for I am not very ambitious of figuring in the midst of the pestilent scribblers who infest that injudicious publication. It appears to me that all the country schoolmasters who have interleaved Greek Grammars, are seizing with avidity, the opportunity which the Classical Journal affords them, of venting their ingenious conjectures & truly original remarks.[64]

Given this attitude, and the *Classical Journal*'s association with Barker, it is understandable that later that same year Blomfield and his friends began to plan their own journal, set up to publish and promote Cambridge work on Classics, and originally entitled 'The Cambridge Literary Journal'. In the event it emerged in April 1813 as the *Museum Criticum*, with the subtitle 'Cambridge classical researches',[65] Monk having concluded a favourable publishing deal with John Murray, publisher of the *Quarterly Review*. While sales were reasonably good, the increasingly long intervals between issues make it clear that the supply of material, editorial time, or both diminished after 1814. The fifth issue appeared in 1815, the sixth in 1816; the seventh not till the end of 1821; the eighth and final issue was not published until 1826. The final delays are explained by Monk's appointment as Dean of Peterborough in 1822; he resigned his Greek chair in the following year.[66]

The Fall

With the closure of the *Museum Criticum* we arrive at 1826, with Housman's 'strokes of doom' ringing in our ears. As Housman suggested, the mid-1820s marked the end of an era in English classical scholarship. Blomfield was made Bishop of Chester in 1824 and soon went on to be an outstanding Bishop of London; Monk was given a rich living and in 1830 became Bishop of Gloucester; both Dobree, who had succeeded Monk as Professor of Greek at Cambridge in 1823, and Elmsley, who had been elected to a chair of ancient history in Oxford in the same year, died in 1825. But Housman's focus on individuals left unmentioned another contemporary event, one which was highlighted by Martin Clarke in his pioneering account of British classical education (Clarke 1959, 73):

It is a curious fact, and one which should not be forgotten by those who put their trust in courses and examinations, that the date at which, according to A. E. Housman, the great age of

---

[64] Blomfield to Elmsley, 19 Feb. 1812: Elmsley papers, Westminster School.
[65] Gaisford, told of the original title, had suggested avoiding the use of 'Cambridge' and calling it 'Repertorium literarium': Blomfield to Elmsley, 1 Dec. 1812. Elmsley papers, Westminster School.
[66] On the history of the *Museum Criticum*, see Chapter 7.

scholarship in England came to an end, coincided almost exactly with the foundation of the Classical Tripos at Cambridge.

The first examination did indeed take place in 1824, though the decision to establish the tripos had been made two years earlier. But what are we to make of this coincidence, if it is one? Clarke, having drawn attention to it, does not return to the topic, but the implication of his remark is that this was in some sense a symptom of decline.[67] My own view is that it should be seen as the culmination of a long Trinity-based campaign for the recognition of Classics in a mathematics-dominated university, led initially by Monk in the 1810s and then taken over by Christopher Wordsworth after he arrived as Master of Trinity in 1820. It could thus be seen as a result of the phenomenon of Porsoniasm, rather than a sign of decline. On the other hand, the severely restricted form in which the tripos was established was due to the demands of the mathematicians, led by the fellows of St John's (2001a). The domination of its question papers by textual analysis and translation might be seen as a victory for Porsonianism; but the mathematical bar on entry to the examination, which operated for over thirty years from its foundation, though in progressively attenuated form, made this a Pyrrhic victory. In a sense, indeed, mathematical restriction and Porsonian scholarship were mutually reinforcing.

In 1826 the final number of the *Museum Criticum* carried the following announcement from the editors:

Although other avocations now compel them to give up the MUSEUM CRITICUM, they have reason to hope, that another series of Numbers of a similar nature, will issue from the Press of this University, under the auspices of an able and judicious scholar.

(*Museum Criticum* 8 (1826), 698)

For 'other avocations', read ecclesiastical preferment. The 'able and judicious scholar' was Hugh James Rose of Trinity, whose *Inscriptiones Graecae Vetustissimae* had appeared in 1825, the year in which he had narrowly failed to succeed Dobree as Regius Professor of Greek (see further Chapter 7).

What emerged, though not till 1831, was the *Philological Museum*, edited by two other fellows of Trinity, Julius Hare and Connop Thirlwall—now remembered mainly for his *History of Greece* (1835–44); Fynes Clinton and Cornewall Lewis both contributed. The new journal was very different from its predecessor, and the contrasting adjectives in the titles—'critical' vs 'philological'—sum up neatly the contrasting conceptions of classical scholarship embodied in their editorial policies (Stray 2004f). The new 'philological' scholarship, moreover, formed part of a wider cultural movement. For over a decade, Hare and Thirlwall, inspired by Coleridge, had been pressing the claims of German romanticism and German scholarship, especially that of Niebuhr. This 'romantic tide' swept over Trinity in the 1820s, its ambitiously theorized

---

[67] Brink made Clarke's statement the epigraph to his chapter on Victorian classical education (Brink 1986, 114), but did not pursue the point in his own discussion.

conception of language and belief highlighting the narrowness of the Porsonian vision of classical scholarship.[68]

The editorial history of the *Philological Museum* has similarities with that of the *Museum Criticum*—Hare went to a rich country living in 1832, leaving Thirlwall to cope by himself. Contributions were few, and Thirlwall was forced to fill up the last issue with his own translations from published German articles. He then left Cambridge after a dispute with the Master of Trinity about compulsory chapel, was soon given a rich living, and in 1840 made Bishop of St David's (Chapter 7). The *Philological Museum* reflected and encouraged the growth of interest in the new, broader conception of scholarship, of which other indications can be seen in the 1830s. In 1836, a translation of Schleiermacher's prefaces to the Platonic dialogues was brought out by William Dobson, who had been an undergraduate at Trinity from 1827 to 1831. Dobson lost his fellowship through marriage and became a headmaster. Other lost leaders included Christopher Wordsworth's sons John and Christopher. John collated Aeschylus in Florence in the early 1830s; his notes were used by Conington for his edition of the *Choephori*. In 1839 he was working on a classical dictionary designed to replace Lempriere, drawing on Pauly's encyclopaedia, whose first volume had just appeared; but he died prematurely at the end of the year.[69] His younger brother Christopher had brought out a book on Athens and Attica based on his travels, and also published Pompeian inscriptions. He also had plans to broaden the Cambridge classical curriculum, which he thought emphasized 'manner at the expense of matter'—a clear sign of revolt against the Porsonian style. But he became a headmaster, and later a bishop. Once again, as Housman might have said, the grave closed over one man, another was lost to the church. In his article on the rise and decay of English scholarship, George Burges listed alphabetically seventeen scholars who, he wrote, 'form the chain between the present and the past'; the list ends with 'the two Wordsworths'.[70] In 1825 tactical voting had denied the Cambridge Greek chair to both the leading contestants, Hare and Rose; it went to the less talented James Scholefield, who clung to the Porsonian style, and the chair, till his death in 1853.[71]

So far we have seen a clear pattern of the foreshortening of careers by preferment, marriage, or death. In fact the influence of conventional religion was two-fold, since it not only removed the orthodox but banished the heterodox—men like Frederick Paley, who became a Catholic, and Charles Badham and John William Donaldson, whose theology was to varying degrees unconventional. Beyond the pale of the Anglican community, however, something was stirring, and a catalyst was provided by the founding of the University of London—the godless college in Gower Street—in 1826 (that Housman moment again!). The new institution gave an opening for men

---

[68] On the romantic vision of language and its implications, see Aarsleff 1967, Burrow 1967, Preyer 1985, Dowling 1986, 3–45, Schaffer 1991.

[69] For Wordsworth's planned dictionary, see 2007h.

[70] Burges 1838-9,145–6. The reference must I think be to John and Christopher Wordsworth, and not to their younger brother Charles.

[71] It was Scholefield who was mentioned above as the object of the young Macaulay's denunciation.

who were unwilling to sign the Thirty-Nine Articles. It also had close connections with another new body, the Society for the Diffusion of Useful Knowledge: the Society's *Penny Cyclopaedia* (1833–42), for example, was edited by George Long, the university's first professor of Greek and later its second professor of Latin.[72] The *Cyclopaedia*, published in parts, in small-printed double columns with large numbers of woodcuts, formed the model for a massive classical encyclopaedia edited by William Smith, a dissenter who had studied at London University; it consisted of three large dictionaries which appeared between 1840 and 1857 (Chapter 11). One of Smith's leading collaborators was Leonhard Schmitz, a pupil of Niebuhr who settled in Britain and became a major conduit for German scholarship; he edited the *Classical Museum*, which ran from 1843 to 1849. The two men and their collaborators, who included liberal Oxbridge men like Jowett but largely came from University College and King's College, London and the dissenters' colleges, belonged to a new London-based world of scholarship which emerged in the generation after the Porsonian era.[73]

By this time denunciations of the Porsonian style were being issued both within and without Cambridge. In his *Letters from Cambridge* (1828), E. S. Appleyard of Trinity criticized Porson for 'dulness [*sic*]' and 'frivolity', and suggested that 'If he correct the text...he ought also to explain it occasionally where explanation is required'; Appleyard, who wrote anonymously, was aware that Porson was regarded as 'the tutelary saint of Trinity' ([Appleyard]1828, 74–5). In a pamphlet published in 1833 containing a comprehensive indictment of the University, R. M. Beverley openly deplored the influence of Porson, who

with his stupendous knowledge of all the intricacies of criticism, has, with the swagger of a bully, tyrannized in the art of restoring the text of the Greek tragedies. It has been the fashion since his time to study the Greek tragedies with extreme attention to words and metres, so that in reality *hyper-criticism* is the fashion at Cambridge. They have indeed wire-drawn the art, and brought it to that perfection that it will not be possible to add much more to this elaborate trifling. If a Cambridge scholar wishes to gain repute, he is sure to publish a Greek tragedy, (the three hundred and fifty-seventh edition perhaps) and in some pert coxcomb notes to sneer at former editors about a particle or a metre.   (Beverley 1833, 33)

Among those who published rebuttals of Beverley's pamphlet was the geologist Adam Sedgwick, fellow of Trinity, Even Sedgwick, however, in a commemoration sermon delivered in the previous year, had felt obliged to admit that

for the last fifty years our classical studies...have been too critical and formal...we have sometimes been taught, while straining after an accuracy beyond our reach, to value the husk more

---

[72] Long also edited the SDUK's *Quarterly Journal of Education* (1831–5): see 2008b.

[73] This broader conception of scholarship, it should be added, had similarities with what was emerging in Oxford, where ancient history was added to the classical curriculum in 1830. W. D. Anderson claimed that 'Although rebellion [sc. against Porsonianism] was inevitable, it came only after the middle of the nineteenth century. The rebel was F. A. Paley': Anderson 1975, 262. A more nuanced view would take into account Paley's Aeschylean editions of the 1840s, as well as (e.g.) Bernard Drake's *Eumenides* (Drake 1853) which included (pp. 47–74) a critical analysis of K. O. Müller's dissertations on the play, originally published in English translation in 1835.

than the fruit of ancient learning... [like] a traveller in classic land... who counts the stones on the Appian way instead of gazing on the monuments of the 'eternal city'.[74]

In 1840 J. W. Donaldson, a Trinity classicist who saw his life's mission as the salvation of Anglican Christianity through a fusion of faith and philology, declared that 'Porson's great reputation during his lifetime converted all the promising young scholars of the time into servile imitators of the great critic; and the "Porsonian school of critics", as they have been termed, threw many impediments in the way of sound and comprehensive scholarship' (Donaldson 1840). Three years later, an anonymous reviewer praised Newton and Bentley, before describing Porson as 'inferior...to Bentley...not...in intrinsic powers, but in the whole scope and tendency of his erudition'. The reviewer went on:,

It became alas, the ambition of learned men, whom we name not, as several of them are still alive, to be regarded as of the Porsonian school! And a literary training came into vogue, which, if it had attained its highest successes, must have turned its votaries into learned scholiasts... doing nothing but comment eternally on the works of the ancient authors, without adding a thought of their own that was worthy to be known or remembered...

He went on to deplore 'The frigidity of their criticisms, the prosaic vulgarity of their illustrative translations, their heavy mechanical conceptions of metre...the utter barrenness of their annotations.' The human variety of ancient authors, he claimed, mean nothing to the Porsonian critic: 'His dissecting knife lays bare with equal coolness the foulness of one passage, and the fire or mysticism of another...we might pronounce him to be a man without a heart' (Anon. 1843, 432). The analysis strikingly prefigures that of Browning's *Grammarian's Funeral*, published twelve years later:

> He settled Hoti's business—let it be!—
> Properly based Oun—
> Gave us the doctrine of the enclitic De,
> Dead from the waist down.   (ll. 129–32)

and so Yeats's later invocation of the trope in *The Scholars*: 'What would they say / Did their Catullus walk that way?'

The Flame and the Shrine

The memory of Porson was preserved in Trinity, if nowhere else, and especially by Henry Luard (1825–91), mathematician, loyal college man, and antiquarian, and university registrary. Luard published an essay on Porson (Luard 1857), an edition of his correspondence (Luard 1867), and an entry in the ninth edition of *Encyclopedia Britannica* in 1875. Until M. L. Clarke's biography appeared (Clarke 1937), the only book-length treatment of Porson was the rather cumbrous life by John Selby Watson,

[74] Sedgwick 1833, 32. The issue re-emerged in a controversy between Richard Shilleto and John Grote in 1851, and was referred to in 1877 by Henry Jackson, who had been taught by Shilleto: see Chapter 1, and 1997a.

classical scholar, headmaster, and murderer, published in 1861.[75] The Porsonian style was continued by Richard Shilleto, the leading classical coach at Cambridge, who died in 1876; both his published work and his privately-circulated satirical comments on current academic events recall Porson's own productions.[76] As archetypal scholar, Porson also featured as a character in academic spoofs. In 1875 a Cambridge tripos verse composed by Edward Selwyn consisted of a dialogue between Porson, a student and a 'psychopompos' in Hades; in 1888 R. Y. Tyrrell published 'The old school of Classics and the new', a dialogue between Bentley, Madvig, Porson, Shakespeare, and Euripides.[77] At this point the Classical Tripos had just been reorganized into two parts, the second consisting of specialized sections on literature, philosophy, history, archaeology, and philology. In an article on 'The development of classical learning' published in 1884, Arthur Tilley of King's College commented that:

The old type of 'scholarship', the name by which we have been accustomed to know 'a minute acquaintance with the niceties of the dead languages', is rapidly passing away from us. No longer is the skilful emendation of a Greek play the royal road to a bishopric; no longer do grave statesmen and men of learning beguile their leisure moments with doing Humpty Dumpty into Latin verse; a classical quotation in the House of Commons is almost an event; a false quantity falls there on unheeding ears. Yet, on the other hand, we have Greek plays, and museums of casts from ancient sculpture, and Hellenic societies, and projects of a Hellenic School at Athens; and Professor Jebb says that 'probably the study of classics in the largest sense has never been more really vigorous than it is at the present day'.

To many these signs of a new era in English scholarship are most distasteful. They cannot bear to think that a man who has loose notions about prosody, or who has no more veneration for Porson than Byron had, should rejoice in the honoured name of 'scholar'.[78]

In 1906 five Cambridge men competed to succeed Richard Jebb in Porson's chair. A Trinity tutor who had sat through the candidates' praelections concluded that:

Not one of the 5 gave any indication of possessing, or interest in, the old Cambridge exact scholarship. Is Porsonian scholarship, then, dead? I must admit that a couple of names do come to mind among the living.[79]

---

[75] Watson 1861. For Watson, see Bainbridge 1985; 2004e. For a criticism of Watson's account by one of Porson's descendants, see 2013a, 211.

[76] Shilleto's edition of Thucydides I appeared in 1872; Book II, unfinished at his death, was completed anonymously by F. A. Paley and was published in 1880. Shilleto's attack on Grote's rehabilitation of Cleon in his *History of Greece* combined a Porsonian focus on linguistic minutiae with a proudly-declared political conservatism (1997a).

[77] Copies of Selwyn's tripos verses are preserved in Cambridge University Archives and elsewhere (e.g. Trinity College Library, C.17.16). Tyrrell's piece (Tyrrell 1888) was designed to criticize the recent publications of Schliemann and his ally A. H. Sayce. The most recent appearance of Porson's ghost is in Nuttall 2003, 205.

[78] Tilley 1884, 163. 'Humpty Dumpty' probably refers to Henry Drury, editor of *Arundines Cami*, in which he included his own Latin elegiac version of the rhyme (Drury 1841, 110–11). Jebb is quoted from the preface to his *The Attic Orators* (London 1876), 1.xv.

[79] John Image to William Smith, 28 Jan. 1906: Trinity College Library, O.1.17.2–3. (For the context, see 2005a, 4–6.) Image did not reveal the names that came to his mind.

Conclusion

The cult of Porsoniasm was the product of a confluence of disparate elements. Porson himself, with his political radicalism, his elusive attachment to established religion, and his notorious lack of social graces, was an unlikely hero for the Anglican divines who followed his scholarly example. But this was of course not the first time that a radical leader had become the hero of a more conventional cult through which his charisma was routinized.[80] As for the rise of the cult, this was clearly associated with the emergence of Trinity as a large classical college in a mathematical university; all this supported by merit-based entry and intense rivalry with St John's. Paradoxically, the domination of Oxford by classics in a university of smallish colleges where power lay at college level may have discouraged anything like the Porsonian phenomenon, producing diffusion rather than the concentration of work and cult in a single large college. The absence of the high-pitched intensity of Cambridge university exams was also perhaps relevant (for an extended comparative discussion, see 2001b, 2005c). As for the fall—Housman was right to declare that death and preferment took their toll. But other forces were at work too, as I have suggested, including the rise of broader conceptions of scholarship, and newer institutions in this country which helped to promulgate them.

In explaining both rise and fall, I have tried to go beyond the individualist tradition of Wilamowitz, Sandys, Housman, Pfeiffer, and Brink by focusing on institutions and groups. The wider contexts of contemporary literature, politics, and religion also need to be taken account of—especially since we are dealing with a period before the rise of the academic profession, the shift from clergyman to don (Engel 1983). Central to this is the complicated and neglected field of early nineteenth-century periodicals (the *Wellesley Index*'s coverage begins only in 1824)[81]—a mixture of general, literary, religious, and scholarly journals. It was within this arena that reputations were made and broken, careers made, and styles of work cultivated. Much of this activity was carried on by groups and networks, rather than by isolated individuals or the members of stable institutional formations; and it may be useful to conclude by revisiting the comparison between the two Cambridge-based movements, Porsoniasm and Ritualism.

The similarities have already been mentioned: the local base with Oxonian attachments (Peter Elmsley; Gilbert Murray), the identification by others as group, school,

---

[80] There is room for a re-examination of Porson himself: for example, the links between his style of classical scholarship and his fondness for mathematics. It was suggested in 1850 that 'those who are well acquainted with his writings will recognize, in everything that he has done, the delicate accuracy of the Cambridge mathematical tripos. Even the characteristic neatness of his handwriting may be referred, in part, to the same habit of mind.' (Anon. 1850, 625.)

[81] *The Wellesley Index to Victorian Periodicals, 1824–1900*, 5 vols (Toronto: University of Toronto Press, 1966–89; CD-rom version 1999). The *Edinburgh Review*, exceptionally, is indexed from its foundation in 1802. The pre-1824 issues of the *Quarterly Review* are now indexed in Jonathan Cutmore's excellent *Quarterly Review Archive* at www.rc.umd.edu/reference/qr/index.html; cf. Cutmore 2007, 2008, 2018.

or movement.[82] The modern tendency to undercut reification has focused attention on the Ritualists while leaving the Porsonians unexplored. Had they included a woman— a veritable Porsonulette—or roamed beyond the texts of drama, the situation would surely be different. Beard's demystifying analysis of Jane Harrison's self-promotion (Beard 2000) at once maintains a local hero cult and recasts it by highlighting penumbral figures: notably Eugenie Strong, who like Beard herself worked on Rome rather than on Greece. An interesting parallel is Henderson's celebration of J. E. B. Mayor (Henderson 1998), though in this case the aim is rehabilitation rather than exposure: taking the subject *more* seriously than his contemporaries did.[83] As for the differences: in comparison with the dynamic interactions of the Ritualists, the Porsonians might be seen as a relatively static group. I hope to have shown, however, that both the internal structure of the Porsonian school and its external relations are best seen as dynamic processes. The school had both 'inside outsiders' and 'outside insiders', and its members both collaborated and disagreed. It was appropriate to the status of Porsoniasm as a hero cult that collaboration took place not in the members' own work, as with the inclusion of an excursus by Murray and a chapter by Cornford in Harrison's *Themis* (Harrison 1912), but in the editing of Porson's *Nachlass*.[84] But shared reverence for Porson and respect for his achievement did not prevent, indeed it promoted, the emergence of mutual suspicion and jealousy as well as loyalty and collaboration. Comparison of such academic and intellectual clusters, both within and between fields of knowledge, is the essential first step in assembling a general analysis of such phenomena. The extent and quality of work on this area in the history of science makes it a fruitful source for such analysis: philology and syphilology may seem unlikely bedfellows, but their similarities and differences are alike instructive.

[82] In a discussion of Thomas Gaisford, Lloyd-Jones refers to 'what is not quite accurately called the school of Porson', but does not explain what the alleged inaccuracy is (Lloyd-Jones 1982, 89). Page declared that 'at Cambridge a cult of Porson was founded by Kidd, Dobree, Monk, and Blomfield', but added that 'We hear much of a *Porsonian School*, though it would be hard to find any member of it worth mention today except Dobree and *longe intervallo* Blomfield' (Page 1960, 230). Even vaguer than Murray's description of Ritualism as a 'movement' was J. U. Powell's reference to 'a constellation of scholars', its brightest star being Porson; '[t]he other names in the constellation' he listed as Monk, Blomfield, and Elmsley (Lehnus 2012, , 268–9).

[83] Here Henderson is close to the radical conservatism displayed by Beard in her barnstorming account of William Ridgeway (Beard 2005), which is curiously different from, if not actually contradictory to, her approach to Harrison. *Parcere subiectis et debellare superbos*? Henderson's study of Mayor can also be linked to his later work on Latin and Greek editions (Henderson 2006, 2007), as explorations of books which have been important to him. They are, in other words, studies in autobiobibliography (another hapax? No, it has been used by Jaroslav Pelikan to characterize Augustine's *Confessions*: Pelikan 1999, p. xiv).

[84] The collaboration of Monk and Blomfield in editing the *Museum Criticum* (1813–26) is of a different kind.

5

Renegotiating Classics
The Politics of Curricular Reform
in Late Victorian Cambridge

From the symbolic repertoire that we call 'Classics', many different conceptions of antiquity have been assembled. These versions of Classics can be identified at a number of levels—personal, institutional, national. This chapter is devoted to an institutional version: the teaching and learning of classics in the University of Cambridge in the second half of the nineteenth century. It is at this institutional level that we can see the larger national traditions and the variety of individual visions and preferences mediated by the curricular forms which develop within the former, and influence the latter. In late Victorian Cambridge, the study of Classics, formerly subordinated to that of mathematics, became an autonomous subject. Subsequently its content was first expanded, and then divided: doubly divided, in fact, into sequential parts and into specialized sections. The classical curriculum which resulted from these changes owed much to the ideology of research, and to the influence of German scholarship. Yet its history was also full of roads not taken, of options chosen then abandoned. Moreover, the options chosen were informed by visions of what might be, but also influenced by competing visions of alternative futures, as well as by the brute facts of human and financial resources; and above all, by the constraints of institutional politics. What was hoped for was abandoned, again and again, in favour of what would work, or what could be achieved within a rigid system of voting. The commonest results were compromises; the exceptions stemmed from the invasion of the institutional arena by external forces too powerful to resist. In Cambridge, as in Oxford, the crucial interventions were made by the state, in the form of Royal Commissions which investigated the two universities in 1850, 1872, and 1922.

The Cambridge Version

In early nineteenth-century Europe, there were clear differences between national forms of Classics. In France, the Roman world and its language constituted a dominant influence, but were linked to a corpus of French classical writers. Where other countries studied two classical languages, here there were three: Latin, Greek, and French.

Germany (not yet a nation) was the proud possessor of the massive and productive realm of *Altertumswissenschaft*. The relaxed amateur scholarship of the English gentleman provided a striking contrast. In place of the pedagogical mission of the German seminar, the patronage of professors, and the cumulative contents of journals, its ancient universities provided clerical and collegiate environments in which social and religious conformity constrained the pursuit of knowledge.[1] In the years after the battle of Waterloo, when enrolments to Oxford and Cambridge rose steeply, the mental and moral discipline of young men was thought more important than the creation of new knowledge.[2]

Though the two universities were alike in being wings of the Anglican Church, their teaching and learning had developed in different ways, as we saw in Chapter 2. Given the embedded position of the study of Latin and Greek in the elite culture of early nineteenth-century England, the mathematical domination of the Cambridge curriculum constituted a striking anomaly.[3] In the eighteenth century, this had probably depressed admissions in favour of Oxford.[4] The classical honours examination founded in 1822 (the Classical Tripos), was introduced as a purely voluntary examination, open only to those students who had passed the (pre-existing) Mathematical Tripos at a high level. Further, that well-known symbol of gentlemanly culture, original composition in Latin and Greek, was barred from the examination (see Chapter 2). That was not the only exclusion, however: there were also no questions on ancient history. The tripos focused on the ancient literary authors, encouraging analysis of their manner rather than their matter.[5] It was this close, disciplined study of literary texts as linguistic corpuses which was above all prized in Cambridge, where it was commonly known as 'pure classics' or 'pure scholarship'. Its heroic exemplar was Richard Porson (1759–1808), whose pupils James Monk (1784–1858: Regius Professor of Greek 1808–23) and Charles Blomfield (1786–1857), as we saw in Chapter 4, carried on the tradition into the 1820s. In the next generation, the torch was borne by Richard Shilleto (1809–1876), whose marriage for long barred him from a college fellowship; he became the leading private tutor ('coach') for Cambridge classical students. Porson and his pupils concentrated largely on the study of Greek drama, but 'pure scholarship' ranged very widely. There was a striking contrast, discussed in Chapter 2, with the Oxford curriculum, in which set books were studied for their literary qualities, and the linguistic and literary

---

[1] For the international and institutional comparisons, see Chapter 2, and 1998a, 23–9.

[2] Sheldon Rothblatt has emphasized the relationship between this atmosphere of alarm and the emergence of standardized written examinations in the two universities: see Rothblatt 1975.

[3] For the background, see Gascoigne 1989, 270–99.

[4] '[In the 18th century] Oxford had definitely become the home of the humanist, Cambridge already specialized in mathematics. But the mathematical tripos, while conferring a lasting prestige on Cambridge, was no doubt answerable to a considerable extent for the falling off in the number of students entering the university, for non-mathematicians were not only discouraged from presenting themselves, but when in residence often formed a neglected and discontented body.' Venn 1908b, 14.

[5] Some authors were of course historians. In the first thirty-seven years of the tripos examination, passages from Thucydides were set for translation and comment thirty-eight times, Herodotus thirty-five, Livy thirty-four, and Tacitus thirty-seven: see Mayor 1860.

Honour Moderations course ('Mods') led on to *Literae Humaniores* ('Greats'), which combined ancient history with philosophy (ancient and modern). As a result, there was in the Cambridge curriculum a potential tension between the study of 'the best authors' (as the examination rubrics specified) and the analysis of Greek and Latin in all their varieties.

In the second half of the century, both universities were prodded towards reform by Royal Commissions established in 1850 and in 1872. In consequence, they converged in some ways on the German model. The universities gained resources, largely through the transfer of funds from the colleges. Chairs were founded (that of Latin at Oxford, in 1854), and restrictions of religion and celibacy removed. New degree courses were founded, old ones reorganized. In many ways, however, Oxford and Cambridge continued to follow distinctive paths. In particular, the power of the colleges and their tutors, as against that of the professoriate and the university, was greater at Oxford than at Cambridge. The internal decision-making structures of the two universities were very similar. A Senate or Congregation initiated proposals which could then be vetoed in a larger body made up of Masters of Arts. This meant that though the latter body was unable to take initiatives, it could block proposals for change. In the second half of the century, reforming initiatives by liberal dons were again and again defeated by conservative MAs, many of them clerics; special trains brought in the 'black battalions' in their hundreds to vote against reform.

From Expansion to Division, 1866–1882

Where Classics was concerned, many of the reforming proposals were hatched in Trinity, both the largest college and the home of several leading liberal dons. Among the staunchest opponents of change in the Classical Tripos, however, was the college's Master, the formidable and autocratic William Whewell (1784–1866). It is hardly a coincidence that in the reformist atmosphere of the mid-1860s, the major proposal for change in this area was advanced by two Trinity dons, William Clark (1821–78) and Robert Burn (1829–1904), soon after Whewell's death in March 1866. The tripos, founded in 1822, had in its early years been dominated by the study of language and literature; an ancient history paper was added only in 1849, and was not taken very seriously by undergraduates. Clark and Burn now proposed to enlarge the historical element in the examination, and also to insert papers on ancient philosophy. After a series of debates, three extra papers, two on philosophy and rhetoric and one on philology, were added in 1869.[6]

---

[6] Winstanley 1947, 212–23, gives an account of this and later developments up to 1880, drawing on polemical pamphlets (known in Cambridge as 'flysheets') in the university archives (DC 1350). In this and other areas, Winstanley's detailed discussion is invaluable, and has not been superseded by Searby 1997 and Brooke 1993. On the introduction of the papers in ancient philosophy, see Todd 1999.

Several contentious issues emerged in the debates of the late 1860s. One was the status of 'fixed' or 'set subjects'—i.e., prescribed texts, or historical periods. The defenders of the Cambridge ideology of linguistic problem-solving saw this as an invitation to cram factual knowledge as opposed to skill. Another issue concerned the status of verse composition. This exercise was now widely criticized in schools and universities, yet it was clear that it was almost impossible to gain a first-class degree unless one did well in composition. The reformers of the late 1860s at one point suggested making composition and philology alternatives. When the conservatives denounced this, they included both, but urged that composition marks should only be taken into account when the other papers had been marked. A final, more general issue had to do with the way in which knowledge and students were assessed. In the early days of the tripos, a narrow range of knowledge had been evaluated by means of a single grading system. By the 1870s, however, the range of papers was so much enlarged that some dons doubted whether this could be maintained. Students were now being tested on performance in language, literature, history, and philology—how could a single unitary mark be given?

The solution eventually found was prompted by a *deus ex machina* in the shape of a university-wide move to the division of triposes into two parts, to facilitate the taking of 'double honours'—i.e. degrees gained in two subjects. Even after the Classical Tripos was freed from the mathematical restriction in 1854, some men had taken both examinations, but their numbers dropped steadily as the content of the courses, and the length of their examinations, were increased. This decline was documented in 1876 in a memorial sent to the university by the headmasters of the leading public schools.[7] Concerned at the erosion of general culture by the advance of specialization, they urged that something be done to enable the taking of 'double honours' to continue. The university responded by splitting the Classical Tripos into two parts, a pattern which already obtained in some other courses.[8] The first part continued the amateur tradition of 'liberal education' by focusing on language and literature. The second part consisted of five specialized sections: literature and criticism, philosophy, history, archaeology, and language (i.e., comparative philology). Of these, all were optional except the first, which until 1895 was compulsory; a maximum of two optional sections could be offered. If this latter restriction made pragmatic sense, the compulsory status of literature surely reflected a compromise between reforming dons and the defenders of 'pure scholarship'.

---

[7] In 1857, a third of the classical first-class men had previously sat the mathematical examination; 17% did so in 1872, none in 1877. Some men may have sat both examinations in the hope of improving their chances of a college fellowship. The headmasters' memorial reported that between 1824, the year of the first classical examination, and 1850, the average number sitting both examinations was nearly thirty; the average from 1851 to 1876 was less than half this figure. *Report of the Annual Conference of Head Masters, held at Rugby School, Dec. 21st and 22nd, 1876* (Rugby 1877) 52–60, at 54. The trend is even more striking if viewed in relation to total numbers gaining honours in classics; the annual average, which had been about thirty in the 1840s, had more then doubled by the 1870s.

[8] Winstanley 1947, 203–4. The Mathematical Tripos had been divided since 1846.

In the 1880s appointments were made to staff the new areas. Charles Waldstein (1856–1927) was employed as lecturer in classical archaeology from 1880. He was given an entrée by Henry Sidgwick (1838–1900), who arranged for him to lecture on Greek art for a term, using Sidgwick's own rooms at Trinity College, which he had vacated on his marriage that year; he was then paid for a year through the generosity of Henry Bradshaw of King's (Prothero 1886, 249–51). Subsequently hired by the university as a lecturer, in 1883 he was appointed to the newly-created readership in classical archaeology.[9] This post he held until he was succeeded by Arthur Cook (1868–1952) in 1907. A readership in comparative philology was established at the same time (John Peile 1884; Peter Giles 1891–1911). A lectureship in Roman history was also set up (J. S. Reid 1883, A. A. Tilley 1887), and changed to 'ancient history' in 1899 (Leonard Whibley 1899–1910). Another lectureship, in comparative philology, was later renamed 'epigraphy and dialects' (E. S. Roberts 1883, S. G. Campbell 1906). These posts were set up in connection with the Special Board of Classics; another lectureship in ancient history was established by the Board on History and Archaeology in 1901 (N. Wedd 1901) but suppressed in 1912. By this time a chair of ancient history had been established (1898: J. S. Reid 1899). William Ridgeway (1853–1926) was appointed to the Disney chair of Archaeology in 1892 and reappointed several times, and later gained the Brereton readership in classics when it was founded in 1906.[10] Ridgeway was in a sense another foreign import—from Ireland—but less exotic, and certainly less smooth, than Waldstein.[11] The compulsory literature section was comfortably overstaffed by the literary scholars in post in the seventeen colleges of the university. The philosophy section was almost Trinity's private domain, the leading teachers of the subject all being fellows of the college: Henry Jackson, R. D. Archer-Hind, R. K. Gaye, F. M. Cornford. Some of the literary scholars were also competent in philology: J. P. Postgate of Trinity, for example, also held the chair of Comparative Philology at University College London from 1880 to 1909.

Several posts in this period were funded, as in Waldstein's case, by private donation. The poverty of the university, in an era before government grants began, was compensated for by the private generosity of its members. The Latin chair was founded (fifteen years after its opposite number at Oxford) by a subscription from ex-pupils of Benjamin Kennedy, Regius Professor of Greek 1867–89. In some areas, university teaching was provided by colleges; Henry Jackson's position as praelector at Trinity College (1875) enabled him to give lectures for the university as a whole. The chairs of

---

[9] For a detailed account of the development of Section D, see Beard 1999.

[10] The Disney chair was poorly endowed; the appointment to the Brereton readership was probably made in part to supplement Ridgeway's income.

[11] For Ridgeway, see Naiditch 1991, 147 n. 77; Beard 2005. The Disney chair was linked not to the Board of Studies in Classics, but to that in History and Archaeology, and Ridgeway long felt marginalized by the linguistic and literary classical dons. He was a vigorous controversialist and an implacable opponent of the two major liberal campaigns of late-Victorian Cambridge: to abolish the university's compulsory Greek requirement for all students, and to admit women to membership. The drawing by Frances Darwin, reproduced in Stewart 1959, facing p. 16, admirably catches his elemental force.

ancient philosophy and comparative philology were established only when a benefaction made this possible in 1931.

Assessment and Choice: Knowledge, College, and Gender

The Cambridge system of teaching and learning gives us, through its printed records, the opportunity to trace patterns of choice and achievement. It also offers a self-portrait, by presenting data in a way which reflects local views of the nature of knowledge and achievement. The form of the tripos lists, as well as their content, merits attention. Successful candidates in the Mathematical Tripos were traditionally listed in a single rank order, a form which implied both a purely meritocratic ordering and a unified conception of knowledge. Even at a time when noblemen and members of King's College had special privileges in the university, the rank order of the tripos trumped such social distinctions. This is vividly depicted in an account of the degree ceremony from the 1820s, which explains that the Senior Wangler is presented for his degree before all other candidates: the moment he reaches the Vice-Chancellor, 'there succeeds an involuntary burst of applause from every part of the gallery, the fair ladies themselves, even, exhibiting a lively interest thus publicly conferred upon science—the Senior Wrangler taking precedence even of the very nobility' (Wright 1827, 1.101). From the first examination for the Classical Tripos in 1824, a similar system had been employed, the first-class list being headed by the Senior Classic. (The relative status of the two triposes was indicated in the University Calendar, in which the Senior Wrangler's name was capitalized—a distinction denied the Senior Classic.) The system agreed for Part II of the Classical Tripos was a compromise between this kind of ranking and the differentiated list encouraged by the heterogeneity of the new multi-sectional structure. The single rank order vanished, and successful candidates were listed alphabetically in three divisions in each class.[12] It was agreed that the names of those in the first class should be annotated, to show in which subjects candidates were classed, and also in which they had gained special distinction. This new institutional rhetoric represented and announced a new relationship between teachers, learners, examiners, and knowledge. The introduction of specialized options made both a single merit ranking and a plain alphabetical list unviable; the compromise solution reported on specialized accomplishment, while retaining a focus on merit in its differential treatment of the first class.[13]

A further complicating factor after 1882 was the incorporation of examination results for women. Since 1873 small numbers of female candidates had answered tripos

---

[12] An alphabetical listing of the third class had been introduced in 1849, but abandoned in 1858, apparently because it was found to discourage effort among mediocre students: Mayor 1860, 1–2.

[13] Winstanley 1947, 220. Benjamin Kennedy, Regius Professor of Greek, would have preferred to retain a merit order to aid the selection of graduates for teaching jobs, but was in a minority and gave way.

questions informally, their papers being marked by some of the examiners acting as individuals.[14] In 1881, however, the senate agreed that women could sit the examinations (separately) and have their results published. Decorum forbade the mixing of names in a single list, and so the women's names followed the men's, in an identical format. Nevertheless, an occasion was bound to arise when direct comparison could be made, and it was not long before this occurred. In 1887 the men's first-class list contained no names in its first division; in the women's list it contained, in solitary splendour, the name of Agnata Frances Ramsay (Figure 5.1).[15]

Between 1882 and 1914, 3,941 candidates sat the Part I examination: 3,490 men and 451 women. Of these, 461 (378 men and 83 women) went on to sit the Part II examination. In looking at this last group, we are thus considering a tiny minority of those who went through the tripos, who were themselves a minority of the student

HONOUR TO AGNATA FRANCES RAMSAY!
(CAMBRIDGE, JUNE, 1887.)

Figure 5.1 'Honour to Agnata Frances Ramsay', a cartoon by George Du Maurier (1834–96): *Punch*, 2 July 1887.

[14] See in general McWilliams Tullberg 1975/1998. Typically, four of six examiners consented to reading the women's papers.

[15] Even more sensationally, in 1890 Philippa Fawcett's place in the Mathematical Tripos was announced as being 'above the Senior Wrangler'.

population.[16] There were ninety-one candidates for Part I in 1882; numbers quickly settled into a range of 110–25, with only occasional peaks and troughs. The women's numbers were much smaller than those of the men, but while men were increasingly unlikely to go on to Part II, for the women this became increasingly common. The percentage for men halved during this period, from 15 per cent to 7.5 per cent, while for women it doubled from 10 per cent to 20 per cent. The results make it clear that women struggled through the obstacle course of Part I, for which they had been less intensively prepared than the men, to the relatively open field of Part II, especially the optional (non-literary) sections. Whereas most men who went on to Part II had gained a first class in the earlier examination, the women tended to do relatively poorly in Part I, and then to raise their class in Part II.

The published lists tell us something of the sections chosen, but only within narrow limits. As I mentioned above, where candidates gained first classes, the sections for which they gained them were listed next to their names. Until 1895, they had to take Literature and one or two other sections; after then, one or two sections from the whole range. Except where a candidate has three sections listed before 1895, or two after then, we cannot assume that he or she took only those listed. The data do tell us something about patterns of choice (and students will often have chosen what they were good at). Nevertheless, it must be borne in mind that they provide only illustrative evidence. An example of how misleading they might be if used as direct evidence is that in this period, only one person (J. W. Headlam) gained a first on a combination of the philosophy and history sections of Part II. Yet the 1883 report of the classical board, quoted above, indicates that this was the most popular combination for those who read for two sections. The combination, we may conclude, was a popular choice, but one in which it was very difficult to gain a first (Table 5.1). (The further conclusion might be drawn that it became less popular as this fact became known.)

The totals are greater than the number of candidates because first classes were in some cases gained in more than one section. Between 1882 and 1894, sixty-seven students gained firsts on their performance in one section, forty-nine in two, and twelve in three sections.

A few striking patterns emerge. The success rate of men in Part II dropped as that of women rose. The popularity of Literature waned dramatically when it became optional in 1895, the post-1895 totals being down by half in proportion to total figures.

---

[16] Precise figures are difficult to find. McWilliams-Tullberg 1975, 222 stated that between 1851 and 1906, 41% of men took honours degrees, 34% pass degrees, 25% no degree at all. Similar figures are given by Leedham-Green 1996, 186: 44.4% honours degrees, 32.9% pass degrees, 22.7% none at all. McWilliams Tullberg (ibid.) added that between 1887 and 1912, pass degrees declined from 48% to 45% as a percentage of all degrees awarded. Brooke 1993, 294 states that 'In the late nineteenth century the proportion slowly declined': but then gives figures for Gonville and Caius College which suggest an increase in the percentage of pass degrees from c.1890 to c.1910, from 24% to 32% of the total. A recent calculation by Elisabeth Leedham-Green, to whom I am indebted for reporting it to me, suggests however that between 1859 and 1899 the percentage of degrees oscillated as follows: honours, 44–55%; pass, 45–56%. These figures cannot be reconciled with those above.

Table 5.1 Firsts in Part II, 1882–1914: sections and sexes

	A	B	C	D	E	
	Lit	Philos	Hist	Arch	Lang	Total
1882–1894						
men	57	39	36	20	28	180
women	1	10	0	0	2	13
1895–1914						
men	16	34	32	24	8	114
women	1	11	4	9	2	27
Totals:	men	294	women		40	334

Language (i.e., comparative philology) suffered a similar fate. On the other hand, the success rate in Archaeology rose considerably, especially for women. If the incidence of firsts is correlated with the candidates' colleges, equally clear patterns emerge. Trinity, by far the largest college, scores eighty-three. Only two other colleges of the nineteen which then existed score more than twenty: Kings (thirty) and Newnham (twenty-five). The King's score is an indication of the success of college reforms in the period. What had been a small and academically undistinguished college had been changed beyond recognition by the activity of such men as Augustus Austen Leigh, Oscar Browning, and George Prothero. Newnham's twenty-five firsts were a remarkable achievement for a small female college whose students had an uphill battle to pass Part I.

Bearing in mind that the later period had a decreased recruitment to Part II overall, a few detailed trends can be seen. The only college to resist the collapse of Literature numbers is Trinity, but even there the fall is noticeable: twenty-three firsts before 1895, ten afterwards. The college's leading position in philosophy was however maintained (twenty-nine firsts before, twenty afterwards). It gained almost two-thirds of all the philosophy firsts in the whole period—the outstanding example of the domination of special subject teaching by a single college. Some of these changes surely have to do with patterns of staffing. Jane Harrison's influence at Newnham, after her return there in 1898, can be assumed to have something to do with the college's string of firsts in archaeology, beginning in 1901 with her 'first first'—Jessie Crum.[17] One also has to allow for the changing rate of enrolments to colleges. Trinity was far bigger than its nearest rival St John's, and in this period grew while St John's shrank: between 1880 and 1910 Trinity's numbers rose from 567 to 700, while St John's declined from 354 to 253. The declining admissions to St John's (down from 104 in 1880 to 73 in 1900) probably

---

[17] On Crum's achievement and its context, see 1995. Her success was the more remarkable since it was gained after one year of study, rather than the usual two. Jessie Crum married Hugh Stewart, reader in Modern Languages and fellow of Trinity. Later she assembled a *Portrait in Letters* of her teacher Harrison (Stewart 1959). Her daughter Katharine married the Marxist Greek scholar George Thomson (1903–87) of King's College, later professor of Greek at Birmingham; their daughter Margaret Alexiou was Seferis Professor of Modern Greek at Harvard from 1984 to 2000. Thus do academic dynasties unfold.

reflected the impact of a drop in income from rural rents, which meant that the college could no longer support at its previous level the poorer students which it had tradition-ally attracted.[18] Caius and King's both doubled in size, but from very different bases: Caius from 162 to 213, King's from 71 to 165 (Brooke 1993, 593–4). Allowing for such differences throws a rather different light on the tripos figures; but the biases toward particular sections of Part II are likely to reflect those of staffing, which are to some extent independent of size. The obituary of J. S. Reid in the Caius college magazine claimed that the notably improved college showing in the tripos results c.1878–99 was due to the teaching of Reid, E. S. Roberts, and William Ridgeway, all fellows in the period.[19]

Dora Ivens and Ella Edghill: Student Choice and Academic Politics

It is not often that we can glimpse the sequences of student choice and advice from teachers which lie behind the published examination results; but the veil is sometimes lifted by differences of opinion. In her unpublished memoirs, Dora Pym, née Ivens, recalled that she had had to struggle against her teachers at Girton, where she matricu-lated in 1910, to choose literature and criticism for her Part II subject. Her director of studies, Katharine Jex-Blake, told her, 'You'll only get a second if you take Section A ... It is really textual criticism, not the literature you think. You have not read enough to tackle it. In history or archaeology you could certainly get a first.'[20] Ella Edghill of Newnham (matriculated 1901) had a similar problem, but in her case dons outside her own college became involved. On 25 June 1904, the young Trinity classical don Russell Gaye (1877–1909) wrote to his senior colleague Henry Jackson about 'a fairly strong prejudice scattered about the University against Section B [philosophy]'.[21] Gaye had taught Edghill for Part I, in which she had gained a first. She now wrote to him to ask for his advice, since pressure was being put on her at Newnham to take Section D [archaeology], for which she felt 'no inclination', whereas she had a 'very strong leaning towards B'. Gaye had replied urging her to declare her choice of B, and this she had done. The response from some of the Newnham dons was to urge her to consider choosing Literature and Criticism. The campaign was led by Margaret Verrall, who with her husband Arthur Verrall, a classical colleague of Gaye's and Jackson's at Trinity, was applying similar pressure to their daughter Helen.[22] Another source of pressure at

[18] Cf. Miller 1961, 98; Linehan 2011, 382. The college was also crippled by the massive loans taken out to build its new chapel, completed in 1869; the loans were not paid off till 1895. The admissions to the various colleges are graphically illustrated in Venn 1908b.

[19] The Caian 34 (1925–7), 134–42. The writer was 'P.G.', presumably Peter Giles. Ridgeway's obituary follows (ibid., 143–55).

[20] D. Pym 'Patchwork from the Past' (unpublished typescript, 5 vols), vol. 4, 464; quoted by permission of the author's daughter, Mary Pym.

[21] Trinity College Library, Add. MS C. 31.7.

[22] Mrs Verrall, born Margaret Merrifield, had collaborated with Jane Harrison on *Mythology and Monuments of Ancient Athens* (London, 1890).

Newnham was Mrs Verrall's colleague Jane Harrison, who wrote to Edghill saying that 'We are all very anxious that Mr Sheppard's disaster—one can call it nothing less—should not prejudice anyone against Section A [i.e., Literature and Criticism].'[23] How strong these pressures were it is difficult to say, but in a later letter to Jackson (28 June 1904), Gaye wrote that 'Miss Edghill is not anxious that [the Newnham people] should know that she has consulted me, and she seems to be a little afraid of Mrs Verrall.'[24] He goes on to agree with Jackson that a special aptitude is needed for B, and adds 'I myself discouraged one Newnham pupil this year from taking it, as I saw she would be unsuitable.'

There is no further trace of the matter in Jackson's correspondence: we only have these letters because Gaye was out of Cambridge at the time. But the university calendar provides the end of the story; Ella Edghill gained a first in philosophy in 1905, Helen Verrall in 1906.[25] Evidently, both students stuck to their guns and resisted the pressure of their college teachers. The letters do, however, also throw light on another subject choice, that of 'Mr Sheppard'. This was John Tresidder Sheppard of Kings, subsequently Provost of the College 1933–54, who after two vain attempts to secure the Greek chair became a college administrator and a popularizer of Greek literature, especially drama. In 1901 he had been placed in the first division of the first class in Part I, and was also awarded the medal given to the best student of the year; but in his Part II examinations in 1904 he could only manage a second. The results would have been announced not long before Gaye wrote to Jackson on 24 June, so his 'disaster' will have been fresh in the minds of Cambridge classicists. In his case, we are able to see through the absence of section identifications for non-first class candidates in the published results, since he must have gone in for the Literature section.

In his letters to Jackson, Gaye denounced what he saw as an attempt to browbeat a student for the sake of the reputation of a section: 'It seems to be monstrous that it should be urged on anyone as a sort of duty to take a particular examination in order to regain for it the popular favour which it is imagine to have lost owing to one failure.' One can only agree; but the pride of a college may have been involved, as well as that of a subject. King's had no first at all in Literature after it became optional in 1895.[26] More generally, the college had slipped from thirty-five firsts in the period 1882–95 to seventeen in the nine years since then.

Like King's, Newnham had no firsts in Literature throughout the period. Newnham's strengths lay in philosophy and, increasingly, in history and archaeology. The figures

[23] See the next paragraph for 'Mr Sheppard's disaster'.

[24] Trinity College Library, Add. MS C. 31. 8.

[25] Edghill subsequently translated the *Categoriae* and the *De Interpretatione* for Ross's Oxford Aristotle series; she was presumably brought to Ross's attention by Gaye, who translated the *Physica* for the same series with R. P. Hardie.

[26] It had not gained a first in Literature since that of R. J. G. Mayor in 1892 (the last student to gain a first in three sections). Mayor belonged to a well-known academic family which included his uncles J. B. Mayor, Professor of Classics at King's College London 1870–9, and J. E. B. Mayor, Professor of Latin at Cambridge 1872–1910.

for Girton, the other women's college, show a similar pattern, except that it had two firsts in Literature. This might be expected, given the ideological differences between the two colleges. Roughly, the Girtonian philosophy was that women should tackle men on their own ground, whereas Newnham held rather to the doctrine of 'separate spheres' (Sutherland 2001). Girton thus challenged the men on their home ground of linguistic and literary knowledge, whereas Newnham opened up the new front of archaeology. It is therefore appropriate that the first great female triumph in the Tripos, when, as we have seen, Agnata Ramsay of Girton scored the highest marks of any student in 1887, should have occurred in the Part I examination. This was male territory: the literary and linguistic test for which the public schools still prepared boys at length. Female students came to Cambridge much less well equipped. They had begun Latin and Greek later, at the age of twelve to fifteen rather than seven to eight, and had attended schools which typically had an academic timetable confined to the morning session.

What must have seemed to the traditionalists the ultimate indignity was reached during the First World War, which bit deeply into the year-groups of young men, and at the universities thus drastically reduced the number of candidates for degrees. In the 1915 tripos examination, the first since the outbreak of hostilities, there were three firsts, two of them female; in 1916 seven, of which five were female; in 1917, two female firsts and no others. In 1918 no class list was published; the Part I list for that year contains only eleven candidates, eight of them women.

Specialization and Academic Community

The patterns of choice I have examined above may suggest what kind of academic community it was that emerged at Cambridge over this period. This can be looked at from several different angles. First of all, the new sections created demands for staffing. Ironically, the low level of demand from students fitted perfectly with the low level of income available for staffing, in a period of rural depression when university funds were low. The colleges' resources were still greater than those of the university, but their income was largely based on rural rents, which had been reduced sharply by the agricultural depression of the 1870s and 1880s. A fellow of King's, for example, had received in the 1870s a dividend of around £300 per annum; by the early 1890s it was down to about £80. Secondly, the teaching of Part II began to be organized on an inter-collegiate basis. This stemmed from an initiative of Henry Sidgwick and his Trinity colleagues in the later 1860s. By 1900, several colleges had agreed to open their lectures to each other's students. Yet in 1903, Francis Cornford could still complain of the absurdity of thirteen independent bodies drawing up lecture lists without any consultation, so that there was 'nothing to prevent the simultaneous delivery to small audiences of four or five courses (say) on the Isthmian Odes' (Cornford 1903, 26).

Thirdly, the products of Part II were themselves, some of them, appointed to college fellowships and university lectureships. Among them we can detect some well-known academic names. In 1884 we have the Platonic scholar James Adam and the classical archaeologist Ernest Gardner. In 1887 the list includes Peter Giles, later reader in comparative philology. In 1892 we find T. R. Glover, who held a chair in Canada before returning to Cambridge, where he became Public Orator; and Francis Cornford, who in 1931 became the first occupant of the chair of ancient philosophy. James Headlam, whom we have already encountered, appears in the 1887 list next to his cousin Clinton. Clinton Headlam subsequently examined for the tripos and gained a college fellowship, but did not follow an academic career.[27] James Headlam was one of a group of men who gained six-year fellowships and then sought permanent appointments. Headlam (King's 1890–6) went into school inspecting, as did others, such as W. H. D. Rouse (Christ's 1888–94)[28] and J. C. Stobart (second class, 1901), the author of two widely-read books on classical culture (Stobart 1911, 1912). Such careers remained common in a period when college finances were depressed by declining rural rents; when state aid had not been set up as a regular part of university finance; and when the modern faculty system was still in the future (it did not appear until after the 1922 Royal Commission).[29]

As far as Cambridge academic recruitment is concerned, it should be remembered that demand exceeded supply, and that there were few jobs available. James Headlam was among the unsuccessful candidates for the new chair of ancient history to which J. S. Reid was appointed in 1898: the others were W. E. Heitland, W. Ridgeway, E. S. Shuckburgh, A. H. Tilley, and L. Whibley, all of Cambridge; A. H. J. Greenidge and G. B. Grundy of Oxford, and the private tutor Eustace Miles. Reid was the obvious candidate, not only because he had held the university's lectureship in ancient history since its foundation in 1879, but because, unlike most of the others, he worked mainly in Roman history, for which the chair was created. The field was unusually large: the Greek chair had four applicants in 1867, three in 1889 and five in 1906; the Latin chair, two in 1869, three in 1872, and three in 1911. The large field in 1898 reflects the paucity of such posts and the pressure on them from those in the field.

Between 1882 and 1904, 208 students gained first-class degrees in Part II of the Classical Tripos. Of these, forty taught at Cambridge, thirty-six at other universities, sixty-seven became schoolteachers, twenty-nine went into the church, twenty-nine to the civil service, ten to the law, twenty-seven into other employment. Some graduates fell into more than one category. Recruitment to the church declined slightly over the period; to the law, more noticeably (none after 1896). The clerical figures can be seen, in a longer perspective, as the remnant of what had once been a majority trend, but had been sharply reduced in the period 1855–85, when first-class graduates who would

---

[27] The Headlams can nevertheless claim to have been another academic dynasty. James's younger brother Arthur was a fellow of All Souls, Oxford; his more famous cousin Walter gained a fellowship at King's College on the same day that James did; James's daughter Agnes became the first female professor (of International Relations) at Oxford.

[28] For Rouse's career, see 1992.

[29] The faculties formalized the system of non-collegiate teaching and administration. In the 1890s, only about half the college fellows at Cambridge held university posts.

earlier have become ordained began to look for academic posts instead (Haig 1986a). The occupational categories are not mutually exclusive. In this period it was common to be ordained, or called to the bar, then go into schoolmastering, or perhaps missionary work which led to an academic post in a missionary college. Some became civil servants but published in Classics (e.g. Sir Edward Marsh, the translator of Horace). Some entered the church and carried on with scholarship (e.g. R. G. Bury, editor of Plato and translator of Sextus Empiricus). This was also a period when the boundaries between school and university work were not so clearly drawn as they are now (a point made in Chapter 1). James Headlam and Edwin Brooks both held the chair of Greek and Ancient History at Queen's College (London), an institution founded in 1848 for the education of governesses, which in the 1890s was about to become a secondary school.

'The damming of the advance': The Politics of Stalemate

The history of the tripos is marked by a series of compromises. Many of them signalled political stalemates, and led to the operation of curricular schemes which fell between several stools and contained the seeds of future dissension. It was the intervention of the state through a series of Royal Commissions (1850, 1872, 1922) which made strategic changes possible. It should also be noted, however, that it was an initiative by another external body, the Headmasters' Conference, which led to the division of the tripos in 1879. Comparing the results of that change with the professed concerns of the headmasters, we might wonder if they had a hidden agenda. The division of the tripos did not lead to a large-scale taking of 'double honours'; its major effect was to enable public schoolboys to prolong a traditional classical education from school to university, avoiding the newer fields of scholarship. In an unpublished paper written in Cambridge during his student career in the mid-1880s, James Headlam put his finger on the problem:

The Classical Tripos more than any other is marred by a difficulty which is the great hindrance to really satisfactory educational work. It has to meet the requirements of two quite different classes of students[.] On the one hand there are those undergraduates who are of sufficient intelligence and ambition not to remain satisfied with the ordinary degree, but have no great love for learning or turn to any particular branch of it. These are the men who are referred to by those who tell us that the Universities exist for the purpose of giving a good Education such as to train men to be 'English Gentlemen'.... On the other hand, we find a considerable number of men every year who really merit the name of Scholar...

He goes on to emphasize that he does not 'undervalue the use of the carefulness and accuracy of verbal criticism and composition; for those who can bear it is good. But it is food not for babes but for strong men, and . . . the majority of the candidates for the Classical Tripos are not strong men.'[30] On other hand, Headlam was optimistic about

---

[30] Untitled MS, *c* 1885, pp. 8–9, 13; cited by kind permission of Mrs. Lorna Headlam-Morley.

the future of Part II: 'The appointment of Dr Waldstein to be Reader in Classical Archaeology is the inauguration of a new era in Cambridge and in English Studies and it is to be hoped that great results may ensue from it.'[31]

Headlam was not alone in looking forward to a 'new era'. A decade later, however, it was accepted by most Cambridge classical dons that Part II was a failure, attracting hardly any candidates. Their attempts to make Part I ineligible for a degree by itself, thus forcing students to go on to Part II (or to another tripos) were repeatedly blocked in the university senate, as were a series of other schemes. One of these would have inserted elements of Part II in Part I; another proposed setting up a Part III. A sense of stalemate dogged the tripos as the century ended, and it was closely bound up with a history of stultifying academic infighting. Time after time non-resident MA's were brought in by special train to vote down proposals which threatened to make Part II necessary for a degree, to make Greek optional, or to admit women to full membership of the university.[32] It was this situation which prompted Francis Cornford to write his celebrated 'guide for the young academic politician' *Microcosmographia Academica*, first published in 1908.[33]

In May 1900, not long before he died, Henry Sidgwick received a letter from his protégé Charles Waldstein. In it Waldstein declared that if one looked at the history of the university over the last twenty years,

the wonderful new life which has come, the variety of new studies so needful to make the university respond to the highest civilisation of our own times and our country, are due to your efforts and to those who have stood by you. Under this influence the old studies have been imbued with a higher spirit as well as with greater depth.

But he went on to add, 'I say this in spite of the temporary checks and reactions which within the last few years have apparently dammed the advance.'[34] Waldstein's words sum up the mixture of triumph and despair which must often been felt by the reforming classicists of the period.

How are we to account for the 'damming of the advance'? Both internal and external pressures played a part. The internal obstacle to change was the university's system of government, in which non-resident MAs could veto reform proposals. This obstacle was removed only by the 1922 Royal Commission. Thus in the 1890s, the reformers—which by then meant, practically all the university teachers of classics—were hamstrung. Declining college revenues cut down the effective options, while creating an atmosphere

---

[31] Ibid., 12. 'English Studies' refers to English education, not to the study of English: the English tripos was not established until 1917.

[32] For Compulsory Greek, see Raphaely 1999; for women, McWilliams Tullberg 1975.

[33] The immediate cause was probably the debates of 1905–6 on Compulsory Greek, when Cornford and his fellow-reformers were routed (the issue had first been debated in 1870). For the complete text, together with an introductory essay by a historian and university politician, see Johnson 1994.

[34] C. Waldstein to H. Sidgwick, 30 May 1900, Trinity College Library, Add MS C. 75[181]; cited by permission of the Master and Fellows of Trinity College. Waldstein's letter was occasioned by his discovering that Sidgwick was ill; he died of cancer on 28 August that year.

of nervousness at possible state financial intervention which reinforced conservative countermoves. It is, in retrospect, remarkable that the reformers achieved as much as they did. The external obstacle to change was, as Headlam indicated in his analysis, the continuing flow of traditionally-educated public schoolboys. In the late Victorian period, the public schools were at the height of their influence, and continued to be sought after by parents eager to gain and transmit social status. The role of Classics as a symbol of this status meant that its content received little attention (1998a, 167–201). The major incentive was to get boys into Oxford and Cambridge, where the majority of entrance scholarships were still restricted to Classics. Public schoolboys learned translation and composition from the ages of eight to eighteen, then went up to university, spent three more years on it (Part I at Cambridge) and gained a degree. Most of them had neither desire nor incentive to attempt Part II.

Conclusion

The period I have been examining saw the emergence in Cambridge of a distinctive pattern of curricular organization which endures today. The two-part tripos persists, though its content and fine structure have changed. The five Part II sections (now called Groups) are still in place, supplemented since the 1980s by a 'wild-card' option, Group X. This course is inter-disciplinary, focusing each year on a different theme. It thus looks back, in a sense, to the time when Classics was a single field, and before it was dissected by the disciplinary ditches of specialization (see Chapter 2 for a comparison with Greats). Its existence offers a useful reminder that the history of the tripos does not hinge only on the 'great divide' of 1882, when 'liberal education' began to give way to 'learning'. The two conceptions of classical study had coexisted, to a degree, in what E. S. Roberts of Caius called the 'middle tripos' of the previous decade, a good example of an abandoned path to the future. Not all Cambridge dons of the late nineteenth century accepted that the division of the tripos had been an unqualified success. In his obituary of Roberts, his colleague J. S. Reid commented that:

Undoubtedly a great deal of Roberts's activity in after life was determined by the desire to remedy the defects of the Classical training through which he himself had passed. But he realised, I know, that the changes which came about were not all pure gain. We felt the Classical Tripos of our time to be somewhat narrow and cramping, but dissatisfaction still exists among the candidates, and with some reason. The possibility of wide reading in ancient literature is not greater now than it was then, but less. And I know I am giving expression to Roberts's own feeling when I say that (contrary to a common opinion) the mastery of language which was then more rigorously demanded than now did not obstruct in the case of the better men a due appreciation of the literary side of the ancient writings. The Tripos seems to me to have been at that time the gateway to fruitful literary study, more than is the case now.[35]

---

[35] J. S. Reid, memoir of E. S. Roberts: *The Caian*, special number (Cambridge, 1912), 5. Both men gained their firsts in 1869; as did Percy Gardner, whose later disagreement about the 'middle tripos' (c.1872–82) with T. E. Page (first class, 1873) is discussed in 1998a, 205–10.

The tension between generalist and specialist conceptions of classics was a political one. The history of the tripos is marked by a series of debates in which a variety of interests—intellectual, religious, institutional—were at stake. Changes were often achieved at the expense of compromises which in the long term proved damaging; most obviously the retention of degree status for Part I. This history, as I hope to have demonstrated, was neither an unproblematic evolution towards 'the twentieth-century curriculum' nor a process of 'transmission' from the past. The Cambridge classical curriculum was not 'transmitted'; rather it was shaped and reshaped, in successive generations, in an ongoing debate between interest groups—teachers, pupils, administrators, alumni. Student choices—choices between remaining content with Part I, or going on to Part II; in the latter case, choices between optional subjects—set up patterns of evidence from which the historian can profit. As we have seen, the ways in which these data are recorded and presented constitute evidence in themselves. The classical curriculum was thus the negotiated product of a politics of knowledge; its history was one of parties as well as parts, sects as well as sections. Within the university, reformers had to cope with entrenched interests and the 'black battalions', as well as with dissension in their own ranks; without it, the persistence of status-ridden public schools was a potent influence. Only state intervention, or the massive shock of war, could kick-start the university's political process into producing large-scale changes.

PART II
Scholarship and Publishing

6

Politics, Culture, and Scholarship
Classics in the *Quarterly Review* 1809–24

On 15 November 1810, William Gifford, editor of the *Quarterly Review*, wrote to a hoped-for contributor, George Ellis: 'redit labor actus in orbem. The wheel is come round, and we are again in the press. In what state is your first article?'[1] On 29 December, sending back a review to Walter Scott, he warned him, 'you must not keep it beyond a fortnight—our labour, you know, like the husbandman's redit actus in orbem, and I wish to put your review as forward as possible.'[2] On both occasions, Gifford was quoting from Virgil's account in the *Georgics* of the farmer's year: *Redit agricolis labor actus in orbem*, 'The work of farmers, once performed, comes round again.'[3] It was to a classical quotation that Gifford went to encapsulate the recurrent demands of a periodical publication. In so doing, he will have reached not for a dictionary of quotations, but simply into his memory, which like that of many other educated men of the times was well stocked with Latin and (to a lesser extent) Greek phrases which summed up situations, feelings, and rules of conduct.[4] Such phrases were convenient resources with which to introduce or drive home a point. Boswell, discussing Johnson's use of quotations, commented that 'a highly classical phrase [may be used] to produce an instantaneous strong expression.'[5] Editing a quarterly journal involved a seasonal cycle of work which might aptly be compared to that of the husbandman; but even within a season, the editor's dealings with several contributors necessitated the repetition of letters of request, encouragement, reminder, or rebuke. It is appropriate, then, that the invocation of Virgil's classical reference to the farmer's round should itself 'come round again', made first to Ellis and then to Scott.

The *Quarterly Review* during Gifford's editorship was published at a time when classical scholarship was still deeply embedded in English high culture, though its

---

[1] British Library, Add. MS BL 28099, (ff. 85–86). Like the other Murray correspondence cited in this chapter, this letter will be published in Cutmore 2018.

[2] National Library of Scotland, Add. MS NLS 3879, ff. 289–92.

[3] Virgil, *Georgics* II, 401. His remarks were doubly apt: in December 1810 he was not only moving toward a new issue, but beginning a new (third) annual cycle of four quarterly issues.

[4] Classical phrases and references, some in Greek but most in Latin, occur in many of Gifford's letters.

[5] Boswell 1927, 1. 484. Not all members of polite society could be assumed to understand such phrases: Johnson complained of David Garrick that 'He has not Latin enough. He finds out the Latin by the meaning, and not the meaning by the Latin' (ibid., 1. 603).

authority had declined in the previous two centuries.[6] The use of Latin as an international language of scholarly communication had withered, surviving only in the ritual and ceremony of church and university. In the 1690s, Newton had written his *Principia* in Latin, but in the same decade, Locke had complained of the difficulty of finding tutors who had a good command of the language. Challenges to the authority of Classics as the exemplar of polite learning had not been wanting in the following century, and from the 1750s demands for the teaching of more 'useful' subjects, including English, had mounted. The new bourgeois groups who rose on the back of the industrial revolution, however, looked for badges of respectability at a time when classical knowledge, or the appearance of it, still constituted the prime source of such things. In the reformed public schools such as Rugby under Thomas James (1778–94) and Shrewsbury under Samuel Butler (1798–1836), the sons of these families were stripped of their provincial accents and armed with useful social connections and with classical learning. In many cases, this would not have enabled them to do more than read a few easy sentences of Latin, and to spout a small number of classical tags learned by heart. But such activities carried with them the assumption that Latin and Greek belonged to gentlemen, marking them off from their inferiors, who communicated only via the ambiguously named 'common language', English. Until well after the period with which we are concerned, English, modern languages, mathematics, and natural science hardly appeared in the curricula of public schools. When science teaching began there, it was through public lectures by visiting teachers. French was taught by laughable 'Monsewers' as a social grace, rather like fencing. As for English, it was not taken seriously until late in the nineteenth century.[7]

The mounting waves of protest against Classics in the 1750s coincided with the visit to Athens of James Stuart and Nicholas Revett, whose accounts of Greek architecture were to spark off a neo-Hellenic revival.[8] As romantic Hellenism gathered force in the 1780s and 90s, ancient Greece took over from Augustan Rome as a dominant cultural exemplar in Britain. In the early nineteenth century, the writing of Keats, Byron, and Shelley drew on this inspiration to create powerful English poetry based on Greek models. The world of Pope and Latinate satire was left behind in favour of the new paradigm, though the three poets I have named covered a wide range of styles and genres. The climactic event of the worship of Greece, in one way, was the arrival of what are now commonly called the Elgin Marbles at the British Museum in 1816. They are controversial today, as the battle goes on between those who would return them to Greece and those who either believe their return would set a dangerous precedent, or that they might suffer from conditions in Athens. But they were controversial in a different way in 1816, when some critics did not believe they were worth buying

---

[6] Se Chapter 12, together with 1998a, 7–29 and Waquet 2001.

[7] It did not enter the Oxford curriculum until the 1890s, and in Cambridge had to wait until the 1910s.

[8] *The Antiquities of Athens, Measured and Delineated by James Stuart and Nicholas Revett*: vol. I (1762); vol. II (1787). A three-volume edition appeared in 1794, a fourth volume in 1816 and a fifth in 1830.

or displaying.[9] Stuart and Revett had been funded by the Society of Dilettanti, a club of gentlemen founded in 1734 whose activities combined travel with antiquarian collecting.[10] The activities of Lord Elgin in Greece were characteristic of dilettante practice, as was the collecting of Edward Clarke of Cambridge, who brought back to England what he claimed was a statue of Ceres; his accounts of his travels were reviewed in the *Quarterly*.[11] This was in effect the tradition of the virtuoso continued; what we might now recognize as 'scientific' archaeology, with systematic excavation, record-keeping and dating, came only with the work of Charles Newton in the 1850s.

Schools and Universities

As in the life of the educated gentleman, so in the endowed and public schools which usually provided his schooling, classical learning was a fossilized relic of the Latinate literary republic of Europe. Typically it involved the memorizing of passages of Horace and Virgil and of Latin grammars written in dog-Latin, and the constant practice of composition in Latin. Greek was begun later on in a boy's school career but learned in the same way, the Greek grammar also being written in Latin. Boys who went on to Oxford or Cambridge from the public schools often had behind them ten or more years of exposure to classical literature. But it should be emphasized that almost all of this was an exposure to texts taught not as literature to be explored, discussed, and appreciated, but as linguistic corpora to be learned by heart and to be analysed ('parsed') according to mechanical rules of grammar and syntax which were themselves learned by rote. The Eton Latin grammar (*Introduction to the Latin Tongue*, 1758) and its Greek counterpart (1768) lay at the heart of this process; the prestige of Eton ensuring that they were used by most English schools. The widespread use of the Latin grammar had led to its being pirated in the 1790s, but from the 1820s it was subjected to an increasing barrage of criticism. Not only were it and its Greek sibling written in Latin, they were confused and internally contradictory; reform was however blocked by institutional pride, and they were not abandoned until the 1860s (1989, 2016b). During the period we are concerned with, translations of the Eton Latin grammar into English began to appear, in part reflecting the growth of a wider reading public, and of aspirant social groups eager to acquire gentlemanly knowledge. The changes in the quarter-century after 1820 were nicely captured by De Quincey in 1846:

Everything in our days is new ... *readers* ... being once an obedient trace of men, most humble and deferential in the presence of a Greek scholar, are now being intractably mutinous, keep

---

[9] J. W. Croker, 'Lord Elgin's collection of sculptured marbles', *Quarterly Review* 14 (Jan. 1816), 513–47.
[10] And with drinking. In 1743 Horace Walpole condemned the society's affectations and described it as 'a club, for which the nominal qualification is having been in Italy, and the real one, being drunk'. W. S. Lewis et al. (eds), *Horace Walpole's Correspondence* (London, 1937–83), 18.211.
[11] G. Ellis, 'Dr Clarke's *Travels in Russia*', QR 4 (Aug. 1810), 111–53; R. Heber, 'Clarkes's *Travels: Greece, Egypt, and the Holy land*', QR 9 (Mar. 1813), 162–206; R. Heber, 'Clarke's *Travels: Vols. III and IV*', QR 17 (Apr. 1817), 160–217.

their hats on whilst he is addressing them, and listen to him or not, as he seem to talk sense or nonsense!...the] vast multiplication of readers within the last twenty-five years has changed the prevailing character of readers. The minority has become the overwhelming majority; the quantity has disturbed the quality. Formerly, out of every five readers, at last four were, in some degree, classical scholars; or if *that* would be saying too much,—if two of the four had 'small Latin and less Greek'—, they were generally connected with those who had more or, at the worst, who had much reverence for Latin, and more reverence for Greek...But now-a-days the readers come chiefly from a class of busy people who care very little for ancestral crazes.

(De Quincey 1846, 111)

From this schooling, boys in their late teens could go on to Oxford and Cambridge, which in 1824 were still the only universities in England. The two universities were non-identical twins, alike in many ways but (as discussed in Chapter 2) with significant differences in religious affiliation and curricular emphasis. Gifford's early university connections were with Oxford, notably with Edward Copleston of Oriel, but through Copleston he made contact with like-minded men in Cambridge. James Monk and Charles Blomfield were both high churchmen, and in this and in their commitment to classical scholarship were apt candidates for recruitment to the *Quarterly*. If we include probable as well as definite identifications, Monk contributed two reviews, Blomfield ten; among other things, they reviewed each other's editions of Greek plays.[12] It seems likely that Monk was contacted first and then brought in Blomfield. Their correspond-ence in this period shows that Monk often urged Blomfield, whom he regarded as a more accomplished and effective writer, to provide articles and reviews Monk thought should be published; and this helps to explain the disparity in the numbers of their reviews. In 1813, Monk wrote to Blomfield, as we saw in Chapter 4, asking him to collaborate on an article ('We will make out an article between us').[13]

'We will make out an article between us': this was clearly a common procedure with *Quarterly* reviews, and it bedevils attempts at attribution. But Monk's estimate of his and his friend's powers ('I shall principally rely upon you. Nature has given me the dangerous powers of satire with a very sparing hand') was a just one, and this helps in the task of identification. Consider the article entitled 'Barker—*Aristarchus Anti-Blomfieldianus*', which appeared in volume 24 of the Review (pp. 376–400 of the January 1821 issue, actually published in April). This reviewed E. H. Barker's incoherent diatribe against Blomfield after the latter's crushing review of Valpy's edition of Estienne's Greek Thesaurus.[14] The review seems to have been a joint effort by Monk and Blomfield. We can assume that the eulogies of Blomfield (e.g. on p. 377) are by Monk; but our

---

[12] J. H. Monk, 'Blomfield—*Aesch. Prometheus Vinctus*', QR 5 (Feb. 1811), 203–29; C. J. Blomfield, 'Monk's *Alcestis*', QR 15 (Apr. 1816), 112–25. For Monk and Blomfield, cf. Chapter 4.

[13] Monk to Blomfield, 15 July 1813.

[14] Valpy printed a sixteen-page reply to Blomfield which was attached to his current advertisements for books. These were bound up with copies of the *Review*; he thus managed to have his response distributed by the enemy. Few bound-in items of this kind have survived, but Valpy's text is preserved as a separate item: British Library 816.l.47(76).

knowledge of their respective talents encourages us to ascribe the finer passages of sarcasm to Blomfield: for example, 'In the same spirit of knight-errantry in behalf of dunces in distress, does Mr Barker stretch his protecting shield over *Ignatius Liebel*' [a sycophantic poetaster](p. 394). The best guess that can be made, then, is that the review was drafted by Monk and then embellished and spiced up by a more enter-taining writer—in this case Blomfield.[15]

Oxford and Cambridge, London and Edinburgh

The role of Classics in Oxford and Cambridge, and the differences between the two universities (both discussed in Chapter 2), formed part of the background to the development of the *Quarterly Review*. Not only were they important sources of both contributors and readers, they played an important part in the *Quarterly's* battle with the *Edinburgh Review*. Just after the *Quarterly* was founded, its great rival in Edinburgh launched an onslaught on Oxford, criticizing its curriculum, its teaching and its religious restrictions.[16] Payne Knight's scathing review of Thomas Falconer's edition of the Greek geographer Strabo and Sydney Smith's broader attack on Oxford, including a criticism of its failure to teach political economy, brought a powerful response from Edward Copleston in the following year. In a series of three pamphlets, he seized on flaws in his opponents' case and was regarded in Oxford as having crushed its opponents.[17] In fact the *Edinburgh* reviewers had a strong case, but they did not make the most of it. Among the points at issue was the use of Latin in scholarly editions, a remnant of the once widespread use of the language for communication between European scholars. Latin continued to be used for editorial introductions and for textual notes until the middle of the nineteenth century, and mistakes in its use in such contexts were often seized upon by critics. The *Edinburgh Review's* onslaught on Oxford in 1809 was typ-ical of this tendency, as were Copleston's replies. The *Quarterly* review of the *Edinburgh* response to Copleston made great play with the defective command of Latin shown by the *Edinburgh* writers; it was written by John Davison, Henry Drummond, and Copleston himself.[18]

Copleston's role as the champion of the more conservative and higher Anglican of the ancient universities against the Scottish onslaught made him the ideal advisor for Gifford in the university world. It is not surprising, then, that Gifford used him as a source of counsel and as a conduit to other contributors, and that he was willing to

---

[15] Cf. the attack on Henry Brougham in 1818 (*QR* 18 July 1818, 492–569), where Monk's text was spiced up by George Canning and others: see Cutmore 2008, 155.

[16] R. Payne Knight, 'The Oxford edition of Strabo', *Edinburgh Review* 14 (July 1809), 429–41; Sydney Smith, 'Edgeworth's *Professional Education*', *ER* 15 (Oct. 1809), 40–53.

[17] *A reply to the calumnies of the Edinburgh review against Oxford* (1810); *A second reply* (1810); *A third reply* (1811). Payne Knight, Smith and John Playfair replied with 'Calumnies against Oxford', *ER* 16 (Apr. 1810), 158–87.

[18] 'Replies to calumnies against Oxford', *Quarterly Review* 4 (1810), 177–206.

share his deepest secret, the identity of other contributors. The recruits brought in via Copleston included Monk and Blomfield. Blomfield had been a regular classical reviewer for the *Edinburgh Review* since 1809, but broke off relations in 1813. On 31 August 1813, he complained to a fellow-classicist, Peter Elmsley, that he had asked Jeffrey to return an article Blomfield had sent him: 'I told him candidly that I could not lend my feeble aid to a Journal, the tone of which was so offensive to men of religious feeling.' Despite this, Blomfield went on, Jeffrey had printed his article 'in the 42nd number'.[19]

In other fields, too, the picture of Classics one gains from the *Quarterly Review* in this period suggests the continuation of an eighteenth-century tradition on the eve of new developments. There is almost no sign of the crucial contemporary movement, the emergence of *Altertumswissenschaft* (the systematic study of the ancient world) in Germany, sparked off at the end of the previous century by Friedrich August Wolf (Grafton 1983). Wolf's study of the Homeric epics employed techniques originally developed for biblical criticism, and the philological seminar which became a characteristic feature of classical training in German universities was modelled on the seminars founded for the training of ministers. The appearance of the 'higher criticism' of ancient literature was viewed with alarm in conservative quarters in Britain, since it was clear that techniques formulated to assess the literature of the Greeks and Romans could also be applied to sacred literature. These alarms, however, belonged largely to the years after 1824. During the early years of Gifford's editorship, the continental blockade severely hindered scholarly contact with the continent, and this in turn was reinforced by isolationist feelings in England after the Revolution, the Terror, and Napoleon's conquests.

The history of the *Museum Criticum* (for which see Chapter 7) and of the *Classical Journal* (which ran until 1829) shows that there were relatively specialized outlets for classical publishing available during Gifford's reign at the *Review*. This raises the question of the relationship between this more specialized publishing and the *Quarterly* and other general reviews. The question is not an easy one to answer, except by saying that the reviews confined themselves to reviewing, though magazines did not. The more specialized journals included original articles, translations, prize poems, notes on texts, inscriptions, lists of recent books, and a whole host of other features whose nature placed them beyond the remit of the *Quarterly* and the *Edinburgh*. A comparison of the reviews published in the two groups of journals reveals very little difference. Reviews of classical editions typically consisted of opening remarks, sometimes including a survey of previous editions; a statement of the leading features of the book under review, and the reviewer's opinion of these; and finally a long (sometimes very long)

---

[19] The article in question must be the July 1813 *Edinburgh* review of Hermann's edition of Photius (pp. 329–40). The tentative attribution in the *Wellesley Index to Victorian Periodicals* is therefore confirmed. Ironically, Wellesley made its attribution on the ground that Blomfield was a regular contributor: in fact, the refusal of Jeffrey to return this article to its author was, together with religious differences, the cause of Blomfield's *ceasing* to be a regular contributor.

list of comments on textual details.[20] A modern reader may wonder how many contemporaries stayed the course to the end of such reviews; and it is clear that Gifford and Murray were also concerned. It was important to include articles on classical topics, if only because the *Edinburgh* did so; and this in turn reflected the continuing centrality of classical learning in gentlemanly culture. Literary articles were also needed for a fundamental reason that Elmsley's and Southey's friend Grosvenor Bedford made very clear: 'To avoid even the appearance & to repel any charge that may be made against the work on the score of ministerial influence all pains will be taken to make it [the *Quarterly*] complete as to scholarship, literature & science.'[21] Anything more than a sprinkling, however, was too much, and this applied especially to reviews of editions of classical texts. It was surely the realization of this limiting factor, inter alia, which prompted Monk and Blomfield to set up their own journal.

On 25 September 1810, Murray wrote to Gifford:

Greek Articles are not read generally even by those who are capable of understanding them— I don't think you or Mr E[llis] or Mr C[anning] would read them in any other Journal—they should therefore be refused. I can concede to very important Works ... by the very first classical scholars.—A Greek article should be very able indeed so as to excite attention at the Universities where almost alone it is read ... If possible too—*one* good religious article in each number would render us more service than two or three—but we should always have one.[22]

Murray reiterated the point to George Ellis on 2 October 1810, in relation to articles on religious subjects: 'If we could compound for *one* Religious Article in each Number it would be serviceable ... and more than one (and that a *very* able) *learned* Article clogs us sadly.'[23] Murray's remarks make it clear that the problem was not confined to classical topics: he saw his market as lying partly within, partly without the universities, and was concerned not to include more academic articles than a wider readership would tolerate. And this resonates with the tensions between the Porsonians and their rivals: for this was, as we saw in Chapter 4, partly founded on the distinction between the Cambridge academic base of the *Museum Criticum* and the metropolitan location of the *Classical Journal*, run by a printer (albeit one with high cultural pretensions) and supported by scholars from outside the universities, such as Edmund Barker and George Burges.

Especially in the case of Greek topics, the use of Greek type (in printers' terminology, an 'exotic' type) constituted a clear visual signal that some readers would be unable

---

[20] For an example, see Blomfield's review of Monk's *Alcestis* (Apr. 1816), discussed later in this section. See also Chapter 6.

[21] Bedford to Elmsley, 26 Jan. 1809 (Elmsley papers). The three men had been fellow-pupils at Westminster School.

[22] BL Add. MS 28099, ff. 83–4.

[23] BL Add. MS 28099, ff. 67–8. The balance between minority interests could itself be a subject of negotiation: Elmsley reported to Butler on 14 November 1811 that he had 'promised Jeffrey an article on Catholics, as the price of his inserting a long paper of mine on the Preface to the Hecuba'. (BL Add MS 34583/342)

to appreciate large parts of a review. The second half of Blomfield's review of Monk's edition of Euripides' *Alcestis* in April 1816 was devoted to comment on textual detail. At the end of his article Blomfield declared, 'We make no apology to our readers for the length and minuteness of these criticisms. Those who take no interest in such matters have only to transfer their paper-knife to the next article.'[24] Blomfield was well aware that he was catering for a small minority. Four years earlier he had written to Elmsley, 'I believe that Jeffrey's notions with regard to classical criticism are nearly such as you describe them; for having observed that my article would occupy 30 pages, he adds, "while on a liberal computation, there are about as many persons who will understand it".' In the same letter, he confirmed that he had published the fragments of the minor Greek writer Sophron in Valpy's *Classical Journal*, and added, 'I wish to continue the Fragments of Sophron, but I have no leisure to transcribe them for the press; nor do I think that when they are printed more than ten people will understand them.' [25] Here Blomfield was in fact echoing the language of an earlier letter from Elmsley: 'there are about ten men in England who really study the *minutiae* of Greek, and of these few, four or five do not write.'[26] The theme had been adumbrated, in fact, in the first classical review to be published in the *Quarterly Review*: James Pillans' review of two works on the Georgics (*QR* 1.1 (Feb. 1809), 69–77). Pillans opened by confronting the problem head on: 'Though the reading population of this country has been long on the advance, the number of classical scholars by no means increases in the same proportion. An indifference to classical learning seems to be gaining ground in society....' His response is to link classical learning as a traditional cultural formation with the *Review*'s task of defending tradition: 'we feel, in common with every Englishman, a partiality approaching to veneration for that discipline which is consecrated by long usage, and guarded by bulwarks coeval almost with the constitution of the country....'.

Classics, *Quarterly Review* Style

What kind of classical work was represented in Gifford's *Quarterly Review*, and what relation did it bear to the classical teaching and research of the period? What Gifford included is of course far from being a simple reflection of classical work. Nor could a reflection in any case be a simple one, given the variety of the strands of Classics—antiquarianism, Porsonian text criticism, archaeology, the study of myth, travel, composition, and translation—practised between 1809 and 1824. We can assume, though

---

[24] 'The Alcestis of Euripides' (QR 15, Apr. 1816, 112–25, at p. 125). The 'minute criticisms' occupy pp. 117–25. The theme was taken up by John Symmons of Oxford, reviewing Blomfield's *Agamemnon* in July 1820 (QR 25, 505–29, at p. 529): 'We are afraid we have tired the general reader by the minuteness of our philological remarks.'

[25] Blomfield to Elmsley, 6 May 1812 (Elmsley papers). Cf. his letter to Elmsley of February 1812, cited in Chapter 4.

[26] Elmsley to [Blomfield], 8 Feb. 1813 (Bodl. Lib. MS. Autogr d 24, ff. 150r–151v). Blomfield is not addressed by name, but he is clearly the recipient. Compare A. Blomfield, *A Memoir of Charles James Blomfield* (London: John Murray, 1863) 1. 12, who quotes from the letter.

it does not get us very far, that 'Quarterly Review Classics' was influenced, though not created, by the books which came to the attention of Gifford and his co-reviewers and to John Murray. Here the varieties of classical practice were filtered out which tended not to result in publication. An obvious example is the great mass of verse compositions in Latin and Greek which were produced at Oxford, Cambridge, and elsewhere. Some of these were written for prize competitions, of which there were several at Cambridge; the relative paucity at Oxford reflected the embedded strength of the subject and hence the lesser need of encouragement.[27] During Gifford's editorship only two volumes of such work were reviewed, the first being *Musae Cantabrigienses* of 1810, reviewed by Thomas Falconer with the help of Edward Copleston, both from Oxford (*QR* 4.8 (Nov. 1810), 382–92). This was a collection of successful entries for the Browne Medal, founded by Sir William Browne in 1774 and restricted to Greek and Latin odes and epigrams. The title of the book does not mention Browne's name, nor does its title page identify the editors; they were in fact C. J. Blomfield, soon to become a regular reviewer, and his friend and co-founder of the *Museum Criticum*, Thomas Rennell. The publication of the book in 1810 might be seen as part of the self-conscious assertion of the Cambridge tradition of scholarship in the wake of Porson's death in 1808.[28] If so, it is ironic that Porson himself despised most modern attempts at Latin and Greek composition, or at least their publication; he praised an earlier Greek scholar, Richard Dawes, for choosing 'rather to read good Greek than to write bad' (Clarke 1937, 104).

The second collection of compositions to be reviewed (*QR* 8.16 (December 1812), 395–406 was of a very different kind: a volume of compositions by pupils of the Royal High School, Edinburgh, edited by their headmaster James Pillans (who afterwards confessed that the publication was premature). The book was sympathetically reviewed in the *Edinburgh Review* in November 1812 by Francis Jeffrey, and this may have prompted Gifford to commission an article in response. The review in the *Quarterly* listed the Edinburgh schoolboys' errors at length: 'We had at first determined to collect all the errors against syntax and prosody contained in this little volume; but we found the task Herculean' (p. 402).[29]

One of the most obvious filters through which books were selected for review was Gifford's own tastes. Like Porson he came from humble origins and owed his education to a series of rich patrons. The two men also shared a taste for satire and polemical writing. Their politics, however, were very different. Porson was a supporter of the

---

[27] In 1809, Oxford had two classical prizes or scholarships, while Cambridge had seven; by 1824 the totals had risen to three and ten respectively. See further Chapter 2.

[28] It is interesting that the book was published by Valpy, who in the same year brought out the first issue of the *Classical Journal*, soon to become the rival of Monk and Blomfield's *Museum Criticum* and the stamping ground of their bête noire, the irritating E. H. Barker. See further Chapter 4.

[29] The reviewer was probably Walter Scott. The mistaken attribution to Robert Southey in *DNB* was taken over by *ODNB*, but the article is not included in the definitive listing of Southey's contributions (Curry and Dedmon 1974). The reviewer, though finding much to criticize, was careful to include a meed of praise; the review can hardly be called 'savage', as Pillans's *ODNB* article has it.

French Revolution and a member of the London Corresponding Society, whereas Gifford made a reputation as a vitriolic tory satirist with the *Baviad* (1791) and the *Maeviad* (1795),[30] culminating in his editorship of the *Anti-Jacobin* in 1797–8. His scholarly work centred on his editing of English authors (Ford, Massinger, Jonson, and Shirley); his translations were made from Roman satirists (Juvenal 1802, Persius 1817; the latter author he had taken as his model in the *Baviad*). The picture of Gifford we gain from this is very much that of a late eighteenth-century figure, his tastes formed by the Augustan period with its liking for Latin authors and satire, before the surge in romantic interest in Hellenism from the 1780s. One might, with caution, link the contrasting literary tastes of Gifford and Porson to their university allegiances: an American visitor who studied classics at Cambridge in the 1840s suggested that 'The Cantabs are stronger in Greek, the Oxonians in Latin' (Bristed 2008, 126). Gifford's predilections are seen most clearly in the reviews he wrote himself, which are all concerned with Roman satirists (Persius and Juvenal).[31] It was in precisely in this area that Gifford himself had published. His own hopes of bringing out a translation of Juvenal by subscription in 1781 had been dashed. He eventually published it in 1802, with some success, though it was unfavourably noticed in the *Critical Review*, prompting his *An Examination of the Strictures of the Critical Reviewers on the Translation of Juvenal* (1803). Gifford may therefore have felt some fellow-feeling toward the anonymous author of *Specimens of a New Translation of Juvenal*, which appeared in 1812. If so, it did not stand in the way of his denouncing it as a 'petty publication' whose author was not up to the task. Nor was he very complimentary to the unfortunate author when, two years later, he published his complete translation. From Gifford's review, it is clear that the anonymous *Specimens* were the work of Charles Badham; a fact of which we should otherwise be ignorant.[32]

The *Quarterly*'s treatment of Classics of course depended in large part on its choice of reviewers. Both Murray and Gifford, with the help of Walter Scott, began with lists of possible contributors, and as we might expect, these included friends and acquaintances. A good example is John Ireland, later to be Dean of Westminster 1815–42, a schoolboy friend of Gifford's and the executor of his will. Ireland was not productive as a classicist, and the *Quarterly* articles attributed to him deal exclusively with religious issues; but he founded prizes at Oxford (the Ireland Prize, 1825) and at Westminster School to promote the practice of classical composition. Ireland's conservatism will have endeared him to Murray, and the same is true of the antiquarian Samuel Seyer of

---

[30] These 'epics' were self-deprecatingly named after two notorious poetasters of the late Roman Republic, Bavius and Maevius (Virgil, *Eclogues* 3.90–1; Horace, *Epodes* 10).

[31] 'The Satires of Aulus Persius Flaccus', *QR* 1 (May 1809), 355–62; '*Specimens of a new translation of Juvenal*', *QR* 8 (Sept. 1812), 60–5; 'Badham's *Translation of Juvenal*', *QR* 11 (July 1814), 377–98.

[32] Gifford may have seen Badham's signed reply, 'Dr Badham's defence against the *Quarterly Review*' in the *New Review* 1 (1813), 351–4. Charles Badham is a famous name among classicists; but this is not the celebrated Greek scholar of that name (1813–84) who ended up as Professor of Classics in Sydney, nor his brother the naturalist Charles David Badham (1805–57), author of *Prose Halieutics*, but their father Charles Badham (1780–1845), professor of physic at Glasgow.

Bristol. A cleric and son of a cleric, Seyer ran a school in Bristol, was an accomplished local historian, and wrote a number of Latin textbooks. He was an Oxonian, but graduated three years before Gifford matriculated; he may however have come to Gifford's attention through his *Latium Redivivum*, published (by Murray) in 1808, the year in which the lists of potential *Quarterly Review* contributors were drawn up. In his book, Seyer proposed the restoration of Latin as the language of international diplomacy, in part as a way of rolling back the advance of French, the language of the Revolution and of Napoleon's empire.[33] Seyer is not known to have contributed to the *Quarterly*, and the same is true of the Norfolk antiquarian William Stevenson, also on Gifford's list: he was probably included as a frequent contributor to the *Gentleman's Magazine*. Murray's own preliminary list of contributors includes 'Pillans', and this is presumably James Pillans of Edinburgh, later to contribute three articles, of which the first has been discussed above. Pillans is an interesting figure in this context, since he was an Edinburgh Whig. He had recently worked at Eton College as an usher, and this may have brought him into contact with Murray; but his review of a translation of Juvenal for the *Edinburgh Review* for April 1808 will also have attracted Gifford's attention.

Two Oxford scholars figure in the lists: Thomas Gaisford and Peter Elmsley. The latter was a prolific contributor of reviews, though as we have seen his liberal views and his connections with *Edinburgh* were a potential problem for Gifford and Murray. Gaisford was quite different, a hardworking scholar who devoted his career to bringing out editions of difficult authors, but he had no wider ambition than this, and as we have seen in Chapter 3, actively avoided ecclesiastical preferment as a distraction from scholarship.

Among those listed by Walter Scott was a man on whose judgement Gifford came to rely: Edward Copleston of Oriel College, Oxford, a classical scholar and, as we have seen, the great champion of his university (and Gifford's) against 'the calumnies of the *Edinburgh Review*'. It is likely that other Oxonian reviewers were recommended by Copleston. Similarly, at Cambridge Gifford was as we have seen in touch with Monk and Blomfield, both of Trinity. The impression one gains from Gifford's letters, however, is that his links with his own alma mater were always stronger.

The classical articles in the Quarterly, *1809–1824*

Fifty or so articles published during Gifford's tenure can be described as 'classical'; almost 15 per cent of the total. There are several cases which are more or less marginal: for example, the review in the first issue of Jerningham's *The Alexandrian School; or a Narrative of the First Church Professors in Alexandria*, deals with ancient history, but its concerns are essentially with church history, as the book's subtitle makes clear: '*with Observations on the Influence they still Maintain over the Established Church*'. A review

---

[33] His textbooks included a Latin grammar of 1781, published anonymously. It can be shown to be Seyer's by comparison with the second edition of 1804. Both editions survive in single copies: the first is British Library 12935.bb.40, the second is Trinity College Library, Cambridge, Stray c.387.

in September 1812 of Woodhouselee's anonymous *Historical and Critical Essay on the Life and Character of Petrarch* is concerned with the Renaissance, and not directly with the classical world. In July 1814 Charles Blomfield reviewed W. M. Leake's *Researches in Greece*; almost the whole review is devoted to the status and nature of modern Greek, with only an initial paragraph or two discussing the wider aspects of Leake's book.[34] This review reflected Blomfield's current interest in contemporary Greek, which unusually he saw as a resource for understanding the classical language; his interest however appears to have waned later in 1814.[35] This may explain Gifford's assignment of a later review in this area (May 1820, a review of Coray's Ἑλληνικη Βιβλιοθήκη *With Observations relating to the Modern Greek Language*) to Robert Walpole. 'Coray' was Adamantios Koraës, a crucial figure in the development of modern Greek language and literature, then living in Paris.

The articles which can be called 'mainstream classics' fall into several distinct clusters. First, there are reviews of editions and translations of Greek or Latin authors. (The distinction is not always easy to maintain, as some translations included critical notes.) There are about two dozen of these, that is about half the total number of classical articles. Some patterns are very clear. Greek authors preponderate—eleven authors and eighteen articles, compared to five Latin authors and as many articles. This is not surprising in a period when romantic Hellenism was in full swing; but another factor may be the strength of the Cambridge contingent in the *Quarterly* reviewing team. The most reviewed author is Euripides, with three reviews of editions of single plays and one of a collection of three. This was an Oxford edition of 1811 of the kind known as 'variorum': that is, it includes selections of notes and other material by several scholars who had previously published on the plays. In this case one of them is highlighted; a leading English classical scholar of the eighteenth century, Jeremiah Markland (1696–1776). The variorum style was by 1811 rather old-fashioned, and it may be significant that this edition was produced on large paper. It was intended, that is, as much for country gentlemen who liked to have visually and socially impressive large-format volumes as for classical scholars in the universities. As a whole, this volume sits slightly oddly among the other editions reviewed in the *Quarterly*, which are fairly recent. In its backward-looking quality and in its use of a variorum format, it belongs to a period when the presses of both ancient universities were out of touch with the leading contemporary scholarly views. The best-known example is the edition of Aeschylus which Porson refused to undertake in 1782 (see Chapter 4). Samuel Butler, headmaster of Shrewsbury, agreed to undertake the task on the Press's terms; the result was a massive four-volume variorum edition, based on Thomas Stanley's text

---

[34] The attribution is confirmed by Blomfield's remark in a letter of 7 Oct. 1814 to Peter Elmsley: 'I have sent to Gifford a long article on the Romaic language for the next Quarterly, in which several persons are decently abused' (Elmsley papers).

[35] Blomfield to Elmsley, 13 Dec. 1814: 'You see I have been dabbling in modern Greek, which I have found rather interesting, but, I think, quite useless to a critical scholar. I used formerly to entertain a different opinion' (Elmsley papers).

of 1663, which began to appear in 1809, when it was severely criticized by Blomfield in the *Edinburgh Review*.[36]

After his death in 1808, as we saw in Chapter 4, a cult of Porson had developed and his pupils and followers published his adversaria, notes, and essays as well as editions of their own in the Porsonian style. They also made clear their reverence for the great man in reviews and other publications, and both reviewed and were reviewed in the *Quarterly*.[37] The attitude taken to Porson is indeed of use on determining authorship in some cases: adulation is to be expected from Monk or Blomfield, but not from Elmsley. In his review of Monk's *Hippolytus* in September 1812, Blomfield provided a summary of the school's characteristics: a conservative attitude to emendation, the use of analogical reasoning, and a condensed and cogent style of annotation. He concluded that 'the Porsonian school' is 'but another term for the *best* school of Greek criticism' (p. 216).

Classics, the *Quarterly* and the *Edinburgh Review*

The *Quarterly Review* was founded as a conservative rival to the *Edinburgh Review*, and it is easy to find evidence for a rough division of the literary world between the reformist supporters of the *Edinburgh* and the conservative contributors to and readers of the *Quarterly*. For example, James Monk wrote to John Murray in 1817 that the dissenter Sir James Smith, against whom he had published a pamphlet, 'has links with some Edinburgh Reviewers'.[38] It would be a mistake, however, to see them as separate and polarized entities (Cutmore 2018). For one thing, there were authors who contributed to both. Elmsley contributed six articles to the *Edinburgh* between April 1803 and February; he then published a review in the *Quarterly*, in July 1812. The review of Monk's Euripides *Hippolytus* (September 1812), previously regarded as being probably by Elmsley, was in fact by Blomfield, who wrote to Elmsley on 1 December 1812:

My dear Sir

The facts relative to my review of Monk's Hippolytus are these. I drew it up in considerable haste early in the Summer, & wrote twice to Jeffrey, requesting him to insert it in the last No. of the Edinburgh. Not receiving any answer to my application, and having understood from you, that you had relinquished the intention, which you once entertained, of reviewing it, I sent it to Gifford through the medium of a friend of mine at Cambridge who is a regular contributor to the *Quarterly*.

---

[36] 'The Cambridge edition of Aeschylus', *ER* 15 (Oct. 1809), 152–63; (Jan. 1810), 315–22. Butler, as we saw in Chapter 4, responded to the review with a pamphlet in the form of a letter to Blomfield.

[37] Review of Burges's Euripides *Troades*, possibly by Monk, in Feb. 1810; of Blomfield's Aeschylus *Prometheus Bound*, certainly by him, in Feb. 1811; of Markland's edition of three Euripides plays, by Elmsley, in June 1812; of Monk's Euripides *Hippolytus*, by Blomfield, in Sept. 1812; and of Blomfield's Aeschylus *Agamemnon* by John Symmons in July 1821.

[38] John Murray archive, NLS, Monk to Murray, 25 Aug. 1818.

My *only* motive for concealment is, that, as I am known to be a personal friend of the author, I might be suspected of partiality in the laudatory parts of my review.[39]

As we have seen, Blomfield abandoned the *Edinburgh Review* in 1813, having had one article published which he wished to withdraw, and another ignored which he wished to publish.[40] The cooling-off may have been mutual: the letter from Blomfield quoted earlier shows that Elmsley did not see Jeffrey as an enthusiastic publisher of classical reviews, at least of the kind he had received from Blomfield and Elmsley: detailed evaluations of editions, including lengthy discussion of textual minutiae. Elmsley may have abandoned the *Edinburgh Review* because he realized that Jeffrey was not keen to continue publishing reviews which attracted only a small minority of the *Review*'s readership, and which would entail an uphill struggle against the *Quarterly*. His motivation, however, probably had more to do with his political and religious beliefs than with his scholarship. By the time the *Edinburgh Review* launched its onslaught on Oxford in 1809, Elmsley had already published in it, though not recently (his three articles had all appeared in 1803), and he went on, as the *Review* continued to criticize his old university, to publish in it again, in November 1810 and November 1811). His articles were all reviews of classical editions—no mention in them of wider issues of education or religion—and this might be thought to lessen his offence. In fact, he was probably felt to be allying his Oxford-based scholarship with precisely those who had criticized it. No wonder Copleston, busily engaged in defending Oxford against the Scottish onslaught, described his fellow-Oxonian's link with the *Edinburgh Review* as 'an unnatural confederacy' (Gifford to Copleston, 18 March 1811; cf. Cutmore 2018). Elmsley's situation was difficult in any case, since he was known to be a Whig and to have the liberal politician George Grenville as a patron. This may be why he turned in 1811 to the writing of articles on ecclesiastical policy; but his offering to Gifford, on the burial of dissenters, was rejected as being sluggish and boring (Gifford to Copleston, 7 December 1811; Cutmore 2018); it would also have offended the more evangelical readers of the *Quarterly*. Elmsley then offered an article to Jeffrey, on Clarendon's view of Catholics, which was published in February 1812. This was a sensitive issue, as the liberal minority in Oxford, to which Elmsley belonged, was pressing for the admission of Catholics, a policy which became the touchstone of liberalism in the university.[41]

[39] Elmsley papers. The friend in Cambridge was presumably George D'Oyly. In an earlier letter (24 July) Blomfield had reported that 'I had some thoughts of giving a summary account of your Oedipus, but I can get no answer from Jeffrey. I believe he is about to get rid of the concern altogether.' Similar information reached Elmsley from Grosvenor Bedford, who wrote to him:

> I hear that the Edinburgh Review is about to close in consequence of the great luminaries, Jeffery, Brougham & Horner all finding themselves too much employed in the law to spare time for conducting it. If so, the Quarterly will get an immense start, for the British appears to me as orthodox and as dull as the British Critic.   (Elmsley papers, n.d. [1812])

[40] On 24 July 1812 Blomfield wrote to Elmsley, 'I had some thoughts of giving a summary account of your Oedipus, but I can get no answer from Jeffrey. I believe he is about to get rid of the concern altogether.'

[41] W. R. Ward, *Victorian Oxford* (1965), 37–8; M. G. Brock, 'The Oxford of Peel and Gladstone', in M. G. Brock and M. C. Curthoys, eds, *The History of the University of Oxford, Vol VI: Nineteenth-Century Oxford, Part 1* (1998), 51–2.

His views contributed to his failure to gain two posts in 1812: first, the Regius chair of Greek at Oxford, which went, as we have seen in Chapter 3, to the safely conservative Thomas Gaisford, and second, the Preachership of Gray's Inn, which despite the conservative vote being split was gained by William Van Mildert, later Bishop of Durham.[42] In October 1813, Elmsley wrote to Samuel Butler that he had not sent articles to the *Edinburgh* for two years: 'The irreligious tone and the Jacobinism of some of its articles have compelled me to withdraw from it' (Butler 1896, 1.88). In the same letter, he told Butler that having contributed an article to the *Quarterly*, 'I have private and personal reasons for not contributing to it again, at least for the present.' He had asked Murray for permission to turn one of his articles into a pamphlet but was refused; Murray had a rule against allowing reprinting and was unwilling to break it. Elmsley thereupon declared that he would not write for the *Quarterly Review* again.[43] To Monk and Blomfield's dismay, he at first extended this prohibition to their *Museum Criticum*, since it was published by Murray. They were however able to persuade him that Murray had no say in the journal's content, and by November 1813, Monk was able to report to Murray that 'Elmsley promises material for no. 3'.[44]

Peter Elmsley, the most distinguished Oxonian classicist of his generation, received no further preferment (he had been given a small rural living in 1797). Not until 1823, two years before his death, was he appointed Camden Professor of Ancient History and Principal of St Alban's Hall. In the previous year, his appointment as Regius Professor of Divinity at Oxford had been blocked by the prime minister Lord Liverpool, an opponent of Catholic Emancipation and a close friend of Canning, and he himself refused the see of Calcutta, thus becoming 'probably the only recusant Greek play bishop'.[45] Elmsley's career and writing provides an interesting case study of the relations between scholarship, politics, and religion in the early nineteenth century, and the two *Reviews* clearly formed part of that complicated nexus.

Telescopes across the Tweed: the *Quarterly Review* and the *Edinburgh Review*

On 31 August 1813, Blomfield complained to Elmsley about Francis Jeffrey's refusal to return a review and his subsequent publication of it in the *Edinburgh* (see note 23 above):

I consider this conduct of Jeffrey as extremely indelicate, to use no harsher term—but I have now no redress...Immediately upon my discovering the circumstance, I wrote to Gifford, begging him not to scruple withholding my remarks on your Heraclidae to a future No. of the

---

[42] Varley 2002, 49. In 1815, his niece married Thomas Gaisford.

[43] Murray to Elmsley, 7 July 1813 (Cutmore 2014), Elmsley to Murray, 25 June and 11 July 1813, John Murray archive, NLS.

[44] Monk to Murray, 13 Nov. 1813, John Murray archive, NLS. Elmsley's article, 'Notes on the Ajax of Sophocles', duly appeared in the third issue of *Museum Criticum*, pp. 351–69, and continued in the fourth issue, pp. 469–88; both issues were published in 1814.

[45] C. Collard, 'Peter Elmsley', in Todd 2004, 286–8, at 287.

Quarterly, in case he should feel any difficulty from the appearance of my contribution in the TransTweedian journal...

Gifford clearly had no such qualms (or no substitute article to hand), since Blomfield's review of Elmsley's *Heracleidae* duly appeared in the July number of the *Quarterly*.[46] He may indeed have been keen to match the *Edinburgh Review*'s performance, as his letters suggest this was a constant concern. In a letter to Copleston of 26 February 1811 (Cutmore 2018), Gifford reported that 'I have for the next a Review of Blomfield's Aesch[ylus] somewhat elaborate; but the article in the last Edinburgh has forced us to exert ourselves a little.' This is a case of special interest, since the two reviews were of the same book: Blomfield's edition of Aeschylus' *Prometheus Vinctus*. Competition could not be harder-pressed than this. Blomfield and Copleston, as we have seen, were corresponding with one another (they were first in touch in January 1812), and to a degree were able to coordinate their reviewing, the former being in touch with policy in Edinburgh and the latter with *Quarterly Review* plans.

One way to assess the interaction of the two journals in the classical field is to look at the rate and nature of their production. Of the 452 articles published in the *Edinburgh* before the *Quarterly* first appeared, sixteen were on classical subjects—about 3.5 per cent. During the period of Gifford's editorship of *Quarterly Review*, a further 613 articles appeared in the *Edinburgh Review*, of which twenty were classical; again, about 3.5 per cent. Compare this with the *Quarterly Review* figures: about fifty classical articles out of a total of 733 (14.5 per cent). As so often, however, overall figures offer only crude pictures of policy and preferences. A closer look at the *Edinburgh*'s record reveals that no classical reviews appeared between July 1813 and January 1820. It seems clear that with the departure of Blomfield and Elmsley, Jeffrey abandoned the classical field altogether for more than six years. When he returned to it, he published on Classics at a rate of about 5.5 per cent—hardly more than a third of the *Quarterly Review*'s percentage, but still a significant amount. Of *Edinburgh Review*'s first sixteen classical articles, six were on Latin topics; of the twenty which Jeffrey brought out during Gifford's reign at the *Quarterly*, none. In the *Quarterly*, by contrast, of the two dozen or so reviews of editions and translations, six were on Latin topics. It could be argued that Jeffrey trimmed to sail parallel to Gifford's course: in other words, that he veered towards a preponderance of Greek topics to match the *Quarterly*'s tendency. But any such argument has to allow for the vagaries of the availability of books and of reviewers; the varying ability of the latter to submit reviews on time; and the kind of internal conflict, as between Murray and Gifford, which is evident in Gifford's letters. We can be more confident about the large-scale patterns, such as the disappearance of classical reviews from the *Edinburgh* between July 1813 and January 1820.

---

[46] The letter, in the Elmsley papers, incidentally confirms a suggested attribution to Blomfield, since the 'TransTweedian' piece he is referring to is surely the review of Hermann's Photius in the *Edinburgh Review* in July 1813.

Most of the discussion so far has been concerned with the reviews of editions, especially those of Greek tragedians. The other classical reviews covered a wide range, but one area which deserves separate mention is the activity of British gentleman abroad, going on the Grand Tour, writing accounts of their travels and bringing back antiquities. Among those with connections to the *Quarterly* were the Cambridge-educated philhellenes William Haygarth, Thomas Smart Hughes, and Robert Walpole. Haygarth, who provided three reviews, was a friend of Byron whose first visit to Athens led to his publishing a long poem on Greece.[47] His interest in the historiography of Greece and Rome was evidenced not only in a history of the Roman Empire (left unpublished at his death), but also reviews of Mitford on Greece and Bankes on Rome. Mitford's conservatism and distrust of democracy made him congenial to the *Quarterly* reviewers, but this did not stop Haygarth protesting at the unattractiveness of his prose style.[48] Thomas Hughes, similarly, went to Greece and published an account of his travels. Robert Walpole followed the same pattern, but also investigated the Herculaneum papyri, on which he published with Sir William Drummond.[49]

The best-known example of this kind of travel was the extensive tour carried out by the antiquary and mineralogist Edward Daniel Clarke of Jesus College, Cambridge (1769–1822), mentioned above. Much of continental Europe being inaccessible in wartime, he and his companions travelled north in 1799, via Sweden and Russia, to Constantinople, the Troad, and finally to mainland Greece, returning to England in 1802. Between them Clarke and his pupil John Cripps brought back more than 150 cases of antiquities. Clarke collected a thousand ancient coins, which were eventually sold to Richard Payne Knight; some valuable Greek MSS, which were bought by the Bodleian Library; and a vast statue weighing nearly two tons from Eleusis, which he (mistakenly) believed was of the goddess Ceres. The statue was badly eroded, and dismissed by some critics as being hardly worth preserving. Clarke's account of his travels was published in six large-format volumes between 1810 and 1823, and was very successful. The interest shown in his account is reflected in the *Quarterly Review* record: Volume 1 was reviewed in 1810, Volume 2 in 1813, and Volumes 3–4 in 1817. The first two of these reviews followed hard on the heels of reviews in the *Edinburgh*, and the first one was clearly designed to match the *Edinburgh* offering.[50]

If Clarke's 'Ceres' attracted derision in some quarters, the statuary brought back by Lord Elgin from the Parthenon (the 'Elgin marbles') provoked a controversy at the highest levels, as I mentioned above. A Select Committee of the House of Commons

---

[47] *Greece: a poem, in three parts; with notes, classical illustrations, and sketches of the scenery* (1814).

[48] Compare the opinion of the Oxford chronologist Henry Fynes Clinton in 1821: 'defective styles are seldom improved. The practice of forty years, and of ten octavo volumes, has not purified the style of Mr Mitford', Clinton 1854, 170.

[49] Their *Herculanensia* appeared in 1810. For a later attempt to decipher the papyri by Elmsley and Humphry Davy, see Chapter 4.

[50] See Gifford's reference to it in his letter to Scott of 27 Oct. 1810 (Cutmore 2018): 'You are right—the enemy feels us—tant mieux. There is more than one thing which he will not like in this Number. George's sly sneer at the "perfumes of Astrachan" is excellent.'

was appointed in 1816, recommended purchase, and the marbles were bought for the nation in the same year for the enormous sum of £35,000. Elgin's removal of them from Athens was itself controversial, but some claimed in addition that they were not distinguished works of art and so not worth acquiring.[51] Croker's review of the Select Committee report and other documents (May 1816) followed an *Edinburgh* review by Jeffrey of the previous October. That, however, had as its subject the *Remains of John Tweddell*. The Elgin and Tweddell stories had by then become deeply entangled. Tweddell, a young, talented and politically radical fellow of Trinity College, Cambridge, had set out for Athens in 1796, made hundreds of drawings of antiquities, and died of a fever in 1799. Some of his drawings were destroyed in a fire, but others were entrusted to the care of Elgin, who appears not to have brought them back to Britain. Tweddell's brother and memorialist accused Elgin of shabby conduct, and the object of the two *Quarterly Review* articles on the topic seems to have been to publicize Elgin's side of the case. The first article was largely by Blomfield, the second by Croker, but it is clear that Elgin was also invited to contribute, and that Blomfield and Croker were shown each other's texts at some point; a procedure at which the latter protested (Cutmore 2018). One might think that Blomfield would take the side of the dead Tweddell, a fine classical scholar and fellow of his own college; but Tweddell's political radicalism would not have appealed to him. Yet Blomfield's hero Richard Porson had also been politically radical in the 1790s—and notorious for his drinking in the 1800s. In fact Tweddell had recanted his Jacobinism after the Terror, and Blomfield's discussion proceeds comfortably, his major criticism being directed at the over-enthusiastic annotation provided by Tweddell's brother.[52]

Conclusion

In 1903, as we have already seen, A. E. Housman declared that the great age of English scholarship which had been initiated by Bentley toward the end of the seventeenth century 'was ended by the successive strokes of doom which consigned Dobree and Elmsley to the grave and Blomfield to the bishopric of Chester'.[53] What Housman called 'scholarship' was the kind of scholarship that mattered to him: the study of the linguistic aspects of classical texts. As we have seen, this kind of scholarship was cultivated by the Porsonians, led by Monk and Blomfield, and it figures prominently in the classical articles in the *Quarterly*. The narrowing of interest promoted by Porson led to a split between this 'critical' or 'pure' scholarship and the study of ancient history and archaeology. These were cultivated by travellers like Clarke and Tweddell, and they were also practised at Oxford, whose classical curriculum took on a broader form

---

[51] Among those taking this view was Richard Payne Knight. On the whole affair, see St Clair 1998, Webb 2002, Beard 2002, 18–20, 155–73.

[52] Blomfield suggests (p. 232) that 'Dr Spurzheim would infallibly discover in Mr Tweddell's occiput a new organ—that of *annotativeness*'.

[53] A. E. Housman, *M. Manilii Astronomicon, Liber Primus* (1903), xlii.

than that at Cambridge, as we saw in Chapter 2. Peter Elmsley, fine textual scholar though he was, also had interests in these wider topics (and in a sense can be counted as a traveller, given his journeys to France, the Netherlands, and Italy to inspect manuscripts). The history of the involvement of classicists in Gifford's *Quarterly Review* is in part that of the contrasting styles of the two universities: in Oxford, his own alma mater and the home of his advisor Edward Copleston, Gifford may have felt more comfortable; though as we have seen he was active in recruiting like-minded reviewers from Cambridge.

Another and sharper contrast of styles obtained between the two English universities and their five Scottish counterparts. North of the border, philosophy and political economy loomed large, while Greek was taught to mixed-age classes, some of whose members were complete beginners. This contrast needs to be remembered when evaluating the political and religious contrasts between the two *Reviews*. In this essay I have hardly scratched the surface of what was clearly a complex history of interaction between the *Edinburgh Review* and *Quarterly Review*, one which involved both differences of belief and commercial rivalry. As far as classical reviewing was concerned, however, the overall pattern is clear. Gifford was concerned from the beginning to match and surpass the *Edinburgh* in his classical contributions, and this doubtless had something to do with the close links between the scholarship of Oxford and Cambridge and the conservative political-religious establishment. The attacks on Oxonian scholarship in 1809, just as he entered on his reign at *Quarterly Review*, will have spurred him on in this quest. He appears to have been successful for a considerable period, since as we have seen his rivals abandoned any attempt to compete in this sphere between 1813 and 1820.

7

From one Museum to Another
The *Museum Criticum* (1813–26) and the *Philological Museum* (1831–3)

A conventional narrative of nineteenth-century British periodicals traces a development from general reviews to specialized academic journals. The narrative begins with the great reviews, like the *Quarterly* and its rival the *Edinburgh*, *Blackwood's Magazine*, the *Athenaeum*, *Fraser's Magazine*, *Macmillan's Magazine*, and the *Fortnightly Review*. A transition is seen in the foundation of the *Academy*, the organ of the Oxford-based Association for the Organization of Academical Study, which campaigned for the development of research along German lines. The *Academy*, which unusually carried only signed articles, was established in 1869 to provide a forum for general academic discussion, though it soon split into specialized sections; it began as a monthly, but moved to fortnightly publication in 1871 and weekly in 1874 (Roll-Hansen 1957). In 1868 the *Journal of Philology* was founded in Cambridge; it closed down in 1921. The *Journal of Hellenic Studies* (1880) and *Classical Review* (1887) survive and flourish today (see Chapter 8). The era of the academic journal, as this suggests, began in the 1880s, and the emergence of the New Journalism and of mass newspapers in the same decade accentuated the polarization between scholarly and mass publishing.

While this picture is broadly accurate, it leaves out of account half a century of scholarly publication. From the 1810s to the 1860s, several classical journals were established, though most of them were short-lived: the *Classical Journal* (1810–29); the *Museum Criticum* (1813–26); the *Philological Museum* (1831–3); the *Classical Museum* (1844–50), the *Journal of Classical and Sacred Philology* (1854–9); the relative longevity of the *Journal of Philology* (1868–1921) indicates a change in the availability of stable readerships for such periodicals. The list below summarizes the publication histories of these journals, their locations, and also failed projects of foundation or continuation.

Nineteenth-century English Classical Journals, Actual and Projected

Projected journals are in square brackets. C = Cambridge, L = London, O = Oxford.

Classical Journal 1810–29. 20 vols, 40 issues. L
Museum Criticum 1813–26. 2 vols, 8 issues. C

[H. J. Rose 1826–7] C
[G. C. Lewis 1830] O
Philological Museum 1831–3. 2 vols, 6 issues. C
    [B. Jowett, H. G. Liddell, R. Scott, A. P. Stanley: 'Museum Academicum' 1841–2]
O *Classical Museum* 1843–9. 7 vols, 28 issues. L
*Terminalia; or Notes on the Subjects of the Literae Humaniores and Moderation
    Schools* 1851–2. 2 issues. O
Journal of Classical and Sacred Philology 1854–9. 4 vols, 12 issues. C
Journal of Philology 1868–1921. 35 vols, 70 issues. C (O)
Transactions of the Oxford Philological Society 1879–90. 11 issues. O
Journal of Hellenic Studies 1880–. Annual. L
Proceedings of the Cambridge Philological Society 1882–. Annual. *Memoranda* 1872–9,
    Transactions 1881–. C
Classical Review 1887– . 10 issues annually. C/O/L
Classical Quarterly 1909– . 4 issues annually. C/O/L

The list above shows a clear pattern of development, from a series of short-lived publications, through the long-lived but mortal *Journal of Philology*, to the *Journal of Hellenic Studies*, *Classical Review*, and *Classical Quarterly*, all of them still published. This fits neatly with the chronology of the emergence of a modern academic discipline and professional community, encouraged by several changes in the second half of the century: reforms at Oxford and Cambridge after the Royal Commissions of the 1850s and 1870s, the declining intake of graduates into Anglican orders and the concomitant growth of an academic profession, and the expansion of provincial universities (Engel 1983, Haig 1986a). Yet this pattern is perhaps too neat: and it will be useful to look briefly at two awkward cases, at opposite ends of the century. First, the earliest journal listed was also one of the longest-lasting; a striking exception to the pattern which dominates the list as a whole, of a succession of short-lived publications. The reason is simply that it was run by the publisher Abraham Valpy, whose ambition was to be a printer-scholar in the manner of Aldus Manutius. The dilemma faced by the founders of several other journals, of retaining a printer's or publisher's support, was solved by Valpy's being his own printer and publisher. Valpy's brother and father were classical scholars, and his monogram, a claim to up-to-date scholarship derided by others, was a large digamma, which appeared on his title pages and also, apparently, on his coach. Another of Valpy's grand projects was a large-scale version of Estienne's Greek Thesaurus (1816–26). Edmund Henry Barker was associated with both publications, and because of this there was, as we have seen in Chapters 4 and 6, rivalry with the *Museum Criticum* of James Monk and Charles Blomfield, fellows of Barker's old college and guardians of the Porsonian flame. The variable quality and omnium-gatherum antiquarianism of the *Classical Journal* contrasted with the hard-nosed textual criticism of the Cambridge dons, who saw themselves as more professional than the learned but uncontrolled Barker. But as we have seen in Chapter 6, the longevity of the *Museum Criticum* was in large part a symptom of decline rather than persistence, since its last two issues appeared at much longer intervals than their predecessors while its editors were preoccupied with church careers.

The second case is that of the *Journal of Philology*, founded in 1868. Since a scholarly community was surely well established by 1921, why did the journal collapse in that year? The answer is that the journal was kept going by a bulk subscription for members of the Cambridge Philological Society, and this was cancelled in 1921.[1] The journal had gone into debt in the 1870s, and had been rescued by the Society's subscription, and by recruiting an Oxford editor, Ingram Bywater, who brought with him several dozen subscriptions from his colleagues. There were several reasons for the cancellation. First, the Society's own *Proceedings*, published since 1882, had by this time become an open classical journal (and thus a competitor), rather than just an in-house record.[2] Second, the *Journal of Philology* had after its foundation quickly become irregular of issue, and from the late 1890s very much so. In several years after that no issues appeared at all.[3] Third, Philological Society members outside Cambridge received only the *Journal* in exchange for their subscription, so there was widespread resentment when publication was late or non-existent in a given year. Macmillan, the journal's publisher, raised the price during the First World War and yet at times did not supply an issue; nor did they respond to a call for a cumulative index to be produced. Fourth, its founding editor and moving spirit, Henry Jackson, professor of Greek at Cambridge since 1906, had by 1919 become a helpless invalid (he died in 1921), so the journal's end must have seemed very close in any case.[4] Finally, the Society had for some time been pressing the publisher, Macmillan, to provide a cumulative index, but to no avail; the Society organized one itself and it appeared in 1923. (See further Chapter 8.)

This example highlights several issues which will recur. One is the relationship between journals and scholarly societies, for whom journals are both functional communication media and sources of pride and prestige. Another is the involvement of

---

[1] The Society's secretary J. P. Postgate reported in 1881 that the Society 'has preserved the Journal of Philology from a collapse which without the subscriptions of its members would have overtaken it long ago': 'The work of a philological society', *Trans. Camb. Phil. Soc.* 1:1872–80 (1881), 5. For the journal's history, see W. Ridgeway, 'Preface', in *An Index to the Journal of Classical Philology 1868–1920* (Cambridge: Cambridge Classical Society, 1923), 2–4; P. G. Naiditch, 'Bibliography and the history of classical scholarship', *Classical Views* 42 (1998), 645–62, at pp. 649–50, 660–2. Ridgeway's preface is printed with the Index at the end of vol. 35 of the *Journal* in the 2012 CUP digital reprint.

[2] The Society's Transactions were absorbed in 1936 by Cambridge Classical Studies, a series whose bibliographical history is unclear. The earlier volumes were numbered: no.1 (1936) was H. D. P. Lee's edition of Zeno of Elea. No. 6 (1940) was A. H. Armstrong's 'The architecture of the intelligible universe in the philosophy of Plotinus'. Also apparently in the series (but not numbered) was Ch. Wirszubski's *Libertas* (1950). The editors were F. M. Cornford (probably the moving spirit, replaced on his death in 1943 by R. Hackforth), F. E. Adcock, and D. S. Robertson. J. A. Crook was an editor of the series 1970–84 (Crook papers, St John's College library, Cambridge, E3/6).

[3] Richard Jebb ascribed this to the lack of a 'working editor' responsible for regular publication. See his letter to George Macmillan about the editorship of *JHS*, 26 March 1880: Jebb 1907, 217–18.

[4] Jackson belonged to a small group of liberal academics who in 1864 had founded the Ad Eundem Club, a dining club which promoted discussion between Oxford and Cambridge dons and met alternately at either place. Like the Journal, the Club in effect died with Jackson.

commercial printers and publishers. They are in business to make a profit, but that has not always been their only motivation. The firm of Macmillan had had strong Cambridge connections since Alexander and Daniel Macmillan set up shop at 1 Trinity Street (the present site of the Cambridge University Press bookshop) in 1843; in the next generation, George Macmillan, a founder of the Hellenic Society and later its secretary, kept up the classical publishing for the firm, which sold the *Journal of Hellenic Studies* on behalf of the Society.[5] Similarly, the firm of John Murray published the *Classical Review* and *Classical Quarterly* from the latter's foundation in 1909 until in 1938 rising costs meant that even the generous terms the firm offered were unaffordable for the journal's owners, the Classical Association, and they were transferred to Oxford University Press, which was willing to publish them at a loss (2003a, 113; 2013b).[6]

In this chapter I consider the linked histories of the *Museum Criticum* and the *Philological Museum*.[7] They make an interesting pair since both were edited by fellows of Trinity College, Cambridge, where the two sets of editors overlapped in the 1820s. Yet though the *Philological Museum* was heralded in advance as a continuation of the *Museum Criticum*, the two journals in fact reflected very different styles of scholarship.[8] As the detailed accounts of the two journals below will show, the *Philological Museum* was to a large extent a mouthpiece for the new comparative philology developed, especially in Germany, by Bopp, Rask, and Grimm, and which reached Britain in the 1820s. What needs to be emphasized at the outset is that this philology had close links with the hermeneutic analysis of biblical texts, and that its practitioners tended to be liberal Christians who reacted against dogmatic theology. In Britain, the followers of the new philology formed a loose grouping known as the Liberal Anglicans, and exerted considerable intellectual and religious influence in the 1830s and 1840s (Forbes 1952). One of their intellectual heroes was Barthold Niebuhr, whose methodologically sceptical *History of Rome* was seen by conservative Anglicans as an implied challenge to orthodox belief; what could be said of Livy might also be said of the Bible. The first two volumes of Niebuhr's *History* were translated into English by Julius Hare and Connop Thirlwall, the editors of the *Philological Museum*.[9] The collision

---

[5] The first volume which did not carry an announcement of the link was vol. 65, 1945 (issued in 1947).

[6] The journals are now published by Cambridge University Press.

[7] Why the prevalence of 'Museum' in these titles'? Models can be found in journals of the eighteenth century (for example *The Museum, or the Literary & Historical Register* (1746–7) and *Museum Helveticum Adjuvandas Literas in Publicos Usus Apertum* (1746–53))—both predating the foundation of the British Museum in 1753. A short-lived enterprise by Thomas Burgess, the *Museum Oxoniense*, ran from 1792 to 1797. The (German) *Rheinisches Museum* was founded in 1827, between the two *Museums* discussed here; since it was supported by B. G. Niebuhr, much admired by the editors of the *Philological Museum*, its title may have constituted their immediate exemplar. Conveniently enough, 'Museum' was identical in English and German.

[8] The tension between Porsonian and 'philological' scholarship was paralleled in Germany by the conflict between the followers of Gottfried Hermann and August Boeckh: see Sandys 1908, 89–101; Most 1997.

[9] B. G. Niebuhr 1828–31 *The History of Rome* Vols 1–2 (London). Vol. 3, translated by L. Schmitz and W. Smith, appeared in 1842. The first volume received a hostile mention in the *Quarterly Review*

of their views with orthodox conservative Anglicanism is dramatically symbolized by the dismissal of Thirlwall from his post of assistant tutor at Trinity in 1832 by the High Anglican master, Christopher Wordsworth. Thirlwall had argued that compulsory chapel was inimical to genuine Christian faith, and finding that Wordsworth believed that the choice was between 'compulsory religion or no religion at all', commented that 'the difference...is too subtle for my grasp'.[10] The move 'from one *Museum* to another' is thus one which reflects wider movements not only in scholarship, but also in religion and politics.

I. *Museum Criticum,* or Cambridge Classical Researches, 1813–26

The *Museum Criticum* encapsulates the dominant style of English classical scholarship in the early nineteenth century: the close linguistic analysis of (mostly Greek) texts practised by Richard Porson, Regius Professor of Greek at Cambridge from 1792 until his death in 1808, discussed in Chapter 4. As its subtitle 'Cambridge Classical Researches' suggests, the *Museum* was edited from Cambridge: more precisely, from Porson's college, Trinity. The editors were his disciples James Henry Monk (1784–1856: Regius Professor of Greek at Cambridge 1809–23; Bishop of Gloucester 1830), and Charles James Blomfield (1786–1857: Bishop of Chester 1824, of London 1828). Monk and Blomfield were not only both fellows of Trinity but were bosom friends; each acted as godfather to the other's son, and each of the boys took his godfather's Christian name. Among their major concerns, as we saw in Chapter 4, were the publication of Porson's notes on Greek literary texts and the continuation of his style of linguistic analysis; but as well as republishing articles by Porson, they also published notes on classical texts by his great predecessor Richard Bentley. The emphasis of their scholarship was largely on the minutiae of linguistic usage—grammar, syntax, metre—and the favoured genre for treatment, as with Porson himself, was Greek drama. The first issue of the *Museum* included several articles on Sophocles and Aeschylus by Monk and Blomfield. Later, articles were commissioned from other Porsonian scholars, including the most talented of his followers, the Oxford classicist Peter Elmsley.[11]

It is remarkable that in the generation to which Monk and Blomfield belonged, the study of classical texts, especially of Greek drama, flowered in Cambridge in a way

(Barrow1829), 8–9) to which Hare replied with *A Vindication of Niebuhr's History of Rome, from the Charges of the Quarterly Review* (Hare 1829). Hare's pamphlet carried a postscript by Thirlwall; the copy in Trinity College Library, given by the author to William Whewell bears the MS inscription by a later owner, W. Aldis Wright of Trinity, 'Hare's bark and Thirlwall's bite'.

[10] C. Thirlwall, *A Letter to the Rev. Thomas Turton...on the Admission of Dissenters to Academical Degrees* (Cambridge, 1834); quoted by W. W. R. Ball, *Cambridge Notes*, 2nd edn (Cambridge, 1921), 60.

[11] The absence of Peter Dobree's name from this list was explained in Chapter 4.

which had almost no parallel at Oxford.[12] Among the causes of this disparity, and for the concentration of scholars in Trinity College, are surely the radical internal changes which had taken place in the college in the 1780s and 1790s. In 1786 a protest over the misconduct of fellowship elections led to the institution of a public written examination for candidates (Winstanley 1935, 243–5). In 1790 annual examinations were introduced for first and second year undergraduates (Monk himself, as Head Lecturer of the college, extended the practice to the third year in 1818). Thus by the time Monk, Blomfield, and their friends entered Trinity in the 1800s, a merit-based system was in place, in what had since the 1780s been the largest college in Cambridge.[13] The group of talented scholars who emerged from this system, united by their admiration for Porson's work, formed the basis for the activities of the *Museum Criticum*.

The journal was originally planned by a group of five Cambridge graduates: James Monk, Charles and Edward Blomfield, John Kaye, and Thomas Rennell. Edward Valentine Blomfield (1788–1816), Charles's younger brother and a fellow of Emmanuel College, was a talented scholar who translated August Matthiae's *Ausführliche griechische Grammatik* of 1807 (*A Copious Greek Grammar*, 2 vols, Cambridge 1818)—a work described by E. S. Shuckburgh in 1886 as 'still unrivalled in its way';[14] he encountered Matthiae's book during his travels in Germany in 1813. At this point the continental blockade made it very difficult for English scholars to obtain German books, but Blomfield had good contacts with German scholars, and travelled extensively in the country until his premature death in 1816. He contributed an 'Account of the present state of classical literature in Germany' to the second issue of the *Museum* (1. 273–8). The Preface to the first issue was provided by Thomas Rennell (1787–1824) of King's College. Blomfield wrote to Monk on 30 April 1813, 'I return you Rennel's [*sic*] Introduction, to which I have no particular objection to make, except that I think it considerably too pompous. Rennel seems to imitate Johnson, and wraps up his meaning so that it is not always easy to be extricated.'[15] Rennell was a friend of Monk's, and with him had edited *Musae Cantabrigienses* (1810); in 1811 he became editor of the *British Critic*, described in his *DNB* entry as 'the organ of his friends'; he was appointed vicar of Kensington in 1816. Like Edward Blomfield, he died prematurely of fever. John Kaye (1788–1853), fellow of Christ's College, was an influential figure in the University of Cambridge over a long period. He had been a candidate for the Regius chair of Greek on the death of Richard Porson in 1808, but withdrew in favour of Monk. He became master of his college in 1814 and Vice-Chancellor of the university the following

---

[12] The exceptions at Oxford were Thomas Gaisford (Regius Professor of Greek 1812–55) and Peter Elmsley. As we have seen in Chapter 3, Gaisford bemoaned the lack of serious interest in Greek scholarship in Oxford.

[13] See in general Robson 1967, and on examination reforms 2005b. Detailed evidence is not easy to find for the 1790s, but the establishment of posts of assistant tutor at Trinity may be relevant. For the possible role of a gift made in 1810 by John Piggott, see Chapter 4.

[14] E. S. Shuckburgh, 'Edward Valentine Blomfield', *Dictionary of National Biography* vol. 5 (1886).

[15] Quoted by permission of the Master and Fellows, Trinity College, Cambridge.

year; he was appointed Bishop of Bristol in 1820 and of Lincoln in 1827, remaining Master of Christ's until 1830. He and Monk played an important part in setting up the Classical Tripos (the honours examination in classics) in 1822 (2001a).

By the end of 1812, however, the planning of the *Museum* was effectively in the hands of Monk and Kaye; they were living in Cambridge, while Blomfield had a country living to cope with.[16] On 19 November Blomfield wrote to Elmsley that 'The journal will principally be managed by Messrs Monk and Kaye.'[17] The two men met on Christmas Eve to plan the first issue:[18]

Rennell and your Brother are gone out of College. Kaye and myself yesterday Morning drew up a plan of the first Number—& got the Vice Chancellor's leave to print at the University Press: & I wrote to Lunn[19] for the loan of the foreign books imported during 1812. The plan is—

1. An introduction; containing a statement of the plan. Rennell [iii–viii]
2. The fragments of Sophocles. C. J. Blomfield
3. Notes on the Electra of Sophocles. Monk [60–78]
4. Account of the old Greek Historians. Kaye [79–101]
5. The fragments of Sappho. [1–31]
6. Account of the Gr. Painters. E. V. Blomfield
7. Emendations on Markland's 3 Plays. C. J. Blomfield
8. Bibliographical account of Editions of Aeschylus. Ditto [105–14]
9. Chishall's Notes on Horace. Rennell [no. 2, 150–76]
10. Notice of Books, published and imported during 1812.

White's Synopsis.[20] Elmsley

Brotier's Tacitus. Kaye [137–8]

Porson's Adversaria. Blomfield & Monk [115–22]

Glasgow Caesar do.

Blomfield's 2 Plays. Monk. Very short

Clarke's MSS. Blomfield [128–32]

[Barker's] 3rd vol of [Class Jnl] do. do.

Burney's Philemon do. [122–8]

[Butler's] Cicero. Blomfield

---

[16]   For an informed sketch of the state of classics in Trinity in relation to the journals, including the role of 'scholarly invective and preening', see McKitterick 1998, 292–3. A good general account of Greek scholarship in the period, including assessments of Monk, Blomfield, Elmsley et al., is given by Clarke 1945, 85–111.

[17]   Elmsley papers, Westminster School; quoted by permission of the Headmaster. See Horsfall 1974.

[18]   Monk to Blomfield, 25 December 1812. I have added page nos. for those items that actually appeared in the first issue. Of the articles not listed by Monk, the 'Tryphonis Grammatici Opuscula' (pp. 32–59) were edited by Blomfield from a transcript by his brother of a manuscript lent by Monk. Blomfield may have incorporated in his discussion of Burney's *Philemon* notes sent by Robert Walpole (1781–1856). It is beyond the scope of this article to identify contributors to later issues, though scattered clues can be found. For example, the anonymous author of 'Syntaxeos Atticae Canones Dawesiani XI'(1, 518–35) was the Yorkshire scholar and schoolmaster James Tate: see L. P. Wenham, *James Tate, Master of Richmond School* (North Yorkshire County Record Office, 1991), 369.

[19]   William Lunn, a London bookseller who imported classical books from the continent.

[20]   This was probably *Crisews Griesbachianæ in Novum Testamentum synopsis edidit Josephus White*, Oxford 1811.

Very soon, the energetic Monk had become de facto editor. He wrote to Blomfield on 7 January 1813, 'If you approve, I will undertake the editorship of the first No. not because I am fit for this task, but because I seem the only person likely to undertake it.' The deferential tone is typical of his letters to Blomfield; who accepting his share of the editorial throne, wrote on 30 April 1813, 'I think you must by this time be pretty well aware on the shoulders of which two of our quinquevirate the burthen will principally rest.' But Monk it was who took the initiative; and it was he who clinched the crucial publishing deal with John Murray, which guaranteed sales and distribution for the journal.[21] The account he gave Blomfield on 8 February 1813 is worth quoting:

Now for the 'Museum Criticum'. Murray, the publisher of the Quarterly Review, who has taken a splendid shop in Albemarle Street, which is frequented more than Paynes by men of Fashion & of Literature, has signified to me his wish to engage in selling this work, of the success of which he is sanguine. I desired him to name his proposals. He offers to undertake it on the same terms as the Quarterly Review: i.e. to defray the whole expence of publication, & then to divide the profits with the editors: & as the future sales will probably increase, he is willing to leave it to our option to make a fresh bargain at the end of 2 years. Now on many accounts this is surely a desirable plan. The sale will be trebled by interesting a bookseller in it. I said I doubted how far you might have committed yourself to Mawman.[22] He said that unless a bargain had been concluded, he would willingly obviate that objection by putting the name of Mawman, or one of the sellers, on the title page. The thing now rests with you. Your engagement, if any, with M. must be kept. But if I understood you, it was only that he should sell the [journal] as he sells the first Eds. of the Plays on commission. This will not interfere with the new plan which will make our work far more respectable, & far less troublesome. If we agree, he will advertize it in the next Quarterly in little more than a week, which would otherwise cost 4 Guineas.

In offering these generous terms to Monk, Murray will have been aware that there was an established rival in the field: the *Classical Journal*, published since 1810 by Abraham Valpy. While the *Museum* was directed from Trinity College, the *Journal* was largely edited by a former Trinity man, a younger contemporary of Monk and Blomfield, who was a source of constant irritation to Monk in particular. This was Edmund Henry Barker (1788–1839), whom we have already met in Chapter 4, and who had won a classical prize at Cambridge but had left Trinity in 1809 without taking a degree.[23] Having contributed to the early numbers of the *Journal*, he had soon assumed an editorial role.[24] Monk's letters to Blomfield contain several complaints about Barker's

---

[21] It is not clear when Monk and Murray first came into contact: possibly when Monk wrote a review of George Burges's edition of Euripides' *Troades* (*Quarterly Review* 3 (February 1810), 167–85), if he was indeed the author.

[22] Joseph Mawman, a prominent London bookseller and publisher, was London agent for Cambridge University Press from 1799 until his death in 1827; he was a keen traveller, and published the travel books of several Cambridge men (McKitterick 1998, 257).

[23] At that time the only honours examination was in mathematics; but Barker's reluctance to take a BA was apparently due to religious scruples.

[24] Valpy was an Oxford graduate who had started his journal soon after leaving his alma mater. He saw himself as a modern Aldus Manutius; his Delphin edition of classical texts ran to 114 volumes. On Barker, see 2004a, McKitterick 2007.

activities. In his letter of 7 January 1813, quoted in Chapter 4, he denounced Barker and urged that he be given a 'good bastinado, not a school flogging'. Blomfield was able to administer a 'bastinado' in 1820, in a review of Barker's edition of Henri Estienne's *Thesaurus Graecae Linguae* (10 vols, 1816–28), also published by Valpy, which attracted more than 1000 subscribers. Blomfield pointed out in the *Quarterly Review* that Barker was inserting so much additional miscellaneous matter that its subscribers would have to wait fifty-five years for its completion.[25] The review led to the disappearance of Barker's name from the title page and the curtailment of his contributions. Barker's infuriated reply, *Aristarchus Anti-Blomfieldianus,* was in effect circulated by his opponent, being bound up, together with advertisements, with a later number of the *Quarterly Review.* Monk and Blomfield replied in the seventh issue of the Museum with a brief dismissal headed simply 'E. H. Barker O.T.N.', in which they took pains to deny that the *Museum* was undertaken 'in opposition to the *Classical Journal*'. However they could not resist adding that 'Had we been inclined to amuse our readers with the ridicule of literary vagaries and extravagances, or with the exposure of blunders and ignorance, never was there a more ample field for such sport than that afforded by certain writers in the Classical Journal.'[26]

The coverage of the *Classical Journal* overlapped with that of the *Museum,* but it included general literature and antiquarian reports on inscriptions and books, as well as publishing Oxford and Cambridge prize poems and examination papers. It might be thought that the rivalry between the two journals could be characterized as being that between an academic and a general review. Such a judgement would however be anachronistic, since the consciously academic community it presupposes, separated from ecclesiastical careers and institutions, did not emerge in England until the second half of the nineteenth century. It is also directly contradicted by the evidence of Monk's intentions. On 8 February 1813 he wrote to Blomfield:

The Notice of the Edd. of Aesch[ylus] must of course be English & a popular article, one which may always be referred to: even by booksellers: at least by amateurs.

I certainly wished all the notices of books—i.e. all the reviews to be in English. If you have sufficient cause, let those of the Philemon and the Cad. class. be exceptions, but I don't think it on the whole desirable. I leave it with you.

The notes on the Electra will be in English, unless you positively object.

In Germany it was common for learned periodicals in this period to be published in Latin.[27] In pressing for the use of English, Monk may have been influenced by the practice of the *Classical Journal,* but he will also have been aware that a large sale for the

---

[25] 'Stephens, *Thesaurus Græcæ Linguæ*', *Quarterly Review,* 22 (1820), 302–48.

[26] *Museum Criticum,* 2.510–12.

[27] Toward mid-century, German journals sometimes offered a choice between German and Latin: see Whitaker 2015.

Museum could not be hoped for if it was written in Latin. His reference to 'a popular article' and to reference by booksellers suggests his concern for a wider market than the small circle of Oxford and Cambridge academics that could be guaranteed to buy a rarefied classical journal. Securing this larger market became a more serious problem through the nineteenth century as specialization increased; both the *Classical Museum* in the 1840s, and the *Journal of Classical and Sacred Philology* in the 1850s, failed to secure a long-term readership. Not till the advent of the *Journal of Philology* (1868–1921) did a classical journal achieve this.

Monk's concern for a general readership is evident, as is his watchful eye on both print runs and the competition, in the 13 November 1813 letter to John Murray quoted above: 'please print covers for MC no 2, October 1813 and send 200 to Deighton for Cambridge sale; the remaining 550 to go to you. Elmsley promises material for no 3. In Cambridge it has done well and has utterly extinguished the C[lassical] J[ournal]. The only fault which I have found with the first no is, that it is not sufficiently amusing—and this fault we shall strive to amend.'[28] Monk was in fact mistaken about the print run: it was 1,000 for the first issue and 750 thereafter, not 750 and 500 as he thought. He seems not to have realized his error until 1821. Oxford sales he thought hardly worth trying for: 'Of the Oxonians I have little hope—they scarcely buy a copy of Elmsley's or of Gaisford's publications, though they are their own scholars' (Monk to Murray, 29 January 1815).

While sales figures were reasonably good, the increasing gaps between issues make it clear that the supply of material, editorial time, or both diminished after 1814. They must also have tried the patience of would-be regular purchasers. The fifth issue appeared in 1815, the sixth in 1816; the seventh at the end of 1821 and the eighth and final issue not till 1826. The two-volume issue of 1826 was not very successful; John Murray's printing ledgers show that the remaining stock of the journal was sold off to H. G. Bohn in 1839, leaving a loss of £155. 17s. 6d.

The long delay in producing the final issue is sufficiently explained by Monk's appointment as Dean of Peterborough in March 1822; he resigned his Greek chair in June of the following year, and was an active dean, raising £6,000 for new building. The mid 1820s, as we have seen, marked the end of an era in English classical scholarship. Blomfield was made Bishop of Chester in 1824; Elmsley and the other leading Porsonian scholar Peter Dobree, who had succeeded Monk as Professor of Greek at Cambridge in 1823, died in 1825. By the summer of 1826, the scholars who might have edited and contributed to the *Museum Criticum* were either dead, or engaged on what they saw as matters higher even than the study of Greek.

---

[28] Monk wrote to Murray on 19 November 1821, 'It is gratifying to find we have sold 250 more of each no. than we thought.' A note in the Murray archives suggests that the first issue sold 768 copies, the next three issues between 570 and 630 copies.

II. The *Philological Museum*, 1831–3

The final number of the *Museum Criticum* carried the following announcement from the editors: 'Although other avocations now compel them to give up the MUSEUM CRITICUM, they have reason to hope, that another series of Numbers of a similar nature, will issue from the Press of this University, under the auspices of an able and judicious scholar.'[29] The phrase 'other avocations' referred, as we have seen, to ecclesiastical preferment. The reference to 'another series of Numbers' was to what emerged as the *Philological Museum*; the 'able and judicious scholar' was Hugh Rose, fellow of Trinity, an unsuccessful candidate for the Regius chair of Greek in 1825. Christopher Wordsworth junior, son of the Master of Trinity, wrote in his diary on 2 April 1826, 'Rose...is going to undertake the Editorship of the Museum Criticum & had been to Oxford to engage contributors for the purpose—but he was disappointed.'[30] Gaisford reported to Fynes Clinton in 1830 that:

Mr Rose, the coryphaeus, has lately obtained a valuable living in Suffolk from the Archbishop of Canterbury; and that kind of preferment in any place would operate as a considerable damper to literature, and especially in a county so far from Metropolitical & Academical opportunities as Suffolk.[31]

Rose had in fact been attempting to prolong the life of the *Museum Criticum* even before its final issue appeared. On 19 February 1827 he wrote to the Museum's publisher John Murray as follows:

I have waited since...May 1825 for your decision on the Museum Criticum. I have written numberless letters in a tone of the utmost courtesy— & I have in return been treated with perfect contempt. I really can submit to this no longer. I had arranged with Mr Mawman as to the publication of the Mus. Crit. & suspended that arrangement in consequence of a verbal message from you thro' Mr Mitchell. I now beg to inform you that I shall proceed upon it, as after waiting 7 or 8 months you have not taken any notice of one of my letters on the subject.[32]

Rose was a religious and political conservative who went on to be a leading theologian, something which has obscured his work as a classicist. It is difficult to guess whether his work on inscriptions might have led to Porsonian minutiae or, perhaps, to something broader. It is not clear what success he had on other fronts; in the

---

[29] *Museum Criticum*, Vol. 2, p. 698.

[30] C. Wordsworth jr, diary 1825–7, 47. Trinity College Library, O.11.9; J. H. Ovenden and E. Wordsworth, *Christopher Wordsworth, Bishop of Lincoln* (London, 1890), 31. The entry is undated, but is for the Sunday after Easter Sunday, which had fallen on 26 March.

[31] Gaisford to Fynes Clinton, 7 Feb. 1830. Gaisford papers, Christ Church, Oxford. The young George Cornewall Lewis was also interested in reviving the *Museum Criticum*: See p. 157.

[32] Murray archive, National Library of Scotland. '1825' is probably a dittography from a dating earlier in the letter: read '1826', as the reference to '7 or 8 months' suggests. There is no evidence that Rose returned to Joseph Mawman (n. 22 above), whose death on 13 September 1827 would in any case have closed that avenue to publication. 'Mr Mitchell' was probably the classical scholar Thomas Mitchell, a family friend of John Murray.

autumn of 1827 he told William Whewell of Trinity that 'Wordsworth has offered a translation of Virgil—a little perhaps out of our way, but such an offer could not be refused.'[33] Wordsworth had begun his translation in 1823, but abandoned it after translating three books. After some prompting, he sent in an extract, which appeared in the second issue of the *Philological Museum* in January 1832.[34]

In 1829 an Oxford man, George Cornewall Lewis, also planned a revival, as we learn from a letter from Thomas Gaisford of Christ Church to his young Christ Church colleague Henry Fynes Clinton:

Dear Fynes

This note will be delivered to you by Mr Lewis a student of Christ Church and the translator of Boeckh's book on the economy of Athens. He is desirous of reviving the Museum Criticum, and has requested me to ask you whether you would occasionally contribute a paper to that miscellany. He can best explain himself viva voce.[35]

Lewis called on Clinton on New Year's Day 1830; in his autobiography, Clinton noted that he had promised 'a contribution to the "Museum Criticum" in the autumn' (Clinton 1854, 283). On 7 February 1830 Gaisford wrote to Clinton again:

I believe Mr Lewis (for I know him only by a very short correspondence & by one or two publications) to be a very zealous young man, and if destined to an academical life might pursue philological labours with success and advantage: but I suspect that the revival of the Museum Criticum will not be a very prosperous speculation. Rose's attempts at a revival of the *Museum Criticum*, as we have seen, had been hampered by his ecclesiastical preferment. His is an interesting case, since he had persisted in pursuing classical scholarship since his failure to gain a Trinity fellowship in 1817; his experience thus, unusually, bridged the worlds of the university and the church.

Rose's attempts at a revival of the journal had indeed been hampered by his ecclesiastical preferments; but a letter written in April 1832 to another Trinity man, William Henry Fox Talbot, shows that he had been involved in the founding of a continuator:

I rejoice to hear that you approve of the two numbers of the Philological Museum w[hi]ch have appeared & trust that you will find the same reason to approve of the work in future. I have Endeavoured of the last 5 or 6 years to set this publication on foot, tho' without success till this last Autumn. Now there appears to be somewhat of a revival of feeling for Ancient Literature & I trust that the Museum may serve to cherish it. At the present moment, I am so much engaged that Mr Hare, my brother Editor, is acting almost alone—& he will, I am sure, have great pleasure in receiving any communication from you.[36]

---

[33] Rose to Whewell, 11 Nov. 1827. Whewell papers, Trinity College Library, Cambridge, A 211/137. For Wordsworth's translation of part of the Aeneid, see Graver 1986; Gillespie 2011, 131–2, 152–5.

[34] Reprinted in *Philological Museum* (1833)1: 382–6. The first issue was reprinted as pp. 1–208 of this volume. In my copy, a list of 'contents of the second number' is bound in between pp. 426 and 427, with a pencil instruction, 'don't include this page'. The third issue begins on p. 427.

[35] Christ Church Library, MS 498.56, n.d. but 1829.

[36] Rose to Fox Talbot, 2 April 1832. The letter is transcribed in *Correspondence of William Henry Fox Talbot* (http://foxtalbot.dmu.ac.uk). Fox Talbot is remembered as a pioneer of photography, but he was also a keen philologist, and in 1838–9 published *Hermes, or Classical and Antiquarian Researches*. His contributions

The new journal was founded as the *Philological Museum*. It is usually seen as the brainchild of two other fellows of Trinity: Julius Hare, co-author with his brother Augustus of the anonymous *Guesses at Truth* (1827), and his friend Connop Thirlwall, later Bishop of St David's, but now remembered mainly for his *History of Greece* (1835–44). Rose's letter, however, shows that he and Hare were the founding editors, and so Thirlwall was presumably brought in as a replacement for Rose.

Despite the blessing it received in advance in the *Museum Criticum* from Monk (who surely wrote the farewell statement quoted above) and its home in Trinity, the new journal was not 'of a similar nature' to its predecessor. The *Museum Criticum* had embodied the values and methods of the Porsonian school: a focus on Greek drama, and on the linguistic minutiae of classical texts. The contrasting adjectives in the journals'—'critical' vs 'philological'—sum up the contrasting conceptions of classical scholarship embodied in the journals' policies; and the change from the Latin 'criticum' to the English 'philological' also reflects a change, from an exclusive focus on Latin and Greek to a wider concern with language in general.[37]

Hare opened his Preface to the first issue by deploring the recent lack 'among the multitude of journals publisht in England' of any 'wholly, or even mainly, devoted to classical literature'.[38] After recalling the demise first of the *Museum Criticum* (in 1826) and then of the *Classical Journal* (in 1829), he went on to regret that the leading English journals no longer devoted space to the discussion of philological questions. The sole recent achievement in England in this area, he suggested, was 'one great work on ancient chronology', of which he declined to speak, since 'its author is one of our fellow-labourers'. The reference was to the Oxford classical scholar Henry Fynes Clinton, whose massive *Fasti Hellenici* had been published in three volumes between 1824 and 1830.[39] Among Clinton's contributions to the *Museum* was a set of additions and corrections to this work (1. 294–404). The singling out of a work on chronology already indicates how far the new journal was intended to move beyond the bounds set by the *Museum Criticum*. Hare ended his Preface by declaring that:

No inquiry that comes under the head of philology, no topic connected with it, will be altogether excluded. [The editors'] main attention will however be directed toward the two colossal edifices that stand forth amid the ruins of the ancient world: their main object will be, in so far as in them lies, and as the kind help of their friends will enable them, to illustrate the language,

to the *Philological Museum* were signed HFT. Fox Talbot's half-sister married Thomas Gaisford's son Thomas. Rose had been given the living of Hadleigh in Suffolk in 1832, but was dogged by ill health and resigned the living; he died in 1838 at the age of forty-three.

[37] The article on Monk in W. Jerdan (ed.), *National portraits* 5, 1832, 6 refers to the *Philological Museum* as 'Museum Philologicum'.

[38] 'Publisht' is characteristic of Hare's idiosyncratic spelling, adopted in the 1820s and adhered to until his death—itself an example of the embedding of philological investigation in the moral life. In his and his brother Augustus's *Guesses at Truth* (London, 1827, 1.337), language is described as the 'moral barometer' of a nation's life; a sentiment taken from the writing of the conservative ideologue Joseph de Maistre.

[39] By Oxford University Press: Vol. 2 in 1824, Vol. 1 in 1827, and Vol. 3 in 1830.

the literature, the philosophy, the history, the manners, the institutions, the mythology, and the religion of Greece and Rome. Biblical criticism will now and then be introduced; and so will dissertations on Oriental literature, when they are not, as such things mostly are, either too heavy or too light.   (1. iii–iv)

It is apparent from this manifesto that the *Philological Museum* was intended to open wider vistas on the ancient world than had the *Museum* it succeeded. And while the *Museum Criticum* had consistently reported developments in continental scholarship and had reviewed foreign books, Hare and Thirlwall wanted to go further, as can be seen from the note Hare prefixed to the translation of Savigny's article on the Ius Latini and the Ius Italicum (1.150–73). There he declared that 'It is one of the main objects of the Philological Museum to acquaint the English student of classical literature with the new views that have been taken, and the new discoveries that have been made, of late years by the scholars upon the continent, that is to say, by a very pardonable synecdoche, the scholars of Germany.' This policy was certainly followed out in later issues, which include contributions by Niebuhr (nos. 2, 3, 6), Boeckh (nos. 3, 4, 5, 6) and Schleiermacher (no. 6—two articles) among others. But as those names suggest, the new journal looked to a particular school of German classical scholarship: not the critical study of linguistic texts practised by Gottfried Hermann and his followers, but the study of texts in their social, political, and religious contexts, favoured by August Boeckh.[40] At the same time, the expansion of philological work from Germany to England was also reflected. The journal's title, in English rather than the Latin used by the *Museum Criticum*, hints both at this widened field and perhaps at a new openness to a more general readership.

Both Hare and Thirlwall were, unusually for English academics of their period, fluent in German. Hare had had a cosmopolitan upbringing. His parents had eloped to Italy and lived there for twenty years before moving to Germany. He was also socially well connected, his uncle being the orientalist Sir William Jones (1746–94). At the age of two, he had been left by his parents in the care of Clotilda Tambroni (1758–1817), professor of Greek at Bologna, the leading Greek scholar in Southern Europe and a correspondent of Porson.[41] Thirlwall, two years his junior, was like him a childhood prodigy, reading Latin at three and Greek at four. When he was eleven his father published a book of his poems, *Primitiae*.[42] Hare and Thirlwall were both schoolboys at Charterhouse (as was George Grote, whose history of Greece was to eclipse Thirlwall's); both went to Trinity College, and both were elected to fellowships there in 1818.

Hare became a classical lecturer at the college in 1822, at the invitation of his friend William Whewell; Thirlwall reluctantly read for the bar, but returned to Cambridge in

---

[40] For Hermann, see Schmidt 1990; on Boeckh, see U. von Wilamowitz-Moellendorff, *History of Classical Scholarship*, ed. H. Lloyd-Jones (London, 1982), 120–3. For the Hermann-Boeckh dispute, see Most 1997.

[41] For Hare, see Distad 1979; for Thirlwall, Thirlwall 1936.

[42] In later years, the embarrassed author sought out copies of the book and destroyed them.

1827 and held several college posts in succession in the next five years, as well as exam-ining for the Classical Tripos (the first examination for which had been held in 1824). Together they translated most of Niebuhr's *Römische Geschichte*, and Hare later defended Niebuhr against the Anglican critics of his historical scepticism.[43] Thirlwall had met Baron Bunsen in Rome in 1818 and formed a close friendship with him; he was thus close to a crucial node in the transmission of German thought to England. By the time Thirlwall returned to Trinity in 1827, Hare had established himself as a dedi-cated and inspiring teacher.[44] Frederick Denison Maurice, who went up to Trinity in 1823, remembered a mode of teaching that combined the characteristic Cambridge attention to linguistic detail—the Porsonian method—with an eye to larger questions. In the first term, they read Sophocles' *Antigone*, and:

The lecturer seemed most anxious to impress us with the feeling that there was no road to the sense which did not go through the words. He took infinite pains to make us understand the force of nouns, verbs, participles, and the grammar of the sentences. We often spent an hour on the strophe or anti-strophe of a chorus ...

You will think that so much philological carefulness could not have been obtained without the sacrifice of higher objects. How could we discover the divine intuitions of the poet, while we were tormenting ourselves about his tenses? I cannot tell; but it seems to me that I never learnt so much about this particular poem, about Greek dramatic poetry generally, about all poetry, as in that term.[45]

This catches very well the intense interest in words that is evident in Hare's contribu-tions to the *Philological Museum*, but also the degree to which this interest transcended the narrower textual focus of the Porsonians. As Arnaldo Momigliano put it, Hare and Thirlwall and their friends 'were fighting within the walls of the old universities for a reform of the prevailing methods of teaching the classics. They wanted the empirical knowledge of the classical languages characteristic of the English school to be replaced by scientific investigation of the classical literatures as pursued in German univer-sities.'[46] That year, 1823, marked a turning point indeed, since in it James Monk, an older fellow of Trinity and, as we have seen, editor of the Porsonian *Museum Criticum*, resigned the chair of Greek. The tide, Hare may have thought, was turning in favour of a wider conception of 'philology'. But Monk's successor was Peter Paul Dobree, another Porsonian disciple. Dobree was a retiring man who published little; much of the work he did produce involved the editing of Porson's unpublished notes.[47]

---

[43] B. G.Niebuhr, The *Roman History* (Cambridge, 1828, 1832). A third volume, translated by Leonhard Schmitz and William Smith, appeared in 1842. Hare's A *Vindication of Niebuhr's History of Rome from the Charges of the Quarterly Review* was published in 1829.

[44] For Hare's time in Trinity in the 1820s, see Distad 1979, 43–57.

[45] F. D. Maurice, *The Life of Frederick Denison Maurice, Chiefly Told in His Own Letters* (London, 1884), vi–x.

[46] See Momigliano 1966, 62.

[47] Notably his *Ricardi Porsoni Notae in Aristophanem, quibus Plutum Comoediam partim ex ejusdem recensione partim e manuscriptis emendatam et variis lectionibus instructam praemisit, et collationum*

Up to this point the Cambridge curriculum had centred on the study of mathematics, which formed the basis of the only honours examination, the Senate House Examination. In 1824, however, this was, however informally, renamed the Mathematical Tripos, on the foundation of a new university examination in classics, the Classical Tripos.[48] Hare and Thirlwall might have hoped that this would give some purchase for their broader conception of scholarship. But it proved to offer a very restrictive curriculum, dominated by translation from Greek and Latin. Another central element of classical practice in Cambridge, original composition in the classical languages, was excluded in deference to the mathematicians who dominated Cambridge academic life (1999b, 2001a). Finally, in 1825 Hare's academic ambitions received a setback, which will have reminded him that, within a university which was still part of the Anglican Church, purely academic distinction was liable to take second place to the politics of religion. He applied for the Regius chair of Greek, vacated by the death of Dobree. Most of the candidates were Trinity men (including, as we have seen, Hugh Rose), but theological divisions counted against Hare, a Broad Churchman, as the Master of Trinity, Christopher Wordsworth, was a High Anglican; and in the final vote tactical voting led to the appointment of a relatively undistinguished candidate, James Scholefield, who remained in post until his death in 1853.[49]

One of the major forces underlying the broader conception of scholarship which Hare and Thirlwall had hoped to import to Cambridge via the *Museum* was the comparative philology which flourished in continental Europe.[50] Developed in the 1810s and 20s by the Dane Rasmus Rask and the Germans Franz Bopp and Jacob Grimm, it was taken up in the 1820s and 1830s not only by Hare and Thirlwall, but also by J. M. Kemble, R. G. Latham, J. W. Donaldson and others. It flourished in the new University of London, where Bopp's favourite pupil Friedrich Rosen was appointed Professor of Oriental Languages, and later of Sanskrit; Rosen's colleague Thomas Key, Professor of Latin, drew on his analysis of 'crude forms' (the root elements of words, to which inflections were added). Key was a member of an informal philological society founded in 1830 in what later became University College, London. In the same year, a society was founded in Cambridge by Whewell and others

---

appendicem adjecit Petrus Paulus Dobree of 1820. For Dobree's relations with Monk, which were at times strained, see Chapter 4.

[48] 'Tripos' from the three-legged stool on which an 'old bachelor' (BA of some standing) sat while interrogating candidates at the degree examination. For the history of the mathematics course, see Gascoigne 1989, Warwick 2003; on examinations, 2005b.

[49] There is an account of the election in a letter from John Croft (one of the electors) to Joseph Romilly, 2 May 1853 (Cambridge University archives, CUR 39.4, 31). The archival entry for the election at O.XIV.53 p. 33 gives only the name of Scholefield and those of the electors. Someone (probably Joseph Romilly, the University Registrary) has added a note: 'N.B./ The Candid[ate]s were Ja. Scholef[iel]d (1813), J. C. Hare (1816), H. J. Rose (1817), W. S. Walker (1819)'. But in his diary for 1825-7, Christopher Wordsworth Jr mentions two others, Robinson and Waddington: both of them praelected, but neither gained any votes (Trinity College Library, O.11. 9, p. 6).

[50] See Aarsleff 1967; and for the role of philology in the defence of Anglican belief, Dowling 1986, 3-45.

whose members' work provided material for the *Philological Museum*. This was the Cambridge Etymological Society, whose short life ended two years later. Its members not only provided individual papers, but also contributed to a collaborative project for a multilingual etymological dictionary. The dictionary was never completed, but several hundred pages of manuscript lists survive, with other records of the Society, in Whewell's papers at Trinity College.[51]

Like Monk and Blomfield, Hare and Thirlwall eventually left Cambridge for ecclesiastical posts. But the final days of the *Philological Museum* were rather different from those of its predecessor. Hare went to a rich country living in Hurstmonceux, Sussex, in 1832, leaving Thirlwall in sole charge of the *Museum*. In 1834, after a disagreement over compulsory chapel with the conservative Master Christopher Wordsworth, Thirlwall was removed from his tutorial post and left Cambridge. But by this time the *Philological Museum* had already been brought to a close. After Hare's departure Thirlwall found it increasingly difficult to find contributions, and was forced to translate German works to fill the pages. Sending a copy to Bunsen in October 1833, he explained that:

I could have wished...that so large a part of the contents had not come from my hand. For though they may be accepted as proofs of my good will toward the undertaking, they at the same time betray the melancholy fact that I am unable to fill up the volume by any other means. Nothing but the pressure of scarcity would have induced me to insert the smaller articles toward the end, which I wrote after having been disappointed of contributions on which I had relied when I undertook to bring out a new number. I am sorry to say that it is not only the latest number, but that according to present appearances it is also likely to be the last of the series. The publishers find the sale so slow that they fear a considerable loss on the two volumes now completed. The prospect of a continuation seems to depend on the disposition there may be in the directors of our University press to bear part of the expenses. It still remains to be seen if they can be prevailed upon to do so; but it is a thing rather to be wished than hoped for.[52]

Thirlwall's pessimism was justified; the Vice-Chancellor, to whom he applied for help, refused to consider subsidizing an anonymously-edited journal, thus sounding the *Museum*'s death knell.

The *Museum* represented an attempt to promulgate a broader vision of classical learning than that which dominated the teaching and examinations of Cambridge. Did it have any effect on the Cambridge curriculum, or on the reading of undergraduates? One piece of evidence suggests that did not. In 1837, J. M. Kemble contributed a review of three publications on Oxford and Cambridge to the *British and Foreign Review*.[53]

---

[51] Whewell papers, Trinity College Library, R. 6. 5, 1–5.

[52] Thirlwall to Bunsen, 10 October 1833, in *Letters of Thirlwall*, 109. (The *Museum*'s publishers were Deighton of Cambridge.)

[53] Kemble edited the journal from 1835 to 1844.

In it he denounced the concentration on the minutiae of linguistic scholarship which ignored the broader cultural aspects of classical antiquity. His text is worth quoting at length:

The consequence in nine cases out of ten is, that we can construe difficult sentences that would have broken the heart of an Alexandrine grammarian...but the spirit of the original never transfers to us....We count the anapaests of the *Electra*, and flatter ourselves that we feel the poetry of Sophocles. This is nothing but the result of our *cramming* for examinations. We well remember an instance in point. A few years ago some gentlemen, feeling that the higher aims of philology were too much lost sight of in our merely grammatical system, projected a Review which might remedy this defect in the scheme. A few numbers appeared under the title of 'The Philological Museum', and were devoted to the loftier questions of philosophy, mythology and art, arising from the study of particular Greek and Latin authors, or to points of history, law, &c, belonging to various classical periods; nor, in a fair proportion, were various critical treatises wanting. The pages of the Review were adorned by the compositions of Mr Thirlwall and other eminent scholars both of Germany and England; yet after seven or eight numbers it died, out of sheer inanition. Shortly before this consummation, on mentioning the Review in the presence of an undergraduate of considerable classical pretensions, we were annoyed at hearing him say, 'Oh, I never read that; it is of no *use*; there's nothing in it that ever comes into an examination:' he afterwards took the highest classical honours that Cambridge has to bestow.

(Kemble 1837, 188–9)

Oxford was better represented than in the *Museum Criticum*; George Cornewall Lewis and Henry Fynes Clinton in particular wrote articles, the former providing ten pieces in all. Thomas Arnold was sent a copy of the first number and invited to contribute; he replied that his philological knowledge was too superficial and that he preferred to spend his time on religion and politics.[54] In a later letter, he wondered if the Germanic scepticism about historical sources was being carried too far.[55] Other contributors came from the emerging field of English philology, including J. M. Kemble and Hare himself.

The identification of contributors, who signed with initials, has been a matter of some dispute. Hans Aarsleff, who included a useful discussion of the journal in his pioneering book on nineteenth-century English linguistics, attempted to match initials to members of the Philological Society of London; but any such attempt must fall short of proof to varying degrees.[56] Aarsleff's list can be supplemented and corrected by that in Robert Bowes's *Catalogue of Cambridge Books*, a work based on local as well

[54] Arnold to Hare, 9 November 1831. A. P. Stanley, *Life and Correspondence of Thomas Arnold*, 2nd edn (London, 1844), 1. 304.
[55] Arnold to Hare 16 March 1832. N. M. Distad, 'The Philological Museum of 1831–1833', *Victorian Periodicals Newsletter* 18 (December 1972), 27–30, at p. 29.
[56] Aarsleff, *Study of Language*, p. 217; letter to author, 4 July 1989.

as bibliographical knowledge.[57] Combining these and other sources, the identified contributors can be listed as follows:

Table 7.1 Contributors to the *Philological Museum*

CT	Connop Thirlwall	EWH	Edmund Walker Head
GCL	George Cornewall Lewis	HA	Henry Alford
HFC	Henry Fynes Clinton	HFT	Henry Fox Talbot
HM	Henry Malden	IAC	John Cramer
IMK	John Mitchell Kemble	JCH	Julius Charles Hare
JK	John Kenrick	JW	John Wordsworth
TFE	Thomas Flower Ellis	W	William Whewell[58]
WW	William Wordsworth	WW-s	William Wilkins
WSL	Walter Savage Landor		

Of the remaining two contributors, 'TFB' may be Thomas Foster Barham (1794–1869), but evidence is lacking. 'MCY' remains unidentified: no Cambridge alumnus had those initials, and the only Oxford graduate who did, Maurice Charles Yescombe, BA 1820, has left no record of philological achievement.

Of the identified contributors, Clinton, Cramer, and Head were Oxford men, probably brought in by Lewis: Cramer and Clinton were, like Lewis, Christ Church men; and Head was a close personal friend of Lewis's. Hare, Thirlwall, Alford, John Wordsworth, Ellis, Whewell, and Malden were fellows of Trinity; Fox Talbot had been a scholar and was a Porson prizeman. Wilkins was a fellow of Caius and had been architect of a court at Trinity. William Wordsworth was the brother of the Master of Trinity. Landor was a friend of Hare's, who had met him through the publisher John Taylor. Kenrick was a dissenter who taught at Manchester College. He had studied in Germany and translated C. G. Zumpt's Latin grammar into English; he also edited the fifth edition (1832) of the Greek grammar of August Matthiae, which had been translated by Edward Blomfield. The group thus testifies to the talent Trinity had produced in the previous decade or so; but the Oxford contribution, though smaller, is not insignificant (especially if we remember Cornewall Lewis's ten articles).

Conclusion

Both the similarities and the differences between the two *Museums* deserve to be noticed. Both were edited from Trinity; both closed down when their editors left there. In each case, the editors left Cambridge for ecclesiastical preferments—though in Thirlwall's case this followed his removal from office at Trinity. Their university was a

---

[57] R. Bowes, *Catalogue of Cambridge Books* (Cambridge, 1894), 320.
[58] Whewell had also contributed an (anonymous) letter to the *Museum Criticum* (1. 514–19). For the attribution, see Todhunter 1876, 1.30.

branch of the Church of England, and the career paths of Monk and Blomfield, Hare and Thirlwall, led out of academe and into the hierarchy of the Church—to an arch-deaconry for Hare and to bishoprics for the other three. Thirlwall became famous for his *History of Greece* (8 vols, 1835–40), though it was soon overshadowed by that of his friend George Grote; Hare published nothing on classical topics after his preferment. That is also true, with minor exceptions, for Monk and Blomfield, but the other feature which distinguishes them from their two successors is that they were 'Greek-play bishops': it was their expertise in editing Greek texts which brought them to the atten-tion of the leaders of the Church.[59] And this brings us back to the ties between classical scholarship and Anglicanism. The most striking difference between the two journals relates to the changing conception of the nature and scope of classical scholarship in the 1820s and 1830s. The Porsonian stress on the detailed analysis of texts (almost all those of Greek drama) gave way to a broader conception influenced by the compara-tive philology of Bopp, Rask, and Grimm and the historiography of Niebuhr.[60] The *Philological Museum*'s contributors included members of the Liberal Anglican group who tried to use classical scholarship in the service of Anglicanism; the world of the journal, though it continued to publish detailed critical scholarship, was thus signifi-cantly different from that of its predecessor.[61] Another contemporary movement of ideas is reflected in the change from Latin to English in the two titles ('Museum' being conveniently ambiguous). We have seen that for Monk the question was open, though he preferred to use English in order to gain a wider readership for the *Museum Criticum*. The use of the vernacular in academic contexts was a feature of heated schol-arly debate in the first half of the nineteenth century. Conservative Anglicans objected strongly to it, Christopher Wordsworth (son of the Master of Trinity) going so far as to declare that its use in academic annotation indirectly threatened Christian faith.[62]

In assessing this mixture of similarity and difference, we need to remember that the older and younger editors were only half a generation apart (born in 1784 and 1786, and 1795 and 1797, respectively), and that they overlapped at Trinity in the first half of the 1820s. What did the older and younger men think of each other? Monk wrote to his fiancée Jane Hughes on 1 March 1818 that 'Thirlwall, who was a Charterhouse man, is the best scholar that I have ever examined—and certainly the best that has been in the University since Charles Blomfield.'[63] But when Monk resigned the Greek chair in 1823, Thirlwall wrote to Hare, 'I hope Monk will have a worthier successor.'[64] Thirlwall's

---

[59] For the Greek play bishops, see Stray 1998a, 39, 41, 61; Burns and Stray 2011.

[60] Though as we have seen, the new wave had little impact on the Cambridge examination system.

[61] The risks attendant on this strategy are illustrated by the career of Thirlwall's Trinity College pupil J. W. Donaldson (1811–61). Donaldson sought to defend the Church through his scholarship, seeing him-self as a 'Protestant philologer'; his heterodoxy brought about his dismissal as headmaster of King Edward VI School, Bury St Edmunds. See C. A. Stray, 'John William Donaldson', in Todd 2004, 253–5.

[62] C. Wordsworth, 'On the practice of publishing ancient authors with English notes', *British Magazine* 13 (1838), 243–6; 1998a, 100. For Wordsworth see 2016b

[63] Monk papers, Trinity College Library, Cambridge; quoted by permission of the Master and Fellows.

[64] Letter of 29 May 1823, in Thirlwall 1881, 69.

dismissive statement surely referred to the style and scope of Monk's scholarship rather than (or as well as) its quality. The account of Hare's teaching quoted above also suggests that while it was firmly based on a Porsonian focus on linguistic detail, it went beyond this to broader concerns. The two *Museums*, then, taken together, reflected a moment of transition between two styles of classical scholarship, but one in which the old style was not so much rejected, as carried over into the new.

The *Museum Academicum* (1841–2)

In 1841 a plot to revive the *Philological Museum* was hatched by a group of young Oxonians: Benjamin Jowett, Henry Liddell, Robert Scott, and Arthur Stanley. All four were to become celebrated: Liddell as Dean of Christ Church, Scott as master of Balliol, and both as editors of the famous Greek lexicon; Jowett as Master of Balliol after Scott; Stanley as Dean of Westminster and biographer of his old headmaster, Arnold of Rugby. The project seems to have been born in the spring of 1841. In June Jowett wrote to Robert Scott, then Vicar of Duloe, a Balliol living in Cornwall:

Stanley has, I believe, written to you about a scheme in which he is deeply interested, viz. the establishment of a philological journal. At the present time, I think it would be of incalculable advantage if it took off in any measure the minds of both readers and writers in some degree from Theological Controversy. The only chance of it's succeeding (I do not mean in a pecuniary way, for this I suppose we must not think of) would be in its uniting of persons interested in philology and ancient history. At Cambridge Stanley thinks that Vaughan, the 2 Lushingtons &c would be likely to join, and that his connexion Archdeacon Hare would be willing to assist, and has probably papers intended for the Philological Museum. The London University people Mr Long and Dr Smith &c had a similar scheme, but would be quite willing instead to unite in an Oxford philological journal. They had got a promise of assistance from Prof Welcker of Bonn and some other German philologists, all of whom they would be willing to transfer to us. So that I really think there would be a fair prospect of success in the best sense of the word.[65]

Jowett's letter shows that Stanley had already been in touch with George Long, Professor of Greek at University College London, and William Smith, whose *Dictionary of Greek and Roman Antiquities* had been appearing in monthly parts since January 1840 (Chapter 9). It also makes plain the depth of the current preoccupation with the Tractarian controversy in Oxford, fuelled by the appearance in February 1841 of Newman's Tract 90. 'Archdeacon Hare' was Julius Hare, editor of the *Philological Museum* and Stanley's uncle (hence 'his connexion'). In November Hare seems to have promised his nephew material left over from the *Philological Museum* for the new

---

[65] Jowett to Scott, June 1841. Scott papers, Pusey House, Oxford, packet 1. The men referred to were Charles Vaughan and Edmund and Henry Lushington (all of Trinity); George Long and William Smith (see the next paragraph); and Friedrich Welcker, a German classical scholar known for his engagement with archaeology as well as literary study.

journal, tentatively entitled *Museum Academicum* but usually referred to by Stanley as 'Blatt' (German for a magazine). He also offered to solicit material from his former co-editor Connop Thirlwall, and wrote to Henry Fynes Clinton, author of *Fasti Hellenici* (1824–34), whom we met in Chapter 3:

I feel sure that you are still among the few persons now remaining in England who take a lively interest in classical philology...I cannot doubt that you will rejoice to hear that a scheme is now on foot to establish a journal of the same kind as the Philological Museum. The editor is of your university, which is nowadays eclipsing ours in public notoriety; and I believe he is a relation or connexion of yours, Arthur Stanley, of University....My reason for writing to you is to express a hope that you will lend him your assistance, which I myself found of such great value, when I was engaged in a similar undertaking.[66]

Hare apparently also offered to write to John Kenrick, a well-known ancient historian who like Hare himself had been greatly influenced by German scholarship; but Kenrick was a Unitarian, and Stanley was alarmed at the mention of his name and asked his uncle not to write to him:

The mention of Kenrick suggests a difficulty which has more than once almost caused me to give up the whole thing in despair—viz. first, a belief that no Newmanist of this place would take any part in a publication, if a Unitarian minister's name was to appear amongst its originators. In which case I should be much afraid of its blessing as far as Oxford is concerned, instead of abating discussion; especially as the so-called liberal party of this place, which is the worst specimen of that name I ever saw, would be thus called to lay their hands more upon it.

(Stanley to Hare, 24 November 1841)

In the following month, Stanley told Hare that he hoped the journal would be launched in the following May; but on 2 May 1842, he reported:

the melancholy fact that on the 1st of May which should have witnessed its birth, it has received what I believe to be its deathblow. The booksellers who originally proposed to undertake it, and who began by making really magnificent offers to us, are so much alarmed by a letter from Deighton, stating the loss he had sustained from the Philological Museum, that they decline having any thing to do with it, & after an epistolary consultation with my coeditors, which ended on Saturday, we have come to the conclusion that nothing can be done, & that we must let it die or [yet] sleep till more propitious times arrive.

(Stanley to Hare, 2 May 1842)

J. and J. J. Deighton were a long-established Cambridge firm of printers and publishers; they had produced the *Philological Museum*, and evidently made a considerable loss. Once the Oxford firm who had agreed to bring out Stanley's journal (we do not know who they were) learned this, they evidently backed out of their agreement with him.

---

[66] Julius Hare to Henry Fynes Clinton, 4 Dec. [1841]. Christ Church Library, MS 500. Stanley and Clinton were in fact unrelated.

The account of the 'Blatt' project given above is as far as I am aware the first to be published. Stanley's first biographer, R. E. Prothero, quoted an undated 1841 letter from Stanley to his sister (Prothero 1893, I: 306) in which he lamented that:

The business of the 'Philological Museum' brought home to me the miserably unsatisfactory character of the so-called Liberals here, and the impossibility of acting with the Newmanites, in whose moral feelings I should so much more sympathise.

Prothero himself remarked only that Stanley's 'attempt to create fresh interest by founding a philosophical [sic] and classical journal proved unsuccessful' (Prothero 1893, 1:304). A discussion of Jowett's relations with Scott by John Prest quoted from Jowett's letter to Scott of June 1841, cited above, adding 'This is presumably the origin of the Classical Museum' (Prest 1966, 5–6; cf. Naiditch 1991, 132 n. 23). A recent biography of Stanley (Witheridge 2013) makes no mention of the project; Stanley's biographers have been more interested in his involvement in current theological debates over Tractarianism, to which Stanley himself alludes, or in the biographical activity into which he plunged after the death of his mentor Thomas Arnold on 12 March 1842. The failure of the project must have been reported informally at the time; a glimpse can be had in the correspondence of Charles Bristed, an American who went from Yale to Trinity College, Cambridge in 1840 (Bristed 2008). In December 1842, he wrote to his old teacher Theodore Woolsey of Yale that 'The classical journal which was to have been published at Oxford is blown up.'[67]

The Classical Museum (1843–9)

The baton now passed to London, and to the Classical Museum, which began to appear in 1843 without any editorial input from the Oxford scholars, though they did later contribute to it. The new Museum was recognisably a continuator of the Philological Museum, drawing on continental scholarship both directly and indirectly (Naiditch 1991, 132–9).[68] Yet it also bore the scars of the controversy Stanley and his friends had sought to avoid, since its editors announced in the first issue (June 1843) that 'Biblical criticism and all subjects of a religious or theological nature will be excluded' (Classical Museum 1, 'Preface', vi; 'Advertisement', ii). William Smith, later to be editor of the Quarterly Review, and knighted shortly before his death in 1893, was a nonconformist who taught in low-church colleges (see Chapter 9). His collaborator, the one-armed Alsatian Leonhard Schmitz, was an Edinburgh headmaster, and thus similarly free from the glories and perils of Anglican preferment. Reflecting their locations and contacts, the journal was printed by Pillans of Edinburgh and published by Taylor and Walton, publishers to the University of London. Schmitz and Smith were in no danger of being promoted out of the editorial seats; yet the Classical

---

[67] Bristed to Woolsey, 1 Dec. 1842. Woolsey Family Papers, Yale University Library, MS 562, Folder 131.
[68] Thirlwall was invited to contribute to the Museum, but declared that he was too busy working on his History of Greece (Thirlwall 1881, 183).

Museum closed after seven years, apparently because it had not attracted enough subscriptions to be viable.

As I suggested above, we tend to think of nineteenth-century periodicals in relation to scholarship as moving from a gentlemanly amateurism to a specialized academic activity. The history of the two *Museums* usefully complicates this picture by showing that in an age of general literary reviews, specialized journals were published, which nevertheless had significant links with wider literary and religious movements. Conversely, at the end of the century, when academic classical journals like the *Journal of Hellenic Studies* (1880) and the *Classical Review* (1887) were well established, editors could be found searching, usually in vain, for general 'literary' material for their columns. By the 1920s, the *Classical Review* found it impossible to find such material (2003a, 112). As J. C. Stobart complained in the preface to his *The Glory that was Greece* (Stobart 1911, vi), scholars were now so specialized that they had lost sight both of each other and of the general public.

Bibliographical Appendix

1 *The* Museum Criticum

The *Museum Criticum* is often referred to as having been published in two volumes, which appeared in 1814 and 1826, or together in the latter year.[69] Its original publication, however, was in eight separate issues, printed by the Cambridge University printer John Smith. The first issue probably appeared in the second half of May 1813. H. R. Luard stated in his memoir of Blomfield that 'In May, 1813, the first number ... came forth.'[70] Monk wrote to John Murray on 14 May that printing would take place the following day, and asking him to send covers, as 'the university will empty soon'. On Sunday 16 May, he wrote to Elmsley that 'the Museum Criticum ... will appear this week'; and on 2 July, that sales were good 'considering that the Museum was only published 4 or 5 days before the university emptied'. The reference to 'emptying' is difficult to pin down, as Full Term did not end until the end of June. But we know that Edward Blomfield left Cambridge for Germany on 2 June, and that Monk himself left Cambridge on the 7th (Trinity College exit book). On the 18th, he wrote to Elmsley that 'no 1 is I hear liked at Cambridge and sells well'. The *Courier*, which Murray used to advertise his publications, carried a notice of its appearance under the heading 'Published this day' on 11 June, but this may have been a late notice (other cases are noticed later in this section). No. 2 was published, according to the *Courier*, on 20 November 1813 (Monk wrote to Murray on the 27th that it had been on sale for five days). No. 3 was announced in the *Courier* on 1 April 1814; No. 4, on 9 December 1814. On 4 November, however, Monk had told Murray that 'the books will reach you by tomorrow's waggon'. These four issues were republished in a single volume in 1814. The fifth issue was announced on 30 June 1815; Monk had asked Murray to print covers on the 8th. The sixth was probably published in May 1816: on 15 April Monk told Murray that the issue was complete except for part of an

---

[69] See e.g. Aarsleff 1967, 220, a brief discussion of the *Philological Museum* which underestimates its difference from its predecessor.
[70] *Journal of Classical and Sacred Philology* 4 (1858), 198.

article by Peter Elmsley. The seventh was, according to Monk, 'selling apace' by 19 November 1821. The *Courier* advertisement of 24 December seems to have been a dilatory insertion by Murray, to whom Monk complained on the 12th, 'I have looked in the Courier for the advertisement of the MC every day in vain.' The eighth and final issue was promised 'in a week or two' by Monk on 23 October 1823, and was 'printing' on 29 November (Blomfield to Elmsley: Elmsley papers, Westminster School), but not till 2 May 1826 did Monk tell Murray that it was 'quite ready'. As with the first issue of thirteen years earlier, he was keen that it should be brought out before the University broke up, so it probably appeared in the second half of May 1826. In the same year a revised version of the 1814 volume was reprinted as Volume 1 of a two-volume set, Volume 2 containing issues nos. 5–8.[71]

2 *The* Philological Museum

Six issues of the *Museum* were published by Deighton of Cambridge, 1,015 copies of each issue being printed by John Smith, the Cambridge University printer. In the preface to the first issue, Hare announced that it was proposed to bring out three numbers a year, 'on the first of November, of February, and of May'. It is known that the first was printed in August 1831; publication however was delayed, being announced on 5 Jan. 1832 (*Morning Post*, 5 Jan., 1d). The next four issues were printed in January, April, July, and December 1832, and the final issue in April 1833 (Distad 1972, 29). The second issue was published on 24 March 1832, the third on 20 May; the exact publication dates of the other issues are unknown.[72] The first three issues were reprinted in one volume in 1832, the last three in a second volume in 1833 (hence the conventional dating, 1832–3).

---

[71] The first serious attempt to date the issues was made by Paul Naiditch (Naiditch 1991, 131–2). The more precise datings given here are drawn from the correspondence of J. H. Monk and C. J. Blomfield: Monk papers, Trinity College, Cambridge; Elmsley papers, Westminster School.

[72] The publication dates for the second and third issues are established by entries in the *Athenaeum* 230 (24 March 1832), 198; 239 (26 May 1832), 343, though 'Published this day' has to be taken with a grain of salt.

8

The *Classical Review* and its Precursors

The previous two chapters explored two different kinds of site for classical publishing in the first half of the nineteenth century: articles published in the great reviews (in this case the *Quarterly Review*) and two of the journals dedicated in different ways to the study of the ancient world, the *Museum Criticum* and the *Philological Museum*. This chapter is largely devoted to an account of the founding of a later journal, the *Classical Review* (1887–); but I begin by providing some context. As we have seen in Chapters 6 and 7, until the 1860s the history of classical periodicals is for the most part one of short-term success followed by collapse, and of abortive attempts at continuation or revival. The *Classical Journal* was aimed at antiquarians and country gentlemen; its subscribers were in all likelihood those who also bought the *Edinburgh Review*, its right-wing rival the *Quarterly Review*, the *British Critic*, *Athenaeum*, and other general periodicals. The two *Museums* aimed at a scholarly market, though the subscription lists in the *Classical Museum* included a sprinkling of headmasters and bishops with scholarly pretensions.

We pick up the story with the foundation in 1854 of the *Journal of Classical and Sacred Philology*. Its prime mover was J. E. B. Mayor, a young fellow of St John's College who had just returned to Cambridge from schoolteaching, having published in 1853 an edition of Juvenal which would later grow to two volumes and swell to bursting with parallel passages (Henderson 1998). Mayor was joined by three Cambridge contemporaries, all Trinity men, whose scholarship was both classical and biblical: Fenton Hort, Brooke Westcott, and Joseph Lightfoot.[1] All four had belonged to an informal essay-reading club variously called the Philological Society and Hermes, whose meetings began in May 1845 and apparently ended in May 1848, when some of the members graduated.[2] The journal was printed at Cambridge University Press and sold by a cluster

[1] For their work, see Thompson 2008, 5–121.
[2] Westcott 1903, 1. 45–7. Hort, Westcott, and Lightfoot later formed a remarkable triumvirate within New Testament scholarship, and the first two produced a revised text of the New Testament in 1881. 'Hermes' had been used as the title of several books on philological topics, including James Harris's *Hermes* (1751), John Jamieson's *Hermes Scythicus* (1814) and W. H. Fox Talbot's *Hermes, or Philological Researches* (1838–9). The use of 'Hermes' for the Philological Society has nevertheless has provoked uninformed denunciation from American fundamentalists, who have convinced themselves that the three men were worshippers of Hermes Trismegistus (for a hilariously absurd example, see Riplinger 2008).

of firms, led by Deighton and Macmillan, both of Cambridge. It folded after five years.[3] When the journal was being planned, Mayor had told William Smith, formerly editor of the *Classical Museum* (1843–9), about the project. Smith replied:

> I was very glad to have your announcement of your journal, and hope that it will go on pros-
> perously. I believe the only way to keep it afloat is for a set of men to work at it, for if you
> depend upon stray contributors, you will very rarely get good articles. This was found to be the
> case with the Classical Museum, which we gave up, not for want of friends, for it paid its expenses,
> but because the articles were for the most part so poor that I was really quite ashamed.[4]

The foundation of the *Journal* came just at the point when the conditions for an academic career began to be established, as the first-class graduates who would previously have gone into the church began increasingly to look for university and public-school careers instead (Haig 1986a). In the 1860s and 1870s the long-established *Athenaeum* (1828) and the new *Academy* (1869) provided forums for scholarly discussion, the latter being founded by the supporters of research at Oxford (Roll-Hansen 1957, Beer 2004). The *Academy*'s remit however covered all academic subjects; and besides, some scholars saw it as lacking impartiality. Richard Jebb and his friends, for example, saw it as siding with their bêtes noires J. P. Mahaffy, A. H. Sayce and Heinrich Schliemann (2013a, 126, 131–2). Both journals were however weeklies, and so well placed to carry ongoing discussions. The *Journal of Philology* (1868) was an increasingly erratic biannual, while the *Journal of Hellenic Studies* (1880) appeared annually. The *Classical Review* (1887–), which appeared every month except in August and September, was much better placed to function as an arena of debate than these journals, especially as it carried a large number of reviews.[5]

The *Journal of Philology* (1868–1921)

So far we have seen several unsuccessful attempts to revive or continue failed journals; we now come to a successful attempt, the launch in Cambridge in 1868 of the *Journal of Philology*, already mentioned in Chapter 7. The new journal was represented at the time as a continuation of the *Journal of Classical and Sacred Philology*; this must have been helped by the fact that the older publication had often been referred to as 'the Journal of Philology', which also served as its spine title (see e.g. Donaldson 1856, 144).[6]

---

[3] The final issue was dated December 1859, but the prospectus in the first issue of the *Journal of Philology* stated that it had appeared in March 1860 (*JPh* 1 (1868), [v]).

[4] The letter is a fragment and breaks off here, so has no signature, but is in Smith's hand and carries his address, 31 Regents Villas, St Johns Wood. Smith to Mayor, 18 Feb. 1854: Mayor papers, Trinity College Library, Cambridge, B.15.2.

[5] The *Journal of Philology* did not carry reviews; the *Journal of Hellenic Studies* began to do so only after the *Classical Review*'s first issues were published. For the *Review*'s role in scholarly debate over Bacchylides, see 2009; for a twentieth-century controversy over reviews, 2015. I take this opportunity to correct an egregious error in 2009, 156: the *Edinburgh* and *Quarterly* reviews were both quarterlies and not monthlies.

[6] The editorial preface to the first issue declared that the Journal 'may be regarded as a second series of the *Journal of Classical and Sacred Philology*': *JPh* 1 (1868), [v]; in November 1867 W. G. Clark told

As its title suggests, the ally counted on by its successor to appeal to a substantial market was (a sign of the times) not biblical scholarship but comparative philology; and like its American contemporary *Transactions of the American Philological Association* (1869), it carried articles on languages other than Latin and Greek, and on philology in general. The late 1860s saw a reform of the Cambridge Classical Tripos which added history and philosophy to its range, the beginnings of intercollegiate lectures in Classics, and the foundation in 1867 of a chair of Sanskrit (whose first incumbent, E. B. Cowell, was a founder of the Cambridge Philological Society). It must have seemed a good time to break the curse which had afflicted previous journals.

The *Journal of Philology* was typical of later Victorian journals in benefiting from organized support from professional academics, but its chequered history illustrates the difference between support and control. The *Journal* was a private enterprise based on an agreement between its publisher, Macmillan, and its founding editors, W. G. Clark and Aldis Wright of Trinity College and J. E. B. Mayor of St John's. In 1872 the recently-founded Cambridge Philological Society purchased a discounted bulk subscription to provide copies for its members. Soon afterwards, Clark was struck down by depression and left Cambridge, while Mayor failed to pull his weight, so that Wright was left effectively in sole charge (Wright, 'Notice', *JPh* 8 (1879) 176), and publication became irregular. By 1878 the journal was in debt to Macmillan to the tune of £150, and the Cambridge Philological Society looked to Oxford for additional subscribers to keep it afloat. Negotiations were opened with the Homerist D. B. Monro of Oriel College, who brought in about forty-five subscribers, and Ingram Bywater of Exeter College was appointed sub-editor, to work with Wright and a Cambridge sub-editor, Henry Jackson of Trinity. It was hoped that the debt could be cleared through the new subscriptions and by selling off back issues.[7] The new arrangements improved the financial health of the journal and restored regularity of issue, but around 1900 publication became irregular once more: no issues appeared in 1902, 1905, 1909, and 1911 (Naiditch 1998, 662). Despite continual requests from subscribers for an index to the journal, neither Macmillan nor the Philological Society provided one.[8] Bywater and Wright died in 1914, to be replaced by H. W. Garrod of Oxford and Arthur Platt of University College London; Henry Jackson became chief editor, but was aging and infirm. In the same year Macmillan raised the cover price, and this, combined with the

---

J. S. Blackie, 'We are going to revive the Journal of Classical and Sacred Philology. Mayor, Wright & I are to be joint editors.' National Library of Scotland, MS 2628 f. 201. Elsewhere it was sometimes referred to as the 'Cambridge Journal of Philology', for example by the Oxford scholar Henry Nettleship, *Academy* 13 Aug. 1870, 303.

[7] Minute books of the Cambridge Philological Society 1874–1923, Cambridge University Library, Add. MSS 7579–81, 14 Feb.–23 May 1878.

[8] In 1909 Bywater wrote to Jackson, 'I think that the time has come for us to have a proper index to the 30 volumes of the Journal, as it requires a very good memory to remember its contents.' Bywater to Jackson, Trinity College Library, Add. MS a.290/165.

failure to produce any issues in 1916–17, was the final straw.[9] The Philological Society had felt for some time that the *Classical Quarterly*, founded in 1909 and admirably regular in its publication, would be a better journal to offer its members, and in 1921 it cancelled its bulk subscription to the *Journal of Philology*, which ceased publication.[10]

The *Classical Review*

The history of the *Review* begins in 1884. At this point the German review journal *Philologische Wochenschrift* (Philological Weekly) was three years old, and was about to be joined by a rival, after its editors defected to another firm to found the *Wochenschrift für klassische Philologie*;[11] the founding of the earlier journal may have provided the impetus for the establishment of the *Review*. In January 1884 Joseph Mayor of King's College London, younger brother of the Cambridge professor of Latin J. E. B. Mayor, proposed a quarterly review journal to Cambridge University Press, to be called the 'Chronicle of Classical Philology'. Joseph Mayor is now almost forgotten by classicists, except perhaps for his edition of Cicero's *De Natura Deorum*.[12] He also published on moral philosophy, and edited the unpublished works of his mentor John Grote, the Cambridge philosopher and brother of the historian of Greece. Mayor's marriage to Grote's niece in 1864 deprived him of his fellowship at St John's College, Cambridge; he served as headmaster of the Kensington Proprietary School (1864–8), then moved to King's College London as professor of Classical Literature (1870–9), before transferring to an unsalaried chair of moral philosophy. His concern to provide his pupils with guides to scholarly literature led him to produce a *Guide to the Choice of Classical Books*, which went into several editions.[13] In the later 1870s he contributed to the *Contemporary Review*, founded in 1866, one of the leading general journals in Britain, and in 1877–8 was editor of its section on current literature, at a salary of £300 p.a. He saw its function as providing 'a thorough review of classified current literature', very much prefiguring the function of the *Classical Review*.[14] He even became a director, in a turbulent period when the editor of the *Review* ran it into debt. At this point he often refers in his diary to his work for 'C R'. In 1883 he resigned his King's College chair, and so was well placed, in early retirement and, with his experience of editing and procuring reviews, to be founding editor of (another) C R—the *Classical Review*.

---

[9] Bywater and Wright, as we have seen, were replaced in 1914 by H. W. Garrod and Arthur Platt; Jackson died in 1921.

[10] See the characteristically frank account by Sir William Ridgeway (Ridgeway 1923). The journal's long-serving editor Henry Jackson died in the same year.

[11] At the same time, *Philologische Wochenschrift* added the prefix '*Berliner*' to its title.

[12] For Mayor, see the entries in Todd 2004 and *ODNB*. Neither mentions his involvement with the *Contemporary Review*.

[13] First edn 1874, second edn 1879, new supplement 1896. The first two were published by George Bell, the supplement by David Nutt, who had been supplying review copies for the *Classical Review*.

[14] J. B. Mayor, diary 1868–82, Trinity College Library, uncatalogued, entry for 11 Mar. 1877.

On 30 January1884, Mayor wrote to Charles Clay, a printer who had been a partner in Cambridge University Press since 1854 and in 1874 had been appointed Secretary to the Syndics, the Press's managing committee.[15] The letter evidently arose from a previous discussion.

You wished me to put down on paper what my ideas were with regard to a new classical journal.

I think every body must feel the very unsatisfactory state of things at present. It is a mere toss up whether a classical book is reviewed at all, whether it is reviewed by a competent man, & whether it is reviewed within a month, or at the end of a couple of years. There is really no criticism & no chronicle of classical work.

It seems to me that there must be a large number of people who feel this & would be ready to support a periodical of the following nature, which might be called a Chronicle of Classical Philology, & appear say once a quarter.

1 All books published in English, which bear on the Latin Greek or Hebrew (?) language and literature, to be reviewed within 6 months from the time of their publication.

2 A summary to be given of the best foreign reviews of classical books in each quarter, and independent notices of the most important books.

3 Modern languages, Assyriology and Egyptology to be entirely excluded, and no original articles submitted.

4 I think the chronicle should be cheap (say 4/- a year) so as to be taken in by all schoolmasters & students interested in Classics.

5 I should be ready to be joint editor with others – but not to have the sole responsibility.

I throw these out as some suggestions for your consideration.

The central proposal in the prospectus was for the publication of summaries of foreign periodicals. In order to understand the importance of this proposal, we need to remember how hard it was to keep abreast of journal publishing in Classics. In London the only serious depository was the British Museum Library, but it was not easy to gain access to recent accessions, and accessioning was a slow process. While Richard Jebb was working on his edition of Bacchylides in the early 1890s he more than once wrote to Frederic Kenyon, of the British Museum, to ask for notification of recent articles relevant to his project (2013a, 214–16, 222–3). In 1898 A. E. Housman wrote to W. G. Hale, Professor of Latin at Chicago, that he had not seen his paper on the Vatican MS of Catullus:

Nor have I seen Schulze's paper. In Chicago no doubt you see all the periodicals as they appear: in London there is no place of the sort. This College [University College London] takes in eight or nine, but Hermes is not among them: the British Museum tries hard and with some success to withhold from readers everything less than a year old.[16]

[15] Cambridge University Press archives, Cambridge University Library, Pr B 13.c.80–1.

[16] Housman to Hale, 21 Nov. 1898; Burnett 2007, 1.113–14. Hale's note on the Catullus MS appeared in *CR* 12 (Dec. 1898), 447–9; Schulze's in *Hermes* 33 (1898) 511–12.

It must have been this proposal on which the Trinity College classicist Arthur Verrall commented to his ex-teacher Richard Jebb in February:

I cannot say I feel sanguine about the 'scholars' review'. The same thing, or something very like it, has been planned or tried so often. One attempt, perfectly honest I believe in its original conception, ended in the Academy!   (Verrall to Jebb, 4 February 1884: 2013, 217)

The *Academy*, as we have seen, was viewed with suspicion by both men, as a journal where J. P. Mahaffy and his allies published scathing reviews of books by Jebb and his friends. Nothing seems to have happened as a result of Mayor's proposal, but two years later he pursued the theme, while sending Clay a German review of his edition of Cicero *De natura deorum*, which the Press had been bringing out since 1880: the third and final volume had been published in 1885.

It shows an absurd state of things when the works of English scholars are reviewed abroad & not in England. I believe you sent copies of each of my volumes as it came out to the 'Spectator', & yet, as far as I know, there has been no notice of any of them.[17] ... if they are in the habit of treating the more solid books which issue from the University Press in the same way, I think it would be worth while in the name of the Syndicate to say that if they did not show more respect to the University, no more books from the Press would be sent to them. I think it is a great pity that the Universities have not got a critical review of their own....[18]

Later the same month, Mayor's thoughts were turning back to the idea of a new journal:

the number of readers interested in higher classics is comparatively small ... unless some pressure is put upon the editors of periodicals, they do not think it worth while to notice such books, but simply get what they can by selling them to 2nd-hand booksellers; from which I draw the inference that it is not worth while sending copies of these books to them, unless they promise to review them, But I think that the proper & dignified course for the Universities to adopt is to start a learned review themselves, or to graft it on the Journal of Philology, which I believe would get a much wider circulation, if it undertook to give an estimate, however brief, of every classical work as it appeared.[19]

We do not know what Clay's response was, but in the next few months, Mayor evidently set to work to gather support for the new journal. A major concern was to assemble a group of supporters who would subscribe to, contribute to, and in some cases edit the journal. Mayor is likely to have had the need for such a group impressed on him by his brother John, who as we saw above had had the same message from William Smith, and will also have remembered the recent financial problems of the *Journal of Philology*. Joseph Mayor will also have seen the editorial statement in the final 1883 issue of the

[17] Mayor's edition was not reviewed in the *Spectator*. The first volume was reviewed in the *Academy* of 24 Jan. 1881, 83; the complete edition in the *Athenaeum* of 2 Oct. 1886, 426, and in the *Saturday Review* of 11 Dec. 1886, 187–8.
[18] Cambridge University Library, UA Pr.B.13.B.70, 3 March 1886.
[19] Cambridge University Library, UA Pr.B.13.B.71, 29 March 1886.

Philologische Wochenschrift (no. 52, 29 December 1883, cols.1663–4), where the change of title to *Berliner Philologische Wochenschrift* was announced, and it was claimed that more than 300 scholars were at the disposal of the journal, among whom were some of the most important authorities. The process of assembling a community of scholars, however, brought with it problems arising from existing tensions between opposed factions. Among those Mayor contacted in August 1886 was Richard Jebb, then Regius Professor of Greek at Glasgow, to whom he broached the subject on the 7th.[20] A subsequent letter to Jebb gives a glimpse of these problems:

I am very glad to find you so strongly in favour of the proposed classical Review. I quite agree with you as to the necessity of keeping clear of the Academy clique, especially Sayce, Mahaffy and the Simcoxes.[21] Since you wrote I have heard from Nutt's, offering to give any help in the way of getting German books & contributing to expenses. Our next difficulty will be in finding enough subscribers to pay our way, especially if we are to pay for the reviews, as I suppose we must do in the end, even if patriotic individuals are willing to write for nothing at first. I forget whether I told you that we hope we may get a room lent, where we may keep the foreign reviews for the use of our subscribers. (Mayor to Jebb, 17 August 1866: Jebb papers, Trinity College Library, Cambridge)

The running battles between the followers of Sayce and Mahaffy and of Jebb have already been mentioned; since Sayce worked on the Hittites, the two camps were informally known as the Jebusites and the Hittites, after tribes who featured in the Old Testament (2013a, 76).

The letter also throws light on a central part of Mayor's plan: the importation of foreign books for review. David Nutt, founded in 1829, was a London bookselling firm which specialized in importing continental scholarly works; since 1878 it had been run by the founder's son Alfred Nutt, who expanded its publishing activities and was a productive scholar in folklore and Celtic studies. The idea of a library and reading room grew naturally from the proposal to import foreign periodicals: the imported volumes would gradually build into a specialized reference library.

By November, Mayor had assembled a group of supporters, but felt he needed more. He wrote to Jebb on 4 November 1886 (Jebb Papers, Trinity College Library):

I inclose you two copies of our draft circular. We want to get about 20 more names before sending out to the public. Would you mind writing to Butcher to ask whether he would become a contributor and what department he would undertake, perhaps Homer along with D. B. Monro? I should also be very much obliged if you would suggest any improvements either in the content or form of the circular. I am in hopes the Pitt Press Syndicate[22] will undertake the publication—if not, there is no doubt that Messrs Nutt will be very glad to do it.

---

[20]   Mayor's letter is reprinted in 2013a, 141–2; later letters about the scheme are at pp. 143, 151–2.

[21]   The brothers Augustus and William Simcox of Queen's College Oxford, to which Sayce also belonged; Augustus was a contributor to the *Academy*.

[22]   The Syndics of Cambridge University Press, who published the Pitt Press series of school books. For a brief account of their dealings with Mayor, see McKitterick 2004, 111–12.

Holden and Wayte[23] rather hang back from editorial responsibility, mainly on the ground of their work for the University of London. I am quite ready to act along with A. M. Cook,[24] but I should prefer to share the work with some more. Can you think of anyone in London? As far as ability and knowledge goes A. Goodwin professor at University College would do, but everyone says he is very queer.[25] What do you think of Leaf?[26] We hope now to start either in January or February. If the latter, we should miss out one month in the summer so as to make up the 10 numbers for the year. My brother promises a review of Friedländer's Martial for the first number.[27] I hope you would also be able to give a report on what has been done on Sophocles.

On the next day, Mayor heard from Clay that CUP would publish the Review if a bond of £150 could be raised and 500 subscribers guaranteed. In his response, Mayor raised the question of Nutt's role in the *Review*; apparently the Press had removed his name from the draft circular which was to be sent to prospective subscribers. The Syndics had at first proposed that Nutt should be allowed a free page of advertising in exchange for his providing copies of foreign books and journals, but then hardened their position. Mayor told Clay on 2 December that:

From an interview held last week at the Pitt Press with a sub-committee appointed by the Syndicate, I further gathered that the Syndics considered it inexpedient for the University Press to connect itself with any one London firm to the exclusion of others, and that in fact they preferred that the Press should trust to itself for procuring foreign books.

I have spoken to several of those who are interested in the proposed review, and I find a very general feeling, that the active cooperation of one of the foreign booksellers in London is essential to the success of the review, and that as Mr Nutt devotes himself especially to the sale of classical books, and has shown his readiness to assist in every way, he should be asked to be publisher of the review, since the Cambridge Press Syndicate do not see their way to entering into any sort of partnership with him.[28]

In December Mayor was able to report to Jebb that more than eighty contributors had been recruited, but he was determined to keep up the campaign, and in January 1887 was still pressing Jebb to act as an agent for Scotland:

Please don't forget to ask Sellar Ramsay Campbell & any other Scotch professors you may think desirable. I think we have swept Trin. Coll. Dublin, with the exception of the 'Hittites'.[29]

[23] Hubert Holden and William Wayte, both among the original supporters of the *Review*, were examiners for the University.

[24] Alfred Marshall Cook is now remembered, if at all, as the author of classical textbooks produced in collaboration with his colleague at St Paul's School, E. C. Marchant (Todd 2004, 200–1). The original proposal for a review journal had come from him (2013c, 141).

[25] Alfred Goodwin was Professor of Latin at UCL from 1876 till his premature death aged forty-two in 1892. He also held the chair of Greek in 1879–80 and 1889–92.

[26] Walter Leaf, Homeric scholar and banker: see Todd 2004, 567–8.

[27] The review appeared on pp. 56–8 of the second issue (April 1887).

[28] Mayor to Clay, 2 Dec. 1886. Cambridge University Library, UA Pr.B.13.C.80–1. 'The Pitt Press' refers to the building which functioned as the headquarters of CUP.

[29] J. P. Mahaffy and his supporters.

Cecil Smith[30] of the Brit. Museum agrees to act as sub-editor & will look after archaeology. I think he will be of great use to us.[31]

In the same month, Alfred Nutt issued a circular announcing the launch of the *Review*, in which he gave a list of 116 contributors and invited subscriptions. He named Mayor as editor, with three assistant editors: Alfred Church, Professor of Latin at University College London; Arthur Cook of St Paul's School, the original proposer of the *Review*; and Cecil Smith of the British Museum. On 6 January, another circular, marked 'private and confidential', was sent out to contributors over Mayor's signature. They were offered a payment of 10s a page for their work, but Mayor explained that sales would probably not cover expenses, and invited them to defer claims for payment till the end of the year. Books reviewed were to be kept by reviewers, but periodicals were to be returned to Nutt. Mayor went on to list topics (Greek literature, Latin literature, philology, history, and antiquities), most of the ancient authors and subdivisions carrying the names of contributors who had been assigned to them. His brother John, for example, was assigned Seneca, Quintilian, Pliny, Aulus Gellius, Juvenal, Persius, and Martial; an expansive range probably suggested by the generous and optimistic J. E. B. Mayor himself. Finally, he gave a list of ninety periodicals to be reviewed; about half of them were German-language periodicals.[32]

The building of a scholarly community to support the journal inevitably ran into trouble when it encountered conflicts between members of that community. The Jebb/Mahaffy antagonism was the most serious obstacle Mayor encountered, and he was obliged to soothe Jebb on several occasions, taking the line that a studied neutrality made criticism of Mahaffy more effective:

I have refused to admit Mahaffy when Palmer wrote to ask that his name might be admitted to our list, and I got Fowler to add the last clause in his notice of 'Alexander's Empire' (p. 204) in which he speaks of his want of taste. Altogether my opinion about M. & his set is just the same as your own, but I feel very strongly that it is better for us to treat them with distant courtesy rather than to taboo them or to attack them directly. Any judgment we pass on their crotchets e.g. on Paley's Homeric view, is I think likely to have more weight than it would have if we declared open war against them. Besides, I think it would have a bad effect on foreign readers. Even as a question of your own personal interest I think it is better that you should feel more of the support of a review which is felt to be generally impartial, than of one which is looked upon as a blind partisan.

I hope what I have said will satisfy you that there is no fear of the Rev. becoming a 2nd Academy, & no possibility of our doing any thing which could justify you in leaving us. I have

---

[30] The tenth and final issue of the first volume of *CR* (Dec.1887) initiated a section on archaeology, with contributions by Smith, who soon afterwards changed his name to Harcourt-Smith. He was promoted to Keeper of Greek and Roman Antiquities at the British Museum in 1904, and was director of the Victoria and Albert Museum 1909–24.

[31] Mayor to Jebb, 17 Jan. 1887. Jebb papers, Trinity College Library, Cambridge.

[32] Both circulars, of 3pp and 7pp respectively, were headed 'The Classical Review'. The only copies I know of are bound at the front of the first volume of the *Review* in Trinity College Library, Cambridge. (My thanks to Neil Hopkinson for sending me copies.)

to thank you more than any one else for your encouragement in making the start & I shall continue to look to you as one of our best supports.[33]

In the previous month a prospectus had been issued which emphasized the need for a review journal to report and comment on publications, and was careful to renounce competition with the *Journal of Philology* and its 'original articles' of 'deep research'. The names of thirty supporters appeared beneath it: thirteen from Oxford, nine from Cambridge, the rest either from elsewhere or retired Oxbridge academics. The contact names given are those of Henry Nettleship of Oxford and James Smith Reid of Cambridge. Localism is avoided in the rhetoric; a journal which was based in one place would attract resentment in the other. (The prospectus is reproduced below, in the Appendix to this chapter.)

The first issue of the *Review* appeared in March 1887, by which time nearly 150 contributors had been enlisted. The issue led off with a few short articles, most of the rest being reviews. This pattern persisted for almost a century, the original plan of concentrating on reviews not being realized until the mid-1970s. The issue was welcomed in the *Saturday Review* in an article which included criticisms of specific contributions and thought the issue rather thin, but declared that the launch of the *Review* 'could be an important development for English scholarship'. In February 1888 the same journal reviewed the first volume of *CR*, concluding that it had been 'well conceived, well managed, and well executed'.[34]

Mayor soon began negotiating an American connection, collecting support from several scholars, including W. W. Goodwin of Harvard. By September the New York publisher Putnam's was being invited to co-publish, with a commitment to take 150 copies; an extra sheet was to be added, to be edited by a US scholar. In the end Ginn of Boston became the US co-publishers and William G. Hale (Chicago), Thomas D. Seymour (Yale) and John W. White (Harvard) joined the editorial board. Mayor's letters to R. C. Jebb indicate that this plan, like the expansion strategy of the *Journal of Philology* a decade earlier, was driven by financial need. In October 1887 Mayor reported on a meeting between Alfred Nutt and some of the contributors at which Nutt told them that the journal had 687 subscribers, and that he sold about 100 additional copies per month, but would probably end the year with a loss of £50. Mayor added, 'We can hardly understand this as he calculated that the sale of 500 copies would pay expenses. However he says that advertising has brought in very little'.[35] The contributors agreed to Nutt's proposal that postage should be charged for, and the price raised

---

[33] Mayor to Jebb, 30 Sept. 1887: Jebb Papers. Mahaffy's colleague Arthur Palmer was Professor of Latin at Trinity College Dublin 1880–97. For Mahaffy's exclusion, cf. 2013c, 149. W. W. Fowler's review of Mahaffy's *Alexander's Empire* (*CR* 1, July 1887, 203–4) ends thus: 'It is all the more to be regretted that we are occasionally offended by faults of taste, which betray a tendency to loose historical thinking, and a desire to make the book readable by means which a judicious writer would on second thoughts reject.'

[34] 'An English classical review', *Saturday Review*, 5 March 1887, 345–6; 'The Classical Review', *Saturday Review*, 11 February 1888, 172–4.

[35] Mayor to Jebb, 21 Oct. 1887. Jebb papers, Trinity College Library.

from 10s to 12s per issue, on condition that the size be increased to forty-eight pages. (Perhaps the reviewer's view, referred to above, that the first issue was rather thin, should be taken literally.)[36]

An editorial statement in the February 1889 issue, announcing the new American link, concluded that 'for a fruitful study of Greek and Roman antiquity the practical judgment of the English is no less needful than the unwearied research and the daring speculation of the Germans, or the lucidity and mental vivacity of the French'. [37] This is interesting both for the assimilation of England (read: Britain) and the USA as 'English', and for the initiation of a topos which reappears during World War 1, where however the triad identified is England, the USA, and Germany.[38] Such comparisons were common in the 1880s and 1890s, as new alliances were built across the Atlantic and as the adulation of Germany faded in the wake of the battle of Sedan in 1870 and the Kulturkampf of the 1890s. The conflicted attitude among American classicists toward both English and German scholarly models is memorably illustrated by Paul Shorey's address on the occasion of the American Philological Association's fiftieth anniversary (Shorey 1919). In seeking to provide 'a little more justice to American scholarship than it usually receives either from American themselves or from foreigners' (p. 34), Shorey (1857–1934), the first Professor of Greek at the University of Chicago, characterizes English scholarship as 'brilliantly amateurish' (p. 48) and German philology as tending toward 'the abuse of conjecture and the pyramiding of hypothesis' (p. 44). His conclusion—a tripartite comparison of three professors of Greek, Richard Jebb of Cambridge, Ulrich von Wilamowitz-Moellendorff of Berlin, and Basil Gildersleeve of Johns Hopkins—leads to a prophecy, addressed to both England and Germany, that 'we shall outstrip you both when time is ripe' (58–61).

As the *Review*'s size leapt from 336 pages in 1888 to 482 pages in 1889, its focus on reviews soon made an impact on other journals. For example, in 1890 Basil Gildersleeve, founder and editor of the *American Journal of Philology* (1880–) wrote to Herbert Weir Smyth of Harvard:

Have you anything for me?... A review would be especially welcome—as the supply of that department of the Journal has been somewhat interfered with by the transfer of so much work to the Classical Review.[39]

Gildersleeve's concern will have been sharpened by his knowledge that he himself had previously built transatlantic bridges for classical scholarship. His visit to Britain in 1880 had been planned to recruit scholars for Johns Hopkins, but he had also used it to

---

[36] The first issue was 32pp, later issues of Vol. 1 ranging between 32pp and 64pp. The issues of vol. 2 (1888) were 32pp except for no. 7 (July), which was 48pp; from vol. 3.1 (January 1889) they were all of 48pp.

[37] Editorial note, *CR* 3 (Feb. 1889), 1.

[38] See e.g. Gilbert Murray, 'German scholarship', *Quarterly Review* 223 (April 1915), 330–9.

[39] Gildersleeve to Smyth, 16 Oct. 1890. Weir Smyth papers, Harvard University. Courtesy of the Harvard University Archives.

encourage contributions to his journal (Briggs 1987, 2015). In the 1880s several British classicists contributed to *AJP*, Robinson Ellis of Oxford being the most prolific.

The foundation of the *Review* is also worth considering in relation to non-classical journals. Of the thirty scholars whose names were listed in the November 1886 prospectus (see Appendix), the philosopher John Cook Wilson and the Homerist David Binning Monro were also contributors to the first issue of the *English Historical Review*, published in 1886. They were both Oxford men, and this is not surprising, since the *EHR* was an Oxford product. The story of its foundation makes an interesting comparison to that of the *CR*, and suggests the outlines of a general account of the emergence of academic journals in late nineteenth-century Britain.[40] Both journals owed their foundation to developing bodies of knowledge, though the study of Classics had a much longer history, reflected, as we have seen, in a long string of mostly short-lived journals. Both also derived from academic institutions: as we have seen, the *Classical Review* was started by a Cambridge man, and was nearly published by CUP; the *English Historical Review* was founded from Oxford, which had built up a much stronger historical school than its rival. In 1884, when James Bryce of Oxford was seeking support in Cambridge for the new journal, the Cambridge philosopher Henry Sidgwick told him that he did not believe there was a single man in Cambridge competent to deal with modern history in an intelligent way.[41] Like *CR*, *EHR* was offered to and rejected by CUP; unlike *CR*, it was also rejected by OUP. Both journals, not coincidentally, ended up being published by commercial firms: Longmans (EHR) and Nutt (CR).[42] Both the university presses were very wary of publishing journals in this period; OUP demanded a bond of £200 for its first journal, the *Annals of Botany* (1887).[43] To concerns over financial loss were superadded worries about controversial content: history, for the presses, was dangerously near to politics.[44]

In the cases of both journals, markets and readership had to be considered. This was partly because the founders had clear ideas about what kind of journal, and readers, they wanted. But it was also necessary because they had to secure enough readers to survive; and this meant convincing a publisher to keep producing. The most long-lived classical journal in the first half of the century was started by its publisher; the rest had scholarly editors who had to persuade publishers to keep going. The *Journal of Philology* had solved the problem, after a fashion, through a group subscription.

[40] See Goldstein 1986, Kadish 1988.

[41] Of those who worked on ancient history, Sidgwick thought Richard Jebb who would be by far the most effective potential contributor. Sidgwick to Bryce, 19 Apr. [1884], Trinity College Library, Add. MS c.105/33. For Jebb's non-classical publications, see 2013c, 275–94.

[42] In both cases, it is clear that the rivalry between the two universities, and their presses, was a factor in planning publication and editing. Similar patterns of mutual suspicion can be seen in the campaigns to found the Hellenic Society (1879) and the British School at Athens (1886): see e.g. 2013c, 123.

[43] Eliot 2013a, 553; for CUP, see McKitterick 2004, 111.

[44] A few days after Mayor wrote to Charles Clay about his proposed classical journal, Oscar Browning wrote to Clay proposing a historical journal (Browning to Clay, 4 Feb.1884: Cambridge University Press archives, Pr B 113.c.14). The proposal was rejected on the ground that history was too close to politics and so controversial: see Howsam 2009, 59; cf. Howsam 2004.

The Hellenic Society's *Journal of Hellenic Studies* took the same road *ab initio* in 1880. The *Classical Review* would follow it with the Classical Association (founded 1903), which in 1909 bought the journal from Nutt (2003a, 111–13). But in the 1880s that road was not open; nor was it to *EHR*, since the Historical Association was not founded till 1906.

Among the constraints on the planning and production of a new journal was the competition from other journals. In 1906 the *Review*'s publisher, David Nutt, announced a sister journal, the *Classical Quarterly*, which was planned to publish articles rather than reviews. This prompted the resignation of J. P. Postgate as editor of the *Classical Review*. In July 1906 he wrote to his Trinity College colleague Henry Jackson, recently elected Regius Professor of Greek, to inform him of the resignation, intended to provide 'a fresh start'. He went on to suggest that Jackson might succeed him as editor. Acknowledging that Jackson was one of the editors of the *Journal of Philology*, Postgate asked him whether there was room for two journals: 'whether [intere]st in the Classics, especially in the higher research, is sufficient to supply and to support two periodicals of this character'.[45] In his reply, Jackson argued for a division of labour between the two journals:

I think that the divis[ion] of the Review into [Review] & Quarterly is quite [sensib]le, but that to make [the Qu]arterly a success, it should take a line quite different from that of the J of Phil. I think that the C.R. should depend upon literary, critical, aesthetic, articles, such as might be written by Verrall, Butcher, Glover, Waldstein, Headlam, Adam, Cornford. [*deleted*: In a word, I think there is room for the three periodicals, & I doubt the possibility of combining the CR and J of Phil.] & that the in[tro]duction into the CQ of our dull (J of Ph) articles [wd griev] ously interfere with the [ ].....

There is room for

(1) J of Ph. High & dry scholarship.
(2) CQ literary criticism, aesthetics, paradoxa.
(3) CR reviews of books, notes, ephemera, education.

...(1) and (2) cannot be combined.[46]

Two years later, both *CR* and *CQ* were bought from Nutt by the Classical Association, which also planned to start a journal of Roman studies. Pipped at the post by the upstart new Roman Society, founded in 1910, with its *Journal of Roman Studies* (1911), the Association was obliged to negotiate with both Hellenic and Roman societies a division of labour among *CQ*, *JHS* and *JRS* (2003a, 110–12). *CR* floated serenely above this strife, since as a review journal it laid no claim to a specific province of Classics. It also appears to have had few internal difficulties, of the kind that had led in 1895 to the resignation of the editors of *JHS* (2013a, 212–13). It may be that the difficulties involved in publishing reviews were not as great as those with articles.

---

[45] Postgate to Jackson, 30 July 1906. Trinity College Library, Add. MS c.40. 98. The letters are water-damaged; my reconstructions are in square brackets.
[46] Jackson to Postgate, 6 July 1906. Trinity College Library, Add. MS c.40.98/2.

Nowadays we tend to think of journals as associated with university presses—as the *American Journal of Philology* and *Classical Philology* have been since their beginnings. But by 1900 OUP and CUP had almost without exception rejected all such proposals, irrespective of subject. In both cases, their previous local involvement in journal printing had lost them money. The Classical Association's journals were published by David Nutt and then by John Murray, and OUP did not take them over till the late 1930s, and then only as a rescue operation. In 2015 not only *CR* and *CQ*, but also *JRS* and *JHS*, are all published by CUP. I have stressed the involvement of publishers, because while journals are complex entities which play an important part in academic and intellectual life, they also have to be considered as material objects which cost money to assemble, produce and distribute.

Conclusion

The conditions for success and failure of journals should now be clearer, though it remains hard to tell just why, for example, the *Museum Criticum* apparently sold well. Its rival the *Classical Journal* was brought to an end when its publisher Valpy was closing down his operations more generally. The journals which sought to break free of Porsonianism and antiquarianism and to import German scholarship (*Philological Museum*, *Classical Museum*, the *Museum Academicum* of Stanley and his friends) were either short-lived or failed even to get off the ground. As we have seen, publishers and printers were needed as well as editors, contributors, and readers, and some prospect of profit, or guarantee against loss, was required to secure their involvement. From the 1870s, organized scholarly communities were deployed to this end—first the Cambridge Philological Society with the *Journal of Philology*, then the Hellenic Society with the *Journal of Hellenic Studies*, and later on the Classical Association and the Roman Society with their own journals. Three years after the *Journal of Philology* was founded, the University Tests Acts were repealed, so that most academic positions could be held without religious restrictions. Celibacy rules for college fellowships were relaxed a decade later. Here we have powerful supports for the making of a disciplinary community which might supply both contributors and readers. Another tactic was to engage allies who brought in new readers—thus the *Journal of Philology* with its Oxonian editor in 1878, and the *Classical Review*'s expansion to the US a decade later. By the early twentieth century, there were enough journals for friction to develop between them. Gildersleeve's *American Journal of Philology*, on the other hand, stood almost alone in the US, though the foundation of *Classical Philology* in 1906, though publicly welcomed by Gildersleeve, was a clear challenge to his journal. All these journals in effect grew from and created informal communities; the difference in the later decades of the century was that these were becoming organized. There were even family links between journals, as we have seen: A. P. Stanley was J. C. Hare's nephew, and asked his uncle for material left over from the *Philological Museum* for his planned new journal; and J. E. B. Mayor warned his younger brother Joseph that if the *Classical*

Review did not have a firm basis in a group of contributors, it would go the way of the *Journal of Classical and Sacred Philology.*[47]

Appendix

The Classical Review *prospectus, November 1886*

[Cambridge papers, MR1, Cambridge University Library]
The need of an organ in the English press for the review of classical books has long been felt among scholars. At the present time there is no periodical which makes it its object to record what is being done in the domain of classical philology, as there is for history and for different branches of natural science. The consequence is that classical works are criticized only fitfully, in papers mainly interested in other matters. The style of criticism has to be adapted to the taste of the general reader, and there is no place in which the student can be sure of finding a full and accurate list of the classical works which issue from the press, still less of learning their precise purpose and character. Such a state of things is discouraging alike to writers and reviewers. It is not worth an editor's while to assign much space to notices of books which will interest only a small section of the community, and the reader, however able and conscientious he may be, must feel that anything like thorough and searching criticism would be labour thrown away.

To meet this want it is proposed to establish a Classical Review, in which all English books dealing with classical antiquity should be noticed, if possible, within three months of publication, and full information should be given respecting the work which is going on outside England. The difficulty of obtaining such information must often have been felt by scholars, who have found too late that they have wasted time over work which had already been adequately done. As regards foreign books therefore the Review will contain (1) a monthly list of new books, (2) a resume of the contents of the different philological reviews, (3) independent notices of the more important works, (4) a classified index of the criticisms of the year. It is also hoped that arrangements can be made for enabling the subscribers to consult the various foreign reviews.

The Review will include the Christian writers of antiquity, as far as this can be done without trenching upon the ground of Theology or Church History; while it is not proposed to admit original articles involving deep research, such as make now the staple of the Journal of Philology, the promoters hope that it may be possible to carry out the suggestion of an eminent headmaster, and insert papers from time to time on subjects which are not included in the ordinary handbooks, but which are yet capable of being treated in a popular manner so as to interest younger students.

Other proposed features of the Review are Records of Exploration and Discovery, Notes and Queries, and Correspondence from foreign Universities.

The promoters have already received encouraging offers of contributions from the scholars whose names appear below, and they would gladly hear from others who may be disposed to help in any of the ways above specified. They venture to think that the names appended are a sufficient guarantee that the proposed Review will be fairly representative of the best English scholarship.

---

[47] For discussions of nineteenth-century periodicals, see Beetham 1990, Pykett 1990, Mussell 2007.

As the realization of the proposed scheme must depend on the number of the subscribers or guarantors, the promoters would make an earnest appeal for support to all who desire that English scholars should no longer labour under the disadvantage of having no classical Review of their own.

The Review is intended to appear once a month, with the exceptions of August and September. The cost to subscribers will be 10s for the ten numbers, to non-subscribers 1s 6d for each no.

It is requested that the names of intending subscribers may be sent with as little delay as possible to Prof Nettleship, Oxford, or Dr Reid, Cambridge.

List of contributors: E. A. Abbott A. M. Cook Robinson Ellis L. F. [*sic*] Farnell C. E. Graves F. Haverfield H. A. Holden H. Jackson R. C. Jebb W. M. Lindsay D. S. Margoliouth J. E. B. Mayor J. B. Mayor D. B. Monro H. Nettleship J. E. Nixon J. H. Onions A. Palmer A. F. [*sic*] Pelham [J.P.] Postgate [J.S.] Reid H. P. Richards [H.J.] Roby W. G. Rutherford [J.E.] Sandys T. C. Snow G. C. Warr W. Wayte E. R. Wharton A. S. Wilkins [J.] Cook Wilson.

9

Sir William Smith
and his Dictionaries

A Study in Scarlet and Black

The word 'Victorian' has conjured up a variety of responses since the end of the Victorian age. For Lytton Strachey, in 1918, it meant an old order to be rejected and caricatured: the first word of his title, *Eminent Victorians*, was to be pronounced very much with tongue in cheek.[1] Almost a century later, we are able to view the Victorians with more detachment. Academic and intellectual fashions, of course, continue to influence what is written and published about the Victorians: sex, race, and empire are popular, 'dead white males' rather less so. Yet those males created most of the monuments we now celebrate as among the outstanding achievements of the Victorian age. The vast sewage system of London (1859–89), constructed by William Bazalgette, continues to serve its purpose, with some repair and modernization. Others, like James Murray's *New* (later *Oxford*) *English Dictionary* (1884–1933) and Leslie Stephen's *Dictionary of National Biography* (1885–1900), have been or are being revised and replaced. In each case, new material is continually being absorbed and processed; in each case the process of updating has brought with it a renewed respect for the magnitude of the original achievement.

Something of the same respect is provoked when one surveys the lesser-known, but still remarkable, achievements of William Smith, who from 1838 till his death in 1893 wrote, edited, or contributed to dozens of reference works and textbooks, including the three large classical dictionaries which first appeared between 1840 and 1857, and for which he is now best remembered.[2] The impression one has of these massive volumes as being solidly embedded in Victorian teaching and learning was already suggested

---

[1] See the 'definitive' edition, with an introduction by Paul Levy and afterwords by various authors (Strachey 2003).

[2] *Dictionary of Greek and Roman Antiquities* (1840–42); *Dictionary of Greek and Roman Biography and Mythology* (1844–49); *Dictionary of Greek and Roman Geography* (1852–57). The present essay has its origin in introductions to reprint editions of all three dictionaries by I. B. Tauris (London 2006–08); I am grateful to David Stonestreet for commissioning them, and to Gill Furlong, Ian Jackson, Nick Lowe, David McKitterick, John and Virginia Murray, Joanne Simmons, David Southern, and Graham Whitaker for help of various kinds.

by one of Smith's colleagues, who wrote in 1852 that 'Dr Smith's Dictionaries no sooner appeared, than they entered, as by native affinity, into the education of the national mind.'[3]

Who was 'Dr Smith', and how did he become such a prolific author and editor? William Smith was born in London on 20 May 1813, the eldest son of a tallow chandler and his wife, both Congregationalists.[4] He attended Madras House, Hackney, a school founded by the dissenter John Allen in 1817,[5] and was then articled to a solicitor, but in 1829 entered the University of London (from 1836, University College, London). Here he excelled in classics, winning first prizes in the senior Latin and Greek classes. In 1835 he attended the lectures of Franz Bopp's favourite pupil Friedrich Rosen, Professor of Sanskrit, from whom he learned comparative philology. From 1836 to 1839 he taught at the school attached to University College, and was then appointed Professor of Classics at Highbury College, founded for the education of dissenters. In 1842 he applied for the Latin chair at UCL, vacated by his teacher Thomas Key; in the event George Long, previously Professor of Greek, was elected. In 1851 Smith moved to New College in Swiss Cottage, the product of the merger of Highbury with two other dissenters' colleges, Homerton and Coward.[6]

Smith's first publications appeared in 1838, while he was still in his twenties: Volume 10 of the *Penny Cyclopaedia* (1833–42), published by the Society for the Diffusion of Useful Knowledge, carried several articles by him on Persian and Chinese topics. This was hardly his native ground, and suggests that he was recruited initially as a hack, perhaps to replace a deceased or dilatory contributor.[7] His first book was an elementary textbook, *Latin Exercises for Beginners* (1838); this was followed by an edition of selections from Plato (Smith 1840). He also seems to have been the author of *A New Latin Reading-book: Consisting of Short Sentences, Easy Narrations and Descriptions Selected from Caesar's Gallic War… with a Dictionary* (1841).[8] Smith's procedure, a common one in this period, was to cobble together material from German scholars and to make of them a usable textbook. The same applies—as the full title shows—to another production of

[3] Revd John Harris, Principal of New College, London, where William Smith taught, in a testimonial supporting Smith's application for the chair of Greek at Edinburgh. The testimonials are held by the British Library, 8366 bb 33: 12–19.

[4] See R. E. Clements' article in *ODNB*, which is better on Smith's biblical work than on his classical books.

[5] As the name suggests, the school was run on the Madras or monitorial system of Andrew Bell, older pupils instructing their juniors. Allen's son Alexander, a year younger than Smith, carried on the school after his father's death in 1839, until his own death in 1842; he contributed to Smith's first dictionary.

[6] Bryant 1986, 106–7. Smith had by then already been appointed Professor of Classics at Homerton College. His introductory lecture, published together with those of his professorial colleagues, was largely devoted to a potted history of classical scholarship: W. Smith, 'A lecture introductory to the course of the Greek and Latin languages and literature', in *New College, London: Introductory Lectures* (London 1851). The title in the British Library catalogue, 'History of Classical Learning', is taken from the running heads.

[7] Smith's authorship is given in the marked set of the *Cyclopaedia* in the British Library (733L). I have been unable to consult the set annotated by its editor, George Long (Brighton Public Library), which was mislaid during a move to new premises.

[8] The book is anonymous, but is assigned to 'Wm. Smith' in *The London Catalogue of Books, 1816–1851* (London 1851).

the same year, which also collected short works by a classical author: *Tacitus. Germania, Agricola, and the First Book of the Annals. With Notes from Ruperti, Passow, Walch, and Bötticher's* Remarks on the style of Tacitus. This volume, which reached a third edition in 1855, was brought out by the publishers to the University of London, Taylor and Walton, as Smith's previous books had been. In this case, Smith used his younger brother Philip and Charles Mason to translate the German material: both were to contribute to his classical dictionaries. Also in 1840, he provided an introduction for a translation of Gustav Wiggers' *A Life of Socrates* (again published by Taylor and Walton). Here too additional matter was inserted, in this case a translation of Schleiermacher's essay on Socrates by Connop Thirlwall. Two years later appeared the third and final volume of Niebuhr's *History of Rome*, translated by Smith and his friend Leonhard Schmitz, a German classical scholar who had settled in Britain.

It was probably through the SDUK, publishers of the *Cyclopaedia*, that he made contact with Schmitz, a pupil of Barthold Niebuhr and a leading transmitter of German scholarship to Britain. The two men later collaborated on the *Classical Museum* (1843–49: discussed in Chapter 7), a major conduit for this transmission. Schmitz was titular editor, but Smith seems to have played a considerable role in dealing with contributors.[9] The first two volumes of Niebuhr's history (1828–31) had been translated by Julius Hare and Connop Thirlwall, of Trinity College Cambridge, who as editors of the *Philological Museum* (1831–33) had tried to bring the spirit of German *Altertumswissenschaft* to the benighted English.[10] Smith's involvement in the Wiggers and Niebuhr volumes was a clear sign of his commitment to this broader style of scholarship.

The *Dictionary of Greek and Roman antiquities*

In the *Publishers' Circular* of 1 January 1840 appeared the following announcement (p. 11): 'This day is published, price One Shilling, the first part of A Dictionary of Greek and Roman Antiquities'. The notice went on to explain that 'The Roman Antiquities of Adam, and the Greek Antiquities of Potter, contain the same kind of information which it is proposed to give in this Dictionary in alphabetic order', adding that it was now possible to gain 'more correct knowledge and more comprehensive views'. The writer (presumably Smith) went on, 'If we look only at what has been collected within the British Museum in the present century, we find abundant material for explaining innumerable allusions in the Greek and Roman writers, which have hitherto been imperfectly understood'. The announcement ended by explaining that the Dictionary was 'to be continued in monthly parts, and to form one Octavo volume', and added

---

[9] Arthur Hugh Clough dealt with Smith rather than with Schmitz about his article on hexameters: *The Correspondence of A. H. Clough*, ed. F. L. Mulhauser (Oxford 1957) 1.142: Clough to T. Burbidge, 31 December 1844.

[10] On the *Philological Museum*, see Chapter 7.

that 'Two further works are to follow: A Dictionary of Greek and Roman Biography and Mythology; A Dictionary of Ancient Geography.'

Several features of this announcement deserve to be noticed. First of all, it is clear that all three dictionaries were planned from the beginning to constitute an encyclopaedic reference work on classical antiquity. They could thus be compared with August Pauly's *Real-Encyclopädie der classischen Altertumswissenschaft, in alphabetischer Ordnung*, which had begun to appear in the previous year. The reference to 'alphabetical order' in Pauly's title is significant. Like the work on which it was modelled, Karl Philipp Funke's *Real Schullexikon* of 1800–05, Pauly's book (eventually completed after his death in six volumes) was organized in this way, and not as a series of subject references. The *Bibliotheca Latina* (1697) and *Bibliotheca Graeca* (1705) of Johann Fabricius, both of which were part encyclopaedia, part bibliography, had been arranged largely in chronological order of literary periods. Samuel Hoffmann's *Lexicon bibliographicum* (Hoffmann 1832) used an alphabetical order, but its entries were on authors. An alternative tradition is exemplified in the *Encyclopaedia Metropolitana* (30 vols, 1829–45), based on a plan of Coleridge's and in a sense representing the romantic reaction to the Enlightenment tradition of the *Encyclopaedia Britannica*. It contained four divisions: pure sciences, mixed sciences, history and biography, miscellaneous and lexicographical.[11] Smith's 'encyclopaedia' combined a general coverage, in the first Dictionary, with a more specialized treatment in its two successors (Biography and Mythology, Geography). One might assume that Smith and his publisher planned them in order to capitalize on the success of the first book; but the announcement quoted above makes it clear that the series was conceived as a whole. Smith's subsequent publications in this area, however, followed predictable commercial paths: specialization, conflation, and abridgement.

Secondly, the Dictionary was to be issued in parts: it was completed in twenty-eight parts in April 1842, and put on sale as a large octavo volume in that month at £1 15s 6d. Parts 1–10, 11–20 and 21–8 were also sold as sewn sections at 10s each.[12] The two later dictionaries appeared in quarterly rather than monthly parts—Smith doubtless learning from bitter experience—but the system was otherwise adhered to throughout. Serial publication was not uncommon in this period, but the crucial exemplar for Smith was surely the SDUK's *Penny Cyclopaedia*, which was still being issued in monthly parts when his first dictionary began to appear, and to which he was himself, as we have seen, a contributor.[13] The price of the *Cyclopaedia* had by this time risen from a penny to fourpence a part, but was nevertheless still cheap and hence accessible to a wide audience; and the same must, to a lesser extent, have been true of the Dictionaries.

---

[11] See Yeo 2001, and on nineteenth-century forms of knowledge-dissemination, Rauch 2001. Neither makes any mention of Smith.

[12] George Long's interleaved and annotated copy in Brighton Public Library is in this (3-volume) form.

[13] It should be added that John Murray, with whom Smith was in touch from the mid-1840s, had also been producing illustrated part-works. For the firm's Family Library (1829–34), a conservative riposte to the SDUK's publishing, see Bennett 1976.

A third feature of the announcement worth noting is the reference to 'more correct knowledge and more comprehensive views'. Smith is claiming not only superior accuracy, but a wider view of the subject. The two books he refers to could safely be mentioned, as both were old and outdated: John Potter's *Archaeologia Graeca, or the Antiquities of Greece* had first appeared in 1697, Alexander Adam's *Roman Antiquities* in 1791. They struggled on until 1850 and 1857 respectively in editions published by Blackie and armed with illustrations, but were no longer serious contenders in the struggle for readers.[14] In a rather different category was John Lemprière's *Classical Dictionary* of 1788, whose publication history, with a variety of revisions and reprintings, has continued to the present day.[15] Smith's claim to 'more comprehensive views' is not aimed at these books, but at the continuing emphasis in English classical schooling on the rote learning of Latin and Greek, to the exclusion of any knowledge of literature, philosophy, history, or archaeology.

A classical dictionary which might have offered Smith stiff competition should be mentioned at this point, in part because it had been commissioned by John Murray; this helps indeed to explain his later interest in Smith's dictionaries. In 1838, Murray had asked John Wordsworth, the poet's nephew and a fellow of Trinity College, Cambridge, to write a dictionary 'of about the same size as Lemprière's Classical Dictionary', and terms were finally agreed in March 1839.[16] Wordsworth died prematurely on 31 December 1839—the day before Smith's first dictionary began to appear—and Murray asked another fellow of Trinity, J. W. Donaldson, to take it over. Donaldson declined on the ground that it was 'too large a work for one man to finish. But in collaboration it might be done...'.[17] Thus Murray must have been considering who might be asked to edit, rather than write, a dictionary, just as Smith (who seems to have begun work on his first dictionary in 1839) was getting under way with his own project, and just as Pauly's multi-authored work was beginning to appear.

Had Smith been free of other commitments, Murray might perhaps have engaged him as editor at that point. As it was, Smith was engaged with Taylor and Walton, and Murray did not come on board until 1845, when Smith's books first appear in Murray's

---

[14] Potter's book seems to have acquired engravings in 1832; Adam's sported 'more than 100' wood and steel engravings in its 14th edition of 1843—perhaps in response to the appearance of Smith's first dictionary.

[15] Among the more notable of its revisers, in an American edition of 1847, was Mozart's librettist Lorenzo da Ponte, then in his second incarnation as Professor of Italian at Columbia University. An earlier revision which Smith will have known was that by Da Ponte's colleague Charles Anthon and the indefatigable Edmund Barker (who has featured in Chapters 3 and 7). The survival of Lemprière's book may be due to its being a dictionary of names found in classical literature; a status which has made it relatively independent of changing academic fashion.

[16] Wordsworth to Murray, 14 November 1838, 10 March 1839 (John Murray archive). This and other material from this source is quoted by permission of the John Murray Archive. The second half of Wordsworth's copy of Lemprière, interleaved and heavily annotated, survives in the Bishops' Wordsworth Library, now at Lancaster University Library Rare Books Archive (Wordsworth A/1). Wordsworth's notes include memoranda on books to read, how to make entries, and what kind of paper to use for interleaving.

[17] Donaldson to Murray, 16 April 1840.

printing ledgers.[18] The correspondence between the two men preserved in the Murray Archive begins in 27 January 1845; it suggests however that they had been in contact for some time.[19] On that date, Smith told Murray that the contributor engaged to produce an article on Horace had not delivered, and asked him to secure the services of Henry Milman. The two men had clearly been corresponding already about the *Dictionary of Greek and Roman Biography and Mythology*, which had begun to appear in the previous year, and to which Milman contributed several articles.

The nineteen contributors to the *Dictionary* did not constitute a coherent or closely-knit group: Smith had to find expertise where he could. Five were fellows of Trinity College, Cambridge; four were Oxford dons; the rest had other institutional affiliations, or none. Several of the major contributors belonged to a loose network of scholars based in or linked to the new London University. The most prolific single contributor was Smith himself, but four others stand out. His younger brother Philip, who contributed 139 articles, was like William a professor of Classics in a dissenting college; he later became headmaster of the dissenters' grammar school, Mill Hill.[20] Leonhard Schmitz (264 articles), whom we have met already, was Rector of the Royal High School in Edinburgh, where he was later a candidate for the chair of Greek. George Long's early life had paralleled Smith's: he was articled to a solicitor, went to classes at the London University and left the law for classical scholarship. Long, who contributed 188 articles, was unusual in his expertise in Roman law and in ancient geography, a dual specialism on which Smith drew extensively for his dictionaries. Finally, James Yates (192 articles) was a Unitarian minister who had been a classical tutor at the dissenters' Manchester College in York. He was notable for his interest in ancient crafts, especially weaving, and this is reflected in the range of his contributions to the *Dictionary*. He also supplied drawings for about half of the woodcuts which were among the *Dictionary*'s most striking features.[21] Many of these were prepared by George Scharf, first secretary of the National Portrait Gallery, formerly one of the first pupils of the junior school at University College, a keen follower of archaeological excavations and well known to the firm of Murray.[22]

[18] The Murray Archive, now at the National Library of Scotland, contains a set of agreements with contributors (including Smith himself) and receipts for payment 1840–2. Though not complete, they show that Smith received over £700 for his work on the book. NLS, MS 42609. My thanks to David McClay and Mick Morris for access to the file.

[19] In 1843 Murray had taken over the firm on the death of his father, John Murray II, and had gone into popular publishing with the Colonial and Home Library. It is likely that he first made contact with Smith at about this time.

[20] An even more famous lexicographer, Sir James Murray, was a master at the school from 1860 to 1885. Mill Hill thus had the distinction, surely unique, of being associated with two men called 'Dictionary'.

[21] See his article in *ODNB*, which estimates that he wrote about one-eighth of the total text. Yates's knowledge of weaving was displayed in his *Textrinum Antiquorum: An Account of the Art of Weaving among the Ancients*, published in 1843, a year after the *Dictionary*, and by the same publishers.

[22] See *ODNB* on Scharf (who is Sir George, not his eponymous father). I have learned from discussions with Kai Kin Yung, whose definitive study of Scharf is forthcoming.

Later Editions

The post-publication history of the *Dictionary of Antiquities* differs from that of its two companions, in that it was revised after its first publication. The other *Dictionaries* were abridged, and the abridgements were revised more than once; only Smith's first dictionary was revised in its full form.[23] (The others, at two and three volumes, would have presented a bigger challenge.) The third edition of 1890–1 was the product of large-scale revision: forty-four scholars were enlisted, two-thirds of the articles were heavily revised and a third completely rewritten (Sandys 1891, 425). The leading scholars of the day contributed long articles: Henry Nettleship, Professor of Latin at Oxford, wrote on *satura*, while Richard Jebb, Professor of Greek at Cambridge, provided articles on *theatrum* and *tragoedia*.[24] The editors were two Eton and King's men, William Wayte (vol. 1) and George Marindin (vol. 2).[25]

In the forty-three years since Smith's own revision of 1848, significant changes had taken place in the content and organization of classical scholarship. The Oxford curriculum had been divided into Honour Moderations (Mods) and Literae Humaniores (Greats), while in Cambridge the Classical Tripos had been reorganized into two parts, Part II being divided, as we saw in Chapter 5, into five specialist courses. A whole range of archaeological discoveries, notably Schliemann's finds at Troy and Mycenae, had opened up new areas of research far from the text-based scholarship of the first half of the century.[26] One of the most exciting of recent discoveries prompted the addition of an appendix to the second volume: a set of essays on the 'Athenian Constitution' attributed to Aristotle, a work acquired on papyrus by the British Museum in 1890 and published in 1891.

The *Dictionary of Greek and Roman Biography and Mythology*

In the Preface to his second dictionary, dated October 1844, Smith explained the need for such a work and the principles on which it had been assembled. The researches of

---

[23] The first edition of the *Dictionary* was abridged in 1845 as *A School Dictionary of Greek and Roman Antiquities*. The second edition of 1848 was later abridged as *A Smaller Dictionary of Greek and Roman Antiquities* (1853).

[24] A useful survey of the contents was given by Sandys in his review (see n. 25, above).

[25] John Murray III had close links with Eton, and published classical textbooks commissioned by its headmaster Edmond Warre. Marindin also edited the *Classical Review* (in this period published by Murray) from 1894 to 1897 (see 2009), and acted as a reader for the firm well into the 1920s. In 1898 another Eton master, Francis Warre Cornish, brought out *A Concise Dictionary of Greek and Roman Antiquities*; this 'concise' version ran to over 800 pages and contained 1,100 woodcuts 'taken from the best examples of ancient art'.

[26] Schliemann 1873, 1877. The earlier book has an interesting link to Smith, as it was edited for John Murray by Philip Smith, himself a leading contributor to his brother William's dictionaries. Philip Smith's letters to Richard Jebb, which survive in the latter's papers at Trinity College, Cambridge, reveal a marked scepticism about some of Schliemann's claims.

modern classical scholars, especially those on the continent, had advanced knowledge in a myriad of special fields: the need now was for the results of all this work to be brought together in an accessible form. Some of the points made by Smith deserve to be highlighted. His reference to 'biography, literature and mythology' (p. vii) makes it clear that he intended the Dictionary to provide an account of classical literature. He goes on to explain that 'More space, relatively, has been given to the Greek and Roman Writers than to any other articles, partly because we have no complete history of Greek and Roman Literature in the English language' (p. viii). The Dictionary can be used not just to dip into individual articles, then, but also to follow the history of classical literary production. The scope and completeness of the work are emphasized in two ways. First, considerable space has been given to 'those persons who do not occupy so prominent a position in history' as the leading writers (p. viii); since their lives often throw light on literary works. Second, the lives of Christian writers are included, Smith being convinced that 'they constitute an important part of the history of Greek and Roman literature' (p. viii). Finally, the biographical coverage does not stop with the fall of the Roman Empire, but continues, though in attenuated form, to the fall of Constantinople in 1453.

When he began to plan this, the largest of his classical reference works, Smith already had behind him the experience gained in editing his first dictionary; the stock of reference information it provided; and the group of nineteen contributors he had assembled to write it. In the new work he was joined by thirty-five contributors, many of them carrying on from previous work on the *Dictionary of Antiquities*. Running such a large team was not without difficulty, and the need to juggle word limits with dilatory contributors was a constant headache. In the case of Henry Milman, brought in, as we have seen, as a replacement for a failed contributor, we find Smith writing to Murray on 10 March 1845 that a sheet (sixteen pages) would make the article disproportionately long, and asking him to tell Milman to provide ten pages only. But he continued:

If, however, Mr Milman should wish for more than 10 pages, I shall not much mind his having a sheet, as I have found it already impossible in such a work to have all the articles of a proportionate length. I shall want Horace early in May.

The concern for the ideal and the acceptance of what was pragmatically possible must have been continually in tension, as deadlines for printing quarterly parts of the *Dictionary* regularly loomed ahead.[27]

Another source of pressure was that while working on the biographical dictionary, Smith was already looking ahead to future condensed works. On 24 February 1845 he wrote to John Walton, of Taylor and Walton, suggesting a scale of payments for contributors for the projected concise dictionary of classical antiquities: 30 shillings a page, made up of 21 shillings (a guinea) for the author and 9 shillings for the editor. Smith added that he would be able to use the large biographical dictionary as a source for the biography and mythology articles, but it would be a lot of work to reduce 3,000

---

[27] Compare the 'continual return of labour' referred to by William Gifford in Chapter 6.

pages to 500 or 600. Other projects tempted him, but some had to be abandoned for lack of time, as the Biographical Dictionary dominated his life. On 11 May 1847, he thanked Murray for the new volumes of Grote's history:[28] 'Gibbon's is the only history of ancient nations worthy to be compared.' Smith added that he would like to review it for the *Quarterly Review*, though he was very busy on a new edition of 'the antiquities dictionary'. On 7 October, however, he told Murray that he must abandon all hope of reviewing Grote:

So many of my collaborateurs have failed to send me the articles for the Dictionary which they had promised that an amount of work has been thrown upon me, which I shall find it difficult to get through. Mr Walton urges me to proceed as quickly as possible with the printing of the new edition of the Antiquities, as the old edition is quite out of print.

Smith's contributors derived in large part from the team recruited for his first dictionary, including his brother Philip. The historian of Mill Hill School, of which Philip Smith was headmaster 1853–60, reports that he was prone to reading a chorus of Sophocles or a scene from Terence, 'illustrated by continual reference to "my article Sappho"' (James 1909, 179). The team included five Germans, nine Oxford men, five from Cambridge, six from London, and three masters from Rugby School. As with the *Dictionary of Antiquities*, colleagues at or connected with University College, London (as it had been since 1836) feature prominently, as do contacts from the world of dissenting Christian scholars. The Baptist Joseph Means, theologian and classicist, had been a member of the first London University entry in Classics in 1828; while writing for the *Dictionary*, he was headmaster of Chatham Proprietary School. Means had contributed topographical and other articles to the *Penny Cyclopaedia* and to the SDUK's short-lived *Biographical Dictionary*.[29] He was a leading member of the General Baptist Assembly, but his theological views at one point led him to retreat from it. A similar experience was that of Samuel Davidson, a learned and prolific writer on biblical subjects, who was dismissed in 1857 from the chair of biblical literature at the Lancashire Independent College in Manchester which he had held since 1842. The UCL staff who contributed included John Thomas Graves, Professor of Jurisprudence since 1839. Graves was a friend of his colleagues Henry Malden and Augustus De Morgan, and served with the latter on the SDUK committee. The articles he contributed including those on the jurists Cato, Crassus, Drusus, and Gaius, and on the legislation of Justinian.[30] Other contributors are more obscure. Edward Elder, a graduate of Balliol College, Oxford, rescued Durham Cathedral School from decline as its headmaster in the 1840s, but failed in a similar attempt at Charterhouse in the following decade, and

---

[28] Volumes 3 and 4 of Grote's *History of Greece* had been published in April.
[29] This was edited by George Long, editor of the *Penny Cyclopaedia*, and was issued between 1842 and 1844, 4 vols in 7. When it ceased to appear it had reached the end of the letter A.
[30] Graves was a talented mathematician (his mathematical collection is now at UCL); his papers include a collection of nearly 3,000 anagrams on the name of Augustus De Morgan.

later went mad. Of William Plate LLD little is known except that he published a map of Arabia in 1847, and was an expert on chess.

The two dictionaries were for the most part favourably received. As a reviewer in the *Gentleman's Magazine* pointed out in 1851:

During the last twenty years an important change has come over the spirit and character of English scholarship. The 'curriculum' of our great public schools has been extended: the course of study at our universities has become more genial and comprehensive. Scholarship is now aiming at something higher than mere purism in diction...Accordingly Dr. Smith's Encyclopaedias were planned and have been executed at exactly the right moment. They synchronise with the general advance of classical scholarship in this country.   (Anon. 1851)

The reviewer went on to point out that no exact models for Smith's work existed in Germany,

though Hoffman and Eschenburg [Hoffmann 1838–45, Eschenburg 1787] had made considerable advances in the same track. For the only German work which resembles these dictionaries, and which includes the three departments of archaeology, biography and geography—Pauly's Encyclopaedia—is merely a work, though a very valuable work, of reference. To graces of form or diction it makes no pretension...Dr. Smith has consulted the interest of his work in making it as popular and readable as was consistent with sound information.

Favourable reviews of the *Dictionary of Antiquities* were published, as its parts appeared, in the *Church of England Quarterly Review*, a journal founded in 1837 which for some years carried classical articles, by George Burges and Frederick Paley among others. Parts 1–6 were praised in 1840: 'it is no small advantage to have articles requiring illustration set off by exquisite wood cuts...the first six parts, extending to C, give a very high promise of the rest'.[31] In the following year, parts 17–21 were also favourably noticed: 'This excellent work is going on well...no expenses have been spared to obtain the best writers...exquisite woodcuts.'[32] The commendatory tone was maintained in 1842 in notices of parts 22–6, with a comment that 'from the more frequent recurrence of the initials L S [i.e. Leonhard Schmitz] we augur well for its improvement'.[33] A longer review was promised of the completed book, but never appeared.

In the USA, Cornelius Felton, Professor of Classics at Harvard, reviewed the first two dictionaries. Smith's first dictionary, he commented, was so popular in England that it was immediately stereotyped in the USA.[34] In his remarks on the *Biographical Dictionary*, he points to the coverage of Byzantine history, which has 'nothing corresponding in any previously existing classical Dictionary'. Looking forward to the *Geographical Dictionary*, Felton concludes that the series 'will constitute by far the most important contribution to classical learning which our age can boast' (433).[35]

---

[31] *Church of England Quarterly Review* 7 (1840) 238.
[32] *Church of England Quarterly Review* 10 (1841) 491.
[33] *Church of England Quarterly Review* 11 (1842) 255, 490.
[34] It was published in New York by Harper and Brothers in 1845.
[35] C. C. Felton, in *North American Review* 70 (April 1850) 424–33.

In 1854 a long and detailed review of all three dictionaries by William Mure appeared in the *Quarterly Review*.[36] Though this was Murray's house journal, the review was no puff: Mure gives a careful comparison between Smith's books and Pauly's encyclopaedia, whose seventh and final volume had been published two years earlier. Mure marginally preferred Pauly's single alphabet to Smith's tripartite division, but allowing for availability and speed of publication, concluded (p. 118) that 'we award the palm of superiority to the Dictionaries'.[37] As we have seen, Smith drew attention in the preface to his first dictionary to the evidence available in the British Museum. This was a major source of illustrations, mostly woodcuts. These illustrations, several hundred of them, were a novelty in the world of classical dictionaries. There had been none in the most popular reference work of the late eighteenth and early nineteenth centuries, John Lemprière's *Bibliotheca Classica* (1788); nor had any illustrations adorned Pauly's *Real-Encyclopädie*. The use of this material through extensive use of engravings, combining popular appeal, scholarly accuracy and a conception of antiquity which went beyond texts, is exemplified in Smith's use of coinage. The *Dictionary of Antiquities* had included only few illustrations of coins. The *Biographical Dictionary* extended the use of coins considerably, a practice which was further developed in the *Geographical Dictionary*, in which nearly 400 coins were depicted. Given access to a large collection like that of the British Museum, which Smith used, this offered a straightforward and distinctive way of representing individuals and gods featured on coins, and also the cities which struck their own coinage. A flattering imitation of Smith's format can be seen in Seth Stevenson's *Dictionary of Roman Coins*: Stevenson's original prospectus announced that the book would be 'printed uniformly with the Dictionaries of Greek and Roman Antiquities and of Greek and Roman Biography and Mythology'.[38] Even where the Smith visual format was not followed, his use of coins was adopted, for example in J. B. Bury's *History of Greece* (1900). In 1919, when the theologian Friedrich von Hügel sent a copy of Bury's book to his niece, he urged her to 'try, by very frequent looking at the coin illustrations, to connect the chief Greek cities with their coins. It is in this way that the geography of ancient Greece sticks in my head ... let the coins help you very largely!' (Greene 1928, 67–8).

Later 'editions' of the *Dictionary* appear to be simple reprints, but it was drawn on for a series of smaller works, such as the *Smaller Classical Mythology, with Translations from the Ancient Poets and Questions upon the Work* (1867). In 1850 Smith had brought out a *New Dictionary of Classical Biography, Mythology and Geography*; this was

[36] [W. Mure], 'Classical dictionaries', *Quarterly Review* 95(1854) 89–118. Mure had published on Egyptian subjects, but was best known for his five-volume history of Greek literature, which appeared between 1850 and 1857.

[37] Sales figures are not easy to establish. Murray's stock book ledger (NLS catalogue no. 680), kindly inspected on my behalf by Mick Morris, lists (p. 237) sales for the *Dictionary of Greek and Roman Antiquities* for 1852–54 as 297, plus direct sales from Murray's shop of 2074. Total sales of the *Dictionary of Greek and Roman Biography* for 1855 are given as 250 sets.

[38] About half of this book was completed when Stevenson died in 1853; completed by others, it was finally published by George Bell in 1889.

presumably the basis of his *Smaller Dictionary of Classical Biography, Mythology and Geography* (1853), which went into several editions before being revised by Marindin in 1894. In 1910 this revision, further edited by E. H. Blakeney, was republished in Everyman's Library, and in 1952 was renamed *Everyman's Smaller Classical Dictionary*. Its most recent incarnation, to date, has been in cheap paperback format as *The Wordsworth Classical Dictionary* (1996)—a title which harks back, unconsciously, to John Wordsworth's unfinished dictionary of the 1830s.

In the 1840s Smith must have had his hands full with the *Antiquities*, and especially with the large and long-running Biography and Mythology dictionary. The only other publication to emerge under his name was *Chronological Tables of Greek and Roman History* (1849), an offshoot of his larger editorial labours. He was also involved with Schmitz's *Classical Museum* (1843–49). In the following decade he flexed his muscles, even while editing the *Dictionary of Geography*, to encompass not only the history of Greece (*A History of Greece, from the Earliest Times to the Roman Conquest; with Supplementary Chapters on the History of Literature and Art: Illustrated by One Hundred Engravings on Wood* [1854]) but also the Latin language. His *A Latin-English Dictionary, based upon the Works of Forcellini and Freund* (1855), which had reached a ninth edition by 1870, is discussed below.

The *Dictionary of Greek and Roman Geography*

This, the last of Smith's three classical dictionaries, was as suggested above also the furthest removed from the linguistic and textual focus of the Porsonian school (see Chapter 4). By this time John Murray, who had sunk a large amount of money in the previous dictionaries, may have become nervous, since he did not take a financial share; the book was published at Smith's risk, Murray taking five per cent of the profits.[39] (This also suggests that Smith had done well out of the earlier books.) Such concerns will not have been lessened by the fact that, like its predecessors, the book outgrew its original projected size. The first part, issued on 1 January 1852 at 4/-, announced on its title page that it was 'To be continued in quarterly parts, and to form one volume octavo'—rather than the two fat volumes which eventually appeared in 1854 and 1857.[40] The schedule was maintained for the first seven parts, after which it slipped until it was hauled back on course in December 1854 with part 11. From Part 14 the size and price were increased, 'With a view to the completion of the work next Autumn', the final and even bulkier part was published on 1 May 1857 at 12/-. Among the reasons for delay was the difficulty of finding reliable contributors. Smith had encountered the problem earlier while working on the *New Dictionary of Classical*

---

[39] References in Murray's records in the 1860s and 1870s suggest that he then held shares of between a third and a half in some of Smith's books.

[40] A complete set of the original seventeen paper-bound parts survives in the library of the University of Virginia, where it was kindly inspected for me by Charles Monaghan.

Biography, Mythology and Geography; he wrote to Murray in February 1850 that he was working as fast as he could on the book, but that:

I had hoped to obtain assistance from Mr Long, Dr Schmitz and one or two other friends in the geography department; but they all failed, pleading the difficulty and unremunerative nature of the work. Thus with the exception of a little help from my brother, the whole work has been thrown on my hands, which I did not anticipate when I hoped to have the work ready by the spring of this year. In writing the geographical articles, I have frequently to read many pages in the ancient writers and in modern travels in order to draw up an article of half a dozen lines; and I do not exaggerate when I say that a page of the Dictionary frequently takes me a long day's work. I cannot tell you how vexed I am that I should have failed in having the book ready by the time you anticipated. If there is one thing which I pride myself on, it is punctuality; and during the many years I was engaged upon the Dictionaries of Antiquities and Biography, I never once disappointed Messrs Taylor and Walton.[41]

Smith eventually secured the help of Long and Schmitz, along with his brother Philip, for the Geography Dictionary; these veterans of the earlier books were joined by fourteen new contributors in volume 1, and nine in volume 2. In some cases, Smith was obliged to make compromises: in September 1856, he wrote to George Cornewall Lewis that in compiling the book, 'I should have been glad of more help than I have had, and I have sometimes been obliged to employ persons, whose knowledge and scholarship were not quite as perfect as I could have wished.'[42] We can assume that he was not referring to the longest and most central articles. 'Athenae', which Smith wrote himself, runs to fifty-three pages; 'Roma', by T. H. Dyer, to 133. This massive article ends with an interesting survey of recent work on the archaeology of Rome which discusses the nationalist politics of excavation; Dyer subsequently published it in book form.[43]

The *Dictionary of Greek and Roman Geography* was perhaps the boldest and most innovative of the series. In it Smith ventured onto ground which had received very little systematic study; he also adopted a very liberal conception of its subject matter. To begin with, places which occur in the Bible are included, 'to make the work a Dictionary of Ancient Geography in the widest acceptation of the term', as Smith wrote in his preface.[44] He went on to declare, 'This work is an historical as well as a geographical one.' To turn to the entry on a Roman city or a Greek *polis* is to find not just an account of location, physical and economic geography, but also a summary history, complete with detailed references to classical authors. Smith's strategy on the choice of illustrations is simple but effective: as well as the predictable use of maps, he incorporates, as we have seen, woodcuts of coins struck by the countries, cities, and towns treated in the *Dictionary*. Many of these feature references to the tutelary deity or hero, or the foundation myth of a city, and thus lead the reader from place and locality to the

[41] Smith to Murray, 15 February 1850 (John Murray archive).
[42] Smith to Lewis, 13 September 1856: National Library of Wales, Harpton Court papers, C 2395.
[43] Dyer's *Ancient Rome* was published by John Murray in 1864.
[44] Here, then, we can already see Smith moving from the classical world to the biblical subject matter of his later dictionaries.

history and politics of local identity. This is very much helped by Smith's decision to extend his treatment, where necessary, beyond the end of the Roman Empire: as he explains in his preface, 'it has sometimes been necessary to trace the history of a town through the middle ages, in order to explain the existing remains of antiquity'.

The *Dictionary* was followed in 1861 by an abridgement by W. L. Bevan, *The Student's Manual of Ancient Geography*. A more ambitious and longer delayed follow-up was the *Atlas of Ancient Geography*. This is first mentioned in the correspondence between Smith and Murray in 1852, and Smith's preface to the first volume of the *Dictionary* announced that it would follow Volume 2. *An Atlas of Ancient Geography, Biblical and Classical* eventually appeared in five parts in 1872–4 and then in a single volume in 1874, with a reprint in 1875 (Talbert 1994, 1996). It was edited by Smith and by George Grove (later famous for his *Dictionary of Music*, 1878–89, but previously an assistant editor for Smith's *Dictionary of the Bible* of 1860–3). Its assembly was not only slow work but also expensive, partly because of the expense of the engraving, which was done to a very high standard in Paris; John Murray lost several thousand pounds on the project. The *Atlas* was later abridged and revised by the Oxford ancient historian G. B. Grundy as *A Smaller Classical Atlas* (1904; 2nd edn 1917; final printing 1967). It was for long a useful adjunct to the massive dictionaries which still provide a valuable reference resource, and which together constitute, as Smith himself said, 'an Encyclopaedia of Classical Antiquity'.[45]

Further Projects, Realized and Unrealized

The *Dictionary of Geography* was the last of Smith's large classical dictionaries to be published, but other projects were mooted. In the 1850s he was often in touch with Sir George Cornewall Lewis, who was keen for Smith to bring out a further dictionary on the natural history of the ancient world. The two men exchanged information on this for some time: Lewis sent Smith an article on amber which he had published, Smith provided him with useful books and references. Another enthusiastic supporter was T. H. Huxley, whom Smith met on holiday on the isle of Arran. The project collapsed when it became clear that it was impossible to find competent contributors to cover the whole range.

At about the same time, Smith began to plan a reference work which would have dwarfed his other books: the *Biographia Britannica*. Named after a famous dictionary of the mid-eighteenth century, it was to be conducted on a very large scale.[46] Had it got off the ground, it would have anticipated, and quite possibly prevented, the publication of the *Dictionary of National Biography*. The project is mentioned in Smith's letters to Murray in 1856, and in passing in 1865. In 1862 Murray had written to a Mrs Tindal, who had offered information on an ancestor for the 'New Biographia

---

[45] Preface to the *Dictionary of Greek and Roman Geography*, vol. 1, dated December 1853.
[46] The *Biographia Britannica* (7 vols, 1747–66) had been produced by a group led by William Oldys. For details and some context, see Thomas 2005, 11–14.

Britannica', that 'Dr. Smith...is so absorbed...with the engagements which will employ him for the next 12 months that he is not able to make more than preliminary arrangements for the work.'[47] In the end, Murray decided that the financial outlay was too large to risk (Huxley 1923, 181).

Another project, in this case successfully realized, was for a large Latin-English dictionary. This was published in 1855 and reached a 22nd edition in 1904, which was in turn kept going till a 26th impression in 1926. In the early 1850s Smith and Murray negotiated with Longman for the right to use Riddle's well-established dictionary as a basis, but the talks petered out. They then thought of importing the plates of the American Ethan Andrews' 1850 dictionary, based on Freund, but the fee demanded by its publishers Harper and Brothers put them off. In the end Smith hired two assistants to go back to Freund's original and remove errors, but they were not very effective, and he ran into flak from Sampson Low, Andrews' publishers, who circulated a flysheet which compared the two books and indignantly alleged plagiarism. Pages from Riddle and Smith were reproduced, the latter with text rubricated to show what had been omitted in the alleged plagiarism.[48] Smith's old teacher Thomas Key also weighed in with a review in the *Westminster Review* of July 1856 which stands out even in the sulphurous annals of *odium philologicum*. Referring to Smith's Tacitean selections of 1840, Key claimed that it was a collection of works by German scholars translated by the editor's friends, 'saving the title page, which was the genuine contribution of Dr Smith himself' (89). His comparison of Freund, Andrews, and Smith is a pure hatchet job, closing with such remarks as this: 'That promise of future scholarship which Dr Smith gave in his early years, we find upon closer examination was soon blighted by a spirit which has reduced him at last to the most unscrupulous class of book-manufacturers' (112). Nowhere did Key reveal that he was himself engaged in the preparation of a large Latin-English dictionary (Glucker 1981).

In the 1860s and 1870s, Smith branched out in several directions. His lexicographical empire was extended from the classical to the biblical world, with *A Dictionary of the Bible, Comprising its Antiquities, Biography, Geography and Natural History* (3 vols, 1860–3). In the following decade came *A Dictionary of Christian Antiquities* (2 vols, 1875–80), described as 'a continuation of *The Dictionary of the Bible*.'[49] He also published widely-used courses in Latin and Greek, *Principia Latina* (6 parts, 1860–77) and *Initia Graeca* (3 parts, 1864–70).[50] Smith seems not to have initiated new projects

---

[47] John Murray to Mrs Tindal, Oak Knoll Books catalogue 264 (2005), no. 446: drawn to my attention by Ian Jackson.

[48] Flysheet bound in with a copy of *Oxford Essays* 1856, in the author's possession. The rubricated page—a study in scarlet and black—is reproduced on the cover of 2007a.

[49] Like its predecessor, this was to be overshadowed in 1898 by the publication of James Hastings' five-volume *Dictionary of the Bible*.

[50] Both of these were complete courses, but the survival patterns of second-hand copies suggest that the initial volumes, which included grammars, were the most widely sold. It was surely the initial volume of *Principia Latina* to which Bertrand Russell referred, when in his eighties, in 1955, he tried to secure a copy of the book from which he had learned Latin seventy years earlier: '*Principia Latina*, on which I wasted so much fruitless labour': Feinberg and Kasrils 1969, 1.41.

in the 1880s; not surprisingly perhaps, as he was now moving into his seventies, and had been editor of John Murray's *Quarterly Review* since 1867 (he contributed a dozen articles to the *Review* between 1856 and 1881). Reissues and reprints however continued to appear, and some of his dictionaries were revised by other hands. Wayte and Marindin's revision of the *Dictionary of Greek and Roman Antiquities* had its final printing in 1914; five years later, *A Classical Dictionary of Biography, Mythology and Geography* was reprinted for the last time.

Marginality and Centrality

By the 1860s Smith had become a familiar figure, known through and in some sense identified with his books (one finds references in contemporary letters to meeting 'Dr. Dictionary Smith').[51] This change was in a way paralleled in the history of his books, which moved from the cheap part works whose accessibility, as we have seen, had been welcomed, to massive and expensive bound volumes. In 1857, when the last of the three was published (and they thus became finally unavailable for subscription), an otherwise enthusiastic reviewer complained at their cost, describing them as

too expensive for any but those who are blessed with abundant means. The published price of the three Dictionaries is within a trifle of *Twelve pounds*, which is to many as effectual a prohibition against their use, as the Index Expurgatorius itself to a Roman Catholic community.

(Millard 1857)

An important aspect of Smith's establishment status was the 'Dr Smith' brand name, reinforced by the uniform binding of his textbooks, black boards with red-edged pages. One of those who used them was the Australian Arthur Piddington (1862–1945), who remembered in his memoirs that:

The very sight of that series of manuals, with their stiff black buckram covers and red edged leaves, makes me think to this day what a helotism for children is uninspired teaching. Years afterwards, when I met Dr Smith in London, and found him dressed from head to foot in black, with ruddy neck and ears and face and hands, a qualm of antipathy rose in me at the semblance between book and author, and I couldn't even tell him that I had been taught from his grammar-books.[52]

Both Smith and his books, then, were studies in scarlet and black.

---

[51] Harriet Grote, wife of the historian of Greece, wrote to her husband on 24 April 1867, 'Remember me kindly to dear Dr William Smith (the Dictionary)': Lewin 1909, 2. 266. Lewin himself explains (ibid. 344) that Smith was known as 'Dictionary Smith'. Writing to Henry Reeve on 22 June 1882, Sir Henry Taylor remembered a dinner at The Club: 'Literature and Learning represented by yourself, Dr. Dictionary Smith, Lecky and Lord Afton...': Laughton 1898, 2. 306.

[52] Piddington 1929, 153. Smith was large and substantially-built, and the boys of Mill Hill School, which he visited to conduct viva voce examinations, nicknamed him 'Pudding': James 1909, 142. For a more sympathetic view, see the pleasantly evocative piece by 'W', 'The grammar hour', *The Academy*, 15 September 1900, 25–6, in which the author praises Smith's fresh and interesting choice of literary examples in his *Manual of English Grammar*. 'to me', writes W, 'his book remained always two books—a Grammar to be shirked, and an anthology to be loved'.

The Smith conjured up by Piddington's story is very much the establishment figure of his later years. In 1852 he had applied for the chair of Greek in Edinburgh; he was strongly supported but lost out to J. S. Blackie.[53] In the following year he was appointed a classical examiner at the University of London, and in 1854 elected a member of the Athenaeum. From 1867 till his death in 1893 he edited John Murray's famous journal the *Quarterly Review*. Smith was appointed a member of the Royal Commission on Copyright in 1875; he was knighted at Windsor in 1892, the year before his death. Yet he began his career as a rather marginal figure, and this marginality is reflected in the choice of collaborators for his dictionaries. Like many other dissenters, he took advantage of the new London University, which opened its doors in 1828, enrolling in its junior classes in the following year. Some boys were able to go on to Cambridge, the training-ground of several of the London University professors—George Long, Thomas Key, Henry Malden, and Augustus De Morgan were all Trinity men—but a Cambridge degree was not accessible to a dissenter like Smith.[54]

An incident occurred in 1869 which throws an interesting light on Smith's journey from his Nonconformist youth to his established position in metropolitan literary society. In the previous year, Matthew Arnold had begun publishing in the *Cornhill Magazine* the articles which were later to appear as *Culture and Anarchy*. In the October issue of the *Quarterly Review*, of which Smith was editor, Oscar Browning was very rude about Arnold's recent *Schools and Universities on the Continent*, and in passing remarked that Smith's excellent dictionaries and manuals had no equal on the continent.[55] Arnold was infuriated both by Browning's criticisms and by his being allowed to puff Smith's books in Smith's journal, and he allowed himself some cutting remarks on the subject in the preface to the first edition of *Culture and Anarchy*, which was published in January 1869. In the following month, however, as Arnold wrote to his mother:

Dr Smith... came up to me with... his hand held out, saying he forgave me all I had said about him and the Quarterly... for the sake of the truth and usefulness of what I had said about the Nonconformists. He said he was born a Nonconformist, was brought up with them, and had seen them all his life—so he was a good judge.[56]

---

[53] He led in the first ballot, but was defeated by Blackie in the second. Smith issued three series of testimonials, eighty-five in all (see n. 3, above). For the context, see the excellent account in Wallace 2006, 160–81.

[54] Alexander Gooden, the son of Roman Catholic parents, had won the same Latin and Greek prizes as Smith two years before him, in 1832, and went on to Trinity. He graduated in 1840 as Senior Classic, his parental religion apparently abandoned. See Smith and Stray 2003.

[55] Daremberg and Saglio's *Dictionnaire des antiquités grecques et romaines* (Paris: Hachette, 6 vols in 10) was published between 1877 and 1904. It did not deserve Browning's contemptuous dismissal; for a characteristically detailed and generous assessment of letters A–C which emphasized that it included topics not treated by Smith, see Mayor 1887. On the assembly of Daremberg and Saglio's dictionary, see the section devoted to it in *Anabases* 4 (2006), 159–255.

[56] Matthew Arnold to Mary Penrose Arnold, 20 February 1869: *The Letters of Matthew Arnold*, ed. C. Y. Lang, vol. 3 (Charlottesville, VA: University Press of Virginia, 1998), 316. Browning's article was 'Mr. Matthew Arnold's report on French education', *Quarterly Review* 125 (1868) 473–90. After Smith's display of magnanimity, Arnold felt obliged to cut his critical remarks from the preface. The excised text is printed in Super 1965, 530–1; cf. Coulling 1974, 208–9.

A major target of Arnold's articles had been the narrow-minded world of the dissenting lower middle classes; Smith's response shows that he himself, born into that world, had come to reject its tenets.

The Afterlife of Smith's Dictionaries

By 1913, only sixty-four copies remained in stock of the *Dictionary of Biography and Mythology*, and the plates were sold off; the final printing of Wayte and Marindin's revision of the *Dictionary of Greek and Roman Antiquities* was in 1914; five years later, *A Classical Dictionary of Biography, Mythology and Geography* was reprinted for the last time. The last of the large dictionaries to survive was the Geography dictionary, but in 1942, the remaining twenty-eight copies were sold or wasted and the plates melted and sold for scrap—perhaps helping the war effort.[57] The many surviving copies, in libraries and in private hands, continued to be read and used in a variety of ways. Lew Wallace drew heavily on the second edition of the book for historical detail in his classic novel of the Roman world, *Ben-Hur* (1878). It was especially valuable as a source of detail in his account of Judah's scene in the galley rammed by the Naxian pirates, and the chariot race in the Maxentian Circus at Antioch.[58] When the 1925 MGM film of the book was being made, Smith's dictionary was again drawn on for the design of costumes and chariots, which were tried out by firefighters and National Guardsmen.[59] More recently Steven Saylor, the author of several historical novels set in the Roman world, has declared that the *Dictionary of Greek and Roman Antiquities*, which he first encountered in 1993, is his most valuable research tool.[60] Saylor's use of Smith is of course entirely legitimate, as was Lew Wallace's in the 1870s. The same can be said of G. O. Trevelyan's *Cambridge Dionysia* of 1858, which incorporates an account of the author's reading the article in the *Dictionary of Antiquities* on the Dionysia: 'But the Greek words bothered me, and I was too lazy to rise for a lexicon' (Trevelyan 1905, 42).

In 1918 the archaeologist F. W. Hasluck told his colleague R. M. Dawkins that:

The Pliny source I got out of Bayle's Dict. Historique. I discovered (or rather, Hill showed me) the use of out-of-date encyclopedias, while doing the Lemnian earth:[61] it is an inexpensive way of

---

[57] Ironically, the plates of a relative failure, the *Classical Atlas*, survive to this day. They were sent to Bartholomew's in Edinburgh, rescued from asset-stripping in the 1990s and are now held in the map library of the National Library of Scotland. (My thanks for this and other information to Richard Talbert, who was instrumental in saving the plates.)

[58] Reference to Smith's dictionaries however did not prevent Wallace from describing the galley rowers as slaves: see James 2001.

[59] See David Mayer's introduction to the World's Classics edition (Oxford 1998), xvii–xx.

[60] In an interview given in 1998, Saylor said that 'It lists everything known about the Romans at the time (1869), every citation, every author. It's an incredible source for me.' (Interview with Sarah Cuthbertson, available online at www.historicalnovelsociety.org.)

[61] Hasluck and Hasluck 1929, 2.671–88, based on Hasluck 1909–10. 'Hill' is the numismatist Sir George Hill (1867–1948).

getting a bibliography of forgotten sources on revived subjects. You suppress the encyclopaedia's name of course, & only cite its sources—as if you had read them all through when you were a boy.[62]

The same technique was employed by Robert Graves during the preparation of his *The Greek Myths* (1955). In his introduction, Graves writes that:

It is strange that the standard work in English, Smith's Dictionary of Greek Mythology and Biography [*sic*], first published in 1844, has not been brought up to date since archaeology and anthropology were both in their cradles. The editors still regarded the cities of Troy and Cnossus as minstrels' fancies; did not suspect the matriarchal origins of Greek society; and largely believe that the World had been created in 4004 BC. My publishers have asked me to write a mythological dictionary on modern lines...[63]

What Graves does not mention is that the sources used for his book were culled from Smith's dictionaries, as is clear from a comparison of his reference listings with Smith's own. Graves did not plagiarize the texts of Smith or his contributors, but did allow his readers to attribute to him a learning he did not himself possess.

In the young E. M. Forster's case, the attraction of Smith's dictionaries lay not in their text but in their illustrations, and specifically in those which showed the undraped male penis: 'he used to look the "dirties" in Smith's *Classical Dictionary* and was annoyed when, in Kingsley's *Heroes*, they were covered up with drapery.'[64] William Smith himself had been concerned at the reaction of the public to some of the undraped figures in woodcut illustrations.[65] The only evidence that the text, as opposed to the illustrations, of the dictionaries was found offensive is to be found in A. P. Herbert's splendid account of the prosecution of the Headmaster of Eton under the Obscene Publications Act of 1857. The magistrate denounced the filthy loves of gods and goddesses and found the defendant guilty, recommending that 'a thorough survey be made of the whole body of classical literature in order that our schools and colleges may be made safe for aristocracy' (Herbert 1935, 164–70).

World War II saw not only the final destruction of plates of the dictionaries, but the buying in by John Murray of the Smith family's copyright (for which they paid £1,000 in 1943). Four years later, a new era in classical reference dawned with the publication of the *Oxford Classical Dictionary*, which had first been projected in 1933. Reviewing it in the *Times Literary Supplement*, under the heading 'The new Smith', R. W. Chapman, who had graduated from Oxford in Classics in 1906, gave it a favourable reception, but remarked that 'it will not be, like Smith, a household name.'[66] The increasing specialization

---

[62] Hasluck to Dawkins, 21 November 1918: Hasluck 1926, 162.

[63] Graves 1955. The passage does not appear in the 1958 edition. Graves employed two young Oxford graduates to collect the material for the book.

[64] Furbank 1978, 1.36. 'Dirty' was Forster's childhood name for his penis.

[65] On 23 October 1851 he sent some prospective illustrations to John Murray with covering note: 'I would direct your attention to those which I have marked, X, namely on pp. 265, 38, 59, 162. I fear some readers will object to the prominence of the naked figure' (John Murray Archive.)

[66] *TLS*, 2 April 1949, 219. The editorial preface to *OCD* also invoked the comparison with Smith's dictionaries. Chapman's review was anonymous, and so readers were not to know that an OUP publication was being reviewed by a former Secretary to the Delegates of OUP.

206 CLASSICS IN BRITAIN

of classical scholarship was evident in the list of editors (nine) and contributors (161). The latter included several emigré scholars from Hitler's Germany, and the *Dictionary* thus, though in a very different context, echoed Smith's own use of German contributors nearly a century earlier.

Conclusion

The development of Smith's classical dictionaries reflects changing conceptions of classical scholarship in early Victorian England. The public-school curriculum was dominated by the rote learning of Latin and Greek grammar, the repeated study of a limited range of authors with little regard for their literary qualities or historical contexts, and the practice of Latin and Greek composition, in prose and in verse. The German style, brought to England in the 1820s by Hare and Thirlwall, was taken up by Smith in the following decade, and by his and Schmitz's *Classical Museum* in the 1840s (see Chapter 7). The *Museum*, together with Smith's classical dictionaries, acted as a conduit for the new style; but it also reflected the broadening of the social and institutional basis of scholarship beyond the Anglican enclaves of Oxbridge to the dissenting and secular circles of London and the provinces. Smith's training in London put him in touch with these circles. It also, crucially, introduced him to the SDUK, and to the cheap part-work publication of illustrated reference works which formed the model for his own dictionaries. It was the fusion of the German intellectual tradition with this accessible style of publication which formed the essence of 'Dr Smith's dictionaries'.

Anyone who surveys the sheer bulk of books put out under the 'Dr Smith' brand is entitled to be sceptical of the quantity and quality of his own involvement, even if few will go as far as the resentful Thomas Key in accusing him of belonging to 'the most unscrupulous class of book-manufacturers'. But nobody who reads his correspondence with Cornewall Lewis, Huxley, and Grote, all of whom admired his scholarship, can fail to be impressed by the man.[67] William Smith was not just a good scholar: he was naturally suited by talent and temperament to the task of editing. As Henry Malden, who taught him at London University, wrote in a testimonial for the Edinburgh chair in 1852, he was not only good at Greek, but had 'extensive and well digested collateral and illustrative reading... a remarkably good temper [and was] punctual and diligent, and even laborious, in the discharge of his duties'.[68]

---

[67] Grote and Cornewall Lewis supported Smith's application for the post of classical examiner at the University of London in 1853. He came top of twenty-seven candidates, polling a majority of the votes cast. (Smith to John Murray, 7 April 1853: John Murray Archive.)

[68] The phrase occurs in Malden's testimonial in support of Smith's application for the Edinburgh Greek chair in 1852 (see n. 3, above). My own experience of editing collaborative books only increases my admiration for him.

10

Jebb's Sophocles
An Edition and its Maker

Jebb's Sophocles, an edition of a classical author which has itself become a classic, was assembled by Richard Jebb between the early 1880s and the mid-1890s. Most of the work was done in Springfield, Jebb's house in Cambridge; a stone's throw away, in Newnham College, the young ladies called the Sophocles edition 'Big Jebb', to distinguish it from the abridged versions which followed (and which are discussed below).[1] The big-headed portrait of Jebb in Figure 10.1 was published in a Glasgow student magazine during his tenure of the Greek chair there (1875–89). Jebb was in fact a small man, and conscious of it. In 1891 he wrote to his sister about his young nephew, 'So Dick is going to be very tall! I have always wished that I was. It is a distinct advantage; women respect one more—except the very tall ones.'[2] But in other senses Jebb was a big man. His Sophocles brought him celebrity (see Figure 10.2), and he died in 1905 loaded with honours: Member of Parliament for his university for fourteen years, knighted, a member of the Order of Merit, the most celebrated British classical scholar of his day. Jebb's reputation was international even in his lifetime but he had especially close links with the United States. In 1874 he married Caroline Slemmer, widow of the commander of Fort Laramie during the Civil War; he subsequently made several visits to the USA, giving the Phi Beta Kappa lecture at Harvard in 1885 and the Turnbull lectures at Johns Hopkins in 1892, and became friendly with their professors of Greek, William Goodwin and Basil Gildersleeve. Between these two visits, in 1891, Jebb was offered the Greek chair at William Harper's new university at Chicago; having been elected Regius Professor of Greek at Cambridge in 1889, he refused the offer. In 1898 he was contacted by the founder of a Greek reading club set up by a group of lawyers in Rochester, New York, asking his permission for it to be called the R. C. Jebb Greek Reading Club. Permission granted, he was begged for a portrait photograph, which was duly sent, and hung up in the clubroom. After his death in December 1905,

---

[1] Girtonians also referred to the *editio maior* as 'Big Jebb', as Dora Pym recalled in her memoirs (Pym [1972] 304). The authority of the edition is reflected in her comment that 'everyone knew that what Jebb said Sophocles meant was correct' ('Dora's story', separately paginated at the end of Pym [1972] vol. 3, at p. 24).

[2] Jebb to Eglantyne Jebb, 16 Aug. 1891. Unless otherwise noted, letters quoted in this essay are held in the Jebb family papers, now held at Trinity College Library, Cambridge.

Figure 10.1 The new professor. Richard Jebb as portrayed in the Glasgow University student magazine *The Bailie* 9, no. 270, 19 December 1877. Jebb was Regius Professor of Greek at Glasgow from 1875 to 1889.

Jebb duly suffered from the Strachey effect: the early twentieth-century disparagement of the Victorians. A. E. Housman, appointed Professor of Latin at Cambridge in 1911, drew examples of sloppy reasoning from the Sophocles edition in his lectures on Textual Criticism, causing some local scandal. In one lecture, he imagined Sir Richard being caught near the Houses of Parliament with bulky-looking pockets, taken to a police station on suspicion of stealing silver spoons, and being defended in court by a

Figure 10.2 'AJAX MP': a cartoon by Spy (Sir Leslie Ward, 1851–1922), *Vanity Fair*, 20 October 1904 (Men of the Day no. 935). Jebb served as one of Cambridge University's two MPs from 1891 till his death in 1905.

red-nosed drunk named Porson. The prosecuting counsel, of course, was Housman himself.[3] In his inaugural lecture as professor of Greek at Sydney in 1938, Housman's ape Enoch Powell went even further, declaring that:

The most celebrated editor of Sophocles...whose work is in the hands of almost every student and who for half a century enjoyed the adulation of his countrymen...is a man prepared,

---

[3] See Diggle 2007. My thanks to James Diggle for allowing me to read his text before publication.

whenever it suits his prejudices, to bamboozle the reader deliberately by any variety of false argument or dishonest trick which occurs to him.[4]

As this in its own lurid way suggests, the man and the edition need to be taken together: *le commentaire, c'est l'homme même.* The Sophocles reveals its editor, just as—to take two other famous products of nineteenth-century Cambridge—the Lucretius of the 1860s reflects the powerfully decisive scholarship of Hugh Munro, and the Juvenal of the 1870s the uncontrolled search for truth of John Mayor.

My concern in this chapter is to situate Jebb and his work in a number of contexts. We can begin in Springfield, the house where the Sophocles edition was assembled, and which is not only near Newnham College, but barely fifty yards from the modern Faculty of Classics building.[5] During Jebb's time as Professor of Greek at Glasgow (1875–89) he benefited from the short Scottish academic year. It was a hard slog from October to March, with large classes to teach—often over a hundred students, between fifteen and thirty years old, many of them complete beginners.[6] December and January were low points, the days short and the nights cold. But every April he could escape to Cambridge for six months and devote himself to his writing. The Jebbs leased Springfield in 1881, and a few years later added the large room Jebb used as his study. His friend Oscar Browning of King's College remembered that:

When he was Greek Professor at Glasgow, and returned for his summer vacation at Cambridge, I was certain to find him in the afternoon in his spacious library writing his edition of Sopho-cles, always with a pencil, the portrait of his beautiful wife looking down upon him with encouragement.[7]

By 1889, when he moved back to Cambridge on his election to the Regius chair, Jebb had already produced the three Theban plays, at a rate of one play every two years. He maintained this rate throughout the edition, except that the *Oedipus Coloneus* (in any case, the longest play) took three years—he was delayed by his summer trip to the USA to give the Phi Beta Kappa lectures at Harvard.

Jebb's editing of Sophocles had begun in the late 1860s, with editions of *Electra* and *Ajax* in Rivingtons' school series Catena Classicorum. The *Electra* was one of the first batch of three books issued in 1867. It must have sold well, because Rivingtons decided to electrotype it (a new form of stereotyping), an indication that they expected large sales in future.[8] This was a time when the reform of classical teaching was being vigorously debated in Cambridge. Proposals for changes in the Classical Tripos issued by Jebb's Trinity colleagues Robert Burn and William Clark in the previous year had

---

[4] From Powell's inaugural lecture at Professor of Greek at Sydney, 7 May 1938; most easily accessible in J. E. Powell, *Reflections of a Statesman* (London 1991) 92.

[5] Jebb's house and the Faculty building are both on Sidgwick Avenue, a road built in 1890 whose construction Jebb resisted, as it removed a large amount of his front garden.

[6] See Morris 2007 for more information on this teaching environment.

[7] Oscar Browning, *Memories of Sixty Years at Eton, Cambridge and Elsewhere* (London 1910) 44.

[8] An appropriate decision perhaps: electrotyping becomes *Electra*.

led to a flurry of leaflets to which Jebb himself contributed. At the same time he, his friend Henry Sidgwick, and a few other young fellows of Trinity were setting up a college teaching system to improve on the rather desultory lectures previously available, and to replace the existing system of private tuition ('coaching'). The reforms extended to the provision of intercollegiate teaching, and the different but overlapping audiences are neatly encapsulated in the diagrams invented at just this point by the logician John Venn of Caius College, who used them in his own intercollegiate lectures. All this indicates that in the mid to late 1860s Jebb was thinking seriously about how Classics might best be taught at different levels.

A notable result of this rethinking in the two Sophocles editions was the translation of Greek passages into an English very different from the cumbrous translationese which was then so common. As his colleague James Duff remembered after his death, Jebb was 'not content to translate noble Greek into barbarous English', giving an example of translationese from an edition of Demosthenes: 'this woman in the first instance merely quietly to drink and eat dessert they tried to force, I should suppose'. Duff remarked that 'Jebb's two volumes were a revelation to the boys whose good fortune it was to read them ... They were quite unlike the commentaries we had been in the habit of using'.[9] A reviewer of the large *OT* edition in the *Journal of Education* remembered that:

Jebb's earlier Ajax and Electra made an epoch in school editions... the schoolboy... now learned for the first time that Sophocles had a style which did not suggest either an Act of Parliament or a leader in the Daily Telegraph. He found, to his astonishment, that Sophocles as rendered by Prof. Jebb, had something in common with Milton and Shakespeare.[10]

English played a large part in Jebb's books. Traditionally, all notes, or at least textual notes, had been given in Latin; and when in the early nineteenth century editions began to appear with English notes, they were very controversial. The Classics occupied a semi-sacred position, between the sacred sphere of the Bible and the everyday world of the vernacular; to use English in editions of classical authors thus threatened a fatal breaching of the walls between the worlds (cf. 2016b). It is thus not surprising that editions which adopted English announced this on their title pages—even as late as 1853, when Bernard Drake's *Eumenides* and John Mayor's *Juvenal* were published by Macmillan. In that same year, the twelve-year old Richard Jebb was sent to St Columba's College near Dublin. In the following March, he asked his father to send him editions of Euripides and Horace with English notes; in May, he was severely

---

[9] Duff, letter to Caroline Jebb after Jebb's death, quoted by her: Jebb 1907, 92–3. Duff's 'we' shows that he was referring to his own experience, as a schoolboy in the 1870s.

[10] Review of *Sophocles, Oedipus Tyrannus*, ed. R. C. Jebb (Cambridge 1883): *Journal of education* (1 May 1884) 180–1. Dora Pym's autobiography records that as a schoolgirl *c*.1900 she 'read Jebb's translation as poetry (it was the *OC*); it reminded her of passages from Tennyson; then she went back to the Greek, realized Sophocles was a poet too, and read him'. 'Dora's story', separately paginated at end of D. Pym, 'Patchwork from the past' (1972) vol. 3, at p. 24.

admonished by the Warden (headmaster) after his teacher found he was using the Horace edition.[11] The choice of English for notes was thus an issue of which the over-sensitive young Jebb had been made painfully aware.

The launch of the Catena Classicorum series in 1867 was prompted by the expanding market for such books created by the growth of examinations. Both Oxford and Cambridge had set up local examinations in the 1850s, and this had led to the founding of school series by their presses—the Clarendon Press series at Oxford began to appear in 1866 and by 1870 had published over fifty titles; Cambridge's Pitt Press series began to appear in 1875 (2013b, c). The aim was to have editions specified in examination syllabuses for the upper forms of schools. These books opened up a new genre, between the scholarly and the school edition; their authors were often bright young graduates who were allowed by recent Oxbridge reforms to be non-resident while retaining their college fellowships. Teaching in public schools while maintaining their university connections, they were encouraged to think how their university learning might be adapted to school teaching. It was this cross-fertilization of levels which was to produce such classic textbooks as *Bradley's Arnold* (for Latin prose composition) and Sidgwick's *Greek Prose Composition* (for Greek).[12]

So much for the early productions of Sophocles' Jebb; but why Sophocles? After all, Jebb's range was very wide. As well as ancient literature, he published on Bentley and on Milton; on Troy and on Homeric archaeology; on the British Museum catalogue and on secondary education; on modern Greek and on ancient journalism. Within classical literature, he wrote on Thucydides, the Attic orators, Theophrastus, Bacchylides, Homer, and Lucretius, and once contemplated a translation of Juvenal. His work on Greek drama, however, was confined to Sophocles. In the introduction to his book on the Attic orators, Jebb made his preferences clear, rejecting the image of Sophocles as 'cold, pompous, stiff', compared with Euripides' 'warm, flexible, fruitful sympathy with humanity': 'Euripides is human, but Sophocles is more human; Sophocles is so in the only way in which a Greek could be, by being more Greek.'[13] In the following year he clarified his position in a primer on Greek literature:

the plays of Sophocles have this special interest, that they interpret, more spiritually than anything else that we have, the higher moral and mental side of the age of Pericles; they have its noble tone of conciliation between sacred tradition and a progressive culture...there is no other Greek poet whose genius belongs so peculiarly to the best Greek time...in order to fully appreciate Sophocles, we must place ourselves in sympathy with the Greek mind in its most characteristic modes of thought and with the Greek sense of beauty in its highest purity.

(*Primer of Greek Literature* [London 1877] 88)

[11] Jebb, letters to his father of 27 March and 17 May 1854: 2013a, 16–17, 19–20. The master was none other than the great bibliographer Henry Bradshaw, who was later, as a fellow of King's College and University Librarian at Cambridge, on very good terms with Jebb.

[12] T. K. Arnold's *A Practical Introduction to Latin Prose Composition* began to appear in 1839 and was revised by G. G. Bradley in 1852; a later revision by Bradley, in the 1880s, became known as 'Bradley's Arnold'. Sidgwick's *Introduction to Greek Prose Composition* was published in 1876.

[13] *The Attic Orators from Antiphon to Isaeus* (London 1876) 1.c.

In this commitment to Sophoclean perfection and to the Paterian ideal of Greece, Jebb was at variance with several other scholars. His successor at Glasgow, Gilbert Murray, felt much more at home with Euripides. The rumbustious J. P. Mahaffy of Dublin, with whom Jebb fought several pamphlet battles, also preferred Euripides to Sophocles, and was even prepared to discuss Greek homosexuality in print. Closer to home, Jebb's pupil Arthur Verrall produced three editions and two books on Euripides. Even more galling, he constructed in them a rationalist and anti-Christian Euripides whom Jebb must have found embarrassing as well as unbelievable.[14] In a fine essay on Jebb's scholarship published in 1907, Verrall commented that 'He could not speak of Euripides without pain in his voice, and seldom, without necessity, spoke at all. He had no strong desire, I think, to comprehend such a person.'[15] It is difficult to repress the suspicion that Jebb was avoiding the Euripideans as much as Euripides himself. In 1897, Murray sent him a copy of his *History of Ancient Greek Literature*. Acknowledging it, Jebb commented that:

I suppose we belong, in some sense, to rather different schools...I imagine that you have more sympathy than I have with the style of the New Journalism. But it is one of the charms of the classics that they afford room for endless variety of treatment.[16]

Jebb's reference to the New Journalism (a phrase coined by Matthew Arnold in 1887) refers to the popular style of the new mass-audience newspapers of the 1880s, exemplified by the crusading journalist W. T. Stead, from 1883 editor of the *Pall Mall Gazette* and famous for his exposé of the white slave trade. In that same year (the year when his Sophocles series was inaugurated with *OT*), Jebb began to write for the *Fortnightly Review*, whose editor Thomas Sweet Escott had asked him to become a contributor.[17] Escott had written to Jebb in August 1882 praising his monograph on Bentley, whose 'singular thoroughness', he thought:

is a great contrast to many of the monographs & manuals, which are now issued, & it is a valuable contribution to the real knowledge of the public.

It has occurred to me that an exceedingly good article might be written apropos of these same manuals & monographs—calculating how far they do good, & pointing out that they offer a rather dangerous opportunity to smatterers. It seems to me difficult to over rate the mischief which men of the stamp of Mr Mahaffy—who...appears to know nothing thoroughly, or accurately, or in scholar-like fashion—do to the cause of true education & genuine culture.[18]

---

[14] On Verrall, see Lowe 2005.

[15] Jebb, *Life* 429–87, at 467. A partial parallel can be found in the attitude of C. S. Lewis to F. R. Leavis: 'I never heard Lewis speak ill of Leavis, but then he plainly preferred not to speak about him at all.' George Watson, quoted in J. Gross, *The New Oxford Book of Literary Anecdotes* (Oxford 2006) 277.

[16] Jebb to Murray, 30 Sept 1897. MSS G. Murray, Bodleian Library.

[17] Escott had read Classics at Oxford, and was deputy professor of classics at King's College, London 1865–73 before embarking on a career in journalism.

[18] Escott to Jebb, 14 August 1882: for the complete letter, see 2013a, 104–5.

The reference to Mahaffy was of course well chosen, and Jebb replied enthusiastically:

In regard to classical literature, there is a distinct mission for a journal of the highest position and influence:—I mean, to explode the pseudo-popular treatment of it (which, as I conceive, Mr Mahaffy represents) by exhibiting a treatment which is at once sound and, in the best sense, popular.[19]

In December 1883 his edition of *OT* was published; Jebb was convinced it was selling badly because of a whispering campaign orchestrated by Mahaffy, and his senior colleague Hugh Munro felt obliged to consult Cambridge University Press, who reported that it had sold 500 copies in two months—a very respectable sale for a 15/- book. In comparison, Munro told Jebb, Benjamin Kennedy's edition of the play, published two years earlier at 3/-, had sold only 300 copies.[20] This is the Kennedy of the famous Latin Primer; but also, since 1867, the Regius Professor of Greek whose failure to resign or die would, for another six years, keep Jebb from stepping into his place.[21]

It may be that Jebb's two small Sophocles editions, *Electra* in 1867 and *Ajax* in 1868, were intended to begin a complete series of Sophocles plays. If so, his defeat in 1869 of Arthur Holmes, the Cambridge editor of the Catena Classicorum series, for the post of Public Orator of the University, may have something to do with his not contributing further volumes.[22] Jebb's next book, in 1870, was an edition of Theophrastus' *Characters*—not a much-edited author, though Frederick Paley had produced a text with Latin notes in the previous year. Jebb's edition printed the text with a facing translation (Figure 10.3): a format which suggested an attempt to aim at a general but not just a popular market; the notes are banished to the back of the book. His subtitle is 'An English translation from a revised text': as he explained in his preface, 'A translator of the Characters is forced to become also an editor. The text is corrupt, and has long been a field for the ingenuity of critics.' Compare the layout of the revised edition published by his friend and colleague John Sandys in 1909, after Jebb's death (Figure 10.4). Here the original and facing translation are joined by notes below in two columns. It is significant that the notes are all keyed to the translation, not to the Greek text: the major orientation is still to the general reader. As for the change of format, I am tempted to see it as influenced by the format of Jebb's Sophocles, and thus as a quiet posthumous tribute from a friend. There were a few passages which Jebb was not prepared to publish in translation, and which he therefore omitted; in his preface he faces the issue head-on, offering three arguments to be considered by what he calls 'that large majority who prefer the integrity to the purity of a text'. The manuscript tradition and variant

---

[19] (Jebb to Escott, 21 August 1882; BL, Add MS 58783.1. Full text at 2013c, 105–6.)
[20] Munro to Jebb, 7 Feb. 1884.
[21] There were then no academic pensions; which helps to explain why Kennedy died in office in his mid-eighties in 1889, as did John Mayor, Professor of Latin, in 1910.
[22] It may also have had something to do with Holmes' suicide in 1875.

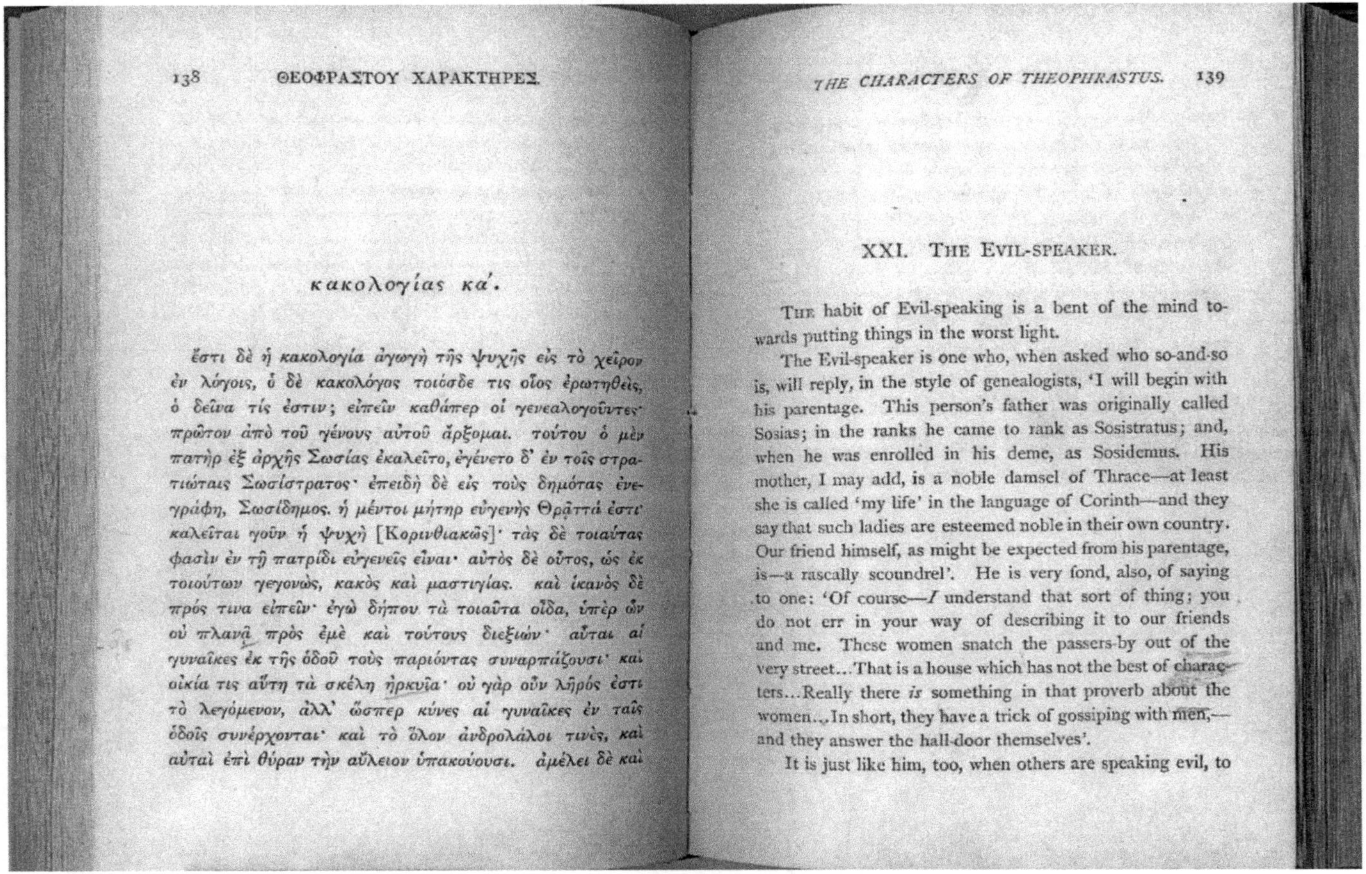

138 ΘΕΟΦΡΑΣΤΟΥ ΧΑΡΑΚΤΗΡΕΣ.

κακολογίας κα´.

ἔστι δὲ ἡ κακολογία ἀγωγὴ τῆς ψυχῆς εἰς τὸ χεῖρον ἐν λόγοις, ὁ δὲ κακολόγος τοιόσδε τις οἷος ἐρωτηθεὶς, ὁ δεῖνα τίς ἐστιν; εἰπεῖν καθάπερ οἱ γενεαλογοῦντες· πρῶτον ἀπὸ τοῦ γένους αὐτοῦ ἄρξομαι. τούτου ὁ μὲν πατὴρ ἐξ ἀρχῆς Σωσίας ἐκαλεῖτο, ἐγένετο δ' ἐν τοῖς στρατιώταις Σωσίστρατος· ἐπειδὴ δὲ εἰς τοὺς δημότας ἐνεγράφη, Σωσίδημος. ἡ μέντοι μήτηρ εὐγενὴς Θρᾶττά ἐστι· καλεῖται γοῦν ἡ ψυχὴ [Κορινθιακῶς]· τὰς δὲ τοιαύτας φασὶν ἐν τῇ πατρίδι εὐγενεῖς εἶναι· αὐτὸς δὲ οὗτος, ὡς ἐκ τοιούτων γεγονὼς, κακὸς καὶ μαστιγίας. καὶ ἱκανὸς δὲ πρός τινα εἰπεῖν· ἐγὼ δήπου τὰ τοιαῦτα οἶδα, ὑπὲρ ὧν οὐ πλανᾷ πρὸς ἐμὲ καὶ τούτους διεξιών· αὗται αἱ γυναῖκες ἐκ τῆς ὁδοῦ τοὺς παριόντας συναρπάζουσι· καὶ οἰκία τις αὕτη τὰ σκέλη ἠρκυῖα· οὐ γὰρ οὖν λῆρός ἐστι τὸ λεγόμενον, ἀλλ' ὥσπερ κύνες αἱ γυναῖκες ἐν ταῖς ὁδοῖς συνέρχονται· καὶ τὸ ὅλον ἀνδρολάλοι τινὲς, καὶ αὐταὶ ἐπὶ θύραν τὴν αὔλειον ὑπακούουσι. ἀμέλει δὲ καὶ

THE CHARACTERS OF THEOPHRASTUS. 139

XXI. THE EVIL-SPEAKER.

THE habit of Evil-speaking is a bent of the mind towards putting things in the worst light.

The Evil-speaker is one who, when asked who so-and-so is, will reply, in the style of genealogists, 'I will begin with his parentage. This person's father was originally called Sosias; in the ranks he came to rank as Sosistratus; and, when he was enrolled in his deme, as Sosidemus. His mother, I may add, is a noble damsel of Thrace—at least she is called 'my life' in the language of Corinth—and they say that such ladies are esteemed noble in their own country. Our friend himself, as might be expected from his parentage, is—a rascally scoundrel'. He is very fond, also, of saying to one: 'Of course—*I* understand that sort of thing; you do not err in your way of describing it to our friends and me. These women snatch the passers-by out of the very street...That is a house which has not the best of characters...Really there *is* something in that proverb about the women...In short, they have a trick of gossiping with men,—and they answer the hall-door themselves'.

It is just like him, too, when others are speaking evil, to

Figure 10.3 *The Characters of Theophrastus, an English Translation From a Revised text, with Introduction and* Notes, by R. C. Jebb (London: Macmillan, 1870).

Image courtesy of the Master and Fellows of Trinity College, Cambridge.

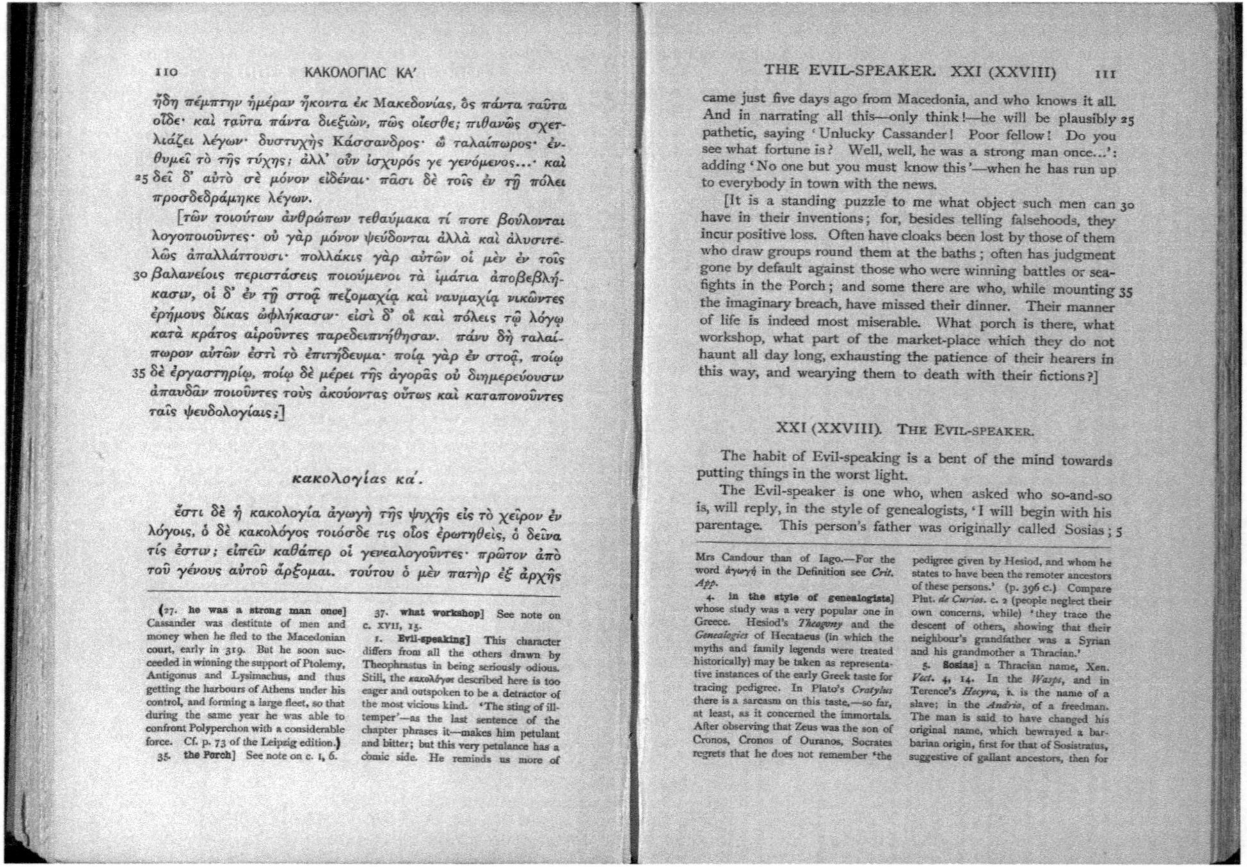

ἤδη πέμπτην ἡμέραν ἥκοντα ἐκ Μακεδονίας, ὃς πάντα ταῦτα οἶδε· καὶ ταῦτα πάντα διεξιών, πῶς οἴεσθε; πιθανῶς σχετλιάζει λέγων· δυστυχὴς Κάσσανδρος· ὦ ταλαίπωρος· ἐνθυμεῖ τὸ τῆς τύχης; ἀλλ' οὖν ἰσχυρός γε γενόμενος... καὶ δεῖ δ' αὐτὸ σὲ μόνον εἰδέναι· πᾶσι δὲ τοῖς ἐν τῇ πόλει προσδεδράμηκε λέγων.

[τῶν τοιούτων ἀνθρώπων τεθαύμακα τί ποτε βούλονται λογοποιοῦντες· οὐ γὰρ μόνον ψεύδονται ἀλλὰ καὶ ἀλυσιτελῶς ἀπαλλάττουσι· πολλάκις γὰρ αὐτῶν οἱ μὲν ἐν τοῖς βαλανείοις περιστάσεις ποιούμενοι τὰ ἱμάτια ἀποβεβλήκασιν, οἱ δ' ἐν τῇ στοᾷ πεζομαχίᾳ καὶ ναυμαχίᾳ νικῶντες ἐρήμους δίκας ὠφλήκασιν· εἰσὶ δ' οἳ καὶ πόλεις τῷ λόγῳ κατὰ κράτος αἱροῦντες παρεδειπνήθησαν. πάνυ δὴ ταλαίπωρον αὐτῶν ἐστὶ τὸ ἐπιτήδευμα· ποία γὰρ οὐ στοά, ποία δὲ ἐργαστήριον, ποῖον δὲ μέρος τῆς ἀγορᾶς οὐ διημερεύουσιν ἀπαυδᾶν ποιοῦντες τοὺς ἀκούοντας οὕτως καὶ καταπονοῦντες ταῖς ψευδολογίαις;]

κακολογίας καʹ

ἔστι δὲ ἡ κακολογία ἀγωγή τῆς ψυχῆς εἰς τὸ χεῖρον ἐν λόγοις, ὁ δὲ κακόλογος τοιόσδε τις οἷος ἐρωτηθείς, ὁ δεῖνα τίς ἐστιν; εἰπεῖν καθάπερ οἱ γενεαλογοῦντες· τοῦτον ἀπὸ τοῦ γένους αὐτοῦ ἄρξομαι.

17. **he was a strong man once**] See note on c. XVII. 3.

1. **Evil-speaking**] This character differs from all the others drawn by Theophrastus in being seriously odious. Still, the κακόλογος described here is too eager and outspoken to be a detractor of the most vicious kind. The sting of ill-temper—as the last sentence of the chapter phrases it—makes him petulant and bitter; but this very petulance has a comic side. He reminds us more of

35. **the Porch**] See note on c. 1, 6.

---

came just five days ago from Macedonia, and who knows it all. And in narrating all this—only think!—he will be plausibly pathetic, saying 'Unlucky Cassander! Poor fellow! Do you see what fortune is? Well, well; he was a strong man once...'; adding 'No one but you must know this'—when he has run up to everybody in town with the news.

[It is a standing puzzle to me what object such men can have in their inventions; for, besides telling falsehoods, they incur positive loss. Often have cloaks been lost by those of them who draw groups round them at the baths; often has judgment gone by default against those who were winning battles or sea-fights in the Porch; and some there are who, while mounting the imaginary breach, have missed their dinner. Their manner of life is indeed most miserable. What porch is there, what workshop, what part of the market-place which they do not haunt all day long, exhausting the patience of their hearers in this way, and wearying them to death with their fictions?]

XXI (XXVIII). THE EVIL-SPEAKER.

The habit of Evil-speaking is a bent of the mind towards putting things in the worst light.

The Evil-speaker is one who, when asked who so-and-so is, will reply, in the style of genealogists, 'I will begin with his parentage. This person's father was originally called Sosias;5

Mr Casaubon than of Iago.—For the word ἀγωγή in the Definition see Def. App.

2. **In the style of genealogists** whose study was a very popular one in Greece. Hesiod's *Theogony* and the *Genealogies* of Hecataeus (in which the myths and family legends were treated historically) may be taken as representative instances of the early Greek taste for tracing pedigrees. In Plato's *Cratylus* there is a sarcasm on this taste,—so far, at least, as it concerned the immortals. After observing that Zeus was the son of Cronos, Cronos of Ouranos, Socrates regrets that he does not remember 'the

pedigree given by Hesiod, and whom he states to have been the remoter ancestors of these persons.' (p. 396 c.) Compare Plut. *de Coriol.* c. 1 [people neglect their own concerns, while] 'they trace the descent of others, shewing that their neighbour's grandmother was a Syrian and his grandmother a Thracian, Xen.

5. **Sosias**] a Thracian name, Xen. *Vect.* 4. 14. In the *Wasps*, and in Terence's *Heyra*, k is the name of a slave: in the *Andria*, of a freedman. The man is said to have changed his original name, which betrayed a barbarian origin, first for that of Sosistratus, suggestive of gallant ancestors, then for

---

Figure 10.4 The second edition of Jebb's *Theophrastus*, ed. J. E. Sandys (London: Macmillan, 1909). The text is set in Figgins Pica no. 4, the mid-page headings in the original Cambridge Porson type. Image courtesy of the Master and Fellows of Trinity College, Cambridge.

readings are discussed in a substantial appendix at the back of the book. This is thus an edition which aims both at general readers and at scholars. As Jebb says in his preface:

The first object of this book is to make these lively pictures of old Greek manners better known to English readers. But some critical labour has been given to it, and I venture to hope that in certain points of view it may have interest for scholars.

All in all, the Theophrastus, like the two small Sophocles editions, shows Jebb trying out formats, not afraid to innovate within and between conventional genres, and to address readers in a variety of markets. Jebb claimed that his motive in publishing the book was to show that 'the lighter traits of character are permanent and universal', just like 'the great, the organic lines of human nature' (Jebb 1907, 102). But the project may have been prompted by the debates on the reform of the Classical Tripos, the Cambridge honours course, in the late 1860s to which he himself had contributed, and which in 1871 led to a cautious widening of its scope. His own work in the 1860s was not just literary and not just classical. In 1869, for example, he published a substantial review of Curtius' history of Greece.[23] He had also reviewed several books on French literature and history for the *Saturday Review*, and it is possible that an interest in La Bruyère's *Characters*, which he read in the 1860s, played a part in leading him to Theophrastus.[24]

Jebb's next major project was a substantial work on the Attic orators. He began work on this in the summer of 1870, soon after the publication of the Theophrastus, but he had been thinking about it for some time: in February 1868 he had written to his mother:

Like the other 'assistant tutors', I am taking a class of college pupils beside my lectures this term ... My subject is the Greek Orators,—the same with which I propose to set the Cam on fire in my later years.[25]

This was the first substantial free time for a busy college tutor after his election as Public Orator of the university in November 1869; an election which made his plan to write on the orators particularly timely. Jebb's preface is interesting for its argument that the orators should be studied as part of the development of Greek as a whole. He is also concerned to offer students something better than the study of plain texts with a few scattered notes on historical allusions. In a comment which significantly echoes the preface to the Theophrastus, Jebb writes, 'A careful analysis, whether copious or not, is necessarily to some extent a commentary, since the analyst must exhibit his view of the relation in which each part of the writer's meaning stands to the rest' (*Attic Orators*, 1.xi). Jebb ends by arguing that the study of classics:

is about to enter on a larger and more truly vigorous life than it has had since the Revival of Letters. That study has become, in a new and fuller sense, scientific. The comparative method,

---

[23] *Cambridge University Gazette*, 3 Feb. 1869, 71–2.
[24] La Bruyère also featured in Jebb's account of the reception history of Sophocles: see Easterling 2005, 41.
[25] Jebb to his mother, 4 February 1868: 2013a, 49.

in its application to language, to literature, to mythology, to political and constitutional history, has given to the classics a general interest and importance far greater than they possessed in the days when the devotion which they attracted was most exclusive.   (*Attic Orators*, 1.xv)

It is to this new age, which he calls an age of transition, that Jebb offers his study of the Attic orators, as part of what he describes as 'that close study of the *best* Greek literature which ought ever to be united with attention to the place of Greece in the universal history of the mind'.[26]

Here Jebb is still under the influence of Pater. He is thus ideologically Oxonian rather than Cantabrigian, and one can see why Frank Turner in 1981 referred to 'the Oxford tradition of Arnold, Jebb and Jowett'.[27] For all of them, ancient Greece offered a vision of original perfection, located in the warm and glowing south, which might be used to improve and direct the progress of modernity. The rigours of the Glasgow winters may have strengthened this vision for Jebb. As we have seen from the preface to *Attic orators*, Sophocles was a prime exemplar of Greek culture: 'In Sophocles, as in a great sculptor, a thousand fine touches go to that which, as the greatest living creator in fiction has proved, he can still help to teach—the delineation of the great primary emotions' (*Attic orators* 1.c.). He is referring back to the mention of 'the great, the organic lines of human nature', the phrase used of his Theophrastus; but also to George Eliot, who had used the phrase when she and Jebb met in 1873.[28] Jebb restated his position in the following year in his *Primer of Greek Literature*, but with a striking addition, which I quoted from above:

Historically, the plays of Sophocles have this special interest, that they interpret, more spiritually than anything else that we have, the higher moral and mental side of the age of Pericles; they have its noble tone of conciliation between sacred tradition and a progressive culture, between authority and reason, between the letter and the spirit of religion.

(*Primer of Greek Literature*, 88)

Thus writes the descendant of bishops, who instead of being ordained has become an academic. He is working out a place for himself in the world and a way of explaining it. The rate of ordination at Oxford and Cambridge declined sharply from the 1850s, and by the 1880s the first-class graduates who thirty years before would have gone into the church and risen through it were going elsewhere, becoming dons, lawyers, or schoolmasters (Haig 1986a). For Jebb, Sophocles represented the role of spirituality in culture—something worthy, perhaps, to take the place of a religion which could no longer claim his full adherence.

Against this secularizing tide stood three outstanding Cambridge scholars who devoted their mastery of Greek to the study of the New Testament: Hort, Westcott, and Lightfoot. Joseph Lightfoot, Jebb's tutor at Trinity, ended his career as Bishop of

---

[26] Ibid., xv. His willingness to change formats continued at this stage: in the first edition of *Selections from the Attic Orators* (London 1880) the critical notes preceded the Greek text, in the second edition of 1888 they were placed beneath it (see Jebb's note in his preface, p. xviii).

[27] Turner 1981, 33.   [28] He had earlier made the same point in different words: Jebb 1907, 156.

Durham. As an undergraduate in the 1850s, Lightfoot had founded a student philological society; after graduation he became one of the editors of the *Journal of Classical and Sacred Philology* (Chapter 8). As an editor of several books of the New Testament he was acute, well read, alert to the importance of archaeology and respected by German scholars. Lightfoot was surely an important role model for Jebb. And if we go back further among the Trinity fellowship, the obvious candidate for a mentor is Hugh Munro, editor of Lucretius. Munro was until his death in 1885 an important source of advice for Jebb, whose papers include several letters in which Munro offers sensible and calming counsel to his nervous and sensitive young friend (2013a, 127–8, 129–30). Munro's edition of Lucretius, published in 1864, had been an event in the history of English classical scholarship, its learning, independence and decisive judgement providing a welcome sign that editions produced in this country could be more than rehashes of German scholarship.[29]

A notable feature of the Lucretius lay in its inclusion of a translation next to (though not facing) the text (see Figure 10.5), and this may well have influenced Jebb's thinking. In the first edition, the notes were in a separate volume, but Munro changed the format in subsequent editions. By the time Jebb begun his Sophocles series in 1883, he thus had three formats to compare and think about.[30] He must also have seen his Trinity colleague Henry Jackson's edition of Book V of the *Nicomachean Ethics*, which appeared in 1879; of this a reviewer commented, 'The translation *en regard*, a model of close and accurate scholarship, is in itself a commentary...'.[31]

One more potential exemplar for Jebb's Sophocles needs to be mentioned: the Cambridge Shakespeare published by Macmillan in nine volumes between 1863 and 1866.[32] The editors were all Trinity men: John Glover, William Aldis Wright, and Jebb's classical colleague William George Clark.[33] The original idea seems to have been Clark's, but Aldis Wright emerged as the leader of the enterprise.[34] Jebb must have

[29] It was surely this that Housman referred in the preface to his Manilius vol. 1 (1903) when he wrote of '1825, when our own great age of scholarship, begun in 1691 by Bentley's Epistola ad Millium, was ended by the successive strokes of doom which consigned Dobree and Elmsley to the grave and Blomfield to the bishopric of Chester. England disappeared from the fellowship of nations for the next forty years.' Blomfield's preferment was in 1824, Munro's *Lucretius* appeared in 1864.

[30] The formats of Munro's *Lucretius* are as follows. Ed. 1 (1864): Vol. 1 text, with translation at foot, both sides; Vol. 2 Notes I (1–92) Introduction, then text-critical notes on all books; Notes II (93–415) Explanatory notes on all books. Ed. 2 (1866): Vol. 1 text and notes, Vol. 2 translation. Ed. 3 (1873): Vol. 1 text, text-critical notes, explanatory notes, Vol. 2 translation. Ed. 4 (1886) [posthumous, ed. J. D. Duff]: Vol. 1 text and text-critical notes, Vol. 2 explanatory notes, Un-numbered vol. translation. Later eds. are largely reprints of Ed. 4, except for vol. 2 which has a '5th' ed. in 1928, with a new essay by E. N. da C. Andrade.

[31] *The Fifth Book of the Nicomachean Ethics of Aristotle* (Cambridge 1879), reviewed in *Athenaeum* 2693, 7 June 1879, 721–3, at 722. Jackson's apparatus criticus was printed beneath the text, his notes at the end of the book.

[32] G. Taylor, *Reinventing Shakespeare* (London 1990), 184–9.

[33] Glover and Wright were successively Librarians at Trinity, where the availability of the Shakespearian collection of Edward Capell, an earlier innovative editor of the plays, given in 1779, must have constituted both inspiration and resource (see D. J. McKitterick (ed.), *The Making of the Wren Library, Trinity College, Cambridge* (Cambridge 1995), 78–82).

[34] The most detailed account is in McKitterick 1998, 392–9. The edition was printed at the Press.

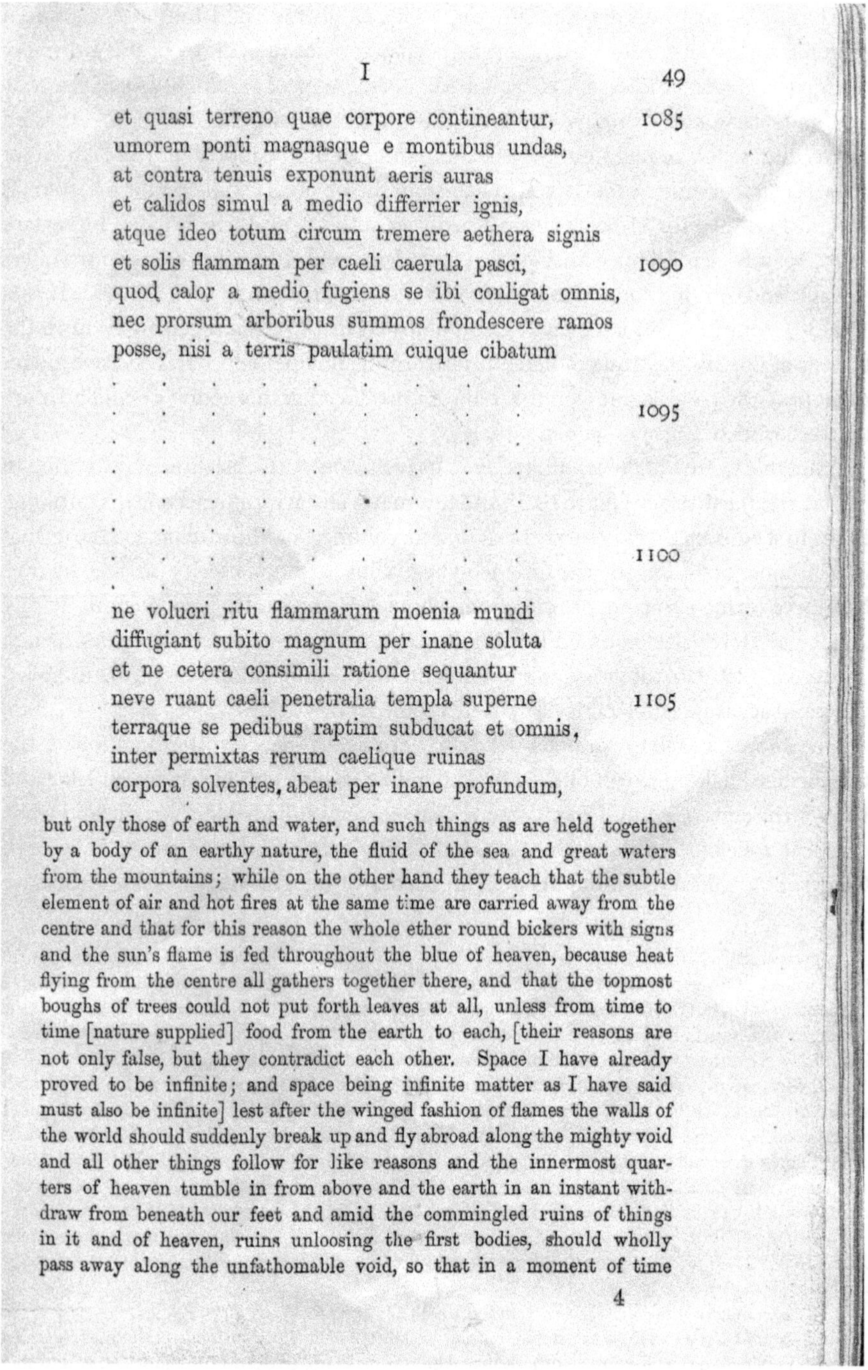

I   49

et quasi terreno quae corpore contineantur,   1085
umorem ponti magnasque e montibus undas,
at contra tenuis exponunt aeris auras
et calidos simul a medio differrier ignis,
atque ideo totum circum tremere aethera signis
et solis flammam per caeli caerula pasci,   1090
quod calor a medio fugiens se ibi conligat omnis,
nec prorsum arboribus summos frondescere ramos
posse, nisi a terris paulatim cuique cibatum

         .   .   .   .   .   .

           1095

         .   .   .   .   .   .

         .   .   .   .   .   .

         .   .   .   .   .   .

           1100

ne volucri ritu flammarum moenia mundi
diffugiant subito magnum per inane soluta
et ne cetera consimili ratione sequantur
neve ruant caeli penetralia templa superne   1105
terraque se pedibus raptim subducat et omnis,
inter permixtas rerum caelique ruinas
corpora solventes, abeat per inane profundum,

but only those of earth and water, and such things as are held together
by a body of an earthy nature, the fluid of the sea and great waters
from the mountains; while on the other hand they teach that the subtle
element of air and hot fires at the same time are carried away from the
centre and that for this reason the whole ether round bickers with signs
and the sun's flame is fed throughout the blue of heaven, because heat
flying from the centre all gathers together there, and that the topmost
boughs of trees could not put forth leaves at all, unless from time to
time [nature supplied] food from the earth to each, [their reasons are
not only false, but they contradict each other. Space I have already
proved to be infinite; and space being infinite matter as I have said
must also be infinite] lest after the winged fashion of flames the walls of
the world should suddenly break up and fly abroad along the mighty void
and all other things follow for like reasons and the innermost quarters of heaven tumble in from above and the earth in an instant withdraw from beneath our feet and amid the commingled ruins of things
in it and of heaven, ruins unloosing the first bodies, should wholly
pass away along the unfathomable void, so that in a moment of time

                                                    4

Figure 10.5 Lucretius, *De rerum natura*, ed. H. A. J. Munro (Cambridge: Deighton Bell, 1864), p. 49. The austere layout is typical of Munro and of his fellow-pupil at Shrewsbury School, J. E. B. Mayor.

known of the progress of the edition; he and Wright both belonged in the mid-1860s to a Trinity discussion group called the Tea Club.[35] The Shakespeare edition was innovatory (for example, in printing line numbers) and authoritative, and gave rise to a popular one-volume text, the *Globe Shakespeare*, which became a bestseller and was still being reprinted a century later. Thus when Jebb was beginning to think of his own academic projects during the early years of his fellowship, an important multi-volume edition and its abridgement were being planned, assembled, and published by men he knew well.

The Sophocles Edition

The seven volumes of Jebb's Sophocles appeared between 1883 and 1896; a planned eighth volume on the fragments never appeared. Walter Headlam, who was given the task after Jebb's death in 1905, himself died in 1908, and the fragments were eventually published by Alfred Pearson in 1917. Ever since Jebb produced the two small editions in 1867–8 he must have been planning to go on to something on a larger scale. This will explain why the publication of Lewis Campbell's two-volume edition, in 1871 and 1881, did not put him off. But in any case Campbell's edition was conceived on a smaller scale, and did not include a translation.

Part of what one remembers after first encountering Jebb's Sophocles is its physical presence: a rather grand tall octavo, bound in the olive green so fashionable in the 1880s and with discreet impressed bands.[36] Such grandeur had to be paid for, and as we have seen, the *OT* was much dearer than Kennedy's (admittedly smaller) edition. In 1902 A. E. Housman, urging his publisher Grant Richards to price the first volume of his edition of Manilius at 4/6, gave as his example of overpricing '12/6 for a single play of Sophocles by Jebb'.[37] The page layout for the text (Figure 10.6) is a treat for the eye. Two different sizes of Porsonic Greek (Pica no. 3/Small Pica no. 2) combine with headings from the same family (Figgins Long Primer no. 4) to give variety.[38] Porson had since the 1850s been the dominant Greek face in Britain. The original typeface had two extra distinctions: it had been cut in 1807, based on the handwriting of Jebb's famous predecessor in the Greek chair, Richard Porson; and it was the typeface which first broke away from the complex ligatured faces used till then.[39] Two sizes of the roman

---

[35] The photograph of Jebb, Aldis Wright, and two other fellows reproduced as the frontispiece in 1999a is probably a Tea Club group portrait.

[36] Benjamin Kennedy's *Revised Latin Primer* of 1888 was published in a similar colour, also with dark bands: Kennedy's daughters, who actually wrote the book, sent the publisher a sample after rejecting all the swatches he had offered them. See 1994a, 19.

[37] Housman to Grant Richards, 8 Nov. 1902: Burnett 2007, 1.136.

[38] These typefaces are illustrated and discussed in Bowman 1992, and more fully in Bowman 1998. The type was bought by OUP in 1864 and first used in 1871; CUP was noted as having an interest in it *c*.1882, and this may refer to its selection for the Sophocles edition (cf. 2013b). My thanks to John Bowman for advice on typefaces.

[39] 'Peter Elmsley and Richard Porson on the one hand and the industrial revolution of printing on the other produced the simplified serifless script that is now standard', wrote Nicolas Barker in his *Aldus*

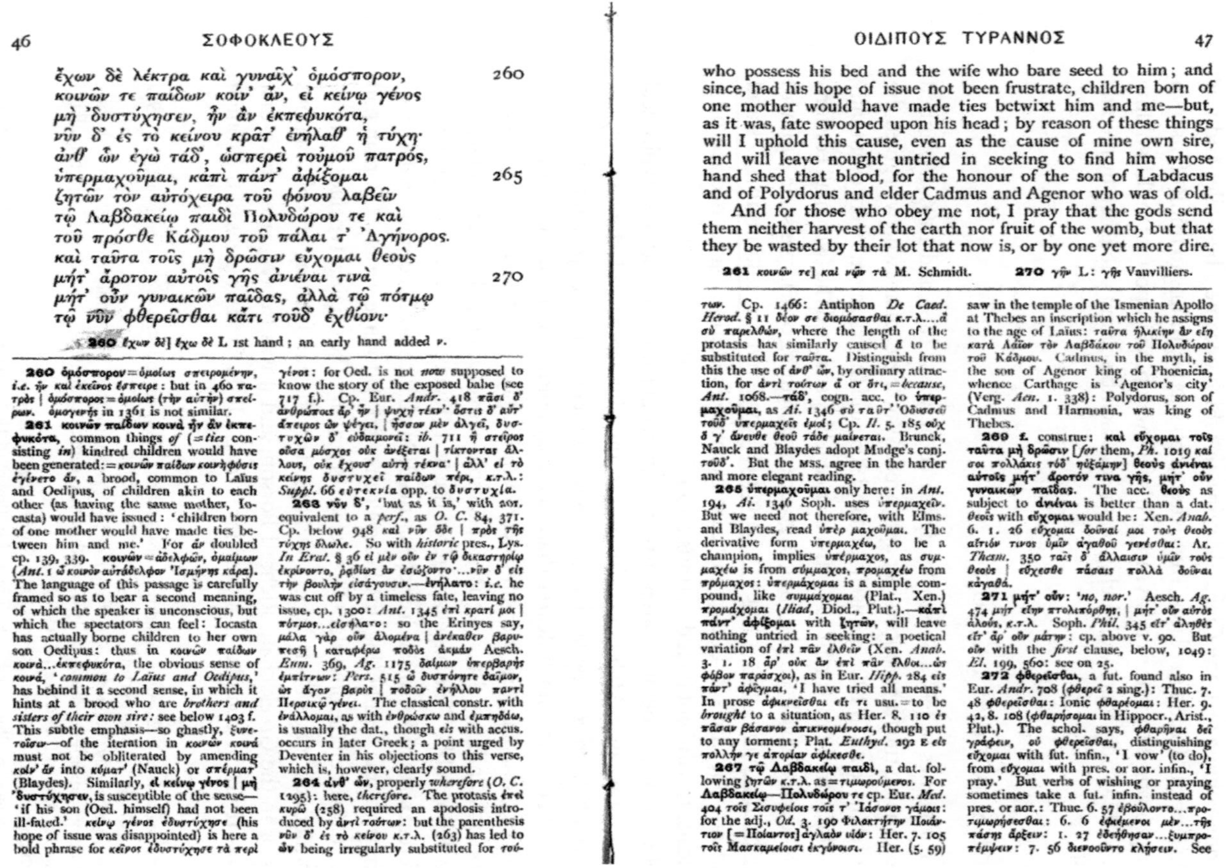

ἔχων δὲ λέκτρα καὶ γυναῖχ᾽ ὁμόσπορον,
κοινῶν τε παίδων κοίν᾽ ἄν, εἰ κείνῳ γένος
μὴ 'δυστύχησεν, ἦν ἂν ἐκπεφυκότα,
νῦν δ᾽ ἐς τὸ κείνου κρᾶτ᾽ ἐνήλαθ᾽ ἡ τύχη·   260
ἀνθ᾽ ὧν ἐγὼ τάδ᾽, ὡσπερεὶ τοὐμοῦ πατρός,
ὑπερμαχοῦμαι, κἀπὶ πάντ᾽ ἀφίξομαι,
ζητῶν τὸν αὐτόχειρα τοῦ φόνου λαβεῖν,
τῷ Λαβδακείῳ παιδὶ Πολυδώρου τε καὶ
τοῦ πρόσθε Κάδμου τοῦ πάλαι τ᾽ Ἀγήνορος.   265
καὶ ταῦτα τοῖς μὴ δρῶσιν εὔχομαι θεοὺς
μήτ᾽ ἄροτον αὐτοῖς γῆς ἀνιέναι τινὰ
μήτ᾽ οὖν γυναικῶν παῖδας, ἀλλὰ τῷ πότμῳ
τῷ νῦν φθερεῖσθαι κἄτι τοῦδ᾽ ἐχθίονι.   270

260 ὁμόσπορον] *...* **261** κοινῶν τε] καὶ τῶν τε L, 1st hand; an early hand added ν.

who possess his bed and the wife who bare seed to him; and since, had his hope of issue not been frustrate, children born of one mother would have made ties betwixt him and me—but, as it was, fate swooped upon his head; by reason of these things will I uphold this cause, even as the cause of mine own sire, and will leave nought untried in seeking to find him whose hand shed that blood, for the honour of the son of Labdacus and of Polydorus and elder Cadmus and Agenor who was of old.

And for those who obey me not, I pray that the gods send them neither harvest of the earth nor fruit of the womb, but that they be wasted by their lot that now is, or by one yet more dire.

261 κοινῶν τε] καὶ τῶν τε L. : τῶν Vauvilliers.   **270** τῷ L : τῷ M. Schmidt.

Figure 10.6 Sophocles, *Oedipus Tyrannus*, ed. R. C. Jebb, 2nd edn (Cambridge: Cambridge University Press, 1887), pp. 46–7. The layout is more lavish and varied than Munro's. The edition, originally published in 1883, was the first volume of a complete edition of the plays of Sophocles which appeared between 1883 and 1896. Image courtesy of the Master and Fellows of Trinity College, Cambridge.

face gain extra variety from the use of bolding for headwords in the notes: a form of typographic cueing which had been pioneered in the first edition of Liddell and Scott in 1843 (see Twyman 1993, and Chapter 3). Like Liddell and Scott, Jebb's Sophocles provides a classic page layout that we now take for granted, but which was in some ways new for its own time. In this respect it can be compared with Venn diagrams, which as I suggested above also emerged from a matrix of institutional and pedagogic reform.

Figure 10.6 shows an opening from the second edition of *OT*; the handwriting is that of Jebb's friend Robert Yelverton Tyrrell, to whom the copy was presented. An intriguing glimpse of the development of the page layout is provided by a proof sheet of *OT* which Jebb approved in the summer of 1883 (Figure 10.7). The asterisk leads to a note on the reverse: 'Approved'. As the position of the asterisk suggests, Jebb chose the left-hand (double-column) example, whose bolded line numbers also differ from those in the single-columned format on the right. The specimen page also shows that Latin is used for the critical notes on the text; but in the second edition of 1887, this was changed to English. (The new format had first been used in the previous year for the second volume, *Oedipus Coloneus*.) In his article on Jebb in the *Dictionary of National Biography*, James Duff reported that Matthew Arnold had urged this on Jebb. Another possible source of influence is Benjamin Jowett, whom Jebb had met in 1880 if not earlier and whose views Jebb took very seriously.[40] In his 'Essay on the Interpretation of Scripture', published in *Essays and Reviews* in 1860, Jowett had remarked that 'The story of the scholar who regretted "that he had not concentrated his life on the dative", is hardly a caricature', and went to note that 'The form of notes to the classics often seems to arise out of a necessity for observing a certain proportion between the commentary and the text.'[41]

Jebb's own published explanation, in his preface, is that though he still believed Latin to be the better language for the purpose, he had concluded that the combination of two languages on the same page 'suffered from a certain want of unity and harmony'. He added that some readers had been 'harassed by the change of mental attitude involved in turning from a Latin to an English note on the same passage'.[42] Pat Easterling has suggested, rightly I think, that the Sophocles edition was conceived as a *Gesamtkunstwerk*, in which Jebb's own literary creativity was at work in a disciplined tension with the task of understanding and explaining that of Sophocles.[43] I should like to extend the point by suggesting that its physical form and its page layout were alike

Manutius and the Development of Greek Script & Type in the Fifteenth Century, 2nd edn (Barker 1992, 2). No evidence is cited, nor have I been able to discover the basis for Barker's statement. It is surprising to see Elmsley listed ahead of Porson, though he did experiment with printed Greek *c*.1803: see Finglass 2007.

[40] Jowett's biographers declared that he had made 'Plato ... an English book': Abbott and Campbell 1897), 2.7.
[41] L. Stephen (ed.), *The Interpretation of Scripture and Other Essays* (London 1907) 1–77, at 46–7.
[42] *Sophocles* Oedipus Tyrannus, ed. R. C. Jebb, 2nd edn (Cambridge 1887), v.
[43] Easterling 2005, 35.

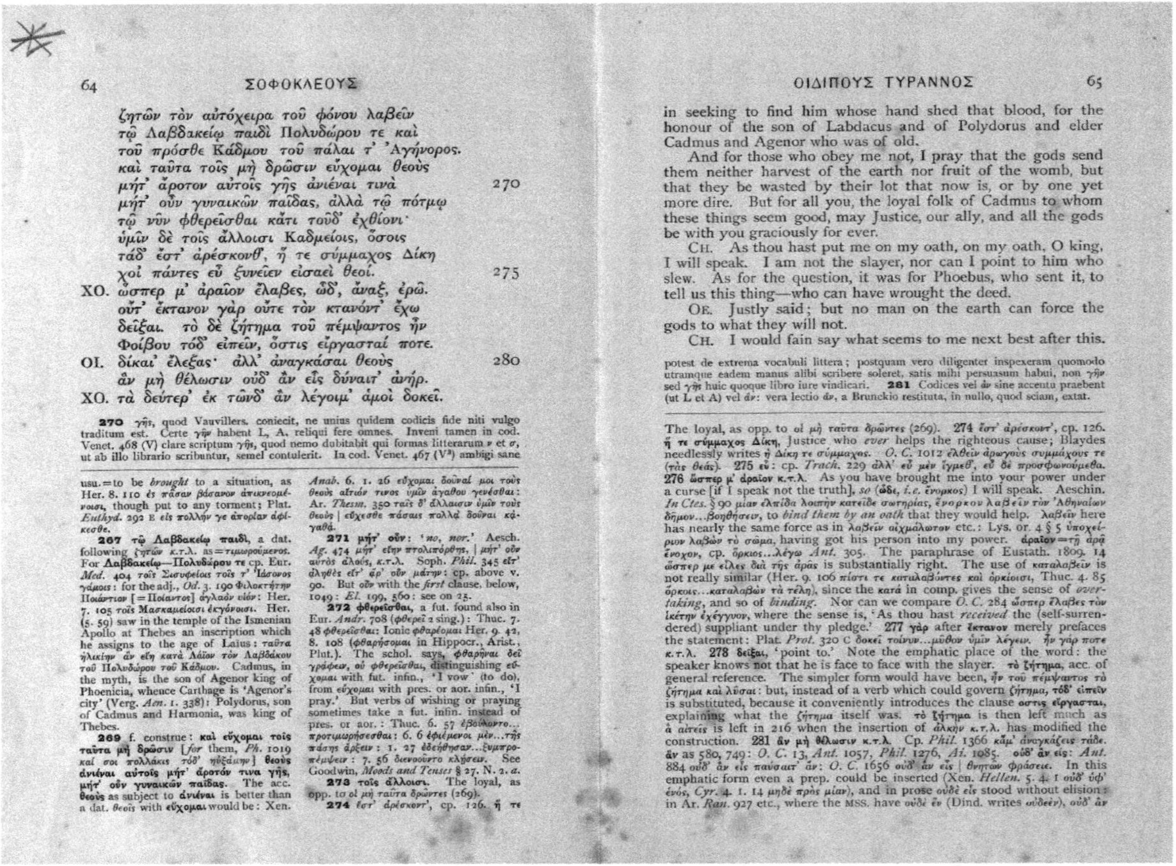

64 ΣΟΦΟΚΛΕΟΥΣ

ζητῶν τὸν αὐτόχειρα τοῦ φόνου λαβεῖν
τῷ Λαβδακείῳ παιδὶ Πολυδώρου τε καὶ
τοῦ πρόσθε Κάδμου τοῦ πάλαι τ' Ἀγήνορος.
καὶ ταῦτα τοῖς μὴ δρῶσιν εὔχομαι θεοὺς
μήτ' ἄροτον αὐτοῖς γῆς ἀνιέναι τινὰ
μήτ' οὖν γυναικῶν παῖδας, ἀλλὰ τῷ πότμῳ
τῷ νῦν φθερεῖσθαι κἄτι τοῦδ' ἐχθίονι·
ὑμῖν δὲ τοῖς ἄλλοισι Καδμείοις, ὅσοις
τάδ' ἔστ' ἀρέσκονθ', ἥ τε σύμμαχος Δίκη
χοἰ πάντες εὖ ξυνεῖεν εἰσαεὶ θεοί.

ΧΟ. ὥσπερ μ' ἀραῖον ἔλαβες, ὧδ', ἄναξ, ἐρῶ.
οὔτ' ἔκτανον γὰρ οὔτε τὸν κτανόντ' ἔχω
δεῖξαι. τὸ δὲ ζήτημα τοῦ πέμψαντος ἦν
Φοίβου τόδ' εἰπεῖν, ὅστις εἴργασταί ποτε.

ΟΙ. δίκαι' ἔλεξας· ἀλλ' ἀναγκάσαι θεοὺς
ἂν μὴ θέλωσιν οὐδ' ἂν εἷς δύναιτ' ἀνήρ.

ΧΟ. τὰ δεύτερ' ἐκ τῶνδ' ἂν λέγοιμ' ἁμοὶ δοκεῖ.

270 γῆς, quod Vauvillers. coniecit, ne unius quidem codicis fide niti vulgo traditum est. Certe γῆν habent L, A, reliqui fere omnes. Inveni tamen in cod. Venet. 468 (V) clare scriptum γῆς, quod nemo dubitabit qui formas litterarum ν et ς, ut ab illo librario scribuntur, semel contulerit. In cod. Venet. 467 (V²) ambigi sane

usu. = to be *brought* to a situation, as Her. 8. 110 ἐς πᾶσαν βάσανον ἀπικνεομένοισι, though put to any torment; Plat. *Euthyd.* 292 E εἰς πολλήν γε ἀπορίαν ἀφίκεσθε.

267 τῷ Λαβδακείῳ παιδί, a dat. following ζητῶν κ.τ.λ. as = τιμωρούμενος. For **Λαβδακείῳ—Πολυδώρου τε** cp. Eur. *Med.* 404 τοῖς Σισυφείοις τοῖς τ' Ἰάσονος γάμοις: for the adj., *Od.* 3. 190 Φιλοκτήτην Ποιάντιον [= Ποίαντος] ἀγλαὸν υἱόν: Her. 7. 105 τοῖς Μασκαμείοισι ἐκγόνοισι. Her. (5. 59) saw in the temple of the Ismenian Apollo at Thebes an inscription which he assigns to the age of Laius: ταῦτα ἡλικίην ἂν εἴη κατὰ Λάϊον τὸν Λαβδάκου τοῦ Πολυδώρου τοῦ Κάδμου. Cadmus, in the myth, is the son of Agenor king of Phoenicia, whence Carthage is 'Agenor's city' (Verg. *Aen.* 1. 338): Polydorus, son of Cadmus and Harmonia, was king of Thebes.

269 f. construe: **καὶ εὔχομαι τοῖς ταῦτα μὴ δρῶσιν** [*for* them, *Ph.* 1019 καί σοι πολλάκις τόδ' ηὐξάμην] **θεοὺς ἀνιέναι αὐτοῖς μήτ' ἄροτόν τινα γῆς, μήτ' οὖν γυναικῶν παῖδας.** The acc. **θεοὺς** as subject to **ἀνιέναι** is better than a dat. θεοῖς with **εὔχομαι** would be: Xen. *Anab.* 6. 1. 26 εὔχομαι δοῦναί μοι τοὺς θεοὺς αἴτιόν τινος ὑμῖν ἀγαθοῦ γενέσθαι: Ar. *Thesm.* 350 ταῖς δ' ἄλλαισιν ὑμῖν τοὺς θεοὺς | εὔχεσθε πάσαις πολλὰ δοῦναι κἀγαθά.

271 μήτ' οὖν: '*no, nor.*' Aesch. *Ag.* 474 μήτ' εἴην πτολιπόρθης, | μήτ' οὖν αὐτὸς ἁλούς, κ.τ.λ. Soph. *Phil.* 345 εἴτ' ἀληθὲς εἴτ' ἄρ' οὖν μάτην: cp. above v. 90. But οὖν with the *first* clause, below, 1049: *El.* 199, 560: see on 25.

272 φθερεῖσθαι, a fut. found also in Eur. *Andr.* 708 (φθερεῖ 2 sing.): Thuc. 7. 48 φθερεῖσθαι: Ionic φθαρέομαι Her. 9. 42, 8. 108 (φθαρήσομαι in Hippocr., Arist., Plut.). The schol. says, φθαρῆναι δεῖ γράφειν, οὐ φθερεῖσθαι, distinguishing εὔχομαι with fut. infin., 'I vow' (to do), from εὔχομαι with pres. or aor. infin., 'I pray.' But verbs of wishing or praying sometimes take a fut. infin. instead of pres. or aor.: Thuc. 6. 57 ἐβούλοντο...προτιμωρήσεσθαι: 6. 6 ἐφιέμενοι μὲν...τῆς πάσης ἄρξειν: 1. 27 ἐδεήθησαν...ξυμπροπέμψειν: 7. 56 διενοοῦντο κλῄσειν. See Goodwin, *Moods and Tenses* § 27. N. 2. *a.*

273 τοῖς ἄλλοισι. The loyal, as opp. to οἱ μὴ ταῦτα δρῶντες (269).

274 ἔστ' ἀρέσκοντ', cp. 126. ἥ τε

65 ΟΙΔΙΠΟΥΣ ΤΥΡΑΝΝΟΣ

in seeking to find him whose hand shed that blood, for the honour of the son of Labdacus and of Polydorus and elder Cadmus and Agenor who was of old.

And for those who obey me not, I pray that the gods send them neither harvest of the earth nor fruit of the womb, but that they be wasted by their lot that now is, or by one yet more dire. But for all you, the loyal folk of Cadmus to whom these things seem good, may Justice, our ally, and all the gods be with you graciously for ever.

CH. As thou hast put me on my oath, on my oath, O king, I will speak. I am not the slayer, nor can I point to him who slew. As for the question, it was for Phoebus, who sent it, to tell us this thing—who can have wrought the deed.

OE. Justly said; but no man on the earth can force the gods to what they will not.

CH. I would fain say what seems to me next best after this.

potest de extrema vocabuli littera; postquam vero diligenter inspexeram quomodo utramque eadem manus alibi scribere soleret, satis mihi persuasum habui, non γῆν sed γῆς huic quoque libro iure vindicari. **281** Codices vel ἂν sine accentu praebent (ut L et A) vel ἄν: vera lectio ἄν, a Brunckio restituta, in nullo, quod sciam, extat.

The loyal, as opp. to οἱ μὴ ταῦτα δρῶντες (269). **274** ἔστ' ἀρέσκοντ', cp. 126. **ἥ τε σύμμαχος Δίκη**, Justice who *ever* helps the righteous cause; Blaydes needlessly writes ἡ Δίκη τε σύμμαχος. *O. C.* 1012 ἐλθεῖν ἀρωγοὺς ξυμμάχους τε (τὰς θεάς). **275 εὖ**: cp. *Trach.* 229 ἀλλ' εὖ μὲν ἵγμεθ', εὖ δὲ προσφωνούμεθα. **276 ὥσπερ μ' ἀραῖον κ.τ.λ.** As you have brought me into your power under a curse [if I speak not the truth], *so* (ὧδε, *i.e.* ἔνορκος) I will speak. Aeschin. *In Ctes.* § 90 μίαν ἐλπίδα λοιπὴν κατεῖδε σωτηρίας, ἔνορκον λαβεῖν τὸν Ἀθηναίων δῆμον...βοηθήσειν, to *bind them by an oath* that they would help. λαβεῖν here has nearly the same force as in λαβεῖν αἰχμάλωτον etc.: Lys. or. 4 § 5 ὑποχείριον λαβὼν τὸ σῶμα, having got his person into my power. **ἀραῖον** = τῇ ἀρᾷ ἔνοχον, cp. ὅρκιος...λέγω *Ant.* 305. The paraphrase of Eustath. 1809. 14 ὥσπερ με εἶλες διὰ τῆς ἀρᾶς is substantially right. The use of καταλαβεῖν is not really similar (Her. 9. 106 πίστι τε καταλαβόντες καὶ ὁρκίοισι, Thuc. 4. 85 ὅρκοις...καταλαβὼν τὰ τέλη), since the κατά in comp. gives the sense of *overtaking*, and so of *binding*. Nor can we compare *O. C.* 284 ὥσπερ ἔλαβες τὸν ἱκέτην ἐχέγγυον, where the sense is, 'As thou hast *received* the (self-surrendered) suppliant under thy pledge.' **277 γὰρ** after **ἔκτανον** merely prefaces the statement: Plat. *Prot.* 320 C δοκεῖ τοίνυν...μῦθον ὑμῖν λέγειν. ἦν γάρ ποτε κ.τ.λ. **278 δεῖξαι**, 'point to.' Note the emphatic place of the word: the speaker knows not that he is face to face with the slayer. **τὸ ζήτημα**, acc. of general reference. The simpler form would have been, ἦν τοῦ πέμψαντος τὸ ζήτημα καὶ λῦσαι: but, instead of a verb which could govern ζήτημα, **τόδ' εἰπεῖν** is substituted, because it conveniently introduces the clause **ὅστις εἴργασται**, explaining what the ζήτημα itself was. **τὸ ζήτημα** is then left much as ἃ αἰτεῖς is left in 216 when the insertion of ἀλκὴν κ.τ.λ. has modified the construction. **281 ἂν μὴ θέλωσιν κ.τ.λ.** Cp. *Phil.* 1366 κἄμ' ἀναγκάζεις τάδε. **ἂν** as 580, 749: *O. C.* 13, *Ant.* 1057, *Phil.* 1276, *Ai.* 1085. **οὐδ' ἂν εἷς**: *Ant.* 884 οὐδ' ἂν εἷς παύσαιτ' ἄν: *O. C.* 1656 οὐδ' ἂν εἷς | θνητῶν φράσειε. In this emphatic form even a prep. could be inserted (Xen. *Hellen.* 5. 4. 1 οὐδ' ὑφ' ἑνός, *Cyr.* 4. 1. 14 μηδὲ πρὸς μίαν), and in prose οὐδὲ εἷς stood without elision: in Ar. *Ran.* 927 etc., where the MSS. have οὐδὲ ἓν (Dind. writes οὐδέν), οὐδ' ἂν

Figure 10.7 Proof sheet for Richard Jebb's edition of Sophocles, *Oedipus Tyrannus*, with alternative page formats, July 1883 (Jebb papers). The asterisk (top left) marks Jebb's preferred format.

Image courtesy of the Master and Fellows of Trinity College, Cambridge.

designed to convey the sense of unity and harmony which Jebb saw as embodied in Sophocles, the representative of 'the best Greek time'. I quoted above the reference in *Attic orators* to the 'thousand fine touches' in Sophocles which help in 'the delineation of the great primary emotions'. The previous sentence reads, 'True simplicity is not the avoidance, but the control, of detail.' Here, surely, is Jebb's credo as he assembled his seven volumes: its text, its visual layout and its physical form were all conceived as a coherent work of art. This was, in fact, meant to be a *Sophoclean* edition of Sophocles.

The length of time over which Jebb worked on the plays, and the fact that he produced revised editions of the first four volumes, means that we must allow for change and development in his practice. Christina Kraus, in a perceptive comparison of Jebb's and Stanford's editions of *Ajax*, has pointed out that Jebb is easier to follow, the relations between notes easier to digest (Kraus 2002, 18–19). Kraus illustrates the point by reprinting Jebb's and Stanford's notes on *Ajax* 161–71. Note that a major distinguishing feature is the contrast between single and double column format—precisely the question Jebb considered in 1883. Note too, however, that reprinting them in a new and uniform type face removes part of what there is to be compared. It is also worth remembering that the *Ajax* was the last edition in the series, and that Jebb had had over a decade to refine his technique. Comparing the 1883 proof of *OT* with the published second edition of 1887 (Figures 10.6–7), it is clear that in rewriting the critical notes in English, he also pared them down. For example, at line 281 'Codices vel ἂν sine accentu praebent (ut L et A) vel ἄν: vera lectio ἂν Brunckio restituta, in nullo, quod sciam, extat' becomes 'ἂν Brunck; the MSS. have ἀν (as L) or ἄν'. In a sense this paralleled the development of Jebb's own English style, from the Paterian grandiloquence of the 1870s to the crisper Addisonian prose of the 1890s. Pat Easterling has succinctly analysed the blend of passion, control, and reserve in the commentary, and her discussion provides an essential complement to Verrall's fine memoir.[44] An interesting piece of evidence recently unearthed by John Henderson is worth mentioning here: a letter from Gilbert Murray to Kenneth Sisam of OUP in which Murray remarks that:

Jebb used to have a story of a coach at Cambridge, called 'Big Smith', or 'the big 'un', who was more popular than much more learned people, on the ground that, 'so-and-so tells you what Hermann thinks and what Blass thinks, | but the Big 'un just tells you what it is'.[45]

The anecdote is a useful reminder of Jebb's awareness of the need to balance the needs of a wide range of readers.

---

[44] Easterling 2005, 35–7; A. W. Verrall, 'The scholar and critic', in Jebb 1907, 427–87.

[45] Henderson 2007, 162: Murray to Sisam, 19 January 1937. The reference suggests an oral telling, which in turns points to the only time the two men are known to have met, in the summer of 1889; Jebb invited Murray to stay with him in Cambridge after the latter was elected to succeed him in the Glasgow Greek chair. 'Big Smith' was James Hamblin Smith of Caius College (1834–1901): 'The principal "Coach" for the ordinary Degree examinations. Known to many generations of students as "Big Smith"' (J. A. Venn, *Alumni Cantabrigienses 1752–1900* vol. 5 (Cambridge, 1953), 559).

The facing translation was originally planned to be in verse, and some of Jebb's friends were disappointed that he changed his mind about this. Arthur Godley, reviewing the *Philoctetes* in the *Oxford magazine* in 1891, was forthright:

Let it be said once for all, a translation such as Professor Jebb's has no place in an edition of a Greek dramatist. It is not in itself literature: no prose translation—let us not be crushed by the contempt of the whole University of Cambridge, nor withered by the wrath of Messrs Butcher, Lang, Leaf and Myers—no prose translation of a poet has, or can have, any literary value.

In other quarters, the appearance of text, translation, and notes on the same opening caused dismay. A reviewer of *OT* in the *Spectator* in 1884 quoted 'a distinguished scholar' as saying of the book, 'When Professor Jebb has finished his Sophocles, we shall have to banish the plays from our schools.' He went on:

It is clear, indeed, that an edition which has the Greek text on the left hand page, a translation on the right, and copious notes which leave absolutely nothing to be explained at the bottom, is not adapted to the wants of the average classroom.[46]

Jebb, however, had this in hand. Even before the *OT* was published he had been discussing with Matthew Bayfield, a Cambridge-trained public school master, how best the large books could be abridged for school use. The abridged edition of *OT* came out in 1885 under Jebb's name; school versions of the other six plays followed only from 1902 under the names of their abridgers. The explanation is to be found in a letter from the publisher Longman to Jebb in 1895, just after his edition of *Electra* had appeared. They had taken over the firm of Rivingtons, which had published Jebb's small editions of *Electra* and *Ajax* in the 1860s, and were concerned at the competition threatened by Jebb's proposed abridged editions.[47] But by 1894 he had already served for three years as MP for the university, and the school editions were not the only projects to be abandoned. The last Sophocles edition, of *Ajax*, was published in October 1896; all that editing had already affected Jebb's sight, and in June 1896 he had been examined and prescribed for by the leading eye surgeon Edward Nettleship (younger brother of the Oxford Professor of Latin).

Jebb soon had need of his new glasses, to cope with a new project even he could not resist. In December the Bacchylides papyrus arrived at the British Museum, and Frederic Kenyon, the Museum's director, encouraged him to publish an edition. Their correspondence hints at patriotic motives: they shared a concern to bring out an edition before the Germans did. But that is another story (told in part in 2009).

---

[46] *The Spectator* (26 Apr. 1884) 534–5. The principle of putting everything in a single opening was further extended by Clyde Pharr in his Virgil edition to include even a vocabulary: *Vergil's Aeneid, I–VI*, ed. C. Pharr (Boston, MA 1930). See the exchange between Pharr and M. B. Ogle in *Classical World* 24 (1930–31) 198–200 (brought to my attention by Ward Briggs). Jebb himself had long been aware of the issue: writing to Macmillan in 1879 about the format of his *Selections from the Attic Orators*, he had specified that the notes should be at the end of the book, adding 'This will please the schoolmasters'. Jebb to Macmillan, 23 February 1879, BL Add MS 55125, ff. 59–60.

[47] Longmans, Green & Co. to Jebb, 8 May 1894; 2013a, 205–6.

Conclusion

Jebb's Sophocles was a grand late-Victorian project fuelled by the editor's idealist conception of classical Greece and of Sophocles, and of his conviction that such a conception was to be held to in a modern age of social, political, and religious transition. As a *Gesamtkunstwerk*, it enshrined but, I have suggested, was also constituted by, the qualities which Jebb saw as typical of classical Greece and as exemplified above all by Sophocles: a spiritual unity and harmony manifested in control at the level of detail. His successor at Glasgow, and in the role of public figure and classical scholar combined, was Gilbert Murray, another Irish immigrant, whose different family background was reflected in his advocacy of rebellion as a test of tradition. Murray urged that Greece not Greek should be fought for; Jebb fought for both. In this essay I have tried to situate Jebb's Sophocles, and Sophocles' Jebb, in a variety of contemporary contexts. These include the emergence of educational publishing markets in the 1860s and of popular journalism in the 1880s; the pedagogical challenges presented by the institutional changes at Trinity in the 1860s and the large and varied classes Jebb encountered at Glasgow in the 1870s; the debates and changes in the Cambridge classical curriculum in both decades; and the models of how and how not to edit provided by Lightfoot, Mayor, Munro, and Verrall. Finally, I have looked at the books as books—thus offering a materialist analysis of what I have suggested was a profoundly idealistic project.

But as well as allowing for the contexts of production, we must also reckon with native talent and its training: the ability to marshal information and the opportunity to deploy it. From the time he spent in the early 1870s writing leaders for the *Times*, to his work in the House of Commons in the 1890s and 1900s, Jebb had both. Let me close with a final glimpse of the cultured commentator, master of the quick summary. In 1891, the year he was elected MP for the university, Jebb attended an exhibition billiards match at the Egyptian Hall in London between John Roberts and W. J. Peall. He pasted the *Times* report of the match into a scrapbook, and wrote underneath:

I saw the play on Saturday evening, March 28; it began about 8.20 pm, and ended at 10.30. During that time, Roberts scored 1108 to Peall's 499: thus scoring more than twice as fast as the winner, to whom he had given half the game.—In his break of 551 Roberts made a large number by nursery cannons at the spot end, varied by pocketing the red.

In its succinct economy, this is typical of Sophocles' Jebb, and worthy of Jebb's Sophocles.

11

Promoting and Defending

Reflections on the History of
the Hellenic Society (1879) and
the Classical Association (1903)

Both the Hellenic Society and the Classical Association were from the start concerned to 'promote the well-being of classical studies'. That phrase is used in Rule 2a of the Classical Association, agreed at its first General Meeting in 1904, and the Hellenic Society's commitment is of course enshrined in its full title: the Society for the Promotion of Hellenic Studies. But my choice of 'promoting and defending', with their implied contrast, reflects the historical reality that Hellenism was not under serious attack in 1879, whereas Classics was in 1903.

In 1879, Hellenism was still a central element in English high culture. It was however not a unitary phenomenon. At Oxford, the high noon of Platonic studies, pushing the traditional study of Aristotle into the background and reinforced by a growing interest in Hegel, was presided over by the diminutive figure of Benjamin Jowett, Regius Professor of Greek 1855–93, renowned for his intimidating silences. His Cambridge counterpart Benjamin Kennedy, Regius Professor of Greek 1867–89, was very different: tall and clumsily built, and prone to intimidate through shouting rather than silence. M. R. James described him as 'resembling an apoplectic macaw',[1] and the Newnham students whose examinations he invigilated wickedly christened him 'the purple boy'.[2] Where Oxford classicists soared into the empyrean of Platonic theory and used it to make imperial proconsuls, the Cantabs took the low road, sticking close to the text, sniping at Jowett's errors of translation and producing backroom boys (cf. Chapter 2). At University College London, there had been a distinctive style based on a receptiveness both to German scholarship, like that of B. G. Niebuhr and K. O. Müller, and to academics whose religion—or lack of it—excluded them from Oxford and

---

[1] James 1926, 182. One's appreciation of James's phrase is increased by the knowledge that Kennedy had a receding chin.
[2] Marshall 1947, 16.

Cambridge.[3] But London was also the capital, and the home of social elites who liked to play with Hellenism. The performance of Greek plays at the homes of wealthy patrons in the West End was referred to, in the early 1880s, as 'South Kensington Hellenism'. Greek dress was all the rage, and the 'Grecian bend' a recent fashion derived from drawings on Greek vases, which forced women to lean forwards on high heels, had given rise to a flurry of songs and cartoons.[4] This scene is now much better known than it was thanks to the work of Fiona Macintosh.[5]

Beneath all this variety, however, a time bomb was ticking away. It had been set off in 1870, when the Royal Commission on endowed schools had asked the Vice-Chancellors of Oxford, Cambridge, and London to make Greek optional for their students so that pupils of schools who did not offer Greek would not be disadvantaged. The debates at Oxbridge flared up sporadically for fifty years, but after the Great War, Compulsory Greek was abolished in both places. The intensity and long drawn out nature of the debate reminds us that Greek was entangled with late Victorian cultural institutions in a number of different ways. For many who after the controversy over *Essays and Reviews* in the early 1860s were losing their Christian faith, Hellenism, already commonly seen as a precursor of Christianity, became a substitute, a spilt religion. But in Oxford and Cambridge, at a time when new honours courses in history, law, and science were growing in popularity, Compulsory Greek became not only a symbol of the entrenched yet contested position of the humanities; it represented the universities' right to control their curricula and entrance requirements independently of the state. In his inaugural lecture as Professor of Greek at Glasgow in 1889, the young Gilbert Murray joined the debate by declaring that 'Greece, not Greek, is the real subject of our study... There is more in Hellenism than a language.'[6] His remark highlighted a tension within classics, and among classicists, which takes us directly to the founding of the Hellenic Society. This represented a determination to pursue a vision of Greece, not Greek: and in particular, the evidence for classical Greek civilization which lay beyond the literary texts and the analysis of their language.

---

[3] For example, the Catholic Frederick Paley and the dissenter William Smith, who made a living from their editions, as Paley did, or their course books and dictionaries, like Smith (Chapter 9).

[4] See for example R. C. Dunham, *The Grecian Bend: What it Is. Profusely Illustrated* (New York: The Grecian Bend Publishing Company, 1868). An example of the pose on Greek vases can be seen in Jane Harrison's *Prolegomena to the Study of Greek Religion* (Cambridge, 1903); it was parodied in a Christmas card sent to Francis Cornford by Frances Darwin (later Cornford) in 1906. See 1991, and Robinson 2002, 211–12.

[5] See e.g. Macintosh 2005.

[6] Murray 1889, 13. The context is worth quoting:

> Some few subjects ought to be studied by everybody: I do not think that Greek is one of them. Greek is a language of unusual difficulty, and a man can undoubtedly reach very high points of culture without any knowledge of Greek. And beyond this there is a distinction to be observed. I believe that for the student of history, of political philosophy, of ethics, of logic, of psychology, and also for the student of most forms of art, the floods of light which ancient Greece can shed upon these subjects is something incalculable and beyond price. But, in considering all these cases, we must remember one important fact, that Greece and not Greek is the real subject of our study.

The Hellenic Society

The immediate genesis of the Society lay in a tour of Greece made in 1877 by four men: the leader, John Pentland Mahaffy (known to his companions as 'The General'), of Trinity College Dublin; his ex-pupil Oscar Wilde, born in Dublin but then at Oxford; another Dubliner, William Goulding; and a fresh-faced young man only three years out of Eton and about to join the family firm.[7] This was George Macmillan of the publishing family, who was to act as secretary to the Society for forty years, to be Honorary Treasurer for another fifteen, and to write the first accounts of its history. On reaching Athens, he wrote home to his sister Olive, 'To you most appropriately I write from this city, where you were of old held in high honour, planted as you were as you may remember in the Acropolis by the hand of Athene herself.' Later in the same letter, he remarked that 'when you have once lived in this climate you see how necessary colour is to architecture, and how unendurable white marble would be in such a glare'—an interesting slant on the polychromy debate.[8]

The address at the Society's inaugural meeting, on 16 June 1879, was given by the grand old man of classical archaeology, Charles Newton. He had joined the British Museum in 1840, and since his appointment as vice-consul at Mytilene in 1852 had been responsible for a long list of classical excavations and acquisitions for the Museum. He had been offered the Oxford Greek chair in 1855, but had turned it down because the salary was so small. Jowett was the second choice; and it is worth considering how different Oxford classics might have been if Newton, who was then under forty, had held the chair for the next quarter of a century. Would he have been able, in the early days of Greats, to get further with reform than Gilbert Murray and E. R. Dodds were in the twentieth century?[9] His idea of Hellenism was very clearly set out in the opening words of his address to the Society:

by Hellenic Studies we do not mean merely the study of Greek texts, grammars and lexicons.... new sources of Hellenic Study are opening up every day. The monuments of the Greeks, their architecture, sculpture and other material remains, deserve our study not less than the texts of the classics.   (Newton 1880, 1)

The Society began life with an impressive line-up of distinguished figures. Joseph Lightfoot, the new Bishop of Durham and Richard Jebb's old tutor at Trinity College, Cambridge, was President. The list of Council members was headed by the Bishop of Lincoln, followed by the Deans of Christ Church and Westminster. The list of

---

[7] Wilde was thinking of converting to Catholicism and intended to go on to Rome; Mahaffy had brought him to Greece to try to deflect him from this course. (Ellmann 1987, 66–70.)

[8] Macmillan to his sister, 17 April 1877, Hellenic Society archive. He is referring to the story that Athena brought the olive tree to Athens. Macmillan published an account of part of his trip (Macmillan 1878). On the polychromy debate, see A. Blühm, *The Colour of Sculpture, 1840–1910* (Zwolle: Waanders, 1996).

[9] For Murray, see 1998a, 282, and in general 2007b; for Dodds, see Dodds 1977, 177–8. Kenneth Dover refused the Greek chair after Dodds's retirement in 1960 because he believed reforms were needed, but thought that as Regius Professor he would be unable to bring them about (Dover 1994, 91).

members began with a single Honorary Member: H.M. the King of the Hellenes. The ecclesiastics were there to bless the infant society and guide it to maturity—all of them being, of course, accomplished classical scholars. The Bishop of Lincoln, Christopher Wordsworth, had toured Greece in the 1830s and reported on it in his book *Athens and Attica* (1836). Soon afterwards he and his brother Charles (by now Bishop of St Andrews) had published parallel Latin and Greek grammars, believing that uniformity in grammar would lead to uniformity in religion (2016). The Dean of Westminster was Arthur Stanley, pupil and biographer of Dr Arnold; the Dean of Christ Church was Henry Liddell, of the famous Greek lexicon. Lightfoot had made it clear that he would not be able to attend many meetings, but he was seen as an important ally in gaining access to manuscripts in Orthodox monasteries. The council was filled up with scholars from Oxford, Cambridge, and the British Museum.

This, then, was a body which combined high cultural prestige with academic interests—two things which cannot have seemed as distinct then as they do now. The amateur scholarly traveller was alive and flourishing and sending back reports on ruins and inscriptions. Like all bodies, the Hellenic Society ran into problems when it began to give its members something in return for their subscriptions. For most of them, this consisted of the meetings and the *Journal*. Indeed some of the Society's council were reluctant to start a journal right away, but gave way when it was pointed out that something had to be offered to the members. As for meetings: it soon became apparent that the audience was a mixed one, and on occasion a scholarly lecture was followed by embarrassingly naïve or irrelevant questions from the floor. The solution adopted was to have general meetings in London and academic meetings in Oxford or Cambridge. But this did not prevent the occasional embarrassment in London. Such things tended to be airbrushed out of the official reports, but occasionally one catches a glimpse. The published report of Arthur Evans's talk on early Cretan seals in November 1896 tells us that 'Mr Hogarth, Sir A. J. Evans, Prof. Ridgeway and others took part in the discussion. which followed'. But a memoir of Lewis Campbell, who chaired the meeting, reveals that when Evans had finished speaking about Cretan seals, an elderly admiral rose to report that in 1828 he had seen a herd of seals off the coast of Crete. The situation was apparently saved by Campbell, who recalled Homer's mention of Proteus and his seals near the mouth of the Nile.[10]

The *Journal of Hellenic Studies* ran into similar problems, its wealthy amateur subscribers finding increasingly that they could not understand its contents, despite the fact that it was lavishly illustrated. Incidentally, its large format, which persists today,

---

[10] Report of Arthur Evans's paper 'On Further Discoveries of the Early Cretan Script', 2 November 1896, *Journal of Hellenic Studies* 17 (1897) xxxiii–iv; *Memorials in Prose and Verse of Lewis Campbell* (printed for private circulation, 1914), 462–3. Proteus and his seals are mentioned at Odyssey 4.365. Curiously enough, the Classical Association's first general meeting (Oxford, 1904) also had the benefit of a naval reminiscence: Admiral Cyprian Bridge, Commander-in-Chief of the China Station, recalled how a knowledge of Latin had been useful in reading ship's documents when his ship had intercepted a suspected blockade-runner. *Proceedings of the Classical Association* (1904), 22–4.

is a function of its archaeological emphasis—large plates meant a large format, and after a few years of producing a smaller-format journal with a supplement of plates, it was found cheaper to produce a single-format volume.[11]

The first rule of the Society declared its aims to be 'To advance the study of Greek language, literature and art, and to illustrate the history of the Greek race.' The order of subjects given was diplomatic: an attempt to appeal to and conciliate the continuing predominance of linguistic and linguistic interests among potential readers. But of the seventeen articles in the first issue, the only one which deals with classical Greek language or literature is that by A. W. Verrall on Ionic elements in Greek tragedy.[12] While the founders were concerned to keep the traditional classical establishment on board, their main concern was to create an outlet for articles on art and archaeology. The fluidity of the situation is evident in the early minute books. In 1880 the editorial committee (meaning in effect Percy Gardner, Disney professor of archaeology at Cambridge, who ran the *Journal* single-handed) proposed that 'papers on pure scholarship should as a rule be subordinated to papers with subjects such as archaeology, palaeography etc. which have hitherto been neglected in England'. The Council however felt this was too stringent a rule: it might, they decided, 'disappoint the expectations of an important section of members'.

In 1880 the only other full-blown classical journal published in Britain was the *Journal of Philology*, whose remit excluded the new areas. From 1887 the *Classical Review* was also in the field (Chapter 8). The first article in its first issue was by A. S. Murray of the British Museum, who had also contributed to the first issue of *JHS*, on Myron's *Pristae*—an interesting article about sawing and seesawing. The foundation of *CR* seems to have encouraged the editors of *JHS* to concentrate on archaeology. Some of the old literary hands disapproved—R. M. Dawkins wrote to the BSA's long-serving and long-suffering secretary John Penoyre in 1911 that 'the journal [*JHS*] is too archaeological... the interests of the SPHS would be better served if it had more literary and historical papers. Droop's old uncle Horton Smith resigned because of this.'[13] The Hellenic Society council minutes of this period make it clear that Droop's old uncle was not the only member who was unhappy about the exclusively archaeological diet.

This is not the place to discuss the British School at Athens in any detail,[14] but it is worth noting that before the First World War there was some unease that *JHS* was taking papers which the *BSA Annual* had wanted, and vice versa. Relations between the

---

[11] The journal has now moved to a smaller format so as to make savings on paper, its previous size involving considerable wastage because of its discrepancy with modern standard paper sizes.

[12] This is at pp. 260–92, leading a final section which also includes short pieces on medieval Greek literature.

[13] Dawkins to Penoyre, 10 April 1911 (British School at Athens archive). J. P. Droop—the name is pronounced 'Drope'—was a classical archaeologist who excavated in Greece. In 1915 he published a handbook, *Archaeological Excavation*, in which he advised against mixed excavations except for married couples: this is in his Chapter 7, known to the BSA's female students as 'Droop's 7th'.

[14] For a detailed account, see Gill 2011, 2–11.

two bodies were at times difficult. In 1899 Jane Harrison proposed to Richard Jebb that they should merge (2013a, 239–40). Nothing seems to have come of this proposal, but it is interesting to know that it was even thought of. Jebb's campaign to found the School, which springs from his visit to Athens in 1878, was at first not supported by the Hellenic Society Council, the obvious source of support. Charles Newton was sceptical; Jebb's great enemy J. P. Mahaffy and his ally A. H. Sayce were opposed. Jebb went round them, enlisting the help of Thomas Sweet Escott, editor of the *Fortnightly Review* (note once again the role of the literary journals). Through Escott he reached the Prince of Wales, and once royal support was secured, the Society's council jumped on board and the School was founded. The foundation meeting of the BSA in 1883 was even grander than that of the Hellenic Society four years earlier: the Prince presided, aristocrats attended, bishops blessed and professors professed themselves totally in favour (2013, 110–18).

The Classical Association

We now move forward twenty years to 1903, and to the foundation meeting of the Classical Association of England of Wales, held in the Gustave Tuck theatre in University College London on 19 December. The venue is significant: the Hellenic Society had been inaugurated at the Freemasons' Tavern, a well-known site for public meetings, the BSA at Marlborough House, the Prince of Wales's official residence. University College was both a lower-key location and a more academic one. It was probably chosen by the prime mover in the Classical Association's foundation, John Postgate of Trinity College Cambridge, who was also Professor of Comparative Philology at UCL. If we consider the three men who played the biggest part in the Association's early years, Postgate, Edward Sonnenschein, and Robert Conway, several points spring to mind. First, they were all Latinists with an interest in comparative philology. Second, they were all educated not at that great bulwark of amateur Victorian Classics, the public boarding school, but at the large urban day schools which were coming to prominence: Postgate at King Edward's, Birmingham, Sonnenschein at University College School, and Conway at City of London School. Third, they all ended up in provincial universities: Postgate at Liverpool, Sonnenschein at Birmingham, and Conway at Manchester. This was a new generation of professional scholars, coping with a new world in which Victorian Hellenism was no longer the only game in town. By 1920, compulsory Greek would be gone, and their universities would be offering degrees in Latin without Greek.

The initial impetus to found the Classical Association came from this new world: from the University of London, whose degrees were taken by a number of provincial colleges. In 1902 it changed its matriculation requirements so that it became possible to avoid Latin altogether. Postgate, who as editor of the *Classical Review* since 1898 had given himself a watching brief on the state of Classics, had a foothold in University

College, where he was Professor of Comparative Philology, and will have been well aware of developments there. In November he published a rousing call to arms in the *Fortnightly Review*—the same journal in which Jebb had urged the foundation of the BSA in 1883. Here is a sample of Postgate's style:

At a time when we appear to be on the eve of extensive reconstructions in the higher educational system of the country, the first duty of those who believe that a due recognition of the claims of Greek and Latin is vital to our intellectual welfare is to know what they want. It is clear that the Classics will not be allowed the lion's share which has been theirs in the past, and the question is, how much must we struggle to retain. (Postgate 1902; cf. 2003a, 5–6)

This is admirable: the kind of tough talking that doesn't date. After several further extensive 'reconstructions', Postgate's message is still worth bearing in mind—not that Classics now has a lion's share in any sphere. What was 'the lion's share' when he wrote? Out of an average teaching week of about twenty-seven hours, boys in the larger public schools spent twelve hours on classics at age thirteen, rising to fifteen hours at age seventeen. The figures for the smaller schools were eight and thirteen and a-half hours respectively. The girls' schools showed more variation, since some of them had morning sessions only; the day schools, as most of them were, offered from two to four hours at age thirteen, from four to seven hours at age seventeen (1998a, 185–7). This entrenched position was bolstered, especially in boys' schools, by two factors. First, Classics was still seen as a status symbol by aspirant upper working-class and middle-class parents; second, the great majority of the entrance scholarships at Oxford and Cambridge were offered for Classics.

Over the next decade the CA built up a substantial membership—450 in 1904, rising to 1,350 in 1908—and planted branches across the country. By the early 1920s there were fifteen of these, the largest with nearly 200 members. Branches were essential for spreading the word on the ground, but they also introduced an extra layer of organization, and potential division, into the Association. Their semi-autonomy was difficult to regulate, and in some cases only around half their members belonged to the national body (2003a, 29–33). This was a problem the Hellenic Society had avoided; there had been a Cambridge branch in its early days, but this was a spontaneous expression of the fact that the Society had stronger support there than in Oxford. Similarly, the choice of Oxford for the Classical Association's first General Meeting in 1904 was based not just on its being the country's premier classical site, but also on its being a *pays de mission*. The two things, of course, went together.

The CA moved ahead on a number of fronts: the pronunciation of Latin, the spelling of Latin words, the curriculum (2003a, 24–9). This last was the most contentious issue, bearing as it did on Postgate's question, 'How much shall we struggle to retain?'— which was a diplomatic way of saying, 'What sections of the classical curriculum shall we jettison?' One contemporary magazine article which discussed the issue was entitled, 'Grammar to the wolves'; and it is clear that the vast amount of grammar, taught repetitively and with little or no eye on literary texts, was a prime candidate for trimming.[15] The problem was that large numbers of public school masters were still confident that, in Matthew Arnold's words, the 'grand old fortifying classical curriculum' had made them what they were.[16] Some might have thought this a prosecution argument—and H. G. Wells was quick to point to the discrepancy between the ideal beauty of Greece and the often ill-favoured Englishmen who urged its glories.

The War was a testing time for classicists. Many of the new generation, of course, didn't survive it—those for whom Achilles didn't 'stand in the trench, flame-capped', and shout for them. Here is another imponderable element in the story: what might have been had those young men survived. Patrick Shaw-Stewart, who wrote the poem I have just quoted from, won most of the classical prizes at Oxford and gained a double first, before being killed in 1917. But he was perhaps lost to scholarship in any case, since he had started working for Baring's Bank before war broke out. Back home, the enemy were the promoters of science, who argued, and with reason, that the bias to humanities, especially Classics, in English education, had left us trailing Germany in science and technology. The humanists' reply was, 'What are we fighting *for*?' Not aniline or explosives, they argued, but the moral ideals which we inherit from classical Greece. The Hellenic Society played its part in this debate by holding meetings at which the issues were debated, and by sending deputations to government. It made things easier for them that at this point our leaders, apart from a few bounders like Lloyd George, had mostly had a classical education. Herbert Fisher, the Minister of Education, was a Balliol man, the friend of J. W. Mackail and Gilbert Murray and Arnold Toynbee. This was an Oxonian group—fairly typical of the continuing linkage between Balliol and empire, Greats and the cabinet.

The British Empire was often likened to its Roman precursor—Charles Lucas's *Greater Rome and Greater Britain* (1912) is one of several such books of the period. But so far Rome has hardly figured in my account. The Latinists—Postgate, Sonnenschein, and Conway—have struck back, but not the Empire. The two empires, Roman and British, came into conflict, in a way, in 1899, when a group of plotters within the Hellenic Society thought of setting up an archaeological school in Rome, but concluded that they could hardly make a public appeal for funds. The British Empire was rather busy at that point in South Africa, and it would not have looked good to ask for money for Roman studies when our boys in Mafeking needed support. In the end, a fair amount was gathered by private appeals, and the British School at Rome was set up in 1900. But it was not until 1910 that the Roman Society was founded, soon to be followed by the first issue of its Journal. Once again, the location and personnel were significant: the inaugural event of the Roman Society took place in the lecture room of the Civil Service Commission, and was chaired by someone who was technically a civil servant—Frederic Kenyon, Director of the British Museum. Over 400 promises of

---

[15] P. A. W. Henderson, 'Grammar to the Wolves', *Blackwood's Magazine* 179 (1906), 667–75. Henderson was Warden of Wadham College, Oxford, 1903–13.

[16] M. Arnold, *Friendship's Garland* (London, 1871), 51.

support had already been sent in. The meeting was crowded, but the list published in the *Times* contains no dignitaries—no royalty, no aristocrats, and almost no ecclesiastics, the nearest being Prebendary H. W. Moss, who was in fact the headmaster of Shrewsbury. It was still almost de rigueur for a public school headmaster to be in orders, as T. E. Page had found to this cost in failing to succeed at Charterhouse, though the first lay head of a major school had been appointed in 1903—Frank Fletcher of Marlborough.[17] What the list *was* full of was professors. The initial letter of appeal sent out to recruit members had urged that the new society should be supported by 'patriot and professor alike'. The Roman Society might not have Hellenism, with its glorious if unrealizable ideals, its democracy, its Kensington fashion and its high-cultural soft porn images à la Lord Leighton. But it had Provincia Britannica, and the Empire, and the disciplinary rigours of Latin grammar.

Classics in 1920

So this is where British Classics stood around 1920, when Compulsory Greek was abolished and a new phase in its twentieth-century history began. At this point the Prime Minister's Committee on Classics in Education, appointed in 1919, was collecting evidence for its report, which was published in 1921. We might pause at this point to note that a full house of classical bodies had now been set up: the Hellenic and Roman Societies, the two schools in Athens and Rome, the Classical Association. Similarly with the journals: though the erratic *Journal of Philology* folded in 1920, by then the *Classical Review* and its younger sibling the *Classical Quarterly* were well established, and since 1909 had belonged to the Classical Association, whose *Year's Work in Classical Studies* had been appearing since 1906; in addition the Athens and Rome Schools each published an *Annual*. Nor should we forget the Association for the Reform of Latin Teaching, the direct method campaign group set up by W. H. D. Rouse and his followers in 1913, which was also alive and well, though a bruising encounter with the Classical Association had led to an armed truce which was only really ended, ironically enough, by the Second World War. They too had a journal, *Latin Teaching*, produced from their earliest days.[18]

A full house indeed—was it perhaps a little crowded? We know that some members of the Hellenic Society were not keen on having a School in Athens. There were also rumblings in the 1900s, as we have seen, to the effect that the *BSA Annual* was taking articles which should really have gone to *JHS*. Then when *JRS* began life in 1910, a series of meetings between the Hellenic Society, the Roman Society, and the Classical Association were needed to hammer out a gentleman's agreement to avoid poaching. The interesting areas were Sicily and Magna Graecia—should they be awarded to the promoters of Hellenic or Roman studies? (In the end it was agreed to deal with them

---

[17] For Page, see Rudd 1981; for Fletcher, Witheridge 2005.
[18] For Rouse and the ARLT, see 1992a. A biography of Rouse by David Jones is in preparation.

on a case-by-case basis.) Part of the agreement was that *JHS* and *JRS* should concentrate on archaeology and history, leaving language and literature to *CR* and *CQ*. So when complaints were heard, as I mentioned above, about the lack of variety in *JHS*, the Council felt that there was little it could do: it was obliged to keep with the agreed bounds. If I had been Droop's old uncle, I would have switched to *CR*, which in those days was to some extent a Review in the Victorian sense, not just a reviewing journal.[19]

In one case the overcrowded house can be identified literally—it was no. 19, Bloomsbury Square, London W1. The Hellenic Society had moved there in 1910 from its original home in 22 Albemarle St, where it had been the tenant of the Royal Asiatic Society. Now the infant Roman Society became its tenant, and shared the use of the telephone and the services of the porter, Mr Wise. Shared domestic facilities are of course the acid test of a marriage—or perhaps this was just cohabitation—and things did not always go smoothly. One of the results was a letter of protest from the Roman Society secretary, accompanied by a chart of telephone and portorial time for 1911 (Figure 11.1a and b).

The social skills demanded of the secretaries a century ago were of course a reflection of contemporary social conventions. Even in 1927, when the Hellenic Society librarian John Penoyre asked for suggestions for an assistant who would also act as secretary to the BSA, he emphasized that 'we want a man with a good degree, interested in archaeology, and a sahib'. Three candidates were interviewed, all from Oxbridge; the victor was from Eton and King's. John Penoyre, like George Macmillan, is one of those people who are almost forgotten, but who held everything together and devoted their lives to classical societies.[20] Appointed secretary and librarian to the Hellenic Society in 1903, and librarian of the Roman Society from its foundation in 1910, he retired thirty-three years later in 1936. He also acted as secretary of the BSA from 1903 to 1919, and the BSR from 1904 to 1912. On his retirement he was presented with a set of the *Encyclopedia Britannica*, a cheque for £200, and a roll with 360 signatures, headed by a set of Greek verses composed by F. G. Kenyon. Penoyre (born John ffolliott Baker Stallard-Penoyre) was a product of Cheltenham College and Oxford, and was a student at the BSA in 1901. He seems to have been well connected; he was certainly a friend of Lord and Lady Roberts. During the First World War he collected cast-off sweaters, telescopes, and binoculars for the troops.[21] His obituary in the *Times* after his death in 1954 reported that 'his exuberant good nature and enthusiasm brought him friends in all classes... his Christmas parties for children were memorable... A solitary journey across the Andes and the Brazilian forests was a real adventure, and not without risk; but armed savages, like Hellenists, were disarmed by his eyeglass and courtly greeting.' (He was lucky to keep his eyeglass—in other words, his telescope.) One of the products of Penoyre's work as librarian was a little booklet called

---

[19] The short articles it carried were discontinued in 1974, the wake of the oil crisis—one of those temporary money-saving decisions which become permanent.

[20] His obituary appeared in *JHS* 74 (1954), 183–4.

[21] He collected 12,000 field glasses: *JHS* 37 (1917), xliii.

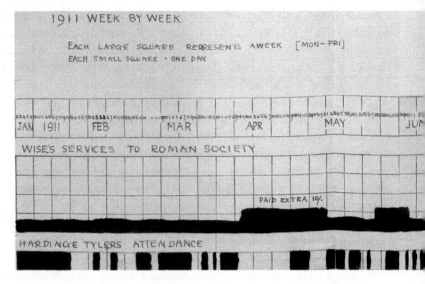

Figures 11.1 (a and b) Hellenic Society and Roman Society: chart of shared telephone and porter's time for 1911. Joint Standing Committee Archive, Society for the Promotion of Roman Studies.

By kind permission of the Society for the Promotion of Roman Studies.

Ante Oculos, subtitled 'Pictures useful for classical teaching in schools', which was published in 1929. It lists illustrated books, slides, and wall pictures available in the UK and in several European countries. In an appendix, Penoyre offers a few 'Notes on Lantern Lecturing', which are still applicable: for example no. 1: 'Do not use too many slides', and no. 11: 'Whatever goes wrong, never lose your temper with the lantern.' When he started circulating the list of Hellenic and Roman slides, he received a letter from the headmaster of Harrow, who told him that getting the optative right was much more important than showing slides of sites and buildings. He added, 'if you have a slide which would help in teaching the optative, I would be glad to borrow it'.[22] The optative in Greek, like the gerund in Latin, clearly had a distinctive symbolic value for the hardline classicist: one is reminded of C. S. Lewis's essay 'The Parthenon and the optative', where the latter stood for real learning and the former 'for all that waffle about the Greeks'.[23]

George Augustin Macmillan, the man Penoyre took over from in 1903, we have already enountered. He was born in 1855, the son of the publisher Alexander Macmillan, and was one of the first five pupils at Summer Fields, a preparatory school in Oxford. From there he went to Eton, and on leaving school in 1874 went into the

---

[22] Joseph Wood to George Macmillan, 27 January 1899 (Hellenic Society archive).
[23] C. S. Lewis, 'The Parthenon and the optative' (1944), reprinted in *On Stories* (New York, 1982), 109–12. This is reminiscent of the views of Walter Shewring, the translator of the *Odyssey*, whose obituary declared that 'As for classical civilisation, he viewed it in general as a much over-rated affair.'

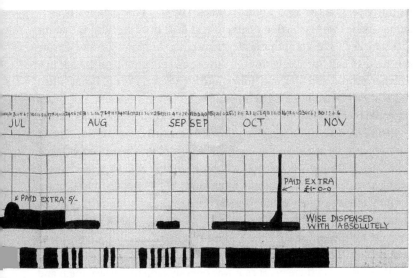

Figures 11.1 (a and b) Continued

family firm. His travels in Greece and his part in founding the Hellenic Society have already been mentioned. His other interests included music (he was Honorary Secretary of the Royal College of Music) and Jersey cattle and blackfaced sheep, which he raised at his home in Yorkshire. He was secretary of the Hellenic Society from its foundation in 1879, and after handing over to Penoyre continued as Honorary Secretary till 1919, when he became Hon. Treasurer, a job only given up in 1934, two years before he died. He was also a member of the BSA managing committee, and had succeeded Richard Jebb as its chairman.

Two things are immediately obvious about these two men. First, their deep and long-term commitment. Penoyre's might seem deeper, but of course he did not have a publishing house to run. Second, the number of posts they held, sometimes simultaneously. This can be dangerous, of course, and not only for the post holder. In the early 1960s, John Sharwood Smith was gathering support for the foundation of the Joint Association of Classical Teachers, and persuaded John Dancy, headmaster of Marlborough College, to chair a small meeting of interested parties. Dancy suggested inviting T. W. (Tommy) Melhuish, and Sharwood Smith asked if he realized what an obstacle to change he could be; he proceeded to list the five important posts Melhuish held. In her contribution to the Classical Association's centenary volume (2003a, 101–3), Clare Roberts sketched the 'almost incestuous' relationships which have obtained between the Hellenic and Roman Societies and JACT. But what makes this almost incest, rather than self-love, is that those involved are not all the same person.

Can one find parallel cases of long-term commitment for the Classical Association? Melhuish and L. J. D. Richardson were its joint secretaries for twenty years; the next longest-serving was Malcolm Schofield, from 1989 to 2003. As for the journals, even

Peter Walcot's thirty years at *Greece & Rome* is dwarfed by C. J. Fordyce's nearly forty at *CR*.[24] What has made the Association distinctive, at least until recently, is that for several decades it lacked what the enthusiastic Victorian headmaster Edward Thring of Uppingham used to call 'the almighty wall': the social effect of being stuck in a building with other people, and files, and books, and a kettle, and so on. Penoyre had a building and a library—two libraries in one, indeed: the Joint Library. This was a place where he could build a nest—perhaps the cast-off sweaters helped. But for almost all of its history, the Classical Association has not had a home. The room it was allotted in the old Institute of Classical Studies building in Gordon Square was in effect taken over by the Joint Association of Classical Teachers, the young activist upstart of the 1960s. To be thus homeless not only curtails some kinds of interaction, it has consequences for writing the history of such bodies. Several sources for the history of the Association have been recovered from shelves and cupboards in various parts of the country. They were there because they were committee files held by individuals, to whom they stuck when those individuals no longer held the jobs to which the files were attached. They were also there because it was nobody's job to retrieve them and care for them. In more than one case, people who told me they could find no trace of the documents I was looking for later found that they *did* have them after all.[25]

The Later History of the Classical Association

I turn now to the second half of the twentieth century, and to a renewed focus on the Classical Association. The Association set up a board of management for *CR* and *CQ* when it bought them in 1909, and another for *Greece & Rome* when it started in 1931. This did not however stop its founder R. H. Barrow arguing in 1949 that it was an entirely independent enterprise; no wonder members of the Association's council complained that *Greece & Rome* seemed to be regarded by Barrow as his own private journal. The two boards merged in 2000, bringing to an end an era of friendly discussion and relaxed lunching. The *Greece & Rome* board lunched at Gianni's restaurant in Tottenham St, Fitzrovia; on one occasion in the early 1990s the secretary reported that 'Gianni has broken his rule for us and we shall be lunching in his private room.' The recent history of the Journals Board has rather resembled that of the early branches in its sometimes problematic semi-autonomy. All the surplus profits of the journals belong to the Association itself, but after seventy or eighty years of effectively independent action, the board understandably came to see itself as running a separate operation for its community of contributors and readers. But in 1987 a sharp-eyed

---

[24] All these figures can be checked in the lists of officers contributed by Philip Hooker to the CA centenary volume (2003, 284–91).

[25] Keeping files in a central location does not, however, necessarily guarantee their preservation. When I was investigating the early history of University College School some time ago, I was told by the then headmaster that a predecessor in the 1930s had decided that the school's future was more important than its past, and had burnt the records.

auditor asked why the journal's accounts were not included in those of the Association, and this led to a long series of negotiations, usually but not always amicable. In the same year, the combative treasurer Richard Wallace wrote to the then secretary, John Percival about the chairman of the Journals Board: 'He's just wrong, and that's that. I am, believe it or not, trying to be conciliatory (but I'm afraid it goes against all my instincts).'[26]

The reader will by now have realized that as well as being confronted by the problem of dealing with two bodies rather than one, I have also had to face the inescapable intrusion of several others. There are two periods in which this has to be dealt with. First, in looking at the classical scene in the early twentieth century, one cannot make proper sense of one body's activities without looking at the others as well. This is because Classics was under attack, the scene was fluid and, as we have seen, both bodies and journals were jostling for position in a cultural space which was itself not clearly defined. In several cases allies were also potential rivals; we have seen this in the case of the classical journals. To take another example, one might expect the promoters of natural science to be the great enemy of classics. To an extent they were, but so, to some extent, were the supporters of modern languages. If a rough division of time and money were agreed between humanities and science, then French and German teachers became, not allies, but competitors for a fixed amount of the timetable or the grant. To return to J. P. Postgate: in an editorial in *CR* in 1903 he warned that:

Classics are now being pressed on one side by the advance of science, on the other by that of modern languages. The latter are its more dangerous opponents. They provide to a certain point the same advantages as the classics; their methods are up to date and their teachers alert and enterprising. How then can they be resisted if confronted only by antiquated methods and a defence which is both backward and supine? High aesthetic and intellectual considerations are all very well; but they are of no avail in a squeeze.[27]

Straight talking again; and his target here is the venerable figure of George Ramsay, Professor of Humanity at Glasgow 1863–1906 and first president of the Classical Association of Scotland, founded in 1902. So we have a complicated situation with several layers: classical bodies, other humanities bodies, scientific associations, government, the universities—not to mention left-wing bodies of varying hues such as the Workers' Educational Association and the Plebs League.

The second period in which a plurality of bodies has to be considered is in the period initiated by the collapse of Compulsory Latin in 1960. As school Classics numbers declined in the 1960s, some institutions which had rather held aloof from that lower level turned their attention to it. The result has been a series of joint projects, funding and other support, in which the Hellenic Society has been very much to the fore. Since its finances became so much healthier in the early 1990s, the Classical Association has

---

[26] R. Wallace to J. Percival, 30 March 1987, quoted by M. Schofield, 'The recent history of the CA', in 2003, 93.

[27] J. P. Postgate, editorial, *Classical Review* 17 (1903), 2.

also been able to give more generously to teachers, schools, and pupils. My impression is that in the 1960s the Hellenic Society council was a fairly rarefied body whose members were not all that knowledgeable about what was going on in schools: one could hardly say that in the twenty-first century. A cynic might claim that the alliances made in the stressful days of the 1960s, when the universities were concerned that the supply of classical pupils might dry up, will fall apart now that the locus of formal education in classics has, if not shifted, at least extended to the university level. My own impression is that the benefits of alliance and co-operation have become so clear that nobody would seriously think of withdrawing from them unless forced to do so. Together they stand.

12

Scholars, Gentlemen, and Schoolboys

The Authority of Latin in Nineteenth- and Twentieth-Century England

Some of the areas to be covered in this chapter can be guessed from its title: first, the transition in scholarship from the amateur gentlemanly style to that of the academic professional; second, the role of pedagogy, the teacher and the pupil in the maintenance and erosion of the authority of Latin. Others cannot be so guessed, so I will list them now: the debates on the pronunciation of Latin, the relationship between Latin and other languages, the role of class and gender, and the way Latin has been imagined in the classroom.

Let me begin with a quotation from James Boswell's life of Samuel Johnson. On the night of 16 July 1783 Johnson suffered a mild stroke, feeling 'a confusion and indistinctness in my head...I was alarmed, and prayed God, that however he might afflict my body, he would spare my understanding. This prayer, that I might try the integrity of my faculties, I made in Latin verse. The lines were not very good, and I knew them to be not very good: I made them easily, and concluded myself to be unimpaired in my faculties' (Boswell 1927, 2.501). A minor but charming feature of this self-test procedure is that the pass mark Johnson awarded himself was based not just on versifying easily, but on noticing that his verses were not very good.[1]

Boswell tells us elsewhere that 'a highly classical phrase (may be used) to produce an instantaneous strong expression'.[2] Both Latin and Greek were, in the late eighteenth and nineteenth centuries, languages of power which could be used both to express thoughts and to impress an audience. It is well known that Johnson thought Greek was like lace—a man should get as much of it as he could. This is sometimes taken to imply that lace was a rare and expensive luxury; but as his biographer Malone pointed out in 1799, in Johnson's lifetime lace was not a scarce commodity, but 'very generally worn'

---

[1] The test may also have had a scarificatory element, as Johnson seems to have regarded Latin versifying as a duty rather than a pleasure: Boswell 1927, 2.495. Two of Johnson's prose declamations, a weekly requirement for him as an undergraduate at Pembroke College, Oxford, survive in the college library.

[2] Boswell 1927, 2.484 (April 1773), where the subject is the use of scriptural phrases in secular conversation.

(Malone 1799, 4.301). The best analogy might be with ice cream rather than caviar. The immediate social world of Johnson and Boswell was one in which a knowledge of Latin at least was expected, and the finer distinctions to be made operated within this larger assumption. Thus, for example, Johnson complained of David Garrick that 'He has not Latin enough. He finds out the Latin by the meaning, and not the meaning by the Latin.'[3] One is reminded of the use of the Loeb Classical Library by semi-learned readers.[4] It seems to have been in the 1750s that the tide changed decisively against Latin as both a language and a source of dominant exemplars. As J. A. W. Gunn put it in his study of eighteenth-century political thought, 'After 1750 concern about the deficiencies of a classical education was increasingly heard, and it undermined the common foundation of the prevailing form of rhetoric' (Gunn 1983, 29). It was just at this time, too, that the practice of printing faulty Latin in grammars for correction by the pupil was first copied in an English grammar: Anne Fisher's *New Grammar* of 1750.[5]

Here, surely, as in the increasingly popular manuals of etiquette, we can see the result of the first industrial revolution, which threw up social groups who could afford to live in style but did not know how to do so. Ironically enough, this same revolution later led to the renewal of decayed rural grammar schools as the alchemical retorts in which the sons of the new rich were turned into classically-educated gentlemen.

The Authority of Latin

All this has to do with cultural authority, its various forms and its social attachments; and my underlying concern in this chapter is with the changing nature of the authority of Latin.[6] Between the late eighteenth and the early twentieth centuries this can be plotted in relation to the social bases and organization of knowledge. Here we are dealing, first of all, with the status of social groups, their competition, their attempts to maintain solidarity among insiders, and to exclude others. The obvious groups to look at are social classes, but gender also needs to be considered. Second, we have to consider the characteristic social forms which learning took. The obvious change in our period is from the amateur learning of the gentleman, who as Macaulay put it read Plato with his feet on the fender, who deployed classical quotations in conversation, who read and contributed to general literary journals which carry articles on classical topics (the *Edinburgh Review*, its tory rival the *Quarterly*, the *Athenaeum*), who made verses and

---

[3] Boswell 1927, i. 603 (May 1775).

[4] Lytton Strachey read Sophocles' *Oedipus Tyrannus* in J. T. Sheppard's edition, which had a facing translation, which he read 'with an occasional puzzled glance at the other side of the page': Holroyd 1967–8, ii.392.1. Cf. Nicolson 1947, 186; 1998a, 285.

[5] Anne Fisher, *A New Grammar: Being the Most Easy Guide to Speaking and Writing the English Language Properly and Correctly*, Newcastle-upon-Tyne 1750. This is in fact the second edition; the first, of which no copy has survived, appeared in 1745. Fisher's book incorporated some 'exercises of false English' supplied by an anonymous teacher in Carlisle in imitation of those in Nathan Bailey's *English and Latin Exercises* (London, 1706), and John Clarke's *New Grammar of the Latin Tongue* (London, 1733), where faulty Latin had to be corrected. See Michael 1970, 196; Görlach 2003.

[6] Some aspects of this topic have been discussed in *Classics Transformed* (1998a); here I cover some of the same ground, but try where possible to use new material and to ask new questions.

compared them with those of his friends, to that of the professional scholar, who explores the texts and lands of antiquity, and reads and writes for scholarly journals, rather than for a wider audience.[7]

Two moments in this history can be illustrated by anecdotes similar to that of Johnson's self-examination. At some point in the late 1840s in Göttingen, a young boy named Max Schneidewin fell down a flight of stairs in his home. His father, a distinguished classical scholar, ran to him, and fearing that he might have suffered injury to his brain, said, 'Max, lieber Max, was is das Geschlecht von Ensis?' His face brightened when Max immediately replied, 'Masculini generis'. We owe this charming anecdote to a visiting American student, George Lane, later Professor of Latin at Harvard 1851–94 and himself author of a standard Latin grammar, who described the event in a letter to his friend Basil Lanneau Gildersleeve.[8] Here Latin and vernacular are juxtaposed, and the boy's response may reflect the language of his school grammar, or of his classroom.[9] Perhaps he was concussed, and thought his master was quizzing him. But once again, we find knowledge of Latin perceived as a central armature of mental functioning and thus as a diagnostic tool for its possible dysfunctioning.

I make no apology for using an anecdote set in Germany, for it was throughout the nineteenth century the powerhouse of classical scholarship in Europe.[10] It provided a source of scholarly authority in classics which needs to be borne in mind even in an account which is confined to England. Housman's rhetorical account in the preface to his Manilius in 1903 (cited earlier in this volume) is well known:

History repeats itself, and we now witness in Germany pretty much what happened in England after 1825, when our own great age of scholarship, begun in 1691 by Bentley's Epistola ad Millium, was ended by the successive strokes of doom which consigned Dobree and Elmsley to the grave and Blomfield to the bishopric of Chester. England disappeared from the fellowship of nations for the next forty years. [English classical scholars]...having turned their backs on Europe and science and the past,...sat down to banquet on mutual approbation, to produce the Classical Museum and the Bibliotheca Classica, and to perish without a name.[11]

[7] The ancestors of such journals in this country were the Museum Criticum of 1813–26 and the Philological Museum of 1831–3, for which see Chapter 7.

[8] Gildersleeve to Max Schneidewin, 25 March 1913: Briggs 1987, 307–8. Both Lane and Gildersleeve had been taught by Schneidewin's father at Göttingen; Lane's son later married Gildersleeve's daughter.

[9] The grammars were in Latin, and Latin and Greek were often taught in Latin too. At Schulpforte, the most famous classical school in Germany, the timetable in 1843 contained sixty-one hours of Latin and only twenty-seven of Greek. A decade later, the fourteen-year old Ulrich von Wilamowitz-Moellendorff and his schoolfellows listened to Greek texts dictated in Greek, and took them down in Latin: 'Er [= Karl Keil, one of the Classics masters at Pforte] diktierte in Unterprima aus Xenophon Griechisch, was sofort in das Latein übersetzt werden sollte.' Greek was no more than an appendix to Latin, Wilamowitz recalled: 'die Griechische war nicht mehr als ein Anhang zum Latein', and the un-Greek syntax was modelled after the unfitting Latin one: 'nachher jene ungriechische, auf den unpassenden lateinisches Leisten geschlagene Syntax' (Wilamowitz-Moellendorff 1928, 79, 71).

[10] A rough indication is provided by the numbers of pages devoted to different European countries by J. E. Sandys in his survey of the nineteenth century in A History of Classical Scholarship, vol. 3 (Sandys 1908): Germany 189, England 56, France twenty-five, the Netherlands sixteen, Italy six.

[11] Housman 1903, pp. xlii–iii, cited in Chapters 2, 4, and 10. Unknown to Housman, an earlier parallel existed: J. H. Monk wrote to John Murray (publisher of the Museum Criticum) on 13 October 1816, 'Of our coadjutors three will fail us—Mr Rennell is I fear too much preoccupied with his parish—Dr Kaye will have

This is a grotesque travesty of the truth. Not only was the *Classical Museum*, as we saw in Chapter 7, edited by a continental scholar, the Alsatian Leonhard Schmitz, it also paid considerable attention to continental publications. From its first appearance in 1844 it printed lists of new books, some of which were then reviewed, and also included articles in translation.[12]

Housman's historical sketch was in fact a plug for his own kind of scholarship, and this is why for him English scholarship stops with the disappearance of the Porsonian school in the mid-1820s, to reappear with the publication of Munro's *Lucretius* in 1864. So much is well known; but what has not been remarked is that whereas the scholarship which dived underground in 1824 was predominantly Greek, what emerged into the light forty years on was an edition of a Latin author.[13] Almost all the work of the Porsonians, as of Porson himself, dealt with Greek drama. The great vindicator of British scholarship of the 1860s, on the other hand, was a Latinist. Hugh Munro was a Scot, schooled at Shrewsbury and trained in Cambridge. As a young man he had dallied with Aristotle, and while still a junior fellow of Trinity College crossed swords on the interpretation of Aristotelian logic with the college's formidable master, William Whewell. But for the rest of his life he concentrated on Latin, and in 1869 became the first incumbent of the Latin chair founded in honour of his old headmaster, Benjamin Kennedy.[14] Housman, who was elected to the same chair in 1911, had also started out by publishing on both literatures, but later concentrated on Latin; when asked why he had done so, he replied that he could not pretend to excellence in both.

Utriusque Linguae: Latin and Greek (and English)

Housman's remark raises the question of the relationship between Latin and Greek scholarship. As a young graduate I noticed that the professors of Greek I had met were usually more interesting people than their Latin colleagues. It would hardly be surprising if there were an element of self-selection involved—an elective affinity between work and person. We should not be rigid about this—an Ovidian scholar is not necessarily a cynical roué, or an exile. It is noteworthy, however, that when Amy Levy, one of the

abundance of employment in the Divinity professorship—and poor Edward Blomfield is no more.' (John Murray archive, National Library of Scotland.)

[12] Thus we have in vol. 3 Wex on the Leges Annales, in vol. 4 Zumpt on Roman religion; in the final volume Hermann on the date of the Laocoon, as well as Platner's reminiscences of Hermann. All these were translated from German, but Dutch articles also appeared, such as Groshans' Zoology of Homer and Hesiod in vol. 4, and Miquel on Homeric flora in vol. 5. These had been previously published, but original articles also appeared by Welcker, Puchta, Bergk, Lersch, Zumpt, and others. Furthermore, starting with vol. 2 reports from foreign correspondents were a regular feature, several of them associated with the university of Bonn, Schmidt's alma mater, where he had been taught by Niebuhr and Ritschl among others. Cf. Naiditch 1991, 133–4.

[13] The site of scholarship was in both cases Cambridge, to which Housman was welcomed on his appointment; he had been an undergraduate at Oxford in the 1880s, but had failed to achieve honours. But even allowing for the occasion, it would be hard to argue against his choice of representative scholars.

[14] Kennedy had himself become Professor of Greek in the university two years earlier.

early women students at Cambridge, drew a sketch representing herself as a dissolute rule-breaker, she put Ovid, Byron, and Lucretius on her bookshelf.[15] Her more famous contemporary, Jane Harrison, shocked William Gladstone when he visited Newnham by telling him that her favourite author was Euripides (Harrison 1925, 44).

It is well known that the great surge of interest in Greece in the later eighteenth and nineteenth centuries constituted a turn away from the predominantly Roman focus of Augustan literature and society (Turner 1989). But by the time Munro was an old man and Housman a young one, though the glories of Classics in English high culture were still predominantly Hellenic, the development of academic specialization had given the study of Latin a new legitimacy. Specialization had advanced most notably as a result of the Royal Commissions of 1850 on Oxford and Cambridge, and in the following decade new honours courses were established in both place in such subjects as law, history, philosophy, and natural science. The effect of this curricular expansion was gradual, and recruitment to the dominant courses—Classics at Oxford, mathematics at Cambridge—remained unaffected for some time. In Oxford, Greats was officially regarded as the university's premier course well after its student numbers had been overtaken in the early 1890s by Modern History. But over time, the formal equivalence of academic courses became established. This new structural development was perhaps reinforced by the growth of comparative philology, which while it could hardly erode the status of Greek as a senior language to Latin, yet could to some extent equalize their status as subjects of philological study. The study of Classics in Oxford and Cambridge between 1870 and 1920 was entangled with that of Sanskrit in a variety of ways.[16]

The story of little Max involved the juxtaposition of Latin with the vernacular. What was the situation in England? In essence, Latin survived as a language of communication, both spoken and written, in academic, ecclesiastical and legal enclaves. Well into the century, small boys learned Latin (and Greek) from grammars written in Latin—often not very good Latin. Latin was also the standard language for notes on classical texts, but English began to be used in the early nineteenth century. This practice was disapproved of by conservative scholars, to whom Latin was not only more precise than English, but belonged to a world of sacred and academic value which they did not want invaded by the common tongue and the common people (2016). Many scholars felt more pragmatically that Latin had a marmoreal quality which made it better suited to learning by heart—a practice which at that time was central to school learning.[17] The phrase 'verb. sap.' both labelled, and in its allusive abbreviation exemplified, a widespread

---

[15] For Levy, see Beckman 2000.

[16] For Cambridge, one thinks of the pioneering teaching of John Peile and Edward Cowell, whose pupils and protégés included the classicists R. S. Conway, Peter Giles and W. H. D. Rouse. To effect a comparison with Oxford, one would need to look not only at Friedrich Max Müller, the public figurehead, but at the work of Henry Nettleship, and at the dissemination of research findings via textbooks by men like John King and Christopher Cookson, the authors of *An Introduction to the Comparative Grammar of Greek and Latin* (Oxford, 1890).

[17] 1998a, 96–102. Contrast the view of Susan Stephens, for whom the ambiguity of Latin 'underscores the limitations of the vulgate for textual criticism': Stephens 2002, 70.

system of linguistic and social exclusion (1998a, 75–80). Flaubert's dictionary of clichés nicely caught the nervous uncertainty of the aspirant bourgeois keen to enter this world of social and cultural authority:

LATIN language natural to man. Harmful to good writing. Is useful only for reading inscriptions on public fountains. Beware of Latin quotations: they always conceal something improper.[18]

The embedded use of Latin persisted longer in Oxford than in Cambridge, for two reasons. First, Oxford clung to oral examination as a public assertion of community for longer than Cambridge did. The written examination, which in this country originated in Cambridge, took hold there in part because of the dominance of Newtonian natural philosophy in the eighteenth century (2005b; Warwick 2003). This is the second reason: the persisting dominance of Classics in the Oxford curriculum, while in Cambridge the Classical Tripos was founded in the 1820s in the shadow of its elder mathematical sister. A remarkable tale told by Arnold Toynbee and buried in the annotatory undergrowth of his vast *Study of History* is set in Balliol College in 1907. Toynbee entered the college in that year, and reports of one of the tutorial fellows that:

the only authors in any tongue that he could any longer bear to read were four Latin poets, namely Virgil, Horace, Ovid, and the humanist-fakir himself. For fear of forgetting one day to slip a printed copy of one or other of the first three of these still unproscribed classics into his pocket, he used to inscribe Latin verses of his own composition on his shirt-cuffs as an iron ration to insure him against the risk of dying of aesthetic starvation. The fate that did overtake him was the sadder one of mental inanition.[19]

In both universities, Latin was used through the nineteenth century on formal and ceremonial occasions, but in the second half of the century, the declining percentage of dons who could confidently understand spoken or written Latin began to take its toll. John William Donaldson, whose radical views of the Bible lost him the headmastership of a grammar school in 1855, had not long before this given praelections in Latin in Cambridge when standing in vain for chairs. Donaldson was admittedly an eccentric figure, but the surviving titles of Cambridge praelections in the 1850s are in Latin, so presumably they were delivered in that language. This is the case for the 1853 contest for the chair of Greek, in which candidates were asked questions in Latin but allowed to answer in English; which they all did. (The official account of the occasion explains: 'licet candidatis Anglice respondere'.)[20] In the next such election, in 1867, there were

---

[18] Flaubert 1954, 83. For an interesting discussion of Latin and law which takes off from this, see Goodrich 2003, who argues (194) that the less Latin is used, the more powerful it becomes: 'Latin may be misused, but it is precisely its misuse that marks its rhetorical force and its likely future.'

[19] Toynbee 1954, 8.711. Balliol was a small college and there are not many candidates. Toynbee's remarkable footnote on J. L. Strachan-Davidson (Toynbee 1954, x. 20) would make him a likely target, but he became Master in June 1907, before Toynbee entered the college. The unnamed tutorial fellow must therefore, I think, be the whimsical and eccentric Francis de Paravicini (1843–1920).

[20] *Prælectio philologica in Scholis Cantabrigiensibus habita...qua Deboræ canticum triumphale denuo interpretatus est J. G. D.* (Cambridge, 1848); *Prælectionis candidatoriæ quam Cantabrigiæ in Scholis Publicis Prid. Kal. Febr. MDCCCLIV habuit J. G. Donaldson...excerpta quædam, quæ ad petitoris rationem*

four candidates, and only one (Richard Shilleto) gave his title in Latin—it may be that he spoke in Latin as well. He received no votes in any of the three rounds of voting. In 1873 the retiring Vice-Chancellor addressed the Senate in English, explaining that he made no apology for this, as their decisions (Graces) were already couched in the vernacular. He was hissed. Five year later, a Grace to have the university statutes given in English was rejected. One of its opponents, E. H. Perowne, declared that the highly inflected nature of Latin made it more suitable for statutes, 'which could not be too exactly worded'.[21] Two years later, in the autumn of 1880, he was himself elected Vice-Chancellor, and spoke in Latin.

Manliness and Accuracy: The Pronunciation of Latin

We have no idea what Perowne's speech sounded like, but it is a safe guess that he used what was commonly called the English pronunciation of Latin, in which vowel sounds followed ordinary English practice. The pronunciation of Latin constituted one of the major battle-grounds between gentlemanly traditionalists and academic reformers in the late nineteenth century.[22] The reformers drew on the comparative philology of Bopp, Rask, and Grimm to argue for a roughly Italianate pronunciation which they saw as an informed approximation to the cultured speech of the late Republic and early Empire. Their manifestos were issued around 1870, one being written jointly by the Professors of Latin at Oxford and Cambridge, Edwin Palmer and Hugh Munro: a rare example of collaboration between the two institutions.[23] The debate was joined in the periodicals, and especially in the *Academy*, a journal founded in 1869 which in any case deserves mention here. At this date no classical journal had been founded which survives today; those which had been started had usually closed down after a few years (see Chapters 7–8). The *Academy* was the product of the Oxford movement for the endowment of research, and was edited by one of the movement's initiators, Edward Appleton (Roll-Hansen 1957). It aimed to provide a general forum for academic discussion, though its pages soon split into specialized sections, and by the 1890s it had been sold off. The *Academy* was thus not only the field in which the competing ideologies of Latin pronunciation engaged, it belonged itself to the developments which had prompted the debates on this topic.

The reformers' argument was fundamentally that it was possible to establish how the Romans had spoken, and that it was right to copy them. Their opponents argued that

---

declarandam pertinent (Cambridge, 1854). This latter was Donaldson's praelection for the chair of Hebrew (for which he received no votes).

[21] *Cambridge University Reporter*, 4 November 1873, 19 November 1878.

[22] 1998a, 126–30, 196–201; Copeman 1996, 199–202, 277–84. The scattered macaronic literature of the nineteenth century, it might be noted, offers some useful clues to contemporary pronunciation of both Latin and Greek when it rhymes classical and vernacular words.

[23] Other collaborative projects were abortive: e.g. a projected edition of Catullus by H. A. J. Munro and J. W. Mackail, a Latin dictionary by H. Nettleship and J. E. B. Mayor, and an edition of Bede by Mayor and another Cambridge man, J. R. Lumby. For the last two projects, see 2011b, and cf. 2011a.

certainty was unattainable; that the use of the reformed pronunciation in schools was pragmatically undesirable; and that some of its sounds were ugly. Max Müller and others especially derided the soft v, pronounced 'w': 'weni widi wici' sounded wimpy. The hard c was another favourite target: 'kikero', they declared, sounded ridiculous.[24] At Cambridge an organized campaign to introduce the new pronunciation was led by Munro as Professor of Latin, backed by Richard Jebb, then Public Orator and so responsible for making Latin speeches to introduce honorands. The lack of progress they achieved is indicated in Jebb's response to an enquiry by an outsider in the following decade:

I am not sure about progress in the schools but it cannot be called a success. At Cambridge Mayor, Munro and Peile used it but Luard, the tory registrary, would not. As Public Orator, I had to give it up—it was not understood by the majority of members of the Senate. As for Postgate's efforts... it won't really work: weni widi wici; kikero; willa for villa—repulsive![25]

One of the most interesting aspects of the debate is the way positions were taken within different institutions. The Headmasters' Conference, typically, debated the issue and took votes which were then ignored by many of its members. The headmaster of Rugby urged his fellow-heads to adopt the new pronunciation, but added that he had no intention of doing so himself.[26] Westminster, with its annual Latin play, was firmly attached to the old pronunciation: to abandon it would have been disloyal. It was not surprising, therefore, that John Sergeaunt of Westminster was among the most vigorous denouncers of the new scheme. In some schools, the lower forms were taught the old, the upper forms the new pronunciation, so that boys going to university would be ready to speak as they might be expected to.

The hesitant progress of reform can be followed in the *Proceedings* of the Classical Association, founded in December 1903.[27] In his presidential address in 1904 Frederic Kenyon, director of the British Museum, identified the introduction of the reformed Latin pronunciation in the schools as an especially significant triumph for the Association, with resistance—in Oxford, although not in Cambridge, Scotland, or the newer Universities—resting 'either upon indolence or upon an irrational prefer-ence for the old mumpsimus'.[28] In 1926, however, the Prime Minister, Stanley Baldwin, confessed that he continued to 'pronounce Latin as it was taught to me fifty years ago':

I have lived for many years in a backwater, and the flood of culture has swept forward far away from me. I speak not as the man in the street even, but as a man in a field-path, a much simpler person, steeped in tradition and impervious to new ideas. To pronounce Latin as our Association

---

[24] Note the acoustic inconsistency (hard-soft).

[25] R. C. Jebb to T. H. S. Escott, 28 Oct 1883. BL, Add MS 58783, ff. 54–8. (The letter is printed in full in 2013a, 122–3.) Cf. Jebb's confident report of 1870 to his old Charterhouse teacher Henry Hayman, then headmaster of Rugby: 1998a, 129 n. 31 (full text in 2013a, 55).

[26] This was some time before 1913: see 1998a, 197 n. 90.

[27] On the history of the Association, see 2003a and Chapter 11.

[28] *Proceedings of the Classical Association* (1914), 51.

has decreed may be to Professor Postgate the breaking of an adhesion; to me it is to convert it into a foreign language.[29]

A prime minister's testimony is of course hardly a representative source; but there were still pockets of resistance in the 1930s, in public schools and especially in prep schools. Writing in the popular classical journal *Greece & Rome* in 1932, Cyril Alington, headmaster of Eton, recommended that the attempt at reform should be given up. Reminding his readers of the depressing results usually obtained while teaching Latin prose to inferior and average pupils, he declared that it was 'pedantic folly' to add another stumbling block to their progress. He himself, he added, had now been asked to change his system of Latin pronunciation seven times.[30] The last refuge of the English pronunciation was the law courts—also the home, of course, of racial and gender discrimination, injustice and absurdity in a variety of manifestations. Here the most engaging evidence is to be found in the writings of A. P. Herbert.[31]

The Varieties of Latin: Culinary, Canine, and Porcine

My third and final anecdote is linked to some of the topics I have been discussing. Like its predecessor, it concerns a father and his child; but in this case, the child was a daughter rather than a son. The father was John Percival Postgate, the Cambridge Latinist who almost certainly, had he applied, would have succeeded J. E. B. Mayor in the university's chair of Latin in 1911 had not Housman been in the field.[32] He is another example of the interaction of classics and comparative philology, holding the chair of the latter subject at UCL from 1880 to 1909. In the 1900s Postgate was a keen advocate of direct method teaching, and he encouraged his children to use Latin at the dinner table. His daughter Margaret recalled in her memoirs two meaty examples. In one case, she asked for a sausage but was refused, since she could not remember the Latin word; she then asked for 'dimidium', and was given half a sausage. On another occasion, she asked for beef from the joint, but simply asked in Latin for 'ox': her father promptly slid the whole joint down the table to her (Cole 1949, 5–7).

The association between food and Latin is in Postgate's case not accidental. His father had been a food purity reformer, and links between Latin and food can be found in several of his publications.[33] The serious point underlying the linkage is surely that the search for purity was in each case concerned with fundamentals—in one case in the material world, in the other in the life of the mind. The use of Latin quotations in

---

[29] *Proceedings of the Classical Association* (1926), 28.

[30] C. A. Alington, 'The pronunciation of Latin', *Greece and Rome* 2 (1932), 2–4; cf. the courteous but crushing reply by F. W. Westaway, *Greece & Rome* 2 (1933), 139–43.

[31] These began with his *Misleading Cases in the Common Law* (1927) and ended with *Bardot MP?* (1964).

[32] R. C. Jebb's disparaging reference to his views on pronunciation are mentioned above.

[33] To the references given at 1998a, 225, add his ' "To Eat" and "To Drink" in Latin' ', *Classical Review* 16 (1902): 110–15; 'Esse, to eat', *Classical Review* 27 (1913): 228–9; 'On the Quantity of Esse, "To Eat"', *Classical Philology* 10 (1915): 315–20.

after-dinner speeches hardly counts here. More to the point, perhaps, is the phenomenon of dog-Latin, which in French is 'Latin de cuisine'.[34] The imposition of composition in Latin prose and verse on thousands of boys in nineteenth-century public schools generated a vast, and mercifully largely vanished, corpus of dog-Latin. The occasional didactic comment has survived: for example, in about 1880 Edmund Morshead of Winchester College wrote on a pupil's composition, 'This *cur* is like itself, canine', adding a drawing of a kennel.[35] For the most part dog-Latin is seen by contemporary commentators as an undifferentiated realm beyond the pale of proper Latinity, though we catch a glimpse of nuance in Thackeray's reference to it in his *English Humorists*: '"Nescio quid est materia cum me", Sterne writes to one of his friends (in dog-Latin, and very sad dog-Latin too)' (Thackeray 1853, 289). Less succulent still is pig Latin, which might be excluded from discussion because it is not Latin, but a systematic mechanical distortion of ordinary English. Iona and Peter Opie commented that '"Pig Latin"...thus: "Unejay ithsmay isay igpay" (June Smith is a pig)...has been spoken by children since before the First World War' (Opie and Opie 1959, 321).[36] I mention it here because of its name: like dog-Latin it is named after the language of the Romans, which it resembles in its capacity to include some and exclude others. 'Latin' has become a generalized metaphor. The parallel uses of 'Greek', on the other hand, evoke its unintelligibility, as in references to the language of Irish immigrants in the USA, or to 'medical Greek'. Within the analytical context provided by these three languages, then, Latin is halfway to gibberish, its difficulty ascribed to social difference rather than intrinsic linguistic features.

This is the view from the bottom of the social hierarchy; things looked different among the middle classes and those who aspired to join them. In the early twentieth century, the high noon of Hellenism was past, and the abolition of Compulsory Greek at Oxford and Cambridge just after the end of the First World War can be taken to symbolize its fall. The national attention focused on the election of a successor to Richard Jebb as Regius Professor of Greek at Cambridge in 1906 makes it perhaps the last occasion on which academic status overlapped to such a degree with high culture and politics (2005a). Jebb, now best remembered for his edition of Sophocles (Chapter 10), was knighted, made a member of the Order of Merit, was a founding fellow of the British Academy, and had served as MP for his university for fourteen years when he died in 1905 (see 2005a, 13–46). The more specialized world of academe which had now emerged, in which scholars were insulated both from the general public and from one another, was symbolized not by the exotic, sometimes toxic, transcendence

---

[34] D. Dalrymple, *Ancient Scottish Poems*, Edinburgh 1770, 243: 'The alternate lines are composed of shreds of the breviary, mixed with what we call Dog-Latin, and the French, Latin de cuisine.'

[35] Morshead's MS is reproduced in 1996, 48. 'Mushri' was the name coined by his pupils for Morshead's idiolect, replacing the more prosaic 'Morsheadic'.

[36] The earliest citation in *OED* dates from 1896, the earlier 'hog Latin' from 1807. Cf. the 'language of Ziph' which De Quincey used at Winchester at the end of the eighteenth century. T. De Quincey, *Collected Works*, ed. D. Masson, vol. 1, London, 1896, pp. 201–3.

of Greek, but by the more down-to-earth formal rigours of Latin. The two were compared in high romantic style by the socialist civil servant and Oxford Professor of Poetry J. W. Mackail in 1904:

The place of Rome, of the Latin temper and civilisation, the Latin achievement in the conquest of life, is definite and assured. It represents all the constructive and conservative forces which make life into an organic structure....Greece represents the dissolving influence of analysis and the creative force of pure intelligence. The return to Greece, it has been said, is the return to nature; it has to be made again and again, always with a fresh access of insight, a fresh impulse of vitality...While Rome has laid down for us a realised standard of human conduct, Greece rears aloft, wavering and glittering before us, an unrealisable ideal of superhuman intelligence.[37]

This fine example of art deco prose came aptly from the son-in-law of Burne-Jones and biographer of William Morris.

The Realm of Latin: Compulsion and Rigour

The abolition of Compulsory Greek initiated a period of forty years in which Compulsory Latin ruled in its stead. Latin was embedded in the curriculum of the grammar schools, the exemplar of academic knowledge and the gateway to university education, professional careers, and middle-class respectability. In the depression years of the late 1920s, Latin symbolized the goal of social ascent and economic security. In the 1930s, it stood for a disciplined democracy which offered a middle road between the tyrannies of right and left which threatened on the world stage. A classics teacher I interviewed in the 1970s, who had grown up in the 1930s, commented that 'Latin produced a self-controlled kind of person, like civil servants'. She might have added, 'like me' (1977).

What lay at the heart of this complex ideological formation was Latin grammar. It represented in condensed form the virtues of Latin: regularity and rule-governedness. So what was the status of Rome, the civilization which used the language? This was a source of much angst to His Majesty's Inspectors of Education in the late 1940s and early 1950s. Latin might be Humanity,[38] but a Latin course which aimed at thoroughness and discipline would not have much room for poetry and history. Teachers were indeed found who were happy to watch pupils dropping out even after only one year of Latin, since even a brief contact with the magical source *must* have done their minds some good. For the good of the small minority of able and committed pupils who went through the course, on to advanced study and then to university, two much larger groups suffered. First, the vast majority of pupils who were forced to learn Latin but whose ability or commitment or both were insufficient. Secondly, and too often forgotten,

---

[37] *Proceedings of the Classical Association* (1904), 14–15, 17. For a discussion of Mackail's address see 1998a, 240–6.

[38] The name given to Latin chairs in the universities of Scotland.

a cadre of teachers who were also trapped in the Latin classroom. The tendency to make Latin compulsory for pupils led to a demand for Latin teachers, and there were not enough qualified graduates to fill this. As a result, many of the unfortunate pupils were taught by staff who were themselves not up to the job. This was a recipe for misery on a large scale. But until well into the 1950s the public faith in Latin meant that pupils' failure to pass examinations was generally regarded as their failure alone, not that of the system, the syllabus, or the teachers.

A good example of the ambivalence felt by some teachers about the tension between grammatical discipline and Roman civilization, between the training of the pupil's mind and the catching of his or her interest, is the preface to a Latin reading book called *Balbus*, written by G. M. Lyne and published in 1934. The title itself belongs to a pedagogic tradition which goes back at least to Thomas Kerchever Arnold's *Introduction to Latin Prose Composition* of 1846, in which Balbus features from the very first exercise.[39] He is the Roman equivalent of Tom, Dick, or Harry, or in nineteenth-century British terms, Brown, Jones, and Robinson.[40] In the early 1930s the placid, one might even say stagnant, waters of Latin textbook publishing were disturbed by an American import called *Latin for Today*—a title which sounds innocuous now, but which must have seemed a little radical then in its rejection of timelessness. *Latin for Today* rejected the standard grammar-translation approach in favour of developing intelligent reading skills; grammar was introduced *pari passu* as the reading exercises progressed. In Arnold's textbook, Balbus is a cipher, any Roman male. In Lyne's book, he appears as a boy and as the leading figure in the reading exercises, which consist of short pieces of synthetic Latin on Roman subjects, interspersed with notes on various aspects of ancient life. The reader (still in the 1930s usually assumed to be male) is expected to identify with Balbus, and to make this easier, the well-known comic artist W. Heath Robinson was commissioned to provide illustrations. Lyne tells us that the humour is meant to be Latin, not English; but a glance at the illustrations suggests that the universal situational humour is rather perfunctorily located in the Roman world by sketches of vaguely classical buildings.

Lyne's preface declares that he wants to show that Latin is not dull by introducing the learner to a 'lighter and more humane aspect' of the subject. The standard intro-ductory fare of 'militaristic sentences' followed by Caesar's commentaries is denounced: it will lose 'the battle for (the pupil's) enthusiasm'. But a different note appears in the section 'On learning Latin' which introduces the main text of the book. This opens by declaring that 'Latin is not dull, nor is it difficult...the really important part...is purely human'. But:

---

[39] No relation to the headmaster of Rugby, with whom he has sometimes been confused.

[40] These three are the travellers who discovered an ancient inscription in George Cornewall Lewis's *Inscriptio Antiqua: in agro Bruttio nuper reperta, edidit et interpretatus est Johannes Brownius* (Oxford, 1862). The text of this scarce pamphlet is reproduced with an introduction in 1996, 63–9.

Nothing worth having is bought without some pain…The grammar must be mastered; there must be some lack of firmness and determination in character of the boy who cannot—or will not—master it. This is probably the chief reason why it is, and no doubt will continue to be, a key subject for matriculation, and an essential one for entry into the professions.

As if to confuse the reader further, Lyne then adds 'But it is foolish to learn it merely to serve an end. If we do this, we shall miss a great deal that it has to offer us.' And to suggest what it has to offer, he quotes several eulogies of Latin, ending with this contribution from 'a well-known ex-headmaster': 'If I were in a runaway motor-car, and the driver had to dodge a dog, put his foot on the right one of three pedals and show presence of mind in handling the steering-wheel, the prayer I should put up would be: I hope this fellow has learnt Latin.' Here we have the apotheosis of the transfer of training doctrine, all the more striking because the ex-headmaster is identified by Lyne as having been trained in science rather than the humanities.

The View from Below

So far I have discussed what adults said and did: but as the doctrine of child interest slowly began to bring to teachers' attention, children too had minds and feelings, which might be challenged and engaged rather than just trained and stuffed with knowledge (in nineteenth century terms, given 'discipline and furniture'). This is discussed in detail in Chapter 18, but I would like to emphasize here that it forms an important element in the reception of Latin. We can call in evidence such familiar rhymes as:

> Latin's a dead language, as dead as dead can be
> It killed the ancient Romans, and now it's killing me.

But such rhymes are hard to locate in time and place.[41] Inscriptions, graffiti, and informal extra-illustration in textbooks are a useful source, since their location sometimes gives clues to what is being responded to. My own copy of *Balbus* is almost unmarked, but one of the illustrations has been coloured in. A copy of Kennedy's *Public School Latin Primer* I have inspected was clearly used to pass messages arranging a meeting in a play break between two schoolgirls.[42] The world of the classical textbook, as this suggests, was not all about Classics. A textbook might be a writing surface, or even a missile. The historian and bishop Mandell Creighton said of copies of his popular school primer on the history of Rome that 'they were just a convenient size and shape to be used by schoolboys to hurl at one another, and their consequent speedy destruction served to promote a rapid sale'.[43]

---

[41] See the discussion in Opie 1959, *passim*.

[42] This copy is held in the Gutman Library at Harvard University.

[43] Creighton 1906, 1.146. The book was first published in 1875 and was still in print in 1912; in 2000 it was reprinted in paperback. In the 1890s the text was used in an English reader for Swahili speakers (SPCK,

In 1960, the universities of Oxford and Cambridge abolished the compulsory Latin requirement, and recruitment to Latin courses in schools immediately dropped sharply. The new courses assembled in the following decade represented attempts to detach Latin from the ideological overtones of mental training and to re-embed it in Roman life. The Cambridge Latin Course, piloted in schools in the late 1960s, followed the *Latin for Today* strategy of thirty years before in leading the pupil through a graded sequence of reading exercises; its original edition actually abjured formal grammar (cf. the Introduction to this volume). Later revisions retreated from this understandably extremist position. A strong narrative thread was maintained, based on life in Herculaneum. The course team went to Herculaneum and took photographs of the site, which were used as slides to reinforce the published text. This itself too the form of brightly coloured and heavily illustrated pamphlets, the illustrations more convincingly authentic than Heath Robinson's perfunctory temples. Reading aloud was encouraged, and reinforced by audio cassettes of passages from the course, read by undergraduates specializing in comparative philology at Cambridge.

In this array of reconstructive materials we seem to have abandoned the traditions of grammatical rigour. Curiously, however, it was possible to recreate the tabulated austerity of the grammar book by re-imagining its form as an analogue of the characteristic grid of the Roman city. In the late 1980s a young girl named Kelsey began the Cambridge Latin Course at school. Her mother was a poet, and wrote this for her:

> Today, a new slave,
> you must fetch and carry, obeying
> plump nouns, obstreperous verbs
> whose endings vacillate
> like the moods of tyrants.
> ...
>
> One day, you may discover
> that even Rome was young.
> And this is literature
> —to hear your own heart-beat echo
> in the bright streets of grammar
> where poets lark and sigh...[44]

Conclusion

The authority of Latin was both social and cultural. Latin was used to reinforce the boundaries of social groups: solidarity within, exclusion without. Within the field of culture, Latin co-existed with other languages—its elder sister Greek, its humble but

1897). Speedy destruction may be partly to blame for the disappearance of early editions: the earliest held by the British Library is the sixth edition of 1880.

[44] Carol Rumens, *Selected Poems*, London 1987, 36. I am grateful to Carol Rumens for discussing the poem and its antecedents with me.

ambitious descendant English. I have tried to sketch some of the features of both of these fields of force. British Latin belonged to European Latin, and its history can be plotted in the terms proposed by Françoise Waquet in her study of European Latin: from empire to royalty to option (Waquet 2001).[45] The period I have been looking at is mostly that of royalty, when Latin was not all-powerful, but still possessed considerable authority. As Constantine saw the sign of victory in the heavens, so classicists saw the sign of Latin's decline when Sputnik passed overhead in 1958. In 2003, even in the lawcourts, the last refuge of 'irrational mumpsimus', Latin is now officially prohibited in favour of the everyday simplicity of the vernacular. A legal journalist who discussed this decision summed up his favourable verdict by declaring, 'Res ipsa loquitur'.

[45] This offers a useful general survey of the uses of Latin in Europe since the Renaissance. For another interesting and wide-ranging discussion, see Farrell 2001.

PART III

Schools and Schoolbooks

13

Paper Wraps Stone
The Beginnings of Educational Lithography

Introduction

In a scene from the semi-documentary film *Etre et Avoir* (2000), set in a junior school in France, two pupils are trying to copy pages of a book on the school's xerox machine. They are clearly unfamiliar with the process, and one of them puts the book on the platen with the text facing up rather than down. To most of us, the xerox copier is so familiar that we take it for granted; but it was, until the advent of the scanner and the digital camera, only the latest in a long line of reproductive machines, beginning (as far as I know) with the copier invented by Erasmus Darwin, a version of which was patented by his friend James Watt in 1778. This was followed by carbon paper—patented by another friend, Ralph Wedgwood, in 1806; lithography, invented in the 1790s by Alois Senefelder; the multigraph or hektograph so popular in the 1880s; by spirit duplicators like the Banda, whose distinctive smell and violet-printed output I remember from my schooldays; and finally the (Gestetner) stencil duplicator.[1] Those more venerable pieces of educational technology the slate and the blackboard have their own independent histories, though little has been written about them.[2]

Blackboards had become standard equipment by 1819 in the Feinaiglian Institution, a school in Dublin (2002); and it is this school to which I want to turn now, to look at an interesting early experiment with lithography.[3] This process had some crucial advantages over other methods of reproduction. First, it was cheaper than letterpress or engraving for short runs.[4] This made it an ideal method for producing small numbers of copies for institutional use—circulars, minutes or, as in this case, teaching material. But it also has implications for the historian, since it means that large numbers of such short-run, in-house productions have almost certainly vanished

---

[1] Rhodes and Streeter 1999. The role of copying equipment in the history of schooling is discussed, though not in depth, by some of the contributors to Grosvenor, Lawn, and Rousmaniere 1999. The multigraph was used to produce the Mushri Dictionary discussed in Chapter 15.

[2] On the slate in the early nineteenth century, see Hall 2003.

[3] When this chapter was first written, the earliest citation for 'blackboard' in *OED* dated from 1823; it has now been predated to 1739.

[4] The output ranges given by Rhodes and Streeter 1999 (carbon paper 1–10 copies; lithography 10–60; stencil duplicators 50–thousands) are wide of the mark. The upper limit for carbon paper is too high, for lithography too low.

without trace. Second, it was more flexible for non-text layouts, and for text layouts above a certain level of complication. This second point explains why so many early lithographed items are of drawings, maps, music, or non-roman texts.[5] Of these last, perhaps the majority were of non-European languages, but a fair number were in Greek, and the two books on which I focus in this chapter are both Greek textbooks.

Hawkesworth's Lucian

In the case of the first book, a selection from Lucian's Dialogues printed in Dublin in 1829, both reasons for using lithography apply: the second in more than one sense, since Greek text is used within a complicated page layout. *A Key to Some of the Dialogues of Lucian* was written in 1829 by the then headmaster of the Feinaiglian Institution in Dublin, John Hawkesworth. Among its other distinctions, this is probably the first book to be lithographed in Ireland.[6]

The school took its name from its founder and first headmaster, Professor Gregor von Feinaigle. Both the academic title and the noble 'von' were in fact self-awarded; he had been born plain Gregor Feinoegl in Ueberlingen on the shores of Lake Constance in 1760. At the age of twenty he entered the Cistercian monastery of Salem, where he was ordained a monk five years later. When the monastery was closed down in 1801 after the Napoleonic invasion, Father Feinoegl had to find a way to make a living, and is next heard of in Karlsruhe in 1804 giving public lectures on mnemonics. From there he went to Paris, where he became well enough known for a comedy to be performed satirizing his exploits. In 1811 he moved to England, and gave successful demonstrations of his mnemonic system at the Royal Institution in London. Here, as in all his lectures, he conducted public demonstrations of mnemonics, interrogating on stage children he had taught for very short periods—days or even hours. In 1812 Feinaigle gave demonstrations in Liverpool, Glasgow, and Edinburgh, and was hired to reform the curriculum at Ampleforth, a Catholic school in Yorkshire. His next and final port of call, in 1813, was Dublin. Here he secured local patronage among the aristocracy and gentry, and his supporters formed a committee to start a school for him, and bought Aldburgh House, the last of the grand eighteenth-century residences of Dublin, built in the 1790s for the Earl of Aldburgh but never lived in. The Feinaiglian Institution was to some extent conducted on Pestalozzian lines, but it was aimed not at the working classes, as Pestalozzi's own school was, but at the wealthier families of Dublin; it offered a wide range of subjects but Classics was the centre of attention, and it soon became the leading secondary school in the city, sending students to Trinity College every year.

---

[5] For accounts of the early use of lithography for texts in non-Latin characters in India and Southeast Asia see Shaw 1998 and Proudfoot 1998.

[6] Hawkesworth 1829. Six copies are known: two each in Ireland (NUI Maynooth, TCD), England (BL, Twyman Collection) and the USA (Columbia, Kansas). On Hawkesworth, his book and the school see 2002, and Twyman 1997.

Fees were high (100 guineas a year to begin with) and classes were small, between ten and twenty boys.

John Hawkesworth taught at the Institution from its foundation, and became its headmaster soon after Feinaigle's death in 1819. The man himself is rather elusive: in the school reports and in his books he is 'Reverend'; but he cannot be found in any clergy lists. He was probably the son of a merchant from Cork, entering Trinity College in 1811 and graduating in 1817. The Lucian comes out of Hawkesworth's teaching, and gives us a glimpse of what it might have been like. As it happens we know something of the room in which he taught from 1820 onwards, since the governors' report of that year announces the completion of 'a new suite of classrooms on an appropriate and peculiar plan' and provides a ground plan (see Figure 13.1).[7] This is clearly a control system very much like the panopticon, or inspection house, which Bentham had first advocated in 1791, and which was realized, for example, in Pentonville Prison. In their report, the Institution's governors went on to boast that:

the rooms…are admirably adapted to the purposes of oral instruction. The pupils are ranged on seats so constructed, as to place every individual in the view of the master (an important circumstance in promoting order and attention on their part,) and at a distance of about 18 feet. This distance has been found by experience to be best calculated not only to promote clearness and distinctness of articulation on the part of the pupils, but also to repress a puerile familiarity often observed to be the immediate forerunner of carelessness and inattention in their classes. The peculiar shape of the rooms is also well adapted to the mutual direction of the voices between the master and Pupils; each teacher is furnished with his black-board and chalk, instruments necessary for fixing the eye of the Pupil, and assisting in those illustrations in which that organ plays an important part.[8]

These rooms were 18 feet 6 inches on the long axis, and about 16 feet at the outer edge. This means that the maximum class size would have been 12–15, assuming that the pupils sat in a single row, as they were clearly intended to.[9] The seventh report, of 1816, gives the names of eighteen members of the fifth class—the class for whom Hawkesworth wrote his book; the class sizes in 1817 varied from twelve to twenty. The form captains were originally called Decurio, or 'leader of ten', but class sizes soon exceeded this (Sandford 1818, 1). It may be that once the new classroom suite was built, class sizes were restricted. We know nothing of the classroom furniture except that master and pupils had seating. It may be that the use of books, such as the *Key*, makes it likely that the boys' bench had a shared desk in front of it.

---

[7] Feinaiglian Institution, *Thirteenth Report* (1820), 13.

[8] Ibid., 14–16. We also know from a pamphlet written by the Institution's 'mmemonic artist' (Sandford 1818, 2) that in 1818 the 'Lecturer is placed in an elevated situation', i.e. on a dais, and that black-boards were in use. This was before the panopticon suite was completed. The only surviving copy of the pamphlet is in the Russell Library, National University of Ireland, Maynooth.

[9] The average seated width of the early nineteenth-century Dublin schoolboy remains an unknown variable.

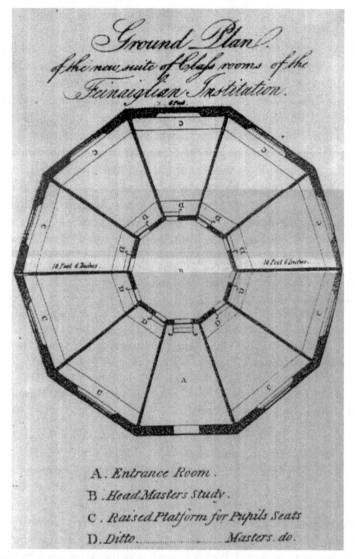

Figure 13.1 The panopticon classroom suite at the Feinaiglian Institution, Dublin. Feinaiglian Institution, *Thirteenth report* (Dublin: printed by R. Graisberry, 1820), p. 13.

Both the title page and the preface of the *Key* breathe the air of familiar internal knowledge: on the former, the letters F I for the school; at the end of the latter, J H for Hawkesworth. The book was clearly printed for use within the institution, so we can assume that the print run was fairly small—scores rather than hundreds. We do not know if pupils were expected to keep their copies or pass them on or resell them after use. The former is more likely, both because it fits with the ethos of the institution and because what evidence we have of manuscript inscription indicates single ownership. A hundred copies would have lasted for five years or more. It is also possible, though unlikely, that Hawkesworth planned to have more copies printed off as necessary, but as used lithographic stones had to be paid for if kept as the equivalent of standing type, a book of this size (384 pages) would have been very expensive to store in that way. On the other hand, according to the Irish Education Enquiry Report of 1826, Hawkesworth's annual income from the school was then £2,000—a very considerable sum.[10]

Lucian had formed part of the school's curriculum for some time. We know that he was being read by 1816, for the *Third Report* of 1815 mentions that 'The Greek class made the strongest impression last time; next time they will be tested on Lucian' (p. 6). And in June of that year the fifth class translated the first thirty chapters of Murphy's Lucian in the public examination. But by 1818 (*Tenth Report*, 1818, 29) they were using Walker's *Selections from Lucian*—presumably the first edition of 1816. Why use Lucian, and why switch from one edition to another? Lucian was quite commonly taught in the early nineteenth century. It was probably Victorian prudery which ejected him from school curricula; understandably, since he wrote biting satires some of which had religious targets, and his narrative works were often erotic. But his writings are in other ways eminently suitable for beginners, since he wrote a large number of lively short narratives with plenty of dialogue in relatively simple Greek. There was a strong Irish tradition of Lucian editions, but the crucial reason for his being read in the Feinaiglian Institution is very simple: Lucian was a staple author in the curriculum and examinations of Trinity College Dublin, the institution at which the brightest of the school's pupils aspired to enrol. This also probably explains the choices of edition, since at some point Walker's edition was specified by the college authorities. It was certainly prescribed in the 1820s, is listed as such in the first published TCD *Calendar* in 1833, and was not abandoned until 1901.[11]

All six copies of Hawkesworth's book appear to be defective in pagination, with pages out of order, or missing, or both. One might think that they have survived partly because their production errors made them difficult to use in Hawkesworth's classroom. On the other hand there are clear signs of use in some copies, and some warning notes were added on the stone, to the effect that some of the pages were out of order. In the Kansas copy there is a manuscript addition at the end of his preface— 'Hooray for Jack!'—followed by a row of exclamation marks. The rear pastedown of this copy tells us that 'O'Brien got a mark from Jack' (i.e., a bad mark). It is striking that both the MS references to Hawkesworth call him 'Jack'. The friendly and relaxed

---

[10] *House of Commons Papers* 1826–7, xii: 566.

[11] In a catalogue issued by the publisher, John Cumming, in 1841, Walker's selection is listed as 'Lucian: All the dialogues read in T.C.D.': *Works on Education: Including Those Read in the University of Dublin*, 5. The catalogue was bound in at the back of some of Cumming's books.

teacher–pupil relationship this suggests is perhaps confirmed by Hawkesworth's preface, which runs as follows:

To the pupils of the 5th Class

Young Gentlemen

I here present you with a Key to some of Lucian's Dialogues, the result of some of my few leisure hours. You will, I trust, find it useful towards the acquirement of a thorough understanding of this Author's Greek; which from your brief acquaintance with the language, you have hitherto found a matter of some difficulty. My object in preparing it has not been to relieve you from the necessity of labour. Labour, you are already old enough to know by experience, is the price which you <u>must</u> pay for every valuable mental acquirement. I have intended rather to provide you with an engine by which you may be enabled to apply your strength with more effect.

You will observe that in the Translation, I have studied only to give you the precise meaning of each Greek word, without any regard to propriety of phrase in English. Whenever the barbarisms into which I continually fall, are totally unintelligible, I subjoin an English phrase, varying as little from the Greek idiom, as possible. The clothing of Lucian's thoughts in a suitable English dress, must be the work of your own judgment, and will furnish a profitable exercise in the use of your own language. In studying Lucian however, your principal object must to learn Greek. I have been careful therefore to give you the grammatical analysis, composition, and origin of every word, so far as I knew or could discover by research. I have also subjoined derivatives in English, Latin and French, with the view of aiding you to retain the Greek words in your memory. You will thus be able to apply to the study of the language, much time which you before lost in tedious and often unavailing research. Part of this time must be devoted to learning the retranslation of Lucian from English into Greek. Without some facility in this practice a scholar can be considered but half-learned; and yet it is a rare acquirement.

When you have studied Lucian thus with care and diligence, you will experience but little difficulty in the reading of any other prose writer in the language, without any such assistance as you are here provided with.

Should this work contribute, in a degree at all corresponding with my expectations, to your proficiency in a language which has always been considered indispensable to a scholar, I shall consider myself amply compensated for the laborious hours its preparation has cost me. This will be my only reward.

I have the honour to be, your very faithful and devoted friend and servant

J. H. Jany 7 1829.

The date tells us that this preface was written first, for the book is signed off 'ΤΕΛΟΣ ['end'] May 27 1829 JH'. The head of the final page is dated the 4th of May. The whole thing thus took Hawkesworth a little under five months to write—an average of about three pages a day.

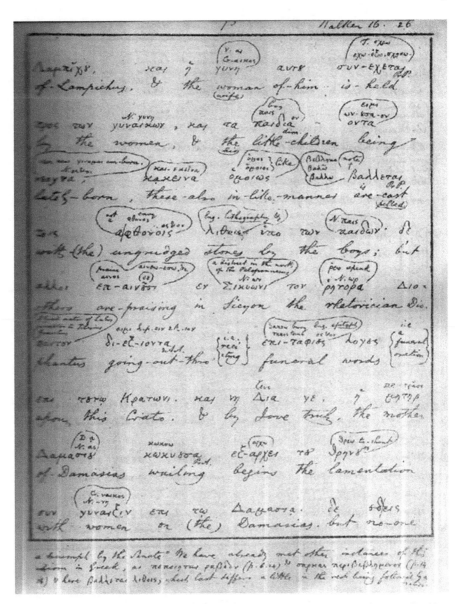

Figure 13.2 John Hawkesworth, *Key to Some of the Selected Dialogues of Lucian* (Dublin, 1829), p. 75. The book was written by Hawkesworth for his pupils at the Feinaiglian Institution, Dublin; it was probably the first book to be lithographed in Ireland.

By kind permission of Michael Twyman.

A sample page (Figure 13.2) will show how Hawkesworth set out text and comment. I have chosen page 75, simply because the word 'lithography' occurs in the fourth line. There are several elements here: the Greek text, a literal translation, notes in balloons explaining etymologies and so on, and the occasional longer background note outside the border Hawkesworth has drawn. In this case it is a note on syntax—a note which in fact began at the foot of page 73. Hawkesworth's expository work on his blackboard is surely the origin of the visual style we can see in his Lucian. Day by day he would put up hints and translations, meanings and etymologies, on the board, only to erase them when he moved on to a different passage. No wonder he seized on a technique which enabled him to capture this pedagogic arsenal in a more permanent form.

It should now be clear why in his preface Hawkesworth emphasized that he was not trying to relieve his pupils from the necessity of labour. This was a sensitive issue in classical teaching, where the use of translations was widely frowned on. In some copies of books used at Eton, we find the Latin translation of a Greek text, printed at the end of the book, razored out by the master. The cribs and ponies produced by Henry Bohn and his rivals and successors were regularly denounced. Not till the Anglo-Irish classical scholar Richard Jebb produced his school editions of Sophocles in the late 1860s did translations begin to become respectable. But even in the 1880s and 1890s, when he was producing his large-format edition of Sophocles with notes and a facing translation, some reviewers suggested (as we saw in Chapter 10) that when his edition was complete it would be impossible to teach Sophocles in schools.

The *Key* was as far as is known Hawkesworth's only essay in lithography; but he did produce other textbooks for the Institution, printed by letterpress. He was probably the anonymous author of an *Introduction to General Grammar* (1826), a work very much in the eighteenth-century Port Royalist tradition. In 1831 he produced an edition of the *Select Satires of Juvenal*, with an English paraphrase and notes; the second edition of his *Progressive Lessons in Latin* appeared in the same year. In 1834 appeared the second edition of *Progressive Lessons of the Grammatical Analysis of English Sentences*. A teaching edition of the Gospel of St John, in Greek, which was published for the school in 1818, is anonymous but may be by Hawkesworth. The fact that two of these books survive only in second editions may indicate that the first editions were very small, though it is quite common for even the most popular of textbooks not to survive in early editions. They were perhaps printed only for use within the school, like the Lucian, but nothing in the later editions suggests that the earlier ones had been lithographed. After several months of writing complicated pages, Hawkesworth may well have thought that enough was enough; and the *Key* remains, warts and all, a remarkable and isolated pioneering effort.[12]

Phillips's *Introduction to Greek Declension*

The second lithographed textbook I want to discuss, *Introduction to Greek Declension and Conjugation*, was printed in 1833 in York, Upper Canada (renamed Toronto in 1834) (Figure 13.3).[13] Like the Lucian, it forms part of the process of expansion traced by Michael Twyman in his *Early Lithographed Books* (Twyman 1990), whereby Alois

[12] Both author and printer were clearly struggling with the new medium, their problems exacerbated by the sheer size of the book. See the lucid discussion in Twyman 1997.
[13] Three copies survive: National Library of Canada, Archives of Ontario, Toronto Public Library.

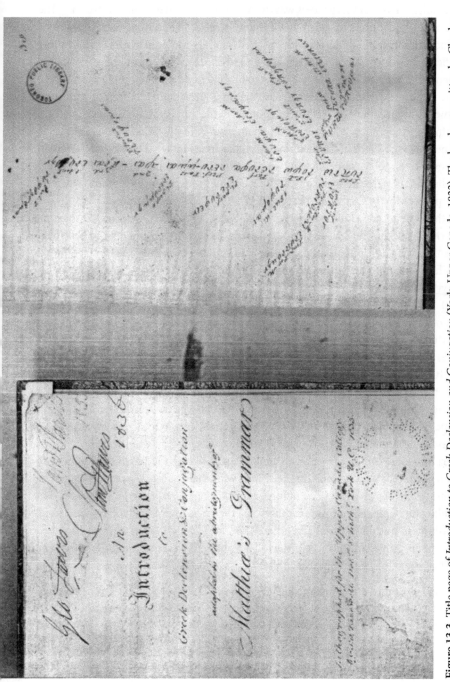

Figure 13.3 Title page of *Introduction to Greek Declension and Conjugation* (York, Upper Canada, 1833). The book was written by Charles Mathews for his pupils at Upper Canada College in York, which was renamed Toronto in 1834. The text was lithographed by Samuel Tazewell (fl. 1820–38).

By kind permission of Michael Twyman.

Senefelder's invention spread to most parts of the globe. A striking feature about some of the earlier phases of this process was the major part played by military printing. The use of an in-house press of course had the advantage of maintaining secrecy about its products; in this case, combined with the need for a large amount of non-text printing: fortifications, winches and pulleys, maps, and so on. The single most important development in Britain in this area was the establishment of a lithographic press at the Quarter-Master General's office in Whitehall in 1808. The foundation of the Royal Engineer Establishment in 1812, at first housed in the same building, led eventually to printing by lithography at its press at Chatham from the early 1820s. The series of military manuals produced at Chatham has been discussed in detail by Michael Twyman (Twyman 1990, 60–5). The engineers went all over the world, and among their colonial establishments were the garrisons at Quebec and Fredericton in Canada, where at some point in the 1820s they began printing maps and surveys by lithography.

In the same decade a London jeweller called Samuel Tazewell emigrated to Kingston, Ontario. Tazewell, who was a skilled engraver, was keen to try lithography and spent some time touring Upper Canada in search of suitable stones. By 1831 he had found what he wanted, imported the necessary equipment from New York, and in August that year announced that his lithographic press was open for business (Gundy 1976, 1988). Late in 1832 he moved to York, the provincial capital of Upper Canada, in the hope of being appointed official lithographer to the government, and began producing maps, plans, and pictures. He was commissioned to print for the government, but after battles with jealous rivals and a complicated history of office intrigue, he gave up in 1834 (the year in which York was renamed Toronto) and in the following year left town and returned to his former trade of jeweller.

When Tazewell reached York in 1832 he will have made contact with the literary and artistic circle of this small colonial town.[14] Among the members of this circle were the staff of the leading local school, Upper Canada College, founded in 1829 by the then governor-general of the province. In 1830 the school had 140 pupils and eight staff. Two of Tazewell's productions can be linked with the College. One is the *Canadian Literary Magazine*, of which three numbers appeared in 1833, printed by letterpress but including lithographed portraits by Tazewell. The magazine was edited by John Kent, English master at the college. The other is the *Introduction to Greek Declension and Conjugation*, printed in April 1833. The full title makes it clear that it was designed to be used in conjunction with August Matthiae's Greek grammar. The short preface adds that:

The only object of the following outline being to preserve the arrangements of Matthiae's Grammars to learners in limine it is intended that examples should be taken from Howard's introductory Greek Exercises, where models are given of every variety of declension, & conjugation.

U.C. College April 1833

[14] An indirect reflection, perhaps, is that Patricia Fleming's bibliography of Upper Canadian imprints (Fleming 1988), which lists the *Introduction* (no. 708), also describes three other publications, of which two are by Joseph Harris, principal of the College (Fleming 1988, 190).

Nathaniel Howard's *Introductory Greek Exercises, to Those of Dunbar, Neilson and Others, to Assist the Learner* (Howard 1819) is a Scottish book, as are the books referred to in its title.[15] Matthiae's book had appeared in a two-volume English translation in 1819, begun by Edward Blomfield of Emmanuel College, Cambridge and finished after his premature death by his brother Charles, later Bishop of London.[16] In 1822 Charles Blomfield, with the help of a schoolmaster, had produced an abridged version in one volume of 188 pages, and it was this which was used in the fourth form at Upper Canada College; Greek had been begun in the third form with Howard's *Exercises*.[17] It may be that the Matthiae was found to be too heavy going, or too expensive, and that the *Introduction* was produced to lead up to it. It would thus have been used by the fourth form. This was taught by the first classical master in 1838–9, Charles Mathews. Little is known of Mathews, except that he corresponded with Wordsworth, and that his translation of Horace: *The Odes and Carmen Saeculare of Horace, Newly Translated into Verse* was published by Longmans in 1867.

On the other hand, the *Introduction* may have been produced for teaching the third form, to lead them gently into the grammar: the reference to 'learners in limine' (on the threshold), points in this direction. This form was taken by the vice principal, at this point Thomas Phillips. Even less is known about Phillips than about his two colleagues; he took over a local parish on his resignation in 1843, and died in 1849. It would have been relatively easy for any of these men to meet Tazewell; York was a small place, and Tazewell was the only lithographer in town. But there is a specific link—the drawing master at the College, John Howard, later a well-known architect.[18] He was hired in the very month that the *Introduction* appeared; soon afterwards he made plans for churches at the request of the local bishop, and these were lithographed by Tazewell. (It is perhaps apt that on Saturday mornings the fourth form were taught first Greek grammar, then perspective and surveying.)

What can be said about the book itself? For the most part there is nothing remarkable about its contents. It provides a 38-page version of a 188-page book (the *Abridgment*) which is itself a summary of a two-volume work of 1,013 pages. (Matthiae himself had produced an abridged version for schools, but this still ran to 642 closely-printed pages.)[19] The exception is the final page, page 38, which provides a Greek verb tree, showing the relationship between stems, moods, and tenses. This is a good

---

[15] Later editions appeared in 1832 and 1843. The non-BL copies listed in COPAC are all in Scotland. George Dunbar's *Introductory Exercises on the Greek Language* (Edinburgh: Stirling and Kenney, 1829) was only one of several Greek textbooks he wrote, of which the *Analecta Graeca Majora* (and *Minora*) were very popular in the USA. William Neilson's *Greek Exercises, in Syntax, Ellipsis, Dialects, Prosody and Metaphrasis* (Dundalk 1804; later editions, Edinburgh and London; final edition, 1853) was another Scottish textbook. For Dunbar, see Morris 2007, 2009.

[16] We have met Blomfield already, in Chapters 4 and 7.

[17] *Regulations and Course of Education, at Upper Canada College and Royal Grammar School; York, Upper Canada. Established January, 1830* (York: printed by Robert Stanton, 1832).

[18] See his entry in *Dictionary of Canadian Biography* 11: 426–8. Howard's daybooks contain references to Tazewell and the church plans in April and June 1833 (mimeographed copy in Toronto Public Library).

[19] See Blomfield's *Abridged Grammar*, Advertisement to 1st and 2nd editions (cited from page v in the 7th edition, rev. J. Edwards, London: J. Murray 1841).

example of the flexibility offered by lithography (Figure 13.3). This is a typical product of the new romantic philology which was imported into Britain from the continent in the 1820s. None of the printed versions of Matthiae, however, carry such a tree. It was certainly widely known from the late 1830s, when Charles Wordsworth's Greek grammar ended with one.[20] We know that young boys at Eton drew them, and then coloured them, in the 1840s—one of the few aspects of classical learning which they actually enjoyed, perhaps.[21]

More can be said of the physical format. Of the three copies known, that in the National Library of Canada lacks page 38, but includes pages 14–15 and 27–30, which are lacking in the other two copies (Archives of Ontario; Toronto Public Library).[22] The parallel with Hawkesworth's problems in Dublin is obvious, though here the job was much simpler—thirty-eight rather than 348 pages. The layout of the title page is very similar to those of the military manuals produced at Chatham by the Royal Engineers from 1822. There is no clear trail of evidence leading from Chatham to Toronto, but it seems fair to suppose that some of the Chatham expertise was transferred to the garrison presses at Quebec and Fredericton soon after this. The title page carries the words, 'lithographed for the Upper Canada College by S. Tazewell Delst. and Lithr. York UC 1833'.[23] That may imply, but it does not explicitly state, that Tazewell himself wrote the text. It is quite likely that Phillips himself did: the Greek script seems flowing and easily-written, and the text was almost certainly written on transfer paper, rather than in reversed script onto the stone.

It is also possible, however, that Tazewell had help from the Royal Engineers. Between 1826 and 1832, when he was setting up his press, they had been building the Rideau Canal between Montreal and Kingston, in part to enable waterborne travel away from the often hostile USA, and he had been called in to lithograph sectional drawings, geological sketches, and plans and pictures of bridges. This had brought him into contact with two of the Royal Engineers. One was Colonel John By, who was in charge of the canal building, and after whom Bytown was named (later renamed Ottawa and made the national capital). The other was Captain Richard Bonnycastle, commanding officer of the Engineers in Upper Canada, whose studies of local limestone, lithographed by Tazewell, were later published in the *American Journal of Science and Arts*. Many if not most of these were transfer lithographs, drawn by the artist or engineer rather than by Tazewell himself. Bonnycastle was the son of John Bonnycastle, Professor of Mathematics at the Woolwich Military Academy and author

[20] C.Wordsworth, *Graecae grammaticae rudimenta* (Oxford: Oxford University Press, 1839), final page (unpaginated). For this book, see 2016.
[21] Copies of these Etonian productions are held in the Briggs Collection, Nottingham University Library.
[22] For the two latter copies, see Fleming 1988, no. 708. The National Library copy seems not to have been known to Fleming.
[23] 'Delst.' is mysterious. One expects a noun, parallel to 'Lith[ographe]r', such as 'Delineator'. The Toronto Public Library copy carries three ownership signatures, all by members of the Jarvis family who attended the College.

of several bestselling textbooks; in 1825 his brother Charles became professor of nat-ural philosophy at the new University of Virginia, whose founder Thomas Jefferson invented an automatic writing device. In the following year, an examination paper in moral philosophy was issued in the University as a lithographed sheet.[24] So we have here a set of links between textbooks, the military, and North America: part of a larger web of such links, perhaps, waiting to be uncovered by further research.

Conclusion

The two textbooks I have been discussing were lithographed early on in the history of the technology in response to two of the major motives which led people to use it: it was a cheap and convenient way to produce short runs, and it enabled non-roman and non-text pages to be flexibly dealt with. In Hawkesworth's case, the second motive was surely the overriding one. In Phillips's case, both motives applied, and it is unlikely that the local printer (the King's Printer, Robert Stanton), had any Greek types. In both cases, however, the projects were driven by pedagogic convenience. Further, both books are linked as we have seen to conventionally-printed works: Hawkesworth's to Walker's edition of Lucian, and Phillips's to the larger and smaller versions of Matthiae's Greek grammar.

It will not have escaped the reader's notice that both books were produced in colo-nial or semi-colonial locations. Technically of course Dublin was not colonial in 1829, as Ireland had joined the Union in 1800, but it was at the edge of the United Kingdom—and Feinaigle was certainly an alien wanderer. York, however, was certainly a colonial settlement, and may well have had problems with book supply, though we know that English (and Scottish) textbooks were imported there. The motivation to make one's own book may therefore have been stronger for Phillips. Is this why examples of educational lithography crop up at the edge and not at the centre, or is it just chance? A lithographed item has recently come to light which was almost certainly produced in London in the mid-1820s: a small (12pp) booklet entitled *A List of English and Latin Words which are Derived from the Same Origin; Intended to Illustrate 'The Companion to the Latin Grammar'* (Figure 13.4).[25] There is no space to discuss it here in any detail; but it is worth noting that this too is an enclitic item, its contents keyed in detail to the pages of another text. So far it has proved impossible to identify the *Companion to the Latin Grammar*; it may be that it was itself a lithographed work, a previous effort by or for the same teacher.

As I have already suggested, the books I have been discussing belong to a specific genre, and one which cuts across printing and production methods: the institutional

---

[24] *Second Examination of the Class of Moral Philosophy. Dec'. 11th. 1826.* Special Collections, Alderman Library, University of Virginia.

[25] The only known copy is in the Twyman Collection.

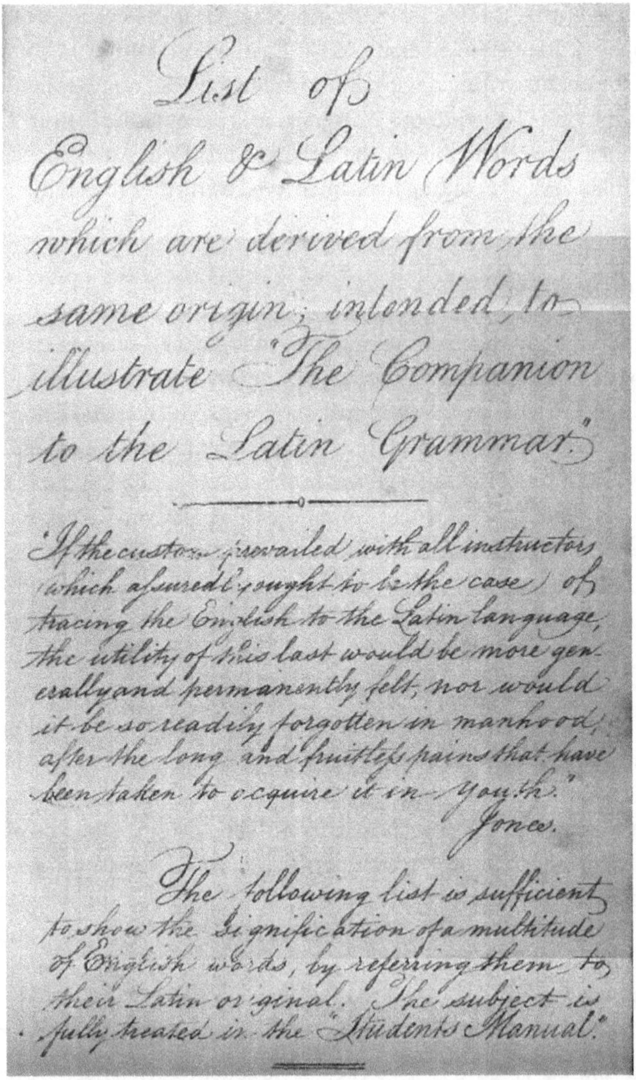

List of
English & Latin Words
which are derived from the
same origin; intended to
illustrate "The Companion
to the Latin Grammar."

"If the custom prevailed with all instructors (which assuredly ought to be the case) of tracing the English to the Latin language, the utility of this last would be more generally and permanently felt, nor would it be so readily forgotten in manhood, after the long and fruitless pains that have been taken to acquire it in youth."
Jones.

The following list is sufficient to show the signification of a multitude of English words, by referring them to their Latin original. The subject is fully treated in the "Students Manual."

Figure 13.4 *A List of English & Latin words which are Derived from the Same Origin; Intended to Illustrate 'The Companion to the Latin Grammar'* (London?, n.d., lithographed).
By kind permission of Michael Twyman.

textbook. Some of these are very well known. The *Introduction to the Latin Tongue* printed in 1758 for Eton College, by the 1790s commonly known as the Eton Latin Grammar, was used in the vast majority of English schools in the early nineteenth century.[26] A Greek grammar followed in 1768, and differences of opinion among the

[26] This is clear from the entries in Carlisle 1818. It was also used in the 1820s at the Royal Grammar School in York (Canada), whose principal was none other than Thomas Phillips: Dickson and Adam 1893, 30–2.

teaching staff led in the 1840s to the use inside the school of several different versions, sections of other books being grafted onto a basic core, in some cases with manuscript additions (1989). I assume that these books were printed by the school printers Pote & Williams.[27] Eton was and is a large school, proud of its history and rich enough to look after it. That is not true of many schools. Dozens if not hundreds of pedagogic ephemera and short-run items must have been lost, though some survive, often unlisted, in school libraries and archives. To interpret their contents, production, and use, a range of knowledge is needed: from the history of pedagogy, and of individual subjects and schools, to the history of printing. Given the limits of individual knowledge and the conventional organization of academic disciplines, this points to the need for collaboration. I am therefore happy to end by acknowledging a long and fruitful collaboration with Michael Twyman, who has not only been generous with both information and ideas, but who also introduced me to the books discussed in this article. [28]

[27] A subgenre which deserves mention here is that of work printed on school presses; some of them set up by the early nineteenth-century schools founded to train the poor for industry. Gowers Walk School in Whitechapel, founded in 1808, began with letterpress but acquired a lithographic press in 1822. 'The managers have bought a *lithographic press*; for observing of late that there was some falling off in a profitable branch of the printing—the epistolary matter—by the preference given *to lithography*, they have provided an apparatus', *Reports of the Free-School, Gower's Walk, Whitechapel* (1842), 153 (printed on the School Press!). Prior Park School near Bath had a productive press (not for training); extensive details are to be found in the auction catalogue from its sale in 1856, when presses, paper, and type were listed (Prior Park archive, in Clifton Roman Catholic diocesan archives, Bristol).

[28] I am also grateful for their help to Mary Allodi (Royal Ontario Museum), Elaine Hoag (National Library of Canada), and Marian Spence (Upper Canada College).

14

John Taylor and 'Locke's Classical System'

John Taylor and his series of classical textbooks, 'Locke's Classical System', are now long forgotten, but they deserve our attention for several reasons. First of all, Taylor's attachment to a particular institution which provided him with both a market and potential authors makes him and his publishing of interest. On 11 December 1827 Taylor was appointed official bookseller and publisher to the new University of London, and his catalogues resound with the names of early professors at the University (which in 1836 became University College, London).[1] Secondly, his infatuation with Locke locates him within a small band who resisted the Anglican idealist onslaught against Lockean empiricism in linguistics in the 1820s and 1830s (Dowling 1986, 3–45).[2] The immediate inspiration for Taylor's system came from a text of Aesop's fables with interlinear translation produced by Locke and his friend Awnsham Churchill in 1703. In a discussion of Locke's Aesop's Fables, Robert Horwitz and Judith Finn stated that 'Locke's Aesop virtually disappeared from view during the eighteenth and nineteenth centuries' (Horwitz and Finn 1975, 72). The story of Taylor's textbook publishing, however, shows that a series of school books based on Locke's Aesop appeared in the 1820s and 1830s, an outcrop of Lockean influence in a century when the distortion of his views was more common than their promulgation. Third, though the evidence is spotty, we can actually get an idea of the commissioning, writing, and selling of the System—something not possible for many such productions of this period. One reason for the publication of some of this evidence is that Taylor published and promoted Keats, Clare, Landor, Lamb, De Quincey, and other literary figures.[3] His educational publishing in fact constitutes a kind of second career. The two books written about him (Blunden 1936, Chilcott 1972) focus on his literary activity, and in so doing epitomize the general tendency to leave textbooks in obscurity. Taylor is thus one of those people about whose textbook-related activities we happen to know just a little,

[1] On the comma, occasionally dropped in the nineteenth century, and its final disappearance, see Naiditch 1988, 110 n. 43.9.

[2] On the vehement attacks on Locke by Julius Hare, see E. H. P[erowne], 'Memoir', in [Hare and Hare] 1897, xxii.

[3] For De Quincey's views on Taylor and on his work on Junius, see D. Masson (ed.), *Collected Writings of Thomas* De Quincey (A. and C. Black, 1897), 3.128–43. De Quincey claimed (p. 130) that Taylor's peculiar and perhaps blind veneration for Locke stemmed from his sharing in all the dominant feelings of the dissenters.

because his high-cultural connections have led students of literature to investigate everything he did.

John Taylor was born in 1781 in East Retford in Nottinghamshire, the son of a printer and bookseller who had just moved there from Newark. He went to school first at Lincoln Grammar School and then at the local grammar school in Retford; this latter during the reigns of two liberal and enlightened headmasters. He was then apprenticed to his father. In 1803, he went to London and worked for the well-known bookseller James Lackington in his vast 'Temple of the Muses' in Finsbury Square. His employer liked him, invited him to dinner several times and promised him positions of trust, but was not prepared to increase his salary, so Taylor left after a few months. His next position was with the publishers Vernor and Hood (the latter being Thomas Hood's father). Here he witnessed the production of one of the first books to be stereotyped in England, Robert Bloomfield's *The Farmer's Boy* (1809). In 1806 he went independent, setting up as a bookseller and binder with his friend James Hessey. In the next few years he established a circle of friends which included Richard Woodhouse, who will reappear later as author of a volume of Locke's System. With several others, in 1811 they founded a debating club which they called the Philological Society. It lasted only a year or so, but doubtless gave Taylor opportunities to discuss two of his great interests: Locke and language. In 1811 Taylor and Hessey published a commonplace book with an introduction by Taylor, with an index based on Locke's ideas.[4] Taylor was no radical or materialist, but he shared Locke's resentment of what they both saw as the intrusion of formal grammar into the inductive learning of language.

Taylor's abiding interest in language is reflected in his declaration to his brother James in 1820 that

the principle of the investigation into language is one of the most important of all that have engaged the attention of men, and the consequences of it to the illustration of antiquities, history, manners and religion are such as I had scarcely foreseen... [but it is] plunging me into such various and abstruse disquisitions. One Word leads on to another till in fact all things are drawn into the Vortex.[5]

Like James Murray of the *OED*, Taylor was 'caught in a web of words'. His investigations into language fed into his discussions about archaic words with Henry Cary, whose translation of Dante he had published. A later book of his, the *Emphatic New Testament*, attempted to mark the text of the New Testament to show how it was to be spoken. In the 1810s he was working on a book called 'Grammar made easy' (never published, if indeed it was finished). He was also investigating a well-known pseudonymous text, the *Letters of Junius*; his book *The Identity of Junius with a Distinguished Living Character Established*, which appeared in 1816, pointed the finger at Sir Philip Francis. It would be easy to see Taylor as a member of the great band of English eccentrics,

---

[4] For Locke's commonplace book method, first published in 1676, and its influence, see Yeo 2004; Allan 2010, 61–70; Stolberg 2014.

[5] Taylor to his brother James, 28 August 1820. Taylor papers, Derbyshire Record Office.

in search of 'the key to all mythologies' and the like; and a reading of his published work on the Great Pyramid might support this. But he should also be remembered as one of the dwindling band of Lockeans who followed their hero in the nineteenth century, when his writing was systematically disparaged by the Anglican apologists who followed Coleridge and his allies. In their determination to remove language from the secular and changeable world of sense and matter, they laid a foundation for the study of 'pure grammar'. The specialized academic community which concentrated on this rarefied realm in the later nineteenth century constructed a historiography which disparaged the efforts of its amateur precursors—men like Taylor. Perhaps the time has come to pay them more attention, if only on the principle that the history of truth cannot be understood without the history of error.

Taylor also published extensively on two other subjects which I can only mention briefly here: currency reform and the pyramids. In the first area, his concern was to distinguish between intrinsic and conventional value, and to insist that only the latter was relevant to currency. This view can be linked with his ideas on language, another conventional system. As for the pyramids, his work now lies in the dustheap of history, along with that of other nineteenth-century speculative writers, though at the time he convinced Piazzi Smyth, the Scottish Astronomer Royal, who became a disciple of his. Underlying Taylor's discussions seems to be an attempt to claim the pyramid planners as ancestors of English measures, and hence a stick with which to beat his bête noire, the French metric system. He thought the Great Pyramid had been built by Noah and his sons, but as an obituarist commented, 'it may be objected that in the infancy of a renovated earth, whose former population had been swept from the surface, labourers in sufficient numbers could not have been collected to raise so gigantic a structure'.[6]

The book trade was in a shaky state in this period, but the onset of continental peace in 1815 seemed to generate an atmosphere of greater confidence. Then in 1817 Taylor met Keats, and two years later Clare, and his career as a publisher of poetry took off. In 1821 Taylor and Hessey bought up the *London Magazine*, whose editor had just been killed in a duel. For the next four years Taylor edited the magazine, and at the same time managed a version of the old Philological Society: round the table at his house sat Thomas Hood, Thomas De Quincey, Charles Lamb, Henry Cary, and several others who wrote for the magazine. He was reputed also to be fond of talking to 'the reverends from Cambridge'; certainly he had a lot to do with the anti-Lockean Julius Hare of Trinity College, who wrote for the magazine and also persuaded him to publish Walter Savage Landor's *Imaginary Conversations*. Taylor defended John Keats from his critics and John Clare from his patrons, while adjusting the latter's English in some cases. It was when Taylor asked him to 'correct' what he had written that Clare replied, 'I may alter

---

[6] 'Biographical sketch of the late Mr. John Taylor', *The Banker's Magazine: Journal of the Money Market and Commercial Digest*, 1864, 824–32. The article may have been written by Taylor's brother James, who was a banker.

but I cannot mend[:] grammer in learning is like tyranny in government—confound the bitch Ill never be her slave.'[7]

By 1825, the magazine was losing its way and sales were declining, and Taylor and Hessey sold out. Hessey became an auctioneer, went bankrupt, and ended up running a private school. Taylor moved sideways but stayed in publishing. This was a time of publishing collapses—one of Taylor's contemporaries told him that 'not more than two or three houses on Paternoster Row are safe'. The biggest collapse was that of Constable; Taylor himself mentions 'Hurst Robinson stopping for 500,000£.'[8] No wonder, then, that in 1827 Taylor told John Clare 'I think in future I shall confine my speculations to works of utility.'[9] In the same year, he began to publish the translations and grammars which made up Locke's System; they sold very well, and after nine months, the first edition of the earliest titles was almost exhausted; In the following January, second editions of the Homer and Virgil were being printed.[10] On 8 December he was appointed the first official bookseller and publisher to the new University of London, which had been founded in the previous year. In 1836 he was reappointed, and the firm became Taylor and Walton; later Taylor, Walton, and Maberly. Taylor retired in 1853 and died in 1864.

In the first half of the nineteenth century, urbanization, Sunday schooling, and technological advances in printing had combined to generate a large popular demand for reading matter and the means to supply it cheaply. Both the size of the market and at least one way to deal with it will have been demonstrated to Taylor by his experience at Lackington's shop. But we also have an interesting additional piece of evidence, an entry in his commonplace book for 19 September, 1815: 'Phillips (Sir Richard) told me yesterday that in the course of last y[ea]r ending Mid[summe]r he sold off 30 000 Goldsmith's Grammar of geography, 10 000 Blair's Class Book, 75 000 Mavor's Spelling.' [11]

It was around this time that the modern textbook was born.[12] This development of the textbook has to do with the interaction between demand, markets, and political and religious authority. By this time the French state had intervened massively in educational provision and prescription (as had Prussia, after its defeat by Napoleon in 1807). Not so England, the land of the free. State intervention began with a whimper in 1833; free elementary education belatedly followed Forster's Act of 1870; state

---

[7] Edward Storey, ed., *The Letters of John Clare* (Oxford, 1985), 231. For an excellent discussion of the issues involved, see Barrell 1983, 110–75.

[8] Both quotations come from a letter to his family written by Taylor on 16 January 1826: Chilcott 1972, 184. On the crash, see Sutherland 1987.

[9] Taylor to Clare, 3 August 1827. BL, Egerton MSS 2247 f. 22.

[10] Taylor to his brother James, 11 Nov. 1827, 31 Jan. 1828. Taylor papers, Derbyshire Record Office.

[11] Quoted by Chilcott 1972, 66, from a note dated 19 September, in Taylor's commonplace books, vol. 3 (New York Public Library, Berg Collection). Sir Richard Phillips was a leading radical publisher and entrepreneur, in business in London since 1795, who wrote or assembled books under several pseudonyms (see Issitt 1998).

[12] An early use is in the title of William Hill's *Grammatical Textbook* (1830). The question of how to date the 'textbook phenomenon' is complicated by the shift from 'text book = a book of useful texts' to text[-]book = book of material for teaching which might also act as a teacher itself. Cf. Stray and Sutherland 2008.

secondary education had to wait until Balfour's Act was passed, in 1902 (Green 1990). This was partly because of the rivalry between denominational and secular educational pressure groups, which produced their own authorized and vetted reading materials. Ireland, however, was a different matter, and there the English were happy to intervene. The (Irish) Kildare Place Society, founded in 1811 to promote interdenominational education, was given government grants between 1815 and 1831 which it used to produce authorized readers, spellers, and other school books (Kingsmill Moore 1904). The Dublin Spelling Book of 1813 and its successors set an example of authoritative, approved, vetted respectable reading for school use. It was assembled by a committee, all of whose members read the proofs. The market extended far beyond this kind of enterprise of course: for example, to the thousands of private schools, and to adults who wanted to teach themselves. This wider market was the home of the various systems which flourished in the 1820s and 1830s: first Hamilton, then Ahn and Ollendorff.[13] The System might be seen as the marketing equivalent of the Library; the set of volumes which like the *Encyclopedia Britannica* in Britain, or the five-foot shelf of books promoted by Mortimer Adler and his allies at the University of Chicago, made up a saleable commodity to attract those hungry for knowledge, upward mobility, or both (Beam 2008). Among the best-known libraries was Dionysius Lardner's Cabinet Cyclopedia, which Taylor published.

Some of the now-forgotten writers and self-publicists in this market were men set adrift by the Napoleonic Wars. Louis Philippe Fenwick de Porquet left Paris in 1814 and built up a textbook empire in London. By 1830 he had established himself as a publisher and bookseller, and wrote from his own warehouse. In addition, he was one of the founders of the *Publishers' Circular* in 1837, and thus links the history of textbook publishing with that of the book trade in general. He makes a interesting contrast to Taylor in that he was a strong monarchist, dedicating several of his books to members of the Royal family and one to the Council of King's College London, the conservative institution set up in 1828 to counter the influence of London University, the 'godless institution in Gower Street'. De Porquet claimed in 1830 that there were 35,000 teachers of French in the country: an estimate which even if excessive, suggests that the true number was at least very large. Could this have been based on his sales figures? James Hamilton, an Irish merchant in business on the continent, was driven to the USA by war, became a teacher of languages, and developed an interlinear translation system, teaching and publishing on both sides of the Atlantic. Hamilton died in Dublin in 1829, ten years after the death of Gregor von Feinaigle in the same city. (Feinaigle, as we saw in Chapter 13, was another of these displaced self-publicists.)

The trend in educational publishing through the nineteenth century was away from institutionally specific books towards the dictates of markets, examinations, and the state (Stray and Sutherland 2008). But in 1827 Taylor's strategy was to gain a stable income not just from school books, but from his University of London connection.

---

[13] For these systems, see Howatt 1984, 129–208.

Taylor had probably been in touch with Henry Brougham, the moving spirit behind the new university, some time before this. Brougham had in fact reviewed his Junius book very favourably in the *Edinburgh Review*.[14] In 1826 Taylor asked Brougham for support from the Society for the Diffusion of Useful Knowledge for his publications, and the following year Brougham supported Taylor's application for the post of official bookseller and publisher to the University. From the new institution Taylor obviously hoped to gain a captive market. In the month after his appointment he told his brother: 'The benefit I may derive from the Univ[y] business in the retail way is variously to be estimated. They calculate on from 1000 to 2000 students annually. If each of these spend 4£ in books the profit on the smaller number will be about 1000£ per annum.'

The connection also gained him authors, including the professors. In a circular of October 1828 Taylor advertised a list of 'works of the professors... designed for the use of students in or preparing for, the University of London'. The list includes works by Lardner, De Morgan, Panizzi, Hurwitz, Turner, Dale, Grant, et al. Following this are advertisements for his own books by other authors, and for Locke's System. It gives a good idea of the different elements of his list. Taylor lived in Gower Street, and presumably met the professors socially. We know that he once went to Stonehenge with George Long, the professor of Greek; and Augustus de Morgan knew him well enough to say that 'he is by temperament a discoverer of hidden things'.[15] On the other hand, it is unclear whether he managed to sell his books for use in the school set up in 1828 as part of the University. At first run by a succession of clerical headmasters, it was taken over in 1832 by the professors of Latin and Greek. The dominant figure was Thomas Key, Professor of Latin, who was sole headmaster from 1842 to his death in 1875. Key had his own ideas about teaching language. His ideas on 'crude forms', taken from Sanskrit grammar and learned from his short-lived colleague Friedrich Rosen, were adopted by several of his colleagues in the school, who produced books using the approach.[16] The best known of these was John Robson, later secretary of the College of Preceptors and of University College; his *Constructive Exercises in Latin*, and a parallel textbook for Greek, were both published by Taylor and Walton.

Taylor, then, was semi-attached to the university, with one foot in its captive market and the other in the larger and more speculative general book market. As his circular shows, he laid some emphasis on his position as publisher to the University. This may have caused some disquiet there at times; a hint of this of this appears in a mention of him in the first issue of the *Quarterly Journal of Education*, which was published by the SDUK. A German journal of philosophy and pedagogy is reported as announcing that 'Locke has revived his ancient way of teaching languages' and is having his books sold by the bookseller of the University of London. The *Journal of Education* writer adds that 'Mr Taylor's interlineary versions are not used in the University of London.

[14] Brougham, 'Junius', *Edinburgh Review* 29 (1817–18), 94–114.
[15] S. E. De Morgan, *Memorials of Augustus de Morgan* (London, 1882), 122.
[16] On Key, see 2011a, and Glucker 1981.

We do not seek to pass any opinion on Mr Taylor's books or plan... The students who enter the University must be qualified to read good authors without the aid of interlineary versions.'[17]

We now come to 'Locke's System' itself.[18] In publishing the series Taylor realized a long-time ambition. In 1821 he had written to his father:

It is now 1/2 past 12 and the Opium Eater has only just left me. No one can attend to this business except myself but it cuts up all my private plans, and will deprive the world I fear of all the excellent treatises on the antiquities of Retford, the origins of language, the true way of reading the classical languages, which I always flattered myself some day I should write.[19]

The System is basically a set of interlinear translations of Latin and Greek authors (later extended to Hebrew and German), together with Latin and Greek grammars. The exemplar Taylor was following was presumably the interlinear Aesop produced by Locke and Awnsham Churchill. The idea was to promote inductive learning without letting formal grammar get in the way. The successive editions of Locke's *Essay on Education* in the 1690s show that he was becoming increasingly tetchy about the obstacle to fluent reading presented by the domination of formal grammar. Locke himself stood in a long line of anti-grammatical protesters: from Haloinus Cominius in the sixteenth century, through Samuel Webbe onwards, there is a line of inductivist writers and practitioners who never gained the central ground in school teaching. The first books to appear were the Homer and Virgil, which were published in February 1827 in impressions of 1000 copies. By August 225 of the Virgil and 175 of the Homer had been sold; by November the impressions were sold out, and what Taylor called 'second editions' were issued soon afterwards. In March a mathematical system had also begun to appear, written by the poet George Darley. Another of Taylor's authors was Dionysius Lardner, who was responsible for the Euclid which appeared in 1829. Of this Taylor said the previous year that 'it is the book which in all likelihood will benefit most by the connection which its author and I have formed with the London Univy'.[20] George Darley, poet and writer on mathematics, was also heavily involved with the Classical System, since he also wrote an explanatory essay which also appeared out in 1829.[21] It is a substantial pamphlet (129 pages, expanded to 143 pages in the second

[17] *Quarterly Journal of Education* 1(1831), 188. The writer was probably George Long, professor of Greek at the University. Long was an active member of the editorial committee of the *Journal*, and became editor after he resigned his chair in August 1831. (For identifications of contributors to the *Journal*, see 2008b.)

[18] See Appendix below for a list of titles.

[19] Taylor to his father, 21 November 1821; quoted by his niece Olive M. Taylor, in her 'John Taylor, author and publisher', *London Mercury* 12 (June–July 1825), 158–66, 258–67, at pp. 262–3. 'The Opium-Eater' was of course Thomas De Quincey.

[20] Taylor to his brother James, 31 January 1828. My thanks to Dr Tim Chilcott for sending me his transcription of the letter, from an original in the Taylor papers, Derbyshire County Record Office, Matlock.

[21] [G. Darley] *An Essay on a System of Classical Instruction... the whole series being designed to exhibit a restoration of the ancient mode of scholastic tuition in England, disembarrassed of its abuses* (Taylor and Walton, 1829; 2nd edn, 1837). The second edition is scarce: there are copies at Trinity College, Cambridge and at the National Library of Poland. For the attribution to Darley see Blunden 1936, 247: one of a number of statements based on Blunden's inspection of letters subsequently sold at Sotheby's, which I have been

edition of 1837), setting out the case for inductive teaching in an expansive style and quoting at length from authorities. Darley also undertook the Aeneid, after Henry Cary's son had made an unsuccessful attempt at the job. Homer was also attempted by young Cary, but again found to be unsatisfactory and finished by Taylor himself. Cary did manage to cope with Xenophon, and Phaedrus's Aesopian fables were given to Taylor's friend the lawyer Richard Woodhouse, whom he had known since the days of the Philological Society in 1811.

This last volume provoked some public criticism when it went on sale in 1828, largely because of the comments which Woodhouse inserted and Taylor presumably allowed to remain. On page 61 is the fable of Mons Parturiens, the mountain which after much bellowing and thundering gives birth to a mouse. A footnote states that 'this fable is applicable to the "Hamiltonian System" and to others of pretension and authority'. James Hamilton, as mentioned above, was the author of a rival series of interlinear translations which became very popular; indeed, an Aesop in his series was published in 1828, the same year as Woodhouse's volume. The criticism of Woodhouse's Aesop came from a somewhat unexpected quarter: a bookseller in Bath. The probable explanation is that Woodhouse had close connections with Bath; both he and Taylor had spent holidays in the nearby village of Claverton. It is likely, therefore, that they took copies of the System to circulate in Bath, and that this provoked the pamphlet printed there soon after the Aesop appeared. This was entitled The *London University Press, or, Remarks upon a late publication, entitled, 'A Popular System of Classical Instruction, combining the methods of Locke, Ascham, Milton &c.'* The pamphlet was probably written by the local bookseller, stationer, and circulating librarian John Upham, for whom it was printed.[22] The burden of Upham's critique is that the editor of Aesop has indulged himself by introducing contentious issues, especially matters of contemporary political debate, in a manner unacceptable in a school book: 'In the name of common sense and common decency, what have boys to do with such terms and topics as the following: —reform—city politics—nostrums—counterfeit present-ments—Love, law and physic et hoc genus omne?' (pp. 7–8) Upham was particularly incensed by the editor's gloss on 'osculum': 'osculum is a diminutive from os, the mouth, often translated as a kiss, as if little mouths were proper for kissing, though Mister Moore quotes an authority to the contrary'.[23] Upham's comment is, 'O tempora, O mores!' (pp. 9–10).

The reference to reform reminds us that political controversy was much in the air at this time. But we should also remember that the Aesopian fable had long been a popular

unable to trace. Darley's biographer C. C. Abbott appears unaware of his involvement with the System, which is not mentioned in his *The Life and Letters of George Darley, Poet and Critic* (Oxford, 1928).

[22] On Upham, see J. Kite, 'Libraries in Bath 1618–1964', Library Association thesis, 1966; J. Tyler, 'A dictionary of printers, booksellers and publishers in Bath...1669–1830', BA Thesis in librarianship, Birmingham Polytechnic, 1972. Upham's library was in operation by 1805, and still running in 1830 (Tyler, 98–100).

[23] Upham may be referring to Thomas Moore's poem 'The Kiss', but this does not mention little mouths. Perhaps the reference is to Moore's edition of the odes of Anacreon.

way of satirizing political opponents. For example, in 1831 the London firm of Roake and Varty published *Aesop in Downing Street*, allegedly produced 'under the superintendence of a society for the diffusion of useful knowledge' (a dig at the SDUK). This includes fables entitled 'The badger and reform: addressed to a certain prime minister'; 'The tools and talents'; and 'The peer and the dustman'. The first of these uses the hierarchy of the animal kingdom as a metaphor for society, and contains the memorable couplet, 'But surely all must think the Ass / At least is of the middle class.'[24] This serves to remind us that in a society where linguistic and social hierarchies to some extent ran parallel, the publication of interlinear translations threatened the barriers between the vernacular of the common people and the classical languages which symbolized the status of their social superiors.

To gain a full understanding of Locke's System, then, we need to locate it at the intersection of several different early nineteenth-century contexts: linguistic and pedagogical theory and ideology, social and economic change, the open market for books, and the various nooks and crannies of institutional demand and prescription. Taylor's case is of some interest because of its relation to the contemporary emergence of the modern textbook, and because it exemplifies the tendency to focus on high culture and to relegate the production of textbooks to the margins of history.

Appendix: Locke's System of Classical Instruction

The titles below are listed in chronological order. This should not be regarded as a comprehensive list, especially as some bibliographical listings of titles are inconsistent or inaccurate. It should however give an idea of the scope of the series. All volumes were in 12mo format and priced at 1s 6d, except for the Hebrew volume, which was priced at 6s 6d, presumably because of the cost of using Hebrew types. The first edition of the Homer volume included an 'explanatory introduction' to the series, from which the *Essay* was probably developed. The list below has been assembled from entries in COPAC, WorldCat, and the European Library. The fullest listing of titles I have found is in S. Low, *The English Catalogue of Books* 1835–63 (London, 1864), 889.

Caesar's Invasion of Britain (selections from *de bello Gallico* 4–5) part 1 1827, part 2 1829
Homer, *Iliad* I part 1 1827, part 2 1828. 1828, 1831[2], 1834[3]
Virgil, *Aeneid* I 1828[2], 1832[4], 1837[5], 1846[6], 1853[10]
Lucian, *Selected Dialogues* 1829, 1838
Herodotus, Selections 1830, 1837[2]
Aesop, *Fables* (Phaedrus) 1830[2], 1835[6], 1838[9]
Anacreon, *Odes* 1833[3], 1837[4]
Ovid, *Metamorphoses* I 1831[2], 1836[6]
Xenophon, *Memorabilia* part 1 1831[2]

---

[24] P. 9. For the genre, see A. Patterson, *Fables of Power: Aesopian Writing and Political History* (Durham NC: Duke University Press, 1991).

Taylor also published in connection with the series a *London Latin Grammar* (1827, 1831[5], 1841[11]) and a *London Greek Grammar* (1828, 1829[2], 1832[3], 1840[5]), and as well as Darley's *Essay* (1829[1], 1837[2]). The series also included works in languages other than Latin and Greek (cf. Sonnenschein's Parallel Grammar series, discussed in Chapter 16):

The Book of Genesis, by Greenfield, with Hebrew Text 1828, 1831[2], 1836[3], 1843[4]
Stories from Italian Writers 1830, 1835[2]
Sismondi, *The Battles of Cressy and Poictiers* 1831
Stories from German Writers 1832

15

Schoolboys and Gentlemen
Classical Pedagogy and Authority
in the English Public School

By the end of the nineteenth century, the authority of classical education had been severely eroded. New areas of knowledge had invaded an enlarged curriculum in the ancient universities (though much less so in the public schools). A mature industrial economy faced increasing competition from rivals abroad; the franchise was being extended to the working classes and would soon also incorporate women. These challenges to the authority of Classics and its bearers prompted a re-articulation of ideas of classical knowledge and pedagogy in which the symbolic centre of classics moved from 'culture' to 'discipline'. The compulsory Greek requirement at Oxford and Cambridge, symbol both of the dominance of Hellenism during the Victorian era and of the universities' autonomy from the state, was repeatedly attacked, especially after 1870, and was finally abolished in 1919–20. In turn, the study of Latin, previously subordinated to Greek, came to be seen as an exemplary disciplinary subject within the widened academic curriculum. In essence, it symbolized the internalized self-control of the new voter, a bulwark against ochlocracy (1998a, and cf. Chapter 12).

In learning grammar by rote in the lower forms of public schools, boys (as they almost all were) were learning both to learn and to obey: the two faces of *disciplina*. The same could be said of the 'nonsense verses' with which many boys began their encounter with verse composition; metrically accurate, but not expected to make any sense.[1] Some of those who went on past this stage, however, found that they were creating poetry, and had found the key to a world of freedom and culture. The tension between order and freedom, discipline and culture, echoed a wider tension between the stability of the social order and the freedom of individual citizens: a structural dilemma characteristic of nineteenth-century liberal democratic states. The emergence in England of a society predicated on the autonomy of the individual is paralleled by the late eighteenth-century move from an Augustan classicism focused

---

[1] The progression from 'nonsense' to 'sense' (making verses which were semantically as well as metrically well-formed) was embedded enough in some schools for two of the lowest forms to be called by these names, as at Eton.

on Rome to what became Victorian Hellenism. The shift from the orderly imaginary of Rome to the wilder freedom of Greece represented, in effect, the adoption of a high-risk strategy oriented to free individuals rather than to stable groups. The ordering of freedom was accomplished, in the new era, by the finely modulated control mechanism of the examination, whose institutional development accelerated in this period (Hoskin 1979; 2005b).

In this chapter, I look at the way social and intellectual styles were reproduced and challenged in everyday institutional settings, concentrating in particular on pedagogic encounters in public-school classrooms. It is notoriously true that evidence of what actually happened in classrooms in history is very difficult to find. A corpus of such evidence has, however, recently come to light in the form of transcripts of classroom conversations in Winchester College in the 1880s and 1890s. In the next section I give three excerpts from these texts, followed by a commentary on the issues they raise. These issues are then pursued in the rest of the chapter.

Horae Mushrianae: A Winchester Classical Classroom in the 1890s

To cast a discussion in the form of text and commentary is of course to opt for a rhetorical format deeply embedded in the history of classical scholarship. There are, however, other reasons for adopting it here. One is that it makes it possible to present the fine texture of classroom interaction, and to show the use of language—vernacular and classical alike—in a setting where most of the formal curriculum involved saturation in linguistic practice in English, Latin, and Greek. But this format also helps to redress the inequality of power between writer and reader by making at least some of the former's evidence publicly available to the latter.

Edmund Morshead, who taught at Winchester from 1873 to 1903, was in charge of 'Junior Division Sixth Book'—that is, the lower sixth form. Morshead's idiosyncratic speech mannerisms led to his pupils' assembling a dictionary of 'Mushri' (his nickname was 'Mush', and his classroom, inevitably, was known as the Mushroom). A surviving photograph, taken surreptitiously through his classroom window in 1898 by one of his pupils suggests an engagement which adds an extra dimension to the conversations quoted below, catching the nuances of stance and expression which we can so rarely find in the printed record (1996, cover image), The Winchester pupils redressed a teacher/pupil imbalance of power by, as it were, writing and publishing their own minutes of their meetings. *Horae Mushrianae* ('Hours with Mushri') forms part of a small corpus of material which Morshead's pupils collected and printed between 1880 and 1901 as appendices to their record of his speech mannerisms, *The Mushri-English Pronouncing* Dictionary (1996a). I shall argue that paradoxically, this personal idiosyncrasy (the display of which is the *raison d'etre* of the *Dictionary*) is typical of a widespread contemporary trend, one which is intimately linked to nineteenth-century

English discourses of authority and freedom.[2] The first extract begins with remarks by Morshead.

I

> Landor's sonnet to Ianthe, line 11,
>> 'The conscious dove
>> Bears in her breast the billet dear to love.'
> In line 11 I have been a trifle too bold; I have not quite kept to the English; but I think the spirit of the passage quite requires some alteration, and this is just what a Latin would have said,—'Pulchraque venustam portat rubecula florem.'
>
> Well, T-lb-t, please keep your remarks till the end of the version; I really can't get on with the bidzness at this rate.—E in venustam short? Is it so? Why then, look it out, P-lt-r ('Short sir!') Formosam! there can be no objection to formosam. ('Please, sir, you said venustam!') I take it I said nothing of the sort. ('Yes you did, sir.') Is it so? so be it, then! I must have said it from the teeth outwards. ('Please, sir.') Why these interruptions? ('Sir, flos is masculine.') I am, I take it, quite aware of that: I said formosum.—I have put rubecula, redbreast, instead of pigeon, because it is so much more poetical, and the spirit of the passage seems to require it. Is it not so?—Mnyum-Mnyum! I take it, it is. (1996, 52–3)

This passage dates from the beginning of the 1880s, and Morshead is taking a class in translation from English into Latin. The English text chosen is a poem by Walter Savage Landor, who was unusual in the nineteenth century in writing a large amount of original verse in Latin. The class would have been told to produce their own versions, after which, as in this case, the master would read out his own translation. This enabled him to display his own talents, but also offered a target to be attacked where errors or infelicities could be spotted by his pupils. In this case, they are able to point out that *venustam* will not scan, since its first syllable is not long but short. The passage shows Morshead attempting to cover his tracks by shifting to alternatives (first *formosam*, then *formosum*), either denying he had uttered an earlier word, or claiming he had spoken it but without meaning to. 'From the teeth outwards', a favourite phrase of his, seems to carry this meaning and is one of those listed in the *Dictionary*. Other idiosyncratic sayings in the passage—'bidzness' [itself one of many variants] for 'business', 'Is it so? So be it then' and 'Mnyum-Mnyum'—are also listed. The second of these is noteworthy, since it is used as a formulaic utterance when deferring to a pupil's opinion, or rather to the authority of a dictionary or grammar, as reported by a pupil. ('Rubecula' does not occur in classical Latin, and would have been found in an English-Latin

---

[2] The *Dictionary* was first produced in manuscript early in 1880. Later that year it was reproduced in a small (32mo) format on a hektograph (also known as a multigraph), a flatbed duplicator which used a gelatine sheet to produce purple-tinted texts. In a sense this could be seen as a functional descendant of the lithographic techniques discussed in Chapter 13. A copy is preserved in Winchester College archives. Enlarged printed editions appeared in 1888 and 1901; this last edition is reprinted with an introduction and appendices in 1996. The theme of 'English freedom' is discussed in the introduction (1996, 2–22); see also Colls and Dodd 1986.

dictionary used for verse composition. It is possible that Morshead is being teased for using late Latin—a revenge for his remarks about *regelatio*—see III below.)

II

> Up to books (Tacitus *Annals* II. 54 § 3)
>
> Br-w-n construes:—'Aquilones depulere, the eagles repulsed them.' Mush. 'Yes! that is, I take it, the Roman Standards!' T-lb-t. 'Sir, I read "aquilones".' M. 'Yes, er! and what does "aquilones" mean?' T. 'NoΘern ... winds.' M. 'Well, er?' T. 'I thought you said "eagles".' M. 'Well, er, and what is the Latin for "eagles"?' T. 'Aquilae.' M. 'Yes, er?' T. 'Does your edition read "aquilae"?' M. 'No, T-lb-t!' T. 'Then, sir, what edition does read "aquilae"?' M. 'Br-w-n's, I presume, er!' (1996, 53)

This scene comes from a lesson ('Up to books') in which Tacitus is being read, the members of the class taking turns to analyse ('construe') each Latin sentence, and then translate it into English. Morshead is represented as accepting, at first, a mistranslation of *Aquilones* (northern winds) as *aquilae* (eagles, hence the Roman legionary standards which bore an image of an eagle). He then tries to throw his pupils off the track by suggesting that the different translations reflect the readings in different editions of the text. Mushric mannerisms in this scene are the use of 'I take it', and the pronunciation of 'northern'. The *Dictionary* records that Morshead pronounced 'northern clime' as 'noΘern climm'. The pervasive influence of classical learning can be seen in the young authors' decision to use the Greek letter theta (θ) to represent the unvoiced 'th' sound, as in 'thick'. Morshead's speech is another strange language, following its own, often mysterious, rules.

III

> Another Version, 1881.
>
> (Scene—The Peg's Class-room, 9 a.m. Enter Mush.)[3] 'We'll take the Latin prose first. I see that you have all used "regelatio" for "thaw". Well, errumn! This "rege-latio" is an English word, first introduced into Latin, I think, by Aggenus Urbicus. Just look it out, er!—(The Looker-out: 'Aggenus Urbicus.')—Yes! I thought so! he died, I take it, a few years before I was born. Hush, please! The entray has been capitally done by everyone except L-c-ck. Yes, L-c-ck, er, there is nothing to laugh at! Run through it, Chittay, and show him how it should be done. Wait a minute. Cr-cksh-nk! will you accentuate, please,* first? Yes, quite right, er; καì is oxytone. I have looked it out in my dictionaray! Hush, please! Now, Chittay, er!—(H. C. τίς πότε καì κτλ)—Come, Chittay, do crawl a bit faster! Come, construe, construe!— (H. C. τίς πότε 'Who in the world–')—Yes that is right! Or you might bring out the meaning by repetition.—(H. C. 'Who-who) (Laughter).—Come, Chittay, do not be an oaf!'—H. C. 'Sir, is that the language of one gentleman to another?' M. 'No, but I take it, it is the language of a schoolmaster to a schoolboy!' *Rare (1996, 53)

---

[3] 'The Peg' was George Ridding, headmaster of Winchester 1866–84.

In this final scene, Morshead is going through Latin prose compositions and an 'entry'—an unseen translation, here from Greek into English, written in a previous lesson. The role of dictionaries as authoritative sources of knowledge looms large. Morshead's pupils have presumably used an English-Latin dictionary to find a word for 'thaw', and choosing to use a noun, found 'regelatio', a word cited only from the end of the fourth-century AD in the works of an obscure writer on agriculture. Morshead has also checked in the dictionary (one can hardly believe he was familiar with the obscure late imperial writer Aggenus Urbicus), but chooses to demonstrate his learning by having the 'looker-out' investigate the word on the spot. This formal role of 'diction-ary monitor' reflects the important part played by the Greek and Latin dictionaries in the life of this sixth-form classroom, in which pupils were assumed to have mastered the elements of grammar and syntax and to be on the verge of serious scholarship (in the photograph referred to above (1996, cover image), the dictionaries can be seen on Morshead's desk). The *Dictionary* reveals that Morshead referred to Liddell and Scott's Greek-English lexicon, the standard work of reference on Greek, as 'Our two friends' (1996, 45; on the lexicon, see 2010). This is the dictionary in which he will have checked the accentuation of καί; and the public admission that he has done so, while it again points to the authority of the book, should also remind us that this whole account is written from a pupil's-eye view. (It is scarcely conceivable that Morshead would have needed to consult a dictionary to check on such a common word.) In this scene, Morshead's idiosyncratic pronunciation is again evident. He liked to pronounce final 'y' as 'ay'—here, in 'entray' and 'dictionaray'. But the issue of linguistic choice is also raised, not just by the whole nature of the translation exercises, but at a different level by his exchange with Chitty. This illuminates the uneasy relationship between a controlling adult and a group of boys who at the age of sixteen were on the verge of both adulthood and scholarship—potentially, but not actually, Morshead's peers. Chitty invokes the norms of gentlemanly politeness, to be rebuffed by Morshead's firm redefinition of the relationship, and hence of the relevant norms of interaction, as that of master and pupil.

The authority of the teacher is clearly a central issue in these scenes. It is asserted by Morshead with the help of standard reference works, the Greek and Latin dictionaries, which are nevertheless equally available, as we have seen, to his pupils. It is challenged in the classroom by use of the public evidence of Morshead's mistakes and self-contradictions. In the Mushroom a triangular relationship obtained between teacher, pupils, and dic-tionaries ('our two friends' in the case of Greek). The role of 'looker-out', which publicly legitimated the practice of reference to an authority beyond Morshead's own, also acknowledged the status of his pupils as apprentice sorcerers, potentially masters of the mysteries of Latin and Greek. In the *Mushri Dictionary*, the challenge is made retrospectively; but it should be remembered that Morshead was teaching at Winchester throughout the publishing career of the *Dictionary*, and that its subversive portrait of him will have been available to successive generations of his pupils.[4] But he

---

[4] Morshead was flattered by the appearance of the early manuscript editions in the school, but not at all pleased when later editions were printed outside Winchester, exposing his mannerisms to a wider world (1996, 32).

also had another claim to authority (and another target for its subversion), through his published translations of classical and modern authors, including Aeschylus' *Agamemnon* (1877) and of the whole Oresteian trilogy (1881). It is these which earned him the sobriquet 'the G. T.' (the Great Translator: a title wickedly described in the *Mushri Dictionary* as 'self-invented': 1996a, 47). The *Dictionary* contains several strange phrases from Morshead's translation of the *Oresteia*, which offered a rich quarry for evidence of his idiosyncratic use of English, and also, by imputation, of mis-understandings of the Greek original. Another title by which he is referred to in the *Dictionary* is 'The Scribe'. This is prompted by his pupils' use of Morshead's written comments on their work—another hostage to fortune—which treats them as if they were recently-discovered papyrus fragments demanding interpretation. The title 'The Scribe' neatly combines mock-respect with gentle derision, since though the scribes who transmitted manuscripts of classical authors had a crucial role in the process, their work was mechanical, and they are known for their proneness to error. Like the teacher's role, theirs is 'special but shadowed'. The authority gained from their know-ledge contrasts with their own low status.[5]

It will be apparent that the conventions of classical learning have been adopted, if only by way of parody, in Morshead's pupils' irreverent account. His own comments on their work are treated as *scholia*: the explanatory comments made by scribes on classical texts. The tables are thus turned, the pupils' work becoming the text, the master's comments the subordinate annotation.[6] Comparable in some ways is the first printed work of Max Beerbohm, written in July 1890 while he was in the sixth form at Charterhouse School. The *Carmen Becceriense* is an account of the mannerisms of the school music master, A. G. Becker, presented as a Latin hexameter poem. The text is equipped with an *apparatus criticus* which guys the conventions of the genre. In par-ticular, it alludes to the school editions of classical authors produced by T. E. Page, the sixth-form classical master at Charterhouse. Beerbohm's notes, which refer to 'my friend Professor Mayor', play on the authority of J. E. B. Mayor, author of a well-known edition of Juvenal, but since Page and Mayor were friends (they had both been taught at Shrewsbury by the famous Benjamin Kennedy), the phrase is probably a direct quote from Page's conversation.[7] The parallel with the reference to Morshead as 'the G[reat] Translator]' is obvious: the status of a teacher as author of published works is deployed in his pupils' interaction with him in school. And there are other parallels, notably in Page's verbal mannerisms. The best known of these was his habit of insert-ing 'please' in many of his sentences—a nice contrast with Morshead, whose brusqueness is characterized in the final extract quoted above by the comment 'Rare' on his use of the word.[8]

---

[5] On 'special but shadowed', see Lortie 1975; on the role of copyists and editors in the transmission of classical texts, see Reynolds and Wilson 1968.

[6] In one case, a disparaging Morsheadic comment is itself treated as a classical text: 'Fragment of a Mushric chorus'. It begins thus: '... Little, and stupid / What there is of it' (1996, 49).

[7] Beerbohm 1964, 1–3; cf. Viscusi 1986, 24.

[8] For Page and his mannerisms, see Rudd 1981, 12–13.

The excerpts above come from classical lessons. How large a part did these play in the total classroom experience of Junior Division Sixth Book? By coincidence, the timetable of the form in 1898—the year in which the photograph of Morshead teaching the form was taken—was printed in A. F. Leach's history of the school, published in the following year. This was almost certainly provided by his eldest son, T. A. Leach, who was in Morshead's form from January 1898 until July 1899.

	7–7.45	10.15–11.15	11.15–12	4.15–5.15	5.15–6.15
Mon	Divinity	German	Livy	Mathematics [or substitute]	Aeschylus
Tues	Divinity	Mathematics [or substitute]	Horace		
Wed	Cicero Latin entry	Plato	Science (Sound)	German	Greek Entry
Thurs	Vergil	Mathematics [or substitute]	Livy		
Fri	Cicero	9.45–11.15 History and Horace	Prose version	Maths	Aeschylus
Sat	English	10–12 Plato and sundries		3.45–4.30 Science	

Young Leach also comments that 'Army Class substitute German for Greek, and cultivate Science and Mathematics at the expense of Plato and Aeschylus.' He explains that an 'entry' is an unseen translation written in class, and an 'entry version' is 'a don's idea of what a perfect version is' (Leach 1899, 534). The phrases I have quoted nicely exemplify the resistant spirit we have already seen in *Horae Mushrianae*. T. A. Leach was in this case able to challenge authority in the public sphere by inserting his subversive statements in his father's book. Here he enters, however briefly, the realm of the 'G. T.'—he is at once within and without the classroom, both schoolboy and author.

In his *Athleticism in the Victorian and Edwardian Public School*, J. A. Mangan asserted that 'Inside the nineteenth-century public school classroom there was a blind belief in a classical prescription for all. Most found it irrelevant. It did nothing to train them for life; in consequence they had very little use for school work.'[9] Leach's timetable reveals that of the twenty-four lessons listed, thirteen are classical. Science and modern languages have made some inroads into what fifty years earlier would have been an almost entirely classical curriculum, but Latin and Greek are still the staple, and the 'tasks' Leach goes on to list are almost all classical (Leach 1899, 533–4). But though the domination of Victorian classrooms by Classics can hardly be denied,

[9] Mangan 1986, 111. I am not here concerned with Mangan's denial of any 'training for life', but there is evidence to the contrary.

it deserves a more nuanced account than Mangan gives. Leach's timetable, after all, comes from the very end of the century: is it representative beyond its time and place? Winchester had in fact concentrated more heavily on Classics than many other public schools. This changed only in 1901, when, for the first time in the school's history, a warden and a headmaster were appointed who were both non-Wykehamists.[10] From that point on, it became respectable to go through the school as something other than a classicist. That Mangan's assertion oversimplifies the situation, even in 1898, is shown by the existence of the Army Class. Even for Junior Division Sixth Book, a 13/24 classical curriculum hardly counts as a 'classical prescription'.[11] As for the 'blind belief' in classics for all, there were liberal, and classically-educated, masters who did not share this 'blind belief'.[12] Indeed, Morshead himself had some pungent things to say about the defenders of classical education in an address he gave in 1906, describing the challenges to classical dominance by scientists as 'an attack by Philistines upon Pharisees, of one sort of unreason upon another: impatience on the one side, bigotry on the other' (Morshead 1906).

Mangan's reference to 'relevance' and 'training for life' raises the question of just what the concerns of pupils were in classrooms like Morshead's. Did they really think in these terms? 'Training for life' is surely more likely to have been something boomed from the pulpit in the school chapel. In the late Victorian decades, the thoughts of pupils are more likely to have been directed to performance at games—as Mangan himself documented in detail. In any case, the schoolboys were not just passive puppets of a disciplinary regime. 'There was a blind belief' is unspecific and lacks a sense of agency, but this agency is certainly not lacking in the pupils quoted in *Home Mushrianae*. Of course those in authority over them had the last word (usually) but the conversations quoted above suggest that pedagogic authority was subject to negotiation. Here the age of the pupils is crucial: these are adolescents on the edge of manhood, whom Morshead's idiosyncrasy will have encouraged to spread their own wings, especially as they were becoming interested in politics. In the early 1880s Gladstone's campaigns were leading to fierce local contests between his Liberal supporters and Conservative voters. Morshead was one of a minority of the Winchester staff who publicly proclaimed their Liberalism; and the election campaign of early 1880 was in fact one of the precipitating causes of the appearance of the *Mushri Dictionary*.[13]

---

[10] Like Eton, Winchester was a collegiate foundation in which authority was divided between a warden (at Eton a provost) and a headmaster. Their appointments indicate that the governors were prepared to depart from the ancient ways.

[11] Unless the phrase means only that pupils did some Classics, however little; in which case it loses most of its meaning.

[12] Examples include E. E. Bowen of Harrow and E. A. Abbott, headmaster of the City of London School and author of *Flatland* (1884). Both men were members of a progressive discussion club known as the 'UU' (United Ushers).

[13] 1996a, 16, 22. For a survey of the scattered evidence for the subversive making of their own sense of Classics by younger pupils, see Chapter 18.

The State, Modernity, and the Masses: Change and Resistance

'Look at those big, isolated clumps of buildings arising up above the slates, like brick islands in a lead-coloured sea.'

'The board schools.'

'Light-houses, my boy! Beacons of the future! Capsules with hundreds of bright little seeds in each, out of which will spring the wiser, better England of the future.'

(Arthur Conan Doyle, *The Naval Treaty*, 1893)

From Morshead's classroom to those of the Board Schools is a long journey; and not only because it takes us, in the 1880s, from the rural fastness of Winchester to the swarming life of the London suburbs. The school buildings are observed by Conan Doyle's Sherlock Holmes from the suburban railway line on which he and Dr Watson are travelling back into the capital from a case in the country. In the Board Schools, the children of the poor were taught a range of subjects which certainly did not include Latin or Greek. Yet these two very different worlds belonged to the same society, late-Victorian England. The contrast serves to remind us that Classics was a major symbol of social distinction. The classical learning of the public schools did, in a sense, train for life, in providing public schoolboys with the shared knowledge of an elite social group; even if that knowledge was to be used in adulthood only to produce a few classical tags. The conversation between Holmes and Watson in the above passage reflects contemporary middle-class concerns with 'darkest England', the sprawling new world of the metropolis.[14] But it also hints at the appearance (much later in this country than on the continent) of mass schooling provided by the state; a development which gave rise to considerable unease. In a country which was home to a powerful ideological tradition celebrating individual and local autonomy (a tradition to which the 'Mushri' phenomenon belonged), such central intervention seemed to many an un-English solution to the problem of securing the survival of England. The ideological campaign for 'national efficiency' conducted in the 1890s represented a compromise formula: centralized intervention was justified if it would improve the efficiency with which the state's human resources were used.[15] The rhetoric of efficiency was used, for example, by Robert Morant, who played a leading role in establishing the pattern of state schooling after the 1902 Education Act. In a report on Swiss education written in 1898, he warned that:

Without control by 'knowledge' in the sphere of public education of all grades...a democratic state must be inevitably beaten in the international struggle for existence, conquered from without by the concentrated brainpower of competing nations, and shattered from within by the centrifugal forces of her own people's unrestrained individualism.   (Quoted by Searle 1971, 210)

---

[14] Among the products of the social concerns of the 1880s is (General) William Booth's *In Darkest England and the Way Out*, published by the Salvation Army, which he had founded (Booth 1890). For a modern discussion see Stedman Jones 1971.

[15] See Searle 1971, and on the relative lateness of English state intervention, Green 1990.

The idiosyncrasy which was celebrated, along with gloriously irrational tradition, in the myth of Englishness assembled in this period, becomes problematic at the point when it spreads from elite sectors to the mass of the population: from Winchester (where Morant himself had been educated) to the Board Schools.

The intervention of the state in education led to a marked contrast between different class-specific varieties of schooling. As free elementary schooling became the mark of the poor, cheap private schools aping the public schools were set up, offering a curriculum which included at least Latin, and sometimes Greek, and which thus marked out both school and pupil as middle class. To be able to send a child (still usually a son) to such a school announced a social status above the world of the Board Schools and their clientele. Conan Doyle was in a minority in eulogizing the future promise of the Board Schools, rather than denouncing their regimented routine or the 'cockney twang' of their pupils.[16]

Winchester sixth-form Classics in the 1880s, then, was one of the peaks of a dominant social and cultural formation, but one whose days were numbered. The collapse of the grand Victorian alliance of Classics and class was symbolized by the abolition of the compulsory Greek requirement by Oxford and Cambridge after the First World War. 'Compulsory Greek' had by then become a kind of Hindenburg Line of culture; a symbolic last ditch to which the defenders of the Classics had retreated. Its abolition after World War I was followed by the expansion of science teaching in the public schools in the 1920s; yet Classics retained a powerful hold over the curricula of public schools, and of the grammar schools which aspired to be like them, well into the 1950s. Alternative curricular tracks were available, but it was common for top-stream pupils to be urged to choose (e.g.) Greek rather than German.[17]

The Languages of Gentlemen: Exclusion, Hierarchy, and Symbolic Markets

At the heart of Morshead's teaching lay the making of delicate linguistic distinctions. The obscure Latin agricultural writer Aggenus Urbicus (sole user of 'regelatio' = thaw) is hardly a respectable source. Morshead's remark about Aggenus' having 'died...just before I was born' was surely intended in part to emphasis the weakness of Aggenus' authority as a source of Latin usage. Elsewhere in the *Dictionary* we are reminded that hierarchies of authorship also operated in English. Expounding Tennyson's 'In Memoriam', Morshead quoted the couplet 'And from his ashes may be made / The violet of his native land' and asked the class for parallels. A pupil offered 'And the roses and the posies / Fertilized by Clementine', and Morshead was ready to take this seriously until he discovered that it was from 'a common music-hall dittay', when he rejected it as beneath contempt (1996, 55). The stratification of English in this period has been

---

[16] Carey 1992, 16. For a more jaundiced view of the Board Schools, see Bullock 1906.
[17] This was still a common practice in public schools in the early 1960s.

well documented, but the role of Latin and Greek in social and linguistic hierarchies has been little discussed.[18] The three languages constituted a market in which each had different claims to distinction and different social and institutional bases.[19] During the first half of the nineteenth century the introduction of English notes in school editions of classical authors had been fiercely resisted. Christopher Wordsworth, headmaster of Harrow, warned in 1838 that the practice 'will produce a general feebleness and indolence in the intellectual habits of the literary student...leading to...mental effeminacy' (Wordsworth 1838, 244: cf. 1989, 2016).

In Morshead's classroom, language was both what was being learned (Latin and Greek) and the shared resource (English) with which pedagogic authority was maintained and contested. To invoke 'the language of one gentleman to another' (1996, 54) was to appeal to the etiquette of the adult male peer-group; to specify 'the language of a schoolmaster to a schoolboy' (ibid.) was to reject the claim to membership of that group implicit in the pupil's demand. Other 'languages', specific to social classes, regions, and occupational groups, were being described in the late nineteenth century. The concern to record dialectal usage, in fact, formed part of the glorification of idiosyncrasy referred to above. The cultural status of such variant forms of English was ambiguous, for though they were to be respected as organic elements of folk life, yet they were clearly marginal to the 'standard English' which had consolidated its dominant position by this period. In the realm of pronunciation, what was called first 'Public School Pronunciation' and then, more neutrally, 'Received Pronunciation', constituted a standard which was in effect maintained by the socialization of the upper middle classes of the Home Counties (1996, 29). It is easy to see that the assertion of gentlemanly idiosyncrasy might, if taken far enough, collide with the norms of standard usage. One of the most intriguing aspects of Morshead's speech mannerisms is that some of his pronunciations resemble Cockneyisms. For example, he pronounced 'There' as 'Theer', the initial 'Th' being unvoiced (θeer). 'Theer' is, however, characteristic of Mrs Peggotty in Dickens' *David Copperfield* (Mugglestone 1995, 242). Morshead may thus have been deliberately employing 'vulgar' pronunciations to assert both his authority and individuality: using, that is, the language of a gentleman and of a schoolmaster.

Subjectivities

What role was the pupil expected to play in classical education? In the first half of the nineteenth century a progressive/developmental emphasis emerged to challenge the prevailing assumption that the pupil was there to be trained through rote learning and physical punishment. The word which summed up the sheer slog of learning, the discipline which combined the acquisition of knowledge with that of mental power, was 'grind'. The men who prepared small boys for public-school and university

---

[18] See Smith 1984, Crowley 1989, and on class and accent, Mugglestone 1995.

[19] For a discussion of the symbolic market of languages, see Ben-Rafael 1994, 38–45.

entrance examinations were familiarly known as 'gerund-grinders' (1995b). What was at issue was not just pedagogic technique but the control of a developing intelligence: the formation of subjectivity. Well into the twentieth century we can trace a continuing tension between the search for pedagogic control and the aspiration to create independent thinkers. It is evident, for example, in the introductory essay to G. M. Lyne's *Balbus* (Lyne 1934), discussed in Chapter 12), where the disciplinary means (mastering the grammar) and the cultural end ('purely human') sit uneasily together.

By 1934, the need for independent yet disciplined thinkers had become a powerful ideological theme in English cultural debate. How else could a liberal democracy survive in a world inhabited by irrational extremisms of left (communism) and right (fascism)? The potential of Latin for the socialization of self-controlled citizens, free voters who constituted bulwarks against ochlocracy, encouraged the continuation of 'grind' and militated against the exploration of literature in search of the 'purely human'. This tension between order and freedom, discipline and culture, can be seen as characteristic of liberal democratic regimes: driven by ideologies of individualism, yet nervous of the consequences of educating and enfranchising the masses. The result was the stultification of Latin teaching and learning.[20]

In Victorian and Edwardian public schools, not only did a focus on grammar reflect a concern with control and the development of self-control, the emphasis on language deflected attention from the varieties of experience to be found in literature. When a literary text was studied, it was usually as a purely linguistic corpus. The classical expression of this strategy is the remark of the 'famous schoolmaster' who remarked to his class at the beginning of term that they were to study the *Oedipus Tyrannus* of Sophocles, 'a veritable treasure-house of grammatical peculiarities'.[21] The obsession with 'peculiarities' may seem to be the opposite of the constant focus on grammatical regularity, but both can be seen as ways of giving the power of classical language without opening the door to its dangers. To go through a literary text looking for linguistic minutiae, after all, is an effective way of diverting attention from the moral issues it may present—including questions of choice and fate, as in the *Oedipus Tyrannus*.[22] Nineteenth-century bourgeois morality had its own problems with the content of classical literature, nicely portrayed in Byron's account of the education of Don Juan. His mother Donna Inez was keen that he should learn Latin, but concerned that he might read of the 'filthy loves of gods and goddesses' (McGann 1986, 21, line 322). Young Juan used an edition of Martial in which the improper lines were conscientiously

---

[20] Both the exemplary role of Classics, and the more general emphasis on the learning of unquestioning obedience, are documented in Evans 1991.

[21] The story first appeared in print in the preface to J. T. Sheppard's edition of the play: J. T. Sheppard, *The Oedipus Tyrannus of Sophocles* (Cambridge: Cambridge University Press, 1920). The 'schoolmaster' may be based on an eccentric Cambridge don, but it is just as likely that his fame is generated within (and subsequently by) the story itself. See further p. 332, n. 21.

[22] Such strategies had a long history, going back at least to the attempts made in early medieval Europe to control the potential of pagan classicism by focusing on grammatical features. See Durkheim 1938, 29, 42; his analysis was summarized and systematized in Archer 1988, 150–1, 162–5.

excised, but were collected together in an appendix. The scholarly urge to completeness effectively subverted the pedagogic concern for propriety.[23] For instance, the widespread use of Caesar's *Bellum Gallicum* as an elementary Latin teaching text in the nineteenth and twentieth centuries may be due, in part, to its lack of sexually embarrassing subject matter. The combination of such a text and a relentless concentration on its linguistic features makes for a powerfully anodyne lesson in discipline.

Conclusion

In exploring the constitution of authority in Victorian classical pedagogy we face two major difficulties. First, the paucity (not peculiar to this period) of evidence on what happened in classrooms. The conversations in *Horae Mushrianae* give a rare opportunity to look at the way pedagogic authority is negotiated; the pupils who appear there were learning about both personal and textual authority. Second, the ideological agenda which orients the analyst's gaze toward those oppressed by elites—women, workers, rebels—diminishes our understanding by ignoring the internal variety of elite culture, as well as the relationship between elite and non-elite groups (Collini 1993). The repression of the writing of American women, workers, and blacks identified, and redressed, by Cary Nelson, has operated just as surely on elite groups (Nelson 1989). The relationships between teacher, pupils, and texts recorded in *Horae Mushrianae* may have been typical of the public-school classical classroom, but it is dangerous to generalize, as I have suggested above in commenting on Mangan's reference to 'a blind belief in a classical prescription'. Henry Nevinson, who had been at Shrewsbury under H. W. Moss in the 18705, recalled that 'To enter Headroom [the sixth-form classroom] was to become a scholar. I doubt if good Greek verse could be written anywhere else. Winged iambics fluttered through the air; they hung like bats along the shelves, and the dust fell in Greek particles.' But Shrewsbury was not typical. Moss's predecessor Benjamin Kennedy had declared that 'My Sixth Form is the hardest Sixth Form in England, and I intend it to be so.'[24] Only by collecting and assessing the scattered evidence can we hope to understand what was common and what was unusual in the classical pedagogy of these schools. Here the *Mushri Dictionary* provides an unusually rich source. Not only is its subject eccentric, its theme is eccentricity; but the embeddedness of idiosyncrasy in the late-Victorian ideology of Englishness means that the *Dictionary* is representative in its very uniqueness. It offers a glimpse of a pedagogic process where pupils were learning, as a group, to be individuals.

---

[23] Byron, *Dun Juan*, canto I, stanzas 40–45. Byron himself had used such a book, an edition of Martial's epigrams (probably the Delphin edition of 1701) at Harrow. Cf. Dover 1988, in a volume which also contains his 'Byron and the Ancient Greeks', and see further Harrison and Stray 2011.

[24] Nevinson 1912, 17. Nevinson, it should be remembered, was a 'soured Salopian': see Leach 1964. His portrait was, however, described by his contemporary Graham Wallas as 'an extraordinarily accurate account of the intellectual atmosphere of the Shrewsbury Sixth at that time': Wallas 1926, 289. Kennedy's remark is quoted in Colman 1950, 8.

16

Edward Adolf Sonnenschein and the Politics of Linguistic Authority in England, 1880–1930

If Edward Adolf Sonnenschein (1851–1929) is remembered today (2004b, 2004c), it is perhaps for his campaign for a linguistic 'entente cordiale', modelled on the Franco-British political 'entente cordiale' of 1904, which would promote the standardized description and teaching of European languages (Walmsley 1991, 2001). This campaign mounted a defence of generalized functional descriptions of linguistic structure against the relativizing formal accounts of vernaculars advocated by Sonnenschein's major opponent, the Danish linguist Otto Jespersen. Sonnenschein's claim was that beneath variation in the surface features of language, a common functional pattern could be found (Walmsley 1991). Jespersen seems to have won this battle, and remains widely known; few now remember Sonnenschein. Let me therefore begin by sum-marizing Sonnenschein's life, in order to locate his campaign in a chronological and institutional context.

Edward Adolf Sonnenschein was born in London in 1851 (2004b). His father Adolf (born Abraham Sonnenschein in Eisgrub, Moravia) was an immigrant, one of the many liberals who had fled the continent after the 1848 revolutions. Adolf established himself in London as a teacher and pedagogic reformer. At one time headmaster of a girls' school, he also taught mathematics, his main subject, at the new Bedford College for women, founded in 1849. He was involved in several educational campaigns and published mathematics and other textbooks. Of special interest in this context is a volume he produced in 1881 which compared the curricular requirements of five European countries; he used this as the basis of proposals for reform in England (Sonnenschein 1881). The pan-European perspective and systematic comparison of national cases foreshadowed—and I believe to a degree inspired—his son's later grammatical campaigns.

Young Edward was sent for his schooling to University College School, then still part of University College London. The secular and liberal atmosphere of this institution made it very popular with the community of continental liberal émigrés in London (Ashton 1986). But it is also worth observing that its headmaster Thomas Key

(1799–1875) was concurrently Professor of Comparative Grammar at the college.[1] He was also one of the founders of the Philological Society of London, and several times its president; though his ludicrous etymologies and disparagement of Sanskrit made him something of an embarrassment at the Society's meetings. The point to be stressed, however, is that UCS was not a conventional public school: all subjects were optional, the characteristic English gentlemanly habit of verse composition was excluded, there was no chapel. This was an atmosphere in which the scientific study of language was encouraged. Edward went on to University College, Oxford, leaving in 1875 with a double first in Classics. He then spent several years in Glasgow, where he combined some lecturing in Humanity (Latin) at the university with the headmaster-ship of a local academy. This combination not only echoes Key's dual role at UCS, but also sowed the seeds of his own later academic involvement in school textbooks.

In 1883 Sonnenschein was appointed Professor of Greek and Latin at Mason College, later to become the University of Birmingham, and stayed in that post until his retirement in 1918. Two years after his arrival in Birmingham, a talk he gave to a local teachers' association led to the foundation of a new body called the Grammatical Society, whose declared aim was to promote uniformity in grammatical terminology. As he explained in a paper published in 1892, 'The need of greater uniformity in the teaching of the grammars of different languages was first forced upon my attention, in a practical form, when I was a schoolmaster. Every classroom had a different set of grammatical terms' (Sonnenschein 1892, 450). Yet as he pointed out, all the languages concerned—Latin, Greek, French, German, English—were members of the great Indo-European family, so that it was unlikely that their grammatical systems were so diverse as the practice of schools implied. The Grammatical Society attracted support both in England and abroad, and plans were soon afoot for the production of grammars with a uniform terminology. By 1890 grammars, readers, and other books had been published for English, German, French, Latin, and Spanish. Conveniently enough, Edward's younger brother William Swan Sonnenschein had gone into pub-lishing, and the books appeared under the imprint of Swan Sonnenschein.[2] In the 1890s he continued in this field, producing for example a Greek grammar in 1892 and a Latin accidence in 1897. By this time, however, Sonnenschein was engaged in a battle on a different front. Mason College was originally conceived as a technical college, and its humanities staff were very much in a minority, while control was vested not with academics but in a council of local notables (Ives, Drummond, and Schwarz 2000). In the late 1890s Sonnenschein led a campaign to make the college a university which would possess academic faculties, increase its humanities staffing, and be run by pro-fessors rather than by bankers and manufacturers. At first rebuffed, he finally secured the support of Joseph Chamberlain (1836–1914), the most powerful political figure in Birmingham, and in 1900 the University of Birmingham received its charter (Ives, Drummond and Schwarz 2000, 73–95).

---

[1] For Key, whom we met in Chapter 14, see Glucker 1981, Marshall 2004.
[2] See Mumby and Stallybrass 1955.

Grammatical Terminology and the Politics of Knowledge

What, the reader may ask, has all this to do with grammatical terminology? The crucial link lies in the changing map of cultural authority in England as it related to language and knowledge. Early in the nineteenth century, scholarship was largely equated with learning in Latin and Greek. It was this scholarship which the radical William Cobbett (1762–1836) had denounced as a symbol of the oppressive social hierarchy represented by the college dons of the Oxbridge Anglican establishment (Smith 1984). This was the period when outstanding Greek scholars were given bishoprics in the Anglican church, which was of course part of the establishment condemned by Cobbett—the 'Greek play bishops' (Burns and Stray 2011). Gradually the authority of the classical languages was eroded. The serious study both of English, and of 'grammar' as a separate object of investigation, reinforced this process of erosion: English became a competitor, though at first handicapped by its association with the middle classes. An education leading to trade rather than to the universities was commonly called 'English, or middle-class education'. Indo-European philology itself undercut the authority of the Classics in two ways. First, its use of Sanskrit threatened to dethrone Greek and Latin from their position as the prime linguistic exemplars of human reason. Second, its very generality encouraged the formation of a content-free intellectual field in which they became examples among a host of others. (In this connexion, it is worth remembering that the Philological Society rarely considered Latin or Greek topics at its meetings.)

The separate realm of grammar thus acquired its students, its societies, and eventually institutional recognition in universities. This development was part of a more general movement towards the construction of a university curriculum of separate specialist subjects, which challenged the old dominance of mathematics at Cambridge and of Classics at Oxford. Faced with the intransigence of defenders of these subjects and fearing to be classed as purveyors of practical or useful knowledge, the university reformers of the mid-century declared that acceptably useless knowledge could be gained outside the old monopolies. What they were creating was an academic ideology—the idea that any subject, studied in the search for truth, had a moral worth. In consequence, towards the end of the century the university community was becoming a collection of specialists, united not by Anglicanism or college loyalties, but by a shared belief in the power of scientific method as employed by professional scholars. Thus the permanent truth of the classical authors was replaced by the progressive truth of science, always provisional but always advancing. Similarly, the universalist claims of Classics were replaced by the method which united specialist fields (see in general 1998a, and cf. Small 1991).

My argument is thus that the detachment of authority from Greek and Latin was reinforced by a shift in authority from the earlier alliance of Anglicanism and established social elites to the specialized knowledge of the professional. Comparative philology became detached from Classics, and within Classics itself, methodical

302 CLASSICS IN BRITAIN

specialization began to supplant the gentleman amateur's immersion in literary texts. Against this background, we should remember that Sonnenschein's campaign at Birmingham secured academic control on a faculty basis, and at the same time an increased representation for the humanities. The linking factor was the argument that a proper university should have a balanced staff and curriculum. Underlying this campaign was an attempt to bring high culture to a city widely seen as a provincial capital of commercialism, where the pursuit of profit ruled out the higher things of life. Much of this missionary activity was conducted under the banner of Hellenism; Sonnenschein, however, belonged to a new generation of classical scholars who concentrated on Latin rather than Greek (1998a, 229–31; 2004a). At the same time, Sonnenschein was proceeding on the grammatical front with his campaign for parallel grammars. These apparently disparate activities should be seen as running (aptly!) in parallel. Both campaigns can be seen as constituting a strategic defensive move at a time when the cultural authority of Classics was under challenge. The nature of that move was to abandon mid-Victorian claims to the special authority of Classics. In a period when the organization of academic knowledge was moving toward a collection of specialisms, such a claim was likely to be devalued. Instead, the argument could be advanced that Greek and Latin were important in a general way, as central elements in a formal pattern which underlay the various languages. Thus in a sense the universalized terminology of grammar is equivalent to the universalized competence of the professional academic role. Grammatical categories are to individual languages as the methodical competence of the professional is to specialized fields of knowledge.

The Classical Association and the Joint Committee on Grammatical Terminology

After the turn of the century Sonnenschein was given the opportunity to prosecute his campaigns on a new basis. During the 1890s a series of subject associations had been set up to promote the teaching of non-classical subjects, including the Modern Language Association. In 1903 the Classical Association of England and Wales was founded to defend Classics against the claims of modern subjects, and Sonnenschein became one of its joint secretaries. Five years later, the Association met at Birmingham, with Sonnenschein playing host; and he used the occasion to launch the Joint Committee on Grammatical Terminology. This included representatives of the associations of school heads, the Modern Language Association, and also the English Association, founded in 1906, as well as the Classical Association. A preliminary report was issued in 1909 and a final report in 1911. The Committee's recommendations were broadly accepted by the associations, and by the (government) Board of Education. Their authority was strengthened by the fact that similar bodies had been set up in France and the USA, and that several other countries had witnessed similar discussions. The conclusions were much the same—the teaching of several languages to children required that grammatical terminology should be simplified and made uniform if confusion and inefficiency were to be avoided. Different countries had their own ways of putting this into practice. The centralized French typically did it by fiat: the ministry of education issued a decree giving a list of approved grammatical terms, and that was that. Equally typical of such a system was that the reformers found the ministry had considerably amended the proposals sent them before issuing the decree. The English situation was very different: the Board of Education at least pretended to be advisory and nondirective; reform, to be effective, needed to be carried out by persuading the schools, the associations, and the examiners.

In the Classical Association, Sonnenschein had a powerful base of operations and in general little opposition. He must have been taken aback, however, when on arriving at a meeting in Bangor to discuss the preliminary report, he found that the local professor of Latin, Edward Arnold, who had been trained in comparative philology at Cambridge, had circulated 200 copies of a pamphlet attacking the report (Arnold 1910): the Association's minutes reported that these were printed 'to aid in the discussion'. Arnold not only disagreed with many of the report's recommendations; he also thought that the Association was being railroaded into supporting a campaign whose course it might later regret. In the English Association, disagreements were more serious. This was in part because Sonnenschein's proposals were based on ideas of functional equivalence, and thus led to the positing of, e.g., more different cases in English than could be identified from surface features. To many supporters of English, his proposals looked like an attempt to impose the formal complexities of Latin and Greek on English. While he was always careful to acknowledge that languages differed, the rationale of the movement for a parallel terminology pushed Sonnenschein irresistibly toward the adoption of a uniform set of terms for each language.

Nesfield vs Sonnenschein

Another and quite different basis for opposition was soon apparent. John Nesfield (c. 1845–1922), firmly established as a writer of grammar and composition books for English which were widely used in English schools, was horrified by the committee's proposals (Walmsley 1989). Nesfield's name is often to be glimpsed on the shelves of that under-rated research resource, the second-hand bookshop. In the early years of the twentieth century, he produced several successful manuals of English grammar and composition which were very popular in India and the Far East as well as in Britain.[3] He was a member of the English Association, but was not at first party to its discussions of the terminology reports. His letters to his publisher, Macmillan, preserved in the firm's archives, suggest that his opposition to Sonnenschein's campaign was based on a conviction that it misrepresented the nature of the English language. But it has to be said that his own books brought him in very large sums of money—thousands

---

[3] Nesfield himself had had experience of teaching in India.

of pounds, when most incomes were measured in hundreds—and he and Macmillan stood to lose heavily if Sonnenschein was successful. Nesfield's problem was that he lacked academic authority. He was simply a textbook writer, albeit one of great experience. He had nothing to counter Sonnenschein's professional status or his connections. His only academic ally was W. W. Skeat (1835–1912), Professor of Anglo-Saxon at Cambridge, who denounced the Sonnenschein scheme in vigorous terms. As he wrote to Nesfield in September 1912:

> I detest the whole concern. The attempt to bring English into the Scheme…is most objectionable. It is riveting upon the poor scholars the old chain, the old notion that English grammar depends upon Latin grammar, and must be expressed in terms of it. It is a survival of the stupid old system that denied the existence of English scholarship, and despised English as dross in comparison with the Classics.

Skeat agreed to write something on these lines for publication, but fell ill and died before he could do so; all Nesfield could do was to print Skeat's letter at the end of his own attack on Sonnenschein, a twenty-page pamphlet entitled *Remarks on the Joint Committee's Report* (Nesfield 1912, xx). Somewhere between 20,000 and 30,000 copies were printed, and bound into copies of Nesfield's textbooks. The pamphlet appeared only in one issue of Nesfield's books for a year or two after 1912.[4]

Nesfield's disagreements with the Joint Committee lay in three areas. First, in the classification of sentences into single, complex, and compound, generally used by Nesfield and others; they proposed to replace the category 'compound' with 'double or multiple sentences'. Second, they laid down that some English words should be classed as both adjectives and pronouns. For example, in the sentence 'This horse is swifter than that', 'this' would be an adjective, 'that' a pronoun. Similar proposals were made about possessives: for example they classed 'my' as an adjective, 'mine' as a pronoun. Finally, instead of the triad of nominative, possessive, and objective cases used by Nesfield, the Committee proposed to use nominative, vocative, accusative, genitive, dative. In their own words, 'as far as possible…the Latin names of Cases [should] be used'. Commenting on this last ruling, Skeat wrote, 'Read, as far as possible, the Latin names of cases should be avoided, rather than imply what is untrue'. It seems clear that English was the big problem; it was, simply, much more resistant to Sonnenschein's Latinate scheme than were the other European languages. At the same time, its status in educational circles was lower. The English Association was set up informally in 1906 by two schoolmasters; compare the foundation of the Classical Association three years before, at a public meeting held at a university and presided over by one of England's

---

[4] The British Library was unable to locate a relevant copy; but luckily, what the library system could not find, the second-hand bookshops provided. There is a serious methodological problem here. By 1900 the publishing of textbooks had become separated from general publishing to the extent that libraries treated them differently. They were often stored separately, at times not even catalogued, and little attention was paid to collecting different editions. The result is that in this field it is at times more difficult to locate relevant copies of nineteenth- and early twentieth-century books than it is for much earlier periods. The recent cataloguing of such books, formerly listed only in a secondary sheaf catalogue, in Cambridge University Library is a welcome sign of change.

senior judges (2003, 9–12). The future of the English Association was in doubt until the end of war in 1918 brought a wave of patriotism to its aid. At one point during World War I, its members almost voted to dissolve it and make it a section of the Modern Language Association.

The status of English and its relative lack of inflections were closely related. Latin still provided the dominant paradigm of linguistic form, and many teachers of French and German were still keen to teach them as if they were dead languages in order to gain reflected status. For them, Sonnenschein's grand alliance offered a place at the top table. The strategy which re-established the prestige of Classics in a new pluralist curriculum, in other words, involved a bargain in a transitional period. The redefined prestige of the old order was to be shared with its challengers in a diplomatic compromise. It was thus in the interests of all parties involved in Sonnenschein's scheme not to rock the boat. The promoters of English had the fewest allies to back them and, as they saw it, the most to lose from disagreement. In at least some schools, Sonnenschein's scheme was welcomed as providing a straightforward pragmatic solution to the problems of grammar teaching. In 1912 a version of it was printed by the headmaster of one of the English public schools. In his preface, he says:

For the sake of clearness it is most desirable that the elementary teaching of grammar and syntax, which is necessarily to a great extent dogmatic, should employ one set of terms, applicable, as far as possible, to all the languages taught. The following scheme is the only one which holds the field. We will therefore adopt it, and all questions in examination papers will be set in accordance with it.[5]

This gives an illuminating view of the whole matter from the classroom battlefront, where accuracy mattered less than clarity, simplicity, and standardization.

So the bandwagon rolled on; yet Nesfield seems to have stuck to his position. The second edition of his *Manual of English Grammar* appeared in 1917 with a preface reiterating his opposition to the Joint Committee's proposals. But after his death in the early 1920s, his publishers trimmed to what was by then presumably the prevailing wind, and his books carried on their title pages the statement 'Revised in accordance with the views of the Joint Committee on Grammatical Terminology'. After the war, English became a school subject of considerable importance, backed up by university courses in Oxford (1896) and Cambridge (1917) and by wartime patriotic impulses (Sampson 1921). One indication of its social ascent was that it began to be used as an indicator of social status itself. In the nineteenth century, it was the Latin quotation which asserted social status; now the received pronunciation of English, based on the upper- and middle-class speech of South-East England, played this same role, and a series of writers, convinced that they were describing a de facto standard, reinforced the prescription of 'talking proper' (Mugglestone 1995). In the curriculum of the grammar schools, Latin, English, and other languages marched on together in a

---

[5] The quotation was transcribed from a copy of an internal school booklet; I regret my inability to recover the original reference and author's name.

conspiracy of dullness; the emphasis on grammatical rigour left little room for creativity or the appreciation of literature.

Conclusion

Sonnenschein's campaigns belong to the transition of English society to modernity as a twentieth-century nation state. As in European countries, this was accompanied by a reassertion of the value of the vernacular. (One thinks, for example, of Kaiser Wilhelm's denunciations of Classics in the 1890s: 'We must bring up little Germans, not little Greeks and Romans': Kandel 1933, 710.) Yet as each country asserted its own identity, they were following parallel paths to statehood and modernity. Their patriotic separatism developed on similar lines, both dividing and uniting them; it is this tension which is reflected in the opposed views of Jespersen and Sonnenschein. Yet both men held to the Romantic notion of organic unity. For Jespersen, the soul of grammar lay in the unity of an individual language; for Sonnenschein, it resided in the unity of ancient and modern languages (Sonnenschein 1927). In trying to understand these differences of opinion, I suggest that we have to work at a variety of levels. At the biographical level: Jespersen was forced, as a youngster, to go in for the law, and was thus obliged to learn Latin. Much later, as an eminent professor, he helped to have it abolished as a university requirement. Sonnenschein was brought up a cosmopolitan by a father whose birthplace was not far from that of Comenius, and who was, I believe, consciously working in the tradition of Comenius and Ratke. Adolf Sonnenschein inherited their vision of a pan-European community of scholarship and passed it on to his son. At the institutional level, I have tried to show how debates about the description of language are bound up with changing patterns of social and cultural authority, as the monopoly of Classics gave way to what I have called academic pluralism. In Sonnenschein's lifetime, the comparative philology he had learned was moving toward what is now linguistics: a separate academic realm controlled by those who have mastered its specialized knowledge. In the nineteenth century, the discovery of pure grammar was welcomed by defenders of the Word of God, who saw in it a weapon against the impure materialism of secularists and radicals (Dowling 1986, 3–45). In the twentieth century, the internalist and synchronic emphasis in Saussure's work, for instance, whatever else it did, certainly created a delimited and stable field of academic enquiry. This can easily lead to an ahistorical and sterile scholasticism. The expansion of work on the history of linguistic ideas is thus a welcome development, in that it encourages us to look back beyond the introspective technicalities of professionalism to the history of both truth and error, both winners and losers. As I have tried to suggest, it also enables us to begin to connect ideas about language with the social and cultural contexts in which they were developed and disseminated.[6]

---

[6]   Such wider perspectives were characteristic of the work of Vivien Law, in whose memory this chapter was originally written (2004d).

17

Primers, Publishing, and Politics

The Classical Textbooks of Benjamin Hall Kennedy

If the connections are to be explored between the histories of the book and of education, then textbooks offer an obvious focus of attention.[1] Such books play a central part in the transmission of culture; indeed, it has been suggested that they provide 'the best evidence for the accommodation of particular ideas to the core of intelligibility' in a society (Cohen 1977, 143, n. 15). Yet the necessarily shared meanings to which this refers should not lead us to assume the existence of a consensus on either curriculum content or pedagogic method. The history of textbook writing, production, commission, and use in England offers ample evidence to the contrary. To take one notable example: the sixteenth-century textbook which is now usually referred to as 'Lily's Latin grammar' was in its early days often called 'the common grammar'; but its general use derived from its being prescribed by royal command. This was a 'commonness' which belonged, with the similar prescription of a primer and the appointment of local magistrates, to a Tudor campaign of centralized control (Simon 1966). Over the next two centuries the book became the basis of a wide range of versions, supplements, and critiques (Allen 1954, 1959). In the mid-eighteenth century an edition prepared at Eton College became in effect the standard textbook of Latin grammar; in this case no direct central prescription was involved, but the increasing prestige of Eton in the second half of the century was certainly buttressed by the marked royal patronage it enjoyed in this period. The book remained the market leader well into the nineteenth century, but by the 1860s had been displaced by newer grammars, including several written by Benjamin Kennedy.

By this time, royal power had long been superseded, and in the industrial society which emerged from the economic revolution of the eighteenth century, the operations of the market in education as well as publishing were little constrained by central intervention in England. State elementary education, as we have seen in earlier chapters, dates only from 1870, secondary education from 1902—much later than the Napoleonic *Université*, or the Prussian system of education set up after Napoleon's victory at

---

[1] For a preliminary enquiry, see 1994a. This chapter might be seen as a modest complement to Johns 1992.

Jena in 1807.[2] It was only in the second half of the century, when a series of Royal Commissions investigated schools and universities, that any impact was made on the operations of these markets. (It is worth noting that the early 1850s, which witnessed the collapse of the cartel in publishing, saw in education a move in the opposite direction: the beginnings of state intervention in what had been a free market.)[3] The Clarendon Commission of 1861, which dealt with the nine leading public schools, prompted the commissioning by those schools' headmasters of Benjamin Hall Kennedy's *Public School Latin Primer* (1866). My discussion will focus on the drafting and reception of this book, and of its successor, Kennedy's *Revised Latin Primer* of 1888.[4] Kennedy was born in 1804 and died in 1889; he was headmaster of Shrewsbury School from 1836 to 1866 and Regius Professor of Greek at Cambridge from 1867 until his death. In his lifetime he was famous as the most successful classical teacher of the century, his pupils including many of the leading scholars of the later Victorian period. Today he is remembered, if at all, for the *Revised Latin Primer,* still in print after several revisions.

Kennedy's two primers are atypical in one important respect: in both cases, we have detailed evidence for their commissioning, writing, revision, and use.[5] Their history involves a number of controversies on a wide range of issues: the relations between ideologies of teaching and learning and commercial imperatives, conceptions of language, and the powerful ideological strain glorifying English freedom from central control (Chapter 16). Much of this history is indeed peculiarly English, but the underlying issues are general ones: how is knowledge to be reformulated in book form as teachable knowledge? Who is to do this? Who decides which book is to be used in teaching? The tension between the market and the state is a familiar theme in the history of American textbooks.[6] Here the constituencies are not states, but the public schools; I begin by sketching in the nature of the schools in relation to textbook publishing in nineteenth-century England. I then turn to Kennedy and his books, before concentrating on his two most influential books, the Latin primers of 1866 and 1888, and concluding with some general points which arise from this case study.

Education and Publishing: The Context

Kennedy's 1866 book was intended, as its title indicates, for use in public schools (that is, in English parlance, private schools with a clientele which was national rather

---

[2] On education and the state in the nineteenth century, see Green 1990.

[3] The cartel led by Longmans collapsed in 1852 after Lord Campbell, appointed to arbitrate between its members and its opponents, denounced protection as indefensible.

[4] As will appear below, the attributions are by no means straightforward. The earlier book, officially produced by a committee, was probably written almost entirely by Kennedy, though his name never appeared on the title page. The later book, which was published under his name, was in fact written by his daughters Marion and Julia.

[5] Some of the evidence is published or privately printed, but much of it, especially in the case of the 1888 Primer, is in the Longman Archives, Reading University Library.

[6] The literature is selectively listed in Woodward, Elliott, and Nagel 1988.

than local). The schools which came to national prominence in the nineteenth century—Eton, Winchester, Harrow, Rugby are among the best known—had been founded to educate poor local scholars, but in the wake of the industrial revolution were reconstructed as boarding schools for the sons of the new urban bourgeoisie. Served by the expanding railway network, which reached Shrewsbury (where Kennedy was headmaster) in 1838 and Rugby a decade earlier, they built up a national catchment. In this development, the state played no part. Napoleonic France had set up the *Université* and mass schooling; Prussia, smarting from its defeat by Napoleon, had responded by founding its own educational system. England had only the competing elementary schools ('British' and 'National') of the Anglican and Dissenting societies.[7] Secondary schooling was a commodity available on a commercial market, and the public schools constituted its elite sector. They transformed the financial capital of parents into cultural capital, detaching boys from their local contacts and their regional accents and making them into gentlemen. The formal curriculum which lay at the centre of this process was almost entirely classical, beginning with several years of rote learning of Latin grammar, from books written in bad Latin, and going on to verse composition which started with nonsense verses—lines which had to conform to metrical rules but were not expected to make sense. In such a system, the Latin grammar was the most important instrument of schooling—expect perhaps for the birch which usually accompanied it.[8]

By the middle of the century, the reformed public schools constituted in effect a national system; but a very disorganized one. The lack of any central regulation meant that not only was there no clear criterion of what counted as a public school, but the schools differed widely among themselves (Honey 1977). While the homogeneity of demand, and the shared concern to keep out the sons of social inferiors, created solidarity, competition between the schools generated marginal differentiation. Each school claimed unique virtues and a proud history of irrational custom, slang, and tradition.[9] Among the ways they buttressed such claims to uniqueness was the publication of their own Latin grammars. A successful school with its own traditions and a scholarly headmaster advertised this by producing its own textbook. The conflicting imperatives of solidarity and differentiation can be seen in the attempts which began in the 1830s to produce a standard grammar. Thomas Arnold of Rugby argued for this in 1835, but the project was taken up by Charles and Christopher Wordsworth, the poet's nephews. The brothers wrote a grammar each, Latin and Greek, to be used in parallel. They had their own agenda, theological rather than educational: uniformity in grammar, they thought, would lead to uniformity in religion. Their books appeared at the end of the 1830s, published by John Murray, and became the market leaders. The biggest

---

[7] A useful comparative analysis is provided by Armstrong 1973.

[8] For details of classical education in this period, see Clarke 1959, 74–97; cf. 1998a for social and cultural context.

[9] The most fully-developed and persistent example of school slang was 'Winchester Notions', recorded in manuscript lists from 1842 and in two printed dictionaries at the end of the century (1996, 1998c).

problem lay with Eton College's reluctance to use a book not written at Eton; and a book not used at the leading English school could hardly be called 'standard'. In the end the Greek grammar was transferred from Murray to Oxford University Press, a condition for Eton's acceptance of the book. Mr Murray's letterbooks show that he was not pleased. 'You brought your Grammar to Albemarle Street', he wrote Charles Wordsworth:

at a time when it was unknown, and when Mr Murray's name was of some use to it. I continued to publish Edition after Edition, not only with no gain, but with a certainty of loss. The fortune of your book is now made; you will not use me as a stepping ladder, and now kick me off? If you do, I will venture to say that Author never so treated Bookseller before . . . Is it right after five years to give it to Messrs Parker of Oxford and Gardner—with the total omission of my name?[10]

Murray's complaint reminds us that by the time the Wordsworths' grammars appeared, a large-scale, competitive market for school books was rapidly being established. The *Publishers' Circular*, first published in 1837, soon afterwards began to issue an educational number twice a year. (The trade committee which ran the *Circular* included a prolific textbook writer, the French emigré Louis Fenwick de Porquet (cf. Chapter 15), who sold his books from his own warehouse.) The expansion of working-class literacy and the competing schools set up by the (Anglican) National Society and the (Dissenting) British Society combined to create a profitable educational market, which was further bolstered by the expansion of examinations in the second half of the century.[11] By this time the mass production methods made possible by mechanical presses, the Fourdrinier machine, and stereotyping were firmly established, so that new markets co-existed with the means to supply them. The financial stability of Oxford University Press in the 1840s and 1850s rested largely on the sales of Charles Wordsworth's Greek grammar and of Liddell and Scott's *Greek-English Lexicon* (1843) (2013b). Textbooks were becoming big business. Their expanding production can be located within the move towards stereotyping and towards cheaper books which by the mid-1850s had inverted the price structure of the 1820s. Yet much remains to be done to map the contours of textbook publishing. We lack both the empirical data on print runs, pricing, and markets which would lay the basis for such a map, and the case studies of particular firms' output in this area which Simon Eliot calls for in his pioneering statistical analysis (Eliot 1994, 107–8). The vagueness of classifications in some contemporary sources hardly helps; lists of 'educational' books are liable to include both school textbooks and books about education.[12]

---

[10] John Murray to Charles Wordsworth, 6 July 1844 (John Murray archives); for a detailed account of the book, see 2016. It may be that Wordsworth's offer of his memoirs of his uncle to Murray a few years later was in part a peace offering; but here again, sharp dealing was involved. See S. Gill 'Copyright and the publishing of Wordsworth', in J. O. Jordan and R. L. Patten (eds) *Literature in the Marketplace* (Cambridge: Cambridge University Press, 1995) 89, n. 9.

[11] On literacy, see Vincent 1989. The Societies published books for use in their schools. On examinations, see Roach 1971.

[12] The history of subject headings itself provides evidence; for example it documents, though indirectly, the changing status of classical education. Candidates for case studies include Macmillan (especially because of the involvement, mentioned below, of Alexander Macmillan with the OUP's School Book

The prospects of large and repeated print runs must have made the educational market attractive to publishers, especially at such difficult times as the aftermath of the 1826 crash (cf. Chapter 14). Hindsight and a close examination of the relevant statistics show that the 'collapse' of 1826 is better seen as a temporary blip, a dip following a rise in the previous year.[13] The perceptions of contemporaries are a different matter, however. For example, it seems that the crash was involved in John Taylor's decision to move out of literary publishing and into the safer waters of education (Chapter 16). At the other extreme, we have the religious-cum-classical project of the brothers Wordsworth, Tory high Anglicans who were published by the conservative John Murray (2016). In between them we could place Longmans, the firm with the largest list of school books, and their author Benjamin Hall Kennedy, who in his grammatical doctrines as in his politics was a liberal reformer.

Kennedy and his Books

Kennedy was appointed headmaster of Shrewsbury School in 1836. He succeeded his own teacher Samuel Butler, who recommended him to his own publisher, Longmans. On Kennedy's appointment, Longmans invited him to publish with them, but his first textbook did not appear till 1844.[14] *Latinae Grammaticae Curriculum, or a Progressive Grammar of the Latin Language*, was based on his experience of taking the lower forms in the school for three years.[15] Like the Wordsworths, Kennedy was concerned to bring the Eton Latin grammar up to date; but his revisions were more radical than theirs. Kennedy was especially proud of his doctrine of the construction of compound sentences, which he called 'as it were, the very sunlight of higher Latin construction... Without this doctrine, the rules of Mood are like a bundle of loose faggots, incoherent and infirm.'[16]

Committee); Rivington, where family ties with public-school staff were used to recruit authors; and Methuen, whose founder Algernon Stedman began as a private tutor, published textbooks, and only later went into general publishing.

[13] Eliot 1994, 16–18. Eliot's conclusions broadly confirm those reached by J. Sutherland 'The book trade crash of 1826', *The Library*, 6th series, 9 (1987): 148–61.

[14] The MS listing of his books in the Longman archives (Reading UL: MS 1393, Pt 2, 111.40) begins with a *Latin Syntax* of 1838. This is probably the authority for R. M. Ogilvie's statement to the same effect in his 'Latin for yesterday' (Ogilvie 1974, 21–44, 17 p. 240); but this is a ghost. The confusion may arise from an entry in the *English Catalogue of Books* for a book of this name by 'Kennedy'. The author may have been James Kennedy, 1793–1864, but I have been unable to locate a copy of the book. Benjamin Kennedy's reputation gained him several mistaken attributions; for example, an Irish translation of Aeschylus' *Agamemnon* by 'Kennedy' (Dublin, 1829), in the *Catalog of the New York Public Library Research Collections*, vol. 403, 526.

[15] Kennedy himself assigned the book to 1843 in his *A Letter to the Rev. W. H. Bateson* (Cambridge: privately printed 1879), which alleges plagiarism by another textbook author (copy in Shrewsbury School Library). Some sections carry signs of local printing—Kennedy probably tried out proof sheets in his teaching. A powerful oral tradition in Shrewsbury School tells of the use of pages of the grammar by boys as 'scent' for the Fox and Hounds, scattered across country for following runners to find. (The 'Fox and Hounds' is the Shrewsbury equivalent of the 'Hare and Hounds'. Cf. p. 330 n. 16.)

[16] B. H. Kennedy, *A Critical Examination of Dr Donaldson's 'Complete Latin Grammar for the Use of Learners'* (London: Longman 1852), 81.

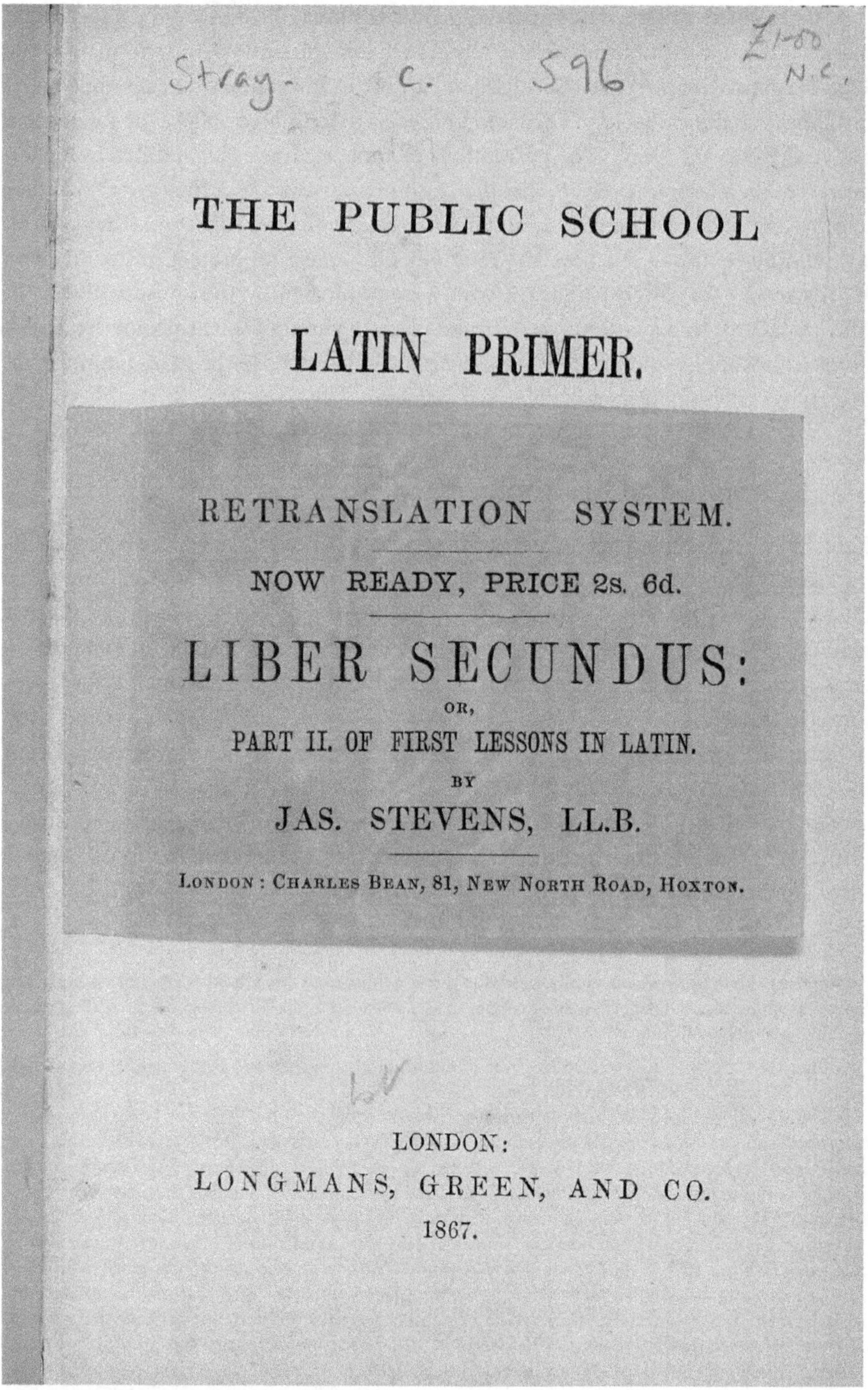

Stray.   c.   596   *£1·00 N.C.*

THE PUBLIC SCHOOL

LATIN PRIMER.

RETRANSLATION   SYSTEM.

NOW READY, PRICE 2s. 6d.

LIBER SECUNDUS:

OR,

PART II. OF FIRST LESSONS IN LATIN.

BY

JAS. STEVENS, LL.B.

LONDON: CHARLES BEAN, 81, NEW NORTH ROAD, HOXTON.

LONDON:

LONGMANS, GREEN, AND CO.

1867.

Figures 17.1 (a and b) Title page of *The Public School Latin Primer*, 2nd printing (London: Longmans, January 1867). Trinity College Library, Cambridge, Stray c.596.

Image courtesy of the Master and Fellows of Trinity College, Cambridge.

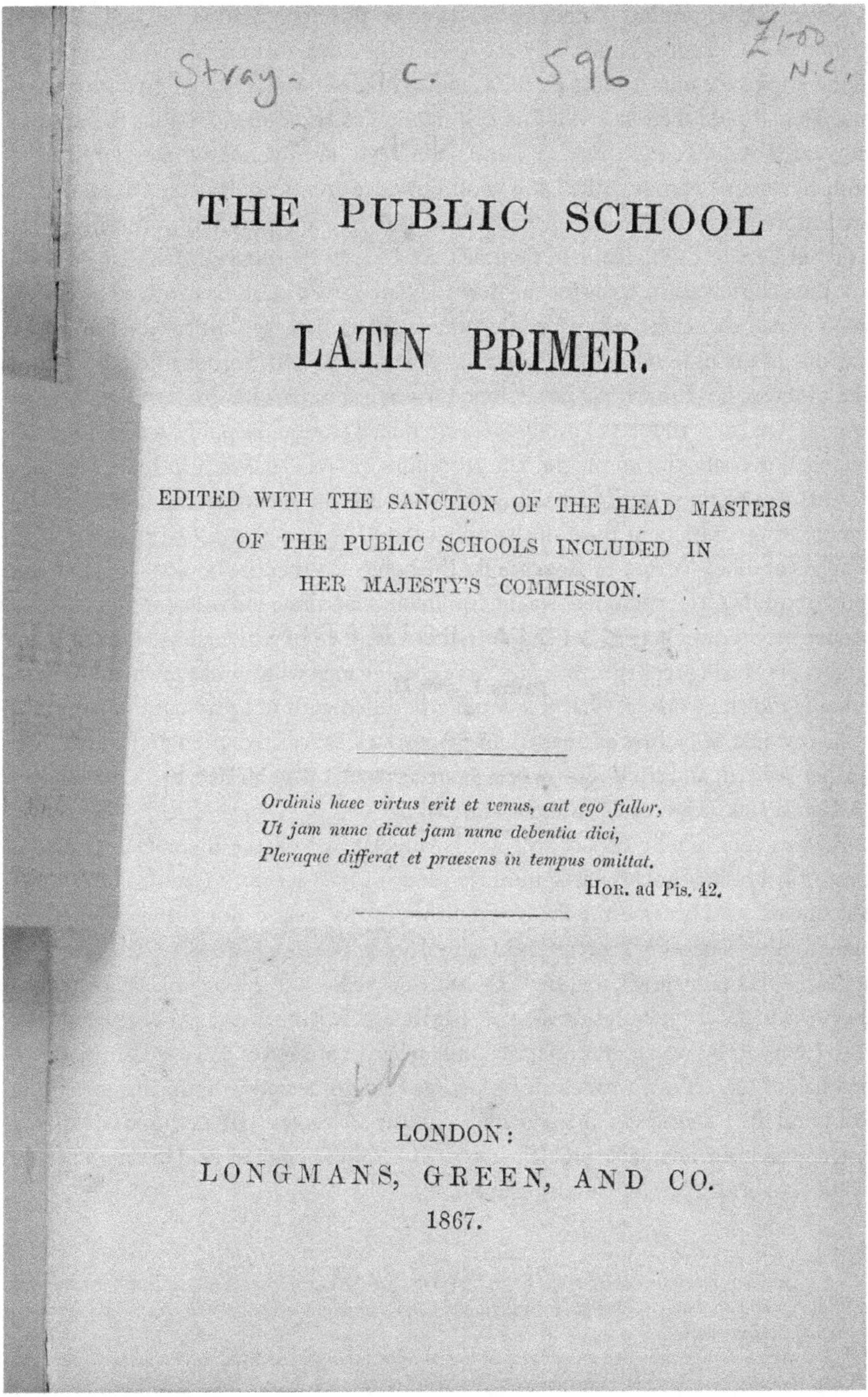

Stray. c. 596 £1·00 N.C.

THE PUBLIC SCHOOL

LATIN PRIMER.

EDITED WITH THE SANCTION OF THE HEAD MASTERS
OF THE PUBLIC SCHOOLS INCLUDED IN
HER MAJESTY'S COMMISSION.

Ordinis haec virtus erit et venus, aut ego fallor,
Ut jam nunc dicat jam nunc debentia dici,
Pleraque differat et praesens in tempus omittat.

Hor. ad Pis. 42.

LONDON:

LONGMANS, GREEN, AND CO.

1867.

Figures 17.1 Continued

Kennedy later produced other books based on this first grammar, as well as Greek grammars and reading books.[17] By 1861, when the Royal Commission was appointed to investigate the nine leading public schools, three of them were using a Latin grammar he had published in 1848. The commissioners recommended that the schools should use standard grammars of Latin and Greek, and Kennedy was asked to write both: he agreed to produce the Latin book, but since profits would accrue to him, felt it was unseemly to provide a Greek textbook as well. He even waived future profits on his Greek grammar so as to leave the field clear for Charles Wordsworth, whose own book was then chosen as the basis for the new standard Greek grammar. In 1863 Kennedy set to work, producing drafts which the other eight headmasters criticized (Shrewsbury was one of the nine schools, so Kennedy was himself both author of the book and one of those of those who commissioned it—hence in part his embarrassment over profits).[18] In 1865, 200 sets of proofs were circulated around the public schools and the ancient universities for comment. The procedure was repeated early in 1866, and publication was planned for Easter that year. But at this point a memorial of protest was circulated by masters in most of the nine schools, together with Oxbridge classical scholars and heads from other schools. They objected that the book as it stood was much too difficult for beginners, was intermittently inaccurate and faulty, and employed a bizarre new terminology. The schoolmasters were men of scholarship, some of them fellows of Oxbridge colleges. But they were also the men who, unlike the headmasters, actually did the work of what was familiarly called gerund grinding: the laborious basic teaching of Latin grammar. Their memorial was rejected, though the book was further revised, and the *Public School Latin Primer* was published by Longmans on 23 August 1866 (Figures 17.1a and b, and 17.2).

All this semi-public debate will not have been lost on the members of Oxford University Press's School Book Committee, set up in 1863 at the instigation of Alexander Macmillan, who became the Press's publisher in that year (Eliot 2013a, 7–9). Their plans for the Clarendon Press series of school books were well advanced (the first titles appeared this same year), and the Committee were keen to get out a Latin primer of their own to pre-empt the headmasters.[19] The Delegates of the Press had been negotiating with Henry Roby, whose grammar Macmillan had published in 1862, and through the first half of 1866 efforts were made by George Kitchin, secretary to the Press, to bring Roby and the Delegates to an agreement. But the Delegates were not used to moving fast, and an insurmountable problem appeared—Roby's book was held in standing type by the Cambridge printer Charles Clay.

---

[17] E.g. *An Elementary Grammar of the Latin Language, for the use of schools* and *Graecae grammaticae institution prima. Rudimentis Etonensibus quantulum potuit immutatis syntaxin de suo edidit B H Kennedy*, both published in 1847.

[18] Kennedy helpfully provided an account of the commissioning and writing in the *Letter to Bateson*. There is also an MS account by him, preserved in a proof copy of the *Revised Latin Primer* in Shrewsbury School Library.

[19] On the School Book Committee, see Sutcliffe 1978, 19–24; 2013c.

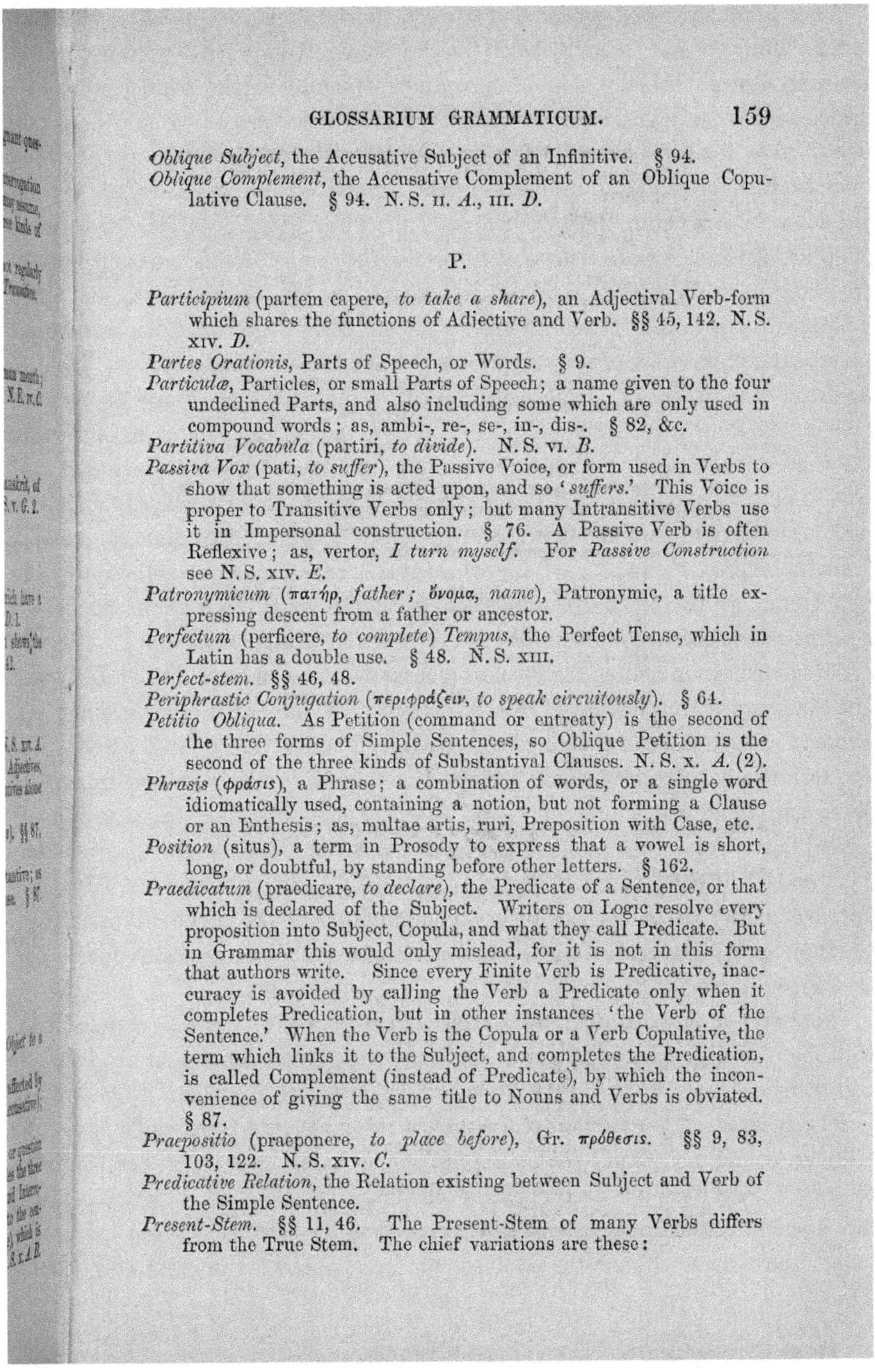

GLOSSARIUM GRAMMATICUM. 159

Oblique Subject, the Accusative Subject of an Infinitive. § 94.
Oblique Complement, the Accusative Complement of an Oblique Copulative Clause. § 94. N. S. ii. *A.*, iii. *D.*

P.

Participium (partem capere, *to take a share*), an Adjectival Verb-form which shares the functions of Adjective and Verb. §§ 45, 142. N. S. xiv. *D.*
Partes Orationis, Parts of Speech, or Words. § 9.
Particulæ, Particles, or small Parts of Speech; a name given to the four undeclined Parts, and also including some which are only used in compound words; as, ambi-, re-, se-, in-, dis-. § 82, &c.
Partitiva Vocabula (partiri, *to divide*). N. S. vi. *B.*
Passiva Vox (pati, *to suffer*), the Passive Voice, or form used in Verbs to show that something is acted upon, and so '*suffers.*' This Voice is proper to Transitive Verbs only; but many Intransitive Verbs use it in Impersonal construction. § 76. A Passive Verb is often Reflexive; as, vertor, *I turn myself.* For *Passive Construction* see N. S. xiv. *E.*
Patronymicum (πατήρ, *father;* ὄνομα, *name*), Patronymic, a title expressing descent from a father or ancestor.
Perfectum (perficere, *to complete*) *Tempus*, the Perfect Tense, which in Latin has a double use. § 48. N. S. xiii.
Perfect-stem. §§ 46, 48.
Periphrastic Conjugation (περιφράζειν, *to speak circuitously*). § 64.
Petitio Obliqua. As Petition (command or entreaty) is the second of the three forms of Simple Sentences, so Oblique Petition is the second of the three kinds of Substantival Clauses. N. S. x. *A.* (2).
Phrasis (φράσις), a Phrase; a combination of words, or a single word idiomatically used, containing a notion, but not forming a Clause or an Enthesis; as, multae artis, ruri, Preposition with Case, etc.
Position (situs), a term in Prosody to express that a vowel is short, long, or doubtful, by standing before other letters. § 162.
Praedicatum (praedicare, *to declare*), the Predicate of a Sentence, or that which is declared of the Subject. Writers on Logic resolve every proposition into Subject, Copula, and what they call Predicate. But in Grammar this would only mislead, for it is not in this form that authors write. Since every Finite Verb is Predicative, inaccuracy is avoided by calling the Verb a Predicate only when it completes Predication, but in other instances 'the Verb of the Sentence.' When the Verb is the Copula or a Verb Copulative, the term which links it to the Subject, and completes the Predication, is called Complement (instead of Predicate), by which the inconvenience of giving the same title to Nouns and Verbs is obviated. § 87.
Praepositio (praeponere, *to place before*), Gr. πρόθεσις. §§ 9, 83, 103, 122. N. S. xiv. *C.*
Predicative Relation, the Relation existing between Subject and Verb of the Simple Sentence.
Present-Stem. §§ 11, 46. The Present-Stem of many Verbs differs from the True Stem. The chief variations are these:

Figure 17.2 *The Public School Latin Primer* (as 17.1), glossary, p. 159.
Image courtesy of the Master and Fellows of Trinity College, Cambridge.

When Kennedy's book appeared, it sparked off a long and furious correspondence in the columns of *The Times*. Between the end of August and early November, thirty-six letters were published.[20] Many of the complaints came from the 'grinders', men who drilled small boys in grammar for entrance to the public schools; the very first letter published by *The Times* was signed, 'A grinder of small boys'.[21] Another wave of protest came from Oxford and Cambridge dons who denounced the inadequacy of the book as a description of Latin. Among these was Henry Roby, whose own book, had Oxford published it, would have been a powerful rival to the *Primer*. Roby's two contributions are pungent and damning: 'The book has amazed me', he declared in his first letter. 'I expected a plain, positive, well-arranged statement of the main facts of Latin grammar. I feared the philosophy of the subject might be ruthlessly slaughtered, but I was in no dread of unnecessary coinages or of errors in the facts. I am clearly no prophet' (1995b, 46). Roby was also the first contributor to the correspondence to break with the convention of writing under a pseudonym; previous writers had included 'BA', 'MA', 'A public schoolmaster', 'DCL', 'An Oxford DD', and so on. This enabled Kennedy—replying in a letter which like all his contributions was signed, 'The Editor of the *Public School Latin Primer*'—to accuse Roby of having an interest, since he was the author of a rival grammar (his 1862 book). Other letters carried similar accusations against the headmasters, who had commissioned a book from one of their own number. 'This way of doing business in matters political or ecclesiastical would be called "a job"', wrote one indignant correspondent (1995a, 67). Eventually one of the other headmasters wrote to say that none of the nine heads had any financial interest in the book. This was technically correct, but only because Kennedy had resigned as headmaster of Shrewsbury at the end of June, and so was no longer one of the Nine. He certainly made a good income out of the book. Initial printings of 2,000 were quickly succeeded by 5,000 and then 10,000 runs, and by February 1867 the total printing was 32,000 and he had £2,000 credit on his account at Longmans. Meanwhile sales of his main rival, Christopher Wordsworth's *King Edward VIth's Latin Grammar*, 'almost suddenly collapsed' (Wordsworth 1899, 168).

There were several distinct issues at stake in this controversy, not all of them to do with the teaching of Latin. In particular, there were tensions between headmasters and their assistants. This was the period in which young graduates of Oxford and Cambridge were allowed to hold fellowships without being resident, and many of the brightest young men went to teach in the public schools. They were liberal-minded reformers, were fresh and accomplished scholars, and were often in charge of lower forms where the grammatical teaching was carried on; the headmasters usually reserved to themselves the teaching of the sixth (senior) forms, where grammatical competence

---

[20] The letters are reprinted with notes and an introduction in 1995a.
[21] A phrase which *The Times* in 1992 refused to print when it was quoted in a letter, on the grounds that it had unacceptable sexual connotations: see 1995a, 17.

was largely taken for granted. The imposition of a bad book on that subject seemed to the liberal scholars a reversion to the old days of autocracy and medievalism. One of them was Edward Bowen of Harrow—best known now for writing the song 'Forty years on'. Bowen was the moving spirit behind the memorial of protest against the *Primer*, and also wrote a pamphlet entitled 'The new national grammar' which criticized it at length.[22] His fundamental objection to the *Primer* was not that it was a bad book, but that it was imposed by authority.[23]

At this point, the wider political context needs to be taken into account. The very first letter printed by *The Times* on 29 August 1866 began as follows 'Sir, A little book, ignored, indeed, by Mudie and by readers at the seaside, has just seen the light, which is intended to make a "rectification of frontiers" for schoolboys as wholesale and as startling as anything recently executed by Bismark himself.'[24] The Prussians had defeated the Austrian army at the battle of Königgratz on 3 July, and had subsequently secured the annexation of Hesse and Hanover by a treaty concluded on the 26th. In England this military expansionism buttressed an ideological opposition between the centralized and regimented Prussians and the free, autonomous Britons who 'never would be slaves'. As another correspondent pointed out, it was ironic that in the much more centralized states of France and Prussia, with their highly organized educational systems, Latin grammars were not standardized, whereas in England the leading public schools, the bastions of British freedom, were now trying to impose a standard textbook.[25]

The protests were of no avail, and the *Primer* rapidly became the de facto standard textbook in the public schools. For twenty years, it reigned as the standard Latin grammar in England. How it was used in the classroom was another matter. In 1884, a public schoolmaster reported that 'many men make no pretence of using the syntax rules of the *Primer*; others teach them by rote, but do not attempt to apply them; others... only trot them out to show how easily you may drive a coach and six through most of them... One master told me he made his boys learn the Syntax as in duty bound, but never attempted explanations, because he found that unexplained the rules were harmless, and did not interfere with his practical teaching.'[26]

Kennedy produced an elementary version of the *Primer*, supplementary exercise books, an advanced grammar to follow it—in fact a whole flotilla of school books. From its first publication, other writers began to revise their books to accommodate his doctrines and to refer to the sections of his grammar. One rival stood against him

---

[22] Bowen 1866; Kennedy replied in another pamphlet (Kennedy 1866).
[23] In the following year he contributed an essay, 'On teaching by means of grammar', to F. W. Farrar's *Essays on a Liberal Education* (Bowen 1867).
[24] 1995a, 16–17. It was this letter which appeared above the signature 'A grinder of small boys'.
[25] The celebrated Greek scholar Charles Badham, who as a pupil of Pestalozzi and friend of Cobet was familiar with continental practice: 1995a, 56–7.
[26] 'The Public School Latin Primer', *Journal of Education* ns 6 (1884), 477–9. This anonymous editorial article was probably written by Francis Storr, the editor at the time.

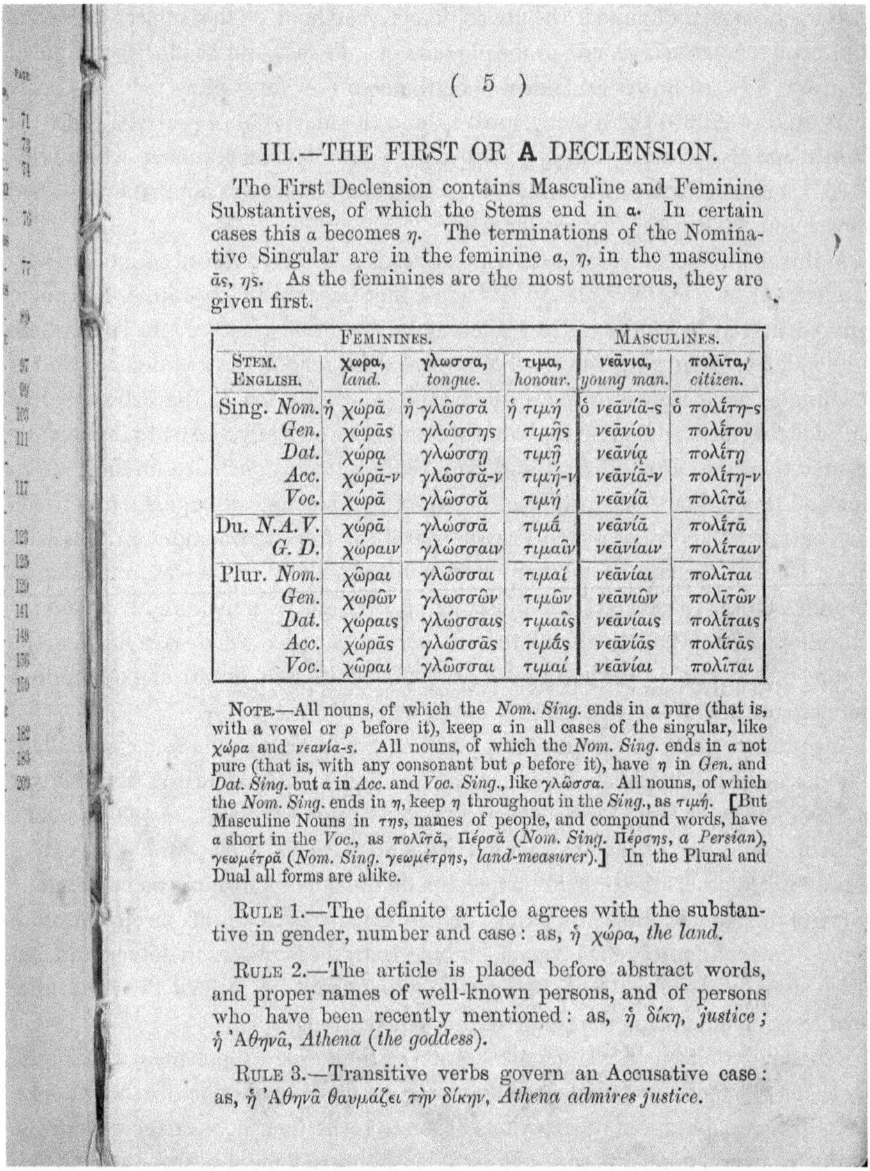

(5)

III.—THE FIRST OR **A** DECLENSION.

The First Declension contains Masculine and Feminine Substantives, of which the Stems end in **a.** In certain cases this a becomes η. The terminations of the Nominative Singular are in the feminine a, η, in the masculine ᾱs, ηs. As the feminines are the most numerous, they are given first.

	FEMININES.			MASCULINES.	
STEM. ENGLISH.	χωρα, *land.*	γλωσσα, *tongue.*	τιμα, *honour.*	νεανια, *young man.*	πολῑτα, *citizen.*
Sing. *Nom.*	ἡ χώρᾱ	ἡ γλῶσσᾰ	ἡ τιμή	ὁ νεᾱνίᾱ-ς	ὁ πολίτη-ς
Gen.	χώρᾱς	γλώσσης	τιμῆς	νεᾱνίου	πολίτου
Dat.	χώρᾳ	γλώσσῃ	τιμῇ	νεᾱνίᾳ	πολίτῃ
Acc.	χώρᾱ-ν	γλῶσσᾰ-ν	τιμή-ν	νεᾱνίᾱ-ν	πολίτη-ν
Voc.	χώρᾱ	γλῶσσᾰ	τιμή	νεᾱνίᾱ	πολῖτᾰ
Du. *N.A.V.*	χώρᾱ	γλώσσᾱ	τιμᾱ́	νεᾱνίᾱ	πολῖτᾱ
G. D.	χώραιν	γλώσσαιν	τιμαῖν	νεᾱνίαιν	πολίταιν
Plur. *Nom.*	χῶραι	γλῶσσαι	τιμαί	νεᾱνίαι	πολῖται
Gen.	χωρῶν	γλωσσῶν	τιμῶν	νεᾱνιῶν	πολῑτῶν
Dat.	χώραις	γλώσσαις	τιμαῖς	νεᾱνίαις	πολίταις
Acc.	χώρᾱς	γλώσσᾱς	τιμᾱ́ς	νεᾱνίᾱς	πολίτᾱς
Voc.	χῶραι	γλῶσσαι	τιμαί	νεᾱνίαι	πολῖται

NOTE.—All nouns, of which the *Nom. Sing.* ends in a pure (that is, with a vowel or ρ before it), keep a in all cases of the singular, like χώρα and νεανία-s. All nouns, of which the *Nom. Sing.* ends in a not pure (that is, with any consonant but ρ before it), have η in *Gen.* and *Dat. Sing.* but a in *Acc.* and *Voc. Sing.*, like γλῶσσα. All nouns, of which the *Nom. Sing.* ends in η, keep η throughout in the *Sing.*, as τιμή. [But Masculine Nouns in της, names of people, and compound words, have a short in the *Voc.*, as πολῖτᾰ, Πέρσᾰ (*Nom. Sing.* Πέρσης, *a Persian*), γεωμέτρᾰ (*Nom. Sing.* γεωμέτρης, *land-measurer*).] In the Plural and Dual all forms are alike.

RULE 1.—The definite article agrees with the substantive in gender, number and case : as, ἡ χώρα, *the land.*

RULE 2.—The article is placed before abstract words, and proper names of well-known persons, and of persons who have been recently mentioned : as, ἡ δίκη, *justice ;* ἡ ᾿Αθηνᾶ, *Athena (the goddess).*

RULE 3.—Transitive verbs govern an Accusative case : as, ἡ ᾿Αθηνᾶ θαυμάζει τὴν δίκην, *Athena admires justice.*

Figures 17.3 (a and b) W. Smith, *Initia Graeca*, 13th edn (London: John Murray, 1882), p. 5. Trinity College Library, Cambridge, Stray c.465.

Image courtesy of the Master and Fellows of Trinity College, Cambridge.

for a long time. This was William Smith, prolific author of course books, dictionaries, and grammars and editor of the *Quarterly Review*. He had his own series of textbooks, headed by *Principia Latina*, *Principia Graeca* and so on—all (as we saw in Chapter 11) with a distinctive dress of black binding and red-edged pages (Figure 17.3). Smith's

[5]

III.—THE FIRST OR A DECLENSION.

The First Declension contains Masculine and Feminine Substantives, of which the Stems end in α. In certain cases this α becomes η. The terminations of the Nominative Singular are in the feminine α, η, in the masculine ᾱς, ης. As the feminines are the most numerous, they are given first.

	FEMININES.			MASCULINES.	
STEM. ENGLISH.	χωρα, land.	γλωσσα, tongue.	τιμα, honour.	νεανια, young man.	πολιτα, citizen.
Sing. *Nom.*	ἡ χώρᾱ	ἡ γλῶσσᾰ	ἡ τιμή	ὁ νεᾱνίᾱ-ς	ὁ πολῑτη-ς
Voc.	χώρᾱ	γλῶσσᾰ	τιμή	νεᾱνίᾱ	πολῖτᾰ
Acc.	χώρᾱ-ν	γλῶσσ-ᾰν	τιμή-ν	νεᾱνίᾱ-ν	πολίτη-ν
Gen.	χώρᾱς	γλώσσης	τιμῆς	νεᾱνίου	πολῑτου
Dat.	χώρᾳ	γλώσσῃ	τιμῇ	νεᾱνίᾳ	πολῑτῃ
Du. *N.V.A.*	χώρᾱ	γλώσσᾱ	τιμᾱ́	νεᾱνίᾱ	πολῑτᾱ
G. D.	χώραιν	γλώσσαιν	τιμαῖν	νεᾱνίαιν	πολῑταιν
Plur. *N. V.*	χῶραι	γλῶσσαι	τιμαί	νεᾱνίαι	πολῖται
Acc.	χώρᾱς	γλώσσᾱς	τιμᾱ́ς	νεᾱνίᾱς	πολῑτᾱς
Gen.	χωρῶν	γλωσσῶν	τιμῶν	νεᾱνιῶν	πολῑτῶν
Dat.	χώραις	γλώσσαις	τιμαῖς	νεᾱνίαις	πολῑταις

NOTE.—All nouns, of which the *Nom. Sing.* ends in α pure (that is, with a vowel or ρ before it), keep α in all cases of the singular, like χώρα and νεανία-ς. All nouns, of which the *Nom. Sing.* ends in α not pure (that is, with any consonant but ρ before it), have η in *Gen.* and *Dat. Sing.* but α in *Acc.* and *Voc. Sing.*, like γλῶσσα. All nouns, of which the *Nom. Sing.* ends in η, keep η throughout in the *Sing.*, as τιμή. [But Masculine Nouns in της, names of people, and compound words, have α short in the *Voc.*, as πολῖτᾰ, Πέρσᾰ (*Nom. Sing.* Πέρσης, a *Persian*), γεωμέτρᾰ (*Nom. Sing.* γεωμέτρης, *land-measurer*).] In the Plural and Dual all forms are alike.

RULE 1.—The definite article agrees with the substantive in gender, number and case : as, ἡ χώρα, *the land.*

RULE 2.—The article is placed before abstract words, and proper names of well-known persons, and of persons who have been recently mentioned : as, ἡ δίκη, *justice* ; ἡ 'Αθηνᾶ, *Athena (the goddess).*

RULE 3.—Transitive verbs govern an Accusative case : as, ἡ 'Αθηνᾶ θαυμάζει τὴν δίκην, *Athena admires justice.*

Figures 17.3 Continued

major problem was that Kennedy had departed from the traditional order in which the cases of the noun were listed, while his own books adhered to it. At first he gave ground by adding an extra page sequence, with the page numbers in square brackets, to his Latin and Greek books. One sequence used the traditional order, the extra pages used

Kennedy's new order.[27] In the 1880s, however, Smith was forced to cave in, and the old order disappeared from his books.

The *Revised Latin Primer* (1888)

By the mid-1880s, Kennedy's *Primer* had reigned supreme for twenty years. But while successive issues and printings of the *Primer* contain minor alteration and corrections, inserted in response to criticism, in essence the book remained unchanged. The protests occasioned by the circulation of proof sheets in 1865 had led to the insertion after the 'Syntaxis memorialis prima' of a 'First memorial syntax' which translated it into English. This represented a concession to the vociferous minority of liberal schoolmasters who were no longer willing to teach Latin in Latin. In 1879 an account of 'compound constructions', previously printed separately, was incorporated into the book. But these extras had been tacked on rather than being integrated, and the book needed a wholesale revision. The string of negatives in the new Preface which appeared in the 1883 issue is eloquent testimony to a mounting wave of criticism: 'The "Public School Latin Primer" was not put forth by its compilers as a First Book for children beginning Latin ... It was not supposed that all sections and parts of sections in the first ninety pages would be learnt in a memorial course; nor was it doubted that some passages in accidence would be sufficiently taught by means of questions and answers ...'[28]

Rival Latin grammars were meanwhile appearing every year, and as the authority of the *Public School Latin Primer* was eroded, the prospect of a return to the confused textbook anarchy of the early nineteenth century loomed larger. The issue was brought to the forefront in 1885 by Edmond Warre, recently appointed headmaster of Eton College, the most prestigious of the public schools. Eton now had nearly a thousand pupils, and Warre, convinced that it constituted a captive market of adequate size, commissioned some of his staff to produce Eton Latin grammars, to be published by John Murray.[29] No more serious threat to the idea of an agreed standard textbook could be imagined, unless it were an attempt to renounce the policy itself. Such a course was in fact advocated at the 1885 meeting of the Headmasters' Conference, the public school headmasters' association, by one of their number, Edward Young of Sherborne School. His motion, however, was defeated, and the Conference then appointed a committee to revise Kennedy's primer. Kennedy himself, now over eighty, had offered to submit his own draft for criticism, but the headmasters were determined to retain the initiative. A sub-committee was appointed to produce a new text, based on the 1866 *Primer*, which would then be submitted to Kennedy for comment. But after six months of struggle, the committee gave up. They had worked through the first sixteen pages of

---

[27] The old order (Nom Gen Dat Acc Abl Voc) is still in use in the USA and in many parts of Europe. The new order changed this to Nom Voc Acc Gen Dat Abl (Allen and Brink 1980).

[28] *The Public School Latin Primer*, London: Longmans, Green 1883, Preface.

[29] Three Eton Latin grammars appeared: preparatory, elementary, and advanced (1992b).

the *Primer*, discarded almost all of Kennedy's text and were unsure how to proceed. In April 1886, the HMC Committee asked the Conference to vote on several proposals about the *Primer*. One of these would have delayed any decision until the next Conference meeting in December; but the majority voted to authorize the Committee to commission a new textbook. On hearing this, Kennedy wrote a dignified letter of protest to the HMC chairman in which he claimed that 'the whole course of my later life has been determined by the faith which I reposed in the stability of the engagement between the nine schools and myself'. He went on to argue that he had lost income by resigning as headmaster of Shrewsbury in 1866 to work on the sequel to the *Primer*, the *Public School Latin Grammar*, and that he had assumed his agreement with the nine headmasters 'would at least have such permanence as would give to me and my children the same benefit that copyright gives to authors and their heirs...'.[30] The Committee replied that they could not be bound by an agreement made with others twenty years ago. Nevertheless this was a shrewd blow, since the Committee will have known that Kennedy was a widower who lived with his two middle-aged spinster daughters; and they agreed that he should prepare a revision for consideration by the full Conference in December.

At the Conference meeting Edward Young returned to the attack, urging his fellow-headmasters to commission their own textbook. In a mordant speech, he referred to what he called 'the diversion which [has] been executed on the flank of the Conference during the last few months by Dr Kennedy' and to 'the almost tender reluctance...to wound...the feelings of the aged Scholar to whom Latin Scholarship in England owed so very much'. Holding in his hand a copy of the revised text which Kennedy had circulated to the headmasters, Young argued that it was so different from the 1866 *Primer* that it could not be accepted as a revision of the earlier book.[31] Eventually it was resolved that the Conference members should be balloted, and that if a majority disapproved of Kennedy's revision, a new textbook should be commissioned. The headmasters now crowned a long career of delay by taking no further action. The balloting of Conference members seems not to have taken place, in fact, until after the publication of the *Revised Latin Primer* in June 1888, when a majority of the twenty-nine (of a total of over eighty) who bothered to comment pronounced themselves satisfied with the book (Figure 17.4).[32]

The satisfaction was general: the *Revised Primer* was without doubt a much better book than its predecessor. The writing is clear, the text well organized, the scholarship up to date; a remarkable achievement for a man in his mid-eighties. But as the Longman archives reveal, the book had in fact been written by Kennedy's two unmarried daughters Marion and Julia, with advice from two of his ex-pupils. The letters which survive from

[30] B. H. Kennedy to G. C. Bell, 7 May 1886; printed in the *Report of the Committee of the Headmasters' Conference*, 1886, 10–13.
[31] *HMC Bulletin* (1886), 5–6. Quotations from the Bulletin, and from the HMC Committee reports, are based on inspection of the complete set at the offices of the Headmasters' Conference.
[32] *Report of the HMC Committee*, November 1888, 1–2.

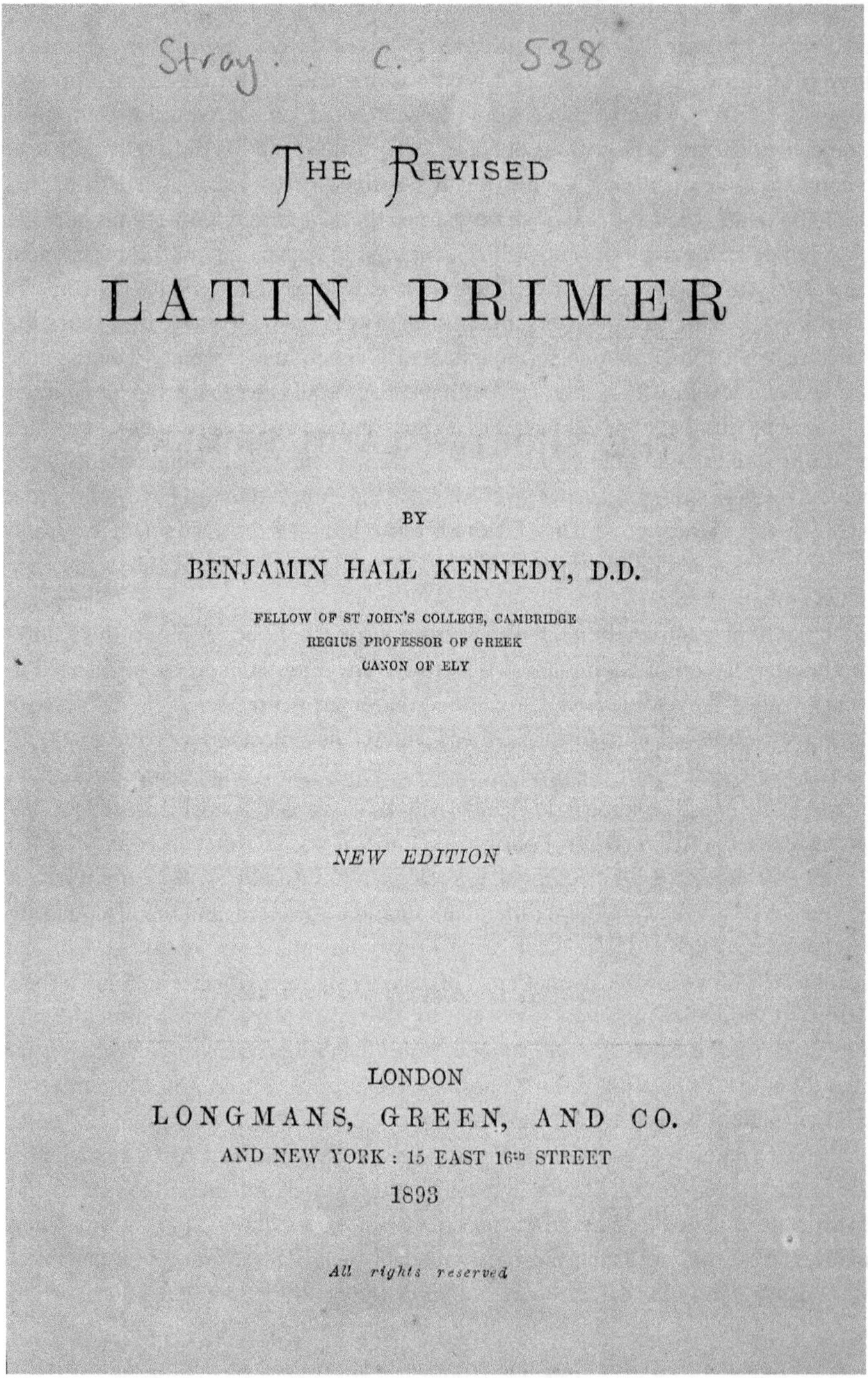

THE REVISED

LATIN PRIMER

BY

BENJAMIN HALL KENNEDY, D.D.

FELLOW OF ST JOHN'S COLLEGE, CAMBRIDGE
REGIUS PROFESSOR OF GREEK
CANON OF ELY

NEW EDITION

LONDON

LONGMANS, GREEN, AND CO.

AND NEW YORK : 15 EAST 16ᵗʰ STREET

1893

Figure 17.4 *The Revised Latin Primer* (London: Longmans, 1893), title page. Trinity College Library, Cambridge, Stray c.538.

Image courtesy of the Master and Fellows of Trinity College, Cambridge.

the period 1885–8 suggest that Marion, his elder daughter, had done most of the work, but conclusive proof emerges from letters to Longmans from her younger sister Julia, written after Marion's death in 1914.[33] A question of copyright had come up, and Julia put on record the history of the *Primer*'s composition. Her and Marion's authorship of the book was then confirmed by affidavits from G. H. Hallam and T. E. Page, the ex-pupils of Kennedy who had helped with the composition.[34] As Julia reluctantly explained, 'My father was only prepared at first for a comparatively slight revision…it was not easy to make him see the extent and far reaching quality of the alterations which were called for, both by the rapid growth of comparative philology and by the newer methods of teaching.'[35]

Ironically, while the 1866 book, largely written by Kennedy, had not carried his name on its title page, its successor did so, despite his not having written it. The *Public School Latin Primer* was known as Benjamin Kennedy's book; to add other names to the *Revised Latin Primer* would have compromised the book's authority, to announce that it was written by two women would have been total disaster. So the hard-working daughters kept loyally silent. When the copyright question was raised in 1914, counsel advised that since their claim had not been publicly asserted, it was very unlikely that a claim to copyright would succeed.[36] Meanwhile the book Marion and Julia had written under their father's name had become the standard Latin grammar in England. The *Eton Latin Grammar* was eventually discontinued, since the Eton masters preferred the Kennedy book, and all the boys coming up to Eton from preparatory schools had been trained on it. After revisions in 1909, 1930, and 1962, it remains a standard textbook today. The continuing decline in the numbers of those learning Latin, however, may yet bring the book's long history to an end.[37]

Conclusion

The history of Kennedy's two primers reveals a complicated web of pressures and tensions, at the centre of which the books themselves hovered, their nature and, at several moments, their very existence uncertain. Commodities in a publishing market, they were also tied to the politics of the market for elite schooling. Their content was assembled, debated, and negotiated at a time when both conceptions of language and ideologies of pedagogy were in flux. Often these two were in direct conflict: the new comparative philology, for example, might tempt a grammarian to begin a book with

[33] Longman archives, MS 1393, Pt 2,110. This contains seventy-five letters to Longmans in 1886–8, nearly all written by Marion Kennedy. The letters on the copyright issue (1914–17) are 2.111. 1–33.

[34] Longman archives MS 1393, 2.111.

[35] Longman archives MS 1393, 2.111. 26: Julia Kennedy to Longmans, 20 February 1915. Benjamin Kennedy had died in 1889, Marion in 1914.

[36] Longman archives MS 1393, 2.111. 35: opinion of E. J. McGillivray, 17 March 1915.

[37] It is also relevant to note that as a result of the generous contract agreed by Longmans in 1888, Kennedy's descendants still receive 60 per cent of the book's profits, the firm 40 per cent.

an exposition of the laws of sound, but this was not what many schoolmasters would wish to use to initiate young pupils. All these tensions were further complicated by the ambiguous status of the primers: commissioned by educational bodies, commercially published, with profits accruing to the 'editor' or 'author' and his family. A final layer of confusion—and embarrassment—was provided by Kennedy's membership, until the summer of 1866, of the body which commissioned the *Public School Latin Primer* from him: the headmasters of the nine Clarendon schools. Behind them, in turn, stood the state, intervening by Royal Commission.

This case is one of several which could be used to explore the interaction of education and publishing. Others might be explored in parallel to the histories of individual firms which Simon Eliot has called for. The targeting of set book markets after the rise of the examination system, for example, would repay investigation. It is clear from Longmans' house magazine *Notes on Books* that some publications were aimed at candidates for specific examinations, and the growth of the University of London as a central examining body was accompanied by the production of books which reprinted past questions and gave hints on how to pass examinations.[38] Finally, there are particular events whose repercussions might be traced. The passing of Forster's Education Act in 1870 encouraged some publishers to produce educational series, though they may have overestimated demand and drawn back within a few years (Eliot 1994, 48). A series of such case studies would be needed before we could begin to assemble a longer-term analysis of the kind recently produced by Lee Erickson for literary genres (Erickson 1996).

In this particular case, we are fortunate to have a considerable body of evidence.[39] The historian of textbooks is rarely so lucky; and the marginal status of the textbook in the history of the book compounds the difficulty. The accession, collection, treatment, and study of textbooks has in general differed from that afforded other books. They have been thrown, drawn on, bitten, more consistently then most books, by readers who are not usually purchasers. They have also suffered from the ideological bias of collectors, since they make an unlikely target for the searcher after elegant books in perfect condition. The net/non-net distinction which emerged at the end of the nineteenth century only reinforced the barrier between collectable books and books for use. It is not surprising, then, to find that textbooks are often not acceded to libraries, or if acceded, not catalogued, or if catalogued, not entered in the main catalogue which is the only one most readers know about.[40] To follow the changes made in successive

---

[38] This quarterly publication is an invaluable source of information on the firm's publications; it ran from 1855 to 1909. Full runs are held at Reading University Library and the Bodleian Library.

[39] No Longman correspondence files survive for the 1866 Primer; they were presumably among the material destroyed by bombing during World War II.

[40] In the autumn of 1991, the *History of Reading News* (vol. 16, 1) reported that the 40,000 textbooks of the early American collection of the US Department of Education's Research Library 'are uncatalogued and lie tightly shelved in a dusty storage room. Many urgently need rebinding.'

issues of the *Public School Latin Primer* is a difficult task, since very few libraries have more than one or two issues.[41]

Textbooks have arguably been as powerful as other books in their effect on the consciousness of readers. This is not to claim that their authors' messages have been effectively transmitted. It is, I hope, clear from the history of Kennedy's primers that Murray Cohen's notion of a 'core of intelligibility' must be treated with great caution. The most common charge brought against the *Public School Latin Primer* was that it was unintelligible, yet it went on, with only slight revision, to become a standard text-book for over twenty years. To a degree, of course, what teachers offer to their pupils is liable to be regarded by the latter as part of an arbitrarily meaningless adult world, a world they do not *expect* to make sense. In the case of Classics, at least, this has not prevented pupils having fun with it, playing with its nonsense, or making their own meaning from it (see Chapter 18). The historical world of the classroom offers its own delights to the researcher, but also formidable challenges, since the evidence is so sparse and difficult to interpret. That world, too, needs to be explored by those who would pursue the joint histories of the book and of education.

---

[41] The following libraries have three or more issues: the British Library; the Bodleian Library; the Brotherton Library, University of Leeds; Trinity College, Cambridge; and the Gutman Library, Harvard University.

18

The Smell of Latin Grammar
Contrary Imaginings in English Classrooms

I know men who say they had as lief read any book in a library copy as in one from their own shelf. To me that is unintelligible. For one thing, I know every book of mine by its *scent*, and I have but to put my nose between the pages to be reminded of all sorts of things. My Gibbon, for example, my well-bound eight-volume Milman edition, which I have read and read and read again for more than thirty years—never do I open it but the scent of the page restores to me all the exultant happiness of that moment when I received it as a prize. Or my Shakespeare, the great Cambridge Shakespeare—it has an odour which carries me yet further back in life; for these volumes belonged to my father, and before I was old enough to read them with understanding, it was often permitted me, as a treat, to take down one of them from the bookcase, and reverently to turn the leaves. The volumes smell exactly as they did in that old time, and what a strange tenderness comes upon me when I hold one of them in hand. For that reason I do not often read Shakespeare in this edition. My eyes being good as ever, I take the Globe volume, which I bought in days when such a purchase was something more than an extravagance; wherefore I regard the book with that peculiar affection which results from sacrifice.

George Gissing, *The Private Papers of Henry Ryecroft* (1903), Chapter 1, section xii[1]

During the Cold War of the 1950s, the climate of educational opinion in Britain was much influenced by the ideological alarms then current in the United States. Established American patterns of progressive education were challenged by right-wing propagandists who called for a 'return to learning', while the American scientific community began to look for ways to stimulate scientific creativity in children. In Britain, 'learning' was still firmly embedded in school curricula, and Latin, still widely regarded as a prime source of mental discipline, continued to be compulsory for

---

[1] H. H. Milman's edition of Gibbon was published in 2 volumes in 1838–9; Gissing probably had a copy of the 8-volume edition of 1887, which also included notes by F. Guizot and William Smith. The 'Cambridge Shakespeare' was edited in 9 vols (1863–6) by W. G. Clark and John Glover (vol. 1), and by Clark and W. Aldis Wright (vols 2–9). The 'Globe volume' is the one-volume Globe edition edited by Clark and Wright, published by Macmillan in 1864.

Oxford and Cambridge entrance until the end of the 1950s, when the pressure for science teaching generated by the Cold War led to its abolition as a general entrance requirement. At the same time, the purely subject-based General Certificate of Education, set up in 1951, was promoting the fragmentation of educational experience into separate subjects; a pattern subsequently legitimized by the idea of 'subject mindedness'. Individual pupils, that is, were thought to gravitate instinctively toward particular subjects. Hence the uniquely early and extreme process of specialization found in England and Wales.[2]

It was against this background that Liam Hudson began his research into the psychology of the English schoolboy in 1957; research which was reported in his book *Contrary Imaginations* (Hudson 1962). Hudson explored the mental sets of English schoolboys by inviting them to suggest uses for common objects: barrels, bricks, tins of boot-polish, blankets, and paper-clips. The responses appeared to reveal two opposed modes of coping with the world—'contrary imaginations'—which Hudson labelled convergence and divergence. The former was associated with defensive caution and impersonality, the latter with imaginative creation and personal association. Hudson found that most arts pupils were divergers, most science pupils convergers. But the classicists in his group appeared to belong with the convergers. Hudson's research had several limitations. Although he was among the most creative and interesting of English psychologists, he evinced no interest in the ideological context of his work: the Cold War alarms about creativity and scientific manpower which I mentioned above. More to the point here, he also took for granted the status of 'subjects' as variables in pupils' experience. The question is never asked, just why should classicists' responses appear to be closer to those of scientists than to those of arts students?[3] One obvious answer is simply that in the 1950s, in the public and grammar schools whose pupils Hudson interviewed, Latin was taught primarily as a rigorous linguistic discipline, and that the boys who continued with it were those to whom this appealed. The 'convergers', in short.[4] Not all those who learned Latin, however, were blissfully convergent in their identification with the impersonal rigours of grammar. Some pupils had, in a sense very different from Hudson's, 'contrary imaginations'.[5] Like the divergers he interviewed, they made sense of Latin, but not necessarily the sense their teachers—or the ancient Romans—would have hoped for. We might in fact see the teacher–pupil

[2] The differences from other national patterns were addressed by Basil Bernstein in his essay 'On the classification and framing of educational knowledge' (Bernstein 1971). His analysis, however, itself reflected the English curricular pattern in residualizing the role of content: see 1990.

[3] Hudson's sample, as well being entirely male, was also confined to selective schools. There are themes in his discussion (e.g. defence systems in relation to the use of boundaries) which overlap with the contemporary work of Bernstein, whose conceptions of 'open' and 'closed' social forms and modes of individual consciousness are close to Hudson's characterization of 'convergence' and 'divergence' as 'open' and 'closed' defence systems. (Hudson confirmed to me in correspondence that the overlap had not occurred to him.)

[4] Looking back in l968 (Hudson 1968, 104), Hudson comments briefly on the changes in subject provision in the interim, but does not draw conclusions about his earlier work.

[5] The difference, and the point I am making here, is symbolized by shifting the accent in 'contrary' from the antepenultimate to the penultimate syllable.

relationship as one which involves the imposition of convergence on divergence. The rule-bound nature of convergence is inherently congenial to the authoritarian dimension of the teacher's task. This is not to deny that some teachers try to encourage divergence, at times by personal example. But Hudson's account of 'frames of mind' deals only with pupil 'imaginations' as individual characteristics. It ignores both interaction among pupils and their relationship with teachers and with adult authority in general. The 'imaginations' evidenced in this latter sphere have often been 'contrary' in a stronger sense, making a different, even deviant, sense of the knowledge wielded by adults.

The recognition of such contrary meaning-construction by pupils inevitably affects the way we conceive of, and analyse, the process of cultural transmission. It demands a dialectical account which incorporates 'reception' as an active process. We thus need to break away from the conceptions of transmission which deny or ignore the possibility of such activity.[6] One way to explore the process of transmission/reception is to look at the coding and recoding of its 'messages'. Even within a single language community, where we speak of a 'message in clear' we should rather refer to a 'message in a shared code'. Natural languages are complex coding devices which organize meaning for transmission—and reception. In the history of European culture, Latin has constituted a coding device of special importance. In the discussion which follows, I want to explore the variety of symbolic overtones which this particular code has acquired in nineteenth- and twentieth-century English education, by concentrating on the role of textbooks. Such books as Latin grammars are material embodiments of meaning, coded in complex ways which relate to subject matter, pedagogic ideologies, publishing markets, and the institutional contexts in which they are used. This complexity, as we shall see, is deepened by the various ways in which pupils perceive them and add their own layers of meaning through 'contrary imaginations'.[7] The evidence I draw on is both sparse and scattered. Notoriously, the life of the schoolroom tends to escape the historian's eye. We often have to rely on the memories of adults, which rarely take us into the minutiae of classroom interaction. When they do, the focus is usually on social relations rather than relations to curricular knowledge. In most cases, this is surely because the latter so often functions as a routine backdrop to the concerns of childhood.

What do people remember from their schooldays? In some retrospective accounts, the physical setting of the classroom is powerfully recalled. 'Class-rooms were then more severe and were almost devoid of adornment...There was something in those

---

[6] Three major conceptions can be distinguished: (1) The long-established focus on the transmitter, which meant that any alteration in the message was seen as the corruption of an original purity (Grafton 1990); (2) The romantic reaction to this approach which in a sense denied the existence of transmission by stressing the constantly creative power of individuals; (3) The structuralist approach, which makes transmission a product of the formal properties of the message. See Roman Jakobson's analysis of 'shifters' (words which change form in reported speech): Jakobson 1971.

[7] A preliminary sketch of this area is attempted in 1994a. For a useful approach to transmission along these lines, see Thompson 1990, 122–62.

days more solid, more true to that time-honoured timber, those plain, unforgettable desk-lids, whereon more than one budding youngster had carved his initials for ever.' Thus Harold Cooke, in 1925, recalling his days at the Perse School, Cambridge in the 1890s. The Latin texts he remembers were Caesar's *de bello Gallico* and Cicero's *de amicitia* and *de senectute*. 'How appreciate either the Latin or the thought...? We had had no sufficient experience to give them the mildest importance; they were almost, I think, without meaning. Old age meant to us but old men—and what time had we then for old men?' Cooke's criticism of the Caesar is more specific: 'As for Caesar we thought him too cold or—shall we say?—"icily regular". We cursed his eternal third person.' Here, among other things, is a view of Latin teaching from below which explicitly renounces the impersonality of 'convergence'.[8]

Kingsley Martin's memories of his first school reinforce Cooke's account of resentment and sheer lack of meaning:

All the way up the school we learnt Latin and Greek. The lower classes were far too crowded and noisy for any real work. We learnt, I suppose, a little Latin and less Greek in five lack lustre years. We had splashed ink on each other's white collars. Paper darts had floated about the room when the master's back was turned...We were bored beyond belief. An agony of boredom. We ragged when we dared and dozed when we could.[9]

The objects which Hudson chose for suggestions by pupils were clearly meant to be utilitarian devices with a low symbolic loading. Compared to the brick or the blanket, the Latin textbook comes heavily laden with connotations from its subject matter (Latin, and by implication the Romans), the world of books and libraries, and the authority of adult knowledge.[10] These fuse into a complex unity of which one element may predominate in a particular situation. The connotations of 'Rome' (law and order, empire, cruelty to Christians, aqueducts, for example) may well be submerged in the mind of a pupil whose experience of Latin teaching is dominated by rote learning and the 'grammar grind'.[11] Even this fairly flexible conception, however, fails to do justice to the range of children's responses, in which all the senses may be involved—even that mentioned in the title of this chapter.[12] But textbooks, after all, are objects, with weight,

[8] Cooke 1925, 14, 12. 'Icily regular' is from Tennyson's *Maud*, lines 82–3, where Maud's features are described as 'Faultily faultless, icily regular, splendidly null , / Dead perfection, no more'. Cooke's memory of 'carving old Gaul into quarters' (12) is perhaps a simple lapse rather than a rebellious rejection of the tripartite division described by Caesar.

[9] Martin 1966, 52–3. In the fifth form, however, Martin discovered Greek poetry and was taught by a master who conveyed a sense of literary value: ibid. 55.

[10] Cf. the remarks of David Hamilton on 'educational tools': 'Like most cultural artefacts, educational tools can be harnessed to a range of different social purposes', Hamilton 1990, 75.

[11] The classical scholar Sir Kenneth Dover reported that he once asked his mother what she thought of when the Romans were mentioned. She replied 'cruelty'. Dover added that if he had asked for a second connotation, it would probably have been 'aqueducts' (Dover 1992, ix).

[12] The remembrance or odours past has not been extensively researched. The French social history which seeks ever for the bizarre and grotesque, as in the smell of burning cats (Darnton 1984), has begun to explore the field: see e.g. Corbin 1986. In a paper on sixteenth-century university teaching, Anthony

size, colour, and smell, handled, thrown and in general, as we shall see, used for other purposes than learning.

My title comes from a childhood memory of both smell and colour, recorded in a memoir of Benjamin Kennedy, headmaster of Shrewsbury School from 1836 to 1866 and the author of several successful Latin grammars.

A grey-haired man in latter middle age remembers the arrival of Dr Kennedy at his home on a visit to his father, who was one of the Doctor's old pupils, and how the great man produced a copy of his Latin Grammar and presented it to the awestruck little boy. It was bound in bright green cloth, and smelt strongly of bookseller's paste, a smell which the small boy firmly believed to be that of 'Latin', and disliked accordingly.[13]

This anecdote is valuable for several reasons. For one thing, it tells us what the book looked like when new; something it is not always easy to guess from surviving copies of such much-used books. Library copies, for their part, have often been rebound, thus destroying coloured binding along with other features such as spine titles.[14] But 'bright green' records not only a colour, but the impact this made on a child who had clearly begun to learn, and to dislike, Latin.[15] The book whose smell How remembered was based on Kennedy's first textbook, the *Latinae Grammaticae Curriculum* of 1844, which had itself been used, though not literally, as 'scent': torn up and scattered as trail by the Fox and Hounds.[16] The use of the definite article and capitals by Young

Grafton evokes the smell of the classroom by pointing out that one teacher apparently took a bath only once a year: Grafton 1981, 37. For an anthropological analysis of religious odours, see Kenna 2005.

[13] How 1904, 120–1. The book was probably Kennedy's *Child's Latin Primer* of 1847. The 'grey-haired man' was surely Frederick How himself, born in 1851 and thus fifty-three when his book appeared; this dates the episode to the second half of the 1850s. How was born in Whittington, twenty miles from Shrewsbury, while Kennedy was headmaster of Shrewsbury School. His father William Walsham How, an ex-pupil of Kennedy's, was Rector of Whittington 1851–79.

[14] The Classics Library at the University of Illinois at Urbana-Champaign contains a tattered copy of Percival Leigh's *Comic Latin Grammar* (London: C. Tilt, 1840). The book is shelved in a box, which also contains on a slip of paper the plaintive request, 'Please do not destroy the lovely designs on the covers by rebinding this book.'

[15] Several of Kennedy's schoolbooks were bound in green. The *Revised Latin Primer* (1888) was published in covers of an olive green chosen by the Kennedy and his daughters; the 1930 revision by James Mountford appeared in a rather poisonous light green. The *Shorter Latin Primer*, which was published in the same year as the *Revised Primer*, was given a brown cover, presumably to distinguish it from its elder sibling. It is possible, though less likely, that what young How smelled c.1860 was in fact the dye used for the book's covers. This may have been 'Paris green', otherwise known as 'emerald' or 'Schweinfurt' green: a highly toxic pigment (copper aceto-arsenite), discovered in Sweden in 1778 and first manufactured in Austria in 1814. For its toxicity, see e.g. Draper 1872.

[16] The story comes from G. W. Fisher's *Annals of Shrewsbury School*, which was based on extensive local knowledge and questioning of old boys. '[Kennedy's] eyes... were opened to some evils connected with the runs in 1843 or 1844 by the disappearance of a large number of copies of the new Latin Grammar, which had taken the form of scent...' (Fisher 1899, 394). The records of the Royal Shrewsbury School Hunt contain no documentary evidence for the story, though much to confirm that Kennedy was often hostile to the Hunt. Though Kennedy himself several times dated it to 1843, the copies in the British Library and the Bodleian Library are dated 1844: they bear the marks of sectional printing in Shrewsbury. It may even be that it was the depredation by the Hunt of stocks of the earlier (unbound?) local printing which led to the London publication by Longmans in 1844.

and Fisher ('the Latin Grammar') hints at the symbolic role of the books as bearers of both social and cultural authority in schools where the learning of Latin occupied much of the timetable in the lower forms. The shredding by pupils of pages written by their headmaster must have been a peculiarly satisfying element in the activities of the Hunt.

The tearing of pages from books by pupils had a long history and was indeed taken into account by the writers of schoolbooks. Thus alphabets often had their first pages inserted twice, so that an initial attack would still leave a complete text. In the preface to his *The English Schoole-Maister* (1596), Edmund Coote had claimed that the book was so carefully planned that each chapter could be understood by a pupil even if he had torn out all the preceding matter. Lindley Murray declared in the preface to the 1797 abridgment of his 1795 English grammar that his 'chief view in presenting the book in this form, is, to preserve the larger work from being torn and defaced by the younger scholars....'[17] Selective removal of pages was also practised by teachers; for example, Latin translations were cut out, leaving a plain Greek text for the pupil to tackle.[18]

The physical properties of classical textbooks were also drawn on in different ways in dealing with corporal punishment. At Temple Grove, one of the leading nineteenth-century preparatory schools, the Latin grammar was customarily clenched between the teeth of small boys while they were being beaten.[19] During Edward Thring's reign as headmaster of Uppingham, it was a 'customary precaution' to insert 'Farrar's flexible "Greek Verb Card" between two pairs of winter pants'.[20]

Apart from Cooke's reference to Caesar, almost all the evidence discussed here has to do with language learning rather than with literature. This reflects the bias of the sources and hence of English classical education. In the nineteenth century in particular, literature was something pupils encountered, for the most part, only after several years of linguistic grind. Even in the higher forms of public schools, classical authors were often studied as linguistic corpora, to the exclusion of any analysis of literary value. It is this tradition, raised to a reactive self-consciousness by the pressure of criticism, which is summed up in the anecdote of the 'famous schoolmaster' who told his

[17] Murray, *An Abridgment of Murray's English Grammar*. (Boston: Lincoln and Edmunds, 1829), iii.

[18] Clarke 1959, 84 (early nineteenth century). The survival of the practice is attested by a carefully mutilated copy of T. Johnson's *Novus graecorum epigrammatum et poimation delectus*... (Eton: E. Williams, 1827). This is now in Trinity College Library, Cambridge, Stray *c.*479.

[19] Young 1936, 96: 'It was the custom under flogging to bite the Latin Grammar.' The reference is one of those which eluded Sir George Kitson Clark, who produced an annotated edition of Young's book (Clark 1977, 104, 326 n. 10. The source is almost certainly A. E. H. Anton's *About Others and Myself* (London: John Murray, 1920), 46: 'The boy was laid face downwards across the Doctor's table, when two of the class held each a leg, and two others held each an arm, and the head boy of the class placed a Latin Grammar in his mouth to bite, to relieve his feelings during the Operations.' 'The Doctor' was Dr J. H. Pinckney, headmaster 1817–35, referred to as a 'sycophantic Doctor of Divinity' in Disraeli's *Coningsby*.

[20] Thornely 1936, 187. The 'Greek Verb Card' is F. W. Farrar's *Greek Grammar Rules, Drawn up for the Use of Harrow School* (London: Longmans, 1866), a 19-page booklet with flexible card covers, which went into twenty-two printings.

pupils, 'Boys, this term we are to read the Oedipus Tyrannus of Sophocles, a storehouse of grammatical peculiarities.' The earliest printed version of this much-repeated tale dates from about 1915. It thus probably reflects the reassertion of the values of the 'grand old fortifying curriculum' against reformist proposals on method and the claims of newer subjects, both much discussed in the 1900s.[21]

Yet even a grammar could in fact contain a considerable amount of literature. Here the economics of marketing interacted with ideas of subject and content, since there were obvious advantages to having a single book containing both grammar and literary excerpts. The variations can be seen if we begin in the early nineteenth century. The market leader in 1800 was undoubtedly the Eton grammar (*A Short Introduction to the Latin Tongue, for the Use of Youth*), an edited appropriation of the Lily/Colet corpus dating from 1758. By the 1790s it was becoming known as simply 'the Eton grammar' and pirated editions were appearing.[22] The grammar taught Latin in Latin (more precisely, it taught classical Latin in dog Latin). Thousands of small boys learned it by rote and were beaten for their mistakes. Success in class was measured by the ability to repeat the rules accurately and apply them to new material. To investigate the principles underlying the rules was a dangerous exercise: it might smack of a challenge to authority, and in any case many of the rules were wrong or self-contradictory. The same could have been said of the previous Eton grammar. In about 1750 the young John Horne Tooke burst into tears when demoted for failing to explain a construction. The master wanted to hear a rote repetition of the rule from the grammar; Tooke wanted to explain the rationale of the construction, but could not. Tooke was unusual; for most boys, the repetition, like the flogging, was just a fact of life.[23]

We can imagine that the author of *The Diversions of Purley* was already fascinated by words. For such children, Latin indeed offered a 'treasure house of peculiarities' to be explored. Some of the ways this store could be drawn upon can be glimpsed in the writing of W. H. Auden, a lover of rare words whose schooling coincided with the First World War. In his 'Letter to Lord Byron', Auden remembers that school was more real than the war:

> The Great War had begun: but masters' scrutiny
> And the fists of big boys were the war to us...

---

[21] The earliest published source is Sheppard 1920, ix. The book was finished by 1915, but publication was delayed by the war. Sheppard's own teacher, Arthur Pearson, held different attitudes; a more likely source was King's College, of which Sheppard was a fellow, and where there were old-fashioned eccentrics like J. E. Nixon teaching in the 1890s.

[22] Only three copies of the 1758 edition survive, in the libraries of University College London, the University of Manchester, and the University of Illinois.

[23] Tooke accepted the flogging for failing to answer 'with perfect sang froid and without a murmur'. It was when another boy recited the grammar rule and had this accepted that Tooke wept. To his credit, the master recanted and gave Tooke an inscribed Virgil in apology: Jerdan 1852–3, 2. 296–7. The grammar in this case would not have been the Eton grammar, which was first printed in 1758, unless sheets were used in the school before that date; a practice for which there is evidence elsewhere.

But occasionally the classroom and the war came together:

> ...once when half the form put down *Bellus*
> We were accused of that most deadly sin,
> Wanting the Kaiser and the Huns to win.
>   (Auden 1976, 96)[24]

When he comes to describe his life as an undergraduate, Auden again invokes Latin; in this case, Amor rather than Bellum:

> We were the tail, a sort of poor relation
> To that debauched, eccentric generation
> That grew up with their fathers at the War,
> And made new glosses on the noun Amor.
>   (Auden 1976, 98)

Here the recording of linguistic usage, normally the reflex of social and cultural history, is made a metaphor for that history. In this case, the remembered content of education becomes part of a metaphorical armature, a way of seeing and evaluating the world rather than simply a stock of information.

Auden will have known of the references his poem's addressee made to his own classical education, via the account of the upbringing of Don Juan. One of Juan's mother's concerns was precisely that he might seek 'Amor' amid the accounts of 'Bellum'. Donna Anna worried that her son might come to moral harm through his classical reading, which told inter alia of 'the filthy loves of gods and goddesses'. Such alarms prompted the assembly of a multitude of school selections and anthologies, and also of bowdlerized editions of the Classics. At school, Byron used the Delphin edition of Martial which was fatally torn between the demands of scholarship and pedagogy. The obscene lines were removed from the text, only to be collected in an appendix at the back of the book.

The tensions between scholarly accuracy and completeness, on the one hand, and pedagogic and parental concerns for morality, on the other, can be found throughout the century. Some authors were trickier than others.[25] Editions of Juvenal might omit altogether the three most embarrassing satires, but most of the others had obscene lines. The keen pupil could easily find where cuts had been made, since the even march of line numbers down the side of the page was abruptly disturbed by excisions. The search for a large edition without cuts was then the obvious next step. Aristophanes presented an interesting problem: he was obscene at times, but politically conservative. This endeared him to the right-wing scholars of the 1830s, some of whom saw the teaching of Classics as a bulwark against religious and political liberalism.[26]

---

[24] Presumably the translation of 'war' as 'bellus' rather than the correct 'bellum' was equated with a lack of patriotism by the master.

[25] For bowdlerizations of classical texts, see Dover 1980; Harrison and Stray 2011.

[26] For example, Christopher Wordsworth: see 1989.

In the earlier decades of the nineteenth century the timetable of the lower forms in large public schools was dominated by the 'gerund grind'[27] the teaching of Latin grammar; followed by the composition of 'nonsense', verses which were required only to scan metrically, not to make sense.[28] Much of pupils' time at the public schools was spent learning verses by heart. For those who went on to become scholars, this will have provided a large memorized corpus which could be drawn on in teaching and research. There are well-documented examples of enormous feats of memory in this area. But for the great majority of boys, what stayed in the memory was likely to be no more than a few tags and some climactic or succinct lines. In the 1860s an anonymous magazine writer claimed that though Old Etonians were fond of quoting Virgil in the House of Commons, all the quoted lines came from Book I of the Aeneid.[29] In many cases, however, quoted lines may have been remembered not from the original text, but from a grammar in which they were used as examples.

The texts of the great Victorian novelists abound in direct classical quotations, as well as oblique references and passages which might hint at Latin, less often Greek, originals. The case of Trollope is an interesting one. He had been scorned at Harrow as a boy—his father ran out of money, and young Anthony was remembered as clumsy, dirty, and subsisting partly on charity. In young adulthood, however, Trollope taught himself Latin, drew on Cicero's moral philosophy in his writings and later wrote a book on Caesar.[30] David Skilton has drawn attention to Trollope's use of classical quotations, some of which come from the Eton grammar (Skilton 1988). In the case of *Framley Parsonage*, several chapter headings can be traced to two facing pages of the grammar: the section on the primary concords. This use of the grammar's examples raises the possibility that some writers, having carried such quotations in their memory since schooldays, used them to construct themes, even plots, for their novels. One might even speculate that the notion of 'primary concords' itself could have stimulated plot construction.

In a rather different way, some other sections of the grammar were drawn on by children and adults. The first line of the verses 'on the gender of nouns', 'propria quae maribus tribuuntur mascula dicas', stayed in many memories, the section being commonly known as 'propria quae maribus'.[31] Similarly a later section 'Of heteroclite

---

[27] The evidence in the first edition of *OED* suggests that the phrase 'gerund grind' gave way to 'grammar grind' during the 1890s; the latest citation of the former is from 1887, the only citation of the latter from 1898. The relevant fascicles were completed in March 1899 and July 1900 respectively. The articles have not been fully revised, but the *OED* files now contain citations for 'grammar-grind' from 1848, as Edmund Weiner kindly informs me.

[28] This was followed in turn by 'sense', in which the verses were required to make sense as well as to scan. Hence the names of two successive forms at Eton: 'Nonsense' and 'Sense': Clarke 1959, 56. At St Paul's in the 1870s, 'nonsense' verses were still being written in the middle forms: Brown 1911, 27. The nonsense-sense sequence dates back to the Roman Empire: see e.g. Gehl 1993, 86–7.

[29] 'Eton quotations', *Academia*, 22 January 1868, 93.

[30] The importance of Cicero for Trollope was emphasized by Ruth ap Roberts (ap Roberts 1971, 58–71). For Trollope and Classics, see Jones 1944, Tracy 1982.

[31] Chilton Mewburn, who had been at St Paul's in the 1840s, reported in 1910 that he could still remember that line, but added that he 'could reel off far more of the Comic Latin Grammar which appeared about that time'. The lines he quotes from this latter source are macaronic, e.g. 'Omnes drownderunt qui swim away non potuerunt'. Mewburn 1911, 10–11.

nouns', beginning with the line 'Quae genus aut flexum variant, quaecunque novato', was known as 'Quae genus'. The phrase was familiar enough to be used by William Combe in his Dr Syntax story 'The history of Johnny Quae Genus, the little foundling of the late Dr. Syntax' (1822). Schoolboys too made use of it; at the Yorkshire school reputed to be the original of Dotheboys Hall, this verse was current in the early nineteenth century:

> Propria quae maribus had a little dog
> Quae genus was its name;
> Propria quae maribus piddled in the entry,
> Quae genus bore the blame.[32]

The basic verbal forms chanted by generations of children could also be used as a kind of macaronic armature, as in the well-known song from John O'Keeffe's comic opera *The Agreeable Surprise*:

> Amo, amas, I loved a lass,
> As a cedar tall and slender;
> Sweet cowslip's grace
> Is her nominative case,
> And she's of the feminine gender.
>> Rorum, corum, sunt Divorum!
>> Harum scarum, Divo!—
>> Tag rag, merry derry, periwig and hatband!
>> Hic hoc horum Genitivo! [33]

Later versions offer an interesting reflection of changing knowledge and awareness:

> Amas, amat
> I laid her flat
> And found out her feminine gender (*c.*1885).
> Amo, amas, I loved a lass
> And she was tall and slender
> Amo, amat, I laid her flat
> And squashed her big suspender. (1956) [34]

Here the change from 'gender' to 'suspender' perhaps indicates not only an increased boldness of reference to underwear, but also the marginalization of the formal grammar teaching which lay at the heart of the traditional 'fortifying curriculum'.

The macaronic element in the verses quoted above reminds us that the relationship between Latin and the vernacular is likely to be crucial to the way pupils make sense of the former. Around the middle of the nineteenth century the use of English in classical textbooks became increasingly common. In part this sprang from the earlier growth of a working-class readership, and then from the expansion of middle-class or 'English'

---

[32] See *Notes and Queries*, 5th ser. iii (1875), 325/2.
[33] J. O'Keeffe, *The Agreeable Surprise* (1782), II. ii.
[34] These two variants were kindly sent me by the late Iona Opie.

education in the 1840s. The latter brought in its wake the local examinations of the 1850s, the first of a series of organized examinations which led to the standardization of the format of school books. At much the same time, the growth of comparative philology led to the work of Anglo-Saxon scholars like Kemble, Thorpe, and Donne (Frantzen 1990). English was becoming respectable, but still carried a dual connotation of inferiority. Its literature was widely seen as a female pursuit, its language as anarchic—lacking the formal rigour of Latin—and as 'common'. Uniting the Englishman against the foreigner, it also, to the regret of some, potentially united Englishmen of different classes. Here Latin, and even more Greek, offered a symbol of distinction which English was not to acquire until the canonization of the received pronunciation gave it an internal hierarchy (Crowley 1989).

The other change which powerfully affected the role of 'contrary imaginations' was the growth of a developmental notion of learning. This undercut the assumptions of totalized rote learning by viewing the (gradually emerging) nature of the individual child as a central focus of pedagogic attention. Early signs of this approach can be seen in the publications of Mrs Barbauld and Lady Fenn.[35] In the series publishing which became common in the expanding textbook market from the later 1830s, the peda- gogical notion of developmental sequence reinforced the marketing advantages of the graded series. The connection was clear in the marketing of the books of Thomas Kerchever Arnold, author of what later became 'Bradley's Arnold', whose advertise- ments listed his many books in the order in which a pupil might use them.[36] In the first half of the twentieth century, developmentalism persisted in an uneasy tension with a stubbornly maintained ideology of mental discipline in Latin textbooks. The possibility that learning Latin could be fun was systematically explored only at the margins of conventional schooling.[37]

The dissemination of doctrines of child psychology and teaching method in the late nineteenth century coincided with the separation of 'don' and 'beak'; the fission of the previously unitary world of university and public school teachers. From the early 1880s university reforms permitted men to hold fellowships and marry, and one result was the cessation of the movement of gifted scholars to schools which had begun in the 1850s. The learned schoolmasters of the turn of the century—men like Thomas Ethelbert Page of Charterhouse, Edward Austen Leigh of Eton, and Edmund Morshead

[35] A. L. Barbauld, *Lessons for Children* (London: J. Johnson, 1778–89), which appeared in four graded parts; E. Fenn ('Mrs Teachwell'), *Cobwebs to Catch Flies, or Dialogues in Short Sentences Adapted to Children from the Age of Three to Eight Years* (London: J. Marshall, 1783).

[36] For example, the list of Arnold's 'classical works' at the back of his *Gradus ad Parnassum novus anticlepticus* (London: Rivington, 1852), 'Arranged under Numbers for Progressive Translation'. 'Bradley's Arnold', one of the best-known classical textbooks of the period, is a revised version by G. G. Bradley (1881) of Arnold's *A Practical Introduction to Latin Prose Composition* (London: Rivington, Part 1, 1839; Part 2, 1843).

[37] The major campaign to attack the 'grammar grand' was that of W. H. D. Rouse, the prophet of direct method teaching in Classics (1992). Well known, but little used in schools, was Mrs Frankenburg's *Latin with Laughter* (Frankenburg 1931). The tension between discipline and developmentalism is evident in the introductory essay 'On learning Latin' in G. M. Lyne's *Balbus* (Lyne 1934), quoted in Chapter 14.

of Winchester—were the last of their breed. In some cases, we may suspect that eccentricity was cultivated as a protest against the growing routinization and stand-ardization of the teacher's task.[38]

The 'famous schoolmaster' of the period, quoted above, is only one of a whole range of teachers described and constructed by pupils to make sense of their school experi-ence. Some of these are anonymous, or are given fictional names, for several different reasons. In a lecture on the teaching of Latin given in the 1880s, Edwin Abbott, the liberal headmaster of City of London School, often quotes a schoolmaster of his acquaintance whom he calls simply 'Praeceptor'. In fact, as can be seen from a compari-son with Abbott's other publications, 'Praeceptor' is Abbott himself.[39] A schoolmaster who was much fictionalized was Horace Elam of St Paul's School, a genuine eccentric who seems to have combined a commitment to the classical literature he taught with a cynical despair at both pupils and textbooks. In Compton Mackenzie's *Sinister Street* (1913), he appears as Mr Neech; lightly disguised, his name provides the tide of Ernest Raymond's semi-autobiographical novel *Mr Olim*. Raymond tells how Elam ordered his form to open a 'battered green book' at any page: 'they are all as bad as each other'. For 'Olim' the instructional layout and format of the book fatally obstructed the pupil's access to the power and beauty of classical literature. He adds that 'Olim' wrote his own book on composition, but that no publisher would accept it.[40] In one case, the school-master/author appeared, remarkably, to be indistinguishable from his textbooks. This was the famous Dr (later Sir) William Smith, whose Principia Latina series was among the most widely used of the later Victorian decades. A. B. Piddington, who had used them, remembered both man and books, as we saw in Chapter 9. The recollections of Benjamin Kennedy's pupils agree in emphasizing another kind of identification, that of their teacher with his subject: 'He is not merely translating Demosthenes: he is Demosthenes speaking extempore in English.' This was the Victorian schoolmaster seen as a powerful natural force; in Kennedy's case, the power being the complement of a notable lack of method and judgement. The intensity of his identification with classical authors stemmed in part from his own naivety.[41]

To add to the boredom and grinding routine of the British classroom between the wars, textbooks were still being produced which took for granted a generous time allotment and which saw little value in any aspect of learning Latin except the gram-matical grind which led to mental discipline. A representative series was *Macmillan's*

---

[38] Morshead's speech mannerisms were recorded in the several editions of the *Mushri-English Pronouncing Dictionary*, printed between 1879 and 1901 and edited by his pupils C. D. Locock and F. W. Montagu. See Stray 1995b, and the discussion in Chapter 12.

[39] Abbott 1884. Abbott is remembered today as the author of *Flatland* (also 1884), issued under a pseudonym ('A Square'). Because of this, and his full name (Edwin Abbott Abbott), Abbott is referred to by some of his modern admirers as 'EA²'.

[40] Cf. Mackenzie 1963, 103–8; Raymond 1961). The 'battered green book' was 'Bradley's Arnold' (n. 36 above).

[41] Heitland 1889, 10. His naivety, attested to by several stories, is kindly described in Heitland's memoirs as 'a simplicity truly child-like': Heitland 1926, 98.

Latin Course, written by A. M. Cook and W. E. Pantin of St Paul's School. A one-volume version was denounced, along with its rival, Bell's *Concise Latin course*, by a practising teacher who had tried both: 'these are very similar in some points. Neither has any illustrations. I disliked both books intensely. The majority of the boys found little inspiration in them and I was not satisfied until I got rid of them.'[42] The expectation of illustrations is a notable feature of this complaint. It reflects not only the influence of developmentalism, but also the broadening of ideas of Classics beyond the purely linguistic: from Latin to Roman, from text to historical context.

These broader conceptions, however, rarely penetrated the recesses of preparatory schools, the last redoubts of disciplinary Latin teaching. Here the grammar grind persisted, and pupils responded by making their own, contrary, sense of Latin, its text-books, and their authors. Given the marginalization of literary by linguistic teaching, it is ironic that a common strategy was to accord literary status to the memorial sections of grammars. The best known example is provided by the memorial rhymes of Kennedy's *Public School Latin Primer* of 1866 and its successor, the *Revised Latin Primer* of 1888. Thomas Thornely, writing in the 1930s, remembered them from his Uppingham schooldays and compared them favourably with modem poetry:

Who would presume to attach a definite meaning to a good deal of modem verse, that yet falls as pleasantly on the ear as the sound of leaping waters? And whose heart has not been stirred in early youth by the solemn chant of the Latin prepositions that govern the ablative?

> A, ab, abaque, coram de,
> Palans, clam, cum ex et e,
> Tenus, sine, pro et prae.

In this meaningless collocation of syllables we seem to hear the low rumbling thunder of the 'Dies Irae', and are naturally led to contrast it with the light tripping of the banded prepositions that favour the accusative.   (Thornely 1936, 157)

Note that the 'meaning' the verses have for Thornely is purely a function of the chanted sound. Others, too, carried in memory into old age the verses they used to chant in unison. Frank Jones, at one time an advocate of direct method teaching of Latin, remarked caustically that an ex-public schoolboy of his acquaintance 'always signal-izes the attainment of a certain stage of intoxication by reciting the gender rhymes he learnt at school. It restores his self esteem' (Jones 1924, 97). Edward Hornby, who was at Winchester at the end of the First World War, remarks of Kennedy's gender rhymes that 'These little gems of poetry have remained in my head for the last 67 years'. He goes on in a way which recalls Thornely's comments on meaninglessness:

The verses fall into two categories, those basically in English are rules; they are interesting but seem to mean little, I will give you an example.

---

[42]   F. S. Fothergill, 'Latin in the secondary school', MEd. thesis, University of Durham, 1934, 107. When he wrote this, Fothergill had been teaching for nine years at Darlington Grammar School.

> Third Nouns Masculine prefer
> endings o, or, os and er;
> add to which the ending es,
> if its Cases have increase.

Not great stuff you may say but listen to the mellifluous tones of some of the Exceptions.

> many neuters end in er,
> siler acer, verber, ver
> tuber, uber and cadaver
> piper, iter and papaver.

My favourite excerpt is this. A Rule followed by some beautiful poetry.

> Third Nouns Feminine we class
> ending is, x, aus, and as,
> s to consonant appended,
> es in flexion unextended

We used to commit these to memory...while queuing to go to the...lav after breakfast...
We chanted them to the tune of Hymn No. 520, 'Love Divine All Loves Excelling'.[43]

Kennedy's primers became an institution, regarded by several generations of school-children with a mixture of loathing and affection. The *Shorter Latin Primer* was often transformed by graffito into the Shortbread Eating Primer, in a tradition of what could grandiosely be labelled 'symbolic appropriation'.[44] The most famous nineteenth-century practitioner was that indefatigable [extra-]illustrator William Thackeray (Figure 18.1). In his 'De juventute', Thackeray recalls how he and his friends at Charterhouse in the 1820s used to draw pictures on the pages of the Latin grammar.[45]

A rather different kind of illustration is given in Ronald Searle's drawings, his contribution to Geoffrey Willans's Molesworth books (see e.g. Willans 1953). Based on a series of *Punch* articles and set in the world of the 1930s prep school, these portray a classroom situation in which pupils do not expect Latin to make ordinary sense. The attitude toward the adult world is very much what Dover recalls from the period in his discussion of expurgation: 'When I was at school in the 1930s we all regarded expurgation as one of the many foolish things done by grown ups...It seemed to be part of the natural order...we treated it with amused tolerance' (Dover 1988, 285). Latin was not the key to Roman

---

[43] Hornby 1985, 27–8. I have quoted this privately-printed memoir at some length since it is not easily accessible. Three hundred copies of this and of its predecessor, *The Adventures of Edward Hornby* (1954), were printed as Christmas gifts for the author's friends. Edward Hornby kindly sent me a copy of the earlier volume and supplementary information.

[44] The reference to food may be linked with the extensive use of the 'Shorter' version of the *Primer* in girls' schools.

[45] 'De juventute' first appeared in the *Cornhill Magazine* in October 1860 (July–December 1860, 501–12); the illustration is on p. 508. It was clearly composed for the article, and looks nothing like the grammar Thackeray would have used as a boy, the book written by his headmaster John Russell for the monitorial system then in force at Charterhouse. Catherine Peters is thus wrong to label it a 'Charterhouse drawing' (Peters 1987, 17). *Thaddeus of Warsaw*, a novel by Jane Porter, first appeared in 1803; Sir Aylmer de Vallence (d. 1309) was Earl of Pembroke.

for my own part, but I don't like to mention the *real* figure for fear of
perverting the present generation of boys by my monstrous confession)—
we may have eaten too much, I say. We did; but what then? The
school apothecary was sent for: a couple of small globules at night, a
trifling preparation of senna in the morning, and we had not to go to
school, so that the draught was an actual pleasure.

For our amusements, besides the games in vogue, which were pretty
much in old times as they are now (except cricket, *par exemple*—and
I wish the present youth joy of their bowling, and suppose Armstrong
and Whitworth will bowl at them with light field-pieces next), there
were novels—ah! I trouble you to find such novels in the present day!
O Scottish Chiefs, didn't we weep over you! O Mysteries of Udolfo,
didn't I and Briggs minor draw pictures out of you, as I have said? This
was the sort of thing: this was the fashion in *our* day:—

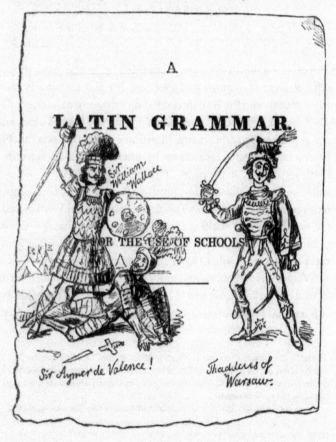

Figure 18.1 William Thackeray, 'Roundabout Papers no.VIII', from the *Cornhill Magazine*,
October 1860, p. 508. The image, drawn by Thackeray himself, does not correspond to any
particular primer.

literature and civilization, but a world in itself. To pupils, 'the Latin language...existed to provide Subjunctives, and Past Participles, and (oh golly!) Gerunds'.[46] The gerund, the feature of Latin most remote from English usage, is also singled out for attention, and invention, by Willans.[47] In Searle's drawings it becomes an exotic creature, brought within the constraining rules of Latin grammar by Benjamin Kennedy, who is portrayed in hunting gear.[48]

Yet though the proponents of mental discipline saw Latin as pre-eminently orderly, many pupils, as I have suggested, found in it a disorderly arbitrariness which prompted them to reorder it in their own, contrary, fashion. Both this attitude and the personification of Latin words to which it gave rise are caught in Carol Rumens's poem 'A Latin primer: for Kelsey', which I quoted earlier (p. 256):

> Today, a new slave,
> you must fetch and carry, obeying
> plump nouns, obstreperous verbs
> whose endings vacillate
> like the moods of tyrants.
>
> (Rumens 1987, 36)

At the end of the 1950s, the compulsory Latin requirement at Oxford and Cambridge was abolished, and recruitment to Ordinary Level examinations immediately began to fall. Among the responses to this situation was the creation of a curriculum project whose remit was to construct a new O-level course for the post-compulsory world of Latin. One of the major premises of this project was that the ordinary sense made by pupils should be built into the teaching material itself. What was eventually produced was thus not a textbook, but a series of brightly-coloured booklets. Each contained a narrative, illustrated with line drawings, while formal grammar was banned. The introductory booklet led the reader into the world of ancient Pompeii, where the everyday life of a family was followed.[49]

This new kind of material reversed all the traditional expectations of what teaching material was like. It was visually attractive and appealed to pupil interests. Instead of presenting a dull authoritarian face on which the pupil might draw a subversive cartoon or graffito, it provided its own drawings, as well as quoting Pompeian graffiti. Instead of asserting, through page after page of dull print and serried tables of linguistic forms, that Latin was hard to learn and remote from ordinary experience, it suggested that Latin might be easy to learn, and something embedded in Roman

[46] L. Hale, *A Fleece of Lambs* (London: J. Cape, 1961), 38. As the use of 'golly' suggests, this novel is set in a girls' school.
[47] Molesworth first appeared in *Punch* on 9 August 1939; even more popular was Jefferson Farjeon's Smith Minor, who first saw the light there on 10 July 1940. Another series of the kind was H. P. Ellis's 'Assistant masters: are they insane?', begun on 30 November 1938 (Price 1957, 270). The genre has not been taken seriously by writers on school-based fiction; an account might begin with Smith Minor's eponymous ancestor, at school in 1884, whose letters are printed in Maurice Baring's *Lost Diaries* (Baring 1913).
[48] It has proved impossible to reproduce Ronald Searle's drawing here; it can be found in 1994b, 218, and in Searle and Willans' *The Compleet Molesworth* (London: Max Parrish, 1958), 136 (or Willans 1953).
[49] This was the course used by Carol Rumens's daughter Kelsey.

experience. In short, it substituted an alien everyday for the everyday alienness of Latin grammar (Forrest 1996; 1998a, 296). In so doing, it presented the language as something which made ordinary sense, and brought to an end a long history of contrary imaginings. Latin would never smell the same again.

Ghosts in the Classroom: Kennedy's Latin Primer in Britten's *The Turn of the Screw*

By the time Molesworth had burst into print, the *Revised Latin Primer* had already appeared in an even more distinguished setting: at the Aldeburgh Festival in 1954, in the British premiere of Benjamin Britten's mysterious opera *The Turn of the Screw*.[50] The opera features not only Kennedy's gender rhymes, but also the teaching rhyme designed to distinguish between several words which are spelled the same but pronounced differently (2001c).

Malo: I would rather be	mālo (v) *I prefer*
Malo: in an apple-tree	mālum (n) *apple tree*
Malo: than a naughty boy	mălus (adj) *bad*
Malo: in adversity.	(ditto)

My focus here, however, is on the use Britten and his librettist Myfanwy Piper made of a gender rhyme from Kennedy's *Primer*.

It is not often that textbooks feature in opera. The only example I know of apart from the *Turn of the Screw* is Ravel's *L'Enfant et les Sortilèges* (1925), in which the contents of his room turn against a naughty boy. Among them is his mathematics textbook, which sings, 'If one tap takes x minutes to fill a bath, how long will two taps…' and so on. If we were to look for further examples, the obvious starting point would be to find operas which include scenes in the schoolroom, as does *The Turn of the Screw*. The plot is based on a story of the same title by Henry James, published in 1898.[51] The plot is simple: a governess is hired to teach a brother and sister in a remote country house in East Anglia. It gradually emerges that a previous governess, Miss Jessel, had been seduced by the manservant, Peter Quint. Both are now dead and their ghosts appear to haunt the house, as well as having the two children, Miles and Flora, under their spell. The housekeeper takes Flora away to safety; the governess tries in vain to save Miles from Peter Quint. At the end of the opera Miles dies and the governess laments her failure to save him. Both James's original story and Britten's opera have been much discussed. A particular focus of debate has been the question of whether Peter Quint and Miss Jessel are real in the story, or just imagined by the children.[52]

[50] The opera had been premiered early that year at the Fenice Theatre in Venice.

[51] James in turn claimed to have taken the plot from a story told him by Edward Benson, Archbishop of Canterbury; it has however been suggested that he had some of Freud's writings in mind, or that he was thinking of his mentally disturbed sister Alice.

[52] For detailed discussions of both James's story and Britten's opera, see P. Howard (ed.) *Benjamin Britten: The Turn of the Screw*, Cambridge, 1985.

After her arrival, the new governess puts Miles and Flora through their paces in the schoolroom. Their treatment faithfully reflects both the overall stress on memorization and the characteristically gendered curriculum of the nineteenth-century schoolroom: Flora is tested on her geography, while Miles is asked about Latin. As Scene 6, The Lesson, opens, we hear Miles singing a gender rhyme from Kennedy's *Latin Primer*:

> Many nouns in *is* we find
> To the masculine are assigned:
> Amnis, axis, caulis, collis,
> Clunis, crinis, fascis, follis,
> Fustis, ignis, orbis, ensis,
> Panis, piscis, postis, mensis,
> Torris, unguis, and canalis,
> Vectis, vermis, and natalis,
> Sanguis, pulvis, cucumis,
> Lapis, casses, manes, glis…

What is going on? Most obviously, the kind of schooling one might expect in a private schoolroom in the 1890s (James's story was published in 1898). Indeed, one could have found this kind of memorizing all over Europe in the nineteenth century; the story of Max Schneidewin has been told in Chapter 12.

Miles is tested on Latin; his sister mostly on geography—lakes and rivers, capes and bays. But the children's names suggests that there is something deeper going on. Miles and Flora are Latin nouns: soldier and flower. Or one might think of them as M and F: masculine and feminine. This is an opera which encourages speculation—and also includes it. Early on it becomes clear that Miles has been expelled from his former school, for some unnamed, or unnameable, offence. The implication is that some kind of moral corruption is suspected. Gradually, the sunny innocence of the classroom scenes takes on a different meaning, as the ghosts of Peter Quint and Miss Jessel appear; as innocence comes to be seen as only apparent, it is redefined as a cover for something nasty in the woodshed.

The point of James's story is that it is radically undecidable: there is no way, for example, of establishing if the ghosts are really there. This is one of the problems in producing the opera—it is too easy to make the ghosts real or unreal, rather than leaving the question open. In Britten's case, however, we can look behind the scenes by considering the drafting of the libretto, which was written by Myfanwy Piper.[53] Several drafts are preserved in the Britten–Pears Library, and they tell a curious tale. Britten wanted Miles to have a simple song which would run through the opera as a kind of leitmotiv. Piper's early drafts all feature a song which she herself thought the best thing she had written for the opera:

> O say I am a fool
> and a fool is a knave

[53] Myfanwy Piper's libretto drafts are quoted by kind permission of her daughter, Mrs Clarissa Lewis.

> O say I am a fool
> and a fool is not a knave
> but I am a Daniel and a Lion too
> My mother laid three brown eggs
> and one was white and round
> she dropped them from her handkerchief
> she had so far to go

Flora had a related song:

> My mother laid three pigeon eggs
> and one was white as snow
> she dropped them from her handkerchief
> she had so far to go.
> The first one fell down, down, down
> The second one was me
> But the one that was as white as snow
> grew into a lilac tree

These persist through the early drafts, but then Piper writes in her notebook:

I'd like if possible some kind of repetition—of the fool song. I think it is the only good thing I have written so far and cling to it a bit because it expresses for me the particular odd musical old-fashioned imaginativeness, bible-knowledge and poetry that such a small boy might have had. But there easily might be something far better. The things one clings to are usually terrible stumbling blocks.

An example of a stumbling block, perhaps, is this early draft for the Prologue, cast as a dialogue for three male and two female voices:

> Imagine it, a child haunted
> Quite a turn of the screw
> What do you say to two children?
> Two turns of the screw of course.

Here Piper adds in manuscript, 'Worse and worse'. When I first read this, I thought it might be her comment on the way the libretto was going: in fact it comes from the opening of Henry James's original story. A little earlier, she had inserted in the schoolroom scene a passage where the governess recites the mnemonic 'A ab asque / Coram de', and then 'Mensa, mensam, mensae, mensa'. She then gets Miles to repeat all this. But evidently Piper had second thoughts, for this whole passage is struck through.

The fair copy of the libretto, with which Myfanwy Piper's file ends, does not include either of the songs I quoted, but the gender rhyme has appeared. How did it get there? It seems that it was suggested by Britten, who borrowed a copy of Kennedy's *Shorter Latin Primer* from a local boy, Richard Kihl, who had used it at Sizewell Hall School near Aldeburgh. The book is still in Britten's library, and there is a pencil line next to the gender rhyme.[54] We don't know quite how Britten and Piper collaborated, except that they corresponded, and phoned each other to discuss drafts. So in a way the evidence is frustrating, as it shows in detail the earlier phases of the construction of a text which clearly changed significantly in its later phases.

The role of the *Primer* in the opera, then, is to provide a symbol of conventional masculine school learning. The choice of a gender rhyme can be explained by its being a rhyme, ready made for singing. The MALO rhyme also sung by Miles adds a layer of mystery, since it talks of apples and evil, and so hints at the Fall and original sin. Yet if we apply its surface message to Miles, it is clear that he prefers sitting in an apple tree (scrumping perhaps) to being naughty.

'Arseholes, scrotum, penis': The Gender Rhymes as Camp Semaphore?

Allowing for the built-in undecidability of the opera, this seems fairly straightforward. But a radical reinterpretation of the Latin was advanced in 2002 by Valentine Cunningham.[55] The heading will give some idea of its nature: 'O arsehole, scrotum, penis, bless ye the Lord': Valentine Cunningham reveals what the Latin bits in The Turn of the Screw really mean.'

Cunningham begins by declaring that:

Doubt and mystery are the very essence of this Jamesian venture into issues of child corruption, and they are central to Britten's version of it, so much so that Britten beefed up the mysteriousness by adding in the Latin sections, and never translating them into English.

It would however surely be very clumsy to add a translation—how would this be done on stage? It would also be atypical of the classroom context, in which as far as I know pupils would not have been expected to recite the English. Giving the English after each Latin word would also have disturbed the chanting rhythm.

Cunningham continues:

What is startling is that these passages have never been properly decrypted in the whole course of the Britten Screw's history. The army of Britten scholars and musicologists has kept them at arm's length. Even those many music historians eager to demystify Britten's life in his works, and uncover the homosexual narrative at their heart, have lacked curiosity about what is actually being sung at these textually darkened moments. They have left their Latin dictionaries in Britten's closet.

---

[54] Kieron Clarke, of the Britten–Pears Library, informed me that the pencil line is typical of Britten's marking of printed texts. Richard Kihl remarked to me, 'Ben never did return the book'.

[55] Cunningham's article nn (in the *Guardian* of 5 January 2002) was published to coincide with a production of the opera at Covent Garden.

Quoting (not always accurately) the gender rhyme, he goes on to claim that:

Clunis is anus, arsehole (its plural, clunes, means buttocks). Caulis (cabbage stalk) was Latin slang for a penis, follis (bellows, punch bag) slang for scrotum, vectis (crowbar) a low term for penis, cucumis (cucumber) another jokily penile term. And the list goes on, packed with suggestive phallic objects: fascis (bunch of sticks), fustis (knobbed stick); ensis (sword), torris (firebrand), canalis (water pipe). The diminutive of vermis (worm) was vermiculus, another slang term for penis.

In advancing this interpretation, Cunningham was relying on the standard work on this subject, J. N. Adams's *The Latin Sexual Vocabulary* (Adams 1982). But a check on the words he cites in that book reveals that the evidence of sexual connotations is either very rare indeed or non-existent. This is not, however, the only point to consider: we also have to ask, was Britten aware that they might exist? Of his classical schooling we only know that he was not all that good—in the third form he was bottom of a form of nine, and was scared of Latin unseens. Cunningham goes on to claim that:

Britten... was knowingly signalling to his gay friends, men like W. H. Auden, who had all been through the Kennedy mill and many of whom, like Auden, had taught in boys' schools.

Now Auden was fond of word play, and liked using rare English words, but I know of no evidence that he knew of any sexual connotations in Latin. The standard Latin dictionary for Auden and Britten, as it was for Kennedy, was that of Lewis and Short, in which none of Cunningham's proposed sexual meanings can be found.[56]

But even more is to come: not only was Britten a homosexual who delighted in inserting secret messages in his writing, so was Benjamin Kennedy. According to Cunningham:

These glosses are Kennedy's cover, as well as extending his coy jesting... Kennedy was playing schoolmaster funnies, a camp semaphore to other Latin masters in the linguistic know, and not least to the many boy-fanciers among them (they were always getting sacked for paedophiliac excesses). The allusiveness, just safe enough, was cannily endorsed by Britten.

After reading just about everything Kennedy wrote, going through surviving papers and discussing him with his great-grand daughter for nearly twenty years, I have come across no evidence which would support Cunningham's claim. The word clunis (buttock) is translated 'hind-leg' in the gender rhymes, a typical piece of Victorian prudery. 'Haunch' would have done perfectly well, and indeed is used in the main body of the book's text (the rhymes are tucked away at the back). I conclude that Cunningham's view of Kennedy (for which no evidence is offered) is simply wrong. The fact is that Kennedy was listing words ending in -is which were third-declension masculines (a large minority of the hundred or so third-declension nouns in Latin). The nature of the Latin language is independent of ideological agendas, whether Kennedy's, Britten's,

[56] C. T. Lewis and C. Short *A Latin Dictionary...*, OUP 1879; now superseded by the *Oxford Latin Dictionary*, which appeared in eight fascicles from 1968 to 1982, when it was published as a single volume.

or Cunningham's. And though we all doubtless all have our agendas, this does not excuse the promulgation of views for which there is no evidence.[57] Cunningham's own agenda was the fashionable one of looking for a gay subtext. But as Britten's biographer Donald Mitchell has reminded me, Britten and Pears were extremely nervous at the prospect of any publicity in this area. Homosexual allusion is something they would have tried to avoid.

Back to the text: can we learn anything from the order in which the words are given? To begin with, it is clear that Kennedy tries to combine two principles to make the lines memorable: alphabetical order and rhyme. In the first two lines he manages to combine them; after that, rhyme takes over and words out of alphabetical order are inserted. The last line ends with three marginal words: *casses* and *Manes* are only found in the plural, and *glis*, dormouse, doesn't really belong here, since the I is long. I assume that Kennedy simply wanted to fill up the line.[58]

I have been referring to 'Kennedy': but we need to remember that the Revised and Shorter Primers were largely written by Kennedy's daughters (Chapter 17): and this should remind us that Cunningham, who is so keen to expose a gay underworld of persecuted men, ignores the role of women. Both Benjamins, Kennedy and Britten, worked with women on their texts. Cunningham's article is a good example of what happens if one allows oneself to be hijacked by a fashionable theory. He mentions, for example, that Henry James called *The Turn of the Screw* a 'queer story'. The implication is that James was signalling its homosexual implications. But this was in the 1890s, and *OED* has no examples of the use of 'queer' in this sense before 1914. The evidence offered above also shows that texts do not just belong to history: they have their own histories of construction and development. The story of the development of the libretto of *The Turn of the Screw* shows us a text in progress: at first quite gradually, then with a leap which remains, for now, in the dark. Appropriate, perhaps, for a ghost story.

---

[57] When I inspected Myfanwy Piper's libretto drafts in the Britten–Pears Library at Aldeburgh, I was told that I was the first to do so. I assume therefore that Cunningham did not look at them.

[58] His *Public School Latin Primer* of 1866 has 'lapis, sanguis, cucumis / Pulvis, casses, manes, glis'. There is no obvious reason for the alteration of order.

Bibliography

Aarsleff, H. (1967) *The Study of Language in England, 1780–1860*, Princeton.

Aarsleff, H. (1971) 'Locke's Reputation in Nineteenth-Century England', *The Monist* 55: 392–422.

Abbott, E. and Campbell, L. (1897) *Life and Letters of Benjamin Jowett*, 2 vols, London.

Abbott, E. A. (1884) *The Teaching of Latin*, London.

Ackerman, R. A. (1969) 'The Cambridge Group and the origins of myth criticism', PhD, Columbia University.

Ackerman, R. A. (1971) 'Some letters of the Cambridge Ritualists', *Greek, Roman and Byzantine Studies* 12: 113–36.

Ackerman, R. A. (2007) 'The Cambridge Ritualists', *ODNB* online.

Adams, J. N. (1982) *The Latin Sexual Vocabulary*, London.

Allan, D. (2010) *Commonplace Books and Reading in Georgian England*, Cambridge.

Allen, C. G. (1954) 'The sources of "Lily's Latin Grammar": a review of the facts and some further suggestions', *The Library*, 5th ser. 9: 85–100.

Allen, C. G. (1959) 'Certayne Briefe Rules and "Lily's Latin Grammar"', *The Library*, 5th ser. 14: 49–53.

Allen, W. S. and Brink, C. O. (1980) 'The old order and the new. A case history', *Lingua* 50: 61–100.

Anderson, R. D. (2004) *European Universities from the Enlightenment to 1914*, Oxford.

Anderson, W. D. (1975) 'Arnold and the Classics', in *Matthew Arnold*, ed. K. Allott, London, 259–85.

Andrews, E. A. (1850) *A Copious and Critical Latin-English Lexicon, Founded on the Larger Latin-German Dictionary of Dr Wilhelm Freund*, London.

Annan, N. G. (1999) *The Dons*, London.

Anon. (1843) 'Kenrick's Egypt of Herodotus', *Eclectic Review* ns 14: 431–43.

Anon. (1845) 'Extracts from the Portfolio of a Man of the World', *Gentleman's Magazine* 24 ns (October), 336–8.

Anon. (1850) 'University reform – Cambridge', *Fraser's Magazine* 41: 617–29.

Anon. (1851) 'Smith's dictionaries of antiquities and biography', *Gentleman's Magazine* 34 ns: 619–27.

Anon. (1952) 'Dean Gaisford and the Meerman Collection', *Bodleian Library Record* 4: 7–8.

ap Roberts, R. (1971) *Trollope, Artist and Moralist*, London.

[Appleyard, E. S.] (1828) *Letters from Cambridge, Illustrative of the Studies, Habits and Peculiarities of the University*, London.

Archer, M. S. (1983) 'Process without system', *European Journal of Sociology* 24: 196–221.

Archer, M. S. (1988) *Culture and Agency: The Place of Culture in Social Theory*, Cambridge.

Armstrong, J. A. (1973) *The European Administrative Elite*, Princeton.

Arnold, E. V. (1910) *Considerations on the Report of the Joint Committee on Grammatical Terminology*, Bangor.

Ashton, R. (1986) *Little Germany: Exile and Asylum in Victorian England*, Oxford.

Auden, W. H. (1976) 'Letter to Lord Byron', in *Collected Poems*, ed. E. Mendelson, London, 77–100.

Avlami, C. and Alvar, J. (eds) (2010) *Historiographie de l'antiquité et transferts culturels: Les histoires anciennes dans l'Europe des XVIIIe et XIXe siècles*, Amsterdam.

Babbage, C. (1864) *Passages from the Life of a Philosopher*, London.

Baertschi, A. and King, C. (eds) (2009) *Die modernen Väter der Antike. Die Entwicklung der Altertumswissenschaften in Akademie und Universität im Berlin des 19. Jahrhunderts*, Berlin.

Bainbridge, B. (1985) *Watson's Apology*, London.

Bake, J. (1839) *Scholica hypomnemata 2*, Leiden.

Baldick, C. (1983) *The Social Mission of English Criticism, 1848–1932*, Oxford.

Baring, M. (1913) *Lost Diaries*, London.

Barker, E. H. (1820) *Aristarchus Anti-Blomfieldianus*, London.

Barker, E. H. (1852) *Literary Anecdotes and Contemporary Reminiscences of Professor Porson and Others*, London.

Barker, N. (1992) *Aldus Manutius and the Development of Greek Script & Type in the Fifteenth Century*, 2nd edn, New York.

Barrell, J. (1983) *English Literature in History 1730–80: An Equal, Wide Survey*, London.

Barrow, J. (1829) 'Dr Granville's travels in Russia', *Quarterly Review* 39: 1–41.

Barrow, J. (1855) Obituary of Thomas Gaisford, *Literary Churchman*, 16 June 1855, repr. *Journal of Classical and Sacred Philology* 2 (Nov. 1855), 343–7.

Barton, R. (2006) 'The X Club (active 1864–92)', *ODNB* online.

Beard, M. (1999) 'The invention and reinvention of "Group D"', in Stray 1999, 95–134.

Beard, M. (2000) *The Invention of Jane Harrison*, Cambridge MA.

Beard, M. (2002) *The Parthenon*, London.

Beard, M. (2005) 'While RIDGEWAY lives, Research can ne'er be dull', in Stray 2005a, 111–41.

Beard, M. and Henderson, J. (1995) *Classics: A Very Short Introduction*, Oxford.

Beard, M., King, G., and Stray, C. A. (1998) *The Birds and the Bees: Women in Classics, Cambridge 1871–1948*, Cambridge.

Becker, H. and H. E. Barnes (1938) *Social Thought from Lore to Science*, Boston.

Beckman, L. H. (2000) *Amy Levy: Her Life and Letters*, Athens OH.

Beer, G. (2004) 'The *Academy*: Europe in England', in G. Cantor and S. Shuttleworth (eds), *Science Serialized: Representations of the Sciences in Nineteenth-century Periodicals*. Cambridge MA, 181–98.

Beerbohm, M. (1911) *Zuleika Dobson*, London .

Beerbohm, M. (1964) 'Carmen Becceriense, cum prolegomenis et commentario critico, edidit H. M. B.', in J. G. Riewald (ed.), *Max in Verse: Rhymes and Parodies*, London, 1–3.

Beetham, M. (1990) 'Towards a theory of the periodical as a publishing genre', in Brake et al. 1990, 19–32.

Bell, R. (1846) *Life of Rt. Hon. George Canning*, London.

Ben-Rafael, E. (1994) *Language, Identity and Social Division: The Case of Israel*, Oxford.

Bennett, S. (1976) 'John Murray's family library and the cheapening of books in nineteenth-century Britain', *Studies in Bibliography* 29: 139–66.

Bentley, E. C. (1937 [1913]) *Trent's Last Case*, Harmondsworth.

Berlinerblau, J. (1999) *Heresy in the University: The Black Athena Controversy and the Responsibilities of American Intellectuals*, New Brunswick, NJ.

Bernstein, B. (1971) 'On the classification and framing of educational knowledge', in Young, M. F. D. (ed.), *Knowledge and Control*, London, 47–69.

Beverley, R. M. (1833) *A letter to His Royal Highness the Duke of Gloucester, Chancellor, on the Present Corrupt State of the University of Cambridge*, London.

Bill, E. G. W. and Mason, J. F. A. (1970) *Christ Church and Reform 1850–1867*, Oxford.

Billings, J. (2015) *Genealogy of the Tragic: Greek Tragedy and German Philosophy*, Princeton.

Blair, A. M. (2010) *Too Much to Know: Managing Scholarly Information before the Modern Age*, New Haven and London.

Blomfield, C. J. ['BJC'] (1807–8) 'On the dancing of the ancients', *Athenaeum* 2: 597–601, 3: 511–14.

Blomfield, C. J. (1809–10) 'The Cambridge edition of Aeschylus', *Edinburgh Review* 15: 152–63, 315–22.

Blomfield, C. J. (1816) 'Monk's Alcestis', *Quarterly Review* 15: 112–25.

[Blomfield, C. J.] (1820) 'Stephens's Thesaurus', *Quarterly Review* 22: 302–48.

Bonnet, C., Krings, V., and Valenti, C. (2010) (eds), *Connaître l'Antiquité: individus, réseaux, stratégies du XVIIIe au XXIe siècle*, Rennes.

Booth, W. (1890) *In Darkest England and the Way Out*, London.

Boswell, J. (1927) *Life of Johnson*, Oxford.

Bowen, E. E. (1866) *The New National Grammar*, London.

Bowen, E. E. (1867) 'On teaching by means of grammar', in Farrar, F. W. (ed.), *Essays on a Liberal Education*, London, 179–204.

Bowman, J. H. (1992) *Greek Printing Types in Britain in the Nineteenth Century: A Catalogue*, London.

Bowman, J. H. (1998) *Greek Printing Types in Britain from the Late Eighteenth to the Early Twentieth Century*, Thessaloniki.

Breay, C. (1999) 'Women and the Classical Tripos 1869–1914', in Stray 1999, 49–70.

Briggs, W. W. (ed.) (1987) *The Letters of Basil Lanneau Gildersleeve*, Baltimore.

Briggs, W. W. (2015) 'B. L. Gildersleeve and the *American Journal of Philology*', in Stray and Whitaker 2015, 3–15.

Brink, C. O. (1986) *English Classical Scholarship: Historical Reflections on Bentley, Porson and Housman*, Cambridge.

Bristed, C. A. (2008 [1852]) *An American in Victorian Cambridge: Charles Astor Bristed's Five Years in an English University*, ed. C.A. Stray, Exeter.

Brock, M. G. (1997) 'The Oxford of Peel and Gladstone, 1800–1833', in Brock and Curthoys 1997, 7–71.

Brock, M. G. (2000) 'A "plastic structure"', in Brock and Curthoys 2000, 3–66.

Brock, M. G. and M. C. Curthoys (eds) (1997) *The History of the University of Oxford VI: Nineteenth-century Oxford, Part 1*, Oxford.

Brock, M. G. and M. C. Curthoys (eds) (2000) *The History of the University of Oxford VI: Nineteenth-century Oxford, Part 2*, Oxford.

Brockliss, L. W. B. (1997) 'The European university in the age of revolution, 1789–1850', in Brock and Curthoys 1997, 77–133.

Brooke, C. N. L. (1993) *History of the University of Cambridge, Vol IV: 1870–1990*, Cambridge.

Brown, R. P. (1911) 'The closing years of Dr Kynaston', in Gardiner, R. B. and Lupton, J. (eds) *Res Paulinae: The Eighth Half-Century of St Paul's School 1859–1909*, London, 21–34.

Bruni, F. and Pettegree, A. (eds) (2016) *Lost Books: Reconstructing the Print World of Pre-industrial Europe*, Leiden.

Bryant, M. (1986) *The London Experience of Secondary Education*, London.

Bullock, S. (1906) 'The Burden of the Middle Classes', *Fortnightly Review* 80 (ns): 411–20.

[Burges, G.] (1838–9) 'English scholarship, its rise, progress and decline', *Church of England Quarterly Review* 4: 91–125; 5: 145–75, 399–426.

[Burges, G.] (1840) 'The living lamps of learning', *Church of England Quarterly Review* 7: 84–106.

Burnett, A. (2007) (ed.), *The Letters of A. E. Housman*, 2 vols, Oxford.

Burns, A. and Stray, C. A. (2011) 'The Greek-play bishop: polemic, prosopography and nineteenth-century prelates', *Historical Journal* 54.4, 1013–38.

Burrow, J. W. (1967) 'The uses of philology in Victorian England', in R. Robson (ed.) *Ideas and institutions of Victorian Britain*, London, 180–204.

Butler, S. (1810) *A Letter to the Rev. C. J. Blomfield...containing Remarks on the Edinburgh Review of the Cambridge Aeschylus...*, Shrewsbury.

Butler, S. (1896) *The Life and Letters of Dr. Samuel Butler*, 2 vols, London.

Butler, S. (ed.) (2016) *Deep Classics: Rethinking Classical Reception*, London.

Butterfield, D. and Stray, C. A. (eds) (2009) *A. E. Housman: Classical Scholar*, London.

Calder, W. III (2002) 'Wilamowitz's correspondence with British colleagues', *Polis: The Journal of the Society for Greek Political Thought* 19.1–2: 125–43.

Cameron, D. (1995) *Verbal Hygiene*, London.

Campbell, L. (1901) *On the Nationalisation of the Old English Universities*, London.

Canfora, L. (1980) *Ideologie del classicismo*, Turin.

Carey, J. (1992) *The Intellectuals and the Masses: Pride and Prejudice among the Literary Intelligentsia 1880–1939*, London.

Carlisle, N. (1818) *A Concise Description of the Endowed Grammar Schools in England and Wales*, London.

Chadwick, J. (1958) *The Decipherment of Linear B*, Cambridge.

Chilcott, T. (1972) *A Publisher and his Circle: The Life and Work of John Taylor, Keats's Publisher*, London.

Christ, K. (2006) *Klios Wandlungen: Die deutsche Althistorie vom Neuhumanismus bis zur Gegenwart*, Munich.

Clark, G. K. (ed. (1977) *Portrait of an Age: Victorian England*, Oxford.

Clark, W. (2006) *Academic Charisma and the Rise of the Research University*, Chicago.

Clarke, M. L. (1937) *Richard Porson: A Biographical Essay*, Cambridge.

Clarke, M. L. (1945) *Greek Studies in England from 1700 to 1830*, Cambridge.

Clarke, M. L. (1959) *Classical Education in Great Britain 1500–1900*, Cambridge.

Clinton, C. J. F. (1854) *Literary Remains of Henry Fynes Clinton: Consisting of an Autobiography and Literary Journal and Brief Essays on Theological Subjects*, London.

Coates, V. C. G. and Seydl, J. L. (eds) (2007) *Antiquity Recovered: The Legacy of Pompeii and Herculaneum*, New York.

Cohen, M. (1977) *Sensible Words: Linguistic Practice in England, 1640–1785*, Baltimore.

Cole, M. (1949) *Growing up into Revolution*, London.

Collard, C. (2004) 'George Burges', in Todd 2004, 119–20.

Collini, S. (1991) *Public Moralists: Political Thought and Intellectual Life in Britain in Britain 1850–1930*, Oxford.

Collini, S. (1993) 'The Passionate Intensity of Cultural Studies', *Victorian Studies* 36: 455–60.

Colls, R. and Dodd, P. (eds) (1986) *Englishness, Politics and Culture 1880–1920*, London.

Colman, D. S. (1950) *Sabrinae Corolla: The Classics at Shrewsbury School under Dr Butler and Dr Kennedy*, Shrewsbury.

Comaroff, J. L. and Roberts, S. (1981) *Rules and Processes: the Cultural Logic of Dispute in an African Context*, Chicago.

Conington, J. (1872) *Miscellaneous Writings*, ed. J. A. Symonds, London.

Cook Wilson, J. (1889) *On the Interpretation of Plato's Timaeus: Critical Studies, with Special Reference to a Recent Edition*, London.

Cooke, H. P. (1925) *In the Days of our Youth*, London.

Copeman, H. (1996) *Singing in Latin*, 2nd rev. edn, Oxford.

Copleston, E. (1810) *Reply to the Calumnies of the Edinburgh Review against Oxford*, Oxford.

Corbin, A. (1986) *The Foul and the Fragrant*, Oxford.

Cornford, F. M. (1903) *The Cambridge Classical Course: An Essay in Anticipation of Further Reform*, Cambridge.

Cornford, F. M. (1907) *Thucydides Mythistoricus*, Cambridge.

Cornford, F. M. (1908) *Microsmographia Academica*, Cambridge.

Coulling, S. (1974) *Matthew Arnold and his Critics*, Athens OH.

Craster, E. (1952) *History of the Bodleian Library 1845–1945*, Oxford.

Crawford, S., Ulmschneider, K., and Elsner, J. (eds) (2017) *Ark of Civilization: Refugee Scholars and Oxford University, 1930–1945*, Oxford.

Creighton, L. (1906) *Life and Letters of Mandell Creighton*, London.

Crowley, T. (1989) *The Politics of Discourse: The Standard Language Question in British Cultural Debates*, London.

Curry, K. and Dedmon, R. (1974) 'Southey's contributions to The Quarterly Review', *The Wordsworth Circle* 6: 261–72.

Curthoys, J. (2012) *The Cardinal's College: Christ Church, Chapter and Verse*, London.

Curthoys, M. C. (1997) 'The careers of Oxford men', in Brock and Curthoys 1997, 477–512.

Cutmore, J. (ed.) (2007) *Conservatism and the Quarterly Review 1809–24*, London.

Cutmore, J. (2008) *Contributors to the Quarterly Review: A History, 1809–25*, London.

Cutmore, J. (2018) *John Murray's* Quarterly Review: *Letters 1807–1843*, Liverpool.

Darnton, R. (1984) *The Great Cat Massacre and Other Episodes in French Cultural History*, New York.

Daston, L. and Galison, P. (2007) *Objectivity*, Cambridge, MA.

Daston, L. and Most, G. W. (2015) 'History of Science and History of Philologies', *Isis* 106.2: 378–90.

Davie, G. E. (1961) *The Democratic Intellect: Scotland and Her Universities in the Nineteenth Century*, Edinburgh.

Davy, H. (1821) 'Some Observations and Experiments on the Papyri Found in the Ruins of Herculaneum', *Philosophical Transactions of the Royal Society of London* 111: 191–208.

De Quincey, T. (1846) 'The Antigone of Sophocles as represented on the Edinburgh stage in December 1845', part 1, *Tait's Edinburgh Magazine* 17 (February), 111–16, repr. in D. Masson (ed.), *The Collected Writings of Thomas De Quincey* vol. 10 (Edinburgh, 1897), 360–88.

De Ricci, S. (1930) *English Collectors of Books and Manuscripts*, Cambridge.

Dickson, G. and Adam, G. M. (1893) *History of Upper Canada College 1829–1892*, Toronto.

Diggle, J. (2007) 'On Housman's Greek', in Finglass, P. J., Collard, C. and Richardson, N. J. (eds), *Hesperos: Studies in Ancient Greek Poetry presented to M. L. West on his Seventieth Birthday*, Oxford, 145–69.

Distad, N. M. (1972) 'The Philological Museum of 1831–1833', *Victorian Periodicals Newsletter* 5: 27–30.

Distad, N. M. (1979) *Guessing at Truth: The Life of Julius Charles Hare (1795–1855)*, Shepherdstown WV.

Dobree, P. P. (ed.) (1820) *Ricardi Porsoni notae in Aristophanem*, Cambridge.

Dobree, P. P. (ed.) (1822) *Photiou tou patriarchou lexeon synagoge: e codice Galeano descripsit Ricardus Porsonus*, Cambridge.

Dodds, E. R. (1956) 'An Oxford Honour School of Classics', *Oxford Magazine*, 3 May, 372–4.

Dodds, E. R. (1977) *Missing Persons*, Oxford.

[Donaldson, J. W.] (1840) 'Richard Porson', *Penny Cyclopaedia* 18: 420.

Donaldson, J. W. (1856) *Classical Scholarship and Classical Learning*, Cambridge.

Douglas, M. (1966) *Purity and Danger: An Analysis of Concepts of Pollution and Taboo*, London.

Dover, K. J. (1988) 'Expurgation of Greek literature', *The Greeks and their Legacy: Collected Papers II*, Oxford, 270–91.

Dover, K. J. (ed.) (1992) *Perceptions of the Ancient Greeks*, Oxford.

Dover, K. J. (1994) *Marginal Comment: A Memoir*, London.

Dowling, L. (1986) *Language and Decadence in the Victorian Fin de Siècle*, Princeton.

Dowling, L. (1994) *Hellenism and Homosexuality in Victorian Oxford*, Ithaca.

Drake, B. (ed) (1853) *Aeschyli Eumenides*, London.

Draper, F. W. (1872) 'Arsenic in certain green colors', *Third Annual Report of the State Board of Health of Massachusetts*, Boston, 18–57.

Drayton, R. (2005) 'The strange late birth of the British Academy', in M. Daunton (ed.), *The Organization of Knowledge in Victorian Britain*, Oxford, 389–400.

Drury, H. (ed.) (1841) *Arundines Cami*, Cambridge.

Durkheim, E. (1938) *L'Evolution Pédagogique en France*, Paris.

Easterling, P. E. (2005) 'The speaking page: reading Sophocles with Jebb', in Stray 2005a, 1–12.

Eliot, S. (1994) *Some Patterns and Trends in British Publishing 1800–1919* (Occasional Papers of the Bibliographical Society, 8), London.

Eliot, S. (ed.) (2013a) *History of Oxford University Press II: 1780–1896*, Oxford.

Eliot, S. (2013b) 'The evolution of a printer and publisher', in Eliot 2013a, 77–112.

Ellis, H. (2012) *Generational Conflict and University Reform: Oxford in the Age of Revolution*, Leiden.

Ellis, H. (2014) 'Enlightened networks: Anglo-German collaboration in classical scholarship, 1750–1850', in Kirchberger, U. and Ellis, H. (eds), *Anglo-German Scholarly Relations in the Long Nineteenth Century*, Leiden, 23–37.

Ellmann, R. (1987) *Oscar Wilde*, London.

Elmsley, P. (1810) 'Blomfield's Prometheus Vinctus', *Edinburgh Review* 17: 211–42, 491.

Elmsley, P. (1812a) 'Markland's Euripidis Supplices', *Quarterly Review* 7: 441–64.

Elmsley, P. (1812b) 'Monk's Euripidis Hippolytus', *Quarterly Review* 8: 215–30.

Engel, A. J. (1983) *From Clergyman to Don: The Rise of the Academic Profession in Nineteenth-century Oxford*, Oxford.

Erickson, L. (1996) *The Economy of Literary Form: English Literature and the Industrialization of Publishing, 1800–1850*, Baltimore.

Eschenburg, J. J. (1787) *Handbuch der klassischen Literatur*, Berlin/Stettin.

Evangelista, S. (2009) *British Aestheticism and Ancient Greece: Hellenism, Reception, Gods in Exile*, Basingstoke.

Evans, M. (1991) *A Good School? Life in a Girls' Grammar School in the 1950s*, London.

[Evans, T. S.] (1839) *Mathematogonia, or, the Mythological Birth of the Nymph Mathesis*, Cambridge.

Farrell, J. (2001) *Latin Language and Latin Culture: from Ancient to Modern Times*, Cambridge.

Feinberg, B. and Kasrils, R. (1969) *Dear Bertrand Russell... A Selection of his Correspondence with the General Public 1950–1968*, 2 vols, Cambridge MA.

Feingold, M. (1996) 'Reversal of Fortunes: the Displacement of Cultural Hegemony from the Netherlands to England in the Seventeenth and Early Eighteenth Centuries', in Hoak, D. and Feingold, M. (eds), *The World of William and Mary: Anglo-Dutch Perspectives on the Revolution of 1688–89*, Stanford, 234–64.

Feingold, M. (1997) 'The Humanities', in *History of the University of Oxford IV: Seventeenth-century Oxford*, ed. N. Tyacke, Oxford, 211–357.

Felski, R. (2011) 'Context Stinks', *New Literary History* 42.4: 573–91.

Felski, R. (2016) *The Limits of Critique*, Chicago.

Finglass, P. J. (2007) 'A Newly-Discovered Edition of Sophocles by Peter Elmsley', *Greek, Roman and Byzantine Studies* 47: 1–16.

Finglass, P. J. (2009) 'Unpublished conjectures at Leiden on the Greek dramatists', *Greek, Roman and Byzantine Studies* 49: 187–221.

Fisher, G. W. (1899) *Annals of Shrewsbury School*, London.

Flaubert, G. (1954) *Dictionary of Platitudes*, London.

Fleck, L. (1979 [1935]) *Genesis and Development of a Scientific Fact*, Chicago.

Fleming, P. (1988) *Upper Canadian Imprints, 1810–1841: A Bibliography*, Toronto.

Forbes, D. (1952) *The Liberal Anglican View of History*, Cambridge.

Formisano, M. and Kraus, C. S. (eds) (2018) *Marginality, Canonicity, Passion*, Oxford.

Forrest, M. St. J. (1996) *Modernising the Classics*, Exeter.

Forster, E. M. (2005 [1927]) *Aspects of the Novel*, ed. O. Stallybrass, with an introduction by F. Kermode, London.

Fowler, D. P. (2000) *Roman Constructions: Readings in Postmodern Latin*, Oxford.

Fowler, R. (2009) 'Blood for the ghosts: Wilamowitz in Oxford', *Syllecta Classica* 20: 171–213.

Fox, G. (1659) *A Primer for the Doctors and Schollers of Europe*, London.

Frantzen, A. J. (1990) *Desire for Origins: New Language, Old English, and Teaching the Tradition*, New Brunswick NJ.

Freund, W. (1834–45) *Wörterbuch der Lateinischen Sprache, nach historisch-genetischen Principien, mit steter Berücksichtigung der Grammatik, Synonymik und Alterthumskunde bearbeitet. Nebst mehreren Beilagen Linguistischen und archäologischen Inhalts*, Leipzig.

Furbank, P. N. (1978) *E. M. Forster: A Life*, New York.

Gardner, P. (1933) *Autobiographica*, Oxford.

Gascoigne, J. (1989) *Cambridge in the Age of the Enlightenment: Science, Religion and Politics from the Restoration to the French Revolution*, Cambridge.

Geertz, C. (1973) *The Interpretation of Cultures*, London.

Gehl, P. F. (1993) *A Moral Art: Grammar, Society and Culture in Trecento Florence*, Ithaca NY.

Gere, J. A. and Sparrow, J. (eds) (1981) *Geoffrey Madan's Notebooks*, Oxford.

Gibbins, J. R. (2007) *John Grote, Cambridge University and the Development of Victorian Thought*, Exeter.

Gill, D. W. J. (2011) *Sifting the Soil Of Greece: The Early Years of the British School at Athens (1886–1919)*, London.

Gillespie, S. (2011) *English Translation and Classical Reception: Towards a New Literary History*, Malden MA.

Gilliver, P. (2016) *The Making of the* Oxford English Dictionary, Oxford.

Glucker, J. (1981) 'Professor Key and Doctor Wagner: an episode in the history of Victorian scholarship', in Stubbs, H. W. (ed.), *Pegasus: Classical Essays from the University of Exeter*, Exeter, 98–123.

Goldhill, S. (2002) *Who Needs Greek? Contests in the Cultural History of Hellenism*, Cambridge.

Goldhill, S. (2012) *Sophocles and the Language of Tragedy*, Oxford.

Goldhill, S. (2017) *A Very Queer Family Indeed: Sex, Religion, and the Bensons in Victorian Britain*, Chicago.

Goodrich, P. (2003) 'Distrust quotations in Latin', *Critical Inquiry* 29: 193–215.

Görlach, M. (2003) 'A new text type: exercises in bad English', *The Teaching of English in the Eighteenth and Nineteenth Centuries*, ed. Austin, F. O. and Stray, C. A. (special issue of *Paradigm*), 5–14.

Grafton, A. T. (1981) 'Teacher, text and pupil in the Renaissance classroom', *History of Universities* 1: 37–70.

Grafton, A. T. (1983) 'Polyhistor into Philolog: Notes on the Transformation of German Classical Scholarship, 1780–1850', *History of Universities* 3: 159–92.

Grafton, A. T. (1990) 'Notes from underground on cultural transmission', *The Transmission of Culture in Early Modern Europe*, ed. Grafton, A. and Blair, A., Philadelphia, 1–7.

Grafton, A. and Weinberg, J. (2011) *'I have always loved the Holy Tongue': Isaac Casaubon, the Jews, and a Forgotten Chapter in Renaissance Scholarship*, Cambridge MA.

Grafton, A. and Most, G. W. (eds) (2016) *Canonical Texts and Scholarly Practices: A Global Comparative Approach*, Cambridge.

Graver, B. (1986) 'Wordsworth and the language of epic: the translation of the *Aeneid*', *Studies in Philology* 83: 261–85.

Graves, R. (1955) *The Greek Myths*, 2 vols, Harmondsworth.

Green, A. (1990) *Education and State Formation*, London.

Green, V. H. H. (1964) *Religion at Oxford and Cambridge*, London.

Green, V. H. H. (1986) 'Reformers and reform in the University', in Sutherland, L. (ed.), *History of the University of Oxford V: The Eighteenth Century*, Oxford, 607–38.

Greene, G. (ed.) (1928) *Letters from Baron Friedrich von Hügel to a Niece*, London.

Groenewegen, P. (ed.) (1996) *Official Papers of Alfred Marshall, A Supplement*, Cambridge.

Grosvenor I., Lawn, M. and Rousmaniere, K. (eds) (1999) *Silences & Images: The Social History of the Classroom*, New York.

Grote, J. (1851) *A Few Remarks upon a Pamphlet by Mr. Shilleto entitled, Thucydides or Grote?*, Cambridge.

Gundy, H. P. (1976) 'Samuel Oliver Tazewell, first lithographer of Upper Canada', *Humanities Association Review* 27: 466–83.

Gundy, H. P. (1988) 'Tazewell, Samuel Oliver', *Dictionary of Canadian Biography* 7: 845–7.

Gunn, J. A. W. (1983) *Beyond Liberty and Property: The Process of Self-Recognition in Eighteenth-Century Political Thought*, Kingston Ont.

Gunning, H. (1855) *Reminiscences of Cambridge*, 2 vols, London.

Gurd, S. (ed.) (2010) *Philology and its Histories*, Columbus OH.

Grote, J. (1856) 'Old studies and new', in *Cambridge Essays 1856*, London, 74–114.

Grote, J. (1861) *A Few Words on Criticism*, Cambridge.

Güthenke, C. (2009) 'Shop Talk: Reception Studies and Recent Work in the History of Scholarship', *Classical Receptions Journal* 1.1: 104–15.

Güthenke, C. (2015) 'The History of Modern Classical Scholarship (since 1750)', *Oxford Online Research Bibliographies*, Oxford. http://www.oxfordbibliographies.com/view/document/obo-9780195389661/obo-9780195389661-0199.xml.

Güthenke, C. and Holmes, B. (2018) 'Hyper-Inclusivity, Hyper-Canonicity, and the Future of the Field', in Formisano and Kraus, *Marginality, Canonicity, Passion*, pp. 57–73.

Haig, A. G. L. (1986a) 'The church, universities and learning in later Victorian England', *Historical Journal* 29: 187–201.

Haig, A. G. L (1986b) *The Victorian Clergy*, London.

Hall, E. and Harrop, S. (eds) (2010) *Theorising Performance: Greek Drama, Cultural History, and Critical Practice*, London.

Hall, E. M. and Macintosh, F. (2005) *Greek Tragedy and the British Stage 1660–1914*, Oxford.

Hall, N. (2003) 'The role of the slate in Lancasterian schools as evidenced by their manuals and handbooks', in Austin, F. O. and Stray, C. A. (eds), *The Teaching of English in the Eighteenth and Nineteenth Centuries* (special issue of *Paradigm*), 46–54.

Hallett, J. and Stray, C. (eds) (2009) *British Classics Beyond England: Its Impact Inside and Outside the Academy*, Waco TX.

Hamacher, W. (2015) *Minima Philologica*, trans. Diehl, C. and Groves, J., New York.

Hamilton, D. (1990) *Learning about Education: An Unfinished Curriculum*, Milton Keynes.

Hare, A. and J. C. (1897 [1827]) *Guesses at Truth*, London.

Hare, J. C. (1829) *A Vindication of Niebuhr's History of Rome from the Charges of the Quarterly Review*, London.

Harloe, K. (2013) *Winckelmann and the Invention of Antiquity: Aesthetics and Historicism in the Age of Altertumswissenschaft*, Oxford.

Harrison, J. E. (1912) *Themis: A Study of the Social Origins of Greek Religion*, Cambridge.

Harrison, J. E. (1925) *Reminiscences of a Student*, London.

Harrison, S. J. (ed.) (2001) *Texts, Ideas, and the Classics*, Oxford.

Harrison, S. J. and Stray, C. A. (eds) (2011) *Expurgating the Classics: Editing Out in Greek and Latin*, London.

Harvie, C. C. (1976) *The Lights of Liberalism: University Liberals and the Challenge of Democracy 1860–86*, London.

Hasluck, F. W. (1909–10) 'Terra Lemnia', *Annual of the British School at Athens* 16: 220–31.

Hasluck, F. W. and M. M. (1929) *Christianity and Islam under the Sultans*, Oxford.

Hasluck, M. M. (ed.) (1926) *Letters on Religion and Folklore by the Late F. W. Hasluck*, London.

Haugen, K. L. (2011) *Richard Bentley: Poetry and Enlightenment*, Cambridge MA.

H[awkesworth], J. (1829) *Key to Some of the Dialogues of Lucian*, Dublin.

Headlam, W. G. (1892) *On Editing Aeschylus*, London.

Heitland, W. E. (1889) 'Dr Kennedy at Shrewsbury', *The Eagle* (St John's College, Cambridge) 15: 3–12.

Heitland, W. E. (1926) *After Many Years*, Cambridge.

Henderson, J. G. W. (1998) *Juvenal's Mayor: The Professor who Lived on 2^D a Day*, Cambridge.

Henderson, J. G. W. (2006) *'Oxford Reds': Classic Commentaries on Latin Classics*, London.

Henderson, J. G. W. (2007) 'The "Euripides Reds" series: well-laid plans at OUP', in Stray 2007a, 143–75.

Herbert, A. P. (1935) *Uncommon Law: Being Sixty-six Misleading Cases*, London.

Herle, A. and Rouse, S. (eds.) (1998) *Cambridge and the Torres Strait: Centenary Essays on the Anthropological Expedition*, Cambridge.

Hewlett, J. T. J. (1843) *College Life, or the Proctor's Notebook*, 3 vols, London.

Hilbold, I., Simon, L. and Späth, T. (2017) 'Holding the reins: Miss Ernst and twentieth-century Classics', *Classical Receptions Journal* 9.4: 487–506.

Hillard, G. S. (ed.) (1876) *Life, Letters and Journals of George Ticknor*, 2nd edn, Boston.

Hilton, A. J. B. (2011) 'The nineteenth century', in Linehan, P. (ed.), *St John's College Cambridge: A History*, Woodbridge, 220–396.

Hinchcliffe, T. (1992) *North Oxford*, New Haven.

Hoffman, S. F. W. (1832–6) *Lexicon bibliographicum, sive, Index editionum et interpretationum scriptorum Graecorum tum sacrorum tum profanorum*, 3 vols, Leipzig [2nd edn 1838–45].

Holroyd, M. (1967–8) *Lytton Strachey*, 2 vols, London.

Honey, J. R. de S. (1977) *Tom Brown's Universe: The Development of the Victorian Public School*, London.

Honey, J. R. de S. and Curthoys, M. C. (2000) 'Oxford and schooling', in Brock and Curthoys 2000, 545–70.

Hopper, E. (1971) *Readings in the Theory of Educational Systems*, London.

Hornby, E. (1985) *Edward Hornby's Last Bow*, London.

Horsfall, N. H. (1974) 'Classical studies in England 1810–1825', *Greek, Roman and Byzantine Studies* 15: 449–77.

Horsfall, N. M. (1987) Review of Brink 1986, *Classical Review* 37: 122–3.

Horsley, G. H. (2011) 'One hundred years of the Loeb Classical Library', *Buried History* 47: 35–58.

Horwitz, R. and Finn, J. (1975) 'Locke's Aesop's Fables', *Locke Newsletter* 6: 71–88.

Hoskin, K. (1979) 'The Examination, Disciplinary Power and Rational Schooling', *History of Education* 8: 135–46.

Housman, A. E. (ed.), (1903) *M. Manilii Astronomicon liber primus*, London.

Housman, A. E. (1969) *The Confines of Criticism: The Cambridge Inaugural, 1911*, ed. J. Carter, Cambridge.

How, F. W. (1904) *Six Great Schoolmasters*, London.

Howatt, A. P. R. (1984) *A History of English Language Teaching*, Oxford.

Howard, N. (1819) *Introductory Greek Exercises, to those of Dunbar, Neilson and Others, to Assist the Learner*, London.

Howsam, L. (2004) 'Academic Discipline or Literary Genre? The Establishment of Boundaries in Historical Writing', *Victorian Literature and Culture* 3: 525–45.

Howsam, L. (2009) *Past into Print: The Publishing of History in Britain 1850–1950*, London.

Huber, V. A. (1843) *The English Universities*, tr. Newman, F. W., 3 vols, London.

Hudson, L. (1962) *Contrary Imaginations: A Psychological Study of the English Schoolboy*, London.

Hudson, L. (1968) *Frames of Mind: Ability, Perception and Self-perception in the Arts and Sciences*, London.

Hui, A. (2016) 'The Many Returns of Philology: a State of the Field Report', *Journal of the History of Ideas* 78.1: 137–56.

[Huxley, L.] (1923) *The House of Smith Elder*, London.

Issitt, J. (1998) 'Introducing Sir Richard Phillips', *Paradigm* 26: 1–7.

Ives, E., Drummond, D., and Schwarz, L. (2000) *The First Civic University: Birmingham 1880–1980*, Birmingham.

Jacob, C. (ed.) (2007) *Lieux de savoirs, vol.1: Espaces et communautés*, Paris.

Jacob, C. (ed.) (2011) *Lieux de savoirs, vol.2: Les mains de l'intellect*, Paris.

Jakobson, R. (1971) 'Shifters, verbal categories and the Russian verb', in *Selected Writings vol 2: Word and Language*, The Hague, 130–47.

James, M. R. (1926) *Eton and King's: Recollections, Mostly Trivial, 1875–1925*, London.

James, N. G. B. (1909) *History of Mill Hill School*, London.

James, S. (2001) 'The Roman galley slave: Ben-Hur and the birth of a factoid', *Public Archaeology* 2: 35–49.

Jebb, C. (1907) *Life and Letters of Sir Richard Claverhouse Jebb*, Cambridge.

Jerdan, W. (1852–3) *The Autobiography of William Jerdan*, London.

Johnson, D. (1993) 'Aspects of a Liberal Education: Late Nineteenth-Century Attitudes to Race, from Cambridge to the Cape Colony', *History Workshop Journal* 36: 163–82.

Johnson, G. (1994) *University Politics. F. M. Cornford's Cambridge and his Advice to the Young Academic Politician*, Cambridge.

Johnstone, J. (ed.) (1828) *The Works of Samuel Parr*, 8 vols, London.

Jones, F. (1924) 'Reform methods of Latin teaching', in Adams, J. (ed.) *Educational Movements and Methods*, London, 97–116.

Jones, F. P. (1944) 'Anthony Trollope and the classics', *Classical Weekly* 37: 227–331.

Kandel, I. L. (1933) *Studies in Comparative Education*, London.

Kemble, J. M. (1837) 'British and foreign universities: Cambridge', *British and Foreign Review* 5: 168–209.

Kenna, M. E. (2005) 'Why does incense smell religious? The anthropology of smell meets Greek Orthodoxy', *Journal of Mediterranean Studies* 15: 51–70.

Kennedy, B. H. (1866) *A Letter to the Rev. Dr. Moberly*, London.

Kenney, E. J. (1974) *The Classical Text: Aspects of Editing in the Age of the Printed Book*, Cambridge.

Key, T. H. (1845) *The Controversy about the Varronianus between T. H. Key and the Rev. J. W. Donaldson*, London.

Kidd, T. (ed.) (1815) *Tracts and Miscellaneous Criticisms of the Late Richard Porson*, London.

Kingsmill Moore, H. (1904) *An Unwritten Chapter in the History of Education, Being the History of the Society for the Education of the Poor of Ireland, Generally Known as the Kildare Place Society, 1811–1831*, London.

Klaniczay, Gábor, Werner, Michael, and Gecser, Ottó (eds) (2011) *Multiple Antiquities—Multiple Modernities: Ancient Histories in Nineteenth Century European Cultures*, Frankfurt/Main.

Konstantinides, A. (1901–7) *Μεγα Λεξικον της Ἑλληνικης Γλωσσης*, 4 vols, Athens.

Kraus, C. S. (2002) 'Introduction: reading commentaries/commentaries as reading', *The Classical Commentary: Histories, Practices, Theory*, ed. Gibson, R. K. and Kraus, C. S. Leiden, 1–27.

Kraus, C. and Stray, C. (eds) (2015) *Classical Commentaries*, Oxford.

Kuhn, T. S. (1966) *The Structure of Scientific Revolutions*, Chicago.

Kuper, A. (2015) *Anthropology and Anthropologists: The Modern British School*, New York.

Laughton, J. K. (1898) *Memoirs of the Life and Correspondence of Henry Reeve, CB, DCL*, London.

Leach, A. F. (1899) *A History of Winchester College*, London.

Leach, A. F. (1903) 'Education', *Victoria County History of Hampshire*, II, London, 251–408.

Leach, J. H. C. (1964) 'Dust and Greek particles', in Cowburn, I. (ed.), *Salopian Anthology: Some Impressions of Shrewsbury School during Four Centuries*, London, 104–21.

Leedham-Green, E. S. (1996) *Concise History of the University of Cambridge*, Cambridge.

Ledger-Lomas, M. (2013) 'Theology, divinity, and sermons', in Eliot 2013, 403–32.

Lefroy, E. C. (1878) *Undergraduate Oxford*, Oxford.

Lehnus, L. (2012) *Incontri con la Philologie del Passato*, Bari.

Leonard, M. (2015) *Tragic Modernities*, Cambridge MA.

Lerer, S. (2002) *Error and the Academic Self: The Scholarly Imagination, Medieval and Modern*, New York.

Levin, S. (1964) *The Linear B Decipherment Controversy Re-examined*, New York.

Lewin, T. H. (ed.) (1909) *The Lewin Letters: A Selection from the Correspondence and Diaries of an English Family, 1756–1884*, 2 vols, London .

Lewis, G. C. (1855) *An Inquiry into the Credibility of the Early Roman History*, London.

Linehan, P. (ed.) (2011) *St John's College, Cambridge: A History*, Woodbridge.

Livingstone, R. W. (1941) *The Classics and National Life*, Oxford.

Lloyd-Jones, H. (1982) *Blood for the Ghosts: Classical Influences in the Nineteenth and Twentieth Centuries*, London.

Lonsdale, R. (1963/4) 'Dr Burney and the Monthly Review', *Review of English Studies* 14: 346–58, 15: 27–37.

Lortie, D. C. (1975) *Schoolteacher*, Chicago.

Losemann, V. 1977 *Nationalsozialismus und Antike. Studien zur Entwicklung des Faches Alte Geschichte 1933–1945*, Hamburg.

Lovejoy, A. O. (1922) 'The paradox of the thinking behaviorist', *Philosophical Review* 31: 135–47.

Lowe, N. J. (2005) 'Problematic Verrall: The Sceptic at Law', in Stray 2005a, 142–60.

Luard, H. R. (1856) Letter, *Journal of Classical and Sacred Philology* 3: 123–4.

Luard, H. R. (1857) 'Richard Porson', in *Cambridge Essays 1857*, London, 125–71.

Luard, H. R. (ed.) (1867) *The Correspondence of Richard Porson, M.A., formerly Regius Professor of Greek in the University of Cambridge*, Cambridge.

Luna, P. F. (2000) 'Clearly defined: continuity and innovation in the typography of English dictionaries', *Typography Papers* 4: 5–56.

Luna, P. F. (2005) 'The typographic design of Johnson's Dictionary', *Anniversary Essays on Johnson's Dictionary*, ed. Lynch, Jack and McDermott, Anne, Cambridge, 175–97.

Lyne, G. M. (1934) *Balbus: A Latin Reader for Junior Forms*, London.

Macintosh, F. (2005) 'London's Greek plays in the 1880s: George Warr and social philhellenism', in Hall, E. M. and Macintosh, F., *Greek Tragedy and the British Stage 1660–1914*, Oxford, 462–87.

Mackenzie, C. (1963) *My Life and Times: Octave One*, London.

Mackenzie, D. F. (1966) *The Cambridge University Press 1696–1712: A Bibliographical Study*, 2 vols, Cambridge.

Macmillan, G. A. (1878) 'A ride across the Peloponnese', *Blackwood's Edinburgh Magazine* 122: 551–2, 561, 563.

Major, J. R. (1826) *The Hecuba of Euripides, from the Text, and with a Translation of the Notes, Preface, and Supplement of Porson...*, London.

Major, J. R. (1827) *Questions Adapted to Mitford's History of Greece...*, London.

Malinowski, B. (1929) *The Sexual Life of Savages in North-Western Melanesia*, London.

Mancuso, G. (2018, forthcoming) 'Lettere inedite di Gottfried Hermann a Peter Elmsley', *Lexis* 36.

Mangan, J. A. (1986) *Athleticism in the Victorian and Edwardian Public School*, Cambridge.

Marchand, S. (1996) *Down from Olympus: Archaeology and Philhellenism in Germany, 1750–1970*. Princeton.

Marchand, S. (2009) Review of Baertschi and King, Classical Review 61/1 (2011): 294–6.

Marchand, S. (2011) 'German scholarship', *Classical Review* 61: 294–6.

Marett, R. R. (ed.) (1908) *Anthropology and the Classics*, Oxford.

Marshall, F. (2004) 'Edwin Guest: historian, philologist, and founder of the Philological Society of London', *Bulletin of the Henry Sweet Society* 42: 11–30.

Marshall, M. P. (1947) *What I Remember*, Cambridge.

Martin, B. K. (1966) *Father Figures*, London.

Mayor, J. B. (*c.*1860) 'Classical Tripos', Trinity College Library, Cambridge, Add. MS 72 c. 85 12/14 .

Mayor, J. E. B. (ed.) (1869) [T. Baker] *History of the College of St John the Evangelist, Cambridge*, Cambridge.

Mayor, J. E. B. (1887) Review of Daremberg and Saglio, *Dictionnaire des Antiquités...* Vol. 1 pts. 1–2, *Classical Review* 1: 201–2.

McGann, J. J. (ed.) (1986) *Lord Byron. The Complete Poetical Works vol. 5: Don Juan*, Oxford.

McKitterick, D. J. (1998) *A History of Cambridge University Press 2: Scholarship and Commerce 1698–1872*, Cambridge.

McKitterick, D. J. (2004) *A History of Cambridge University Press 3: New Worlds for Learning, 1873–1972*, Cambridge.

McKitterick, D. J. (2007) 'Publishing and perishing in classics: E. H. Barker and the early nineteenth-century English book trades', in Stray 2007a, 7–33.

McManus, B. F. (2007) ' "Macte nova virtute, puer!": Gilbert Murray as mentor and friend to J. A. K. Thomson', in Stray 2007c, 181–200.

McWilliams Tullberg, Rita (1975, rev. edn 1998, Cambridge) *Women at Cambridge: A Men's University—Though of a Mixed Type*, London.

Merivale, C. (1898) *Autobiography of Charles Merivale*, London.

Mewburn, C. (1911) 'The third school', in Gardiner, R. B. and Lupton, J. (eds) *Res Paulinae: The Eighth Half-Century of St Paul's School 1859–1909*, London, 2–11.

Michael, I. (1970) *English Grammatical Categories and the Tradition to 1800*, Cambridge.

[Millard, J.] (1857) 'A dictionary of Greek and Roman geography, by various writers', *Athenaeum* 1563: 1261–2.

Miller, E. (1961) *Portrait of a College: A History of the College of St John the Evangelist in Cambridge*, Cambridge.

Millett, P. (2007) 'Alfred Zimmern's *The Greek Commonwealth* revisited', in Stray 2007b, 168–202.

Milnes, R. M. (1857) 'The Dilettanti Society', *Edinburgh Review* 105: 493–517.

Mitchell, L. (2009) *Maurice Bowra: A Life*, Oxford.

Momigliano, A. (1994) *Studies on Modern Scholarship*, ed. Bowersock, G. W. and Cornell, T. J., with new translations by Cornell, T. J., Berkeley CA.

Momigliano, A. (1966) 'George Grote and the study of Greek history', in *Studies in Historiography* (London), 56–74.

Monk, J. H. and Blomfield, C. J. (eds) (1812) *Adversaria: notæ et emendationes in poetas Græcos quas ex schedis manuscriptis Porsoni deprompserunt et ordinarunt nec non indicibus instruxerunt Jacobus Henricus Monk A.M., Carolus Jacobus Blomfield A.M.*, Cambridge.

Morris, M. (2007) ' "Sneaking, Foul-Mouthed, Scurrilous Reptiles": the battle of the grammars, Edinburgh 1849–50', in Stray 2007a, 55–73.

Morris, M. J. (2009) 'A Manly Desire to Learn': the teaching of the Classics in 19th-century Scotland', PhD thesis, Open University.

Morshead, E. D. A. (1906) *Inaugural Address, delivered on 7th February 1906* (to the Birmingham and Midland Branch of the Classical Association), Birmingham.

Most, G. (1997) 'One hundred years of fractiousness: disciplining polemics in nineteenth-century German classical scholarship', *Transactions of the American Philological Association* 127: 349–61.

Most, G. W. (ed.) (1997) *Collecting Fragments = Fragmente Sammeln*, Göttingen.

Most, G. W. (ed.) (1998) *Editing Texts = Texte Edieren*, Göttingen.

Most, G. W. (ed.) (1999) *Commenaries = Kommentare*, Göttingen.

Most, G. W. (ed.) (2002) *Disciplining Classics = Altertumswissenschaft als Beruf*, Göttingen.

Mugglestone, L. C. (1995) *'Talking Proper': The Rise of Accent as Social Symbol*, Oxford.

Müller, P. (2010) 'Ranke in the Lobby of the Archive: Metaphors and Conditions of Historical Research', in Jobs, S. and Lüdtke, A. (eds), *Unsettling History: Archiving and Narrating in Historiography*, Frankfurt, 109–25.

Mumby, F. A. and Stallybrass, F. H. S. (1955) *From Swan Sonnenschein to George Allen & Unwin, Ltd*, London.

Murray, G. G. A. (1889) *The Place of Greek in Education: An Inaugural Lecture delivered in the University of Glasgow, November 6, 1889*, Glasgow.

Murray, G. G. A. (1915) 'German scholarship', *Quarterly Review* 223: 230–9.

Murray, O. (1997) 'The beginnings of Greats, 1800–1872: ancient history', in Brock and Curthoys 1997, 520–42.

Murray, O. (2000) 'Classics in England' [review of Stray 1998a], *Classical Review* ns 50: 256–9.

Mussell, J. (2007) *Science, Time and Space in the Late Nineteenth-century Periodical Press: Movable Types*, Aldershot.

Näf, B. (ed.) (2001) *Antike und Altertumswissenschaften in der Zeit von Faschismus und Nationalsozialismus*, Mandelbachtal.

Naiditch, P. G. (1988) *A. E. Housman at University College, London*, Leiden.

Naiditch, P. G. (1991) 'Classical studies in nineteenth-century Great Britain as a background to the Cambridge Ritualists', in Calder, W. M. III (ed.) *The Cambridge Ritualists Reconsidered* (*Illinois Classical Studies*, Supplement 2), 123–52.

Naiditch, P. G. (1998) 'Bibliography and the history of classical scholarship', *Echos du Monde Classique/Classical Views* 42 (ns 7): 645–62.

Najman, H. (2017) 'Ethical Reading: the Transformation of the Text and the Self', *The Journal of Theological Studies* 68.2: 507–29.

Nangle, B. C. (1955) *The Monthly Review, second series: Indexes of Contributors and Articles*, Oxford.

Nelson, C. (1989) *Repression and Recovery: Modern American Poetry and the Politics of Cultural Memory 1910–1945*, Madison WI.

Nesfield, J. C. (1912) *Remarks on the Final Report issued in 1911 by the Joint Committee on Grammatical Terminology*, London.

Nevinson, H. W. (1912) *Between the Acts*, London.

Newsome, D. (1974) *Two Classes of Men: Platonism and English Romantic Thought*, London.

[Newton, B.] (1808) *The Names in the Cambridge Triposes, from 1754 to 1807...Prefaced by a Short Letter, on the Comparative Merits of the Two Universities, Oxford and Cambridge*, Bath.

Newton, C. T. (1880) 'Hellenic Studies. An Introductory Address', *Journal of Hellenic Studies* 1: 1–6.

Nicolson, H. (1947) *Some People*, London.

Niebuhr, G. B. (1828, 1831) *The History of Rome*, Cambridge [2 vols; a third volume was published in 1842].

Nimis, S. (1984) 'Fussnoten: das Fundament der Wissenschaft', *Arethusa* 17.2: 105–35.

Nisbet, R. G. M. (2007) 'Half a century of classical research at Oxford', in Stray 2007b, 219–25.

Nockles, P. B. (1997) 'Lost Causes and Impossible Loyalties: The Oxford Movement and the University', in Brock and Curthoys 1997, 195–267.

Nora, P. (ed.) (1984–92) *Les lieux de mémoire*, 3 vols, Paris.

Nuttall, A. D. (2003) *Dead from the Waist Down: Scholars and Scholarship in the Popular Imagination*, New Haven.

Ogilvie, R. M. (1964) *Latin and Greek: A History of the Influence of the Classics on English Life from 1600 to 1918*, London.

Ogilvie, R. M. (1974) 'Latin for yesterday', in Briggs, A., *Essays in the History of Publishing in Celebration of the 250th Anniversary of the House of Longman, 1724–1974*, London, 219–44.

Opie, I. and P. (1959) *The Lore & Language of Schoolchildren*, Oxford.

Orrells, D. (2011) *Classical Culture and Modern Masculinity*, Oxford.

Page, A. (2003) *John Jebb and the Enlightenment Origins of British Radicalism*, New York.

Page, D. L. (1960) 'Richard Porson (1759–1808)', *Proceedings of the British Academy* 45, 221–36.

Page, T. E. (1888) [Review of Orelli's Horace], *Classical Review* 2: 72–4.

Pálsson, G. (1995) *The Textual Life of Savants: Ethnography, Iceland and the Linguistic Turn*, Chur.

Parker, R. (2019) 'The Greeks and the Irrational', in Stray, Pelling, and Harrison 2019.

Parry, R. St J. (1926) *Henry Jackson O.M.*, Cambridge.

Parsons, P. J. (2006) 'The study of ancient tongues: Gaisford and Liddell', in Butler, C. (ed.), *Christ Church, Oxford: A Portrait of the House*, London, 103–6.

Peacock, S. (1988) *Jane Ellen Harrison: The Mask and the Self*, New Haven.

Pelikan, J. (1999) 'Foreword', in Fitzgerald, A. D. (ed.) *Augustine through the Ages: An Encyclopedia*, Grand Rapids MI.

Peters, C. (1987) *Thackeray's Universe*, Oxford.

Pfeiffer, R. (1976) *History of Classical Scholarship from 1300 to 1850*, Oxford.

Philip, I. G. (1997) 'The Bodleian Library', in Brock and Curthoys 1997, 585–97.

Piddington, A. B. (1929) *Worshipful Masters*, Sydney.

Pinney, T. (ed.) (1974) *Letters of Thomas Babington Macaulay*, vol.1, Cambridge.

Pinney, T. (ed.) (1981) *Letters of Thomas Babington Macaulay*, vol. 6, Cambridge.

Pollock, S. (2009) 'Future Philology? The Fate of a Soft Science in a Hard World', *Critical Inquiry* 35: 931–61.

Postclassicisms Collective (forthcoming), *Postclassicisms*, Chicago.

Postgate, J. P. (1902) 'Are the Classics to go?', *Fortnightly Review* ns 72 (November): 886–80.

Prest, J. (1966) *Robert Scott and Benjamin Jowett, Balliol College Record*, Supplement.

Preyer, R. O. (1985) 'The romantic tide reaches Trinity: notes on the transmission and diffusion of new approaches to traditional studies at Cambridge, 1820–1840', in Paradis, J. and Postlewait, T. (eds) *Victorian Science and Victorian Values: Literary Perspectives*, New Brunswick NJ, 39–68.

Price, R. G. G. (1957) *A History of PUNCH*, London.

Pym, D. [1972] 'Patchwork from the past', 5 vols, typescript memoirs; copy in Girton College Library, Cambridge.

Prothero, G. W. (1886) *A Memoir of Henry Bradshaw*, London.

Prothero, R. E. (1893) *The Life and Correspondence of Arthur Penrhyn Stanley, D.D., late Dean of Westminster*, London.

Proudfoot, I. (1998) 'Lithography at the Crossroads of the East', *Journal of the Printing Historical Society* 27: 113–31.

Pykett, L. (1990) 'Reading the periodical: text and context', in Brake et al. 1990, 3–17.

Raphaely, J. (1999) 'Nothing but gibberish and shibboleths? The Compulsory Greek debates, 1870–1919', in Stray 1999a, 71–94.

Rauch, A. (2001) *Useful Knowledge: the Victorians, Morality, and the March of Intellect*, Durham NC.

Raworth, B. C. (1802) *Cambridge University Calendar for the Year 1802*, Cambridge.

Raymond, E. (1961) *Mister Olim*, London.

Rebenich, S. (2002) *Theodor Mommsen: eine Biographie*, Munich.

Reid, W. A. and Filby, J. (1982) *The Sixth: An Essay in Education and Democracy*, Lewes.

Reynolds, L. D. and Wilson, N. G. (1968) *Scribes and Scholars*, Oxford.

Rhodes, B. and Streeter, W.W. (1999) *Before Photocopying: The Art and History of Mechanical Copying, 1780–1938*, New Castle DE.

Richardson, E. (2013) *Classical Victorians: Scholars, Scoundrels and Generals in Pursuit of Antiquity*, Cambridge.

Ridgeway, W. (1923) 'Preface', An Index to the Journal of Philology *(1868–1920)*, Cambridge, 2–4.

Riplinger, G. (2008) *Hazardous Materials: Greek and Hebrew Study Dangers*, Ararat VA.

Roach, J. P. C. (1971) *Public Examinations in England 1850–1900*, Cambridge.

Roberts, S. C. (1954) *The Evolution of Cambridge Publishing*, Cambridge.

Robinson, A. (2002) *Jane Harrison: Life and Work*, Oxford.

Robson, R. (1967) 'Trinity College in the age of Peel', in Robson, R. (ed.) *Ideas and Institutions of Victorian Britain*, London, 313–35.

Roll-Hansen, D. (1957) *The Academy, 1869–1879: Victorian Intellectuals in Revolt*, Copenhagen.

Ross, R. (1909) 'The brand of Isis', in *Masques and Phases*, London, 33–46.

Rothblatt, S. (1968) *The Revolution of the Dons: Cambridge and Society in Victorian England*, London.

Rothblatt, S. (1975) 'The student sub-culture and the examination system in early 19th-century Oxbridge', in Stone, L. (ed.), *The University in Society*, Princeton, 1: 247–304.

Rouse, J. (1987) *Knowledge and Power: Towards a Political Philosophy of Science*, Ithaca NY.

Rudd, W. J. N. (1981) *T.E. Page: Schoolmaster Extraordinary*, Bristol.

Rudwick, M. J. S. (2005) *Bursting the Limits of Time: The Reconstruction of Geohistory in the Age of Revolution*, Chicago.

Rumens, C. (1987) *Selected Poems*, London.

Sampson, G. (1921) *English for the English: A Chapter on National Education*, Cambridge.

Sandford, M. (1818) *Grammar of the Mnemonic and Methodic Art*, Dublin.

Sandys, J. E. (1891) 'The new edition of Dr. Smith's Dictionary of Antiquities', *Classical Review* 5: 425–8.

Sandys, J. E. (1908) *A History of Classical Scholarship*, Vol. 3, Cambridge.

Schaffer, S. (1991) 'The history and geography of the intellectual world: Whewell's politics of language', in Fisch, M. and Schaffer, S. (eds) *William Whewell: A Composite Portrait*, Oxford, 201–32.

Schaffer, S. (2007) 'Newton on the beach: a genealogy of testimony and solitude': unpublished paper, Dept. of History and Philosophy of Science, University of Cambridge.

Schliemann, H. (1873) *Troy and its Remains*, London.

Schliemann, H. (1877) *Mycenae*, London.

Schmidt, E. G. (1990) 'Gottfried Hermann', in Briggs, W. W. and Calder, W. M. III (eds), *Classical Scholarship: a Biographical Encyclopedia*, New York, 160–75.

Schnicke, F. (2015) *Die Männliche Disziplin: zur Vergeschlechtlichung der Deutschen Geschichtswissenschaft 1780–1900*, Göttingen.

Schwindt, J. P. (ed.) (2009) *Was ist eine Philologische Frage?* Frankfurt/Main.

[Scott, R.] (1839) 'Modern criticism on Aeschylus', *Quarterly Review* 64: 370–95.

Scullion, S. (2019) ' "The Road of Excess": Dodds and Greek Tragedy', in Stray, Pelling and Harrison 2019.

Searby, P. (1997) *History of the University of Cambridge, Volume III: 1750–1870*, Cambridge.

Searle, G. R. (1971) *The Quest for National Efficiency*, Oxford.

Secord, J. A. (2001) *Victorian Sensation: The Extraordinary Publication, Reception, and Secret Authorship of* Vestiges of the Natural History of Creation, Chicago

Sedgwick, A. (1833) *A Discourse on the Studies of the University*, Cambridge and London (reprinted 1969, ed. Ashby, E. and Anderson, M., Leicester).

Seeley, J. R. (1867) 'Liberal education in universities', in Farrar, F. W. (ed.) *Essays on a Liberal Education*, London, 145–78.

Shaw, G. (1998) 'Calcutta: birthplace of the Indian lithographed book', *Journal of the Printing Historical Society* 27: 89–111.

Sheppard, J. T. (1920) *The Oedipus Tyrannus of Sophocles*, Cambridge.

Shilleto, R. (1851) *Thucydides or Grote?*, Cambridge.

Short, T. V. (1829) *A Letter on the State of the Public Examinations in the University of Oxford...Reprinted with an Appendix*, Oxford.

Sikes, E. E. (1914) *The Anthropology of the Greeks*, London.

Simon, J. (1966) *Education and Society in Tudor England*, Cambridge.

Skilton, D. (1988) 'Schoolboy Latin and the mid-Victorian novelist: a study in reader competence', *Browning Institute Studies* 16: 39–55.

Small, I. (1991) *Conditions for Criticism: Authority, Knowledge and Literature in the Late Nineteenth Century*, Oxford.

Smith, A. (2012) *Artful*, London.

Smith, B. G. (1998) *The Gender of History: Men, Women, and Historical Practice*, Cambridge MA.

Smith, G. H. (1834) *A Manual of Grecian Antiquities. Compiled for the Use of Schools and Private Students*, London.

Smith, J. (2001) 'Trinity College annual examinations in the nineteenth century', in Smith and Stray 2001, 122–38.

Smith, J. and Stray, C. A. (eds) (2001) *Teaching and learning in 19th-Century Cambridge*, Woodbridge.

Smith, J. and Stray, C.A. (eds) (2003) *Cambridge in the 1830s: the letters of Alexander Chisholm Gooden, 1831–41*, Woodbridge.

Smith, J. and Toynbee, A. (eds) (1960) *Gilbert Murray: An Unfinished Autobiography, with Contributions by his Friends*, London.

Smith, O. (1984) *The Politics of Language 1791–1819*, Oxford.

[Smith, S.] (1809) 'Edgeworth's *Professional Education*', *Edinburgh Review* 15: 40–53; repr. in *Collected Works* (2nd edn, London, 1840), 1: 189–95.

Smith, W. (1840) *The Apology of Socrates, the Crito, and part of the Phædo; With Notes from Stallbaum and Schleiermacher's Introductions*, London.

Smith, W. (1855) *A Latin-English Dictionary, based upon the works of Forcellini and Freund*, London.

Sonnenschein, A. (1881) *Standards of Teaching of Foreign Codes Relating to Elementary Education*, London.

Sonnenschein, E. (1892) 'The parallel study of grammar', *Educational Review* 3: 450–61.

Sonnenschein, E. (1927) *The Soul of Grammar*, Cambridge.

Squibb, G. D. (1972) *Founder's Kin*, Oxford.

St Clair, W. (1998) *Lord Elgin and the Marbles*, London.

Stedman Jones, G. (1971) *Outcast London*, Oxford.

Stephens, S. (2002) 'Commenting on fragments', in *The Classical Commentary*, ed. Gibson, R. K. and Kraus, C. S., Leiden, 67–88.

Stephens, S. and Vasunia, P. (eds) (2010) *Classics and National Cultures*, Oxford.

Stewart, J. G. (1959) *Jane Ellen Harrison: A Portrait from Letters*, London.

Stockhorst, S., Lepper, M., and Hoppe, V. (eds) (2016) *Symphilologie: Formen der Kooperation in den Geisteswissenschaften*, Göttingen.

Stobart, J. C. (1911) *The Glory That Was Greece*, London.

Stobart, J. C. (1912) *The Grandeur That Was Rome*, London.

Stolberg, M. (2014) 'John Locke's "New method of making commonplace books": tradition, innovation and epistemic effects', *Early Science and Medicine* 19: 448–70.

Strachey, L. (2003 [1918]) *Eminent Victorians*, introd. Levy, P., London.

Stray, C. A. (1977) 'Classics in Crisis. The changing forms and current decline of Classics as exemplary curricular knowledge, with special reference to the experience of Classics teachers in South Wales', MSc. Econ. thesis, University of Wales.

Stray, C. A. (1988) 'England, culture and the 19th century', *Liverpool Classical Monthly* 13.6: 85–90.

Stray, C. A. (1989) 'Paradigms of Social Order: The Politics of Latin Grammar in Nineteenth-Century England', *Bulletin of the Henry Sweet Society* 13: 13–24.

Stray, C. A. (1990) 'Beyond classification: Bernstein and the grammarians', *History of Education* 19: 267–8.

Stray, C.A. (1991) 'Locke's System of Classical Instruction', *The Locke Newsletter* 22: 115–21.

Stray, C. A. (1991b) Review of S. Peacock, *Jane Ellen Harrison: The Mask and the Self*, *Liverpool Classical Monthly* 16: 103–11.

Stray, C. A. (1992a) *The Living Word: W. H. D. Rouse and the Crisis of Classics in Edwardian England*, Bristol.

Stray, C. A. (1992b) 'The last Eton grammars', *Paradigm* 8: 1–8.

Stray, C. A. (1993) 'Who wrote Kennedy?', *familiares* V: ii.

Stray, C. A. (1994a) 'Paradigms regained: towards a historical sociology of textbooks', *Journal of Curriculum Studies* 26: 1–29.

Stray, C. A. (1994b) 'The smell of Latin grammar: contrary imaginings in English classrooms', *Bulletin of the John Rylands Library* 76: 201–22.

Stray, C. A. (1995a) *Grinders and Grammars: A Mid-Victorian Controversy*, Reading.

Stray, C. A. (1995b) 'Digs and degrees: Jessie Crum's tour of Greece in 1901', *Classics Ireland* 2: 121–32.

Stray, C. A. (ed.) (1996a) *The Mushri-English Pronouncing Dictionary: A Chapter in Nineteenth-Century Public-School Lexicography*, Reading.

Stray, C. A. (1996b) 'John Taylor and Locke's Classical System', *Paradigm* 1.20: 26–38.

Stray, C. A. (1996c) 'Primers, Publishing and Politics: The Classical Textbooks of Benjamin Hall Kennedy', *Papers of the Bibliographical Society of America* 90.4: 451–74.

Stray, C. A. (1998a) *Classics Transformed: Schools, Universities, and Society in England 1830–1960*, Oxford.

Stray, C. A. (1998b) 'Renegotiating Classics: the politics of curricular reform in late-Victorian Cambridge', *Echos du Monde Classique/Classical Views* 42 (ns 7): 1–22.

Stray, C. A. (1998c) 'Schoolboys and Gentlemen: Classical Pedagogy and Authority in the English Public School', in Livingstone, N. and Too, Y. L. (eds), *Pedagogy and Power: Rhetorics of Ancient Learning*, Cambridge: 29–46.

Stray, C. A. (ed.) (1998d) *Winchester Notions: The English Dialect of Winchester College*, London.

Stray, C. A. (2001a) 'A parochial anomaly: the Classical Tripos 1822–1900', in Smith and Stray 2001, 31–44.

Stray, C. A. (2001b) 'Curriculum and style in the collegiate university: classics in nineteenth-century Oxbridge', *History of Universities* 16: 183–218.

Stray, C. A. (2001c) 'A preference for naughty boys in apple trees', *ad familiares* XX, vi.

Stray, C. A. (2001d) 'Purity in danger: the contextual life of savants', in Harrison 2001, 265–85.

Stray, C. A. (2002) 'A pedagogic palace: the Feinaiglian Institution and its textbooks', *Long Room* 47: 14–25.

Stray, C. A. (ed.) (2003a) *The Classical Association: The First Century 1903–2003*, London.

Stray, C. A. (2003b) 'Sexy Ghosts and Gay Grammarians: Kennedy's Latin Primer in Britten's *Turn of the Screw*', *Paradigm* 2.6: 9–13.

Stray, C. A. (2004a) 'Edmund Henry Barker, 1788–1839', *Oxford Dictionary of National Biography*, Oxford.

Stray, C. A (2004b) 'Edward Adolf Sonnenschein', in Todd 2004, 908–10.

Stray, C. A. (2004c) 'Edward Adolf Sonnenschein', *Oxford Dictionary of National Biography*, Oxford.

Stray, C. A. (2004d) 'Edward Adolf Sonnenschein and the Politics of Linguistic Authority in England 1880–1930', in Linn, A. and McLelland, N. (eds), *Flores Grammaticae: Essays in Memory of Vivien Law*, Münster: 211–19.

Stray, C. A. (2004e) 'John Selby Watson', Todd 2004, 1034–5.

Stray, C. A. (2004f) 'From one Museum to another: the Museum Criticum (1813–26) and the Philological Museum (1831–3)', *Victorian Periodicals Review* 37: 289–314.

Stray, C. A. (2004g) *Promoting and Defending: Reflections on the History of the Hellenic Society and the Classical Association*, London.

Stray, C. A. (ed.) (2005a) *The Owl of Minerva: the Cambridge Praelections of 1906*, Proceedings of the Cambridge Philological Society, supp. vol, 28, Cambridge.

Stray, C. A. (2005b) 'Flying at dusk: the 1906 praelections', in Stray 2005a, 1–12.

Stray, C. A. (2005c) 'From oral to written examinations: Oxford, Cambridge and Dublin 1700–1914', *History of Universities* 20: 76–130.

Stray, C. A. (2005d) 'Scholars, gentlemen and schoolboys: the authority of Latin in nineteenth and twentieth-century England', in Burnett, C. and Mann, N. (eds), *Britannia Latina: Latin in the Culture of Great Britain from the Middle Ages to the Twentieth Century*, Oxford, 194–208.

Stray, C. A. (2006) 'Paper Wraps Stone: The Beginnings of Educational Lithography', *Journal of the Printing Historical Society* ns 9: 13–29.

Stray, C. A. (ed.) (2007a) *Classical Books: Scholarship and Publishing in Britain since 1800*, London.

Stray, C. A. (ed.) (2007b) *Gilbert Murray Reassessed: Hellenism, Theatre, & International Politics*, Oxford.

Stray, C. A. (ed.) (2007c) *Oxford Classics: Teaching and Learning 1800–2000*, London.

Stray, C. A. (2007d) 'Jebb's Sophocles: an edition and its maker', in Stray 2007a, 75–96.

Stray, C. A. (2007e) 'Non-identical twins: Classics in nineteenth-century Oxford and Cambridge', in Stray 2007c, 1–13.

Stray, C. A. (2007f) 'Politics, culture and scholarship: Classics in the *Quarterly Review*', in Cutmore 2007, 87–106.

Stray, C. A. (2007g) 'The Rise and Fall of Porsoniasm', *Cambridge Classical Journal* 53: 40–71.

Stray, C. A. (2007h) 'Sir William Smith and his dictionaries: a study in scarlet and black', in Stray 2007a, 35–54.

Stray, C. A. (2011a) 'Lex Wrecks: a tale of two Latin dictionaries', *Dictionaries* 32: 66–81.

Stray, C. A. (2011b) 'Reading silence: the books that never were', Verlinsky, A. et al. (eds), *Variante loquella. Alexandro Gavrilov septuagenario*, St Petersburg, 527–38.

Stray, C. A. (2013a) *Sophocles' Jebb: A Life in Letters*, Cambridge.

Stray, C. A. (2013b) 'Classics', in Eliot 2013a, 435–70.

Stray, C. A. (2013c) 'Education', in Eliot 2013a, 473–510.

Stray, C. A. (2014a) 'The absent academy: the organisation of classical scholarship in nineteenth-century England', *Hyperboreus* 19: 214–26.

Stray, C. A. (2014b) Review of Richardson 2013, *Bryn Mawr Classical Reviews* 2014.06.05.

Stray, C. A. (2015a) 'A divided text: Shackleton Bailey, W. S. Watt and Cicero's *Epistulae ad Atticum*', in Stray and Whitaker 2015, 115–28.

Stray, C. A. (2015b) 'A Teutonic monster in Oxford: the making of Fraenkel's *Agamemnon*', in Kraus, C. S. and Stray, C. A. (eds), *Classical Commentaries: Studies in the History of an Academic Genre*, Oxford, 39–57.

Stray, C. A. (2016a) 'Disciplinary histories of Classics', *History of Universities* XXIX/1: 112–34.

Stray, C. A. (2016b) 'A semi-sacred monster: Charles Wordsworth's *Graecae Grammaticae Rudimenta*', in *Philologia Classica* (St Petersburg) 11: 101–18.

Stray, C. A. (2019) 'Liddell and Scott in its Victorian contexts', in Stray, Clarke, and Katz 2019.

Stray, C. A., Clarke, M. J., and Katz, J. T. (eds) (2019) *Liddell and Scott: The History, Methodology and Languages of the World's Leading Lexicon of Ancient Greek*, Oxford.

Stray, C. A., Pelling, C. B. R., and Harrison, S. J. (2019) C. B. R. Pelling and S. J. Harrison, *Rediscovering E.R. Dodds: Scholarship, Poetry, and the Paranormal*, Oxford.

Stray, C. A. and Sutherland, G. (2008) 'Mass markets: education', in McKitterick, D. J. (ed.) *Cambridge History of the Book in Britain, vol 6: 1830–1914*, Cambridge, 359–81.

Stray, C. A. and Whitaker, G. (eds) (2015) *Classics in Practice: Studies in the History of Scholarship* (Bulletin of the Institute of Classical Studies, supplement 128), London.

Super, R. H. (1974) *The Collected Prose Works of Matthew Arnold*, vol. 5, Ann Arbor MI.

Sutcliffe, P. (1978) *Oxford University Press: An Informal History*, Oxford.

Sutherland, Gillian (2001) 'Girton for ladies, Newnham for governesses', in Smith and Stray 2001, 139–49.

Sutherland, J. (1987) 'The British book trade and the crash of 1826', *The Library*, 6th ser. 9: 148–61.

Symonds, R. W. (1986) *Oxford and Empire: The Last Lost Cause?* Oxford.

Talbert, R. J. A. (1994) 'Mapping the classical world: major atlases and map series 1872–1990', *Journal of Roman Archaeology* 5: 5–38.

Talbert, R. J. A. (1996) 'Carl Müller (1813–1894), S. Jacobs, and the making of classical maps in Paris for John Murray', *Imago Mundi* 46: 128–50.

Teuffel, W. S. (1871), 'Ueber die Hauptrichtungen in der heutigen classischen Alterthumswissenschaft', *Studien und Charakteristiken zur griechischen und römischen, sowie zur deutschen Literaturgeschichte*, Leipzig, 460–72.

Thackeray, W. M. (1853) *The English Humorists of the Eighteenth Century*, London.

Thirlwall, J. C. (1936) *Connop Thirlwall, Historian and Theologian*, London.

Thirlwall, N. C. (1881) *Letters Literary and Theological of Connop Thirlwall*, ed. Perowne, J. H. and Stokes, L., London.

Thompson. D. M. (2017) *Cambridge Theology in the Nineteenth Century; Enquiry, Controversy and Truth*, Aldershot.

Thompson, H. L. (1899) *Life of Dean Liddell*, London.

Thompson, H. L. (1900) *Christ Church*, London.

Thompson, J. B. (1990) *Ideology and Modern Culture: Critical Theory in the Era of Mass Communication*, Cambridge.

Thornely, T. (1936) *Cambridge Memories*, London.

Tilley, A. A. (1884) 'The development of classical learning', *National Review* 3: 163–76.

Todd, R. B. (1999) 'Henry Sidgwick, Cambridge Classics, and the study of ancient philosophy: the decisive years (1866–1869)', in Stray 1999, 15–26.

Todd, R. B. (ed.) (2004) *Dictionary of British Classicists*, 3 vols, Bristol.

Toynbee, A. J. (1954) *A Study of History*, vols 7–11, Oxford.

Tracy, R. (1982) '"Lana medicate fuco": Trollope's classicism', in Halperin, J. (ed.) *Trollope Centenary Essays*, London, 1–23.

Traweek, S. (1988) *Beamtimes and Lifetimes: The World of High Energy Physicists*, Cambridge MA.

Trevelyan, G. O. (1905) *Interludes in Verse and Prose*, London.

Trevelyan, G. O. (1932) *Life of T. B. Macaulay*, Oxford.

Tuckwell, W. (1907) *Reminiscences of Oxford*, 2nd edn, London.

Turner, F. M. (1981) *The Greek Heritage in Victorian Britain*, New Haven.

Turner, F. M. (1989) 'Why the Greeks and not the Romans in Victorian Britain?' *Rediscovering Hellenism*, ed. Clarke, G. W., Cambridge, 61–82.

Turner, J. S. (2014) *Philology: the Forgotten Origins of the Modern Humanities*, Princeton.

Twyman, M. L. (1990) *Early Lithographed Books*, London.

Twyman, M. L. (1993) 'The bold idea: the use of bold-looking types in the nineteenth century', *Journal of the Printing Historical Society* 2: 107–43.

Twyman, M. L. (1997) 'Ireland's earliest lithographed book?', *Long Room* 42: 27–33.

Tyrrell, R. Y. (1888) 'The old school of Classics and the new. A dialogue of the dead', *Fortnightly Review* 49: 42–59.

Varley, E. A. (2002) *The Last of the Prince Bishops: William Van Mildert and the High Church Movement in the Early Nineteenth Century*, Oxford.

Vasunia, P. (2009) 'Latin and Greek in the Indian Civil Service', in Hallett and Stray 2009, 61–93.

Venn, J. A. (1908b) *Statistical Chart, Showing Admissions to the Various Colleges of the University of Cambridge*, Cambridge.

Verrall, A W. *On Editing Aesechylus: A Reply*, London.

Veysey, L. R. (1965) *The Emergence of the American University*, Chicago.

Viscusi, R. (1986) *Max Beerbohm, or the Dandy Dante: Rereading with Mirrors*, Baltimore.

Walker, W. S. (1852) *The Poetical Remains of William Sidney Walker, Edited with a Memoir by Revd J. Moultrie*, London.

Wallace, S. (2006) *John Stuart Blackie: Scottish Scholar and Patriot*, Edinburgh.

Wallas, G. (1926) *The Art of Thought*, London.

Walmsley, J. (1989) 'The Sonnenschein v. Jespersen controversy', in Fries, U. and Heusser, M. (eds), *Meaning and Beyond*, Tübingen, 253–81.

Walmsley, J. (1991) 'E. A. Sonnenschein and grammatical terminology', in Leitner, G. (ed.) *English Traditional Grammars: An International Perspective*, Amsterdam, 57–80.

Walmsley, J. (2001) 'The "Entente Cordiale Grammaticale", 1885–1915', in Colombat, B. and Savelli, M. (eds), *Métalangage et terminologie linguistique*, Leuven, 499–512.

Waquet, F. (2001) *Latin, or the Empire of a Sign*, London.

Ward, R. (1958) *Georgian Oxford: University Politics in the Eighteenth Century*, Oxford.

Ward, W. R. (1965) *Victorian Oxford*, London.

Warwick, A. (2003) *Masters of Theory: Cambridge and the Rise of Mathematical Physics*, Chicago.

Warwick, A. and Kaiser, D. (2005) 'Kuhn, Foucault, and the power of pedagogy', in Kaiser, D. (ed), *Pedagogy and the Practice of Science*, Cambridge MA, 393–409.

Watson, J. S. (1861) *Life of Richard Porson*, London.

Webb, T. (2002) 'Appropriating the stones: the "Elgin marbles" and the English national taste', in *Claiming the Stones/Naming the Bones: Cultural Property and the Negotiation of National and Ethnic identity*, Barkan, E. and Bush, R. (eds), Los Angeles, 51–6.

Wegeler, C. (1996) '... wir sagen ab der internationalen Gelehrtenrepublik': Altertumswissenschaft und Nationalsozialismus: Das Göttinger Institut für Altertumskunde 1921–1962, Vienna.

Wegmann, N. (2014) 'Philology: An Update', in Bahjor, H. et al. (eds), *The Future of Philology*, Newcastle, 27–46.

Westcott, A. (1903) *Life and Letters of Brooke Foss Westcott*, 2 vols, London.

Whewell, W. (1861) *Platonic Dialogues for English Readers*, London.

Whitaker, G. (2015) 'Alterthumswissenschaft at mid-century', in Stray and Whitaker 2015, 129–69.

Wilamowitz-Moellendorff, U. von (1908) *Greek Historical Writing and Apollo: Two Lectures Delivered before the University of Oxford, June 3 and 4, 1908*, transl. G. Murray, Oxford.

Wilamowitz-Moellendorff, U. von (1928) *Erinnerungen 1848–1914*, 2nd edn, Leipzig.

Wilamowitz-Moellendorff, U. von (1982[1921]) *History of Classical Scholarship*, trans. Harris, A. ed. with intro and notes by Lloyd-Jones, H., London [German original 1921].

Wilson, A. T. and J. S. (eds) (1933) *James M. Wilson: An Autobiography*, London.

Winstanley, D. A. (1935) *Unreformed Cambridge*, Cambridge.

Winstanley, D. A. (1947) *Early Victorian Cambridge*, Cambridge.

Winstanley, D. A. (1950) *Later Victorian Cambridge*, Cambridge.

Witheridge, J. D. (2005) *Frank Fletcher, 1870–1954: A Formidable Headmaster*, Norwich.

Witheridge, J. D. (2013) *Excellent Dr Stanley: The Life of Dean Stanley of Westminster*, Norwich.

Wood, H. G. (1953) *Terrot Reaveley Glover: A Biography*, Cambridge.

Woodward, A., Elliott, D. L., and Nagel, K. C. (1988) *Textbooks in School and Society: An Annotated Bibliography and Guide to Research*, New York.

Wordsworth, Charles (1891) *Annals of My Early Life 1806–1846*, London.

Wordsworth, Charles (1893) *Annals of My Life 1847–56*, London.

Wordsworth, Christopher (1838) 'On the practice of publishing ancient authors with English notes', *British Magazine* 13: 243–6.

Wordsworth, J. (1899) *The Episcopate of Christopher Wordsworth*, London.

[Wright, J. M. F.] (1827) *Alma Mater, or, Seven Years at the University of Cambridge, by a Trinity-man*, 2 vols, London.

Yeo, R. (2001) *Encyclopaedic Visions: Scientific Dictionaries and Enlightenment Culture*, Cambridge.

Yeo, R. (2004) 'John Locke's "New Method" of commonplacing: managing memory and information', *Eighteenth-Century Thought* 2: 1–38.

Young, G. M. (1936) *Victorian England: Portrait of an Age*, Oxford.

Young, G. M. (1948) *Daylight and Champaign*, London.

Index

New English Dictionary 23, 187
New Journalism 146, 213
Newman, Francis 41
Newton, Benjamin 36
Newton, Charles 129, 230, 233
Newton, Isaac 33, 93, 104, 128
Niebuhr, Barthold 48, 101, 103, 149, 159, 160, 165, 189, 228
Nutt, Alfred 177, 179
Nutt, David 177, 178, 183, 184

Oakeley, Sir Herbert 71
Ogilvie, Robert 87
O'Keeffe, John 335
Olim, Mr. *see* Elam, Horace
Opie, Iona and Peter 252
Osbourne, Lloyd 44
Oxbridge 32
Oxford and Cambridge Schools Examinations Board 38
Oxford Classical Dictionary 205
Oxford Dictionary of Quotations, The 76–7
Oxford English Dictionary 187
Oxford Philological Society 85
Oxford University 31–52
  Ashmolean Museum 69
  Balliol College 51, 87, 91, 248
  Bodleian Library 68–9, 73
  Cabinet, links to 51
  Camden chair of ancient history 96, 141
  Catholics, admission of 140
  Christ Church xii, 70–3, 91
  Clarendon Press 53, 55, 56, 67–8
  Corpus Christi chair of Latin 19, 249
  English school 23, 305
  Examination statute (1800) 33, 35, 91
  Hebdomadal Board 31, 70
  Honour Moderations (Mods) 50, 51, 109–10, 193
  Ireland Prize 136
  Literae Humaniores (Greats) 36, 40, 41, 42, 51, 109–10, 247
  Logic-chopping 46
  Magdalen College xii
  Merton College 45
  Modern History course 247
  New College xii, 39
  Oriel College 91
  Poetry, chair of 253
  Regius chair of divinity 141
  Regius chair of Greek 96, 141, 230
  Sanskrit 247
  Tractarian controversy 43, 52, 168
  Tutors vs professors 32
Oxford University Press 182, 212, 310
  Clarendon Press Series 212, 314
  School Book Committee 314

Page, Thomas Ethelbert 20–2, 28, 43, 235, 291, 323, 336
Paley, Frederick 102, 196, 214
Pall Mall Gazette 213
Palmer, Arthur 179
Palmer, Edwin 249
Pálsson, Gisli 15, 30
Panopticon schoolrooms 263–4
Pantin, W.E. 338
Paradigms (Kuhnian) 15
Parallel grammars 300, 302
Parr, Samuel 62, 89
Parr, Mrs 90
Parsons, Peter 79
Passow, Franz 57
Pater, Walter 52, 213, 225
Pattison, Mark 32
Pauly, August, *Real-Encyclopädie der classischen Altertumswissenschaft* 190, 197
Payne Knight, Richard 131, 143
Peall, W.J. 227
Pearson, Arthur 221
Peel, Sir Robert 46
Peggotty, Mrs (*David Copperfield*) 296
Peile, John 112
Penny Cyclopaedia (SDUK) 103, 188, 190, 195
Penoyre, John 232, 237
  Ante Oculos 238
Perceval, Spencer 74
Percival, John 241
Perowne, E.H. 249
Perse School, Cambridge 329
Persius 136
Pestalozzian system 262
Pfeiffer, Rudolf 6, 85, 106
Phillipps, Sir Thomas 69
Phillips, Sir Richard 279
Phillips, Thomas 271
  Introduction to Greek Declension (1833) 268–73
Philological Museum 40, 101–2, 146–70 *passim*, 171, 184, 189
Philological Society (c.1811) 277, 283
Philological Society (1845–8) 171
Philological Society of London 23, 301
Philologische Wochenschrift 174, 176
Philology, comparative 165, 272, 323–4
Photius 89
Piazzi Smyth, Charles 278
Piddington, A.B. 202, 337
Pillans (printers) 168
Pillans, James 134, 135, 137
Piper, Myfanwy 342–5
Pitt Press Series (CUP) 212
Plagiarism 25
Plate, William 196
Plato 43, 51, 228, 244